D0909721

SWEET REVENGE

10 Plays of Bloody Murder

Anthologies edited by Marvin Kaye

Lovers and Other Monsters
Haunted America
Devils & Demons
Ghosts
Masterpieces of Terror and the Supernatural
13 Plays of Ghosts and the Supernatural
Weird Tales™: The Magazine That Never Dies
Witches & Warlocks
Fiends and Creatures
Brother Theodore's Chamber of Horrors

SWEET REVENGE

10 Plays of Bloody Murder

Selected by Marvin Kaye

*With an Introduction by
Marilyn Stasio*

ISBN 1-56865-007-8

ACKNOWLEDGMENTS

THE BASTARD OF BOLOGNA copyright © 1992 Paula Volsky. All rights reserved. Printed by permission of the author. CAUTION: *The Bastard of Bologna*, being duly copyrighted, may not be acted by professionals or amateurs without formal permission and payment of a royalty. Address inquiries to the author's agent, Donald Maass, Inc., 304 West 92 Street, Suite 8 P, New York City, New York, 10025.

SWEENEY TODD, revised and reconstructed, copyright © 1992 Marvin Kaye. All rights reserved. CAUTION: This version of *Sweeney Todd* may not be acted without obtaining formal permission. No royalty fee is required. Address all queries to The Open Book, 525 West End Avenue, Apt. 12 E, New York City, New York, 10024 - 3207.

MURDERER copyright © 1979 Anthony Shaffer. Reprinted by permission of Marion Boyars Publishers, Inc. All performance rights are strictly reserved. Address queries to the author's agent, The Lantz Office, 888 Seventh Avenue, Suite 2500, New York City, New York, 10106.

VICTIM copyright © 1978 Mario Fratti. Reprinted by permission of the author. CAUTION: Professionals and amateurs are hereby warned that *Victim*, being fully protected under the copyright laws of the United States of America, the British Empire, including the Dominion of Canada, and all other countries of the Copyright Union, is subject to a royalty. All rights, including professional, amateur, motion pictures, recitation, public reading, radio and television broadcasting, and the rights of translation in foreign languages are strictly reserved. For performing rights, contact Samuel French, Inc., 45 West 25th Street, New York City, New York, 10010.

CONTENTS

Acknowledgments	*iv*
Preface	*vii*
Introduction by Marilyn Stasio	*xi*
THE SPANISH TRAGEDY	1
Thomas Kyd	
THE WITCH OF EDMONTON	97
Thomas Dekker	
THE REVENGER'S TRAGEDY	187
Cyril Tourneur	
HAMLET [1603 version]	295
William Shakespeare	
THE CHANGELING	373
Thomas Middleton and William Rowley	
THE BASTARD OF BOLOGNA	467
Paula Volsky	
FRANCESCA DA RIMINI [Expanded 1853 Acting Edition]	533
George Henry Boker	
SWEENEY TODD	629
George Dibdin Pitt, revised and restructured by Marvin Kaye	
MURDERER	683
Anthony Shaffer	
VICTIM	743
Mario Fratti	
APPENDIX: *Textual Notes*	815

PREFACE

While I was studying theatre at Penn State, I participated in several heated discussions on the nature of tragedy in the modern drama. In those days, academics seemed to think it important to determine whether Willy Loman could truly be considered a tragic protagonist in the tradition of Oedipus or Hamlet. Since the focus of early drama was skewed towards the nobility, how could Arthur Miller's pathetic little salesman possibly qualify?

I believed he did and maintained that position with some heat, though in those days my main reason for thinking so was chiefly emotional: Willy "felt" tragic to me; he reminded me of my own father. My attitude surely reflected the fact that I grew up in lower middle class America during the nineteen-forties and post-war years when the nation's acknowledged heroes were citizen soldiers and when films glorified and mourned the plight of the common man in such epics as *The Grapes of Wrath* and *The Best Years of Our Lives*.

I still believe Willy qualifies, but now my opinion rests on a formal reassessment of the tragic hero. That aristocratic rank once figured in the equation was merely a function of the West's evolving social system and not an indispensable element. In the modern theatre, only two characteristics are essential.

The tragic protagonist must be a deeply realized character capable of enlisting the intellectual interest and emotive concern of the spectators.

The protagonist cannot merely be a helpless victim. Such a character may evoke the pathos and sympathy of the audience (as often occurs in melodrama) but the essential impact of tragedy depends upon witnessing a fellow human being challenging her or his destiny and failing. Neither can that failure be a function of a meaningless fate; to achieve the tragic effect, the protagonist's defeat must be rooted in her or his own nature's inability to conquer the odds.

In the broadest sense, a tragic hero is handicapped by spiritual blindness, like Oedipus or Melville's Captain Amasa Delano, or else, like Hamlet or Benito Cereno, possesses too clear a vision of what Joseph Conrad darkly calls "the formidable Work of the Seven Days."

This shift towards psychologically-compelling heroes and heroines of whatever social rank has its roots in the protagonists of Jacobean revenge tragedy and may be traced through their tricentenary evolution into such modern-day counterparts as Eugene O'Neill's Emperor Jones, Emlyn Williams's Dan in *Night Must Fall*, John LeCarre's George Smiley and, in debased form, the Raymond Chandler school of cynical errantry, not to mention the quotidian romantic villains of "ladyprose" and television soap operas.

At their best, Jacobean revenge tragedies contain the potential for catharsis, drama's most powerful aesthetic effect. At their worst, they reflect the theatre's old love-hate affair with pure spectacle: Hellmouth and its tricksters, magicians and fire-eaters, ritual dismemberment and resurrection. Though a drama may be tragic without involving bloodshed or death, as, for instance, Ibsen's *Ghosts*, Jacobean revenge tragedy is always bloody and often gruesome. At first, this characteristic appears to be linked to such awesome moments in the Greek drama as Oedipus's blinding or the savage butchery of *The Bacchae*, but those horrors occurred offstage,* whereas English playhouses of the late sixteenth and early seventeenth centuries brought the gore "down center."

The true forefather of revenge tragedy is the Roman playwright, Lucius Annaeus Seneca, whose declamatory plays began to be translated into English in 1559 and continued to appear in print over a period of twenty-two years. The character of all true Jacobean revengers is skillfully limned by the Senecan nurse who cautions Medea to

> Be still for now, I warn thee: thy wrongs confine
> To secret grief. She who bears great abuse
> Silently, and patiently bides her time,
> May be rewarded with revenge. Hidden hatred triumphs;
> To cry one's wounds destroys the power to wound.

---

* It is generally maintained that Seneca's atrocities also took place offstage, but at the climax of *Medea*, the title character specifically slays both of her children in full view of Jason and the audience.

Combined with what the English learned of skulduggery in foreign courts like Spain or Portugal as well as the mountain-bound vendettas of Italy, Seneca's concern with vengeful ghosts and retributive justice inspired gory efforts by many British playwrights, notably Francis Beaumont, Thomas Dekker, John Fletcher, Thomas Kyd, Christopher Marlowe, Thomas Middleton, William Rowley, Cyril Tourneur, John Webster and of course, William Shakespeare.

Despite the ethical censure of the world's chief religions, the theme of revenge still has a strong fascination for modern audiences, whether it manifests itself in a revival of *Hamlet* or the cloning of yet another Clint Eastwood or Charles Bronson vigilante fable.

Anthropologists may attribute this, perhaps, to the animal origins of the species, but mere bestiality cannot explain its profound hold on the imagination. The problem of sin and its punishment is endlessly significant in a society attempting to reshape itself after the madness of Nazism, the bitter repressions of Communism and the criminal aggressions of mideastern dictators.

In the following ten plays—Jacobean revenge tragedies, their theatrical variants and lineal descendants—the seductive, yet corrosive nature of "sweet revenge" is thoroughly explored.

—MARVIN KAYE
New York City 1992

INTRODUCTION

Ever since reading "The Romantic Agony," I have been holding my breath for the *fin de siècle,* a period of history, I did believe, when the demons of the id would leap from our collective subconscious and onto our stages to do fierce battle with the weakened values of an exhausted civilization. Or was I, silly romantic goose, merely longing for theatre as dangerous as the Jacobean tragedies and nineteenth-century melodramas that had thrilled me in my youth?

Now, *there* was theatre that wasn't afraid to do our psychosexual dirty work for us! Unencumbered by the enlightened behavioral theories of later generations, such playwrights as Middleton, Webster, Tourneur and Ford simply looked into our souls and projected our darkest urges into theatrical deeds. And they weren't ashamed to call it evil.

The characters in these lurid dramas offered no rationalization and expected no forgiveness for their crimes. They lusted after their fathers' crowns, their brothers' inheritances, their sisters' bodies, their neighbors' goods, their enemies' heads—and they made no bones about it. They snatched whatever they wanted and yanked out any tongue that dared wag in protest. These unregenerate villains could articulate, in bold and often beautiful language, the elemental bloodlust that motivated their crimes; but in the most horrid cases, they were driven by the pure itch of evil.

By the Victorian period, of course, everyone had calmed down a lot. It was harder to find villains as inventive as Villuppo, or revengers with Vendice's incredible stamina, and a far greater sense of guilt and remorse was expected of these fiends. Plots that once teemed with multiple instances of rape, incest, madness, suicide, mutilation, and murder could now turn on a single criminal act. But all in all, the belief still prevailed that some human acts were bestial and that people who committed them were evil.

I wonder what some of the playwrights whose works of blood and revenge Marvin Kaye has collected in his grand anthology might have made of our modern age's timid interpretations of their violent themes. George Dibdin Pitt would surely snicker, I fancy, at the Stephen Sondheim/Harold Prince 1979 musical version of "Sweeney Todd," which transformed the demonic barber of Fleet Street into a pitiful victim of society. Despite the creaky devices of its period stagecraft and the innocuous virtue of its hero, Pitt's grisly melodrama stirs powerful feelings of revulsion and terror in a modern reader with imagination— and with an uneasy respect for evil. The labyrinthine cellars beneath Sweeney's shop are as twisted and murky as the psychological abyss from which spring all human nightmares, and Sweeney himself is a genuine monster of the id. No one who suspects that evil can take on human features could fail to tremble at his memorable line: "I believe I am not easily forgotten by those who have once seen me."

I miss evil, I really do. The stage, along with our lives, has become so ignoble without it. Without evil, which is rooted in the human heart, the things we fear are too abstract, too clinical, or too base to put us in mind of our own demons, or to animate the heroic side of our nature that longs to exorcise them. Personally, I can work up a purer feeling of horror for Middleton's wretched Beatrice or Oscar Wilde's insatiable Salome than I can for our self-absorbed contemporary heroes who whine for deliverance from such disembodied torments as anxiety, alienation, disease, social inequity and domestic discomfort.

Which is not to say that playwrights of earlier eras were unmindful of the political and sociological origins of violence. On the contrary, not even a radical firebrand like Caryl Churchill has written more persuasively of social injustice than Thomas Dekker, whose poignant characterization of the "witch" of Edmonton could open a dead man's eyes to society's oppression of its disenfranchised poor. "If every poor old woman / Be trod on thus by slaves, reviled, kicked, beaten / As I am daily, she to be revenged / Had need turn witch," declares Mother Sawyer, whose miseries of birth are compounded by the calculated wickedness of her social betters.

Mother Sawyer certainly has good cause, then, to go on a rampage in Edmonton. But despite the compassion that Dekker feels for her, he never suggests that the old woman's crimes were justified by the rotten social conditions that motivated them. Mother Sawyer makes a deliberate pact with the devil in order to avenge herself on her enemies—and she pays a terrible price for the power she bought in the bargain.

Readers who come to this anthology expecting to find amusement in characters who lived by the quaint notions of good and evil, guilt and retribution will probably be shocked by the stormy emotions in these plays. Living as we do in an age where emotional excess is not only unfashionable but also dangerous to one's health, there is, indeed, something disorienting about people who would kill for pleaure and die for passion. The revenger's ideal—of killing with malicious *cunning*—is a concept even more alien to a generation educated to violence through the impersonal images of wars, riots, serial killings and drive-by shootings. Not to mention those mass, mechanical wipeouts enacted on film by cartoon characters and futuristic terminators.

The theatre, at least, still offers a platform for those monsters in our mirrors who would kill with deliberation and style. Now, more than ever, with the *fin de siècle* already upon us, we need such magnificent villains.

—MARILYN STASIO
New York City 1992

THE SPANISH TRAGEDY

OR

HIERONIMO IS MAD AGAIN

Thomas Kyd

Elements of bloodshed and horror appear from time to time in the Medieval drama, but the first important revenge tragedy in English is generally acknowledged to be *The Spanish Tragedy* by THOMAS KYD (1558–1594).

Initially performed and published in 1592, *The Spanish Tragedy* begins, appropriately enough, with the personified appearance of Revenge, who, in a framing story, chronicles for the troubled ghost of a Spanish courtier a sequence of treacherous events that culminate in the incidental avenging of the courtier's death. The play establishes some of the key devices of the genre, including (besides the expected onstage atrocities) a Dumb Show and a play-within-the-play, conventions that Shakespeare profitably adopted in *Hamlet*.

Kyd, at one time believed to have been Christopher Marlowe's roommate, suffered torture and imprisonment on behalf of Marlowe's public blasphemies. Kyd's compositions, except for *Cornelia* (1594), were published anonymously, but may include a lost *Hamlet* script as well as a prequel to *The Spanish Tragedy*, known as *The First Part of Hieronimo*.

DRAMATIS PERSONAE

GHOST OF ANDREA,
a Spanish courtier, ⎫
REVENGE, ⎬ Chorus
⎭
KING OF SPAIN
DON CYPRIAN, DUKE OF CASTILE,
his brother
LORENZO, the Duke's son
BEL-IMPERIA, Lorenzo's sister
VICEROY OF PORTUGAL
BALTHAZAR, his son
DON PEDRO, the Viceroy's brother
HIERONIMO, Marshal of Spain
ISABELLA, his wife
HORATIO, their son
SPANISH GENERAL
DEPUTY
DON BAZULTO, an old man
THREE CITIZENS
PORTUGUESE AMBASSADOR
ALEXANDRO, ⎫ Portuguese
VILLUPPO, ⎬ NOBLEMEN
TWO PORTUGUESE
PEDRINGANO, Bel-imperia's servant

CHRISTOPHIL, Bel-imperia's custo-
dian
LORENZO'S PAGE
SERBERINE, Balthazar's servant
ISABELLA'S MAID
MESSENGER
HANGMAN
SOLIMAN, Sultan of ⎫
Turkey (Balthazar) ⎪
ERASTUS, Knight of ⎪ In
Rhodes (Lorenzo) ⎬ Hieronimo's
THE BASHAW ⎪ Play
(Hieronimo) ⎪
PERSEDA (Bel- ⎪
imperia) ⎭
THREE KINGS and THREE KNIGHTS
in the first Dumb-show
HYMEN and two torchbearers in
the second
ARMY, ROYAL SUITES, NOBLEMEN,
HALBERDIERS, OFFICERS, THREE
WATCHMEN, SERVANTS, ETC.

Scene: Spain and Portugal

ACT ONE

Prologue

Enter the ghost of ANDREA *and with him* REVENGE.

GHOST: When this eternal substance of my soul
    Did live imprisoned in my wanton flesh,
    Each in their function serving other's need,
    I was a courtier in the Spanish court.
    My name was Don Andrea; my descent,
    Though not ignoble, yet inferior far
    To gracious fortunes of my tender youth,
    For there in prime and pride of all my years,
    By duteous service and deserving love,
    In secret I possessed a worthy dame,
    Which hight sweet Bel-imperia by name.
    But in the harvest of my summer joys
    Death's winter nipped the blossoms of my bliss,
    Forcing divorce betwixt my love and me.
    For in the late conflict with Portingale
    My valor drew me into danger's mouth
    Till life to death made passage through my wounds.
    When I was slain, my soul descended straight
    To pass the flowing stream of Acheron;
    But churlish Charon, only boatman there,
    Said that, my rites of burial not performed,
    I might not sit amongst his passengers.
    Ere Sol had slept three nights in Thetis' lap,
    And slaked his smoking chariot in her flood,
    By Don Horatio, our knight marshal's son,
    My funerals and obsequies were done.
    Then was the ferryman of Hell content
    To pass me over to the slimy strond,
    That leads to fell Avernus' ugly waves
    There, pleasing Cerberus with honeyed speech,
    I passed the perils of the foremost porch.
    Not far from hence, amidst ten thousand souls,
    Sat Minos, Aeacus, and Rhadamanth;
    To whom no sooner 'gan I make approach,
    To crave a passport for my wandering ghost,

But Minos, in graven leaves of lottery,
Drew forth the manner of my life and death.
"This knight," quoth he, "both lived and died in love;
And for his love tried fortune of the wars;
And by war's fortune lost both love and life."
"Why then," said Aeacus, "convey him hence,
To walk with lovers in our fields of love,
And spend the course of everlasting time
Under green myrtle-trees and cypress shades."
"No, no," said Rhadamanth, "it were not well,
With loving souls to place a martialist.
He died in war and must to martial fields,
Where wounded Hector lives in lasting pain,
And Achilles' Myrmidons do scour the plain."
Then Minos, mildest censor of the three,
Made this device to end the difference:
"Send him," quoth he, "to our infernal king,
To doom him as best seems his Majesty."
To this effect my passport straight was drawn.
In keeping on my way to Pluto's court
Through dreadful shades of ever-glooming night,
I saw more sights than thousand tongues can tell,
Or pens can write, or mortal hearts can think.
Three ways there were: that on the right-hand side
Was ready way unto the 'foresaid fields,
Where lovers live and bloody martialists;
But either sort contained within his bounds.
The left-hand path, declining fearfully,
Was ready downfall to the deepest Hell,
Where bloody Furies shakes their whips of steel,
And poor Ixion turns an endless wheel;
Where usurers are choked with melting gold,
And wantons are embraced with ugly snakes,
And murderers groan with never-killing wounds,
And perjured wights scalded in boiling lead,
And all foul sins with torments overwhelmed.
'Twixt these two ways I trod the middle path,
Which brought me to the fair Elysian green,
In midst whereof there stands a stately tower,
The walls of brass, the gates of adamant.
Here finding Pluto with his Proserpine,

I showed my passport, humbled on my knee;
Whereat fair Proserpine began to smile,
And begged that only she might give my doom.
Pluto was pleased, and sealed it with a kiss.
Forthwith, Revenge, she rounded thee in th' ear,
And bade thee lead me through the gates of horn,
Where dreams have passage in the silent night.
No sooner had she spoke, but we were here—
I know not how—in twinkling of an eye.

REVENGE: Then know, Andrea, that thou art arrived
Where thou shalt see the author of thy death,
Don Balthazar, the prince of Portingale,
Deprived of life by Bel-imperia.
Here sit we down to see the mystery,
And serve for Chorus in this tragedy.

Scene One

The Spanish court. Enter SPANISH KING, GENERAL, CASTILE, *and* HIERONIMO.

KING: Now say, lord General, how fares our camp?

GENERAL: All well, my sovereign liege, except some few
That are deceased by fortune of the war.

KING: But what portends thy cheerful countenance,
And posting to our presence thus in haste?
Speak, man, hath fortune given us victory?

GENERAL: Victory, my liege, and that with little loss.

KING: Our Portingals will pay us tribute then?

GENERAL: Tribute and wonted homage therewithal.

KING: Then blessed be Heaven and guider of the heavens,
From whose fair influence such justice flows.

CASTILE: *O multum dilecte Deo, tibi militat aether,*
   Et conjuratae curvato poplite gentes
   Succumbunt: recti soror est victoria juris. *

KING: Thanks to my loving brother of Castile.
   But, General, unfold in brief discourse
   Your form of battle and your war's success,
   That, adding all the pleasure of thy news
   Unto the height of former happiness,
   With deeper wage and greater dignity
   We may reward thy blissful chivalry.

GENERAL: Where Spain and Portingale do jointly knit
   Their frontiers, leaning on each other's bound,
   There met our armies in their proud array;
   Both furnished well, both full of hope and fear,
   Both menacing alike with daring shows,
   Both vaunting sundry colors of device,
   Both cheerly sounding trumpets, drums, and fifes,
   Both raising dreadful clamors to the sky,
   That valleys, hills, and rivers made rebound,
   And Heaven itself was frighted with the sound.
   Our battles both were pitched in squadron form,
   Each corner strongly fenced with wings of shot;
   But ere we joined and came to push of pike,
   I brought a squadron of our readiest shot
   From out our rearward to begin the fight:
   They brought another wing t' encounter us.
   Meanwhile, our ordnance played on either side,
   And captains strove to have their valors tried.
   Don Pedro, their chief horsemen's colonel,
   Did with his mounted bravely make attempt
   To break the order of our battle ranks;
   But Don Rogero, worthy man of war,
   Marched forth against him with our musketeers,
   And stopped the malice of his fell approach.
   While they maintain hot skirmish to and fro,
   Both battles join, and fall to handy-blows,

___

* O beloved of God, Heaven defends you. On bended knee, conspiring nations fall.
Victory is righteous law's sister.

Their violent shot resembling th'ocean's rage,
When, roaring loud, and with a swelling tide,
It beats upon the rampires of huge rocks,
And gapes to swallow neighbor-bounding lands.
Now, while Bellona rageth here and there,
Thick storms of bullets rain like winter's hail,
And shivered lances dark the troubled air.
Pede pes et cuspide cuspis;
*Arma sonant armis, vir petiturque viro.**
On every side drop captains to the ground,
And soldiers, some ill-maimed, some slain outright;
Here falls a body sundered from his head,
There legs and arms lie bleeding on the grass,
Mingled with weapons and unbowelled steeds,
That scattering overspread the purple plain.
In all this turmoil, three long hours and more,
The victory to neither part inclined;
Till Don Andrea, with his brave lanciers,
In their main battle made so great a breach,
That, half dismayed, the multitude retired;
But Balthazar, the Portingals' young prince,
Brought rescue and encouraged them to stay.
Here-hence the fight was eagerly renewed,
And in that conflict was Andrea slain—
Brave man at arms, but weak to Balthazar.
Yet while the prince, insulting over him,
Breathed out proud vaunts, sounding to our reproach,
Friendship and hardy valor joined in one
Pricked forth Horatio, our knight marshal's son,
To challenge forth that prince in single fight.
Not long between these twain the fight endured,
But straight the prince was beaten from his horse,
And forced to yield him prisoner to his foe.
When he was taken, all the rest they fled,
And our carbines pursued them to the death,
Till, Phoebus setting in the western deep,
Our trumpeters were charged to sound retreat.

---

* Foot for foot, point for point, arms clash against arms, man attacks man.

KING: Thanks, good lord General, for these good news;
    And for some argument of more to come,
    Take this and wear it for thy sovereign's sake.
    (Gives him his chain)
    But tell me now, hast thou confirmed a peace?

GENERAL: No peace, my liege, but peace conditional,
    That if with homage tribute be well paid,
    The fury of your forces will be stayed;
    And to this peace their viceroy hath subscribed,
    (Gives the KING a paper)
    And made a solemn vow that, during life,
    His tribute shall be truly paid to Spain.

KING: These words, these deeds, become thy person well.
    But now, knight marshal, frolic with thy king,
    For 'tis thy son that wins this battle's prize.

HIERONIMO: Long may he live to serve my sovereign liege,
    And soon decay, unless he serve my liege.

KING: Nor thou, nor he, shall die without reward.
    (A flourish afar off)
    What means this warning of this trumpet's sound?

GENERAL: This tells me that your Grace's men of war,
    Such as war's fortune hath reserved from death,
    Come marching on towards your royal seat,
    To show themselves before your majesty;
    For so I gave in charge at my depart.
    Whereby by demonstration shall appear
    That all, except three hundred or few more,
    Are safe returned and by their foes enriched.

(The ARMY enters; BALTHAZAR, between LORENZO and HORATIO, captive)

KING: A gladsome sight! I long to see them here.
    (They enter and pass by)
    Was that the warlike prince of Portingale,
    That by our nephew was in triumph led?

GENERAL: It was, my liege, the prince of Portingale.

KING: But what was he that on the other side
   Held him by th' arm, as partner of the prize?

HIERONIMO: That was my son, my gracious sovereign;
   Of whom though from his tender infancy
   My loving thoughts did never hope but well,
   He never pleased his father's eyes till now,
   Nor filled my heart with overcloying joys.

KING: Go, let them march once more about these walls,
   That, staying them, we may confer and talk
   With our brave prisoner and his double guard.   *(Exit a messenger)*
   Hieronimo, it greatly pleaseth us
   That in our victory thou have a share,
   By virtue of thy worthy son's exploit.
   (Enter again)
   Bring hither the young prince of Portingale.
   The rest march on: but, ere they be dismissed,
   We will bestow on every soldier
   Two ducats and on every leader ten,
   That they may know our largess welcomes them.
   (Exeunt all but BALTHAZAR, LORENZO *and* HORATIO)
   Welcome, Don Balthazar! Welcome, nephew!
   And thou, Horatio, thou art welcome too.
   Young Prince, although thy father's hard misdeeds,
   In keeping back the tribute that he owes,
   Deserve but evil measure at our hands,
   Yet shalt thou know that Spain is honorable.

BALTHAZAR: The trespass that my father made in peace
   Is now controlled by fortune of the wars;
   And cards once dealt, it boots not ask why so.
   His men are slain, a weakening to his realm;
   His colors seized, a blot unto his name;
   His son distressed, corrosive to his heart:
   These punishments may clear his late offense.

KING: Ay, Balthazar, if he observe this truce,
   Our peace will grow the stronger for these wars.

Meanwhile live thou, though not in liberty,
Yet free from bearing any servile yoke;
For in our hearing thy deserts were great,
And in our sight thyself art gracious.

BALTHAZAR: And I shall study to deserve this grace.

KING: But tell me—for their holding makes me doubt—
To which of these twain art thou prisoner?

LORENZO: To me, my liege.
   HORATIO: To me, my sovereign.

LORENZO: This hand first took his courser by the reins.

HORATIO: But first my lance did put him from his horse.

LORENZO: I seized his weapon, and enjoyed it first.

HORATIO: But first I forced him lay his weapons down.

KING: Let go his arm, upon our privilege.   *(They let him go)*
Say, worthy Prince, to whether did'st thou yield?

BALTHAZAR: To him in courtesy, to this perforce.
He spake me fair, this other gave me strokes:
He promised life, this other threatened death;
He won my love, this other conquered me,
And, truth to say, I yield myself to both.

HIERONIMO: But that I know your grace for just and wise,
And might seem partial in this difference,
Enforced by nature and by law of arms
My tongue should plead for young Horatio's right.
He hunted well that was a lion's death,
Not he that in a garment wore his skin;
So hares may pull dead lions by the beard.

KING: Content thee, marshal, thou shalt have no wrong;
And, for thy sake, thy son shall want no right.
Will both abide the censure of my doom?

LORENZO: I crave no better than your grace awards.

HORATIO: Nor I, although I sit beside my right.

KING: Then by my judgment, thus your strife shall end:
   You both deserve and both shall have reward.
   Nephew, thou tookst his weapon and his horse:
   His weapons and his horse are thy reward.
   Horatio, thou didst force him first to yield:
   His ransom therefore is thy valor's fee;
   Appoint the sum, as you shall both agree.
   But, nephew, thou shalt have the prince in guard,
   For thine estate best fitteth such a guest;
   Horatio's house were small for all his train.
   Yet, in regard thy substance passeth his,
   And that just guerdon may befall desert,
   To him we yield the armor of the prince.
   How likes Don Balthazar of this device?

BALTHAZAR: Right well, my liege, if this proviso were,
   That Don Horatio bear us company,
   Whom I admire and love for chivalry.

KING: Horatio, leave him not that loves thee so.
   Now let us hence to see our soldiers paid,
   And feast our prisoner as our friendly guest.   *(Exeunt.)*

Scene Two

Portugal: the VICEROY's *palace. Enter* VICEROY, ALEXANDRO, VILLUPPO.

VICEROY: Is our ambassador despatched for Spain?

ALEXANDRO: Two days, my liege, are past since his depart.

VICEROY: And tribute-payment gone along with him?

ALEXANDRO: Ay, my good lord.

VICEROY: Then rest we here awhile in our unrest,
   And feed our sorrows with some inward sighs,

For deepest cares break never into tears.
But wherefore sit I in a regal throne?
This better fits a wretch's endless moan.
Yet this is higher than my fortunes reach,
And therefore better than my state deserves,
(*Falls to the ground*)
Ay, ay, this earth, image of melancholy,
Seeks him whom fates adjudge to misery.
Here let me lie; now am I at the lowest.

> *Qui jacet in terra, non habet unde cadat.*
> *In me consumpsit vires fortuna nocendo;*
> *Nil superest ut jam possit obesse magis.* *

Yes, Fortune may bereave me of my crown:
Here, take it now; let Fortune do her worst,
She will not rob me of this sable weed.
O no, she envies none but pleasant things.
Such is the folly of despiteful chance!
Fortune is blind, and sees not my deserts;
So is she deaf and hears not my laments;
And could she hear, yet is she wilful-mad,
And therefore will not pity my distress.
Suppose that she could pity me, what then?
What help can be expected at her hands
Whose foot [is] standing on a rolling stone,
And mind more mutable than fickle winds?
Why wail I, then, where's hope of no redress?
O yes, complaining makes my grief seem less.
My late ambition hath bestained my faith;
My breach of faith occasioned bloody wars;
Those bloody wars have spent my treasure;
And with my treasure my people's blood;
And with their blood, my joy and best beloved,
My best beloved, my sweet and only son.
O, wherefore went I not to war myself?
The cause was mine; I might have died for both.
My years were mellow, his but young and green,
My death were natural, but his was forced.

---

* He who lies on the ground cannot fall. Fortune has consumed her strength to harm me. Nothing is left to hurt worse.

ALEXANDRO: No doubt, my liege, but still the prince survives.

VICEROY: Survives! Ay, where?

ALEXANDRO: In Spain, a prisoner by mischance of war.

VICEROY: Then they have slain him for his father's fault.

ALEXANDRO: That were a breach to common law of arms.

VICEROY: They reck no laws that meditate revenge.

ALEXANDRO: His ransom's worth will stay from foul revenge.

VICEROY: No; if he lived, the news would soon be here.

ALEXANDRO: Nay, evil news fly faster still than good.

VICEROY: Tell me no more of news, for he is dead.

VILLUPPO: My sovereign, pardon the author of ill news,
   And I'll display the fortune of thy son.

VICEROY: Speak on, I'll guerdon thee, whate'er it be.
   Mine ear is ready to receive ill news;
   My heart grown hard 'gainst mischief's battery.
   Stand up, I say, and tell thy tale at large.

VILLUPPO: Then hear that truth which these mine eyes have seen.
   When both the armies were in battle joined,
   Don Balthazar, amidst the thickest troops,
   To win renown did wondrous feats of arms.
   Amongst the rest, I saw him, hand to hand,
   In single fight with their lord-general;
   Till Alexandro, that here counterfeits
   Under the color of a duteous friend,
   Discharged his pistol at the prince's back
   As though he would have slain their general;
   But therewithal Don Balthazar fell down;
   And when he fell, then we began to fly:
   But, had he lived, the day had sure been ours.

ALEXANDRO: O wicked forgery! O traitorous miscreant!

VICEROY: Hold thou thy peace! But now, Villuppo, say,
    Where then became the carcass of my son?

VILLUPPO: I saw them drag it to the Spanish tents.

VICEROY: Ay, ay, my nightly dreams have told me this.—
    Thou false, unkind, unthankful, traitorous beast,
    Wherein had Balthazar offended thee,
    That thou shouldst thus betray him to our foes?
    Was't Spanish gold that bleared so thine eyes
    That thou couldst see no part of our deserts?
    Perchance, because thou art Terceira's lord,
    Thou hadst some hope to wear this diadem,
    If first my son and then myself were slain;
    But thy ambitious thought shall break thy neck.
    Ay, this was it that made thee spill his blood;
    (Takes the crown and puts it on again)
    But I'll now wear it till thy blood be spilt.

ALEXANDRO: Vouchsafe, dread sovereign, to hear me speak.

VICEROY: Away with him! His sight is second Hell.
    Keep him till we determine of his death:
    If Balthazar be dead, he shall not live.
    Villuppo, follow us for thy reward.   *(Exit* VICEROY*)*

VILLUPPO: Thus have I with an envious, forged tale
    Deceived the king, betrayed mine enemy,
    And hope for guerdon of my villainy.   *(Exit.)*

Scene Three

Spain: the palace. Enter HORATIO *and* BEL-IMPERIA.

BEL-IMPERIA: Signior Horatio, this is the place and hour,
    Wherein I must entreat thee to relate
    The circumstance of Don Andrea's death,

Who, living, was my garland's sweetest flower,
And in his death hath buried my delights.

HORATIO: For love of him and service to yourself,
  I shan't refuse this heavy doleful charge;
  Yet tears and sighs, I fear, will hinder me.
  When both our armies were enjoined in fight,
  Your worthy chevalier amidst the thickest,
  For glorious cause still aiming at the fairest,
  Was at the last by young Don Balthazar
  Encountered hand to hand. Their fight was long,
  Their hearts were great, their clamors menacing,
  Their strength alike, their strokes both dangerous.
  But wrathful Nemesis, that wicked power,
  Envying at Andrea's praise and worth,
  Cut short his life to end his praise and worth.
  She, she herself, disguised in armor's mask,
  As Pallas was before proud Pergamus,
  Brought in a fresh supply of halberdiers,
  Which 'bowelled his horse, and knocked him to the ground.
  Then young Don Balthazar with ruthless rage,
  Taking advantage of his foe's distress,
  Did finish what his halberdiers begun,
  And left not, till Andrea's life was done.
  Then, though too late, incensed with just remorse,
  I with my band set forth against the prince,
  And brought him prisoner from his halberdiers.

BEL-IMPERIA: Would thou hadst slain him that so slew my love!
  But then was Don Andrea's carcass lost?

HORATIO: No, that was it for which I chiefly strove,
  Nor stepped I back till I recovered him.
  I took him up, and wound him in mine arms;
  And wielding him unto my private tent,
  There laid him down, and dewed him with my tears,
  And sighed and sorrowed as became a friend.
  But neither friendly sorrow, sighs nor tears
  Could win pale Death from his usurped right.
  Yet this I did, and less I could not do:
  I saw him honored with due funeral.

This scarf I plucked from off his lifeless arm,
And wear it in remembrance of my friend.

BEL-IMPERIA: I know the scarf; would he had kept it still!
For had he lived, he would have kept it still,
And worn it for his Bel-imperia's sake;
For 't was my favor at his last depart.
But now wear thou it both for him and me;
For after him thou hast deserved it best.
But for thy kindness in his life and death,
Be sure, while Bel-imperia's life endures,
She will be Don Horatio's thankful friend.

HORATIO: And, madam, Don Horatio will not slack
Humbly to serve fair Bel-imperia.
But now, if your good liking stand thereto,
I'll crave your pardon to go seek the prince;
For so the duke, your father, gave me charge.

BEL-IMPERIA: Ay, go, Horatio, leave me here alone;
For solitude best fits my cheerless mood.
(*Exit* HORATIO)
Yet what avails to wail Andrea's death,
From whence Horatio proves my second love?
Had he not loved Andrea as he did,
He could not sit in Bel-imperia's thoughts.
But how can love find harbor in my breast
Till I revenge the death of my beloved?
Yes, second love shall further my revenge!
I'll love Horatio, my Andrea's friend,
The more to spite the prince that wrought his end;
And where Don Balthazar, that slew my love,
Himself now pleads for favor at my hands,
He shall, in rigor of my just disdain,
Reap long repentance for his murderous deed.
For what was't else but murderous cowardice,
So many to oppress one valiant knight,
Without respect of honor in the fight?
And here he comes that murdered my delight.

(*Enter* LORENZO *and* BALTHAZAR)

LORENZO: Sister, what means this melancholy walk?

BEL-IMPERIA: That for a while I wish no company.

LORENZO: But here the prince is come to visit you.

BEL-IMPERIA: That argues that he lives in liberty.

BALTHAZAR: No, madam, but in pleasing servitude.

BEL-IMPERIA: Your prison then, belike, is your conceit.

BALTHAZAR: Ay, by conceit my freedom is enthralled.

BEL-IMPERIA: Then with conceit enlarge yourself again.

BALTHAZAR: What, if conceit have laid my heart to gage?

BEL-IMPERIA: Pay that you borrowed, and recover it.

BALTHAZAR: I die, if it return from whence it lies.

BEL-IMPERIA: A heartless man, and live? A miracle!

BALTHAZAR: Ay, lady, love can work such miracles.

LORENZO: Tush, tush, my lord! Let go these quibbles,
And in plain terms acquaint her with your love.

BEL-IMPERIA: What boots complaint, when there's no remedy?

BALTHAZAR: Yes, to your gracious self must I complain,
In whose fair answer lies my remedy,
On whose perfection all my thoughts attend,
On whose aspect mine eyes find beauty's bower,
In whose translucent breast my heart is lodged.

BEL-IMPERIA: Alas, my lord, these are but words of course,
And but devised to drive me from this place.

(She, in going in, lets fall her glove, which HORATIO, *coming out, takes up)*

HORATIO: Madam, your glove.

BEL-IMPERIA: Thanks, good Horatio; take it for thy pains.   *(Exit)*

BALTHAZAR: Signior Horatio stooped in happy time!

HORATIO: I reaped more grace than I deserved or hoped.

LORENZO: My lord, be not dismayed for what is past:
You know that women oft are humorous.
These clouds will overblow with little wind;
Let me alone, I'll scatter them myself.
Meanwhile, let us devise to spend the time
In some delightful sports and revelling.

HORATIO: The king, my lords, is coming hither straight,
To feast the Portingal ambassador;
Things were in readiness before I came.

BALTHAZAR: Then here it fits us to attend the king,
To welcome hither our ambassador,
And learn my father and my country's health.

(Enter the Banquet, Trumpets, the KING, *and* AMBASSADOR)

KING: See, Lord Ambassador, how Spain entreats
Their prisoner Balthazar, thy viceroy's son.
We pleasure more in kindness than in wars.

AMBASSADOR: Sad is our king, and Portingale laments,
Supposing that Don Balthazar is slain.

BALTHAZAR: So am I, slain by beauty's tyranny!
You see, my Lord, how Balthazar is slain:
I frolic with the Duke of Castile's son,
Wrapped every hour in pleasures of the court,
And graced with favors of his majesty.

KING: Put off your greetings, till our feast be done;
Now come and sit with us, and taste our cheer.
(Sit to the banquet)

Sit down, young prince, you are our second guest;
Brother, sit down; and, nephew, take your place.
Signior Horatio, wait thou upon our cup,
For well thou hast deserved to be honored.
Now, lordings, fall to; Spain is Portugal,
And Portugal is Spain; we both are friends;
Tribute is paid, and we enjoy our right.
But where is old Hieronimo, our marshal?
He promised us, in honor of our guest,
To grace our banquet with some pompous jest.

(Enter HIERONIMO, *with a drum, three knights, each his scutcheon; then he fetches three kings; they take their crowns and them captive*)

Hieronimo, this masque contents mine eye,
   Although I sound not well the mystery.

HIERONIMO: The first armed knight, that hung his scutcheon up,
   (*He takes the scutcheon and gives it to the* KING)
   Was English Robert, Earl of Gloucester,
   Who, when King Stephen bore sway in Albion,
   Arrived with five and twenty thousand men
   In Portingale, and by success of war
   Enforced the king, then but a Saracen,
   To bear the yoke of the English monarchy.

KING: My lord of Portingale, by this you see
   That which may comfort both your king and you,
   And make your late discomfort seem the less.
   But say, Hieronimo, what was the next?

HIERONIMO: The second knight, that hung his scutcheon up,
   (*He doth as he did before*)
   Was Edmund Earl of Kent in Albion,
   When English Richard wore the diadem.
   He came likewise and razed Lisbon walls,
   And took the King of Portingale in fight;
   For which and other such-like service done
   He after was created Duke of York.

KING: This is another special argument,
   That Portingale may deign to bear our yoke
   When it by little England hath been yoked.
   But now, Hieronimo, what were the last?

HIERONIMO: The third and last, not least, in our account,
   (Doing as before)
   Was, as the rest, a valiant Englishman,
   Brave John of Gaunt, the Duke of Lancaster,
   As by his scutcheon plainly may appear.
   He with a puissant army came to Spain,
   And took our King of Castile prisoner.

AMBASSADOR: This is an argument for our viceroy
   That Spain may not insult for her success,
   Since English warriors likewise conquered Spain,
   And made them bow their knees to Albion.

KING: Hieronimo, I drink to thee for this device,
   Which hath pleased both the ambassador and me:
   Pledge me, Hieronimo, if thou love the king.
   (Takes the cup of HORATIO*)*
   My Lord, I fear we sit but overlong,
   Unless our dainties were more delicate;
   But welcome are you to the best we have.
   Now let us in, that you may be despatched;
   I think our council is already set.   *(Exeunt omnes.)*

Interlude

ANDREA: Come we for this from depth of underground,
   To see him feast that gave me my death's wound:
   These pleasant sights are sorrow to my soul:
   Nothing but league, and love, and banqueting?

REVENGE: Be still, Andrea; ere we go from hence,
   I'll turn their friendship into fell despite,
   Their love to mortal hate, their day to night,
   Their hope into despair, their peace to war,
   Their joys to pain, their bliss to misery.

ACT TWO

Scene One

The DUKE's *castle. Enter* LORENZO *and* BALTHAZAR.

LORENZO: My lord, though Bel-imperia seem thus coy.
　　Let reason hold you in your wonted joy,
　　In time the savage bull sustains the yoke,
　　In time all haggard hawks will stoop to lure,
　　In time small wedges cleave the hardest oak,
　　In time the flint is pierced with softest shower,
　　And she in time will fall from her disdain,
　　And rue the sufferance of your friendly pain.

BALTHAZAR: No, she is wilder, and more hard withal,
　　Than beast, or bird, or tree, or stony wall.
　　But wherefore blot I Bel-imperia's name?
　　It is my fault, not she, that merits blame.
　　My feature is not to content her sight,
　　My words are rude and work her no delight.
　　The lines I send her are but harsh and ill,
　　Such as do drop from Pan and Marsyas' quill.
　　My presents are not of sufficient cost,
　　And being worthless, all my labor's lost.
　　Yet might she love me for my valiancy:
　　Ay, but that's slandered by captivity.
　　Yet might she love me to content her sire:
　　Ay, but her reason masters his desire.
　　Yet might she love me as her brother's friend:
　　Ay, but her hopes aim at some other end.
　　Yet might she love me to uprear her state:
　　Ay, but perhaps she hopes some nobler mate.
　　Yet might she love me as her beauty's thrall:
　　Ay, but I fear she cannot love at all.

LORENZO: My lord, for my sake leave these ecstasies,
　　And doubt not but we'll find some remedy.
　　Some cause there is that lets you not be loved;

First that must needs be known, and then removed.
What, if my sister love some other knight?

BALTHAZAR: My summer's day will turn to winter's night.

LORENZO: I have already found a stratagem
  To sound the bottom of this doubtful theme.
  My lord, for once you shall be ruled by me;
  Hinder me not, whate'er you hear or see.
  By force or fair means will I cast about
  To find the truth of all this question out.
  Ho, Pedringano!

PEDRINGANO: *Signior!*

LORENZO: *Vien qui presto.*

(*Enter* PEDRINGANO)

PEDRINGANO: Hath your lordship any service to command me?

LORENZO: Ay, Pedringano, service of import;
  And, not to spend the time in trifling words,
  Thus stands the case: it is not long, thou knowst,
  Since I did shield thee from my father's wrath,
  For thy conveyance in Andrea's love,
  For which thou wert adjudged to punishment.
  I stood betwixt thee and thy punishment,
  And since, thou knowst how I have favored thee.
  Now to these favors will I add reward,
  Not with fair words, but store of golden coin,
  And lands and living joined with dignities,
  If thou but satisfy my just demand.
  Tell truth, and have me for thy lasting friend.

PEDRINGANO: Whate'er it be your lordship shall demand,
  My bounden duty bids me tell the truth,
  In case it lie in me to tell the truth.

LORENZO: Then, Pedringano, this is my demand:
  Whom loves my sister Bel-imperia?

For she reposeth all her trust in thee.
Speak, man, and gain both friendship and reward.
I mean, whom loves she in Andrea's place?

PEDRINGANO: Alas, my lord, since Don Andrea's death
I have no credit with her as before,
And therefore know not, if she love or no.

LORENZO: Nay, if thou dally, then I am thy foe,
(*Draws his sword*)
And fear shall force what friendship cannot win.
Thy death shall bury what thy life conceals;
Thou diest for more esteeming her than me.

PEDRINGANO: O, stay, my lord!

LORENZO: Yet speak the truth and I will guerdon thee,
And shield thee from whatever can ensue,
And will conceal whate'er proceeds from thee.
But if thou dally once again, thou diest.

PEDRINGANO: If madam Bel-imperia be in love—

LORENZO: What, villain! If's and and's?   (*Offers to kill him*)

PEDRINGANO: O, stay, my lord! She loves Horatio.

(BALTHAZAR *starts back*)

LORENZO: What, Don Horatio, our knight marshal's son?

PEDRINGANO: Even him, my lord.

LORENZO: Now say but how know'st thou he is her love,
And thou shalt find me kind and liberal.
Stand up, I say, and fearless tell the truth.

PEDRINGANO: She sent him letters, which myself perused,
Full-fraught with lines and arguments of love,
Preferring him before Prince Balthazar.

LORENZO: Swear on this cross* that what thou sayst is true,
    And that thou wilt conceal what thou hast told.

PEDRINGANO: I swear to both, by him that made us all.

LORENZO: In hope thine oath is true, here's thy reward;
    But if I prove thee perjured and unjust,
    This very sword whereon thou tookst thine oath
    Shall be the worker of thy tragedy.

PEDRINGANO: What I have said is true, and shall—for me—
    Be still concealed from Bel-imperia.
    Besides, your honor's liberality
    Deserves my duteous service, even till death.

LORENZO: Let this be all that thou shalt do for me:
    Be watchful when and where these lovers meet,
    And give me notice in some secret sort.

PEDRINGANO: I will, my lord.

LORENZO: Then shalt thou find that I am liberal.
    Thou knowst that I can more advance thy state
    Than she; be therefore wise and fail me not.
    Go and attend her, as thy custom is,
    Lest absence make her think thou dost amiss.   (*Exit* PEDRINGANO)
    Why so, *tam armis quam ingenio*:
    Where words prevail not, violence prevails;
    But gold doth more than either of them both.
    How likes Prince Balthazar this stratagem?

BALTHAZAR: Both well and ill; it makes me glad and sad:
    Glad, that I know the hinderer of my love;
    Sad, that I fear she hates me whom I love;
    Glad, that I know on whom to be revenged;
    Sad, that she'll fly me, if I take revenge.
    Yet must I take revenge, or die myself,
    For love resisted grows impatient.
    I think Horatio be my destined plague:

---

* The cross made by his sword's blade and hilt.

First, in his hand he brandished a sword,
And with that sword he fiercely waged war,
And in that war he gave me dangerous wounds,
And by those wounds he forced me to yield,
And by my yielding I became his slave.
Now in his mouth he carries pleasing words,
Which pleasing words do harbor sweet conceits,
Which sweet conceits are limed with sly deceits,
Which sly deceits smooth Bel-imperia's ears,
And through her ears dive down into her heart,
And in her heart set him, where I should stand.
Thus hath he ta'en my body by his force,
And now by sleight would captivate my soul;
But in his fall I'll tempt the destinies,
And either lose my life, or win my love.

LORENZO: Let's go, my lord; your staying stays revenge.
Do you but follow me, and gain your love:
Her favor must be won by his remove.   *(Exeunt.)*

Scene Two

The DUKE's *castle. Enter* HORATIO *and* BEL-IMPERIA.

HORATIO: Now, madam, since by favor of your love
Our hidden smoke is turned to open flame,
And that with looks and words we feed our thought
(Two chief contents, where more cannot be had);
Thus, in the midst of love's fair blandishments,
Why show you sign of inward languishments.

(PEDRINGANO *showeth all to the* PRINCE *and* LORENZO, *placing them in secret*)

BEL-IMPERIA: My heart, sweet friend, is like a ship at sea:
She wisheth port, where, riding all at ease,
She may repair what stormy times have worn,
And leaning on the shore, may sing with joy
That pleasure follows pain, and bliss annoy.
Possession of thy love is the only port,
Wherein my heart, with fears and hopes long tossed,

Each hour doth wish and long to make resort,
There to repair the joys that it hath lost,
And, sitting safe, to sing in Cupid's choir
That sweetest bliss is crown of love's desire.

(BALTHAZAR *and* LORENZO *above*)

BALTHAZAR: O sleep, mine eyes, see not my love profaned;
   Be deaf, my ears, hear not my discontent;
   Die, heart; another joys what thou deserv'st.

LORENZO: Watch still, mine eyes, to see this love disjoined;
   Hear still, mine ears, to hear them both lament;
   Live, heart, to joy at fond Horatio's fall.

BEL-IMPERIA: Why stands Horatio speechless all this while?

HORATIO: The less I speak, the more I meditate.

BEL-IMPERIA: But whereon dost thou chiefly meditate?

HORATIO: On dangers past, and pleasures to ensue.

BALTHAZAR: On pleasures past, and dangers to ensue.

BEL-IMPERIA: What dangers and what pleasures dost thou mean?

HORATIO: Dangers of war, and pleasures of our love.

LORENZO: Dangers of death, but pleasures none at all.

BEL-IMPERIA: Let dangers go, thy war shall be with me:
   But such a war as breaks no bond of peace.
   Speak thou fair words, I'll cross them with fair words;
   Send thou sweet looks, I'll meet them with sweet looks;
   Write loving lines, I'll answer loving lines;
   Give me a kiss, I'll countercheck thy kiss:
   Be this our warring peace or peaceful war.

HORATIO: But, gracious madam, then appoint the field,
   Where trial of this war shall first be made.

BALTHAZAR: Ambitious villain, how his boldness grows!

BEL-IMPERIA: Then be thy father's pleasant bower the field.
　　Where first we vowed a mutual amity:
　　The court were dangerous, that place is safe.
　　Our hour shall be, when Vesper 'gins to rise,
　　That summons home distressful travellers.
　　There none shall hear us but the harmless birds;
　　Haply the gentle nightingale
　　Shall carol us asleep, ere we be ware,
　　And, singing with the prickle at her breast,
　　Tell our delight and mirthful dalliance.
　　Till then each hour will seem a year and more.

HORATIO: But, honey-sweet and honorable love,
　　Return we now into your father's sight;
　　Dangerous suspicion waits on our delight.

LORENZO: Ay, danger mixed with jealous despite
　　Shall send thy soul into eternal night.   (Exeunt.)

Scene Three

The Spanish court. Enter KING OF SPAIN, PORTINGALE AMBASSADOR, DON CYP-
RIAN, *etc.*

KING: Brother of Castile, to the prince's love
　　What says your daughter Bel-imperia?

CYPRIAN: Although she coy it, as becomes her kind,
　　And yet dissemble that she loves the prince,
　　I doubt not, I, but she will stoop in time.
　　And were she froward, which she will not be,
　　Yet herein shall she follow my advice,
　　Which is to love him or forgo my love.

KING: Then, Lord Ambassador of Portingale,
　　Advise thy king to make this marriage up,
　　For strengthening of our late-confirmed league;
　　I know no better means to make us friends.

Her dowry shall be large and liberal:
Besides that she is daughter and half-heir
Unto our brother here, Don Cyprian,
And shall enjoy the moiety of his land,
I'll grace her marriage with an uncle's gift,
And this it is, in case the match go forward:
The tribute which you pay, shall be released;
And if by Balthazar she have a son,
He shall enjoy the kingdom after us.

AMBASSADOR: I'll make the motion to my sovereign liege,
And work it, if my counsel may prevail.

KING: Do so, my lord, and if he give consent,
I hope his presence here will honor us,
In celebration of the nuptial day;
And let himself determine of the time.

AMBASSADOR: Will 't please your grace command me aught beside?

KING: Commend me to the king, and so farewell.
But where's Prince Balthazar to take his leave?

AMBASSADOR: That is performed already, my good lord.

KING: Amongst the rest of what you have in charge,
The prince's ransom must not be forgot:
That's none of mine, but his that took him prisoner;
And well his forwardness deserves reward.
It was Horatio, our knight marshal's son.

AMBASSADOR: Between us there's a price already pitched,
And shall be sent with all convenient speed.

KING: Then once again farewell, my Lord.

AMBASSADOR: Farewell, my Lord of Castile, and the rest.

(*Exit*)

KING: Now, brother, you must take some little pains
　　To win fair Bel-imperia from her will.
　　Young virgins must be ruled by their friends.
　　The prince is amiable, and loves her well;
　　If she neglect him and forgo his love,
　　She both will wrong her own estate and ours.
　　Therefore, whiles I do entertain the prince
　　With greatest pleasure that our court affords,
　　Endeavor you to win your daughter's thought:
　　If she refuse, all this will come to naught.　　　　　　　　(Exeunt.)

Scene Four

HIERONIMO's garden. Enter HORATIO, BEL-IMPERIA and PEDRINGANO.

HORATIO: Now that the night begins with sable wings
　　To overcloud the brightness of the sun,
　　And that in darkness pleasures may be done:
　　Come, Bel-imperia, let us to the bower,
　　And there in safety pass a pleasant hour.

BEL-IMPERIA: I follow thee, my love, and will not back,
　　Although my fainting heart controls my soul.

HORATIO: Why, make you doubt of Pedringano's faith?

BEL-IMPERIA: No, he is as trusty as my second self.—
　　Go, Pedringano, watch without the gate,
　　And let us know if any make approach.

PEDRINGANO (aside): Instead of watching, I'll deserve more gold
　　By fetching Don Lorenzo to this match.　　　　　(Exit PEDRINGANO)

HORATIO: What means thy love?

BEL-IMPERIA:　　　　　　　　　　I know not what myself;
　　And yet my heart foretells me some mischance.

HORATIO: Sweet, say not so; fair fortune is our friend,
　　And heavens have shut up day to pleasure us.

The stars, thou seest, hold back their twinkling shine,
And Luna hides herself to pleasure us.

BEL-IMPERIA: Thou hast prevailed; I'll conquer my misdoubt,
And in thy love and counsel drown my fear.
I fear no more; love now is all my thoughts.
Why sit we not? for pleasure asketh ease.

HORATIO: The more thou sitt'st within these leafy bowers,
The more will Flora deck it with her flowers.

BEL-IMPERIA: Ay, but if Flora spy Horatio here,
Her jealous eye will think I sit too near.

HORATIO: Hark, madam, how the birds proclaim by night,
For joy that Bel-imperia sits in sight.

BEL-IMPERIA: No, Cupid counterfeits the nightingale,
To frame sweet music to Horatio's tale.

HORATIO: If Cupid sing, then Venus is not far;
Ay, thou art Venus, or some fairer star.

BEL-IMPERIA: If I be Venus, thou must needs be Mars;
And where Mars reigneth, there must needs be wars.

HORATIO: Then thus begin our wars: put forth thy hand,
That it may combat with my ruder hand.

BEL-IMPERIA: Set forth thy foot to try the push of mine.

HORATIO: But first my looks shall combat against thine.

BEL-IMPERIA: Then ward thyself: I dart this kiss at thee.

HORATIO: Thus I retort the dart thou threw'st at me.

BEL-IMPERIA: Nay, then to gain the glory of the field,
My twining arms shall yoke and make thee yield.

HORATIO: Nay, then my arms are large and strong withal:
　Thus elms by vines are compassed, till they fall.

BEL-IMPERIA: O, let me go; for in my troubled eyes
　Now mayst thou read that life in passion dies.

HORATIO: O, stay a while, and I will die with thee;
　So shalt thou yield, and yet have conquered me.

BEL-IMPERIA: Who's there? Pedringano? We are betrayed!

(*Enter* LORENZO, BALTHAZAR, SERBERINE, PEDRINGANO, *disguised*)

LORENZO: My lord, away with her, take her aside.—
　O, sir, forbear; your valor is already tried.
　Quickly despatch, my masters.　　　　(*They hang him in the arbor*)

HORATIO:　　　　　　　　　　　　What, will you murder me?

LORENZO: Ay, thus, and thus: these are the fruits of love.

(*They stab him*)

BEL-IMPERIA: O, save his life, and let me die for him!
　O, save him, brother; save him, Balthazar:
　I loved Horatio; but he loved not me.

BALTHAZAR: But Balthazar loves Bel-imperia.

LORENZO: Although his life were still ambitious, proud,
　Yet is he at the highest now he is dead.

BEL-IMPERIA: Murder! Murder! Help, Hieronimo, help!

LORENZO: Come, stop her mouth; away with her.　　　　(*Exeunt*)

(*Enter* HIERONIMO *in his shirt, etc.*)

HIERONIMO: What outcries pluck me from my naked bed,
　And chill my throbbing heart with trembling fear,
　Which never danger yet could daunt before?

Who calls Hieronimo? Speak, here I am.
I did not slumber; therefore 'twas no dream.
No, no, it was some woman cried for help,
And here within this garden did she cry,
And in this garden must I rescue her.
But stay, what murd'rous spectacle is this?
A man hanged up and all the murderers gone!
And in my bower, to lay the guilt on me!
This place was made for pleasure, not for death.
(He cuts him down)
Those garments that he wears I oft have seen—
Alas, it is Horatio, my sweet son!
O no, but he that whilom was my son!
O, was it thou that calledst me from my bed?
O speak, if any spark of life remain!
I am thy father; who hath slain my son?
What savage monster, not of human kind,
Hath here been glutted with thy harmless blood,
And left thy bloody corpse dishonored here,
For me, amidst these dark and deathful shades,
To drown thee with an ocean of my tears?
O heavens, why made you night to cover sin?
By day this deed of darkness had not been.
O earth, why didst thou not in time devour
The vile profaner of this sacred bower?
O poor Horatio, what hadst thou misdone,
To lose thy life, ere life was new begun?
O wicked butcher, whatsoe'er thou wert,
How could thou strangle virtue and desert?
Ay me most wretched, that have lost my joy.
In leesing my Horatio, my sweet boy!

(Enter ISABELLA)

ISABELLA: My husband's absence makes my heart to throb!—
    Hieronimo!

HIERONIMO: Here, Isabella, help me to lament;
    For sighs are stopped and all my tears are spent.

ISABELLA: What world of grief! My son Horatio!
  O, where's the author of this endless woe?

HIERONIMO: To know the author were some ease of grief.
  For in revenge my heart would find relief.

ISABELLA: Then is he gone? And is my son gone too?
  O, gush out, tears, fountains and floods of tears;
  Blow, sighs, and raise an everlasting storm;
  For outrage fits our cursed wretchedness.

HIERONIMO: Sweet, lovely rose, ill-pluckt before thy time.
  Fair, worthy son, not conquered, but betrayed,
  I'll kiss thee now, for words with tears are stayed.

ISABELLA: And I'll close up the glasses of his sight,
  For once these eyes were only my delight.

HIERONIMO: Seest thou this handkercher besmeared with blood?
  It shall not from me, till I take revenge.
  Seest thou those wounds that yet are bleeding fresh?
  I'll not entomb them, till I have revenged.
  Then will I joy amidst my discontent;
  Till then my sorrow never shall be spent.

ISABELLA: The heavens are just; murder cannot be hid:
  Time is the author both of truth and right,
  And time will bring this treachery to light.

HIERONIMO: Meanwhile, good Isabella, cease thy plaints,
  Or, at the least, dissemble them awhile;
  So shall we sooner find the treason out,
  And learn by whom all this was brought out.
  Come, Isabel, now let us take him up,
  And bear him in from out this cursèd place.
  I'll say his dirge; singing fits not this case.
  O aliquis mihi quas pulchrum ver educat herbas,
  (HIERONIMO *sets his breast unto his sword*)
  Misceat, et nostro detur medicina dolori;
  Aut, si qui faciunt annorum oblivia, succos
  Praebeat; ipse metam magnum quaecunque per orbem

Gramina Sol *pulchras effert in luminis oras;*
Ipse bibam quicquid meditatur saga veneni,
Quicquid et herbarum vi caeca nenia nectit:
Omnia perpetiar, lethum quoque, dum semel omnis
Noster in extincto moriatur pectore sensus.
Ergo tuos oculos nunquam, mea vita, videbo,
Et tua perpetuus sepelivit lumina somnus?
Emoriar tecum: sic, juvat ire sub umbras.
At tamen absistam properato cedere letho,
Ne mortem vindicta tuam tam nulla sequatur. *

(Here he throws it from him and bears the body away.)

Interlude

ANDREA: Broughtst thou me hither to increase my pain?
I looked that Balthazar should have been slain;
But 'tis my friend Horatio that is slain,
And they abuse fair Bel-imperia,
On whom I doted more than all the world,
Because she loved me more than all the world.

REVENGE: Thou talkst of harvest, when the corn is green:
The end is crown of every work well done;
The sickle comes not, till the corn be ripe.
Be still; and ere I lead thee from this place,
I'll show thee Balthazar in heavy case.

---

* *Freely translated:* O let someone make me the herbs produced by Spring, and medicate our grief, or offer potions to help us forget. Let me reap the plants the sun brings forth and drink the poison that the Seer concocts of herbs and arcane power. I will endure all things, even death, provided this pain perishes in a heart already dead. Shall I never see your eyes again? Then let me die with you. Yet I must survive, lest no vengeance pursue your murder.

ACT THREE

Scene One

The Portuguese court. Enter VICEROY OF PORTINGALE, NOBLES, VILLUPPO.

VICEROY: Infortunate condition of kings,
    Seated amidst so many helpless doubts!
    First we are placed upon extremest height,
    And oft supplanted with exceeding hate,
    But ever subject to the wheel of chance;
    And at our highest never joy we so
    As we both doubt and dread our overthrow.
    So striveth not the waves with sundry winds
    As Fortune toileth in the affairs of kings,
    That would be feared, yet fear to be beloved,
    Sith fear or love to kings is flattery.
    For instance, lordings, look upon your king,
    By hate deprived of his dearest son,
    The only hope of our successive line.

NOBLEMAN: I had not thought that Alexandro's heart
    Had been envenomed with such extreme hate;
    But now I see that words have several works,
    And there's no credit in the countenance.

VILLUPPO: No; for, my lord, had you beheld the craft
    That feigned love had colored in his looks,
    When he in camp consorted Balthazar,
    Far more inconstant had you thought the sun,
    That hourly coasts the center of the earth,
    Than Alexandro's purpose to the prince.

VICEROY: No more, Villuppo, thou hast said enough,
    And with thy words thou slayst our wounded thoughts.
    Nor shall I longer dally with the world,
    Procrastinating Alexandro's death.
    Go some of you, and fetch the traitor forth,
    That, as he is condemned, he may die.

(Enter ALEXANDRO *with a* NOBLEMAN *and halberds)*

NOBLEMAN: In such extremes will nought but patience serve.

ALEXANDRO: But in extremes what patience shall I use?
   Nor discontents it me to leave the world,
   With whom there nothing can prevail but wrong.

NOBLEMAN: Yet hope the best.

ALEXANDRO: 'Tis heaven is my hope.
   As for the earth, it is too much infect
   To yield me hope of any of her mold.

VICEROY: Why linger ye? Bring forth that daring fiend,
   And let him die for his accursed deed.

ALEXANDRO: Not that I fear the extremity of death
   (For nobles cannot stoop to servile fear)
   Do I, O King, thus discontented live.
   But this, O this, torments my laboring soul,
   That thus I die suspected of a sin
   Whereof, as heavens have known my secret thoughts,
   So am I free from this suggestion.

VICEROY: No more, I say! To the tortures! When?
   Bind him, and burn his body in those flames,
   (They bind him to a stake)
   That shall prefigure those unquenched fires
   Of Phlegethon, prepared for his soul.

ALEXANDRO: My guiltless death will be avenged on thee,
   On thee, Villuppo, that hath maliced thus,
   Or for thy meed hast falsely me accused.

VILLUPPO: Nay, Alexandro, if thou menace me,
   I'll lend a hand to send thee to the lake
   Where those thy words shall perish with thy works,
   Injurious traitor! monstrous homicide!

(Enter AMBASSADOR*)*

AMBASSADOR: Stay, hold a while;
And here—with pardon of his majesty—
Lay hands upon Villuppo.

VICEROY: Ambassador,
What news hath urged this sudden entrance?

AMBASSADOR: Know, sovereign lord, that Balthazar doth live.

VICEROY: What sayst thou? Liveth Balthazar our son?

AMBASSADOR: Your highness' son, Lord Balthazar, doth live;
And, well entreated in the court of Spain,
Humbly commends him to your majesty.
These eyes beheld; and these my followers,
With these, the letters of the king's commends,
(Gives him letters)
Are happy witnesses of his highness' health.

(The KING *looks on the letters and proceeds)*

VICEROY: "Thy son doth live, your tribute is received;
Thy peace is made, and we are satisfied.
The rest resolve upon as things proposed
For both our honors and thy benefit."

AMBASSADOR: These are his highness' farther articles.

(He gives him more letters)

VICEROY: Accursed wretch, to intimate these ills
Against the life and reputation
Of noble Alexandro! Come, my lord, unbind him.
Let him unbind thee, that is bound to death,
To make a quital for thy discontent. *(They unbind him)*

ALEXANDRO: Dread lord, in kindness you could do no less
Upon report of such a damned fact;
But thus we see our innocence hath saved
The hopeless life which thou, Villuppo, sought
By thy suggestions to have massacred.

VICEROY: Say, false Villuppo, wherefore didst thou thus
Falsely betray Lord Alexandro's life?
Him whom thou know'st that no unkindness else
But even the slaughter of our dearest son
Could once have moved us to have misconceived.

ALEXANDRO: Say, treacherous Villuppo, tell the king:
Wherein hath Alexandro used thee ill?

VILLUPPO: Rent with remembrance of so foul a deed,
My guilty soul submits me to thy doom;
For not for Alexandro's injuries,
But for reward and hope to be preferred,
Thus have I shamelessly hazarded his life.

VICEROY: Which, villain, shall be ransomed with thy death;
And not so mild a torment as we here
Devised for him who, thou saidst, slew our son,
But with the bitt'rest torments and extremes
That may be yet invented for thine end.
(ALEXANDRO *seems to entreat*)
Entreat me not; go, take the traitor hence: (*Exit* VILLUPPO)
And, Alexandro, let us honor thee
With public notice of thy loyalty.
To end those things articulated here
By our great lord, the mighty King of Spain,
We with our council will deliberate.
Come, Alexandro, keep us company.   (*Exeunt.*)

Scene Two

Spain: Near the DUKE's *castle. Enter* HIERONIMO.

HIERONIMO: O eyes! no eyes, but fountains fraught with tears;
O life! no life, but lively form of death;
O world! no world, but mass of public wrongs,
Confused and filled with murder and misdeeds!
O sacred heavens! If this unhallowed deed,
If this inhuman and barbarous attempt,
If this incomparable murder thus

Of mine, but now no more my son,
Shall unrevealed and unrevenged pass,
How should we term your dealings to be just,
If you unjustly deal with those that in your justice trust?
The night, sad secretary to my moans,
With direful visions wake my vexed soul,
And with the wounds of my distressful son
Solicit me for notice of his death.
The ugly fiends do sally forth of Hell,
And frame my steps to unfrequented paths,
And fear my heart with fierce inflamed thoughts.
The cloudy day my discontents records,
Early begins to register my dreams,
And drive me forth to seek the murderer.
Eyes, life, world, heavens, Hell, night, and day,
See, search, shew, send some man, some mean, that may—
(A *letter falleth*)
What's here? A letter? Tush! it is not so!—
A letter written to Hieronimo!   (*Red ink*)
"For want of ink, receive this bloody writ.
Me hath my hapless brother hid from thee;
Revenge thyself on Balthazar and him:
For these were they that murdered thy son.
Hieronimo, revenge Horatio's death,
And better fare than Bel-imperia doth."
What means this unexpected miracle?
My son slain by Lorenzo and the prince!
What cause had they Horatio to malign?
Or what might move thee, Bel-imperia,
To accuse thy brother, had he been the mean?
Hieronimo, beware! Thou art betrayed,
And to entrap thy life this scheme is laid.
Advise thee therefore, be not credulous;
This is devised to endanger thee,
That thou, by this, Lorenzo shouldst accuse:
And he, for thy dishonor done, should draw
Thy life in question and thy name in hate.
Dear was the life of my beloved son,
And of his death behoves me be revenged
Then hazard not thine own, Hieronimo,
But live t' effect thy resolution.

I therefore will by circumstances try,
What I can gather to confirm this writ;
And, heark'ning near the Duke of Castile's house,
Close, if I can, with Bel-imperia,
To listen more, but nothing to bewray.
(*Enter* PEDRINGANO)
Now, Pedringano!

PEDRINGANO: Now, Hieronimo!

HIERONIMO: Where's thy lady?

PEDRINGANO: I know not; here's my lord.

(*Enter* LORENZO)

LORENZO: How now, who's this? Hieronimo?

HIERONIMO: My lord.

PEDRINGANO: He asketh for my lady Bel-imperia.

LORENZO: What to do, Hieronimo? The duke, my father, hath
    Upon some disgrace awhile removed her hence;
    But, if it be aught I may inform her of,
    Tell me, Hieronimo, and I'll let her know it.

HIERONIMO: Nay, nay, my lord, I thank you; it shall not need.
    I had a suit unto her, but too late,
    And her disgrace makes me unfortunate.

LORENZO: Why so, Hieronimo? Use me.

HIERONIMO: O no, lord, I dare not; it must not be.
    I humbly thank your lordship.

LORENZO: Why then, farewell.

HIERONIMO: My grief no heart, my thoughts no tongue can tell.   (*Exit*)

LORENZO: Come hither, Pedringano, see'st thou this?

PEDRINGANO: My lord, I see it, and suspect it too.

LORENZO: This is that damned villain Serberine
That hath, I fear, revealed Horatio's death.

PEDRINGANO: My lord, he could not, 'twas so lately done;
And since he hath not left my company.

LORENZO: Admit he have not, his condition's such,
As fear of flattering words may make him false.
I know his humor, and therewith repent
That e'er I used him in this enterprise.
But, Pedringano, to prevent the worst,
And 'cause I know thee secret as my soul,
Here, for thy further satisfaction, take thou this,
(*Gives him more gold*)
And hearken to me, thus it is devised:
This night thou must (and, prithee, so resolve),
Meet Serberine at Saint Luigi's Park—
Thou knowst 'tis here hard by behind the house—
There take thy stand, and see thou strike him sure,
For die he must, if we do mean to live.

PEDRINGANO: But how shall Serberine be there, my lord?

LORENZO: Let me alone; I'll send to him to meet
The prince and me, where thou must do this deed.

PEDRINGANO: It shall be done, my lord, it shall be done;
And I'll go arm myself to meet him there.

LORENZO: When things shall alter, as I hope they will,
Then shalt thou mount for this; thou knowst my mind.

(*Exit* PEDRINGANO. *Enter* PAGE)

PAGE: My lord?

LORENZO: Go, sirrah,
To Serberine, and bid him forthwith meet

The prince and me at Saint Luigi's Park,
Behind the house; this evening, boy!

PAGE: I go, my lord.

LORENZO: But, sirrah, let the hour be eight o'clock:
Bid him not fail.

PAGE: I fly, my lord.   *(Exit)*

LORENZO: Now to confirm the complot thou hast cast
Of all these practices, I'll spread the watch,
Upon precise commandment from the king
Strongly to guard the place where Pedringano
This night shall murder hapless Serberine.
Thus must we work that will avoid distrust;
Thus must we practise to prevent mishap,
And thus one ill another must expulse.
This sly enquiry of Hieronimo
For Bel-imperia breeds suspicion,
And this suspicion bodes a further ill.
As for myself, I know my secret fault,
And so do they; but I have dealt for them.
They that for coin their souls endangered,
To save my life, for coin shall venture theirs;
And better it's that base companions die
Than by their life to hazard our good haps.
Nor shall they live, for me to fear their faith:
I'll trust myself, myself shall be my friend;
For die they shall—
Slaves are ordained to no other end.   *(Exit.)*

Scene Three

Saint Luigi's Park. Enter PEDRINGANO *with a pistol.*

PEDRINGANO: Now, Pedringano, bid thy pistol hold,
And hold on, Fortune! Once more favor me;
Give but success to mine attempting spirit,
And let me shift for taking of mine aim.

Here is the gold: this is the gold proposed;
It is no dream that I adventure for,
But Pedringano is possessed thereof.
And he that would not strain his conscience
For him that thus his liberal purse hath stretched,
Unworthy such a favor, may he fail,
And, wishing, want when such as I prevail.
As for the fear of apprehension,
I know, if need should be, my noble lord
Will stand between me and ensuing harms;
Besides, this place is free from all suspect.
Here therefore will I stay and take my stand.

(*Enter the* WATCH)

FIRST WATCH: I wonder much to what intent it is
That we are thus expressly charged to watch.

SECOND WATCH: 'Tis by commandment in the king's own name.

THIRD WATCH: But we were never wont to watch and ward
So near the duke his brother's house before.

SECOND WATCH: Content yourself, stand close, there's somewhat in 't.

(*Enter* SERBERINE)

SERBERINE: Here, Serberine, attend and stay thy pace;
For here did Don Lorenzo's page appoint
That thou by his command shouldst meet with him.
How fit a place—if one were so disposed—
Methinks this corner is to close with one.

PEDRINGANO: Here comes the bird that I must seize upon.
Now, Pedringano, or never, play the man!

SERBERINE: I wonder that his lordship stays so long,
Or wherefore should he send for me so late?

PEDRINGANO: For this, Serberine! And thou shalt ha't.
  (Shoots)
  So, there he lies; my promise is performed.

(Enter the WATCH*)*

FIRST WATCH: Hark, gentlemen, this is a pistol shot.

SECOND WATCH: And here's one slain; stay the murderer.

PEDRINGANO: Now by the sorrows of the souls in Hell,
  (He strives with the WATCH*)*
  Who first lays hand on me, I'll be his priest.

THIRD WATCH: Sirrah, confess, and therein play the priest,
  Why hast thou thus unkindly killed the man?

PEDRINGANO: Why? Because he walked abroad so late.

THIRD WATCH: Come, sir, you had been better kept your bed,
  Than have committed this misdeed so late.

SECOND WATCH: Come, to the marshal's with the murderer!

FIRST WATCH: On to Hieronimo's! Help me here
  To bring the murdered body with us too.

PEDRINGANO: Hieronimo? Carry me before whom you will.
  Whate'er he be, I'll answer him and you;
  And do your worst, for I defy you all.   *(Exeunt.)*

Scene Four

The DUKE's *castle. Enter* LORENZO *and* BALTHAZAR.

BALTHAZAR: How now, my lord, what makes you rise so soon?

LORENZO: Fear of preventing our mishaps too late.

BALTHAZAR: What mischief is it that we not mistrust?

LORENZO: Our greatest ills we least mistrust, my Lord,
  And inexpected harms do hurt us most.

BALTHAZAR: Why, tell me, Don Lorenzo, tell me, man,
  If aught concerns our honor and your own.

LORENZO: Nor you, nor me, my lord, but both in one;
  For I suspect—and the presumption's great—
  That by those base confederates in our fault
  Touching the death of Don Horatio,
  We are betrayed to old Hieronimo.

BALTHAZAR: Betrayed, Lorenzo? Tush, it cannot be.

LORENZO: A guilty conscience, urged with the thought
  Of former evils, easily cannot err.
  I am persuaded—and dissuade me not—
  That all's revealed to Hieronimo.
  And therefore know that I have cast it thus—
  (*Enter* PAGE)
  But here's the page. How now? What news with thee?

PAGE: My lord, Serberine is slain.

BALTHAZAR: Who? Serberine, my man?

PAGE: Your highness' man, my lord.

LORENZO: Speak, page, who murdered him?

PAGE: He that is apprehended for the fact.

LORENZO: Who?

PAGE: Pedringano.

BALTHAZAR: Is Serberine slain, that loved his lord so well?
  Injurious villain, murderer of his friend!

LORENZO: Hath Pedringano murdered Serberine?
  My lord, let me entreat you to take the pains

To exasperate and hasten his revenge
With your complaints unto my lord the king.
This their dissension breeds a greater doubt.

BALTHAZAR: Assure thee, Don Lorenzo, he shall die,
   Or else his highness hardly shall deny.
   Meanwhile I'll haste the marshal-sessions,
   For die he shall for this his damned deed.   (*Exit* BALTHAZAR)

LORENZO: Why so, this fits our former policy,
   And thus experience bids the wise to deal.
   I lay the plot; he prosecutes the point.
   I set the trap; he breaks the worthless twigs,
   And sees not that wherewith the bird was limed.
   Thus hopeful men, that mean to hold their own,
   Must look like fowlers to their dearest friends.
   He runs to kill whom I have holp to catch,
   And no man knows it was my reaching scheme.
   'Tis hard to trust unto a multitude,
   Or any one, in mine opinion,
   When men themselves their secrets will reveal.
   (*Enter a* MESSENGER *with a letter*)
   Boy!

PAGE: My lord.

LORENZO: What's he?

MESSENGER: I have a letter to your lordship.

LORENZO: From whence?

MESSENGER: From Pedringano that's imprisoned.

LORENZO: So he is in prison then?

MESSENGER: Ay, my good lord.

LORENZO: What would he with us?—He writes us here,
   To stand good lord, and help him in distress.—
   Tell him I have his letters, know his mind;

And what we may, let him assure him of.
Fellow, begone; my boy shall follow thee.
(*Exit* MESSENGER)
This works like wax; yet once more try thy wits.
Boy, go, convey this purse to Pedringano;
Thou knowst the prison, closely give it him,
And be advised that none be there about.
Bid him be merry still, but secret;
And though the marshal-sessions be to-day,
Bid him not doubt of his delivery.
Tell him his pardon is already signed,
And thereon bid him boldly be resolved:
For, were he ready to be turned off—
As 'tis my will the uttermost be tried—
Thou with his pardon shalt attend him still.
Show him this box, tell him his pardon's in 't;
But open 't not, an if thou lovest thy life,
But let him wisely keep his hopes unknown.
He shall not want while Don Lorenzo lives.
Away!

. PAGE: I go, my Lord, I run.

LORENZO: But, sirrah, see that this be cleanly done.   (*Exit* PAGE)
Now stands our fortune on a tickle point,
And now or never ends Lorenzo's doubts.
One only thing is uneffected yet,
And that's to see the executioner.
But to what end? I list not trust the air
With utterance of our pretence therein,
For fear the privy whisp'ring of the wind
Convey our words amongst unfriendly ears,
That lie too open to advantages.   (*Exit.*)

Scene Five

A *street. Enter* BOY *with the box.*

BOY: My master hath forbidden me to look in this box; and, by my troth,
'tis likely, if he had not warned me, I should not have had so much
idle time; for we men's-kind in our minority are like women in their
uncertainty: that they are most forbidden, they will soonest attempt;
so I now.— By my bare honesty, here's nothing but the bare empty
box! Were it not sin against secrecy, I would say it were a piece of
gentlemanlike knavery. I must go to Pedringano and tell him his pardon is in this box; nay, I would have sworn it, had I not seen the
contrary. I cannot choose but smile to think how the villain will flout
the gallows, scorn the audience and descant on the hangman, and all
presuming of his pardon from hence. Will't not be an odd jest for me
to stand and grace every jest he makes, pointing my finger at this box,
as who would say, "Mock on, here's thy warrant." Is 't not a scurvy
jest that a man should jest himself to death? Alas! poor Pedringano, I
am in a sort sorry for thee; but if I should be hanged with thee, I
cannot weep.   *(Exit.)*

Scene Six

The court of justice. Enter HIERONIMO *and the* DEPUTY.

HIERONIMO: Thus must we toil in other men's extremes,
That know not how to remedy our own;
And do them justice, when unjustly we,
For all our wrongs, can compass no redress.
But shall I never live to see the day,
That I may come, by justice of the heavens,
To know the cause that may my cares allay?
This toils my body, this consumeth age,
That only I to all men just must be,
And neither gods nor men be just to me.

DEPUTY: Worthy Hieronimo, your office asks
A care to punish such as do transgress.

HIERONIMO: So is 't my duty to regard his death
  Who, when he lived, deserved my dearest blood.
  But come, for that we came for. Let's begin,
  For here lies that which bids me to be gone.

(*Enter* OFFICERS, BOY *and* PEDRINGANO *with a letter in his hand, bound*)

DEPUTY: Bring forth the prisoner, for the court is set.

PEDRINGANO: Gramercy, boy, but it was time to come;
  For I had written to my lord anew
  A nearer matter that concerneth him,
  For fear his lordship had forgotten me.
  But sith he hath rememb'red me so well—
  Come, come, come on, when shall we to this gear?

HIERONIMO: Stand forth, thou monster, murderer of men,
  And here, for satisfaction of the world,
  Confess thy folly, and repent thy fault;
  For there's thy place of execution.

PEDRINGANO: This is short work. Well, to your marshalship
  First I confess—nor fear I death therefore—
  I am the man, 'twas I slew Serberine.
  But, sir, then you think this shall be the place,
  Where we shall satisfy you for this gear?

DEPUTY: Ay, Pedringano.

PEDRINGANO: Now I think not so.

HIERONIMO: Peace, impudent; for thou shalt find it so;
  For blood with blood shall, while I sit as judge,
  Be satisfied, and the law discharged.
  And though myself cannot receive the like,
  Yet will I see that others have their right.
  Despatch; the fault's approved and confessed,
  And by our law he is condemned to die.

(*Enter* HANGMAN)

HANGMAN: Come on, sir, are you ready?

PEDRINGANO: To do what, my fine, officious knave?

HANGMAN: To go to this gear.

PEDRINGANO: O sir, you are too forward: thou wouldst fain furnish me with a halter, to disfurnish me of my habit. So I should go out of this gear, my raiment, into that gear, the rope. But, hangman, now I spy your knavery, I'll not change without boot, that's flat.

HANGMAN: Come, sir.

PEDRINGANO: So, then, I must up?

HANGMAN: No remedy.

PEDRINGANO: Yes, but there shall be for my coming down.

HANGMAN: Indeed, here's a remedy for that.

PEDRINGANO: How? Be turned off?

HANGMAN: Ay, truly. Come, are you ready? I pray, sir, despatch; the day goes away.

PEDRINGANO: What, do you hang by the hour? If you do, I may chance to break your old custom.

HANGMAN: Faith, you have reason; for I am like to break your young neck.

PEDRINGANO: Dost thou mock me, hangman? Pray God, I be not preserved to break your knave's pate for this.

HANGMAN: Alas, sir! You are a foot too low to reach it, and I hope you will never grow so high while I am in the office.

PEDRINGANO: Sirrah, dost see yonder boy with the box in his hand?

HANGMAN: What, he that points to it with his finger?

PEDRINGANO: Ay, that companion.

HANGMAN: I know him not; but what of him?

PEDRINGANO: Dost thou think to live till his old doublet will make thee a new truss?

HANGMAN: Ay, and many a fair year after, to truss up many an honester man than either thou or he.

PEDRINGANO: What hath he in his box, as thou think'st?

HANGMAN: Faith, I cannot tell, nor I care not greatly; methinks you should rather hearken to your soul's health.

PEDRINGANO: Why, sirrah, hangman, I take it that that is good for the body is likewise good for the soul; and it may be, in that box is balm for both.

HANGMAN: Well, thou art even the merriest piece of man's flesh that e'er groaned at my office door!

PEDRINGANO: Is your roguery become an office with a knave's name?

HANGMAN: Ay, and that shall all they witness that see you seal it with a thief's name.

PEDRINGANO: I prithee, request this good company to pray with me.

HANGMAN: Ay, marry, sir, this is a good motion. My masters, you see here's a good fellow.

PEDRINGANO: Nay, nay, now I remember me, let them alone till some other time; for now I have no great need.

HIERONIMO: I have not seen a wretch so impudent.
O monstrous times, where murder's set so light,
And where the soul, that should be shrined in heaven,

Solely delights in interdicted things,
Still wand'ring in the thorny passages,
That intercepts itself of happiness.
Murder! O bloody monster! God forbid
A fault so foul should 'scape unpunished.
Despatch, and see this execution done!
This makes me to remember thee, my son.

(*Exit* HIERONIMO)

PEDRINGANO: Nay, soft, no haste.

DEPUTY: Why, wherefore stay you? Have you hope of life?

PEDRINGANO: Why, ay!

HANGMAN: As how?

PEDRINGANO: Why, rascal, by my pardon from the king.

HANGMAN: Stand you on that? Then you shall off with this.

(*He turns him off*)

DEPUTY: So, executioner; convey him hence;
   But let his body be unburied:
   Let not the earth be choked or infect
   With that which heaven condemns, and men neglect.   *(Exeunt.)*

Scene Seven

HIERONIMO'*s house. Enter* HIERONIMO.

HIERONIMO: Where shall I run to breathe abroad my woes,
   My woes, whose weight hath wearied the earth?
   Or mine exclaims, that have surcharged the air
   With ceaseless plaints for my deceased son?
   The blust'ring winds, conspiring with my words,
   At my lament have moved the leafless trees,
   Disrobed the meadows of their flowered green,

Made mountains marsh with spring-tides of my tears,
And broken through the brazen gates of Hell.
Yet still tormented is my tortured soul
With broken sighs and restless passions,
That, winged, mount; and, hovering in the air,
Beat at the windows of the brightest heavens,
Soliciting for justice and revenge.
But they are placed in those empyreal heights,
Where, countermured with walls of diamond,
I find the place impregnable; and they
Resist my woes, and give my words no way.

(Enter HANGMAN *with a letter)*

HANGMAN: O lord, sir! God bless you, sir! The man, sir,
   Petergade, sir, he that was so full of merry conceits—

HIERONIMO: Well, what of him?

HANGMAN: O lord, sir, he went the wrong way; the fellow had a fair
   commission to the contrary. Sir, here is his passport; I pray, you, sir,
   we have done him wrong.

HIERONIMO: I warrant thee; give it me.

HANGMAN: You will stand between the gallows and me?

HIERONIMO: Ay, ay.

HANGMAN: I thank your lord worship.   *(Exit* HANGMAN*)*

HIERONIMO: And yet, though somewhat nearer me concerns,
   I will, to ease the grief that I sustain,
   Take truce with sorrow while I read on this.
   "My lord, I write, as mine extremes required,
   That you would labor my delivery:
   If you neglect, my life is desperate,
   And in my death I shall reveal the troth.
   You know, my Lord, I slew him for your sake,
   And was confed'rate with the prince and you;
   Won by rewards and hopeful promises,

I holp to murder Don Horatio too."
Holp he to murder mine Horatio?
And actors in th' accursed tragedy
Wast thou, Lorenzo, Balthazar and thou,
Of whom my son, my son deserved so well?
What have I heard, what have mine eyes beheld?
O sacred heavens, may it come to pass
That such a monstrous and detested deed,
So closely smothered, and so long concealed,
Shall thus by this be venged or revealed?
Now see I what I durst not then suspect,
That Bel-imperia's letter was not feigned.
Nor feigned she, though falsely they have wronged
Both her, myself, Horatio, and themselves.
Now may I make compare 'twixt hers and this,
Of every accident I ne'er could find
Till now, and now I feelingly perceive
They did what heaven unpunished would not leave.
O false Lorenzo! Are these thy flattering looks?
Is this the honor that thou didst my son?
And Balthazar—bane to thy soul and me!—
Was this the ransom he reserved thee for?
Woe to the cause of these constrained wars!
Woe to thy baseness and captivity,
Woe to thy birth, thy body, and thy soul,
Thy cursed father, and thy conquered self!
And banned with bitter execrations be
The day and place where he did pity thee!
But wherefore waste I mine unfruitful words,
When nought but blood will satisfy my woes?
I will go plain me to my lord the king,
And cry aloud for justice through the court,
Wearing the flints with these my withered feet;
And either purchase justice by entreats,
Or tire them all with my revenging threats.   (*Exit.*)

Scene Eight

The same. Enter ISABELLA *and her* MAID.

ISABELLA: So that you say this herb will purge the eye,
    And this, the head?
    Ah, but none of them will purge the heart!
    No, there's no medicine left for my disease,
    Nor any physic to recure the dead.   *(She runs lunatic)*
    Horatio! O, where's Horatio?

MAID: Good madam, affright not thus yourself
    With outrage for your son Horatio;
    He sleeps in quiet in the Elysian fields.

ISABELLA: Why, did I not give you gowns and goodly things,
    Bought you a whistle and a whipstalk too,
    To be revenged on their villainies?

MAID: Madam, these humors do torment my soul.

ISABELLA: My soul—poor soul, thou talkst of things
    Thou knowst not what—my soul hath silver wings,
    That mounts me up unto the highest heavens;
    To heaven? Ay, there sits my Horatio,
    Backed with a troop of fiery cherubins,
    Dancing about his newly healed wounds,
    Singing sweet hymns and chanting heavenly notes,
    Rare harmony to greet his innocence,
    That died, ay died, a mirror in our days.
    But say, where shall I find the men, the murderers,
    That slew Horatio? Whither shall I run
    To find them out that murdered my son?   *(Exeunt)*

Scene Nine

The DUKE's *castle.* BEL-IMPERIA *at a window.*

BEL-IMPERIA: What means this outrage that is offered me?
   Why am I thus sequestered from the court?
   No notice! Shall I not know the cause
   Of these my secret and suspicious ills?
   Accursed brother, unkind murderer,
   Why bend'st thou thus thy mind to martyr me?
   Hieronimo, why writ I of thy wrongs,
   Or why art thou so slack in thy revenge?
   Andrea, O Andrea! that thou saw'st
   Me for thy friend Horatio handled thus,
   And him for me thus causeless murdered!—
   Well, force perforce, I must constrain myself
   To patience, and apply me to the time,
   Till heaven, as I have hoped, shall set me free.

(Enter CHRISTOPHIL*)*

CHRISTOPHIL: Come, Madam Bel-imperia, this may not be.

(Exeunt.)

Scene Ten

A room in the castle. Enter LORENZO, BALTHAZAR *and the* PAGE.

LORENZO: Boy, talk no further; thus far things go well.
   Thou art assured that thou sawest him dead?

PAGE: Or else, my Lord, I live not.

LORENZO: That's enough.
   As for his resolution in his end,
   Leave that to him with whom he sojourns now.
   Here, take my ring and give it Christophil,
   And bid him let my sister be enlarged,

And bring him hither straight.——   (*Exit* PAGE)
This that I did was for a policy,
To smooth and keep the murder secret,
Which, as a nine-days' wonder, being o'erblown,
My gentle sister will I now enlarge.

BALTHAZAR: And time, Lorenzo; for my lord the duke,
You heard, enquired for her yesternight.

LORENZO: Why, and my Lord, I hope you heard me say
Sufficient reason why she kept away;
But that's all one. My Lord, you love her?

BALTHAZAR: Ay.

LORENZO: Then in your love beware; deal cunningly:
Salve all suspicions, only back me up;
And if she try to come on terms with us—
As for her sweetheart and concealment so—
Jest with her gently; under feigned jest
Are things concealed that else would breed unrest.
But here she comes.
(*Enter* BEL-IMPERIA)
                    Now, sister,——

BEL-IMPERIA: Sister? No!
Thou art no brother, but an enemy;
Else wouldst thou not have used thy sister so:
First, to affright me with thy weapons drawn,
And with extremes abuse my company;
And then to hurry me, like whirlwind's rage,
Amidst a crew of thy confederates,
And clap me up where none might come at me,
Nor I at any to reveal my wrongs.
What madding fury did possess thy wits?
Or wherein is 't that I offended thee?

LORENZO: Advise you better, Bel-imperia,
For I have done you no disparagement;
Unless, by more discretion than deserved,
I sought to save your honor and mine own.

BEL-IMPERIA: Mine honor? Why, Lorenzo, wherein is 't
  That I neglect my reputation so,
  As you, or any, need to rescue it?

LORENZO: His highness and my father were resolved
  To come confer with old Hieronimo
  Concerning certain matters of estate
  That by the viceroy was determined.

BEL-IMPERIA: And wherein was mine honor touched in that?

BALTHAZAR: Have patience, Bel-imperia; hear the rest.

LORENZO: Me, next in sight, as messenger they sent
  To give him notice that they were so nigh:
  Now when I came, consorted with the prince,
  And unexpected in an arbor there
  Found Bel-imperia with Horatio—

BEL-IMPERIA: How then?

LORENZO: Why, then, remembering that old disgrace,
  Which you for Don Andrea had endured,
  And now were likely longer to sustain,
  By being found so meanly accompanied,
  Thought rather—for I knew no readier mean—
  To thrust Horatio forth my father's way.

BALTHAZAR: And carry you obscurely somewhere else,
  Lest that his highness should have found you there.

BEL-IMPERIA: Even so, my lord? And you are witness
  That this is true which he entreateth of?
  You, gentle brother, forged this for my sake,
  And you, my Lord, were made his instrument?
  A work of worth, worthy the noting too!
  But what's the cause that you concealed me since?

LORENZO: Your melancholy, sister, since the news
  Of your first favorite Don Andrea's death,
  My father's old wrath hath exasperate.

BALTHAZAR: And better was 't for you, being in disgrace,
To absent yourself, and give his fury place.

BEL-IMPERIA: But why had I no notice of his ire?

LORENZO: That were to add more fuel to your fire,
Who burnt like Aetna for Andrea's loss.

BEL-IMPERIA: Hath not my father then enquired for me?

LORENZO: Sister, he hath, and thus excused I thee.
(He whispereth in her ear)
But Bel-imperia, see the gentle prince;
Look on thy love, behold young Balthazar,
Whose passions by thy presence are increased;
And in whose melancholy thou mayst see
Thy hate, his love; thy flight, his following thee.

BEL-IMPERIA: Brother, you are become an orator—
I know not, I, by what experience—
Too politic for me, past all compare,
Since last I saw you; but content yourself:
The prince is meditating higher things.

BALTHAZAR: 'Tis of thy beauty, then, that conquers kings;
Of those thy tresses, Ariadne's twines,
Wherewith my liberty thou hast surprised;
Of that thine ivory front, my sorrow's map,
Wherein I see no haven to rest my hope.

BEL-IMPERIA: To love and fear, and both at once, my lord,
In my conceit, are things of more import
Than women's wits are to be busied with.

BALTHAZAR: 'Tis I that love.

BEL-IMPERIA: Whom?

BALTHAZAR: Bel-imperia.

BEL-IMPERIA: But I that fear.

BALTHAZAR: Whom?

BEL-IMPERIA: Bel-imperia.

LORENZO: Fear yourself?

BEL-IMPERIA: Ay, brother.

LORENZO: How?

BEL-IMPERIA: As those
   That what they love are loath and fear to lose.

BALTHAZAR: Then, fair, let Balthazar your keeper be.

BEL-IMPERIA: No, Balthazar doth fear as well as we:
   I would not swell his sore anxiety—
   All barren is the soil of treachery.*

LORENZO: Nay, and you argue things so cunningly,
   We'll go continue this discourse at court.

BALTHAZAR: Led by the loadstar of her heavenly looks,
   Wends poor oppressèd Balthazar,
   As o'er the mountains walks the wanderer,
   Incertain to effect his pilgrimage.   *(Exeunt.)*

Scene Eleven

A street. Enter TWO PORTINGALES *and* HIERONIMO *meets them.*

FIRST PORTINGALE: By your leave, sir.

HIERONIMO: Good leave have you; nay, I pray you go,
   For I'll leave you, if you can leave me so.

---

* *I would not swell . . . soil of treachery* is a free substitution for BEL-IMPERIA's original
retort:

> "*Et tremulo metui pavidum iunxere timorem—*
> *Est vanum stolidae proditionis opus.*"

SECOND PORTINGALE: Pray you, which is the next way to my lord the
    duke's?

HIERONIMO: The next way from me.

FIRST PORTINGALE: To his house, we mean.

HIERONIMO: O, hard by: 'tis yon house that you see.

SECOND PORTINGALE: You could not tell us if his son were there?

HIERONIMO: Who, my Lord Lorenzo?

FIRST PORTINGALE: Ay, sir.

(He goeth in at one door and comes out at another)

HIERONIMO: O, forbear!
    For other talk for us far fitter were.
    But if you be importunate to know
    The way to him, and where to find him out,
    Then list to me, and I'll resolve your doubt.
    There is a path upon your left-hand side
    That leadeth from a guilty conscience
    Unto a forest of distrust and fear—
    A darksome place, and dangerous to pass.
    There shall you meet with melancholy thoughts,
    Whose baleful humors if you but uphold,
    It will conduct you to despair and death;
    Whose rocky cliffs when you have once beheld,
    Within a hugy dale of lasting night,
    That, kindled with the world's iniquities,
    Doth cast up filthy and detested fumes:
    Not far from thence, where murderers have built
    A habitation for their cursed souls,
    There, in a brazen cauldron, fixed by Jove,
    In his fell wrath, upon a sulphur flame,
    Yourselves shall find Lorenzo bathing him
    In boiling lead and blood of innocents.

FIRST PORTINGALE: Ha, ha, ha!

HIERONIMO: Ha, ha, ha! Why, ha, ha, ha! Farewell, good ha, ha, ha!*(Exit)*

SECOND PORTINGALE: Doubtless this man is passing lunatic,
  Or imperfection of his age doth make him dote.
  Come, let's away to seek my lord the duke.   *(Exeunt.)*

Scene Twelve

The Spanish court. Enter HIERONIMO, *with a poniard in one hand and a rope in the other.*

HIERONIMO: Now, sir, perhaps I come and see the king;
  The king sees me, and fain would hear my suit.
  Why, is not this a strange and seld-seen thing,
  That standersby with toys should strike me mute?
  Go to, I see their shifts, and say no more.
  Hieronimo, 'tis time for thee to trudge.
  Down by the dale that flows with purple gore
  Standeth a fiery tower; there sits a judge
  Upon a seat of steel and molten brass,
  And 'twixt his teeth he holds a firebrand,
  That leads unto the lake where Hell doth stand.
  Away, Hieronimo; to him be gone;
  He'll do thee justice for Horatio's death.
  Turn down this path; thou shalt be with him straight;
  Or this, and then thou needst not take thy breath:
  This way or that way?—Soft and fair, not so!
  For if I hang or kill myself, let's know
  Who will revenge Horatio's murder then?
  No, no! fie, no! Pardon me, I'll none of that.
  (He flings away the dagger and halter)
  This way I'll take, and this way comes the king:
  (He takes them up again)
  And here I'll have a fling at him, that's flat;
  And, Balthazar, I'll be with thee to teach,
  And thee, Lorenzo! Here's the king—nay, stay;
  And here, ay here—there goes the hare away.

(Enter KING, AMBASSADOR, CASTILE *and* LORENZO)

KING: Now show, ambassador, what our viceroy saith.
   Hath he received the articles we sent?

HIERONIMO: Justice, O justice to Hieronimo.

LORENZO: Back! Seest thou not the king is busy?

HIERONIMO: O, is he so?

KING: Who is he that interrupts our business?

HIERONIMO: Not I. *(Aside)* Hieronimo, beware! Go by, go by!

AMBASSADOR: Renowned King, he hath received and read
   Thy kingly proffers, and thy promised league;
   And, as a man extremely overjoyed
   To hear his son so princely entertained,
   Whose death he had so solemnly bewailed,
   This for thy further satisfaction
   And kingly love he kindly lets thee know:
   First, for the marriage of his princely son
   With Bel-imperia, thy beloved niece,
   The news are more delightful to his soul,
   Than myrrh or incense to the offended heavens.
   In person, therefore, will he come himself,
   To see the marriage rites solemnized,
   And, in the presence of the court of Spain,
   To knit a sure inseverable band
   Of kingly love and everlasting league
   Betwixt the crowns of Spain and Portingal.
   There will he give his crown to Balthazar,
   And make a queen of Bel-imperia.

KING: Brother, how like you this our viceroy's love?

CASTILE: No doubt, my lord, it is an argument
   Of honorable care to keep his friend,
   And wondrous zeal to Balthazar his son;
   Nor am I least indebted to his grace,
   That bends his liking to my daughter thus.

AMBASSADOR: Now last, dread lord, here hath his highness sent
    (Although he send not that his son return)
    His ransom due to Don Horatio.

HIERONIMO: Horatio! Who calls Horatio?

KING: And well remembered; thank his majesty.
    Here, see it given to Horatio.

HIERONIMO: Justice, O, justice, justice, gentle king!

KING: Who is that? Hieronimo?

HIERONIMO: Justice, O, justice! O my son, my son!
    My son, whom naught can ransom or redeem!

LORENZO: Hieronimo, you are not well-advised.

HIERONIMO: Away, Lorenzo, hinder me no more;
    For thou hast made me bankrupt of my bliss.
    Give me my son! You shall not ransom him!
    Away! I'll rip the bowels of the earth,
    (He diggeth with his dagger)
    And ferry over to th' Elysian plains,
    And bring my son to show his deadly wounds.
    Stand from about me!
    I'll make a pickaxe of my poniard,
    And here surrender up my marshalship;
    For I'll go marshal up the fiends in Hell,
    To be avenged on you all for this.

KING: What means this outrage?
    Will none of you restrain his fury?

HIERONIMO: Nay, soft and fair! You shall not need to strive.
    Needs must he go that the devils drive.   *(Exit)*

KING: What accident hath happed Hieronimo?
    I have not seen him to demean him so.

LORENZO: My gracious lord, he is with extreme pride,
    Conceived of young Horatio his son
    And covetous of having to himself
    The ransom of the young prince Balthazar,
    Distract, and in a manner lunatic.

KING: Believe me, nephew, we are sorry for 't;
    This is the love that fathers bear their sons.
    But, gentle brother, go give to him this gold,
    The prince's ransom; let him have his due.
    For what he hath, Horatio shall not want;
    Haply Hieronimo hath need thereof.

LORENZO: But if he be thus helplessly distract,
    'Tis requisite his office be resigned,
    And given to one of more discretion.

KING: We shall increase his melancholy so.
    'Tis best that we see further in it first,
    Till when, ourself will exempt the place.
    And, brother, now bring in the ambassador,
    That he may be a witness of the match
    'Twixt Balthazar and Bel-imperia,
    And that we may prefix a certain time,
    Wherein the marriage shall be solemnized,
    That we may have thy lord, the viceroy, here.

AMBASSADOR: Therein your highness highly shall content
    His majesty, that longs to hear from hence.

KING: On, then, and hear you, lord ambassador—   (*Exeunt.*)

Scene Thirteen

HIERONIMO's *garden. Enter* HIERONIMO, *with a book in his hand.*

HIERONIMO: Revenging is mine!
    Ay, heaven will be revenged of every ill;
    Nor will they suffer murder unrepaid.
    Then stay, Hieronimo, attend their will:

For mortal men may not appoint their time.
Strike, and strike home, where wrong is offered thee;
For evils ills conductors be,
And death's the worst of resolution.
For he that thinks with patience to contend
To quiet life, his life shall easily end.
"If destiny thy miseries do ease,
Then hast thou health, and happy shalt thou be;
If destiny deny thee life, Hieronimo,
Yet shalt thou be assured of a tomb."
If neither, yet let this thy comfort be:
Heaven covereth him that hath no burial.
And to conclude, I will revenge his death!
But how? Not as the vulgar wits of men,
With open, but inevitable ills,
As by a secret, yet a certain mean,
Which under kindship will be cloaked best.
Wise men will take their opportunity,
Closely and safely fitting things to time.
But in extremes advantage hath no time;
And therefore all times fit not for revenge.
Thus therefore will I rest me in unrest,
Dissembling quiet in unquietness,
Not seeming that I know their villainies,
That my simplicity may make them think
That ignorantly I will let all slip;
For ignorance, I wot, and well they know,
*Remedium malorum iners est.**
Nor ought avails it me to menace them,
Who, as a wintry storm upon a plain,
Will bear me down with their nobility.
No, no, Hieronimo, thou must enjoin
Thine eyes to observation, and thy tongue
To milder speeches than thy spirit affords,
Thy heart to patience, and thy hands to rest,
Thy cap to courtesy, and thy knee to bow,
Till to revenge thou know when, where, and how.   (*A noise within*)
How now, what noise? What coil is that you keep?

---

* As a remedy, it's worthless.

(*Enter a* SERVANT)

SERVANT: Here are a group of poor petitioners
   That are importunate, and it shall please you, sir,
   That you should plead their cases to the king.

HIERONIMO: That I should plead their several actions?
   Why, let them enter, and let me see them.

(*Enter* THREE CITIZENS *and an* OLD MAN)

FIRST CITIZEN: So, I tell you this: for learning and for law,
   There is not any advocate in Spain
   That can prevail, or will take half the pain
   That he will, in pursuit of equity.

HIERONIMO: Come near, you men, that thus importune me.
   (*Aside*) Now must I bear a face of gravity;
   For thus I used, before my marshalship,
   To plead in causes as a barrister.
   Come on, sirs, what's the matter?

SECOND CITIZEN: Sir, an action.

HIERONIMO: Of battery?

FIRST CITIZEN: Mine of debt.

HIERONIMO: Give place.

SECOND CITIZEN: No, sir, mine is an action of the case.

THIRD CITIZEN: Mine an eviction notice by a lease.

HIERONIMO: Content you, sirs; are you determined
   That I should plead your several actions?

FIRST CITIZEN: Ay, sir, and here's my declaration.

SECOND CITIZEN: And here's my band.

THIRD CITIZEN: And here's my lease.

(They give him papers)

HIERONIMO: But wherefore stands yon simple man so mute,
   With mournful eyes and hands to heaven upreared?
   Come hither, father, let me know thy cause.

SENEX: O worthy sir, my cause, but slightly known,
   May move the hearts of warlike Myrmidons,
   And melt the Corsic rocks with ruthful tears.

HIERONIMO: Say, father, tell me, what's thy suit?

SENEX: No, sir, could my woes
   Give way unto my most distressful words,
   Then should I not in paper, as you see,
   With ink bewray what blood began in me.

HIERONIMO: What's here? "The humble supplication
   Of Don Bazulto for his murdered son."

SENEX: Ay, sir.

HIERONIMO: No, sir, it was my murdered son:
   O my son, my son, O my son Horatio!
   But mine, or thine, Bazulto, be content.
   Here, take my handkercher and wipe thine eyes,
   Whiles wretched I in thy mishaps may see
   The lively portrait of my dying self.
   (He draweth out a bloody napkin)
   O no, not this; Horatio, this was thine;
   And when I dyed it in thy dearest blood,
   This was a token 'twixt thy soul and me,
   That of thy death revenged I should be.
   But here, take this, and this—what, my purse?—
   Ay, this, and that, and all of them are thine;
   For all as one are our extremities.

FIRST CITIZEN: O, see the kindness of Hieronimo!

SECOND CITIZEN: This gentleness shows him a gentleman.

HIERONIMO: See, see, O see thy shame, Hieronimo!
   See here a loving father to his son!
   Behold the sorrows and the sad laments,
   That he delivereth for his son's decease!
   If love's effects so strive in lesser things,
   If love enforce such moods in meaner wits,
   If love express such power in poor estates,
   Hieronimo, as when a raging sea,
   Tossed with the wind and tide, o'erturneth then
   The upper billows, course of waves to keep,
   Whilst lesser waters labor in the deep,
   Then shamst thou not, Hieronimo, to neglect
   The sweet revenge of thy Horatio?
   Though on this earth justice will not be found,
   I'll down to Hell, and in this passion
   Knock at the dismal gates of Pluto's court,
   Getting by force, as once Alcides did,
   A troop of Furies and tormenting hags
   To torture Don Lorenzo and the rest.
   Yet lest the triple-headed porter should
   Deny my passage to the slimy strand,
   The Thracian poet thou shalt counterfeit.
   Come on, old father, be my Orpheus,
   And if thou canst no notes upon the harp,
   Then sound the burden of thy sore heart's grief,
   Till we do gain that Proserpine may grant
   Revenge on them that murdered my son.
   Then will I rent and tear them, thus and thus,
   Shivering their limbs in pieces with my teeth.

(Tears the papers)

FIRST CITIZEN: O sir, my declaration!

(Exit HIERONIMO, *and they after)*

SECOND CITIZEN: Save my bond!

(Enter HIERONIMO*)*

SECOND CITIZEN: Save my bond!

THIRD CITIZEN: Alas, my lease! It cost me ten pound
    And you, my lord, have torn the same.

HIERONIMO: That cannot be, I gave it never a wound.
    Show me one drop of blood fall from the same!
    How is it possible I should slay it then?
    Tush, no; run after, catch me if you can.

(*Exeunt all but the* OLD MAN. BAZULTO *remains till* HIERONIMO *enters again
who, staring him in the face, speaks*)

HIERONIMO: And art thou come, Horatio, from the depth,
    To ask for justice in this upper earth,
    To tell thy father thou art unrevenged,
    To wring more tears from Isabella's eyes,
    Whose lights are dimmed with overlong laments?
    Go back, my son, complain to Aeacus,
    For here's no justice; gentle boy, begone,
    For justice is exiled from earth:
    Hieronimo will bear thee company.
    The mother cries on righteous Rhadamanth
    For just revenge against the murderers.

SENEX: Alas, my lord, whence springs this troubled speech?

HIERONIMO: But let me look on my Horatio.
    Sweet boy, how art thou changed in death's black shade!
    Had Proserpine no pity on thy youth,
    But suffered thy fair crimson-colored spring
    With withered winter to be blasted thus?
    Horatio, thou art older than thy father.
    Ah, ruthless fate, that favor thus transforms!

BAZULTO: Ah, my good lord, I am not your young son.

HIERONIMO: What, not my son? Thou then a Fury art,
    Sent from the empty kingdom of black night
    To summon me to make appearance
    Before grim Minos and just Rhadamanth,

To plague Hieronimo that is remiss,
And seeks not vengeance for Horatio's death.

BAZULTO: I am a grieved man, and not a ghost,
That came for justice for my murdered son.

HIERONIMO: Ay, now I know thee, now thou namest thy son.
Thou art the lively image of my grief;
Within thy face my sorrows I may see.
Thy eyes are gummed with tears, thy cheeks are wan,
Thy forehead troubled, and thy mutt'ring lips
Murmur sad words abruptly broken off
By force of windy sighs thy spirit breathes;
And all this sorrow riseth for thy son:
And selfsame sorrow feel I for my son.
Come in, old man, thou shalt to Isabel.
Lean on my arm; I thee, thou me, shalt stay,
And thou, and I, and she will sing a song,
Three parts in one, but all of discords framed—:
Talk not of chords, but let us now be gone,
For with a cord Horatio was slain.   (*Exeunt.*)

Scene Fourteen

The Spanish court. Enter KING OF SPAIN, *the* DUKE, VICEROY *and* LORENZO,
BALTHAZAR, DON PEDRO *and* BEL-IMPERIA.)

KING: Go, brother, it is the Duke of Castile's cause;
Salute the Viceroy in our name.

CASTILE: I go.

VICEROY: Go forth, Don Pedro, for thy nephew's sake,
And greet the Duke of Castile.

PEDRO: It shall be so.

KING: And now to meet these Portuguese:
For as we now are, so sometimes were these,
Kings and commanders of the western Indies.

Welcome, brave Viceroy, to the court of Spain,
And welcome all his honorable train!
'Tis not unknown to us for why you come,
Or have so kingly crossed the seas.
Sufficeth it, in this we note the troth
And more than common love you lend to us.
So is it that mine honorable niece
(For it beseems us now that it be known)
Already is betrothed to Balthazar;
And by appointment and our condescent
Tomorrow are they to be married.
To this intent we entertain thyself,
Thy followers, their pleasure and our peace.
Speak, men of Portingal, shall it be so?
If ay, say so; if not, say flatly no.

VICEROY: Renowned King, I come not, as thou thinkst,
With doubtful followers, unresolved men,
But such as have upon thine articles
Confirmed thy motion, and contented me.
Know, sovereign, I come to solemnize
The marriage of thy beloved niece,
Fair Bel-imperia, with my Balthazar,
With thee, my son; whom sith I live to see,
Here take my crown, I give it her and thee;
And let me live a solitary life,
In ceaseless prayers,
To think how strangely heaven hath thee preserved.

KING: See, brother, see, how nature strives in him!
Come, worthy Viceroy, and accompany
Thy friend with thine extremities;
A place more private fits this princely mood.

VICEROY: Or here, or where your highness thinks it good.

(*Exeunt all but* CASTILE *and* LORENZO)

CASTILE: Nay, stay, Lorenzo, let me talk with you.
Seest thou this entertainment of these kings?

LORENZO: I do, my lord, and joy to see the same.

CASTILE: And knowst thou why this meeting is?

LORENZO: For her, my lord, whom Balthazar doth love,
And to confirm their promised marriage.

CASTILE: She is thy sister?

LORENZO: Who, Bel-imperia? Ay,
My gracious lord, and this is the day,
That I have longed so happily to see.

CASTILE: Thou wouldst be loth that any fault of thine
Should intercept her in her happiness?

LORENZO: Heavens will not let Lorenzo err so much.

CASTILE: Why then, Lorenzo, listen to my words:
It is suspected, and reported too,
That thou, Lorenzo, wrongst Hieronimo,
And in his suits towards his majesty
Still keepst him back, and seekst to cross his suit.

LORENZO: That I, my lord—?

CASTILE: I tell thee, son, myself have heard it said,
When (to my sorrow) I have been ashamed
To answer for thee, though thou art my son.
Lorenzo, knowst thou not the common love
And kindness that Hieronimo hath won
By his deserts within the court of Spain?
Or seest thou not the king my brother's care
In his behalf, and to procure his health?
Lorenzo, shouldst thou thwart his passions,
And he exclaim against thee to the king,
What honor were't in this assembly,
Or what a scandal were't among the kings
To hear Hieronimo exclaim on thee?
Tell me—and look thou tell me truly too—
Whence grows the ground of this report in court?

LORENZO: My lord, it lies not in Lorenzo's power
To stop the vulgar, liberal of their tongues.
A small advantage makes a water-breach,
And no man lives that long contenteth all.

CASTILE: Myself have seen thee busy to keep back
Him and his supplications from the king.

LORENZO: Yourself, my lord, hath seen his passions,
That ill beseemed the presence of a king;
And, for I pitied him in his distress,
I held him thence with kind and courteous words
As free from malice to Hieronimo
As to my soul, my lord.

CASTILE: Hieronimo, my son, mistakes thee then.

LORENZO: My gracious father, believe me, so he doth.
But what's a silly man, distract in mind
To think upon the murder of his son?
Alas, how easy is it for him to err!
But for his satisfaction and the world's,
'Twere good, my lord, that Hieronimo and I
Were reconciled, if he misconster me.

CASTILE: Lorenzo, thou hast said; it shall be so.
Go one of you, and call Hieronimo.

(*Enter* BALTHAZAR *and* BEL-IMPERIA)

BALTHAZAR: Come, Bel-imperia, Balthazar's content,
My sorrow's ease and sovereign of my bliss;
Sith heaven hath ordained thee to be mine,
Disperse those clouds and melancholy looks,
And clear them up with those thy sun-bright eyes,
Wherein my hope and heaven's fair beauty lies.

BEL-IMPERIA: My looks, my lord, are fitting for my love,
Which, new-begun, can show no brighter yet.

BALTHAZAR: New-kindled flames should burn as morning sun.

BEL-IMPERIA: But not too fast, lest heat and all be done.
 I see my lord my father.

BALTHAZAR: Truce, my love;
 I will go salute him.

CASTILE: Welcome, Balthazar.
 Welcome, brave prince, the pledge of Castile's peace!
 And welcome, Bel-imperia!—How now, girl?
 Why comest thou sadly to salute us thus?
 Content thyself, for I am satisfied:
 It is not now as when Andrea lived;
 We have forgotten and forgiven that,
 And thou art graced with a happier love.
 But, Balthazar, here comes Hieronimo;
 I'll have a word with him.

(*Enter* HIERONIMO *and a* SERVANT)

HIERONIMO: And where's the duke?

SERVANT: Yonder.

HIERONIMO: Even so.—
 What new device have they devised, trow?
 *Pocas palabras!** Mild as the lamb!
 Is 't I will be revenged? No, I am not the man.

CASTILE: Welcome, Hieronimo.

LORENZO: Welcome, Hieronimo.

BALTHAZAR: Welcome, Hieronimo.

HIERONIMO: My lords, I thank you for Horatio.

CASTILE: Hieronimo, the reason that I sent
 To speak with you, is this.

---

* Few words.

HIERONIMO: What so short?
  Then I'll be gone, I thank you for 't.

CASTILE: Nay, stay, Hieronimo! Go call him, son.

LORENZO: Hieronimo, my father craves a word with you.

HIERONIMO: With me, sir? Why, my lord, I thought you had done.

LORENZO: No. *(Aside)* Would he had!

CASTILE: Hieronimo, I hear
  You find yourself aggrieved at my son,
  Because you have not access unto the king;
  And say 'tis he that intercepts your suits.

HIERONIMO: Why, is not this a miserable thing, my lord?

CASTILE: Hieronimo, I hope you have no cause,
  And would be loath that one of your deserts
  Should once have reason to suspect my son,
  Considering how I think of you myself.

HIERONIMO: Your son Lorenzo! Whom, my noble lord?
  The hope of Spain, mine honorable friend?
  Grant me the combat of them, if they dare;   *(Draws out his sword)*
  I'll meet him face to face, to tell me so!
  These be the scandalous reports of such
  As love not me, and hate my lord too much.
  Should I suspect Lorenzo would prevent
  Or cross my suit, that loved my son so well?
  My lord, I am ashamed it should be said.

LORENZO: Hieronimo, I never gave you cause.

HIERONIMO: My good lord, I know you did not.

CASTILE: There then pause;
  And for the satisfaction of the world,
  Hieronimo, frequent my homely house,
  The Duke of Castile, Cyprian's ancient seat;

And when thou wilt, use me, my son, and it.
But here, before Prince Balthazar and me,
Embrace each other, and be perfect friends.

HIERONIMO: Ay, marry, my lord, and shall.
Friends, quoth he? See, I'll be friends with you all:
Especially with you, my lovely lord;
For divers causes it is fit for us
That we be friends: the world is suspicious,
And men may think what we imagine not.

BALTHAZAR: Why, this is friendly done, Hieronimo.

LORENZO: And that I hope old grudges are forgot.

HIERONIMO: What else? It were a shame it should not be so.

CASTILE: Come on, Hieronimo, at my request;
Let us entreat your company today.   (*Exeunt*)

HIERONIMO: Your lordship's to command.— Pah! keep your way:
Who caresseth too much betrays,
Or plans to betray: (*Exit.*)

Interlude

Enter GHOST *and* REVENGE.

GHOST: Awake, Erichtho! Cerberus, awake!
Solicit Pluto, gentle Proserpine!
To combat, Acheron and Erebus!
For ne'er, by Styx and Phlegethon in Hell,
O'er ferried Charon to the fiery lakes
Such fearful sights, as poor Andrea sees.
Revenge, awake!

REVENGE: Awake? For why?

GHOST: Awake, Revenge; for thou art ill-advised
To sleep away what thou art warned to watch!

REVENGE: Content thyself, and do not trouble me.

GHOST: Awake, Revenge, if love—as love hath had—
    Have yet the power or prevalence in Hell!
    Hieronimo with Lorenzo is joined in league,
    And intercepts our passage to revenge.
    Awake, Revenge, or we are woebegone!

REVENGE: Thus worldlings ground what they have dreamed upon.
    Content thyself, Andrea; though I sleep,
    Yet is my mood soliciting their souls.
    Sufficeth thee that poor Hieronimo
    Cannot forget his son Horatio.
    Nor dies Revenge, although he sleep awhile;
    For in unquiet, quietness is feigned,
    And slumb'ring is a common worldly wile.
    Behold, Andrea, for an instance, how
    Revenge hath slept, and then imagine thou,
    What 'tis to be subject to destiny.

(Enter a Dumb Show)

GHOST: Awake, Revenge; reveal this mystery.

REVENGE: The two first the nuptial torches bore
    As brightly burning as the midday's sun;
    But after them doth Hymen hie as fast,
    Clothed in sable and a saffron robe,
    And blows them out, and quencheth them with blood,
    As discontent that things continue so.

GHOST: Sufficeth me; thy meaning's understood,
    And thanks to thee and those infernal powers
    That will not tolerate a lover's woe.
    Rest thee, for I will sit to see the rest.

REVENGE: Then argue not, for thou hast thy request.   *(Exeunt.)*

ACT FOUR

Scene One

The DUKE's *castle. Enter* BEL-IMPERIA *and* HIERONIMO.

BEL-IMPERIA: Is this the love thou bearst Horatio?
    Is this the kindness that thou counterfeits?
    Are these the fruits of thine incessant tears?
    Hieronimo, are these thy passions,
    Thy protestations and thy deep laments,
    That thou wert wont to weary men withal?
    O unkind father! O deceitful world!
    With what excuses canst thou show thyself
    From this dishonor and the hate of men,
    Thus to neglect the loss and life of him
    Whom both my letters and thine own belief
    Assures thee to be causeless slaughtered?
    Hieronimo, for shame, Hieronimo,
    Be not a history to aftertimes
    Of such ingratitude unto thy son.
    Unhappy mothers of such children then!
    But monstrous fathers to forget so soon
    The death of those whom they with care and cost
    Have tendered so, thus careless should be lost.
    Myself, a stranger in respect of thee,
    So loved his life, as still I wish their deaths.
    Nor shall his death be unrevenged by me,
    Although I bear it out for fashion's sake;
    For here I swear, in sight of heaven and earth,
    Shouldst thou neglect the love thou shouldst retain,
    And give it over and devise no more,
    Myself should send their hateful souls to Hell
    That wrought his downfall with extremest death.

HIERONIMO: But may it be that Bel-imperia
    Vows such revenge as she hath deigned to say?
    Why, then I see that Heaven applies our drift,
    And all the saints do sit soliciting

For vengeance on those cursed murderers.
Madam, 'tis true, and now I find it so,
I found a letter, written in your name,
And in that letter, how Horatio died.
Pardon, O pardon, Bel-imperia,
My fear and care in not believing it;
Nor think I thoughtless think upon a mean
To let his death be unrevenged at full.
And here I vow—so you but give consent,
And will conceal my resolution—
I will ere long determine of their deaths
That causeless thus have murdered my son.

BEL-IMPERIA: Hieronimo, I will consent, conceal,
And ought that may effect for thine avail,
Join with thee to revenge Horatio's death.

HIERONIMO: On, then. Whatsoever I devise,
Let me entreat you, grace my practices,
For why the plot's already in mine head.
Here they are.

(*Enter* BALTHAZAR *and* LORENZO)

BALTHAZAR: How now, Hieronimo?
What, courting Bel-imperia?

HIERONIMO: Ay, my lord;
Such courting as, I promise you,
She hath my heart, but you, my lord, have hers.

LORENZO: But now, Hieronimo, or never,
We are to entreat your help.

HIERONIMO: My help?
Why, my good lords, assure yourselves of me;
For you have given me cause,—ay, by my faith have you!

BALTHAZAR: It pleased you, at the entertainment of the ambassador,
To grace the king so much as with a show.
Now, were your study so well furnished,

As, for the passing of the first night's sport,
To entertain my father with the like,
Or any suchlike pleasing motion,
Assure yourself, it would content them well.

HIERONIMO: Is this all?

BALTHAZAR: Ay, this is all.

HIERONIMO: Why then, I'll fit you; say no more.
    When I was young, I gave my mind
    And plied myself to fruitless poetry;
    Which though it profit the professor naught,
    Yet is it passing pleasing to the world.

LORENZO: And how for that?

HIERONIMO: Marry, my good lord, thus:
    And yet methinks, you are too quick with us—
    When in Toledo there I studied,
    It was my chance to write a tragedy,
    See here, my lords—   (He shows them a book)
    Which, long forgot, I found this other day.
    Now would your lordships favor me so much
    As but to grace me with your acting it—
    I mean each one of you to play a part—
    Assure you it will prove most passing strange,
    And wondrous plausible to that assembly.

BALTHAZAR: What, would you have us play a tragedy?

HIERONIMO: Why, Nero thought it no disparagement,
    And kings and emperors have ta'en delight
    To make experience of their wits in plays.

LORENZO: Nay, be not angry, good Hieronimo;
    The prince but asked a question.

BALTHAZAR: In faith, Hieronimo, an you be in earnest,
    I'll make one.

LORENZO: And I another.

HIERONIMO: Now, my good lord, could you entreat
  Your sister Bel-imperia to make one?
  For what's a play without a woman in it?

BEL-IMPERIA: Little entreaty shall serve me, Hieronimo;
  For I must needs be employed in your play.

HIERONIMO: Why, this is well. I tell you, lordings,
  It was determined to have been acted
  By gentlemen and scholars too,
  Such as could tell what to speak.

BALTHAZAR: And now
  It shall be played by princes and courtiers,
  Such as can tell how to speak:
  If, as it is our country manner,
  You will but let us know the argument.

HIERONIMO: That shall I roundly. The chronicles of Spain
  Record this written of a knight of Rhodes:
  He was betrothed and wedded at the length
  To one Perseda, an Italian dame,
  Whose beauty ravished all that her beheld,
  Especially the soul of Soliman,
  Who at the marriage was the chiefest guest.
  By sundry means sought Soliman to win
  Perseda's love and could not gain the same.
  Then 'gan he break his passions to a friend,
  One of his pashas, whom he held full dear.
  Her had this pasha long solicited,
  And saw she was not otherwise to be won,
  But by her husband's death, this knight of Rhodes,
  Whom presently by treachery he slew.
  She, stirred with an exceeding hate therefore,
  As cause of this slew Soliman,
  And, to escape the pasha's tyranny,
  Did stab herself; and this the tragedy.

LORENZO: O excellent!

BEL-IMPERIA: But say, Hieronimo,
  What then became of him that was the pasha?

HIERONIMO: Marry, thus: moved with remorse of his misdeeds,
  Ran to a mountaintop, and hung himself.

BALTHAZAR: But which of us is to perform that part?

HIERONIMO: O, that will I, my lords; make no doubt of it.
  I'll play the murderer, I warrant you;
  For I already have conceited that.

BALTHAZAR: And what shall I?

HIERONIMO: Great Soliman, the Turkish emperor.

LORENZO: And I?

HIERONIMO: Erastus, the knight of Rhodes.

BEL-IMPERIA: And I?

HIERONIMO: Perseda, chaste and resolute.
  And here, my lords, are several abstracts drawn,
  For each of you to note your parts,
  And act it, as occasion's offered you.
  You must provide a Turkish cap,
  A black mustachio and a falchion;   (*Gives a paper to* BALTHAZAR)
  You with a cross, like to a knight of Rhodes;
  (*Gives another to* LORENZO)
  And, madam, you must attire yourself
  (*He giveth* BEL-IMPERIA *another*)
  Like Phoebe, Flora, or the huntress Dian,
  Which to your discretion shall seem best.
  And as for me, my lords, I'll look to one,
  And, with the ransom that the viceroy sent,
  So furnish and perform this tragedy,
  As all the world shall say, Hieronimo
  Was liberal in gracing of it so.

BALTHAZAR: Hieronimo, methinks a comedy were better.

HIERONIMO: A comedy?
   Fie! comedies are fit for common wits;
   But to present a kingly troop withal,
   Give me a stately-written tragedy;
   Tragoedia cothurnata, fitting kings,
   Containing matter, and not common things.
   My lords, all this must be performed,
   As fitting for the first night's revelling.
   The Italian tragedians were so sharp of wit,
   That in one hour's meditation
   They would perform anything in action.

LORENZO: And well it may; for I have seen the like
   In Paris 'mongst the French tragedians.

HIERONIMO: In Paris? mass! And well remembered!
   There's one thing more that rests for us to do.

BALTHAZAR: What's that, Hieronimo? Forget not anything.

HIERONIMO: Each one of us
   Must act his part in unknown languages,
   That it may breed the more variety:
   As you, my lord, in Latin, I in Greek,
   You in Italian; and for because I know
   That Bel-imperia hath practiced the French,
   In courtly French shall all her phrases be.

BEL-IMPERIA: You mean to try my cunning then, Hieronimo?

BALTHAZAR: But this will be a mere confusion
   And hardly shall we all be understood.

HIERONIMO: It must be so; for the conclusion
   Shall prove the invention and all was good;
   And I myself in an oration,
   And with a strange and wondrous show besides,
   That I will have there behind a curtain,
   Assure yourself, shall make the matter known;
   And all shall be concluded in one scene,
   For there's no pleasure ta'en in tediousness.

BALTHAZAR: How like you this?

LORENZO: Why, thus my lord:
   We must resolve to soothe his humors up.

BALTHAZAR: On then, Hieronimo; farewell till soon.

HIERONIMO: You'll ply this gear?

LORENZO: I warrant you.

(*Exeunt all but* HIERONIMO)

HIERONIMO: Why so!
   Now shall I see the fall of Babylon,
   Wrought by the heavens in this confusion.
   And if the world like not this tragedy,
   Hard is the hap of old Hieronimo.   (*Exit.*)

                          Scene Two

HIERONIMO's *garden. Enter* ISABELLA *with a weapon.*

ISABELLA: Tell me no more!—O monstrous homicides!
   Since neither piety or pity moves
   The king to justice or compassion,
   I will revenge myself upon this place,
   Where thus they murdered my beloved son.
   (*She cuts down the arbor*)
   Down with these branches and these loathsome boughs
   Of this unfortunate and fatal pine!
   Down with them, Isabella; rent them up,
   And burn the roots from whence the rest is sprung!
   I will not leave a root, a stalk, a tree,
   A bough, a branch, a blossom, nor a leaf,
   No, not an herb within this garden plot,—
   Accursed complot of my misery!
   Fruitless for ever may this garden be,
   Barren the earth and blissless whosoever
   Imagines not to keep it unmanured!

An eastern wind, commixed with noisome airs,
Shall blast the plants and the young saplings;
The earth with serpents shall be pestered,
And passengers, for fear to be infect,
Shall stand aloof, and, looking at it, tell:
"There, murdered, died the son of Isabel."
Ay, here he died, and here I him embrace;
See, where his ghost solicits with his wounds
Revenge on her that should revenge his death.
Hieronimo, make haste to see thy son:
For sorrow and despair hath cited me
To hear Horatio plead with Rhadamanth.
Make haste, Hieronimo, to hold excused
Thy negligence in pursuit of their deaths
Whose hateful wrath bereaved him of his breath.
Ah, nay, thou dost delay their deaths,
Forgives the murderers of thy noble son,
And none but I bestir me—to no end!
And as I curse this tree from further fruit,
So shall my womb be cursed for his sake;
And with this weapon will I wound the breast,
The hapless breast, that gave Horatio suck.   *(She stabs herself.)*

Scene Three

The DUKE's *castle. Enter* HIERONIMO; *he knocks up the curtain. Enter the*
DUKE OF CASTILE.

CASTILE: How now, Hieronimo, where's your fellows,
     That you take all this pain?

HIERONIMO: O sir, it is for the author's credit,
     To look that all things may go well.
     But, good my lord, let me entreat your grace,
     To give the king the copy of the play:
     This is the argument of what we show.

CASTILE: I will, Hieronimo.

HIERONIMO: One thing more, my good lord.

CASTILE: What's that?

HIERONIMO: Let me entreat your grace
   That, when the train are passed into the gallery,
   You would vouchsafe to throw me down the key.

CASTILE: I will, Hieronimo.   (*Exit* CASTILE)

HIERONIMO: What, are you ready, Balthazar?
   Bring a chair and a cushion for the king.
   (*Enter* BALTHAZAR *with a chair*)
   Well done, Balthazar! Hang up the title:
   Our scene is Rhodes. What, is your beard on?

BALTHAZAR: Half on; the other is in my hand.

HIERONIMO: Despatch for shame; are you so long?
   (*Exit* BALTHAZAR)
   Bethink thyself, Hieronimo,
   Recall thy wits, recount thy former wrongs
   Thou hast received by murder of thy son,
   And lastly, not least, how Isabel,
   Once his mother and thy dearest wife,
   All woebegone for him, hath slain herself.
   Behoves thee then, Hieronimo, to be revenged!
   The plot is laid of dire revenge.
   On, then, Hieronimo, pursue revenge.
   For nothing wants but acting of revenge!   (*Exit* HIERONIMO)

Enter Spanish KING, VICEROY, *the* DUKE OF CASTILE, *and their train.*

KING: Now, Viceroy, shall we see the tragedy
   Of Soliman, the Turkish emperor,
   Performed of pleasure by your son the prince,
   My nephew Don Lorenzo and my niece.

VICEROY: Who? Bel-imperia?

KING: Ay, and Hieronimo, our marshal,
   At whose request they deign to do't themselves.
   These be our pastimes in the court of Spain.

Here, brother, you shall be the bookkeeper:
This is the argument of that they show.   *(He giveth him a book)*

(Gentlemen, this play of HIERONIMO, *in sundry languages, was thought good to be set down in English, more largely, for the easier understanding to every public reader)*

(Enter BALTHAZAR, BEL-IMPERIA *and* HIERONIMO)

BALTHAZAR: *Pasha, that Rhodes is ours, yield heavens the honor,*
   And holy Mahomet, our sacred prophet!
   And be thou graced with every excellence
   That Soliman can give, or thou desire.
   But thy desert in conquering Rhodes is less
   Than in reserving this fair Christian nymph,
   Perseda, blissful lamp of excellence,
   Whose eyes compel, like powerful adamant,
   The warlike heart of Soliman to wait.

KING: See, Viceroy, that is Balthazar, your son,
   That represents the emperor Soliman:
   How well he acts his amorous passion!

VICEROY: Ay, Bel-imperia hath taught him that.

CASTILE: That's because his mind runs all on Bel-imperia.

HIERONIMO: *Whatever joy earth yields, betide your majesty.*

BALTHAZAR: *Earth yields no joy without Perseda's love.*

HIERONIMO: *Let then Perseda on your grace attend.*

BALTHAZAR: *She shall not wait on me, but I on her:*
   Drawn by the influence of her eyes, I yield.
   But let my friend, the Rhodian knight, come forth,
   Erasto, dearer than my life to me,
   That he may see Perseda, my beloved.

(Enter ERASTO)

KING: Here comes Lorenzo: look upon the plot,
  And tell me, brother, what part plays he?

BEL-IMPERIA: *Ah, my Erasto, welcome to Perseda.*

LORENZO: *Thrice happy is Erasto that thou livest;*
  Rhodes' loss is nothing to Erasto's joy;
  Sith his Perseda lives, his life survives.

BALTHAZAR: *Ah, Pasha, here is love between Erasto*
  And fair Perseda sovereign of my soul.

HIERONIMO: *Remove Erasto, mighty Soliman,*
  And then Perseda will be quickly won.

BALTHAZAR: *Erasto is my friend; and while he lives,*
  Perseda never will remove her love.

HIERONIMO: *Let not Erasto live to grieve great Soliman.*

BALTHAZAR: *Dear is Erasto in our princely eye.*

HIERONIMO: *But if he be your rival, let him die.*

BALTHAZAR: *Why, let him die—so love commandeth me.*
  Yet grieve I that Erasto should so die.

HIERONIMO: *Erasto, Soliman saluteth thee,*
  And lets thee wit by me his highness' will,
  Which is, thou shouldst be thus employed.   (Stabs him)

BEL-IMPERIA: *Ay me!*
  Erasto! See, Soliman, Erasto's slain!

BALTHAZAR: *Yet liveth Soliman to comfort thee.*
  Fair queen of beauty, let not favor die,
  But with a gracious eye behold his grief
  That with Perseda's beauty is increased,
  If by Perseda his grief be not released.

BEL-IMPERIA: *Tyrant, desist soliciting vain suits;*
   Relentless are mine ears to thy laments,
   As thy butcher is pitiless and base,
   Which seized on my Erasto, harmless knight.
   Yet by thy power thou thinkest to command,
   And to thy power Perseda doth obey;
   But, were she able, thus she would revenge
   Thy treacheries on thee, ignoble prince: *(Stabs him)*
   And on herself she would be thus revenged.   *(Stabs herself)*

KING: Well said!—Old marshal, this was bravely done!

HIERONIMO: But Bel-imperia plays Perseda well!

VICEROY: Were this in earnest, Bel-imperia,
   You would be better to my son than so.

KING: But now what follows for Hieronimo?

HIERONIMO: Marry, this follows for Hieronimo:
   Here break we off our sundry languages,
   And thus conclude I in our vulgar tongue.
   Haply you think—but bootless are your thoughts—
   That this is fabulously counterfeit,
   And that we do as all tragedians do,
   To die today, for fashioning our scene,
   The death of Ajax or some Roman peer,
   And in a minute starting up again,
   Revive to please tomorrow's audience.
   No, princes; know I am Hieronimo,
   The hopeless father of a hapless son,
   Whose tongue is tuned to tell his latest tale,
   Not to excuse gross errors in the play.
   I see, your looks urge instance of these words;
   Behold the reason urging me to this!   *(Shows his dead son)*
   See here my show, look on this spectacle!
   Here lay my hope, and here my hope hath end;
   Here lay my heart, and here my heart was slain;
   Here lay my treasure, here my treasure lost;
   Here lay my bliss, and here my bliss bereft;
   But hope, heart, treasure, joy, and bliss,

All fled, failed, died, yea, all decayed with this.
From forth these wounds came breath that gave me life;
They murdered me that made these fatal marks.
The cause was love, whence grew this mortal hate;
The hate, Lorenzo and young Balthazar;
The love, my son to Bel-imperia.
But night, the coverer of accursed crimes,
With pitchy silence hushed these traitors' harms,
And lent them leave, for they had chosen leisure
To take advantage in my garden plot
Upon my son, my dear Horatio.
There merciless they butchered up my boy,
In black, dark night, to pale, dim, cruel death.
He shrieks; I heard—and yet, methinks, I hear—
His dismal outcry echo in the air.
With soonest speed I hasted to the noise,
Where hanging on a tree I found my son,
Throughgirt with wounds, and slaught'red as you see.
And grieved I, think you, at this spectacle?
Speak, Portuguese, whose loss resembles mine:
If thou canst weep upon thy Balthazar,
'Tis like I wailed for my Horatio.
And you, my lord, whose reconciled son
Marched in a net, and thought himself unseen,
And rated me for brainsick lunacy,
With "God amend that mad Hieronimo!"—
How can you brook our play's catastrophe?
And here behold this bloody handkercher,
Which at Horatio's death I weeping dipped
Within the river of his bleeding wounds:
It as propitious, see, I have reserved,
And never hath it left my bloody heart,
Soliciting remembrance of my vow
With these, O, these accursed murderers!
Which now performed, my heart is satisfied.
And to this end the Pasha I became
That might revenge me on Lorenzo's life,
Who therefore was appointed to the part,
And was to represent the knight of Rhodes,
That I might kill him more conveniently.
So, Viceroy, was this Balthazar, thy son,

That Soliman which Bel-imperia,
In person of Perseda, murdered;
Solely appointed to that tragic part
That she might slay him that offended her.
Poor Bel-imperia missed her part in this:
For though the story saith she should have died,
Yet I of kindness, and of care to her,
Did otherwise determine of her end;
But love of him whom they did hate too much
Did urge her resolution to be such.
And, princes, now behold Hieronimo,
Author and actor in this tragedy,
Bearing his latest fortune in his fist;
And will as resolute conclude his part,
As any of the actors gone before.
And, gentles, thus I end my play;
Urge no more words; I have no more to say.

(He runs to hang himself)

KING: O hearken, Viceroy! Hold, Hieronimo!
    Brother, my nephew and thy son are slain!

VICEROY: We are betrayed; my Balthazar is slain!
    Break ope the doors; run, save Hieronimo.
    (They break in and hold HIERONIMO*)*
    Hieronimo, do but inform the king of these events;
    Upon mine honor, thou shalt have no harm.

HIERONIMO: Viceroy, I will not trust thee with my life,
    Which I this day have offered to my son.
    Accursed wretch!
    Why stayst thou him that was resolved to die?

KING: Speak, traitor! Damned, bloody murderer, speak!
    For now I have thee, I will make thee speak.
    Why hast thou done this undeserving deed?

VICEROY: Why hast thou murdered my Balthazar?

CASTILE: Why hast thou butchered both my children thus?

HIERONIMO: O, good words!
  As dear to me was my Horatio
  As yours, or yours, or yours, my lord, to you.
  My guiltless son was by Lorenzo slain.
  And by Lorenzo and that Balthazar
  Am I at last revenged thoroughly,
  Upon whose souls may heavens be yet avenged
  With greater far than these afflictions.

CASTILE: But who were thy confederates in this?

VICEROY: That was thy daughter Bel-imperia;
  For by her hand my Balthazar was slain:
  I saw her stab him.

KING: Why speakst thou not?

HIERONIMO: What lesser liberty can kings afford
  Than harmless silence? Then afford it me.
  Sufficeth, I may not, nor I will not tell thee.

KING: Fetch forth the tortures; traitor as thou art,
  I'll make thee tell.

HIERONIMO: Indeed,
  Thou mayst torment me as his wretched son
  Hath done in murd'ring my Horatio;
  But never shalt thou force me to reveal
  The thing which I have vowed inviolate.
  And therefore, in despite of all thy threats,
  Pleased with their deaths, and eased with their revenge,
  First take my tongue, and afterwards my heart.

(He bites out his tongue)

KING: O monstrous resolution of a wretch!
  See, Viceroy, he hath bitten forth his tongue,
  Rather than to reveal what we required.

CASTILE: Yet can he write.

KING: And if in this he satisfy us not,
  We will devise th' extremest kind of death
  That ever was invented for a wretch.

(Then he make signs for a knife to mend his pen)

CASTILE: O, he would have a knife to mend his pen.
  Here and advise thee that thou write the troth.—
  Look to my brother! Save Hieronimo!

(He with a knife stabs the DUKE and himself)

KING: What age hath ever heard such monstrous deeds?
  My brother, and the whole succeeding hope
  That Spain expected after my decease!
  Go, bear his body hence, that we may mourn
  The loss of our beloved brother's death,
  That he may be entombed whate'er befall.
  I am the next, the nearest, last of all.

VICEROY: And thou, Don Pedro, do the like for us:
  Take up our hapless son, untimely slain;
  Set me with him, and he with woeful me,
  Upon the mainmast of a ship unmanned,
  And let the wind and tide haul me along
  To Scylla's barking and untamed gulf,
  Or to the loathsome pool of Acheron,
  To weep my want for my sweet Balthazar:
  Spain hath no refuge for a Portingale.

(The trumpets sound a dead march, the KING OF SPAIN mourning after his brother's body and the KING OF PORTINGAL bearing the body of his son.)

Epilogue

Enter GHOST and REVENGE

GHOST: Ay, now my hopes have end in their effects,
  When blood and sorrow finish my desires:
  Horatio murdered in his father's bower;

Vile Serberine by Pedringano slain;
False Pedringano hanged by quaint device;
Fair Isabella by herself misdone;
Prince Balthazar by Bel-imperia stabbed;
The Duke of Castile and his wicked son
Both done to death by old Hieronimo;
My Bel-imperia fallen as Dido fell,
And good Hieronimo slain by himself:
Ay, these were spectacles to please my soul!
Now will I beg at lovely Proserpine
That, by the virtue of her princely doom,
I may consort my friends in pleasing sort,
And on my foes work just and sharp revenge.
I'll lead my friend Horatio through those fields,
Where never-dying wars are still inured;
I'll lead fair Isabella to that train,
Where pity weeps, but never feeleth pain;
I'll lead my Bel-imperia to those joys,
That vestal virgins and fair queens possess;
I'll lead Hieronimo where Orpheus plays,
Adding sweet pleasure to eternal days.
But say, Revenge, for thou must help, or none,
Against the rest how shall my hate be shown?

REVENGE: This hand shall hale them down to deepest Hell,
Where none but Furies, bugs, and tortures dwell.

GHOST: Then, sweet Revenge, do this at my request:
Let me be judge, and doom them to unrest.
Let loose poor Tityus from the vulture's gripe,
And let Don Cyprian supply his room;
Place Don Lorenzo on Ixion's wheel,
And let the lover's endless pains surcease
(Juno forgets old wrath, and grants him ease);
Hang Balthazar about Chimaera's neck,
And let him there bewail his bloody love,
Repining at our joys that are above;
Let Serberine go roll the fatal stone,
And take from Sisyphus his endless moan;
False Pedringano, for his treachery,
Let him be dragged through boiling Acheron,

And there live, dying still in endless flames,
Blaspheming gods and all their holy names.

REVENGE: Then haste we down to meet thy friends and foes:
To place thy friends in ease, the rest in woes;
For here though death hath end their misery,
I'll there begin their endless tragedy.   *(Exeunt.)*

THE WITCH OF EDMONTON

Thomas Dekker

THOMAS DEKKER (1570?–1632) was born in London and, despite being sent to debtor's prison on more than one occasion, was esteemed for his sunny nature. He was the prolific author and collaborator of *The Honest Whore*, *Old Fortunatus*, *The Shoemaker's Holiday*, *The Virgin Martyr*, *Westward Ho* and other popular theatrical comedies and dramas.

The Witch of Edmonton, conjecturally first performed in 1623 (the year the First Folio of Shakespeare was published), was published in 1658. It contains an odd mixture of domestic and revenge tragedy, Shakespearean low comedy in the guise of the hobbyhorse mummers and, of course, Middletonian sorcery in the presence of the witch and a protean Devil who arguably foreshadows certain early moments of Goethe's *Faust*.

Though Dekker probably had collaborators for *The Witch of Edmonton*—John Ford and William Rowley are often proposed—the authorship of individual parts is far from certain. Ernest Rhys, in The

Mermaid edition of Dekker's plays, states that the witchcraft plot is certainly Dekker's.

The Mother Sawyer plot derives from a 1621 pamphlet by Henry Goodcole that chronicled the true story of Elizabeth Sawyer, of Islington, who was executed in 1621 for witchcraft. Its dramatic irony is remarkable. Mother Sawyer has nothing in common with Macbeth's Scottish witches. Dekker treats her with the kind of compassion that Shakespeare showed to his most problematic villain, Shylock.

DRAMATIS PERSONAE

SIR ARTHUR CLARINGTON.
OLD THORNEY, *a gentleman.*
CARTER, *a rich yeoman.*
WARBECK, ⎫
SOMERTON, ⎬ *suitors to Carter's daughters.*
FRANK, *Thorney's son.*
OLD BANKS, *a countryman.*
CUDDY BANKS, *his son.*
RATCLIFFE, ⎫
HAMLUC, ⎬ *Countrymen.*
MORRIS DANCERS.
SAWGUT, *an old fiddler.*
A Dog, *a familiar.*
A *spirit.*
Countrymen, Justice, Constable, officers, servingmen and maids.

MOTHER SAWYER, *the witch.*
ANN, *Ratcliffe's wife.*
SUSAN, ⎫
KATHERINE, ⎬ *Carter's daughters.*
WINNIFRED, *Sir Arthur's maid.*

Scene: The town and neighborhood of Edmonton; in the end of the last act, London

ACT THE FIRST

Scene One

The neighborhood of Edmonton. A room in the house of SIR ARTHUR CLAR-INGTON. *Enter* FRANK THORNEY *and* WINNIFRED, *who is with child.*

FRANK: Come, wench; why, here's a business soon dispatched:
    Thy heart I know is now at ease; thou need'st not
    Fear what the tattling gossips in their cups
    Can speak against thy fame; thy child shall know
    Whom to call dad now.

WIN: You have here discharged
    The true part of an honest man; I cannot
    Request a fuller satisfaction
    Than you have freely granted: yet methinks
    'Tis an hard case, being lawful man and wife,
    We should not live together.

FRANK: Had I failed
    In promise of my truth to thee, we must
    Have then been ever sundered; now the longest
    Of our forbearing either's company
    Is only but to gain a little time
    For our continuing thrift; that so hereafter
    The heir that shall be born may not have cause
    To curse his hour of birth, which made him feel
    The misery of beggary and want—
    Two devils that are occasions to enforce
    A shameful end. My plots aim but to keep
    My father's love.

WIN: And that will be as difficult
    To be preserved, when he shall understand
    How you are married, as it will be now,
    Should you confess it to him.

FRANK: Fathers are
    Won by degrees, not bluntly, as our masters

Or wrongèd friends are; and besides I'll use
Such dutiful and ready means, that ere
He can have notice of what's past, th' inheritance
To which I am born heir shall be assured;
That done, why, let him know it: if he like it not,
Yet he shall have no power in him left
To cross the thriving of it.

WIN: You who had
The conquest of my maiden-love may easily
Conquer the fears of my distrust. And whither
Must I be hurried?

FRANK: Prithee do not use
A word so much unsuitable to the constant
Affections of thy husband: thou shalt live
Near Waltham Abbey with thy uncle Selman;
I have acquainted him with all at large:
He'll use thee kindly; thou shalt want no pleasures
Nor any other fit supplies whatever
Thou canst in heart desire.

WIN: All these are nothing
Without your company.

FRANK: Which thou shalt have
Once every month at least.

WIN: Once every month!
Is this to have an husband?

FRANK: Perhaps oftener;
That's as occasion serves.

WIN: Ay, ay; in case
No other beauty tempt your eye, whom you
Like better, I may chance to be remembered,
And see you now and then. Faith, I did hope
You'd not have used me so: 'tis but my fortune.
And yet, if not for my sake, have some pity
Upon the child I go with, that's your own:

And 'less you'll be a cruel-hearted father,
You cannot but remember that.
Heaven knows how—

FRANK: To quit which fear at once,
As by the ceremony late performed
I plighted thee a faith as free from challenge
As any double thought; once more, in hearing
Of Heaven and thee, I vow that never henceforth
Disgrace, reproof, lawless affections, threats,
Or what can be suggested 'gainst our marriage,
Shall cause me falsify that bridal oath
That binds me thine. And, Winnifred, whenever
The wanton heat of youth, by subtle baits
Of beauty, or what woman's art can practise,
Draw me from only loving thee, let Heaven
Inflict upon my life some fearful ruin!
I hope thou dost believe me.

WIN: Swear no more;
I am confirmed, and will resolve to do
What you think most behoveful for us.

FRANK: Thus, then;
Make thyself ready; at the furthest house
Upon the green without the town, your uncle
Expects you. For a little time, farewell!

WIN: Sweet,
We shall meet again as soon as thou canst possibly?

FRANK: We shall. One kiss—away!

(*Exit* WINNIFRED. *Enter* SIR ARTHUR CLARINGTON)

SIR ARTH: Frank Thorney!

FRANK: Here, sir.

SIR ARTH: Alone? then must I tell thee in plain terms
Thou hast wronged thy master's house basely and lewdly.

FRANK: Your house, sir?

SIR ARTH: Yes, sir: if the nimble devil
  That wantoned in your blood rebelled against
  All rules of honest duty, you might, sir,
  Have found out some more fitting place than here
  To have built a stews in. All the country whispers
  How shamefully thou hast undone a maid,
  Approved for modest life, for civil carriage,
  Till thy prevailing perjuries enticed her
  To forfeit shame. Will you be honest yet,
  Make her amends and marry her?

FRANK: So, sir,
  I might bring both myself and her to beggary;
  And that would be a shame worse than the other.

SIR ARTH: You should have thought on this before, and then
  Your reason would have overswayed the passion
  Of your unruly lust. But that you may
  Be left without excuse, to salve the infamy
  Of my disgracèd house, and 'cause you are
  A gentleman, and both of you my servants,
  I'll make the maid a portion.

FRANK: So you promised me
  Before, in case I married her. I know
  Sir Arthur Clarington deserves the credit
  Report hath lent him, and presume you are
  A debtor to your promise: but upon
  What certainty shall I resolve? Excuse me
  For being somewhat rude.

SIR ARTH: It is but reason.
  Well, Frank, what think'st thou of two hundred pounds
  And a continual friend?

FRANK: Though my poor fortunes
  Might happly prefer me to a choice
  Of a far greater portion, yet, to right

A wrongèd maid and to preserve your favor,
I am content to accept your proffer.

SIR ARTH: Art thou?

FRANK: Sir, we shall every day have need to employ
The use of what you please to give.

SIR ARTH: Thou shall have 't.

FRANK: Then I claim
Your promise.—We are man and wife.

SIR ARTH: Already?

FRANK: And more than so, sir, I have promised her
Free entertainment in her uncle's house
Near Waltham Abbey, where she may securely
Sojourn, till time and my endeavours work
My father's love and liking.

SIR ARTH: Honest Frank!

FRANK: I hope, sir, you will think I cannot keep her
Without a daily charge.

SIR ARTH: As for the money,
'Tis all thine own! and though I cannot make thee
A present payment, yet thou shalt be sure
I will not fail thee.

FRANK: But our occasions—

SIR ARTH: Nay, nay,
Talk not of your occasions; trust my bounty;
It shall not sleep.—Hast married her, i'faith, Frank?
'Tis well, 'tis passing well!—then, Winnifred,
Once more thou art an honest woman. Frank,
Thou hast a jewel; love her; she'll deserve it.
And when to Waltham?

FRANK: She is making ready;
   Her uncle stays for her.

SIR ARTH: Most provident speed.
   Frank, I will be thy friend, and such a friend!—
   Thou'lt bring her thither?

FRANK: Sir, I cannot; newly
   My father sent me word I should come to him.

SIR ARTH: Marry, and do; I know thou hast a wit
   To handle him.

FRANK: I have a suit t'ye.

SIR ARTH: What is't?
   Anything, Frank; command it.

FRANK: That you'll please
   By letters to assure my father that
   I am not married.

SIR ARTH: How!

FRANK: Some one or other
   Hath certainly informed him that I purposed
   To marry Winnifred; on which he threatened
   To disinherit me:—to prevent it,
   Lowly I crave your letters, which he seeing
   Will credit; and I hope, ere I return,
   On such conditions as I'll frame, his lands
   Shall be assured.

SIR ARTH: But what is there to quit
   My knowledge of the marriage?

FRANK: Why, you were not
   A witness to it.

SIR ARTH: I conceive; and then—

His land confirmed, thou wilt acquaint him throughly
With all that's past.

FRANK: I mean no less.

SIR ARTH: Provided
I never was made privy to't.

FRANK: Alas, sir,
Am I a talker?

SIR ARTH: Draw thyself the letter,
I'll put my hand to't. I commend thy policy;
Thou'rt witty, witty, Frank; nay, nay, 'tis fit:
Dispatch it.

FRANK: I shall write effectually.   (*Exit*)

SIR ARTH: Go thy way, cuckoo—have I caught the young man?
One trouble, then, is freed. He that will feast
At other's cost must be a bold-faced guest.
(*Re-enter* WINNIFRED *in a riding suit*)
Win, I have heard the news; all now is safe;
The worst is past: thy lip, wench (*Kisses her*): I must bid
Farewell, for fashion's sake; but I will visit thee
Suddenly, girl. This was cleanly carried;
Ha! was't not, Win?

WIN: Then were my happiness,
That I in heart repent I did not bring him
The dower of a virginity. Sir, forgive me;
I have been much to blame: had not my laxness
Given way to your immoderate waste of virtue,
You had not with such eagerness pursued
The error of your goodness.

SIR ARTH: Dear, dear Win,
I hug this art of thine; it shows how cleanly
Thou canst beguile, in case occasion serve
To practise; it becomes thee: now we share
Free scope enough, without control or fear,

To interchange our pleasures; we will surfeit
In our embraces, wench. Come, tell me, when
Wilt thou appoint a meeting?

WIN: What to do?

SIR ARTH: Good, good, to con the lesson of our loves,
  Our secret game.

WIN: O, blush to speak it further!
  As you're a noble gentleman, forget
  A sin so monstrous: 'tis not gently done
  To open a cured wound: I know you speak
  For trial; 'troth, you need not.

SIR ARTH: I for trial?
  Not I, by this good sunshine!

WIN: Can you name
  That syllable of good, and yet not tremble
  To think to what a foul and black intent
  You use it for an oath? Let me resolve you:
  If you appear in any visitation
  That brings not with it pity for the wrongs
  Done to abusèd Thorney, my kind husband
  If you infect mine ear with any breath
  That is not thoroughly perfumed with sighs
  For former deeds of lust—may I be cursed
  Even in my prayers, when I vouchsafe
  To see or hear you! I will change my life
  From a loose whore to a repentant wife.

SIR ARTH: Wilt thou turn monster now? art not ashamed
  After so many months to be honest at last?
  Away, away! fie on't!

WIN: My resolution
  Is built upon a rock. This very day
  Young Thorney vowed, with oaths not to be doubted,
  That never any change of love should cancel
  The bonds in which we are to either bound

Of lasting truth: and shall I, then, for my part
Unfile the sacred oath set on record
In Heaven's book? Sir Arthur, do not study
To add to your lascivious lust the sin
Of sacrilege; for if you but endeavour
By any unchaste word to tempt my constancy
You strive as much as in you lies to ruin
A temple hallowed to the purity
Of holy marriage. I have said enough;
You may believe me.

SIR ARTH: Get you to your nunnery;
There freeze in your cold cloister: this is fine!

WIN: Good angels guide me! Sir, you'll give me leave
To weep and pray for your conversion?

SIR ARTH: Yes:
Away to Waltham! Pox on your honesty!
Had you no other trick to fool me? Well,
You may want money yet.

WIN: None that I'll send for
To you, for hire of a damnation.
When I am gone, think on my just complaint:
I was your devil; O, be you my saint!   *(Exit)*

SIR ARTH: Go, go thy ways; as changeable a baggage
As ever cozened knight: I'm glad I'm rid of her.
Honest! marry, hang her! Thorney is my debtor;
I thought to have paid him too; but fools have fortune.

(Exit.)

Scene Two

Edmonton. A room in CARTER's *house. Enter* OLD THORNEY *and* CARTER.

O. THOR: You offer, Master Carter, like a gentleman; I cannot find fault with it, 'tis so fair.

CAR: No gentleman I, Master Thorney; spare the Mastership, call me by my name, John Carter. Master is a title my father, nor his before him, were acquainted with; honest Hertfordshire yeomen; such an one am I; my word and my deed shall be proved one at all times. I mean to give you no security for the marriage money.

O. THOR: How! no security? although it need not so long as you live, yet who is he has surety of his life one hour? Men, the proverb says, are mortal; else, for my part, I distrust you not, were the sum double.

CAR: Double, treble, more or less, I tell you, Master Thorney, I'll give no security. Bonds and bills are but terriers to catch fools, and keep lazy knaves busy; my security shall be present payment. And we here about Edmonton hold present payment as sure as an alderman's bond in London, Master Thorney.

O. THOR: I cry you mercy, sir; I understood you not.

CAR: I like young Frank well, so does my Susan too; the girl has a fancy to him, which makes me ready in my purse. There be other suitors within, that make much noise to little purpose. If Frank love Sue, Sue shall have none but Frank. 'Tis a mannerly girl, Master Thorney, though but a homely man's daughter; there have worse faces looked out of black bags, man.

O. THOR: You speak your mind freely and honestly. I marvel my son comes not; I am sure he will be here some time today.

CAR: Today or tomorrow, when he comes he shall be welcome to bread, beer and beef, yeoman's fare; we have no kickshaws: full dishes, whole bellyfuls. Should I diet three days at one of the slender city-suppers, you might send me to Barber-Surgeons' hall the fourth day, to hang

up for a skeleton.—Here come they that—
(*Enter* WARBECK *with* SUSAN, SOMERTON *with* KATHERINE)
How now, girls! every day play-day with you? Valentine's day too, all
by couples? Thus will young folks do when we are laid in our graves,
Master Thorney; here's all the care they take. And how do you find
the wenches, gentlemen? Have they any mind to a loose gown and a
strait shoe? Win 'em and wear 'em; they shall choose for themselves
by my consent.

WAR: You speak like a kind father.—Sue, thou hear'st
    The liberty that's granted thee; what say'st thou?
    Wilt thou be mine?

SUS: Your what, sir? I dare swear
    Never your wife.

WAR: Canst thou be so unkind,
    Considering how dearly I affect thee,
    Nay, dote on thy perfections?

SUS: You are studied,
    Too scholar-like, in words I understand not.
    I am too coarse for such a gallant's love
    As you are.

WAR: By the honor of gentility—

SUS: Good sir, no swearing; yea and nay with us
    Prevail above all oaths you can invent.

WAR: By this white hand of thine—

SUS: Take a false oath!
    Fie, fie! flatter the wise; fools not regard it,
    And one of these am I.

WAR: Dost thou despise me?

CAR: Let 'em talk on, Master Thorney; I know Sue's mind. The fly may
    buzz about the candle, he shall but singe his wings when all's done;
    Frank, Frank is he has her heart.

SOM: But shall I live in hope, Kate?

KATH: Better so
  Than be a desperate man.

SOM: Perhaps thou think'st it is thy portion
  I level at: wert thou as poor in fortunes
  As thou art rich in goodness, I would rather
  Be suitor for the dower of thy virtues
  Than twice thy father's whole estate; and, prithee,
  Be thou resolved so.

KATH: Master Somerton,
  It is an easy labor to deceive
  A maid that will believe men's subtle promises;
  Yet I conceive of you as worthily
  As I presume you to deserve.

SOM: Which is,
  As worthily in loving thee sincerely
  As thou art worthy to be so beloved.

KATH: I shall find time to try you.

SOM: Do, Kate, do;
  And when I fail, may all my joys forsake me!

CAR: Warbeck and Sue are at it still. I laugh to myself, Master Thorney,
  to see how earnestly he beats the bush, while the bird is flown into
  another's bosom. A very unthrift, Master Thorney; one of the country
  roaring-lads: we have such as well as the city, and as arrant rake-hells
  as they are, though not so nimble at their prizes of wit. Sue knows the
  rascal to an hair's-breadth, and will fit him accordingly.

O. THOR: What is the other gentleman?

CAR: One Somerton; the honester man of the two by five pound in every
  stone-weight. A civil fellow; he has a fine convenient estate of land in
  West Ham, by Essex: Master Ranges, that dwells by Enfield, sent him
  hither. He likes Kate well; I may tell you I think she likes him as well:
  if they agree, I'll not hinder the match for my part. But that Warbeck

is such another—I use him kindly for Master Somerton's sake; for he came hither first as a companion of his: honest men, Master Thorney, may fall into knaves' company now and then.

WAR: Three hundred a year jointure, Sue.

SUS: Where lies it?
By sea or by land? I think by sea.

WAR: Do I look like a captain?

SUS: Not a whit, sir.
Should all that use the seas be reckoned captains,
There's not a ship should have a scullion in her
To keep her clean.

WAR: Do you scorn me, Mistress Susan?
Am I a subject to be jeered at?

SUS: Neither
Am I a property for you to use
As stale to your fond wanton loose discourse:
Pray, sir, be civil.

WAR: Wilt be angry, wasp?

CAR: God-a-mercy, Sue! she'll firk him, on my life, if he fumble with her.
(*Enter* FRANK)
Master Francis Thorney, you are welcome indeed; your father ex-pected your coming. How does the right worshipful knight, Sir Arthur Clarington, your master?

FRANK: In health this morning.—Sir, my duty.

O. THOR: Now
You come as I could wish.

WAR (*aside*):   Frank Thorney, ha!

SUS: You must excuse me.

FRANK: Virtuous Mistress Susan,
  Kind Mistress Katherine. *(Kisses them)*—Gentlemen, to both
  Good time o' th' day.

SOM: The like to you.

WAR: 'Tis he.
  A word, friend. *(Aside to* SOM*)* On my life, this is the man stands fair
  in crossing Susan's love to me.

SOM *(aside to* WAR*)*:   I think no less; be wise, and take no notice on't;
  He that can win her best deserves her.

WAR *(aside to* SOM*)*:   Marry
  A serving-man? mew!

SOM *(aside to* WAR*)*: Prithee, friend, no more.

CAR: Gentlemen all, there's within a slight dinner ready, if you please to
  taste of it; Master Thorney, Master Francis, Master Somerton.—
  Why, girls! what huswives! will you spend all your forenoon in tittle-
  tattles? Away! It's well, i'faith.—Will you go in, gentlemen?

O. THOR: We'll follow presently; my son and I
  Have a few words of business.

CAR: At your pleasure.

(Exeunt all but O. THOR *and* FRANK*)*

O. THOR: I think you guess the reason, Frank, for which
  I sent for you.

FRANK: Yes, sir.

O. THOR: I need not tell you
  With what a labyrinth of dangers daily
  The best part of my whole estate's encumbered;
  Nor have I any clue to wind it out
  But what occasion proffers me; wherein
  If you should falter, I shall have the shame,

And you the loss. On these two points rely
Our happiness or ruin. If you marry
With wealthy Carter's daughter, there's a portion
Will free my land; all which I will enstate,
Upon the marriage, to you: otherwise
I must be of necessity enforced
To make a present sale of all; and yet,
For aught I know, live in as poor distress,
Or worse, than now I do. You hear the sum?
I told you thus before; have you considered on't?

FRANK: I have, sir; and however I could wish
To enjoy the benefit of single freedom—
For that I find no disposition in me
To undergo the burthen of that care
That marriage brings with it—yet, to secure
And settle the continuance of your credit,
I humbly yield to be directed by you
In all commands.

O. THOR: You have already used
Such thriving protestations to the maid
That she is wholly yours; and—speak the truth—
You love her, do you not?

FRANK: 'Twere pity, sir,
I should deceive her.

O. THOR: Better you'd been unborn.
But is your love so steady that you mean,
Nay, more, desire, to make her your wife?

FRANK: Else, sir,
It were a wrong not to be righted.

O. THOR: True,
It were: and you will marry her?

FRANK: Heaven prosper it,
I do intend it.

O. THOR: O, thou art a villain!
  A devil like a man! Wherein have I
  Offended all the powers so much, to be
  Father to such a graceless, godless son?

FRANK: To me, sir, this! O, my cleft heart!

O. THOR: To thee,
  Son of my curse. Speak truth and blush, thou monster!
  Hast thou not married Winnifred, a maid
  Was fellow-servant with thee?

FRANK (aside):   Some swift spirit
  Has blown this news abroad; I must outface it.

O. THOR: D' you study for excuse? why, all the country
  Is full on't.

FRANK: With your license, 'tis not charitable,
  I'm sure it is not fatherly, so much
  To be o'erswayed with credulous conceit
  Of mere impossibilities; but fathers
  Are privileged to think and talk at pleasure.

O. THOR: Why, canst thou yet deny thou hast no wife?

FRANK: What do you take me for? An atheist?
  One that nor hopes the blessedness of life
  Hereafter, neither fears the vengeance due
  To such as make the marriage bed an inn,
  Which travelers, day and night,
  After a toilsome lodging, leave at pleasure?
  Am I become so insensible of losing
  The glory of creation's work, my soul?
  O, I have lived too long!

O. THOR: Thou hast, dissembler.
  Dar'st thou persever yet, and pull down wrath
  As hot as flames of Hell to strike thee quick
  Into the grave of horror? I believe thee not;
  Get from my sight!

FRANK: Sir, though mine innocence
Needs not a stronger witness than the clearness
Of an unperished conscience, yet for that
I was informed how mainly you had been
Possessed of this untruth—to quit all scruple,
Please you peruse this letter; 'tis to you.

O. THOR: From whom?

FRANK: Sir Arthur Clarington, my master.

O. THOR: Well, sir.   (*Reads*)

FRANK (*aside*):   On every side I am distracted;
Am waded deeper into mischief
Than virtue can avoid; but on I must:
Fate leads me; I will follow.—There you read
What may confirm you.

O THOR: Yes, and wonder at it.
Forgive me, Frank; credulity abused me.
My tears express my joy; and I am sorry
I injured innocence.

FRANK: Alas! I knew
Your rage and grief proceeded from your love
To me; so I conceived it.

'O. THOR: My good son,
I'll bear with many faults in thee hereafter;
Bear thou with mine.

FRANK: The peace is soon concluded.

(*Re-enter* CARTER *and* SUSAN)

CAR: Why, Master Thorney, d'ye mean to talk out your dinner? The
company attends your coming. What must it be, Master Frank? Or
son Frank?

O. THOR: Son, brother, if your daughter like to have it so.

FRANK: I dare be confident she is not altered
From what I left her at our parting last:—
Are you, fair maid?

SUS: You took too sure possession
Of an engagèd heart.

FRANK: Which now I challenge.

CAR: Marry, and much good may it do thee, son. Take her to thee; get
me a brace of boys at a burthen, Frank; the nursing shall not stand
thee in a pennyworth of milk; reach her home and spare not: when's
the day?

O. THOR: Tomorrow, if you please. To use ceremony
Of charge and custom were to little purpose;
Their loves are married fast enough already.

CAR: A good motion. We'll e'en have an houschold dinner, and let the
fiddlers go scrape: let the bride and bridegroom dance at night together; no matter for the guests:—tomorrow, Sue, tomorrow.—Shall's
to dinner now?

O. THOR: We are on all sides pleased, I hope.

SUS: Pray Heaven I may deserve the blessing sent me:
Now my heart is settled.

FRANK: So is mine.

CAR: Your marriage-money shall be received before your wedding-shoes
can be pulled on. Blessing on you both!

FRANK (aside): No man can hide his shame from Heaven that views him;
In vain he flees whose destiny pursues him.   (Exeunt.)

ACT THE SECOND

Scene One

The fields near Edmonton. Enter MOTHER SAWYER *gathering sticks.*

MOTHER SAWYER: And why on me? why should the envious world
    Throw all their scandalous malice upon me?
    'Cause I am poor, deformed, and ignorant,
    And like a bow buckled and bent together
    By some more strong in mischiefs than myself,
    Must I for that be made a common sink
    For all the filth and rubbish of men's tongues
    To fall and run into? Some call me witch,
    And being ignorant of myself, they go
    About to teach me how to be one; urging
    That my bad tongue—by their bad usage made so—
    Enspells their cattle, doth bewitch their corn,
    Themselves, their servants and their babes at nurse.
    This they enforce upon me, and in part
    Make me to credit it; and here comes one
    Of my chief adversaries.

(Enter OLD BANKS*)*

O. BANKS: Out, out upon thee, witch!

M. SAW: Dost call me witch?

O. BANKS: I do, witch, I do; and worse I would, knew I a name more
hateful. What makest thou upon my ground?

M. SAW: Gather a few rotten sticks to warm me.

O. BANKS: Down with them when I bid thee quickly; I'll make thy bones
rattle in thy skin else.

M. SAW: You won't, churl, cutthroat, miser!—there they be *(Throws them
down)*: would they stuck cross thy throat, thy bowels, thy maw, thy
midriff!

O. BANKS: Sayest thou me so, hag? Out of my ground!   *(Beats her)*

M. SAW: Dost strike me, slave, curmudgeon! Now, thy bones ache, thy joints cramp and convulsions stretch and crack thy sinews!

O. BANKS: Cursing, thou hag! take that and that.

(Beats her and exits)

M. SAW: Strike, do!—and withered may that hand and arm
Whose blows have lamed me drop from the rotten trunk.
Abuse me! beat me! call me hag and witch!
What is the name, where and by what art learned,
What spells, what charms or invocations,
May the thing called Familiar be purchased?

(Enter CUDDY BANKS *and several other* CLOWNS)

CUD: A new head for the tabor, and silver tipping for the pipe; remember that: and forget not five leash of new bells.

FIRST CL: Double bells;—Crooked Lane—ye shall have 'em straight in Crooked Lane:—double bells all, if it be possible.

CUD: Double bells? double coxcombs! trebles, buy me trebles, all trebles; for our purpose is to be in the altitudes.

SECOND CL: All trebles? not a baritone?

CUD: Not one. The morris is so cast, we'll have neither mean nor basc in our company, fellow Rowland.

THIRD CL: What! nor a counter tenor?

CUD: By no means, no hunting counter, leave that to Enfield Chase men: all trebles, all in the altitudes. Now for the disposing of parts in the morris, little or no labor will serve.

SECOND CL: If you that be minded to follow your leader know me—an ancient honor belonging to our house—for a forehorse i' th' team and foregallant in a morris, my father's stable is not unfurnished.

THIRD CL: So much for the forehorse; but how for a good hobbyhorse?

CUD: For a hobbyhorse? Let me see an almanac. Midsummer-moon, let me see ye. "When the moon's in the full, then's wit in the wane." No more. Use your best skill; your morris will suffer an eclipse.

FIRST CL: An eclipse?

CUD: A strange one.

SECOND CL: Strange?

CUD: Yes, and most sudden. Remember the foregallant, and forget the hobbyhorse! The whole body of your morris will be darkened.—There be of us—but 'tis no matter:—forget the hobbyhorse!

FIRST CL: Cuddy Banks!—have you forgot since he paced it from Enfield Chase to Edmonton?—Cuddy, honest Cuddy, cast thy stuff.

CUD: Suffer may ye all! it shall be known, I can take mine ease as well as another man. Seek your hobbyhorse where you can get him.

FIRST CL: Cuddy, honest Cuddy, we confess, and are sorry for our neglect.

SECOND CL: The old horse shall have a new bridle.

THIRD CL: The caparisons new painted.

FOURTH CL: The tail repaired. The snaffle and the bosses new saffroned o'er.

FIRST CL: Kind—

SECOND CL: Honest—

THIRD CL: Loving, ingenious—

FOURTH CL: Affable Cuddy.

CUD: To show I am not flint, but affable, as you say, very well stuffed, a
kind of warm dough or puff-paste, I relent, I connive, most affable
Jack. Let the hobbyhorse provide a strong back, he shall not want a
belly when I am in him—but *(Seeing* SAWYER*)*—'uds me, Mother Sawyer!

FIRST CL: The old Witch of Edmonton!—if our mirth be not crossed—

SECOND CL: Bless us, Cuddy, and let her curse her t'other eye out.—
What dost now?

CUD: "Ungirt, unblest," says the proverb; but my girdle shall serve for a
riding knot; and a fig for all the witches in Christendom!—What
wouldst thou?

FIRST CL: The devil cannot abide to be crossed.

SECOND CL: And scorns to come at any man's whistle.

THIRD CL: Away—

FOURTH CL: With the witch!

ALL: Away with the Witch of Edmonton!

(Exeunt in strange postures)

M. SAW: Still vexed! still tortured! that curmudgeon Banks
Is ground of all my scandal; I am shunned
And hated like a sickness; made a scorn
To all degrees and sexes. I have heard old beldams
Talk of familiars in the shape of mice,
Rats, ferrets, weasels and I know not what,
That have appeared, and sucked, some say, their blood;
But by what means they came acquainted with them
I am now ignorant. Would some power, good or bad,
Instruct me which way I might be revenged
Upon this churl, I'd go out of myself,
And give this fury leave to dwell within
This ruined cottage ready to fall with age,
Abjure all goodness, be at hate with prayer,

And study curses, imprecations,
Blasphemous speeches, oaths, detested oaths,
Or anything that's ill: so I might work
Revenge upon this miser, this black cur,
That barks and bites, and sucks the very blood
Of me and of my credit. 'Tis all one
To be a witch as to be counted one:
Vengeance, shame, ruin light upon that canker!

(*Enter a* BLACK DOG)

DOG: Ho! have I found thee cursing? now thou art
Mine own.

M. SAW: Thine! what art thou?

DOG: He thou hast so often
Importuned to appear to thee, the Devil.

M. SAW: Bless me! the Devil?

DOG: Come, do not fear; I love thee much too well
To hurt or fright thee; if I seem terrible,
It is to such as hate me. I have found
Thy love unfeigned; have seen and pitied
Thy open wrongs; and come, out of my love,
To give thee just revenge against thy foes.

M. SAW: May I believe thee?

DOG: To confirm't, command me
Do any mischief unto man or beast,
And I'll effect it, on condition
That, uncompelled, thou make a deed of gift
Of soul and body to me.

M. SAW: Out, alas!
My soul and body?

DOG: And that instantly,
And seal it with thy blood: if thou deniest,
I'll tear thy body in a thousand pieces.

M. SAW: I know not where to seek relief: but shall I,
After such covenants sealed, see full revenge
On all that wrong me?

DOG: Ha, ha! silly woman!
The Devil is no liar to such as he loves:
Didst ever know or hear the Devil a liar
To such as he affects?

M. SAW: Then I am thine; at least so much of me
As I can call mine own—

DOG: Equivocations?
Art mine or no? speak, or I'll tear—

M. SAW: All thine.

DOG: Seal't with thy blood.
(She pricks her arm, which he sucks. Thunder and lightning)
                        See! now I dare call thee mine!
For proof, command me; instantly I'll run
To any mischief; goodness can I none.

M. SAW: And I desire as little. There's an old churl,
One Banks—

DOG: That wronged thee, lamed thee, called thee witch.

M. SAW: The same; first upon him I'd be revenged.

DOG: Thou shalt; do but name how.

M. SAW: Go, touch his life.

DOG: I cannot.

M. SAW: Hast thou not vowed? Go, kill the slave!

DOG: I wonnot.

M. SAW: I'll cancel, then, my gift.

DOG: Ha, ha!

M. SAW: Dost laugh!
  Why wilt not kill him?

DOG: Fool, because I cannot.
  Though we have power, know it is circumscribed
  And tied in limits: though he be curst to thee,
  Yet of himself he's loving to the world,
  And charitable to the poor: now men that,
  As he, love goodness, though in smallest measure,
  Live without compass of our reach. His cattle
  And corn I'll kill and mildew; but his life—
  Until I take him, as I late found thee,
  Cursing and swearing—I've no power to touch.

M. SAW: Work on his corn and cattle, then.

DOG: I shall.
  The Witch of Edmonton shall see his fall;
  If she at least put credit in my power,
  And in mine only; make orisons to me,
  And none but me.

M. SAW: Say how and in what manner.

DOG: I'll tell thee: when thou wishest ill,
  Corn, man, or beast wouldst spoil or kill,
  Turn thy back against the sun,
  And mumble this short orison:
  "If thou to death or shame pursue 'em,
  Sanctibicetur nomen tuum."

M. SAW: "If thou to death or shame pursue 'em,
            Sanctibicetur nomen tuum."

DOG: Perfect: farewell. Our first-made promises
  We'll put in execution against Banks.   *(Exit)*

M. SAW: *Contaminetur nomen tuum.* I'm an expert scholar;
  Speak Latin, or I know not well what language,

As well as the best of 'em—but who comes here?
(*Re-enter* CUDDY BANKS)
The son of my worst foe.
> To death pursue 'em,
> *Et sanctibicetur nomen tuum.*

CUD: What's that she mumbles? The Devil's paternoster? Would it were else!—Mother Sawyer, good morrow.

M. SAW: Ill   morrow   to   thee,   and   all   the   world   that   flout
A poor old woman,
> To death pursue 'em,
> And *sanctibicetur nomen tuum.*

CUD: Nay, good Gammer Sawyer, whate'er it pleases my father to call you, I know you are—

M. SAW: A witch.

CUD: A witch? would you were else i'faith!

M. SAW: Your father knows I am by this.

CUD: I would he did.

M. SAW: And so in time may you.

CUD: I would I might else! But, witch or no witch, you are a motherly woman; and though my father be a kind of God-bless-us, as they say, I have an earnest suit to you; and if you'll be so kind to do me one good turn, I'll be so courteous as to do you another.

M. SAW: What's that? To spurn, beat me and call me witch,
As your kind father doth?

CUD: My father! I am ashamed to own him. If he has hurt the head of thy credit, there's money to buy thee a plaster (*gives her money*); and a small courtesy I would require at thy hands.

M. SAW: You seem a good young man, and—(*aside*) I must dissemble,
The better to accomplish my revenge.—

But—for this silver, what wouldst have me do?
Bewitch thee?

CUD: No, by no means; I am bewitched already: I would have thee so
good as to unwitch me, or witch another with me for company.

M. SAW: I understand thee not; be plain, my son.

CUD: As a pikestaff, mother. You know Kate Carter?

M. SAW: The wealthy yeoman's daughter? What of her?

CUD: That same party has bewitched me.

M. SAW: Bewitched thee?

CUD: Bewitched me, *hisce auribus*. I saw a little devil fly out of her eye
like an arrow which sticks at this hour up to the feathers in my heart.
Now, my request is, to send one of thy what-d'ye-call-'ems either to
pluck that out, or stick another as fast in hers: do, and here's my
hand, I am thine for three lives.

M. SAW *(aside)*: We shall have sport.—Thou art in love with her?

CUD: Up to the very hilts, mother.

M. SAW: And thou wouldst have me make her love thee too?

CUD *(aside)*: I think she'll prove a witch in earnest.—Yes, I could find in
my heart to strike her three quarters deep in love with me too.

M. SAW: But dost thou think that I can do't, and I alone?

CUD: Truly, Mother Witch, I do verily believe so; and, when I see it
done, I shall be half persuaded so too.

M. SAW: It is enough: what art can do be sure of.
Turn to the west, and whatsoe'er thou hear'st
Or seest, stand silent, and be not afraid.

(She stamps on the ground; the DOG *appears, and fawns, and leaps upon her)*

CUD: Afraid, Mother Witch!—"turn my face to the west!" I said I should always have a back-friend of her; and now it's out. If her little Devil should be hungry, come sneaking behind me, like a cowardly catchpole, and clap his talons on my haunches—'Tis woundy cold, sure—I dudder and shake like an aspen leaf every joint of me.

M. SAW: To scandal and disgrace pursue 'em,
   Et sanctibicetur nomen tuum.   (*Exit* DOG)

How now, my son, how is't?

CUD: Scarce in a clean life, Mother Witch.—But did your goblin and you spout Latin together?

M. SAW: A kind of charm I work by; didst thou hear me?

CUD: I heard I know not the Devil what mumble in a scurvy base tone, like a drum that had taken cold in the head the last muster. Very comfortable words; what were they? and who taught them you?

M. SAW: A great learned man.

CUD: Learned man! learned devil it was as soon! But what? what comfortable news about the party?

M. SAW: Who? Kate Carter? I'll tell thee. Thou knowest the stile at the west end of thy father's peas-field: be there tomorrow night after sunset; and the first live thing thou seest be sure to follow, and that shall bring thee to thy love.

CUD: In the peas-field? Has she a mind to early peas already? The first living thing I meet, you say, shall bring me to her?

M. SAW: To a sight of her, I mean. She will seem wantonly coy, and flee thee; but follow her close and boldly: do but embrace her in thy arms once, and she is thine own.

CUD: "At the stile at the west end of my father's peas-land, the first live thing I see, follow and embrace her, and she shall be thine." Nay, an I come to embracing once, she shall be mine; I'll go near to make at eaglet else.   *(Exit)*

M. SAW: A ball well bandied! Now the set's half won; The father's wrong I'll wreak upon the son.   *(Exit.)*

Scene Two

CARTER's *house. Enter* CARTER, WARBECK *and* SOMERTON.

CAR: How now, gentlemen! cloudy? I know, Master Warbeck, you are in a fog about my daughter's marriage.

WAR: And can you blame me, sir?

CAR: Nor you me justly. Wedding and hanging are tied up both in a proverb; and destiny is the juggler that unties the knot. My hope is, you are reserved to a richer fortune than my poor daughter.

WAR: However, your promise—

CAR: Is a kind of debt, I confess it.

WAR: Which honest men should pay.

CAR: Yet some gentlemen break in that point now and then, by your leave, sir.

SOM: I confess thou hast had a little wrong in the wench; but patience is the only salve to cure it. Since Thorney has won the wench, he has most reason to wear her.

WAR: Love in this kind admits no reason to wear her.

CAR: Then Love's a fool, and what wise man will take exception?

SOM: Come, frolic, Ned: were every man master of his own fortune, Fate might pick straws, and Destiny go a-wool-gathering.

WAR: You hold yours in a string, though: 'tis well; but if there be any equity, look thou to meet the like usage ere long.

SOM: In my love to her sister Katherine? Indeed, they are a pair of arrows drawn out of one quiver, and should fly at an even length; if she do run after her sister,—

WAR: Look for the same mercy at my hands as I have received at thine.

SOM: She'll keep a surer compass; I have too strong a confidence to mistrust her.

WAR: And that confidence is a wind that has blown many a married man ashore at Cuckold's Haven, I can tell you; I wish yours more prosperous, though.

CAR: Whate'er your wish, I'll master my promise to him.

WAR: Yes, as you did to me.

CAR: No more of that, if you love me: but for the more assurance, the next offered occasion shall consummate the marriage; and that once sealed—

SOM: Leave the manage of the rest to my care. But see, the bridegroom and bride come; the new pair of Sheffield knives, fitted both to one sheath.

WAR: The sheath might have been better fitted, if somebody had their due; but—

CAR: No harsh language, if thou lovest me. Frank Thorney has done—

WAR: No more than I, or thou, or any man, things so standing, would have attempted.

(*Enter* FRANK THORNEY *and* SUSAN)

SOM: Good morrow, Master Bridegroom.

WAR: Come; give thee joy: mayst thou live long and happy
   In thy fair choice!

FRANK: I thank ye, gentlemen; kind Master Warbeck, I find you loving.

WAR: Thorney, that creature—much good do thee with her!—
   Virtue and beauty hold fair mixture in her;
   She's rich, no doubt, in both: yet were she fairer,
   Thou art right worthy of her. Love her, Thorney;
   'Tis nobleness in thee, in her but duty.
   The match is fair and equal; the success
   I leave to censure. Farewell, Mistress Bride!
   Till now elected, thy old scorn deride.   (*Exit*)

SOM: Good Master Thorney—

CAR: Nay, you shall not part till you see the barrels run a-tilt,
   gentlemen.   (*Exit with* SOMERTON)

SUS: Why change you your face, sweetheart?

FRANK: Who, I? for nothing.

SUS: Dear, say not so; a spirit of your constancy
   Cannot endure this change for nothing.
   I have observed strange variations in you.

FRANK: In me?

SUS: In you, sir.
   Awake, you seem to dream, and in your sleep
   You utter sudden and distracted accents,
   Like one at enmity with peace. Dear loving husband, if I
   May dare to challenge any interest in you,
   Give me the reason fully; you may trust
   My breast as safely as your own.

FRANK: With what?
   You half amaze me; prithee—

SUS: Come, you shall not,

Indeed you shall not, shut me from partaking
The least dislike that grieves you; I'm all yours.

FRANK: And I all thine.

SUS: You are not, if you keep
The least grief from me: but I find the cause;
It grew from me.

FRANK: From you?

SUS: From some distaste
In me or my behavior: you're not kind
In the concealment. 'Las, sir, I am young,
Silly and plain; more, strange to those contents
A wife should offer: say but in what I fail,
I'll study satisfaction.

FRANK: Come; in nothing.

SUS: I know I do; knew I as well in what,
You should not long be sullen. Prithee, love,
If I have been immodest or too bold,
Speak't in a frown; if peevishly too nice,
Show't in a smile: thy liking is the glass
By which I'll habit my behavior.

FRANK: Wherefore dost weep now?

SUS: You, sweet, have the power
To make me passionate as an April day;
Now smile, then weep; now pale, then crimson red:
You are the powerful moon of my blood's sea,
To make it ebb or flow into my face,
As your looks change.

FRANK: Change thy conceit, I prithee;
Thou art all perfection: Diana herself
Swells in thy thoughts and moderates thy beauty.
Within thy left eye amorous Cupid sits,
Feathering love shafts, whose golden heads he dipped

In thy chaste breast; in the other lies
Blushing Adonis scarfed in modesties;
And still as wanton Cupid blows love fires,
Adonis quenches out unchaste desires;
And from these two I briefly do imply
A perfect emblem of thy modesty.
Then, prithee, dear, maintain no more dispute,
For when thou speak'st, it's fit all tongues be mute.

SUS: Come, come, these golden strings of flattery
 Shall not tie up my speech, sir; I must know
 The ground of your disturbance.

FRANK: Then look here;
 For here, here is the fen in which this hydra
 Of discontent grows rank.

SUS: Heaven shield it! Where?

FRANK: In mine own bosom, here the cause has root;
 The poisoned leeches twist about my heart,
 And will, I hope, confound me.

SUS: You speak riddles.

FRANK: Take't plainly, then: 'twas told me by a woman
 Known and approved in palmistry,
 I should have two wives.

SUS: Two wives? sir, I take it
 Exceeding likely; but let not conceit hurt you:
 You're afraid to bury me?

FRANK: No, no, my Winnifred.

SUS: How say you? Winnifred! you forget me.

FRANK: No, I forget myself!—Susan.

SUS: In what?

FRANK: Talking of wives, I pretend Winnifred,
    A maid that at my mother's waited on me
    Before thyself.

SUS: I hope, sir, she may live
    To take my place: but why should all this move you?

FRANK: The poor girl!—(*Aside*) she has't before thee,
    And that's the fiend torments me.

SUS: Yet why should this
    Raise mutiny within you? such presages
    Prove often false: or say it should be true?

FRANK: That I should have another wife?

SUS: Yes, many;
    If they be good, the better.

FRANK: Never any
    Equal to thee in goodness.

SUS: Sir, I could wish I were much better for you;
    Yet if I knew your fate
    Ordained you for another, I could wish—
    So well I love you and your hopeful pleasure—
    Me in my grave, and my poor virtues added
    To my successor.

FRANK: Prithee, prithee, talk not
    Of deaths or graves; thou art so rare a goodness
    As Death would rather put itself to death
    Than murder thee: but we, as all things else,
    Are mutable and changing.

SUS: Yet you still move
    In your first sphere of discontent. Sweet, chase
    Those clouds of sorrow, and shine clearly on me.

FRANK: At my return I will.

SUS: Return! ah me!
  Will you, then, leave me?

FRANK: For a time I must:
  But how? As birds their young, or loving bees
  Their hives, to fetch home richer dainties.

SUS: Leave me!
  Now has my fear met its effect. You shall not;
  Cost it my life, you shall not.

FRANK: Why? your reason?

SUS: Like to the lapwing have you all this while
  With your false love deluded me, pretending
  Counterfeit senses for your discontent;
  And now at last it is by chance stole from you.

FRANK: What? what by chance?

SUS: Your pre-appointed meeting
  Of single combat with young Warbeck.

FRANK: Ha!

SUS: Even so: dissemble not; 'tis too apparent:
  Then in his look I read it:—deny it not,
  I see't apparent; cost it my undoing,
  And unto that my life, I will not leave you.

FRANK: Not until when?

SUS: Till he and you be friends.
  Was this your cunning?—and then flam me off
  With an old witch, two wives, and Winnifred!
  You're not so kind, indeed, as I imagined.

FRANK *(aside)*: And you are more fond by far than I expected.—
  It is a virtue that attends thy kind—
  But of our business within:—and by this kiss,
  I'll anger thee no more; 'troth, chuck, I will not.

sus: You shall have no just cause.

FRANK: Dear Sue, I shall not.

(Exeunt.)

ACT THE THIRD

Scene One

The village green. Enter CUDDY BANKS *with the morris dancers.*

FIRST CLOWN: Nay, Cuddy, prithee do not leave us now; if we part all this night, we shall not meet before day.

SECOND CL: I prithee, Banks, let's keep together now.

CUD: If you were wise, a word would serve; but as you are, I must be forced to tell you again, I have a little private business, an hour's work; it may prove but an half hour's, as luck may serve; and then I take horse, and along with you. Have we e'er a witch in the morris?

FIRST CL: No, no; no woman's part but Maid Marian and the hobby-horse.

CUD: I'll have a witch; I love a witch.

FIRST CL: 'Faith, witches themselves are so common now-a-days, that the counterfeit will not be regarded. They say we have three or four in Edmonton besides Mother Sawyer.

SECOND CL: I would she would dance her part with us.

THIRD CL: So would not I; for if she comes, the Devil and all comes along with her.

CUD: Well, I'll have a witch; I have loved a witch ever since I pitched at cherry-pit. Leave me, and get my horse dressed; give him oats: but water him not till I come. Whither do we foot it first?

SECOND CL: To Sir Arthur Clarington's first; then whither thou wilt.

CUD: Well, I am content; but we must up to Carter's, the rich yeoman; I must be seen on hobbyhorse there.

FIRST CL: O, I smell him now!—I'll lay my ears Banks is in love, and that's the reason he would walk melancholy by himself.

CUD: Ha! who was that said I was in love?

FIRST CL: Not I.

SECOND CL: Nor I.

CUD: Go to, no more of that: when I understand what you speak, I know what you say; believe that.

FIRST CL: Well, 'twas I, I'll not deny it; I meant no hurt in't. I have seen you walk up to Carter's of Chessum: Banks, were not you there last Shrovetide?

CUD: Yes, I was ten days together there the last Shrovetide.

SECOND CL: How could that be, when there are but seven days in the week?

CUD: Prithee peace! I reckon *stila nova* as a traveler; thou understandest as a freshwater farmer, that never sawest a week beyond sea. Ask any soldier that ever received his pay but in the Low Countries, and he'll tell thee there are eight days in the week there hard by. How dost thou think they rise in High Germany, Italy and those remoter places?

THIRD CL: Ay, but simply there are but seven days in the week yet.

CUD: No, simply as thou understandest. Prithee look but in the lover's almanac: when he has been but three days absent, "O," says he, "I have not seen my love these seven years:" there's a long cut! When he comes to her again and embraces her, "O," says he, "now methinks I am in Heaven;" and that's a pretty step! He that can get up to Heaven in ten days need not repent his journey; you may ride a hundred days in a caroche, and be further off than when you set forth. But, I pray you, good morris mates, now leave me. I will be with you by midnight.

FIRST CL: Well, since he will be alone, we'll back again and trouble him no more.

ALL THE CLOWNS: But remember, Banks.

CUD: The hobbyhorse shall be remembered. But hark you; get Poldavis, the barber's boy, for the witch, because he can show his art better than another.
(Exeunt all but CUDDY)
Well, now to my walk. I am near the place where I should meet—I know not what: say I meet a thief? I must follow him, if to the gallows; say I meet a horse, or hare, or hound? still I must follow: some slow-paced beast, I hope; yet love is full of lightness in the heaviest lovers. Ha! my guide is come.
(Enter the DOG)
A water-dog! I am thy first man, sculler; I go with thee; ply no other but myself. Away with the boat! land me but at Katherine's Dock, my sweet Katherine's Dock, and I'll be a fare to thee. That way? nay, which way thou wilt; thou knowest the way better than I:—fine gentle cur it is, and well brought up, I warrant him. We go a-ducking, spaniel; thou shalt fetch me the ducks, pretty kind rascal.

(Enter a SPIRIT *vizarded. He throws off his mask, etc., and appears in the shape of* KATHERINE)

SPIR: Thus throw I off mine own essential horror,
  And take the shape of a sweet lovely maid
  Whom this fool dotes on: we can meet his folly,
  But from his virtues must be runaways.
  We'll sport with him; but when we reckoning call,
  We know where to receive; the witch pays for all.
  (The DOG *barks)*

CUD: Ay? Is that the watchword? She's come. *(Sees the* SPIRIT) Well, if ever we be married, it shall be at Barking Church, in memory of thee: now come behind, kind cur.

And have I met thee, sweet Kate?
I will teach thee to walk so late.

O, see, we meet in meter. *(The* SPIRIT *retires as he advances)* What!
dost thou trip from me? O, that I were upon my hobbyhorse, I would
mount after thee so nimble! "Stay, nymph, stay, nymph," singed
Apollo.

Tarry and kiss me, sweet nymph, stay;
Tarry and kiss me, sweet:
We will to Chessum Street,
And then to the house stands in the highway.

Nay, by your leave, I must embrace you.
(Exit, following the SPIRIT)
(Within) O, help, help! I am drowned, I am drowned!

(Re-enter CUDDY *wet)*

DOG: Ha, ha, ha, ha!

CUD: This was an ill night to go a-wooing in; I find it now in Pond's
almanac: thinking to land at Katherine's Dock, I was almost at
Gravesend. I'll never go to a wench in the dog days again; yet 'tis cool
enough.—Had you never a paw in this dog trick? A mange take that
black hide of yours! I'll throw you in at Limehouse in some tanner's
pit or other.

DOG: Ha, ha, ha, ha!

CUD: How now! who's that laughs at me? Hist to him! *(The* DOG *barks)*
—Peace, peace! thou didst but thy kind neither; 'twas my own fault.

DOG: Take heed how thou trustest the Devil another time.

CUD: How now! Who's that speaks? I hope you have not your reading
tongue about you?

DOG: Yes, I can speak.

CUD: The Devil you can! You have read Aesop's fables, then; I have played one of your parts then—the dog that catched at the shadow in the water. Pray you, let me catechise you a little; what might one call your name, dog?

DOG: My dame calls me Tom.

CUD: 'Tis well, and she may call me Ass; so there's an whole one betwixt us, Tom-Ass: she said I should follow you, indeed. Well, Tom, give me thy fist, we are friends; you shall be my friend. I love you; but I pray you let's have no more of these ducking devices.

DOG: Not, if you love me. Dogs love where they are beloved; cherish me, and I'll do anything for thee.

CUD: Well, you shall have jowls and livers; I have butchers to my friends that shall bestow 'em: and I will keep crusts and bones for you, if you'll be a kind dog, Tom.

DOG: Any thing; I'll help thee to thy love.

CUD: Wilt thou? That promise shall cost me a brown loaf, though I steal it out of my father's cupboard: you'll eat stolen goods, Tom, will you not?

DOG: O, best of all; the sweetest bits those.

CUD: You shall not starve, Friend Tom, believe that: if you love fish, I'll help you to maids and soles; I'm acquainted with a fishmonger.

DOG: Maids and soles? O, sweet bits! banqueting stuff those.

CUD: One thing I would request you, as you have played the knavish cur with me a little, that you would mingle amongst our morris-dancers in the morning. You can dance?

DOG: Yes, yes, any thing; I'll be there, but unseen to any but thyself. Get thee gone before; fear not my presence. I have work tonight; I serve more masters, more dames than one.

CUD: He can serve Mammon and the Devil, too.

DOG: It shall concern thee and thy love's purchase.
　　There is a gallant rival loves the maid,
　　And likely is to have her. Mark what a mischief,
　　Before the morris ends, shall light on him!

CUD: O, sweet friend, thy paw once again; friends must part for a time.
　　Farewell, with this remembrance; shalt have bread too when we meet
　　again. If ever there were an honest devil, 'twill be the Devil of
　　Edmonton, I see. Farewell, Tom; I prithee dog me as soon as thou
　　canst.   *(Exit)*

DOG: I'll not miss thee, and be merry with thee.
　　Those that are joys denied must take delight
　　In sins and mischiefs; 'tis the Devil's right.   *(Exit.)*

Scene Two

The neighborhood of Edmonton. Enter FRANK THORNEY *and* WINNIFRED *in boy's clothes.*

FRANK: Prithee no more! those tears give nourishment
　　To weeds and briers in me, which shortly will
　　O'ergrow and top my head; my shame will sit
　　And cover all that can be seen of me.

WIN: I have not shown this cheek in company;
　　Pardon me now: thus singled with yourself,
　　It calls a thousand sorrows round about,
　　Some going before, and some on either side,
　　But infinite behind; all chained together:
　　Your second adulterous marriage leads;
　　That is the sad eclipse, th' effects must follow,
　　As plagues of shame, spite, scorn, and obloquy.

FRANK: Why, hast thou not left one hour's patience
　　To add to all the rest? one hour bears us
　　Beyond the reach of all these enemies:
　　Are we not now set forward in the flight,
　　Provided with the dowry of my sin
　　To keep us in some other nation?

While we together are, we are at home
In any place.

WIN: 'Tis foul ill-gotten coin,
Far worse than usury or extortion.

FRANK: Let
My father, then, make the restitution,
Who forced me to take the bribe: it is his gift
And patrimony to me; so I receive it.
He would not bless, nor look a father on me,
Until I satisfied his angry will:
When I was sold, I sold myself again—
Some knaves have done't in lands, and I in body—
For money, and I have the hire. But, sweet, no more,
'Tis hazard of discovery, our discourse;
And then prevention takes off all our hopes:
For only but to take her leave of me
My wife is coming.

WIN: Who coming? Your wife!

FRANK: No, no; thou art here: the woman—I knew
Not how to call her now; but after this day
She shall be quite forgot and have no name
In my remembrance. See, see! she's come.
(*Enter* SUSAN)
                                    Go lead
The horses to th' hill's top; there I'll meet thee.

SUS: Nay, with your favor let him stay a little;
I would part with him too, because he is
Your sole companion; and I'll begin with him,
Reserving you the last.

FRANK: Ay, with all my heart.

SUS: You may hear, if't please you, sir.

FRANK: No, 'tis not fit:

Some rudiments, I conceive, they must be,
To overlook my slippery footings: and so—

SUS: No, indeed, sir.

FRANK: Tush, I know it must be so,
And it is necessary: on! but be brief.   *(Walks forward)*

WIN: What charge soe'er you lay upon me, mistress,
I shall support it faithfully—being honest—
To my best strength.

SUS: Believe't shall be no other.
I know you were commended to my husband
By a noble knight.

WIN: O, gods! O, mine eyes!

SUS: How now! what ail'st thou, lad?

WIN: Something hit mine eye,—it makes it water still—
Even as you said "commended to my husband."
Some bug I think it was.—I was, forsooth,
Commended to him by Sir Arthur Clarington.

SUS: Whose servant once my Thorney was himself.
That title, methinks, should make you almost fellows;
Or at the least much more than a servant;
And I am sure he will respect you so.
Your love to him, then, needs no spur from me,
And what for my sake you will ever do,
'Tis fit it should be bought with something more
Than fair entreats; look! here's a jewel for thee,
A pretty wanton label for thine ear;
And I would have it hang there, still to whisper
These words to thee, "Thou hast my jewel with thee."
It is but earnest of a larger bounty,
When thou return'st with praises of thy service,
Which I am confident thou wilt deserve.
Why, thou art many now besides thyself:
Thou mayst be servant, friend, and wife to him;

A good wife is them all. A friend can play
The wife and servant's part, and shift enough;
No less the servant can the friend and wife:
'Tis all but sweet society, good counsel,
Interchanged loves, yes, and counsel-keeping.

FRANK: Not done yet?

SUS: Even now, sir.

WIN: Mistress, believe my vow; your severe eye,
　　Were't present to command, your bounteous hand,
　　Were it then by to buy or bribe my service,
　　Shall not make me more dear or near unto him
　　Than I shall voluntary. I'll be all your charge,
　　Servant, friend, wife to him.

SUS:　　　　　　　　　　　　Wilt thou?
　　Now blessings go with thee for't! Courtesies
　　Shall meet thee coming home.

WIN:　　　　　　　　　　　Pray you say plainly,
　　Mistress, are you jealous of him? If you be,
　　I'll look to him that way too.

SUS:　　　　　　　　　　　Say'st thou so?
　　I would thou hadst a woman's bosom now;
　　We have weak thoughts within us. Alas,
　　There's nothing so strong in us as suspicion;
　　But I dare not, nay, I will not think
　　So hardly of my Thorney.

WIN:　　　　　　　　　Believe it, mistress,
　　I'll be no pander to him; and if I find
　　Any loose lubric scapes in him, I'll watch him,
　　And at my return protest I'll show you all:
　　He shall hardly offend without my knowledge.

SUS: Thine own diligence is that I press,
　　And not the curious eye over his faults.

Farewell: if I should never see thee more,
Take it for ever.

FRANK: Prithee take that along with thee, *(Handing his sword to*
WINNIFRED) and haste thee
To the hill's top; I'll be there instantly.

SUS: No haste, I prithee; slowly as thou canst—

(Exit WINNIFRED)

Pray let him obey me now; 'tis happily
His last service to me: my power is e'en
A-going out of sight.

FRANK: Why would you delay?
We have no other business now but to part.

SUS: And will not that, sweetheart, ask a long time?
Methinks it is the hardest piece of work
That e'er I took in hand.

FRANK: Fie, fie! why, look,
I'll make it plain and easy to you—farewell!

(Kisses her)

SUS: Ah, 'las, I'm not half perfect in it yet;
I must have it read o'er an hundred times:
Pray you take some pains; I confess my dulness.

FRANK *(aside):* What a thorn this rose grows on! Parting were sweet;
But what a trouble 'twill be to obtain it!—
Come, again and again, farewell!—*(Kisses her)* Yet wilt return?
All questions of my journey, my stay, employment
And revisitation, fully I have answered all;
There's nothing now behind but—nothing.

SUS: And
That *nothing* is more hard than anything,
Than all the everythings. This request—

FRANK: What is't?

SUS: That I may bring you through one pasture more
Up to yon knot of trees; amongst those shadows
I'll vanish from you, they shall teach me how.

FRANK: Why, 'tis granted; come, walk, then.

SUS: Nay, not too fast:
They say slow things have best perfection;
The gentle shower wets to fertility,
The churlish storm may mischief with his bounty;
The baser beasts take strength even from the womb,
But the lord lion's whelp is feeble long.   (*Exeunt.*)

Scene Three

A *field with a clump of trees. Enter the* DOG.

DOG: Now for an early mischief and a sudden!
The mind's about it now; one touch from me
Soon sets the body forward.

(*Enter* FRANK *and* SUSAN)

FRANK: Your request
Is out; yet will you leave me?

SUS: What? so churlishly?
You'll make me stay for ever,
Rather than part with such a sound from you.

FRANK: Why, you almost anger me. Pray you be gone.
You have no company, and 'tis very early;
Some hurt may betide you homewards.

SUS: Tush! I fear none;
To leave you is the greatest hurt I can suffer:
Besides, I expect your father and mine own
To meet me back, or overtake me with you;

They began to stir when I came after you
I know they'll not be long.

FRANK: So! I shall have more trouble—*(The* DOG *rubs against him)*—
thank you for that:
(Aside) Then I'll ease all at once. It is done now;
What I ne'er thought on.—You shall not go back.

SUS: Why, shall I go along with thee? Sweet music!

FRANK: No, to a better place.

SUS: Any place I;
I'm there at home where thou pleasest to have me.

FRANK: At home? I'll leave you in your last lodging;
I must kill you.

SUS: O, fine! you'd fright me from you.

FRANK: You see I had no purpose; I'm unarmed;
'Tis this minute's decree, and it must be:
Look, this will serve your turn.   *(Draws a knife)*

SUS: I'll not turn from it,
If you be earnest, sir; yet you may tell me
Wherefore you'll kill me.

FRANK: Because you are a whore.

SUS: There's one deep wound already; a whore!
'Twas ever further from me than the thought
Of this black hour; a whore?

FRANK: Yes, I'll prove it,
And you shall confess it. You are my whore.
No wife of mine; the word admits no second.
I was before wedded to another; have her still.
I do not lay the sin unto your charge,
'Tis all mine own: your marriage was my theft,
For I espoused your dowry, and I have it.

I did not purpose to have added murder;
The devil did not prompt me till this minute:
You might have safe returned; now you cannot.
You have dogged your own death.   *(Stabs her)*

SUS: And I deserve it;
I'm glad my fate was so intelligent:
'Twas some good spirit's motion. Die? O, 'twas time!
How many years might I have slept in sin,
The sin of my most hatred, too, adultery!

FRANK: Nay, sure, 'twas likely that the most was past;
For I meant never to return to you
After this parting.

SUS: Why, then, I thank you more;
You have done lovingly, leaving yourself,
That you would thus bestow me on another.
Thou art my husband, Death, and I embrace thee
With all the love I have. Forget the stain
Of my unwitting sin; and then I come
A crystal virgin to thee: my soul's purity
Shall with bold wings ascend the doors of Mercy;
For Innocence is ever her companion.

FRANK: Not yet mortal? I would not linger you,
Or leave you a tongue to blab.   *(Stabs her again)*

SUS: Now heaven reward you ne'er the worse for me!
I did not think that Death had been so sweet,
Nor I so apt to love him. I could ne'er die better,
Had I stayed forty years for preparation;
For I'm in charity with all the world.
Let me for once be thine example, Heaven;
Do to this man as I him free forgive,
And may he better die and better live.   *(Dies)*

FRANK: 'Tis done; and I am in! Once past our height,
We scorn the deep'st abyss. There is a spell
To heal her wounds by dressing of the weapon.
Arms, thighs, hands, any place; we must not fail

(Wounds himself)
Light scratches, giving such deep ones: the best I can
To bind myself to this tree. Now's the storm,
Which if blown o'er, many fair days may follow.
(Binds himself to a tree; the DOG *ties him behind and exit)*
So, so, I'm fast; I did not think I could
Have done so well behind me. How prosperous
And effectual mischief sometimes is!—*(Aloud)*
Help! help! Murder, murder, murder!

(Enter CARTER *and* OLD THORNEY*)*

CAR: Ha! whom tolls the bell for?

FRANK: O, O!

O. THOR: Ah me!
The cause appears too soon; my child, my son!

CAR: Susan, girl, child! not speak to thy father? ha!

FRANK: O, lend me some assistance to o'ertake
This hapless woman.

O. THOR: Let's o'ertake the murderers.
Speak whilst thou canst, anon may be too late;
I fear thou hast death's mark upon thee too.

FRANK: I know them both; yet such an oath is passed
As pulls damnation up if it be broke.
I dare not name 'em: think what forced men do.

O. THOR: Keep oath with murderers! that were a conscience
To hold the Devil in.

FRANK: Nay, sir, I can describe 'em,
Shall show them as familiar as their names:
The taller of the two at this time wears
His satin doublet white, but crimson-lined,
Hose of black satin, cloak of scarlet—

O. THOR: Warbeck,
   Warbeck, Warbeck!—do you list to this, sir?

CAR: Yes, yes, I listen you; here's nothing to be heard.

FRANK: Th' other's cloak branched velvet, black, velvet-lined his suit.

O. THOR: I have 'em already; Somerton, Somerton!
   Binal revenge all this. Come, sir, the first work
   Is to pursue the murderers, when we have
   Removed these mangled bodies hence.

CAR: Sir, take that carcass there, and give me this.
   I will not own her now; she's none of mine.
   Bob me off with a dumb show! No, I'll have life.
   This is my son too, and while there's life in him,
   'Tis half mine; take you half that silence for't.—
   When I speak I look to be spoken to:
   Forgetful slut!

O. THOR: Alas, what grief may do now!
   Look, sir, I'll take this load of sorrow with me.

CAR: Ay, do, and I'll have this. (*Exit* OLD THORNEY *with* SUSAN *in his arms*)
   How do you, sir?

FRANK: O, very ill, sir.

CAR: Yes,
   I think so; but 'tis well you can speak yet:
   There's no music but in sound; sound it must be.
   I have not wept these twenty years before,
   And that I guess was ere that girl was born;
   Yet now methinks, if I but knew the way,
   My heart's so full, I could weep night and day.

(*Exit with* FRANK.)

Scene Four

Before SIR ARTHUR CLARINGTON'S house. Enter SIR ARTHUR CLARINGTON, WARBECK *and* SOMERTON.

SIR ARTH: Come, gentlemen, we must all help to grace
The nimble-footed youth of Edmonton,
That are so kind to call us up today
With an high morris.

WAR: I could wish it for the best, it were the worst now. Absurdity's in my opinion ever the best dancer in a morris.

SOM: I could rather sleep than see 'em.

SIR ARTH: Not well, sir?

SOM: 'Faith, not ever thus leaden: yet I know no cause for't.

WAR: Now am I beyond mine own condition highly disposed to mirth.

SIR ARTH: Well, you may have yet a morris to help both;
To strike you in a dump, and make him merry.

(Enter SAWGUT *with the* MORRIS DANCERS *etc.)*

SAW: Come, will you set yourselves in morris array? the forebell, second-bell, tenor, and great-bell; Maid Marian for the same bell. But where's the weathercock now? the hobbyhorse?

FIRST CL: Is not Banks come yet? What a spite 'tis!

SIR ARTH: When set you forward, gentlemen?

FIRST CL: We stay but for the hobbyhorse, sir; all our footmen are ready.

SOM: 'Tis marvel your horse should be behind your foot.

SECOND CL: Yes, sir, he goes further about; we can come in at the wicket, but the broad gate must be opened for him.

(*Enter* CUDDY BANKS *with the hobbyhorse, followed by the* DOG)

SIR ARTH: O, we stayed for you, sir.

CUD: Only my horse wanted a shoe, sir; but we shall make you amends ere we part.

SIR ARTH: Ay? well said; make 'em drink ere they begin.

(*Enter* SERVANTS *with beer*)

CUD: A bowl, I prithee, and a little for my horse; he'll mount the better. Nay, give me: I must drink to him, he'll not pledge else. (*Drinks*) Here, Hobby. (*Holds the bowl to the hobbyhorse*)—I pray you: no? Not drink! You see, gentlemen, we can but bring our horse to the water; he may choose whether he'll drink or no.   (*Drinks again*)

SOM: A good moral made plain by history.

FIRST CL: Strike up, Father Sawgut, strike up.

SAW: E'en when you will, children. (CUDDY *mounts the Hobby*)—Now in the name of—the best foot forward! (*Endeavours to play, but the fiddle gives no sound*)—How now! not a word in thy guts? I think, children, my instrument has caught cold on the sudden.

CUD (*aside*): Black Tom's doing.

ALL THE CLOWNS: Why, what mean you, Father Sawgut?

CUD: Why, what would you have him do? You hear his fiddle is speechless.

SAW: I'll lay mine ear to my instrument that my poor fiddle is bewitched. I played "The Flowers in May" e'en now, as sweet as a violet; now 'twill not go against the hair: you see I can make no more music than a beetle of a cow-turd.

CUD: Let me see, Father Sawgut *(Takes the fiddle)*; say once you had a
   brave hobbyhorse that you were beholding to. I'll play and dance
   too.—   *(Gives it to the* DOG, *who plays the morris)*

ALL THE CLOWNS: Ay, marry, sir!   *(They dance)*

(Enter a CONSTABLE *and* OFFICERS*)*

CON: Away with jollity! 'Tis too sad an hour.—
   Sir Arthur Clarington, your own assistance,
   In the king's name, I charge, for apprehension
   Of these two murderers, Warbeck and Somerton.

SIR ARTH: Ha! Flat murderers?

SOM: Ha, ha, ha! this has awakened my melancholy.

WAR: And struck my mirth down flat.—Murderers?

CON: The accusation's flat against you, gentlemen.—
   Sir, you may be satisfied with this. *(Shows his warrant)*—
   I hope you'll quietly obey my power;
   'Twill make your cause the fairer.

SOM AND WAR: O, with all our hearts, sir.

CUD: There's my rival taken up for hangman's meat; Tom told me he
   was about a piece of villainy.—Mates and morrismen, you see here's
   no longer piping, no longer dancing; this news of murder has slain the
   morris. You that go the footway, fare ye well; I am for a gallop.—
   Come, ningle.

(Canters off with the hobbyhorse and the DOG*)*

SAW: *(strikes his fiddle, which sounds as before)*: Ay? nay, an my fiddle be
   come to himself again, I care not. I think the devil has been abroad
   amongst us to-day; I'll keep thee out of thy fit now, if I can.

(Exit with the MORRIS DANCERS*)*

SIR ARTH: These things are full of horror, full of pity.
　　But if this time be constant to the proof,
　　The guilt of both these gentlemen I dare take
　　On mine own danger; yet, howsoever, sir,
　　Your power must be obeyed.

WAR: O, most willingly, sir.
　　'Tis a most sweet affliction; I could not meet
　　A joy in the best shape with better will:
　　Come, fear not, sir; nor judge nor evidence
　　Can bind him o'er who's freed by conscience.

SOM: Mine stands so upright to the middle zone
　　It takes no shadow to't, it goes alone.   (*Exeunt.*)

ACT THE FOURTH

Scene One

Edmonton. The street. Enter OLD BANKS *and several* COUNTRYMEN.

OLD BANKS: My horse this morning runs most piteously of the glanders,
　　whose nose yesternight was as clean as any man's here now coming
　　from the barber's; and this, I'll take my death upon't, is long of this
　　jadish witch Mother Sawyer.

FIRST COUN. I took my wife and a servingman in our town of Edmonton
　　thrashing in my barn together such corn as country wenches carry to
　　market; and examining my polecat why she did so, she swore in her
　　conscience she was bewitched: and what witch have we about us but
　　Mother Sawyer?

SECOND COUN: Rid the town of her, else all our wives will do nothing else
　　but dance about other country maypoles.

THIRD COUN: Our cattle fall, our wives fall, our daughters fall, and maid-
　　servants fall; and we ourselves shall not be able to stand, if this beast
　　be suffered to graze amongst us.

(*Enter* HAMLUC *with thatch and a lighted link*)

HAM: Burn the witch, the witch, the witch, the witch!

COUNTRYMEN: What hast got there?

HAM: A handful of thatch plucked off a hovel of hers; and they say, when 'tis burning, if she be a witch, she'll come running in.

O. BANKS: Fire it, fire it! I'll stand between thee and home for any danger. (HAM. *sets fire to the thatch. Enter* MOTHER SAWYER *running*)

M. SAW: Diseases, plagues, the curse of an old woman follow and fall upon you!

COUNTRYMEN: Are you come, you old trot?

O. BANKS: You hot whore, must we fetch you with fire in your tail?

FIRST COUN: This thatch is as good as a jury to prove she is a witch.

COUNTRYMEN: Out, witch! beat her, kick her, set fire on her!

M. SAW: Shall I be murdered by a bed of serpents?
Help, help!

(*Enter* SIR ARTHUR CLARINGTON *and a* JUSTICE)

COUNTRYMEN: Hang her, beat her, kill her!

JUST: How now! Forbear this violence.

M. SAW: A crew of villains, a knot of bloody hangmen, Set to torment me, I know not why.

JUST: Alas, neighbor Banks, are you a ringleader in mischief? Fie! to abuse an aged woman.

O. BANKS: Woman? A she hell-cat, a witch! To prove her one, we no sooner set fire on the thatch of her house, but in she came running as if the Devil had sent her in a barrel of gunpowder; which trick as surely proves her a witch as the pox in a snuffling nose is a sign a man is a whoremaster.

JUST: Come, come: firing her thatch? ridiculous!
　　Take heed, sirs, what you do; unless your proofs
　　Come better armed, instead of turning her
　　Into a witch, you'll prove yourselves stark fools.

COUNTRYMEN: Fools?

JUST: Arrant fools.

O. BANKS: Pray, Master Justice What-do-you-call-'em, hear me but in one
　　thing: this grumbling Devil owes me I know no good will ever since I
　　fell out with her.

M. SAW: And break'dst my back with beating me.

O. BANKS: I'll break it worse.

M. SAW: Wilt thou?

JUST: You must not threaten her; 'tis against law: Go on.

O. BANKS: So, sir, ever since, having a dun cow tied up in my backside, let
　　me go thither, or but cast mine eye at her, and if I should be hanged I
　　cannot choose, though it be ten times in an hour, but run to the cow,
　　and taking up her tail, kiss—saving your worship's reverence—my cow
　　behind, that the whole town of Edmonton has been ready to bepiss
　　themselves with laughing me to scorn.

JUST: And this is long of her?

O. BANKS: Who the devil else? For is any man such an ass to be such a
　　baby, if he were not bewitched?

SIR ARTH: Nay, if she be a witch, and the harms she does end in such
　　sports, she may scape burning.

JUST: Go, go: pray, vex her not; she is a subject,
　　And you must not be judges of the law
　　To strike her as you please.

COUNTRYMEN: No, no, we'll find cudgel enough to strike her.

O. BANKS: Ay; no lips to kiss but my cow's—!

M. SAW: Rots and foul maladies eat up thee and thine!

(*Exeunt* OLD BANKS *and* COUNTRYMEN)

JUST: Here's none now, Mother Sawyer, but this gentleman,
    Myself, and you: let us to some mild questions;
    Have you mild answers; tell us honestly
    And with a free confession—we'll do our best
    To wean you from it—are you a witch, or no?

M. SAW: I am none.

JUST: Be not so furious.

M. SAW: I am none.
    None but base curs so bark at me; I'm none:
    Or would I were! If every poor old woman
    Be trod on thus by slaves, reviled, kicked, beaten,
    As I am daily, she to be revenged
    Had need turn witch.

SIR ARTH: And you to be revenged
    Have sold your soul to th' Devil.

M. SAW: Keep thine own from him.

JUST: You are too saucy and too bitter.

M. SAW: Saucy?
    By what commission can he send my soul
    On the Devil's errand more than I can his?
    Is he a landlord of my soul, to thrust it,
    When he list, out of door?

JUST: Know whom you speak to.

M. SAW: A man; perhaps no man. Men in gay clothes,
    Whose backs are laden with titles and with honors,

Are within far more crooke̍d than I am,
And, if I be a witch, more witchlike.

SIR ARTH: You're a base Hellhound.—
And now, sir, let me tell you, far and near
She's bruited for a woman that maintains
A spirit that sucks her.

M. SAW: I defy thee.

SIR ARTH: Go, go:
I can, if need be, bring an hundred voices,
E'en here in Edmonton, that shall loud proclaim
Thee for a secret and pernicious witch.

M. SAW: Ha, ha!

JUST: Do you laugh? Why laugh you?

M. SAW: At my name,
The brave name this knight gives me—witch.

JUST: Is the name of witch so pleasing to thine ear?

SIR ARTH: Pray sir, give way, and let her tongue gallop on.

M. SAW: A witch! Who is not?
Hold not that universal name in scorn, then.
What are your painted things in princes' courts,
Upon whose eyelids lust sits, blowing fires
To burn men's souls in sensual hot desires,
Upon whose naked paps a lecher's thought
Acts sin in fouler shapes than can be wrought?

JUST: But those work not as you do.

M. SAW: No, but far worse
These by enchantments can whole lordships change
To trunks of rich attire, turn ploughs and teams
To Flanders mares and coaches, and huge trains
Of servitors to a French butterfly.

Have you not city witches who can turn
Their husbands' wares, whole standing shops of wares,
To sumptuous tables, gardens of stolen sin;
In one year wasting what scarce twenty win?
Are not these witches?

JUST: Yes, yes; but the law
Casts not an eye on these.

M. SAW: Why, then, on me,
Or any lean old beldam? Reverence once
Had wont to wait on age; now an old woman,
Ill-favored grown with years, if she be poor,
Must be called bawd or witch. Such so abused
Are the coarse witches; t'other are the fine,
Spun for the Devil's own wearing.

SIR ARTH: And so is thine.

M. SAW: She on whose tongue a whirlwind sits to blow
A man out of himself, from his soft pillow
To lean his head on rocks and fighting waves,
Is not that scold a witch? The man of law
Whose honeyed hopes the credulous client draw—
As bees by tinkling basins—to swarm to him
From his own hive to work the wax in his;
He is no witch, not he!

SIR ARTH: But these men-witches
Are not in trading with Hell's merchandise,
Like such as you are, that for a word, a look,
Denial of a coal of fire, kill men,
Children, and cattle.

M. SAW: Tell them, sir, that do so:
Am I accused for such an one?

SIR ARTH: Yes; 'twill be sworn.

M. SAW: Dare any swear I ever tempted maiden
With golden hooks flung at her chastity

To come and lose her honor; and being lost,
To pay not a penny for't? Some slaves have done it.
Men-witches can, without the fangs of law
Drawing once one drop of blood, put counterfeit pieces
Away for true gold.

SIR ARTH: By one thing she speaks
I know now she's a witch, and dare no longer
Hold conference with the fury.

JUST: Let's, then, away.—
Old woman, mend thy life; get home and pray.

(*Exeunt* SIR ARTHUR *and* JUSTICE)

M. SAW: For his confusion.
   (*Enter the* DOG)
                  My dear Tom-boy, welcome!
I'm torn in pieces by a pack of curs
Clapt all upon me, and for want of thee:
Comfort me; thou shalt have the teat anon.

DOG: Bow, wow! I'll have it now.

M. SAW: I am dried up
With cursing and with madness, and have yet
No blood to moisten these sweet lips of thine.
Stand on thy hind-legs up—kiss me, my Tommy.
And rub away some wrinkles on my brow
By making my old ribs to shrug for joy
Of thy fine tricks. What hast thou done? Let's tickle.
Hast thou struck the horse lame as I bid thee?

DOG: Yes;
And nipped the sucking child.

M. SAW: Ho, ho, my dainty,
My little pearl! no lady loves her hound,
Monkey, or paroquet, as I do thee.

DOG: The maid has been churning butter nine hours; but it shall not come.

M. SAW: Let 'em eat cheese and choke.

DOG: I had rare sport
  Among the clowns i' th' morris.

M. SAW: I could dance
  Out of my skin to hear thee. But, my curl-pate,
  That jade, that foul-tongued whore, Nan Ratcliffe,
  Who, for a little soap licked by my sow,
  Struck and almost had lamed it;—did not I charge thee
  To pinch that queen to th' heart?

DOG: Bow, wow, wow! look here else.

(Enter ANN RATCLIFFE *mad)*

ANN: See, see, see! The man i' th' moon has built a new windmill; and what running there's from all quarters of the city to learn the art of grinding!

M. SAW: Ho, ho, ho! I thank thee, my sweet mongrel.

ANN: Hoyda! a pox of the Devil's false hopper! all the golden meal runs into the rich knaves' purses, and the poor have nothing but bran. Hey derry down! are not you Mother Sawyer?

M. SAW: No, I am a lawyer.

ANN: Art thou? I prithee let me scratch thy face; for thy pen has flayed off a great many men's skins. You'll have brave doings in the vacation; for knaves and fools are at variance in every village. I'll sue Mother Sawyer, and her own sow shall give in evidence against her.

M. SAW: Touch her. *(To the* DOG, *who rubs against her)*

ANN: O, my ribs are made of a paned hose, and they break! There's a Lancashire hornpipe in my throat; hark, how it tickles it, with doodle,

doodle, doodle, doodle! Welcome, sergeants! welcome, Devil!—
Hands, hands! hold hands, and dance around, around, around.

(*Dancing. Re-enter* OLD BANKS, *with* CUDDY, RATCLIFFE *and* COUNTRYMEN)

RAT: She's here; alas, my poor wife is here!

O. BANKS: Catch her fast, and have her into some close chamber, do; for
she's, as many wives are, stark mad.

CUD: The witch! Mother Sawyer, the witch, the devil!

RAT: O, my dear wife! Help, sirs!

(ANN *is carried off by* RATCLIFFE *and* COUNTRYMEN)

O. BANKS: You see your work, Mother Bumby.

M. SAW: My work? should she and all you here run mad, is the work
mine?

CUD: No, on my conscience, she would not hurt a devil of two years old.
(*Re-enter* RATCLIFFE *and* COUNTRYMEN)
How now! what's become of her?

RAT: Nothing; she's become nothing but the miserable trunk of a
wretched woman. We were in her hands as reeds in a mighty tempest:
spite of our strengths away she brake; and nothing in her mouth being
heard but "the Devil, the witch, the witch, the Devil!" she beat out
her own brains, and so died.

CUD: It's any man's case, be he never so wise, to die when his brains go a
wool-gathering.

O. BANKS: Masters, be ruled by me; let's all to a justice.—Hag, thou hast
done this, and thou shalt answer it.

M. SAW: Banks, I defy thee.

O. BANKS: Get a warrant first to examine her, then ship her to Newgate;
here's enough, if all her other villainies were pardoned, to burn her for

a witch.—You have a spirit, they say, comes to you in the likeness of a dog; we shall see your cur at one time or other: if we do, unless it be the Devil himself, he shall go howling to the gaol in one chain, and thou in another.

M. SAW: Be hanged thou in a third, and do thy worst!

CUD: How, father! You send the poor dumb thing howling to the gaol? He that makes him howl makes me roar.

O. BANKS: Why, foolish boy, dost thou know him?

CUD: No matter if I do or not: he's bailable, I am sure, by law;—but if the dog's word will not be taken, mine shall.

O. BANKS: Thou bail for a dog!

CUD: Yes, or a bitch either, being my friend. I'll lie by the heels myself before puppison shall; his dogdays are not come yet, I hope.

O. BANKS: What manner of dog is it? Didst ever see him?

CUD: See him? Yes, and given him a bone to gnaw twenty times. The dog is no court-foisting hound that fills his belly full by base wagging his tail; neither is it a citizen's water spaniel, enticing his master to go a-ducking twice or thrice a week, whilst his wife makes ducks and drakes at home: this is no Paris-garden bandog neither, that keeps a bow-wow-wowing to have butchers bring their curs thither; and when all comes to all, they run away like sheep: neither is this the Black Dog of Newgate.

O. BANKS: No, Goodman Son-fool, but the dog of Hellgate.

CUD: I say, Goodman Father-fool, it's a lie.

ALL: He's bewitched.

CUD: A gross lie, as big as myself. The Devil in St. Dunstan's will as soon drink with this poor cur as with any Temple-bar laundress that washes and wrings lawyers.

DOG: Bow, wow, wow, wow!

ALL: O, the dog's here, the dog's here.

O. BANKS: It was the voice of a dog.

CUD: The voice of a dog? If that voice were a dog's, what voice had my
mother? So am I a dog: bow, wow, wow! It was I that barked so,
father, to make coxcombs of these clowns.

O. BANKS: However, we'll be coxcombed no longer: away, therefore, to
the justice for a warrant; and then, Gammer Gurton, have at your
needle of witchcraft!

M. SAW: And prick thine own eyes out. Go, peevish fools!

(*Exeunt* OLD BANKS, RATCLIFFE *and* COUNTRYMEN)

CUD: Ningle, you had liked to have spoiled all with your bow-ings. I was
glad to have put 'em off with one of my dog tricks on a sudden; I am
bewitched, little Cost-me-nought, to love thee—a pox,—that morris
makes me spit in thy mouth.—I dare not stay; farewell, ningle; you
whoreson dog's nose!—Farewell, witch!   (*Exit*)

DOG: Bow, wow, wow, wow.

M. SAW: Mind him not, he is not worth thy worrying;
Run at a fairer game: that foul-mouthed knight,
Scurvy Sir Arthur, fly at him, my Tommy,
And pluck out's throat.

DOG: No, there's a dog already biting,—'s conscience.

M. SAW: That's a sure bloodhound. Come, let's home and play;
Our black work ended, we'll make holiday.   (*Exeunt.*)

Scene Two

A Bedroom in CARTER's *house. A bed thrust forth, with* FRANK *in a slumber.*
Enter KATHERINE.

KATH: Brother, brother! so sound asleep? that's well.

FRANK: *(waking):* No, not I, sister; he that's wounded here
    As I am—all my other hurts are bitings
    Of a poor flea;—but he that here once bleeds
    Is maimed incurably.

KATH: My good sweet brother—
    For now my sister must grow up in you—
    Though her loss strikes you through, and that I feel
    The blow as deep, I pray thee be not cruel
    To kill me too, by seeing you cast away
    In your own helpless sorrow. Good love, sit up;
    And if you can give physic to yourself,
    I shall be well.

FRANK: I'll do my best.

KATH: I thank you;
    What do you look about for?

FRANK: Nothing, nothing;
    But I was thinking, sister,—

KATH: Dear heart, what?

FRANK: Who but a fool would thus be bound to a bed,
    Having this room to walk in?

KATH: Why do you talk so?
    Would you were fast asleep!

FRANK: No, no; I'm not idle.
    But here's my meaning; being robbed as I am,

Why should my soul, which married was to hers,
Live in divorce, and not fly after her?
Why should I not walk hand in hand with Death,
To find my love out?

KATH: That were well indeed,
  Your time being come; when Death is sent to call you,
  No doubt you shall meet her.

FRANK: Why should not I
  Go without calling?

KATH: Yes, brother, so you might,
  Were there no place to go when you're gone
  But only this.

FRANK: 'Troth, sister, thou say'st true;
  For when a man has been an hundred years
  Hard traveling o'er the tottering bridge of age,
  He's not the thousand part upon his way:
  All life is but a wandering to find home;
  When we're gone, we're there. Happy were man,
  Could here his voyage end; he should not, then,
  Answer how well or ill he steered his soul
  By Heaven's or by Hell's compass; how he put in—
  Losing blessed goodness' shore—at such a sin;
  Nor how life's dear provision he has spent,
  Nor how far he in's navigation went
  Beyond commission: this were a fine reign,
  To do ill and not hear of it again;
  Yet then were man more wretched than a beast;
  For, sister, our dead pay is sure the best.

KATH: 'Tis so, the best or worst; and I wish Heaven
  To pay—and so I know it will—that traitor,
  That devil Somerton—who stood in mine eye
  Once as an angel—home to his deservings:
  What villain but himself, once loving me,
  With Warbeck's soul would pawn his own to Hell
  To be revenged on my poor sister!

FRANK: Slaves!
A pair of merciless slaves! Speak no more of them.

KATH: I think this talking hurts you.

FRANK: Does me no good, I'm sure;
I pay for't everywhere.

KATH: I have done, then.
Eat, if you cannot sleep; you have these two days
Not tasted any food.—Jane, is it ready?

FRANK: What's ready? what's ready?

KATH: I have made ready a roasted chicken for you:
(Enter MAID *with chicken)*
Sweet, wilt thou eat?

FRANK: A pretty stomach on a sudden; yes.—
There's one in the house can play upon a lute;
Good girl, let's hear him too.

KATH: You shall, dear brother.   *(Exit* MAID*)*
Would I were a musician, you should hear
How I would feast your ear! *(Lute plays within)*—stay mend your pillow,
And raise you higher.

FRANK: I am up too high,
Am I not, sister now?

KATH: No, no; 'tis well.
Fall-to, fall-to.—A knife! Here's never a knife.
Brother, I'll look out yours.   *(Takes up his vest)*

(Enter the DOG, *shrugging as it were for joy, and dances)*

FRANK: Sister, O, sister,
I'm ill upon a sudden, and can eat nothing.

KATH: In very deed you shall: the want of food
    Makes you so faint. Ha! *(Sees the bloody knife)*—here's none in
      your pocket;
    I'll go fetch a knife.   *(Exit hastily)*

FRANK: Will you?—'tis well, all's well.

(FRANK searches first one pocket, then the other, finds the knife, and then lies down.—The DOG runs off.—The spirit of SUSAN comes to the bed's side: FRANK stares at it, and then turns to the other side, but the spirit is there too. Meanwhile enter WINNIFRED as a page, and stands sadly at the bed's foot.—FRANK affrighted sits up. The spirit vanishes.)

FRANK: What art thou?

WIN: A lost creature.

FRANK: So am I too.—Win?

Ah, my she-page!

WIN: For your sake I put on
    A shape that's false; yet do I wear a heart
    True to you as your own.

FRANK: Would mine and thine
    Were fellows in one house!—Kneel by me here.
    On this side now! how dar'st thou come to mock me
    On both sides of my bed?

WIN: When?

FRANK: But just now:
    Outface me, stare upon me with strange postures,
    Turn my soul wild by a face in which were drawn
    A thousand ghosts leapt newly from their graves
    To pluck me into a winding-sheet!

WIN: Believe it,
    I came no nearer to you than yon place
    At your bed's feet; and of the house had leave,

Calling myself your horse-boy, in to come,
And visit my sick master.

FRANK: Then 'twas my fancy;
Some windmill in my brains for want of sleep.

WIN: Would I might never sleep, so you could rest!
But you have plucked a thunder on your head,
Whose noise cannot cease suddenly: why should you
Dance at the wedding of a second wife,
When scarce the music which you heard at mine
Had ta'en a farewell of you? O, this was ill!
And they who thus can give both hands away
In th' end shall want their best limbs.

FRANK: Winnifred—
The chamber door's fast?

WIN: Yes.

FRANK: Sit thee, then, down;
And when thou'st heard me speak, melt into tears:
Yet I, to save those eyes of thine from weeping,
Being to write a story of us two.
Instead of ink dipped my sad pen in blood.
When of thee I took leave, I went abroad
Only for pillage, as a freebooter,
What gold soe'er I got to make it thine.
To please a father I have Heaven displeased;
Striving to cast two wedding rings in one,
Through my bad workmanship I now have none;
I have lost her and thee.

WIN: I know she's dead;
But you have me still.

FRANK: Nay, her this hand
Murdered; and so I lose thee too.

WIN: O me!

FRANK: Be quiet; for thou my evidence art,
Jury, and judge: sit quiet, and I'll tell all.

(While they are conversing in a low tone, enter at one door CARTER *and* KATHERINE, *at the other the* DOG, *pawing softly at* FRANK)

KATH: I have run madding up and down to find you,
Being laden with the heaviest news that ever
Poor daughter carried.

CAR: Why? Is the boy dead?

KATH: Dead, sir!
O, father, we are cozened: you are told
The murderer sings in prison, and he laughs here.
This villain killed my sister see else, see,
(Takes up his vest, and shows the knife to her father, who secures it.)
A bloody knife in's pocket!

CAR: Bless me, patience!

FRANK *(seeing them)* The knife, the knife, the knife!

KATH: What knife?   *(Exit the* DOG)

FRANK: To cut my chicken up, my chicken;
Be you my carver, father.

CAR: That I will.

KATH: How the devil steels our brows after doing ill!

FRANK: My stomach and my sight are taken from me;
All is not well within me,

CAR: I believe thee, boy; I that have seen so many moons clap their
horns on other men's foreheads to strike them sick, yet mine to scape
and be well; I that never cast away a fee upon urinals, but am as
sound as an honest man's conscience when he's dying; I should cry
out as thou dost, "All is not well within me," felt I but the bag of thy

imposthumes. Ah, poor villain! ah, my wounded rascal! All my grief is, I have now small hope of thee.

FRANK: Do the surgeons say my wounds are dangerous, then?

CAR: Yes, yes, and there's no way with thee but one.

FRANK: Would he were here to open them!

CAR: I'll go to fetch him; I'll make an holiday to see thee as I wish.

FRANK: A wondrous kind old man!

WIN (*aside to* FRANK):   Your sin's the blacker
So to abuse his goodness.—(*Aloud*) Master, how do you?

FRANK: Pretty well now, boy; I have such odd qualms
Come cross my stomach.—I'll fall to; boy, cut me—

WIN (*aside*): You have cut me, I'm sure;—A leg or wing, sir?

FRANK: No, no, no; a wing—

(*Aside*) Would I had wings but to soar up yon tower!
But here's a clog that hinders me.

(*Re-enter* CARTER, *with* SERVANTS *bearing the body of* SUSAN *in a coffin*)

                              What's that?

CAR: That! What? O, now I see her; 'tis a young wench, my daughter, sirrah, sick to the death; and hearing thee to be an excellent rascal for letting blood, she looks out at a casement, and cries, "Help, help! stay that man! him I must have or none."

FRANK: For pity's sake, remove her: see, she stares
With one broad open eye still in my face!

CAR: Thou putted'st both hers out, like a villain as thou art; yet, see! she is willing to lend thee one again to find out the murderer, and that's thyself.

FRANK: Old man, thou liest!

CAR: So shalt thou—in the gaol.—
Run for officers.

KATH: O, thou merciless slave!
She was—though yet above ground—in her grave
To me; but thou hast torn it up again—
Mine eyes, too much drowned, now must feel more rain.

CAR: Fetch officers.

(*Exit* KATHERINE *and* SERVANTS *with the body of* SUSAN)

FRANK: For whom?

CAR: For thee, sirrah, sirrah! Some knives have foolish posies upon them, but thine has a villainous one; look! (*Showing the bloody knife*) O, it is enamelled with the heartblood of thy hated wife, my belovèd daughter! What sayest thou to this evidence? Is't not sharp? Does't not strike home? Thou canst not answer honestly and without a trembling heart to this one point, this terrible bloody point.

WIN: I beseech you, sir,
Strike him no more; you see he's dead already.

CAR: O, sir, you held his horses; you are as arrant a rogue as he: up go you too.

FRANK: As you're a man, throw not upon that woman
Your loads of tyranny, for she is innocent.

CAR: How! how! A woman! Is't grown to a fashion for women in all countries to wear the breeches?

WIN: I'm not as my disguise speaks me, sir, his page,
But his first, only wife, his lawful wife.

CAR: How! how! More fire i' th' bed-straw!

WIN: The wrongs which singly fell upon your daughter
   On me are multiplied; she lost a life,
   But I an husband, and myself must lose
   If you call him to a bar for what he has done.

CAR: He has done it, then?

WIN: Yes, 'tis confessed to me.

FRANK: Dost thou betray me?

WIN: O, pardon me, dear heart! I'm mad to lose thee,
   And know not what I speak; but if thou didst,
   I must arraign this father for two sins,
   Adultery and murder.

(*Re-enter* KATHERINE)

KATH: Sir, they are come.

CAR: Arraign me for what thou wilt, all Middlesex knows me better for
   an honest man than the middle of a marketplace knows thee for an
   honest woman.—Rise, sirrah, and don your tacklings; rig yourself for
   the gallows, or I'll carry thee thither on my back: your trull shall to the
   gaol go with you: there be as fine Newgate birds as she that can draw
   him in: pox on's wounds!

FRANK: I have served thee, and my wages now are paid;
   Yet my worse punishment shall, I hope, be stayed.

(*Exeunt.*)

ACT THE FIFTH

Scene One

The WITCH's *cottage. Enter* MOTHER SAWYER.

MOTHER SAWYER: Still wronged by every slave, and not a dog
   Bark in his dame's defense? I am called witch,

Yet am myself bewitched from doing harm.
Have I given up myself to thy black lust
Thus to be scorned? Not see me in three days!
I'm lost without my Tomalin; prithee come,
Revenge to me is sweeter far than life;
Thou art my raven, on whose coal-black wings
Revenge comes flying to me. O, my best love!
I am on fire, even in the midst of ice,
Raking my blood up, till my shrunk knees feel
Thy curled head leaning on them: come, then, my darling;
If in the air thou hover'st, fall upon me
In some dark cloud; and as I oft have seen
Dragons and serpents in the elements,
Appear thou now so to me. Art thou i' th' sea?
Muster up all the monsters from the deep,
And be the ugliest of them: so that my hound
Show but his swarth cheek to me, let earth cleave
And break from Hell, I care not! Could I run
Like a swift powdermine beneath the world,
Up would I blow it all, to find out thee,
Though I lay ruined in it. Not yet come!
I must, then, fall to my old prayer:
Sanctibicetur nomen tuum.
Not yet come! the worrying of wolves, biting of mad dogs, the
manges, and the—

(Enter the DOG *which is now white)*

DOG: How now! whom art thou cursing?

M. SAW: Thee!
Ha! No, it is my black cur I am cursing
For not attending on me.

DOG: I am that cur,

M. SAW: Thou liest: hence! Come not nigh me.

DOG: Baw, waw!

M. SAW: Why dost thou thus appear to me in white,
  As if thou wert the ghost of my dear love?

DOG: I am dogged, and list not to tell thee; yet,—to torment thee,—my
  whiteness puts thee in mind of thy winding-sheet.

M. SAW: Am I near death?

DOG: Yes, if the dog of Hell be near thee; when the Devil comes to thee
  as a lamb, have at thy throat!

M. SAW: Off, cur!

DOG: He has the back of a sheep, but the belly of an otter; devours by
  sea and land. "Why am I in white?" Didst thou not pray to me?

M. SAW: Yes, thou dissembling hellhound!
  Why now in white more than at other times?

DOG: Be blasted with the news! Whiteness is day's footboy, a forerunner
  to light, which shows thy old rivelled face: villainies are stripped naked; the witch must be beaten out of her cockpit.

M. SAW: Must she? she shall not: thou'rt a lying spirit:
  Why to mine eyes art thou a flag of truce?
  I am at peace with none; 'tis the black color,
  Or none, which I fight under: I do not like
  Thy puritan paleness; glowing furnaces
  Are far more hot than they which flame outright.
  If thou my old dog art, go and bite such
  As I shall set thee on.

DOG: I will not.

M. SAW: I'll sell myself to twenty thousand fiends
  To have thee torn in pieces, then.

DOG: Thou canst not; thou art so ripe to fall into Hell, that no more of
  my kennel will so much as bark at him that hangs thee.

M. SAW: I shall run mad.

DOG: Do so, thy time is come to curse, and rave, and die; the glass of thy
  sins is full, and it must run out at gallows.

M. SAW: It cannot, ugly cur; I'll confess nothing;
  And not confessing, who dare come and swear
  I have bewitched them? I'll not confess one mouthful.

DOG: Choose, and be hanged or burned.

M. SAW: Spite of the Devil and thee,
  I'll muzzle up my tongue from telling tales.

DOG: Spite of thee and the Devil, thou'lt be condemned.

M. SAW: Yes! when?

DOG: And ere the executioner catch thee full in's claws, thou'lt confess
  all.

M. SAW: Out, dog!

DOG: Out, witch! thy trial is at hand:
  Our prey being had, the Devil does laughing stand.

(Runs aside) *(Enter* OLD BANKS, RATCLIFFE *and* COUNTRYMEN*)*

O. BANKS: She's here; attach her.—Witch you must go with us.

(They seize her)

M. SAW: Whither? To Hell?

O. BANKS: No, no, no, old crone; your mittimus shall be made thither,
  but your own jailors shall receive you.—Away with her!

M. SAW: My Tommy! my sweet Tom-boy! O, thou dog!
  Dost thou now fly to thy kennel and forsake me?
  Plagues and consumptions—   *(She is carried off)*

DOG: Ha, ha, ha, ha!
Let not the world witches or devils condemn;
They follow us, and then we follow them.

(Enter CUDDY BANKS)

CUD: I would fain meet with my friend once more: he has had a claw
amongst 'em: my rival that loved my wench is like to be hanged like
an innocent. A kind cur where he takes, but where he takes not, a
dogged rascal; I know the villain loves me. *(The* DOG *barks)* No! Art
thou there? *(Seeing the* DOG*)* that's Tom's voice, but 'tis not he; this is
a dog of another hair, this. Bark, and not speak to me? Not Tom,
then; there's as much difference betwixt Tom and this as betwixt
white and black.

DOG: Hast thou forgot me?

CUD: That's Tom again.—Prithee, ningle, speak; is thy name Tom?

DOG: Whilst I served my old Dame Sawyer 'twas; I'm gone from her
now.

CUD: Gone? Away with the witch, then, too! She'll never thrive if thou
leavest her; she knows no more how to kill a cow, or a horse, or a sow,
without thee, than she does to kill a goose.

DOG: No, she has done killing now, but must be killed for what she has
done; she's shortly to be hanged.

CUD: Is she? In my conscience, if she be, 'tis thou hast brought her to
the gallows, Tom.

DOG: Right; I served her to that purpose; 'twas part of my wages.

CUD: This was no honest servant's part, by your leave, Tom. This remember, I pray you, between you and I; I entertained you ever as a
dog, not as a Devil.

DOG: True;
And so I used thee doggedly, not devilishly;
I have deluded thee for sport to laugh at:

The wench thou seek'st after thou never spak'st with,
But a spirit in her form, habit, and likeness.
Ha, ha!

CUD: I do not, then, wonder at the change of your garments, if you can
enter into shapes of women too.

DOG: Any shape, to blind such silly eyes as thine; but chiefly those
coarse creatures, dog, or cat, hare, ferret, frog, toad.

CUD: Louse or flea?

DOG: Any poor vermin.

CUD: It seems you devils have poor thin souls, that you can bestow
yourselves in such small bodies. But, pray you, Tom, one question at
parting;—I think I shall never see you more;—where do you borrow
those bodies that are none of your own?—the garment-shape you may
hire at broker's.

DOG: Why would'st thou know that, fool? It avails thee not.

CUD: Only for my mind's sake, Tom, and to tell some of my friends.

DOG: I'll thus much tell thee: thou never art so distant
From an evil spirit, but that thy oaths,
Curses, and blasphemies pull him to thine elbow;
Thou never tell'st a lie, but that a devil
Is within hearing it; thy evil purposes
Are ever haunted; but when they come to act—
As thy tongue slandering, bearing false witness,
Thy hand stabbing, stealing, cozening, cheating—
He's then within thee: thou play'st, he bets upon thy part.
Although thou lose, yet he will gain by thee.

CUD: Ay? Then he comes in the shape of a rook?

DOG: The old cadaver of some self-strangled wretch
We sometimes borrow, and appear human;
The carcass of some disease-slain strumpet
We varnish fresh, and wear as her first beauty.

Did'st never hear? If not, it has been done;
An hot luxurious lecher in his twines,
When he has thought to clip his dalliance,
There has provided been for his embrace
A fine hot flaming Devil in her place.

CUD: Yes, I am partly a witness to this; but I never could embrace her; I
thank thee for that, Tom. Well, again I thank thee, Tom, for all this
counsel; without a fee too! There's few lawyers of thy mind now.
Certainly, Tom, I begin to pity thee.

DOG: Pity me! for what?

CUD: Were it not possible for thee to become an honest dog yet?—'Tis a
base life that you lead, Tom, to serve witches, to kill innocent children, to kill harmless cattle, to blight corn and fruit, etc.: 'twere better
yet to be a butcher and kill for yourself.

DOG: Why, these are all my delights, my pleasures, fool.

CUD: Or, Tom, if you could give your mind to ducking,—I know you can
swim, fetch, and carry—some shopkeeper in London would take great
delight in you, and be a tender master over you: or if you have a mind
to the game either at bull or bear, I think I could prefer you to Moll
Cutpurse.

DOG: Ha, ha! I should kill all the game,—bulls, bears, dogs and all; not a
cub to be left.

CUD: You could do, Tom; but you must play fair; you should be staved
off else. Or if your stomach did better like to serve in some nobleman's, knight's, or gentleman's kitchen, if you could brook the wheel
and turn the spit—your labor could not be much—when they have
roast meat, that's but once or twice in the week at most: here you
might lick your own toes very well. Or if you could translate yourself
into a lady's arming puppy, there you might lick sweet lips, and do
many pretty offices; but to creep under an old witch's coats, and suck
like a great puppy! Fie upon't!—I have heard beastly things of you,
Tom.

DOG: Ha, ha!
  The worse thou heard'st of me the better 'tis
  Shall I serve thee, fool, at the selfsame rate?

CUD: No, I'll see thee hanged, thou shalt be damned first! I know thy
  qualities too well, I'll give no suck to such whelps; therefore
  henceforth I defy thee. Out, and avaunt!

DOG: Nor will I serve for such a silly soul:
  I am for greatness now, corrupted greatness;
  There I'll creep in, and get a noble countenance;
  Serve some Briarean footcloth-strider,
  That has an hundred hands to catch at bribes,
  But not a finger's nail of charity.
  Such, like the dragon's tail, shall pull down hundreds
  To drop and sink with him: I'll stretch myself.
  And draw this bulk small as a silver wire,
  Enter at the least pore tobacco-fume
  Can make a breach for:—hence, silly fool!
  I scorn to prey on such an atom soul.

CUD: Come out, come out, you cur! I will beat thee out of the bounds of
  Edmonton, and tomorrow we go in procession, and after thou shalt
  never come in again: if thou goest to London, I'll make thee go about
  by Tyburn, stealing in by Thieving Lane. If thou canst rub thy shoulder against a lawyer's gown, as thou passest by Westminster Hall, do;
  if not, to the stairs amongst the bandogs, take water, and the Devil go
  with thee!

(Exit, followed by the DOG barking.)

Scene Two

London. The neighborhood of Tyburn. Enter JUSTICE, SIR ARTHUR, SOMERTON,
WARBECK, CARTER *and* KATHERINE.

JUST: Sir Arthur, though the bench hath mildly censured your errors, yet
  you have indeed been the instrument that wrought all their misfor-
  tunes; I would wish you paid down your fine speedily and willingly

SIR ARTH: I'll need no urging to it.

CAR: If you should, 'twere a shame to you; for if I should speak my
conscience, you are worthier to be hanged of the two, all things considered; and now make what you can of it: but I am glad these gentlemen are freed.

WAR: We knew our innocence.

SOM: And therefore feared it not.

KATH: But I am glad that I have you safe.

(A *noise within*)

JUST: How now! What noise is that?

CAR: Young Frank is going the wrong way. Alas, poor youth! Now I begin
to pity him.

(*Enter* OLD THORNEY *and* WINNIFRED *weeping*)

O. THOR: Here let our sorrows wait him; to press nearer
The place of his sad death, some apprehensions
May tempt our grief too much, at height already.—
Daughter be comforted.

WIN: Comfort and I
Are far too separated to be joined.
But in eternity: I share too much
Of him that's going thither.

CAR: Poor woman, 'twas not thy fault; I grieve to see thee weep for him
that hath my pity too.

WIN: My fault was lust, my punishment was shame.
Yet I am happy that my soul is free
Both from consent, foreknowledge and intent
Of any murder but of mine own honor,
Restored again by a fair satisfaction,
And since not to be wounded.

O. THOR: Daughter, grieve not
For what necessity forceth;
Rather resolve to conquer it with patience.—
Alas, she faints!

WIN: My griefs are strong upon me;
My weakness scarce can bear them.

VOICES *(offstage)*: Away with her! hang her, witch!

(Enter to execution MOTHER SAWYER; OFFICERS *with halberds, followed by a crowd of* COUNTRYPEOPLE)

CAR: The witch, that instrument of mischief! Did not she witch the Devil into my son-in-law, when he killed my poor daughter?—Do you hear, Mother Sawyer?

M. SAW: What would you have?
Cannot a poor old woman have your leave
To die without vexation?

CAR: Did not you bewitch Frank to kill his wife? He could never have done't without the Devil.

M. SAW: Who doubts it? But is every Devil mine?
Would I had one now whom I might command
To tear you all in pieces? Tom would have done't
Before he left me.

CAR: Thou didst bewitch Ann Ratcliffe to kill herself.

M. SAW: Churl, thou liest; I never did her hurt:
Would you were all as near your ends as I am,
That gave evidence against me for it!

FIRST COUN: I'll be sworn, Master Carter, she bewitched Gammer Wash-bowl's sow to cast her pigs a day before she would have farrowed: yet they were sent up to London and sold for as good Westminster dog-pigs at Bartholomew Fair as ever great-bellied alewife longed for.

M. SAW: These dogs will mad me: I was well resolved

To die in my repentance. Though 'tis true
I would live longer if I might, yet since
I cannot, pray torment me not; my conscience
Is settled as it shall be: all take heed
How they believe the Devil; at last he'll cheat you.

CAR: Thou'dst best confess all truly.

M. SAW: Yet again?
Have I scarce breath enough to say my prayers,
And would you force me to spend that in bawling?
Bear witness, I repent all former evil;
There is no damnèd conjuror like the Devil.

ALL: Away with her, away!   *(She is led off)*

(Enter FRANK *to execution,* OFFICERS, *& etc.)*

O. THOR: Here's the sad object which I yet must meet
With hope of comfort, if a repentant end
Make him more happy than misfortune would
Suffer him here to be.

FRANK: Good sirs, turn from me:
You will revive affliction almost killed
With my continual sorrow.

O. THOR: O, Frank, Frank!
Would I had sunk in mine own wants, or died
But one bare minute ere thy fault was acted!

FRANK: To look upon your sorrows executes me
Before my execution.

WIN: Let me pray you, sir—

FRANK: Thou much-wronged woman, I must sigh for thee,
As he that's only loth to leave the world
For that he leaves thee in it unprovided,
Unfriended; and for me to beg a pity
From any man to thee when I am gone

Is more than I can hope; nor, to say truth,
Have I deserved it: but there is a payment
Belongs to goodness from the great exchequer
Above; it will not fail thee, Winnifred;
Be that thy comfort.

O. THOR: Let it be thine too,
Untimely-lost young man.

FRANK: He is not lost
Who bears his peace within him: had I spun
My web of life out at full length, and dreamed
Away my many years in lusts, in surfeits,
Murders of reputations, gallant sins
Commended or approved; then, though I had
Died easily, as great and rich men do,
Upon my own bed, not compelled by justice,
You might have mourn'd for me indeed; my miseries
Had been as everlasting as remediless:
But now the law hath not arraigned, condemned
With greater rigor my unhappy fact
Than I myself have every little sin
My memory can reckon from my childhood:
A court hath been kept here, where I am found
Guilty; the difference is, my impartial judge
Is much more gracious than my faults
Are monstrous to be named; yet they are monstrous.

O. THOR: Here's comfort in this penitence.

WIN: It speaks
How truly you are reconciled, and quickens
My dying comfort, that was near expiring
With my last breath: now this repentance makes thee
As white as innocence; and my first sin with thee,
Since which I knew none like it, by my sorrow
Is clearly cancelled. Might our souls together
Climb to the height of their eternity,
And there enjoy what earth denied us, happiness!
But since I must survive, and be the monument
Of thy loved memory, I will preserve it

With a religious care, and pay thy ashes
A widow's duty, calling that end best
Which, though it stain the name, makes the soul blest.

FRANK: Give me thy hand, poor woman; do not weep.
Farewell: thou dost forgive me?

WIN: 'Tis my part
To use that language.

FRANK: O, that my example
Might teach the world hereafter what a curse
Hangs on their heads who rather choose to marry
A goodly portion than a dower of virtues!—
Are you there, gentlemen? there is not one
Amongst you whom I have not wronged; *(To* CARTER*)* you most:
I robbed you of a daughter; but she is
In Heaven; and I must suffer for it willingly.

CAR: Ay, ay, she's in Heaven, and I am so glad to see thee so well
prepared to follow her. I forgive thee with all my heart; if thou hadst
not had ill counsel, thou wouldst not have done as thou didst; the
more shame for them.

SOM: Spare your excuse to me, I do conceive
What you would speak; I would you could as easily
Make satisfaction to the law as to my wrongs.
I am sorry for you.

WAR: And so am I,
And heartily forgive you.

KATH: I will pray for you
For her sake, who I'm sure did love you dearly.

SIR ARTH: Let us part friendly too; I am ashamed
Of my part in thy wrongs.

FRANK: You are all merciful,
And send me to my grave in peace. Sir Arthur,
Heaven send you a new heart!—Lastly, to you, sir;

And though I have deserved not to be called
Your son, yet give me leave upon my knees
To beg a blessing.   *(Kneels)*

O. THOR: Take it; let me wet
Thy cheeks with the last tears my griefs have left me.
O, Frank, Frank, Frank!

FRANK: Let me beseech you, gentlemen,
To comfort my old father, keep him with ye;
Love this distressèd widow; and as often
As you remember what a graceless man
I was, remember likewise that these are
Both free, both worthy of a better fate
Than such a son or husband as I have been.
All help me with your prayers.—On, on; 'tis just
That law should purge the guilt of blood and lust.

(Exit, led off by the OFFICERS*)*

CAR: Go thy ways; I did not think to have shed one tear for thee, but
thou hast made me water my plants spite of my heart.—Master
Thorney, cheer up, man; whilst I can stand by you, you shall not want
help to keep you from falling: we have lost our children, both on's, the
wrong way, but we cannot help it; better or worse, 'tis now as 'tis.

O. THOR: I thank you, sir; you are more kind than I have cause to hope or
look for.

CAR: Master Somerton, is Kate yours or no?

SOM: We are agreed.

KATH: And but my faith is passed, I should fear to be married, husbands
are so cruelly unkind. Excuse me that I am thus troubled.

SOM: Thou shalt have no cause.

JUST: Take comfort, Mistress Winnifred: Sir Arthur,
For his abuse to you and to your husband,

Is by the bench enjoined to pay you down
A thousand marks.

SIR ARTH: Which I will soon discharge.

WIN: Sir, 'tis too great a sum to be employed
Upon my funeral.

CAR: Come, come; if luck had served, Sir Arthur, and every man had his
due, somebody might have tottered ere this, without paying fines, like
it as you list.—Come to me, Winnifred; shalt be welcome.—Make
much of her, Kate, I charge you: I do not think but she's a good
wench, and hath had wrong as well as we. So let's every man home to
Edmonton with heavy hearts, yet as merry as we can, though not as
we would.

JUST: Join, friends, in sorrow; make of all the best:
Harms past may be lamented, not redrest.   (Exeunt.)

Epilogue

Spoken by WINNIFRED

I am a widow still, and must not sort
A second choice without a good report;
Which though some widows find, and few deserve,
Yet I dare not presume, but will not swerve
From modest hopes. All noble tongues are free;
The gentle may speak one kind word for me.

THE REVENGER'S TRAGEDY

Cyril Tourneur

Nearly three hundred years before the infamous Grand Guignol opened its doors to horrify Parisians with plays that featured dismemberment, gougings and torture, the anonymously published *The Revenger's Tragedy* appeared in 1607 to shock English playgoers with its wonderfully repellent cast of bastards, bawds, poisoners and rapists.

Its authorship, long disputed, has been assigned with equal fervor to Thomas Middleton and to Cyril Tourneur (1576?–1626). Almost nothing is known about Tourneur's life other than the fact that he worked for a time in the Netherlands, died in Ireland and penned a small number of poems and plays, including another revenge tragedy, *The Atheist's Tragedy* (1611).

The Revenger's Tragedy has accurately been described as a macabre ballet that encapsulates the emotional stress and iniquities of an entire age. Yet, as critic Gamini Salgado points out, it is still rooted in a "deeply moral and deeply traditional" vision, though, as is often the case in theatre, moral order is only reestablished after the spectator-voyeur has supped full of horrors.

The Revenger's Tragedy is second only to Shakespeare's Titus Andronicus for unremitting gruesomeness.

DRAMATIS PERSONAE

DUKE
LUSSURIOS, *the Duke's son.*
SPURIO, *his bastard son.*
AMBITIOSO, *the Duchess' eldest son.*
SUPERVACUO, *the Duchess' second son.*
JUNIOR, *the youngest son of the Duchess.*
VINDICE (Piato),
HIPPOLITO (Carlo), } *Brothers, sons of Gratiana.*
ANTONIO,
PIERO, } *Nobles.*
DONDOLO, *servant to Castiza.*
NENCIO,
SORDIDO, } *followers of Lussurioso.*

    Nobles, Gentlemen, Judges, Officers, Servants.
DUCHESS
CASTIZA, *sister to Vindice and Hippolito.*
GRATIANA, *her mother.*

    Scene: Italy, in and around the DUKE'S *palace.*

ACT ONE

Scene One

Enter VINDICE *carrying a skull; the* DUKE, DUCHESS, LUSSURIOSO *his Son,* SPURIO *the Bastard, with a train, pass over the Stage with Torchlight.*

VINDICE: Duke, royal lecher! Go, gray-haired adultery,
    And thou his son, as impious steeped as he:
    And thou his bastard, true-begot in evil:
    And thou his Duchess, that will do with Devil,
    Four ex'lent characters—O, that marrowless age
    Would stuff the hollow bones with damn'd desires,
    And 'stead of heat kindle infernal fires
    Within the spendthrift veins of a dry Duke,
    A parched and juiceless luxur. O God! One
    That has scarce blood enough to live upon,
    And he to riot it like a son and heir?
    O the thought of that
    Turns my abusèd heartstrings into fret.
    (Addressing skull)
    Thou sallow picture of my poisoned love,
    My study's ornament, thou shell of death,
    Once the bright face of my betrothèd lady,
    When life and beauty naturally filled out
    These ragged imperfections;
    When two heaven-pointed diamonds were set
    In those unsightly rings;—then 'twas a face
    So far beyond the artificial shine
    Of any woman's bought complexion
    That the uprightest man, (if such there be,
    That sin but seven times a day) broke custom
    And made up eight with looking after her.
    Oh, she was able to ha'made a usurer's son
    Melt all his patrimony in a kiss,
    And what his father fifty yearès told
    To have consumed, and yet his suit been cold:
    But oh accursèd palace!
    Thee, when thou wert apparelled in thy flesh,
    The old Duke poisoned,
    Because thy purer part would not consent

Unto his palsy-lust, for old men lust-full
Do show like young men angry, eager-violent,
Out-bid like their limited performances.
O 'ware an old man hot, and vicious!
'Age as in gold, in lust is covetous.'
Vengeance, thou Murder's quit-rent, and whereby
Thou show'st thyself tenant to tragedy,
Oh keep thy day, hour, minute, I beseech;
For those thou hast determined: hum, whoe'er knew
Murder unpaid? Faith, give Revenge her due
Sh'as kept touch hitherto—be merry, merry
Advance thee, O thou terror to fat folks,
To have their costly three-piled flesh worn off
As bare as this—for banquets, ease and laughter
Can make great men as greatness goes by clay,
But wise men little are more great than they.

(*Enter his brother* HIPPOLITO)

HIPPOLITO: Still sighing o'er death's vizard.

VINDICE: Brother, welcome,
   What comfort bring'st thou? How go things at court?

HIPPOLITO: In silk and silver brother: never braver.

VINDICE: Puh,
   Thou play'st upon my meaning. Prithee say
   Hast that bald madam, Opportunity,
   Yet thought upon's? Speak, are we happy yet?
   Thy wrongs and mine are for one scabbard fit.

HIPPOLITO: It may prove happiness.

VINDICE: What is't may prove?
   Give me to taste.

HIPPOLITO: Give me your hearing then.
   You know my place at court.

VINDICE: Ay, the Duke's chamber,
  But 'tis a marvel thou'rt not turned out yet!

HIPPOLITO: Faith, I have been shoved at, but 'twas still my hap
  To hold by th'Duchess' skirt, you guess at that,
  Whom such a coat keeps up can ne'er fall flat,
  But to the purpose:
  Last evening, predecessor unto this,
  The Duke's son warily enquired for me,
  Whose pleasure I attended: he began
  By policy to open and unhusk me
  About the time and common rumor:
  But I had so much wit to keep my thoughts
  Up in their built houses, yet afforded him
  An idle satisfaction without danger;
  But the whole aim and scope of his intent
  Ended in this, conjuring me in private
  To seek some strange-digested fellow forth,
  Of ill-contented nature, either disgraced
  In former times, or by new grooms displaced
  Since his stepmother's nuptials, such a blood,
  A man that were for evil only good;
  To give you the true word, some base-coin'd pander.

VINDICE: I reach you, for I know his heat is such,
  Were there as many concubines as ladies
  He would not be contained, he must fly out:
  I wonder how ill-featured, vile-proportioned
  That one should be, if she were made for woman,
  Whom, at the insurrection of his lust
  He would refuse for once; heart, I think none;
  Next to a skull, tho' more unsound than one
  Each face he meets he strongly dotes upon.

HIPPOLITO: Brother, y'ave truly spoke him.
  He knows not you, but I'll swear you know him.

VINDICE: And therefore I'll put on that knave for once,
  And be a right man then, a man o'th'time,
  For to be honest is not to be i'th'world,
  Brother, I'll be that strange-composèd fellow.

HIPPOLITO: And I'll prefer you brother.

VINDICE: Go to then,
The small'st advantage fattens wrongèd men.
It may point out, occasion, if I meet her,
I'll hold her by the forelock fast enough,
Or, like the French mole, heave up hair and all,
I have a habit that will fit it quaintly.
(*Enter* GRATIANA *and* CASTIZA)
Here comes our mother.

HIPPOLITO: And sister.

VINDICE: We must dissemble.
Women are apt, you know, to take false money,
But I dare stake my soul for these two creatures
Only excuse excepted, that they'll swallow
Because their sex is easy in belief.

GRATIANA: What news from court, son Carlo?

HIPPOLITO: Faith, mother,
'Tis whispered there the Duchess' youngest son
Has played a rape on Lord Antonio's wife.

GRATIANA: On that religious lady!

CASTIZA: Royal blood! Monster, he deserves to die
If Italy had no more hopes but he.

VINDICE: Sister, y'ave sentenced most direct and true,
The law's a woman, and would she were you.
Mother, I must take leave of you.

GRATIANA: Leave for what?

VINDICE: I intend speedy travel.

HIPPOLITO: That he does, Madam.

GRATIANA: Speedy indeed!

VINDICE: For since my worthy father's funeral
   My life's unnatural to me, e'en compelled,
   As if I lived now when I should be dead.

GRATIANA: Indeed he was a worthy gentleman
   Had his estate been fellow to his mind.

VINDICE: The Duke did much deject him.

GRATIANA: Much!

VINDICE: Too much.
   And through disgrace oft smothered in his spirit
   When it would mount; surely I think he died
   Of discontent, the nobleman's consumption.

GRATIANA: Most sure he did.

VINDICE: Did he? 'Lack—you know all,
   You were his midnight secretary.

GRATIANA: No.
   He was too wise to trust me with his thoughts.

VINDICE *(aside)*: I' faith then, father, thou wast wise indeed
   'Wives are but made to go to bed and feed.'
   Come mother, sister: you'll bring me onward, brother?

HIPPOLITO: I will.

VINDICE: I'll quickly turn into another.

(Exeunt.)

Scene Two

Enter the old DUKE, LUSSURIOSO *his Son, the* DUCHESS, SPURIO *the Bastard,
the Duchess' two sons* AMBITIOSO *and* SUPERVACUO, *the third her youngest,*
JUNIOR *brought out with officers for the rape: two Judges.*

DUKE: Duchess, it is your youngest son, we're sorry
    His violent act has e'en drawn blood of honor
    And stained our honors,
    Thrown ink upon the forehead of our state
    Which envious spirits will dip their pens into
    After our death, and blot us in our tombs.
    For that which would seem treason in our lives
    Is laughter when we're dead; who dares now whisper
    That dares not then speak out, and e'en proclaim
    With loud words and broad pens our closest shame.

FIRST JUDGE: Your Grace hath spoke like to your silver years
    Full of confirmèd gravity; for what is it to have
    A flattering false insculption on a tomb,
    And in men's hearts reproach? The bowelled corpse
    May be seared in, but with free tongue I speak,
    'The faults of great men through their sear clothes break.'

DUKE: They do, we're sorry for't, it is our fate
    To live in fear and die to live in hate.
    I leave him to your sentence; doom him, lords—
    The fact is great—whilst I sit by and sigh.

DUCHESS *(kneeling)*: My gracious lord, I pray be merciful,
    Although his trespass far exceed his years,
    Think him to be your own, as I am yours.
    Call him not son in law: the law I fear
    Will fall too soon upon his name and him:
    Temper his fault with pity!

LUSSURIOSO: Good my lord,
    Then 'twill not taste so bitter and unpleasant
    Upon the judges' palate, for offenses
    Gilt o'er with mercy show like fairest women,
    Good only for their beauties, which washed off,
    No sin is uglier.

AMBITIOSO: I beseech your Grace,
    Be soft and mild, let not relentless law
    Look with an iron forehead on our brother.

SPURIO *(aside)*: He yields small comfort yet, hope he shall die,
    And if a bastard's wish might stand in force,
    Would all the court were turned into a corse.

DUCHESS: No pity yet? Must I rise fruitless then?
    A wonder in a woman. Are my knees
    Of such low metal, that without respect—

FIRST JUDGE: Let the offender stand forth:
    'Tis the Duke's pleasure that impartial doom
    Shall take first hold of his unclean attempt;
    A rape! Why, 'tis the very core of lust,
    Double adultery.

JUNIOR: So sir.

SECOND JUDGE: And which was worse
    Committed on the lord Antonio's wife,
    That general honest lady; confess my lord
    What moved you to't?

JUNIOR: Why flesh and blood, my lord.
    What should move men unto a woman else?

LUSSURIOSO: Oh do not jest thy doom, trust not an axe
    Or sword too far; the law is a wise serpent
    And quickly can beguile thee of thy life;
    Though marriage only has made thee my brother
    I love thee so far, play not with thy death.

JUNIOR: I thank you troth, good admonitions, 'faith,
    If I'd the grace now to make use of them.

FIRST JUDGE: That lady's name has spread such a fair wing
    Over all Italy, that if our tongues
    Were sparing toward the fact, judgment itself
    Would be condemned and suffer in men's thoughts.

JUNIOR: Well then 'tis done, and it would please me well
    Were it to do again: sure she's a goddess,
    For I'd no power to see her and to live.

It falls out true in this, for I must die;
Her beauty was ordained to be my scaffold,
And yet methinks I might be easier ceased,
My fault being sport, let me but die in jest.

FIRST JUDGE: This be the sentence—

DUCHESS: O keep't upon your tongue, let it not slip!
Death too soon steals out of a lawyer's lip.
Be not so cruel-wise!

FIRST JUDGE: Your Grace must pardon us,
'Tis but the justice of the law.

DUCHESS: The law
Is grown more subtle than a woman should be.

SPURIO (aside): Now, now he dies, rid 'em away.

DUCHESS (aside): O, what it is to have an old-cool Duke,
To be as slack in tongue as in performance.

FIRST JUDGE: Confirmed; this be the doom irrevocable.

DUCHESS: Oh!

FIRST JUDGE: Tomorrow early—

DUCHESS: Pray be abed, my lord.

FIRST JUDGE: Your Grace much wrongs yourself.

AMBITIOSO: No, 'tis that tongue,
Your too much right does do us too much wrong.

FIRST JUDGE: Let that offender—

DUCHESS: Live and be in health.

FIRST JUDGE: Be on a scaffold—

DUKE: Hold, hold, my lord.

SPURIO *(aside):* Pox on't,
What makes my dad speak now?

DUKE: We will defer the judgment till next sitting;
In the meantime let him be kept close prisoner:
Guard, bear him hence.

AMBITIOSO *(to* JUNIOR*)*: Brother, this makes for thee,
Fear not, we'll have a trick to set thee free.

JUNIOR: Brother, I will expect it from you both,
And in that hope I rest.

SUPERVACUO: Farewell, be merry.

(Exit JUNIOR *with a guard)*

SPURIO: Delayed, deferred! Nay then, if judgment have
Cold blood, flattery and bribes will kill it.

DUKE: About it then, my lords, with your best powers.
More serious business calls upon our hours.

(Exeunt. DUCHESS *remains)*

DUCHESS: Was't ever known step-Duchess was so mild
And calm as I? Some now would plot his death
With easy doctors, those loose-living men,
And make his withered Grace fall to his grave
And keep church better.
Some second wife would do this, and dispatch
Her double-loathèd lord at meat, and sleep.
Indeed 'tis true an old man's twice a child;
Mine cannot speak, one of his single words
Would quite have freed my youngest dearest son
From death or durance, and have made him walk
With a bold foot upon the thorny law
Whose prickles should bow under him; but 'tis not,
And therefore wedlock faith shall be forgot;

I'll kill him in his forehead, hate there feed,
That wound is deepest, though it never bleed.
(*Enter* SPURIO)
And here comes he whom my heart points unto,
His bastard son, but my love's true-begot;
Many a wealthy letter have I sent him
Swelled up with jewels, and the timorous man
Is yet but coldly kind;
That jewel's mine that quivers in his ear
Mocking his master's chillness and vain fear.
H'as spied me now.

SPURIO: Madam? Your Grace so private?
My duty on your hand.

DUCHESS: Upon my hand, sir? Troth, I think you'd fear
To kiss my hand too if my lip stood there.

SPURIO: Witness I would not, madam.

(*Kisses her*)

DUCHESS: 'Tis a wonder,
For ceremony has made many fools.
It is as easy way unto a Duchess
As to a low-born dame—if her love answer—
But that by timorous honors, pale respects,
Idle degrees of fear, men make their ways
Hard of themselves. What have you thought of me?

SPURIO: Madam I ever think of you, in duty,
Regard and—

DUCHESS: Puh, upon my love I mean.

SPURIO: I would 'twere love, but 'tis a fouler name
Than lust; you are my father's wife, your Grace may guess now
What I could call it.

DUCHESS: Why, th'art his son but falsely,
'Tis a hard question whether he begot thee.

SPURIO: I'faith 'tis true, too; I'm an uncertain man,
   Of more uncertain woman; maybe his groom
   A'th'stable begot me—you know I know not—
   He could ride a horse well, a shrewd suspicion, marry,
   He was wondrous tall, he had his length i'faith,
   For peeping over half-shut holiday windows,
   Men would desire him 'light; when he was afoot,
   He made a goodly show under a penthouse,
   And when he rid, his hat would check the signs
   And clatter barbers' basins.

DUCHESS: Nay, set you a-horseback once,
   You'll ne'er light off.

SPURIO: Indeed, I am a beggar.

DUCHESS: That's more the sign thou art great—
   But to our love:
   Let it stand firm both in thought and mind
   That the Duke was thy father, as no doubt then
   He bid fair for't, thy injury is the more,
   For had he cut thee a right diamond
   Thou hadst been next set in the dukedom's ring
   When his worn self, like age's easy slave
   Had dropped out of the setting into th'grave.
   What wrong can equal this? Canst thou be tame
   And think upon't?

SPURIO: No, mad and think upon't.

DUCHESS: Who would not be revenged of such a father
   E'en in the worst way? I would thank that sin
   That could most injure him, and be in league with it.
   Oh what a grief 'tis, that a man should live
   But once i'th'world, and then to live a bastard,
   The curse o'the womb, the thief of Nature,
   Begot against the seventh commandment,
   Half-damned in the conception, by the justice
   Of that unbribèd everlasting law.

SPURIO: Oh, I'd a hot-backed devil to my father!

DUCHESS: Would not this mad e'en patience, make blood rough?
  Who but an eunuch would not sin, his bed
  By one false minute disinherited?

SPURIO *(aside):* Ay, there's the vengeance that my birth was wrapt in.
  I'll be revenged for all; now hate, begin,
  I'll call foul incest but a venial sin.

DUCHESS: Cold still? In vain then must a Duchess woo?

SPURIO: Madam, I blush to say what I will do.

DUCHESS: Thence flew sweet comfort;—earnest, and farewell.

(Kisses him)

SPURIO: Oh, one incestuous kiss picks open Hell.

DUCHESS: Faith now, old duke, my vengeance shall reach high,
  I'll arm thy brow with cuckold's heraldry.

(Exit)

SPURIO: Duke, thou didst do me wrong, and by thy act,
  Adultery is my nature;
  Faith, if the truth were known, I was begot
  After some gluttonous dinner, some stirring dish
  Was my first father; when deep healths went round,
  And ladies' cheeks were painted red with wine,
  Their tongues as short and nimble as their heels,
  Uttering words sweet and thick; and when they rose
  Were merrily disposed to fall again—
  In such a whispering and withdrawing hour,
  When base male bawds kept sentinel at stairhead,
  Was I stol'n softly; oh—damnation met
  The sin of feasts, drunken adultery.
  I feel it swell me; my revenge is just,
  I was begot in impudent wine and lust.
  Stepmother, I consent to thy desires;
  I love thy mischief well, but I hate thee,
  And those three cubs thy sons, wishing confusion

Death and disgrace may be their epitaphs;
As for my brother, the Duke's only son
Whose birth is more beholding to report
Than mine, and yet perhaps as falsely sown,
(Women must not be trusted with their own),
I'll loose my days upon him, hate all I,
Duke, on thy brow I'll draw my bastardy.
For indeed a bastard by nature should make cuckolds,
Because he is the son of a cuckold-maker.

(Exit.)

Scene Three

Enter VINDICE *and* HIPPOLITO, VINDICE *in disguise to attend* LUSSURIOSO *the Duke's son.*

VINDICE: What, brother, am I far enough from myself?

HIPPOLITO: As if another man had been sent whole
    Into the world, and none wist how he came.

VINDICE: It will confirm me bold: the child o' the court;
    Let blushes dwell i'th'country. Impudence!
    Thou goddess of the palace, mistress of mistresses,
    To whom the costly perfumed people pray,
    Strike thou my forehead into dauntless marble,
    Mine eyes to steady sapphires: turn my visage,
    And if I must needs glow, let me blush inward
    That this immodest season may not spy
    That scholar in my cheeks, fool-bashfulness.
    That maid in the old time, whose flush of grace
    Would never suffer her to get good clothes.
    Our maids are wiser, and are less ashamed:
    Save Grace the bawd, I seldom here grace named!

HIPPOLITO: Nay brother, you reach out o'th'verge now—
    (Enter LUSSURIOSO *attended)*
    'Sfoot, the Duke's son; settle your looks.

VINDICE: Pray let me not be doubted. *(He withdraws)*

HIPPOLITO: My Lord—

LUSSURIOSO: Hippolito?—Be absent, leave us.

(Exeunt Attendants)

HIPPOLITO: My lord, after long search, wary inquiries
  And politic siftings, I made choice of yon fellow,
  Whom I guess rare for many deep employments;
  This our age swims within him; and if Time
  Had so much hair, I should take him for Time,
  He is so near kin to this present minute.

LUSSURIOSO: 'Tis enough,
  We thank thee: yet words are but great men's blanks,
  Gold, tho' it be dumb does utter the best thanks.

(Gives him money)

HIPPOLITO: Your plenteous honor—an ex'lent fellow my Lord.

LUSSURIOSO: So, give us leave—   *(Exit Hippolito)*

                         Welcome, be not far off,
  We must be better acquainted. Pish, be bold
  With us—thy hand.

VINDICE: With all my heart, i'faith!
  How dost, sweet musk-cat—when shall we lie together?

LUSSURIOSO *(aside)*: Wondrous knave!
  Gather him into boldness? 'Sfoot, the slave's
  Already as familiar as an ague
  And shakes me at his pleasure. *(To* VINDICE*)* Friend, I can
  Forget myself in private, but elsewhere
  I pray do you remember me.

VINDICE: Oh, very well, sir—I construe myself saucy.

LUSSURIOSO: What hast been,
Of what profession?

VINDICE: A bone-setter.

LUSSURIOSO: A bone-setter?

VINDICE: A bawd, my lord,
One that sets bones together.

LUSSURIOSO: Notable bluntness!
Fit, fit for me, e'en trained up to my hand.
Thou hast been scrivener to much knavery then.

VINDICE: Fool to abundance sir; I have been witness
To the surrenders of a thousand virgins,
And not so little;
I have seen patrimonies washed apieces,
Fruit-fields turned into bastards,
And in a world of acres,
Not so much dust due to the heir 'twas left to
As would well blot dry a petition.

LUSSURIOSO (*aside*): Fine villain! Troth, I like him wondrously,
He's e'en shaped for my purpose. (*To* VINDICE) Then, thou know'st
I'th'world strange lust?

VINDICE: O Dutch lust!* Fulsome lust!
Drunken procreation, which begets so many drunkards;
Some father dreads not—gone to bed in wine—to slide from the
        mother
And cling the daughter-in-law;
Some uncles are adulterous with their nieces,
Brothers with brothers' wives, O hour of incest!
Any kin now next to the rim o'th'sister
Is man's meat in these days; and in the morning,
When they are up and dressed, and their mask on,
Who can perceive this? Save that eternal eye
That sees through flesh and all? Well, if any thing be damned

---

* *Dutch lust:* drunkenness.

It will be twelve o'clock at night; that twelve
Will never 'scape,—
It is the Judas of the hours, wherein
Honest salvation is betrayed to sin.

LUSSURIOSO: In troth it is too, but let this talk glide,
It is our blood to err, tho' Hell gaped wide.
Ladies know Lucifer fell, yet still are proud.
Now sir; wert thou as secret as thou art subtle
And deeply fathomed into all estates,
I would embrace thee for a near employment,
And thou shouldst swell in money, and be able
To make lame beggars crouch to thee.

VINDICE: My lord?
Secret? I ne'er had that disease o'th'mother.
I praise my father: why are men made close
But to keep thoughts in best? I grant you this,
Tell but some woman a secret over night,
Your doctor may find it in the urinal i'th'morning.
But my lord—

LUSSURIOSO: So, thou'rt confirmed in me,
And thus I enter thee.

(Gives him gold)

VINDICE: This Indian devil—gold—
Will quickly enter any man but a usurer;
He prevents that by ent'ring the Devil first.

LUSSURIOSO: Attend me: I am past my depth in lust
And I must swim or drown. All my desires
Are levelled at a virgin, not far from court
To whom I have conveyed by messenger
Many waxed lines, full of my neatest spirit,
And jewels that were able to ravish her
Without the help of man; all which and more
She, foolish chaste, sent back, the messengers
Receiving frowns for answers.

VINDICE: Possible?

'Tis a rare phoenix who e'er she be;
If your desires be such, she so repugnant
In troth my lord, I'd be revenged and marry her.

LUSSURIOSO: Pish! The dowry of her blood and of her fortunes
    Are both too mean—good enough to be bad withal.
    I'm one of that number can defend
    Marriage is good: yet rather keep a friend;
    Give me my bed by stealth, there's true delight
    What breeds a loathing in't, but night by night?

VINDICE: A very fine religion!

LUSSURIOSO: Therefore thus,
    I'll trust thee in the business of my heart
    Because I see thee well experienced
    In this luxurious day wherein we breathe.
    Go thou, and with a smooth enchanting tongue
    Bewitch her ears, and cozen her of all grace.
    Enter upon the portion of her soul,
    Her honor, which she calls her chastity
    And bring it into expense, for honesty
    Is like a stock of money laid to sleep,
    Which ne'er so little broke, does never keep.

VINDICE: You have gi'n't the tang i'faith, my lord.
    Make known the lady to me, and my brain
    Shall swell with strange invention: I will move it
    Till I expire with speaking, and drop down
    Without a word to save me;—but I'll work—

LUSSURIOSO: We thank thee, and will raise thee: receive her name,
    It is the only daughter to Madam
    Gratiana, the late widow.

VINDICE *(aside)*: Oh, my sister, my sister!

LUSSURIOSO: Why dost walk aside?

VINDICE: My lord, I was thinking how I might begin,

As thus: 'Oh Lady!'—or twenty hundred devices;
Her very bodkin will put a man in.

LUSSURIOSO: Ay, or the wagging of her hair.

VINDICE: No, that shall put you in, my lord.

LUSSURIOSO: Shall't? Why, content. Dost know the daughter then?

VINDICE: O ex'lent well by sight.

LUSSURIOSO: That was her brother
  That did prefer thee to us.

VINDICE: My lord, I think so,
  I knew I had seen him somewhere.

LUSSURIOSO: And therefore, prithee let thy heart to him
  Be as a virgin close.

VINDICE: Oh, me good Lord!

LUSSURIOSO: We may laugh at that simple age within him;—

VINDICE: Ha, ha, ha.

LUSSURIOSO: Himself being made the subtle instrument
  To wind up a good fellow.

VINDICE: That's I, my lord.

LUSSURIOSO: That's thou
  To entice and work his sister.

VINDICE: A pure novice!

LUSSURIOSO: 'Twas finely managed.

VINDICE: Gallantly carried;
  A pretty-perfumed villain.

LUSSURIOSO: I've bethought me
   If she prove chaste still and immovable,
   Venture upon the mother, and with gifts
   As I will furnish thee begin with her.

VINDICE: O fie, fie, that's the wrong end my lord.
   'Tis mere impossible that a mother by any gifts
   Should become a bawd to her own daughter!

LUSSURIOSO: Nay then, I see thou'rt but a tyro
   In the subtle mystery of a woman:—
   Why, 'tis held now no dainty dish: the name
   Is so in league with age that nowadays
   It does eclipse three quarters of a mother.

VINDICE: Does't so, my lord?
   Let me alone then, to eclipse the fourth.

LUSSURIOSO: Why well said, come, I'll furnish thee; but first
   Swear to be true in all.

VINDICE: True!

LUSSURIOSO: Nay but swear!

VINDICE: Swear? I hope your honor little doubts my faith.

LUSSURIOSO: Yet for my humor's sake, 'cause I love swearing.

VINDICE: 'Cause you love swearing,—'slud I will.

LUSSURIOSO: Why enough,
   Ere long look to be made of better stuff.

VINDICE: That will do well indeed, my lord.

LUSSURIOSO *(calling Attendants)*: Attend me!

(Exit)

VINDICE: Oh—

Now let me burst, I've eaten noble poison,
We are made strange fellows, brother, innocent villains,
Wilt not be angry when thou hear'st on't, think'st thou?
I'faith, thou shalt. Swear me to foul my sister!
Sword, I durst make a promise of him to thee,
Thou shalt dis-heir him, it shall be thine honor;
And yet, now angry froth is down in me,
It would not prove the meanest policy
In this disguise to try the faith of both;
Another might have had the self-same office,
Some slave, that would have wrought effectually,
Ay, and perhaps o'er-wrought 'em; therefore I,
Being thought traveled, will apply myself
Unto the self-same form, forget my nature,
As if no part about me were kin to 'em,
So touch 'em,—tho' I durst almost for good
Venture my lands in Heaven upon their blood.

(Exit.)

Scene Four

Enter the discontented Lord ANTONIO, *whose wife the Duchess' younger son ravished; he discovering the body of her dead to certain lords:* PIERO *and* HIPPOLITO.

ANTONIO: Draw nearer lords, and be sad witnesses
　　Of a fair comely building newly fall'n,
　　Being falsely undermined: violent rape
　　Has played a glorious act; behold my lords
　　A sight that strikes man out of me.

PIERO: That virtuous lady!

ANTONIO:　　　　　　　Precedent for wives!

HIPPOLITO: The blush of many women, whose chaste presence
　　Would e'en call shame up to their cheeks, and make
　　Pale wanton sinners have good colors.—

ANTONIO: Dead!
  Her honor first drunk poison, and her life,
  Being fellows in one house, did pledge her honor.

PIERO: O grief of many!

ANTONIO: I mark'd not this before—
  A prayer-book, the pillow to her cheek;
  This was her rich confection, and another
  Placed in her right hand, with a leaf tucked up,
  Pointing to these words:
  Melius virtute mori, quam per dedecus vivere.
  True and effectual it is, indeed.

HIPPOLITO: My lord, since you invite us to your sorrows,
  Let's truly taste 'em, that with equal comfort
  As to ourselves we may relieve your wrongs;
  We have grief too, that yet walks without tongue—
  Curae leves loquuntur, majores stupent.

ANTONIO: You deal with truth, my lord.
  Lend me but your attentions, and I'll cut
  Long grief into short words: last reveling night,
  When torchlight made an artificial noon
  About the court, some courtiers in the mask,
  Putting on better faces than their own,
  Being full of fraud and flattery: amongst whom
  The Duchess' youngest son—that moth to honor—
  Filled up a room; and with long lust to eat
  Into my wearing, amongst all the ladies
  Singled out that dear form, who ever lived
  As cold in lust as she is now in death,
  —Which that step-duchess' monster knew too well—
  And therefore in the height of all the revels,
  When music was heard loudest, courtiers busiest,
  And ladies great with laughter—O vicious minute!
  Unfit but for relation to be spoken of,
  Then with a face more impudent than his vizard
  He harried her amidst a throng of panders
  That live upon damnation of both kinds,
  And fed the ravenous vulture of his lust,

—O death to think on't!—She, her honor forced,
Deemed it a nobler dowry for her name
To die with poison than to live with shame.

HIPPOLITO: A wondrous lady, of rare fire compact;
Sh'as made her name an empress by that act.

PIERO: My lord, what judgment follows the offender?

ANTONIO: Faith none, my lord, it cools and is deferred.

PIERO: Delay the doom for rape?

ANTONIO: O, you must note who 'tis should die,
The Duchess' son; she'll look to be a saver,
'Judgment in this age is near kin to favor.'

HIPPOLITO: Nay then, step forth, thou bribeless officer;   *(Draws sword)*
I bind you all in steel to bind you surely.
Here let your oaths meet, to be kept and paid,
Which else will stick like rust and shame the blade:
Strengthen my vow, that if at the next sitting,
Judgment speak all in gold, and spare the blood
Of such a serpent, e'en before their seats
To let his soul out, which long since was found
Guilty in heaven.

ALL: We swear it and will act it.

ANTONIO: Kind gentlemen, I thank you in mine ire.

HIPPOLITO: 'Twere pity
The ruins of so fair a monument
Should not be dipped in the defacer's blood.

PIERO: Her funeral shall be wealthy, for her name
Merits a tomb of pearl; my lord Antonio,
For this time wipe your lady from your eyes,
No doubt our grief and yours may one day court it,
When we are more familiar with Revenge.

ANTONIO: That is my comfort, gentlemen, and I joy
   In this one happiness above the rest.
   Which will be called a miracle at last,
   That, being an old man, I'd a wife so chaste.

(Exeunt.)

ACT TWO

Scene One

Enter CASTIZA, *the sister.*

CASTIZA: How hardly shall that maiden be beset
   Whose only fortunes are her constant thoughts,
   That has no other child's-part but her honor,
   That keeps her low and empty in estate.
   Maids and their honors are like poor beginners,
   Were not sin rich there would be fewer sinners;
   Why had not virtue a revenue? Well,
   I know the cause, 'twould have impoverished Hell.
   (Enter DONDOLO*)*
   How now, Dondolo?

DONDOLO: Madona, there is one, as they say a thing of flesh and blood, a
   man I take him by his beard, that would very desirously mouth to
   mouth with you.

CASTIZA: What's that?

DONDOLO: Show his teeth in your company.

CASTIZA: I understand thee not.

DONDOLO: Why, speak with you, madona!

CASTIZA: Why, say so, madman, and cut off a great deal
   Of dirty way; had it not been better spoke
   In ordinary words, that one would speak with me?

DONDOLO: Ha, ha, that's as ordinary as two shillings, I would strive a
  little to show myself in my place, a gentleman-usher scorns to use the
  phrase and fancy of a servingman.

CASTIZA: Yours be your own sir; go direct him hither.
  (*Exit* DONDOLO)
  I hope some happy tidings from my brother
  That lately traveled, whom my soul affects.
  Here he comes.

(*Enter* VINDICE, *her brother disguised*)

VINDICE: Lady, the best of wishes to your sex;
  Fair skins and new gowns.   (*Gives her a letter*)

CASTIZA: Oh they shall thank you, sir.
  Whence this?

VINDICE: Oh, from a dear and worthy friend,
  Mighty!

CASTIZA: From whom?

VINDICE: The Duke's son!

CASTIZA: Receive that!
  (*A box of the ear to her brother*)
  I swore I'd put anger in my hand
  And pass the virgin limits of myself
  To him that next appeared in that base office
  To be his sins' attorney. Bear to him
  That figure of my hate upon thy cheek
  Whilst 'tis yet hot, and I'll reward thee for't;
  Tell him my honor shall have a rich name
  When several harlots shall share his with shame.
  Farewell, commend me to him in my hate!

(*Exit*)

VINDICE: It is the sweetest box that e'er my nose came nigh,
  The finest drawn-work cuff that e'er was worn;

I'll love this blow for ever, and this cheek
Shall still henceforward take the wall of this.
Oh I'm above my tongue! Most constant sister,
In this thou hast right honorable shown;
Many are called by their honor that have none,
Thou art approved for ever in my thoughts.
It is not in the power of words to taint thee,
And yet for the salvation of my oath,
As my resolve in that point, I will lay
Hard siege unto my mother, though I know
A siren's tongue could not bewitch her so.

(*Enter* GRATIANA)

Mass, fitly here she comes. Thanks, my disguise.
    Madam, good afternoon.

GRATIANA: Y'are welcome sir.

VINDICE: The next of Italy commends him to you,
    Our mighty expectation, the Duke's son.

GRATIANA: I think myself much honored, that he pleases
    To rank me in his thoughts.

VINDICE: So may you, lady:
    One that is like to be our sudden duke—
    The crown gapes for him every tide—and then
    Commander o'er us all, do but think on him,
    How blest were they now that could pleasure him
    E'en with any thing almost.

GRATIANA: Ay, save their honor.

VINDICE: Tut, one would let a little of that go too
    And ne'er be seen in 't: ne'er be seen in 't, mark you.
    I'd wink and let it go.

GRATIANA: Marry, but I would not.

VINDICE: Marry, but I would I hope, I know you would, too,

If you'd that blood now which you gave your daughter;
To her indeed 'tis, this wheel comes about;
That man that must be all this, perhaps ere morning
—For his white father does but mould away—
Has long desired your daughter.

GRATIANA: Desired?

VINDICE: Nay, but hear me,
He desires now that will command hereafter,
, Therefore be wise, I speak as more a friend
To you than him; Madam, I know you're poor,
And 'lack the day, there are too many poor ladies already
Why should you vex the member? 'Tis despised;
Live wealthy, rightly understand the world
And chide away that foolish country girl
Keeps company with your daughter, Chastity.

GRATIANA: Oh, fie, fie, the riches of the world cannot hire
A mother to such a most unnatural task.

VINDICE: No, but a thousand angels can,
Men have no power, angels must work you to't.
The world descends into such baseborn evils
That forty angels can make fourscore devils;
There will be fools still I perceive, still fools.
Would I be poor, dejected, scorned of greatness,
Swept from the palace, and see other daughters
Spring with the dew o'th'court, having mine own
So much desired and loved—by the Duke's son?
No, I would raise my state upon her breast
And call her eyes my tenants, I would count
My yearly maintenance upon her cheeks:
Take coach upon her lip, and all her parts
Should keep men after men, and I would ride
In pleasure upon pleasure.
You took great pains for her, once when it was,
Let her requite it now, tho' it be but some;
You brought her forth, she may well bring you home.

GRATIANA: O heavens! This overcomes me!

VINDICE *(aside)*: Not, I hope, already?

GRATIANA *(aside)*: It is too strong for me, men know that know us
  We are so weak their words can overthrow us.
  He touched me nearly, made my virtues 'bate,
  When his tongue struck upon my poor estate.

VINDICE *(aside)*: I e'en quake to proceed, my spirit turns edge!
  I fear me she's unmothered, yet I'll venture,
  'That woman is all male whom none can enter'—
  What think you now lady, speak, are you wiser?
  What said advancement to you? Thus it said:
  The daughter's fall lifts up the mother's head!
  Did it not madam? But I'll swear it does
  In many places: tut, this age fears no man,
  ' 'Tis no shame to be bad, because 'tis common'.

GRATIANA: Ay, that's the comfort on't.

VINDICE *(aside)*:   The comfort on't!—
  I keep the best for last; can these persuade you
  (Showing her gold)
  To forget heaven and—

GRATIANA: Ay, these are they—

VINDICE: Oh!

GRATIANA: That enchant our sex;
  These are the means that govern our affections—that woman
  Will not be troubled with the mother long
  That sees the comfortable shine of you;
  I blush to think what for your sakes I'll do!

VINDICE *(aside)*: O suffering Heaven, with thy invisible finger
  E'en at this instant turn the precious side
  Of both mine eyeballs inward, not to see myself.

GRATIANA: Look you, sir.

VINDICE: Holla.

GRATIANA: Let this thank your pains.

VINDICE: O, you're a kind madam.

GRATIANA: I'll see how I can move.

VINDICE: Your words will sting.

GRATIANA: If she be still chaste, I'll never call her mine.

VINDICE *(aside)*: Spoke truer than you meant it.

GRATIANA: Daughter Castiza.

(Enter CASTIZA*)*

CASTIZA: Madam?

VINDICE: O, she's yonder.
Meet her. *(Aside)* Troops of celestial soldiers guard her heart,
Yon dam has devils enough to take her part.

CASTIZA: Madam, what makes yon evil-officed man
In presence of you?

GRATIANA: Why?

CASTIZA: He lately brought
Immodest writing sent from the Duke's son
To tempt me to dishonorable act.

GRATIANA: Dishonorable act? Good honorable fool,
That wouldst be honest 'cause thou wouldst be so,
Producing no one reason but thy will;
And't'as a good report, prettily commended
But pray by whom? Mean people, ignorant people,
The better sort I'm sure cannot abide it,
And by what rule shouldst we square out our lives,
But by our betters' actions? Oh if thou knew'st
What 'twere to lose it, thou would never keep it:
But there's a cold curse laid upon all maids,

While others the sun, they clasp the shades!
Virginity is paradise, locked up.
You cannot come by yourselves without fee.
And 'twas decreed that man should keep the key.
Deny advancement, treasure, the Duke's son!

CASTIZA: I cry you mercy. Lady, I mistook you.
　　Pray did you see my mother? Which way went you?
　　Pray God I have not lost her.

VINDICE (*aside*):　　　　　　Prettily put by.

GRATIANA: Are you as proud to me as coy to him?
　　Do you not know me now?

CASTIZA:　　　　　　　　Why, are you she?
　　The world's so changed, one shape into another
　　It is a wise child now that knows her mother.

VINDICE: Most right, i'faith.

GRATIANA: I owe your cheek my hand
　　For that presumption now, but I'll forget it.
　　Come, you shall leave these childish 'haviors
　　And understand your time. Fortunes flow to you,
　　What, will you be a girl?
　　If all feared drowning that spy waves ashore,
　　Gold would grow rich and all the merchants poor.

CASTIZA: It is a pretty saying of a wicked one,
　　But methinks now, it does not show so well
　　Out of your mouth—better in his.

VINDICE (*aside*): Faith, bad enough in both,
　　Were I in earnest, as I'll seem no less.—
　　I wonder, lady, your own mother's words
　　Cannot be taken, nor stand in full force.
　　'Tis honesty you urge; what's honesty?
　　'Tis but Heaven's beggar, and what woman is
　　So foolish to keep honesty
　　And be not able to keep herself? No,
　　Times are grown wiser and will keep less charge.

A maid that has small portion now intends
To break up house and live upon her friends.
How blest are you, you have happiness alone!
Others must fall to thousands, you to one
Sufficient in himself to make your forehead
Dazzle the world with jewels, and petitionary people
Start at your presence.

GRATIANA: Oh, if I were young, I should be ravish'd!

CASTIZA: Ay, to lose your honor.

VINDICE: 'Slid, how can you lose your honor
    To deal with my lord's Grace?
    He'll add more honor to it by his title.
    Your mother will tell you how.

GRATIANA: That I will.

VINDICE: O think upon the pleasure of the palace,
    Securèd ease and state, the stirring meats
    Ready to move out of the dishes
    That e'en now quicken when they're eaten!
    Banquets abroad by torchlight, music, sports,
    Bare-headed vassals, that had ne'er the fortune
    To keep on their own hats, but let horns wear 'em!
    Nine coaches waiting—hurry, hurry, hurry.

CASTIZA: Ay, to the Devil.

VINDICE (aside): Ay, to the Devil.—To the Duke, by my faith.

GRATIANA: Ay, to the Duke: daughter, you'd scorn to think
    O'th'Devil, if you were there once.

VINDICE: True, for most there are as proud
    As he for his heart, i'faith.—
    Who'd sit at home in a neglected room,
    Dealing her short-lived beauty to the pictures
    That are as useless as old men, when those
    Poorer in face and fortune than herself

Walk with a hundred acres on their backs,
Fair meadows cut into green fore-parts? Oh!
It was the greatest blessing ever happened to women
When farmers' sons agreed and met again
To wash their hands and come up, gentlemen.
The commonwealth has flourished ever since;
Lands that were spanned by the rod—that labor's spared—
Tailors ride down and measure 'em by the yard.
Fair trees, those comely foretops of the field,
Are cut to maintain head-tires—much untold.
All thrives but Chastity, she lies a-cold.
Nay, shall I come nearer to you? Mark but this:
Why are there so few honest women, but
Because 'tis the poorer profession?
That's accounted best that's best followed;
Least in trade, least in fashion,
And that's not honesty, believe it; and do
But note the low and dejected price of it:
'Lose but a pearl, we search and cannot brook it,
But that once gone, who is so mad to look it?'

GRATIANA: Troth, he says true.

CASTIZA: False! I defy you both!
I have endured you with an ear of fire,
Your tongues have struck hot irons on my face.
Mother, come from that poisonous woman there.

GRATIANA: Where?

CASTIZA: Do you not see her? She's too inward, then.
Slave, perish in thy office! You heavens, please
Henceforth to make the mother a disease
Which first begins with me; yet I've outgone you.

(Exit)

VINDICE (aside): O angels, clap your wings upon the skies
And give this virgin crystal plaudities!

GRATIANA: Peevish, coy, foolish!—But return this answer;

My lord shall be most welcome, when his pleasure
Conducts him this way. I will sway mine own,
Women with women can work best alone.

(Exit)

VINDICE: Indeed I'll tell him so.
   O, more uncivil, more unnatural
   Than those base-titled creatures that look downward!
   Why does not Heaven turn black, or with a frown
   Undo the world? Why does not earth start up
   And strike the sins that tread upon it? Oh,
   Were't not for gold and women, there would be no damnation—
   Hell would look like a lord's great kitchen without fire in't.
   But 'twas decreed before the world began,
   That they should be the hooks to catch at man.   *(Exit)*

Enter LUSSURIOSO *with* HIPPOLITO, VINDICE's *brother.*

LUSSURIOSO: I much applaud
   Thy judgment. Thou art well read in a fellow,
   And 'tis the deepest art to study man.
   I know this, which I never learnt in schools,
   The world's divided into knaves and fools.

HIPPOLITO *(aside):* Knave in your face, my lord—behind your back,—

LUSSURIOSO: And I much thank thee, that thou hast preferred
   A fellow of discourse well mingled,
   And whose brain time hath seasoned.

HIPPOLITO: True, my lord,
   We shall find season once, I hope. *(Aside)* O, villain!
   To make such an unnatural slave of me,—but—

(Enter VINDICE *disguised)*

LUSSURIOSO: Mass, here he comes.

HIPPOLITO *(aside):* And now shall I have free leave to depart.

LUSSURIOSO: Your absence—leave us.

HIPPOLITO *(aside):*   Are not my thoughts true?
  I must remove; but brother, you may stay;
  Heart, we are both made bawds a new-found way.

(Exit)

LUSSURIOSO: Now we're an even number, a third man's dangerous,
  Especially her brother; say, be free,
  Have I a pleasure toward?

VINDICE: Oh, my lord!

LUSSURIOSO: Ravish me in thine answer; art thou rare?
  Hast thou beguiled her of salvation
  And rubbed Hell o'er with honey? Is she a woman?

VINDICE: In all but in desire.

LUSSURIOSO: Then she's in nothing.
  I 'bate in courage now.

VINDICE: The words I brought
  Might well have made indifferent honest naught.
  A right good woman in these days is changed
  Into white money with less labor far;
  Many a maid has turned to Mahomet
  With easier working; I durst undertake
  Upon the pawn and forfeit of my life
  With half those words to flat a Puritan's wife.
  But she is close and good; yet 'tis a doubt
  By this time. Oh, the mother, the mother!

LUSSURIOSO: I never thought their sex had been a wonder
  Until this minute; what fruit from the mother?

VINDICE *(aside):* Now must I blister my soul, be forsworn
  Or shame the woman that received me first.
  I will be true; thou liv'st not to proclaim;

Spoke to a dying man, shame has no shame.—
My lord—

LUSSURIOSO: Who's that?

VINDICE: Here's none but I, my lord.

LUSSURIOSO: What would thy haste utter?

VINDICE: Comfort.

LUSSURIOSO: Welcome.

VINDICE: The maid being dull, having no mind to travel
   Into unknown lands, what did me I straight
   But set spurs to the mother; golden spurs
   Will put her to a false gallop in a trice.

LUSSURIOSO: Is't possible that in this
   The mother should be damned before the daughter?

VINDICE: Oh that's good manners, my lord; the mother for
   Her age must go foremost, you know.

LUSSURIOSO: Thou'st spoke that true, but where comes in this comfort?

VINDICE: In a fine place, my lord,—the unnatural mother
   Did with her tongue so hard beset her honor
   That the poor fool was struck to silent wonder;
   Yet still the maid, like an unlighted taper,
   Was cold and chaste, save that her mother's breath
   Did blow fire on her cheeks. The girl departed
   But the good ancient madam, half mad, threw me
   These promising words, which I took deeply note of:
   'My lord shall be most welcome—'

LUSSURIOSO: 'Faith, I thank her.

VINDICE: '—When his pleasure conducts him this way.'

LUSSURIOSO: That shall be soon, i'faith.

VINDICE: 'I will sway mine own.'

LUSSURIOSO: She does the wiser, I commend her for't.

VINDICE: 'Women with women can work best alone.

LUSSURIOSO: By this light and so they can! Give 'em
  Their due, men are not comparable to 'em.

VINDICE: No, that's true, for you shall have one woman
  Knit more in an hour than any man
  Can ravel again in seven and twenty year.

LUSSURIOSO: Now my desires are happy; I'll make 'em free men now.
  Thou art a precious fellow, 'faith I love thee;
  Be wise and make it thy revenue. Beg, leg!
  What office couldst thou be ambitious for?

VINDICE: Office, my lord!
  Marry, if I might have my wish, I would
  Have one that was never begged yet.

LUSSURIOSO: Nay, then thou canst have none.

VINDICE: Yes, my lord,
  I could pick out another office yet.
  Nay, and keep a horse and drab upon't.

LUSSURIOSO: Prithee, good bluntness, tell me.

VINDICE: Why, I would desire but this, my lord;
  To have all the fees behind the arras, and all
  The farthingales that fall plump about twelve o'clock
  At night upon the rushes.

LUSSURIOSO: Thou'rt a mad, apprehensive knave;
  Dost think to make any great purchase of that?

VINDICE: Oh, 'tis an unknown thing my lord: I wonder
  'T'as been missed so long!

LUSSURIOSO: Well, this night I'll visit her, and 'tis till then
  A year in my desires. Farewell, attend;
  Trust me with thy preferment.

(Exit)

VINDICE: My loved lord.—
  Oh, shall I kill him o'th'wrong side now? No!
  Sword, thou wast never a backbiter yet.
  I'll pierce him to his face; he shall die looking upon me;
  Thy veins are swelled with lust, this shall unfill 'em;
  Great men were gods, if beggars could not kill 'em.
  Forgive me, Heaven, to call my mother wicked;
  Oh lessen not my days upon the earth,
  I cannot honor her. By this, I fear me
  Her tongue has turned my sister into use.
  I was a villain not to be forsworn,
  To this our lecherous hope, the Duke's son;
  For lawyers, merchants, some divines, and all
  Count beneficial perjury a sin small.
  It shall go hard yet, but I'll guard her honor
  And keep the ports sure.

(Enter HIPPOLITO)

HIPPOLITO: Brother, how goes the world? I would know news
  Of you, but I have news to tell you.

VINDICE: What, in the name of knavery?

HIPPOLITO: Knavery, 'faith;
  This vicious old Duke's worthily abused;
  The pen of his bastard writes him cuckold!

VINDICE: His bastard?

HIPPOLITO: Pray believe it; he and the Duchess
  By night meet in their linen; they have been seen
  By stair-foot panders.

VINDICE: Oh sin foul and deep!

Great faults are winked at when the Duke's asleep.
See, see, here comes the Spurio.

(Enter SPURIO *with two servants)*

HIPPOLITO: Monstrous luxur!

VINDICE: Unbraced: two of his valiant bawds with him.
O, there's a wicked whisper,—Hell is in his ear.
Stay, let's observe his passage.

(They withdraw)

SPURIO: Oh, but are you sure on't?

SERVANT: My lord, most sure on't, for 'twas spoke by one
That is most inward with the Duke's son's lust
That he intends within this hour to steal
Unto Hippolito's sister, whose chaste life
The mother has corrupted for his use.

SPURIO: Sweet word, sweet occasion! 'Faith then, brother,
I'll disinherit you in as short time
As I was when I was begot in haste,
I'll damn you at your pleasure—precious deed!
After your lust, oh 'twill be fine to bleed.
Come, let our passing out be soft and wary.

(Exeunt)

VINDICE: Mark, there, there, that step now, to the Duchess;
This their second meeting writes the Duke cuckold
With new additions, his horns newly revived:
Night! Thou that look'st like funeral heralds' fees
Torn down betimes i'th'morning, thou hang'st fitly
To grace those sins that have no grace at all.
Now 'tis full sea abed over the world,
There's juggling of all sides; some that were maids
E'en at sunset are now perhaps i'th'tollbook.
This woman in immodest thin apparel
Lets in her friend by water; here a dame

Cunning nails leather hinges to a door
To avoid proclamation.
Now cuckolds are acoining, apace, apace, apace, apace!
And careful sisters spin that thread i'th'night
That does maintain them and their bawds i'th'day.

HIPPOLITO: You flow well, brother!

VINDICE: Puh, I'm shallow yet,
Too sparing and too modest; shall I tell thee?
If every trick were told that's dealt by night,
There are few here that would not blush outright.

HIPPOLITO: I am of that belief, too. Who's this comes?

(*Enter* LUSSURIOSO)

VINDICE: The Duke's son up so late? Brother, fall back
And you shall learn some mischief. (HIPPOLITO *withdraws*)—My good
    lord.

LUSSURIOSO: Piato, why, the man I wished for! Come,
    I do embrace this season for the fittest
    To taste of that young lady.

VINDICE (*aside*):   Heart and Hell!

HIPPOLITO (*aside*): Damned villain!

VINDICE (*aside*): I ha' no way now to cross it, but to kill him.

LUSSURIOSO: Come, only thou and I.

VINDICE: My lord, my lord.

LUSSURIOSO: Why dost thou start us?

VINDICE: I'd almost forgot—the bastard!

LUSSURIOSO: What of him?

VINDICE: This night, this hour—this minute, now—

LUSSURIOSO: What? What?

VINDICE: Shadows the Duchess—

LUSSURIOSO: Horrible word!

VINDICE: And like strong poison eats
   Into the Duke your father's forehead.

LUSSURIOSO: Oh!

VINDICE: He makes horn royal.

LUSSURIOSO: Most ignoble slave!

VINDICE: This is the fruit of two beds.

LUSSURIOSO: I am mad.

VINDICE: That passage he trod warily.

LUSSURIOSO: He did?

VINDICE: And hushed his villains every step he took.

LUSSURIOSO: His villains? I'll confound them.

VINDICE: Take 'em finely, finely now.

LUSSURIOSO: The Duchess' chamberdoor shall not control me.

(Exeunt all but HIPPOLITO)

HIPPOLITO: Good, happy, swift! There's gunpowder i'th'court,
   Wildfire at midnight; in this heedless fury
   He may show violence to cross himself.
   I'll follow the event.

(Exit.)

Scene Two

DUKE *and* DUCHESS *discovered in bed. Enter again* LUSSURIOSO *and* VINDICE.

LUSSURIOSO: Where is that villain?

VINDICE: Softly my lord, and you may take 'em twisted.

LUSSURIOSO: I care not how!

VINDICE: Oh, 'twill be glorious
    To kill 'em doubled, when they're heaped; be soft, my lord.

LUSSURIOSO: Away, my spleen is not so lazy; thus and thus
    I'll shake their eyelids ope, and with my sword
    Shut 'em again for ever.—

(Approaching bed)

                        Villain! Strumpet!

DUKE: You upper guard, defend us!

DUCHESS: Treason, treason!

DUKE: Oh, take me not in sleep!
    I have great sins; I must have days,
    Nay, months, dear son, with penitential heaves,
    To lift 'em out, and not to die unclear.
    O, thou wilt kill me both in Heaven and here.

LUSSURIOSO: I am amazed to death!

DUKE: Nay, villain traitor,
    Worse than the foulest epithet, now I'll grip thee
    E'en with the nerves of wrath, and throw thy head
    Amongst the lawyers! Guard!

(Enter NOBLES *and Sons with* HIPPOLITO)

FIRST NOBLE: How comes the quiet of your grace disturbed?

DUKE: This boy, that should be myself after me,
   Would be myself before me, and in heat
   Of that ambition, bloodily rushed in,
   Intending to depose me in my bed.

SECOND NOBLE: Duty and natural loyalty forfend!

DUCHESS: He called his father villain, and me strumpet,
   A word that I abhor to 'file my lips with.

AMBITIOSO: That was not so well done, brother.

LUSSURIOSO: I am abused—
   I know there's no excuse can do me good.

VINDICE *(aside to* HIPPOLITO): 'Tis now good policy to be from sight;
   His vicious purpose to our sister's honor
   Is crossed beyond our thought.

HIPPOLITO: You little dreamt his father slept here.

VINDICE: Oh, 'twas far beyond me,
   But since it fell so, without fright-full words,
   Would he had killed him, 'twould have eased our swords.

(VINDICE *and* HIPPOLITO *flee)*

DUKE: Be comforted our duchess, he shall die.

LUSSURIOSO: Where's this slave-pander now? Out of mine eye?
   Guilty of this abuse.

(Enter SPURIO *with his villains)*

SPURIO: Y'are villains, fablers,
   You have knaves' chins and harlots' tongues, you lie
   And I will damn you with one meal a day.

FIRST SERVANT: O, good my lord!

SPURIO: 'Sblood! You shall never sup.

SECOND SERVANT: O, I beseech you, sir.

SPURIO: To let my sword
   Catch cold so long and miss him.

FIRST SERVANT: Troth, my lord,
   'Twas his intent to meet there.

SPURIO: Heart, he's yonder!
   Ha, what news here? Is the day out o'th'socket
   That it is noon at midnight?—The court up?
   How comes the guard so saucy with his elbows?

LUSSURIOSO: The bastard here?
   Nay then, the truth of my intent shall out.
   My lord and father, hear me.

DUKE: Bear him hence.

LUSSURIOSO: I can with loyalty excuse—

DUKE: Excuse? To prison with the villain!
   Death shall not long lag after him.

SPURIO (aside): Good, i'faith, then 'tis not much amiss.

LUSSURIOSO: Brothers, my best release lies on your tongues;
   I pray, persuade for me.

AMBITIOSO: It is our duties; make yourself sure of us.

SUPERVACUO: We'll sweat in pleading.

LUSSURIOSO: And I may live to thank you.

(Exeunt LUSSURIOSO and guards)

AMBITIOSO (aside): No, thy death shall thank me better.

SPURIO *(aside):* He's gone; I'll after him
  And know his trespass, seem to bear a part
  In all his ills, but with a Puritan heart.

(Exit SPURIO *and villains)*

AMBITIOSO *(aside):* Now brother, let our hate and love be woven
  So subtly together, that in speaking one
  Word for his life, we may make three for his death;
  The craftiest pleader gets most gold for breath.

SUPERVACUO: Set on, I'll not be far behind you, brother.

DUKE: Is't possible a son
  Should be disobedient as far as the sword?
  It is the highest, he can go no farther.

AMBITIOSO: My gracious lord, take pity—

DUKE: Pity, boys?

AMBITIOSO: Nay, we'd be loath to move your Grace too much;
  We know the trespass is unpardonable,
  Black, wicked and unnatural.

SUPERVACUO: In a son, oh monstrous!

AMBITIOSO: Yet, my lord,
  A duke's soft hand strokes the rough head of law
  And makes it lie smooth.

DUKE: But my hand shall n'er do't.

AMBITIOSO: That, as you please, my lord.

SUPERVACUO: We must needs confess
  Some father would have entered into hate
  So deadly pointed, that before his eyes
  He would have seen the execution sound
  Without corrupted favor.

AMBITIOSO: But my lord,
   Your Grace may live the wonder of all times
   In pardoning that offense which never yet
   Had face to beg a pardon.

DUKE: Honey, how's this?

AMBITIOSO: Forgive him good my lord, he's your own son,
   And I must needs say, 'twas the vilelier done.

SUPERVACUO: He's the next heir, yet this true reason gathers,
   None can possess that dispossess their fathers.
   Be merciful.—

DUKE (*aside*):   Here's no stepmother's wit;
   I'll try 'em both upon their love and hate.

AMBITIOSO: Be merciful—altho'—

DUKE: You have prevailed.
   My wrath like flaming wax hath spent itself;
   I know 'twas but some peevish moon in him.—
   Go, let him be released.

SUPERVACUO (*aside*):   'Sfoot, how now, brother?

AMBITIOSO: Your Grace doth please to speak beside your spleen;
   I would it were so happy.

DUKE: Why, go release him.

SUPERVACUO: O my good lord, I know the fault's too weighty
   And full of general loathing, too inhuman,
   Rather by all men's voices, worthy death.

DUKE: 'Tis true too; here then, receive this signet:
   Doom shall pass, direct it to the judges: he shall die
   Ere many days. Make haste.

AMBITIOSO: All speed that may be

We could have wished his burden not so sore,
We knew your Grace did but delay before.

(Exeunt)

DUKE: Here's Envy with a poor thin cover o'er 't
Like scarlet hid in lawn, easily spied through.
This their ambition by the mother's side
Is dangerous, and for safety must be purged.
I will prevent their envies. Sure, it was
But some mistaken fury in our son
Which these aspiring boys would climb upon;
He shall be released suddenly.

(Enter NOBLES*)*

FIRST NOBLE: Good morning to your Grace.

DUKE: Welcome, my lords.

(They kneel)

SECOND NOBLE: Our knees shall take away the office of
Our feet for ever,
Unless your Grace bestow a father's eye
Upon the clouded fortunes of your son,
And in compassionate virtue grant him that
Which makes e'en mean men happy—liberty.

DUKE *(aside):* How seriously their loves and honors woo
For that which I am about to pray them do.
—Rise, my lords, your knees sign his release:
We freely pardon him.

FIRST NOBLE: We owe your Grace much thanks, and he much duty.

(Exeunt)

DUKE: It well becomes that judge to nod at crimes
That does commit greater himself and lives.
I may forgive a disobedient error,

That expect pardon for adultery
And in my old days am a youth in lust.
Many a beauty have I turned to poison
In the denial, covetous of all.
Age hot is like a monster to be seen:
My hairs are white, and yet my sins are green.

ACT THREE

Scene One

Enter AMBITIOSO *and* SUPERVACUO.

SUPERVACUO: Brother, let my opinion sway you once,
　　I speak it for the best,—to have him die
　　Surest and soonest. If the signet come
　　Unto the judges' hands, why then his doom
　　Will be deferred till sittings and court-days,
　　Juries and further; faiths are bought and sold,
　　Oaths in these days are but the skin of gold.

AMBITIOSO: In troth, 'tis true too.

SUPERVACUO:　　　　　　　　　Then let's set by the judges
　　And fall to the officers; 'tis but mistaking
　　The Duke our father's meaning, and where he named
　　'Ere many days', 'tis but forgetting that
　　And have him die i'th'morning.

AMBITIOSO:　　　　　　　　　Excellent!
　　Then am I heir—Duke in a minute.

SUPERVACUO *(aside):*　　　　　　　Nay,
　　If he were once puffed out, here is a pin
　　Should quickly prick your bladder.

AMBITIOSO:　　　　　　　　　Blest occasion!
　　He being packed, we'll have some trick and wile
　　To wind our younger brother out of prison,

That lies in for the rape; the lady's dead
And people's thoughts will soon be burièd.

SUPERVACUO: We may with safety do't, and live and feed:
The duchess' sons are too proud to bleed.

AMBITIOSO: We are i'faith, to say true.—Come, let's not linger,
I'll to the officers; go you before
And set an edge upon the executioner.

SUPERVACUO: Let me alone to grind him.

(Exit)

AMBITIOSO: Meet; farewell.
I am next now, I rise just in that place
Where thou'rt cut off, upon thy neck, kind brother,
The falling of one head lifts up another.

(Exit.)

Scene Two

Enter with the NOBLES, LUSSURIOSO *from prison.*

LUSSURIOSO: My lords, I am so much indebted to your loves
For this—O, this delivery.

FIRST NOBLE: But our duties, my lord,
Unto the hopes that grow in you.

LUSSURIOSO: If e'er I live to be myself, I'll thank you.
O Liberty, thou sweet and heavenly dame!
But Hell, for prison is too mild a name.

(Exeunt.)

Scene Three

Enter AMBITIOSO *and* SUPERVACUO *with* OFFICERS.

AMBITIOSO: Officers, here's the Duke's signet, your firm warrant
   Brings the command of present death along with it
   Unto our brother, the Duke's son; we are sorry
   That we are so unnaturally employed
   In such an unkind office, fitter far
   For enemies than brothers.

SUPERVACUO: But you know
   The Duke's command must be obeyed.

FIRST OFFICER: It must and shall, my lord; this morning then
   —So suddenly?

AMBITIOSO: Ay, alas, poor good soul,
   He must breakfast betimes, the executioner
   Stands ready to put forth his cowardly valor.

SECOND OFFICER: Already?

SUPERVACUO: Already i'faith—O, sir, destruction hies,
   And that is least impudent, soonest dies.

FIRST OFFICER: Troth, you say true, my lord; we take our leaves.
   Our office shall be sound; we'll not delay
   The third part of a minute.

AMBITIOSO: Therein you show
   Yourselves good men and upright officers.
   Pray, let him die as private as he may;
   Do him that favor, for the gaping people
   Will but trouble him at his prayers
   And make him curse and swear, and so die black.
   Will you be so far kind?

FIRST OFFICER: It shall be done, my lord.

AMBITIOSO: Why, we do thank you; if we live to be,
  You shall have a better office.

SECOND OFFICER: Your good lordship.

SUPERVACUO: Commend us to the scaffold in our tears.

FIRST OFFICER: We'll weep and do your commendations.

(Exeunt)

AMBITIOSO: Fine fools in office!

SUPERVACUO: Things fall out so fit.

AMBITIOSO: So happily! Come brother, ere next clock
  His head will be made to serve a bigger block.

(Exeunt.)

Scene Four

Enter in prison JUNIOR.

JUNIOR: Keeper.

KEEPER: My lord?

JUNIOR: No news lately from our brothers?
  Are they unmindful of us?

KEEPER: My lord, a messenger came newly in
  And brought this from 'em.

(Hands him a letter)

JUNIOR: Nothing but paper comforts?
  I looked for my delivery before this,
  Had they been worth their oaths.—Prithee, be from us.
  (Exit KEEPER*)*
  Now, what say you, forsooth; speak out, I pray:

(Reads letter): 'Brother, be of good cheer.'
'Slud, it begins like a whore, with good cheer.
'Thou shalt not be long a prisoner.'
Not five and thirty year, like a bankrupt,—I think so.
'We have thought upon a device to get thee out by a trick.'
By a trick? Pox o' your trick,' an it be so long a-playing!
'And so rest comforted, be merry and expect it suddenly.'
Be merry? Hang merry, draw and quarter merry!
I'll be mad. Is't not strange that a man
Should lie in a whole month for a woman?
Well, we shall see how sudden our brothers
Will be in their promise; I must expect
Still a trick. I shall not be long a prisoner.
(Enter KEEPER)
How now, what news?

KEEPER: Bad news my lord; I am discharged of you.

JUNIOR: Slave, call'st thou that bad news? I thank you, brothers.

KEEPER: My lord, 'twill prove so; here come the officers
Into whose hands I must commit you.

(Exit KEEPER)

JUNIOR: Ha, officers? What, why?

(Enter OFFICERS)

FIRST OFFICER: You must pardon us, my lord,
Our office must be sound; here is our warrant,
The signet from the Duke; you must straight suffer.

JUNIOR: Suffer? I'll suffer you to be gone, I'll suffer you
To come no more; what would you have me suffer?

SECOND OFFICER: My lord, those words were better changed to prayers.
The time's but brief with you, prepare to die.

JUNIOR: Sure 'tis not so.

THIRD OFFICER: It is too true, my lord.

JUNIOR: I tell you 'tis not, for the Duke my father
    Deferred me till next sitting, and I look
    E'en every minute, threescore times an hour
    For a release, a trick wrought by my brothers.

FIRST OFFICER: A trick my lord? If you expect such comfort,
    Your hope's as fruitless as a barren woman:
    Your brothers were the unhappy messengers
    That brought this powerful token for your death.

JUNIOR: My brothers? No, no.

SECOND OFFICER: 'Tis most true, my lord.

JUNIOR: My brothers to bring a warrant for my death?
    How strange this shows!

THIRD OFFICER: There's no delaying time.

JUNIOR: Desire 'em hither, call 'em up, my brothers!
    They shall deny it to your faces.

FIRST OFFICER: My lord,
    They're far enough by this, at least at court,
    And this most strict command they left behind 'em
    When grief swum in their eyes, they showed like brothers,
    Brim-full of heavy sorrow: but the Duke
    Must have his pleasure.

JUNIOR: His pleasure?

FIRST OFFICER: These were their last words which my memory bears
    'Commend us to the scaffold in our tears.'

JUNIOR: Pox dry their tears, what should I do with tears?
    I hate 'em worse than any citizen's son
    Can hate salt water; here came a letter now,
    New bleeding from their pens, scarce stinted yet—
    Would I'd been torn in pieces when I tore it;
    Look, you officious whoresons, words of comfort,
    'Not long a prisoner.'

FIRST OFFICER: It says true in that sir, for you must suffer presently.

JUNIOR: A villainous Duns upon the letter—knavish exposition—
　　Look you then here, sir: 'We'll get thee out by a trick,' says he.

SECOND OFFICER: That may hold, too, sir, for you know
　　A trick is commonly four cards, which was meant
　　By us four officers.

JUNIOR:　　　　　　　　Worse and worse dealing.

FIRST OFFICER: The hour beckons us,
　　The headsman waits, lift up your eyes to Heaven.

JUNIOR: I thank you, 'faith; good, pretty-wholesome counsel;
　　I should look up to Heaven as you said,
　　Whilst he behind me cozens me of my head—
　　Ay, that's the trick.

THIRD OFFICER:　　　　　You delay too long, my lord.

JUNIOR: Stay, good Authority's bastards, since I must
　　Through brothers' perjury die, O let me venom
　　Their souls with curses.

FIRST OFFICER:　　　　　　　Come, 'tis no time to curse.

JUNIOR: Must I bleed then, without respect of sign? Well—
　　My fault was sweet sport, which the world approves,
　　I die for that which every woman loves.

(Exeunt.)

Scene Five

Enter VINDICE *with* HIPPOLITO *his brother.*

VINDICE: O sweet, delectable, rare, happy, ravishing!

HIPPOLITO: Why, what's the matter brother?

VINDICE: O, 'tis able—
  To make a man spring up and knock his forehead
  Against yon silver ceiling.

HIPPOLITO: Prithee tell me,
  Why may not I partake with you? You vowed once
  To give me share to every tragic thought.

VINDICE: By th'Mass, I think I did, too;
  Then I'll divide it to thee. —The old Duke
  Thinking my outward shape and inward heart
  Are cut out of one piece—for he that prates his secrets,
  His heart stands o'th'outside—hires me by price:
  To greet him with a lady
  In some fit place veiled from the eyes o'th'court,
  Some darkened blushless angle, that is guilty
  Of his forefathers' lusts, and great folks' riots,
  To which I easily—to maintain my shape—
  Consented, and did wish his impudent grace
  To meet her here in this unsunnèd lodge,
  Wherein 'tis night at noon, and here the rather
  Because, unto the torturing of his soul,
  The bastard and the Duchess have appointed
  Their meeting too in this luxurious circle,
  Which most afflicting sight will kill his eyes
  Before we kill the rest of him.

HIPPOLITO: 'Twill i'faith, most dreadfully digested!
  I see not how you could have missed me, brother.

VINDICE: True, but the violence of my joy forgot it.

HIPPOLITO: Ay, but where's that lady now?

VINDICE: Oh, at that word
  I'm lost again! You cannot find me yet,
  I'm in a throng of happy apprehensions.
  He's suited for a lady; I have took care
  For a delicious lip, a sparkling eye—
  You shall be witness, brother;
  Be ready, stand with your hat off.

(Exit)

HIPPOLITO: Troth, I wonder what lady it should be?
　　Yet 'tis no wonder, now I think again,
　　To have a lady stoop to a duke, that stoops unto his men.
　　'Tis common to be common through the world,
　　And there's more private common shadowing vices
　　Than those who are known both by their names and prices.
　　'Tis part of my allegiance to stand bare
　　To the Duke's concubine—and here she comes.

(Enter VINDICE *with the skull of his love dressed up in headdress)*

VINDICE: Madam, his grace will not be absent long.
　　Secret? Ne'er doubt us madam; 'twill be worth
　　Three velvet gowns to your ladyship. Known?
　　Few ladies respect that disgrace, a poor thin shell!
　　'Tis the best grace you have to do it well;
　　I'll save your hand that labor, I'll unmask you.

(He reveals the skull)

HIPPOLITO: Why, brother, brother!

VINDICE: Art thou beguiled now? Tut, a lady can
　　At such—all hid—beguile a wiser man.
　　Have I not fitted the old surfeiter
　　With a quaint piece of beauty? Age and bare bone
　　Are e'er allied in action; here's an eye
　　Able to tempt a great man—to serve God;
　　A pretty hanging lip, that has forgot now to dissemble;
　　Methinks this mouth should make a swearer tremble,
　　A drunkard clasp his teeth and not undo 'em
　　To suffer wet damnation to run through 'em.
　　Here's a cheek keeps her color, let the wind go whistle.
　　Spout, rain, we fear thee not; be hot or cold,
　　All's one with us. And is not he absurd
　　Whose fortunes are upon their faces set,
　　That fear no other God but wind and wet?

HIPPOLITO: Brother, y'ave spoke that right;
  Is this the form that living shone so bright?

VINDICE: The very same—
  And now methinks I could e'en chide myself
  For doting on her beauty, tho' her death
  Shall be revenged after no common action.—
  Does the silkworm expend her yellow labors
  For thee? For thee does she undo herself?
  Are lordships sold to maintain ladyships
  For the poor benefit of a bewitching minute?
  Why does yon fellow falsify high ways
  And put his life between the judge's lips
  To refine such a thing, keeps horse and men
  To beat their valours for her?
  Surely, we're all mad people, and they
  Whom we think are, are not,—we mistake those;
  'Tis we are mad in sense, they but in clothes.

HIPPOLITO: 'Faith, and in clothes too we,—give us our due.

VINDICE: Does every proud and self-affecting dame
  Camphor her face for this, and grieve her Maker
  In sinful baths of milk,—when many an infant starves
  For her superfluous outside—all for this?
  Who now bids twenty pound a night, prepares
  Music, perfumes, and sweetmeats? All are hushed,
  Thou may'st lie chaste now! It were fine, methinks
  To have thee seen at revels, forgetful feasts
  And unclean brothels; sure 'twould fright the sinner
  And make him a good coward, put a reveller
  Out of his antic amble,
  And cloy an epicure with empty dishes.
  Here might a scornful and ambitious woman
  Look through and through herself; see, ladies with false forms
  You deceive men, but cannot deceive worms.
  Now to my tragic business. Look you, brother,
  I have not fashioned this only for show
  And useless property; no, it shall bear a part
  E'en in its own revenge. This very skull,
  Whose mistress the Duke poisoned with this drug,

The mortal curse of the earth, shall be revenged
In the like strain, and kiss his lips to death.
As much as the dumb thing can, he shall feel:
What fails in poison, we'll supply in steel.

HIPPOLITO: Brother, I do applaud thy constant vengeance,
The quaintness of thy malice—above thought.

VINDICE: So—'tis laid on: now come, and welcome, Duke,
I have her for thee. I protest it, brother,
Methinks she makes almost as fair a sign
As some old gentlewoman in a periwig.   *(Masks skull)*
Hide thy face now for shame; thou hadst need have a mask now.
'Tis vain when beauty flows; but when it fleets,
This would become graves better than the streets.

HIPPOLITO: You have my voice in that.
(Noises within)
                                   Hark, the Duke's come.

VINDICE: Peace, let's observe what company he brings,
And how he does absent 'em, for you know
He'll wish all private. Brother, fall you back a little
With the bony lady.

HIPPOLITO: That I will.   *(He withdraws)*

VINDICE: So, so;—now nine years' vengeance crowd into a minute.

(Enter DUKE and GENTLEMEN)

DUKE: You shall have leave to leave us, with this charge
Upon your lives: if we be missed by the Duchess
Or any of the nobles, to give out
We're privately rid forth.

VINDICE *(aside)*:   Oh, happiness!

DUKE: With some few honorable gentlemen, you may say;
You may name those that are away from court.

GENTLEMAN: Your will and pleasure shall be done, my lord.

(Exeunt GENTLEMEN*)*

VINDICE *(aside):* 'Privately rid forth!'
    He strives to make sure work on 't.
                                        Your good Grace!

DUKE: Piato, well done. Hast brought her? What lady is 't?

VINDICE: 'Faith, my lord,
    A country lady, a little bashful at first,
    As most of them are; but after the first kiss
    My lord, the worst is past with them; your Grace
    Knows now what you have to do;
    Sh'as somewhat a grave look with her, but—

DUKE: I love that best; conduct her.

VINDICE *(aside):*   Have at all.

DUKE: In gravest looks the greatest faults seem less;
    Give me that sin that's robed in holiness.

VINDICE *(aside):* Back with the torch, brother, raise the perfumes.

DUKE: How sweet can a duke breathe? Age has no fault.
    Pleasure should meet in a perfumèd mist.
    Lady, sweetly encountered; I came from court,
    I must be bold with you.

(Kisses skull)

                              Oh, what's this? Oh!

VINDICE: Royal villain! White devil!

DUKE: Oh!

VINDICE: Brother, place the torch here, that his affrighted eyeballs
    May start into those hollows. Duke, dost know

Yon dreadful vizard? View it well; 'tis the skull
Of Gloriana, whom thou poisonedst last.

DUKE: Oh, 't'as poisoned me!

VINDICE: Didst not know that till now?

DUKE: What are you two?

VINDICE: Villains—all three! The very ragged bone
Has been sufficiently revenged.

DUKE: Oh Hippolito, call treason!

HIPPOLITO: Yes, my good lord—treason! treason! treason!

(Stamping on him)

DUKE: Then I'm betrayed.

VINDICE: Alas, poor lecher! In the hands of knaves,
A slavish duke is baser than his slaves.

DUKE: My teeth are eaten out.

VINDICE: Hadst any left?

HIPPOLITO: I think but few.

VINDICE: Then those that did eat are eaten.

DUKE: O, my tongue!

VINDICE: Your tongue? 'Twill teach you to kiss closer,
Not like a flobbering Dutchman. You have eyes still:
Look, monster, what a lady hast thou made me
My once betrothèd wife!

DUKE: Is it thou, villain? Nay then—

VINDICE *(taking off disguise)*: 'Tis I, 'tis Vindice, 'tis I!

HIPPOLITO: And let this comfort thee: our lord and father
Fell sick upon the infection of thy frowns
And died in sadness; be that thy hope of life.

DUKE: Oh!

VINDICE: He had his tongue, yet grief made him die speechless.
Puh, 'tis but early yet; now I'll begin
To stick thy soul with ulcers, I will make
Thy spirit grievous sore; it shall not rest,
But like some pestilent man, toss in thy breast.
Mark me, duke,
Thou'rt a renownèd, high and mighty cuckold.

DUKE: Oh!

VINDICE: Thy bastard, thy bastard rides a-hunting in thy brow.

DUKE: Millions of deaths!

VINDICE: Nay, to afflict thee more,
Here in this lodge they meet for damnèd slips;
Those eyes shall see the incest of their lips.

DUKE: Is there a Hell besides this, villains?

VINDICE: Villain?
Nay, Heaven is just, scorns are the wages of scorns:
I ne'er knew yet adulterer without horns.

HIPPOLITO: Once ere they die 'tis quitted.

VINDICE: Hark, the music;
Their banquet is prepared, they're coming.

DUKE: Oh, kill me not with that sight!

VINDICE: Thou shalt not lose that sight for all thy dukedom.

DUKE: Traitors, murderers!

VINDICE: What! Is not thy tongue eaten out yet?
Then we'll invent a silence. Brother, stifle the torch.

DUKE: Treason, murder!

VINDICE: Nay, 'faith, we'll have you hushed now with thy dagger.
Nail down his tongue, and mine shall keep possession
About his heart; if he but gasp he dies,
We dread not death to quittance injuries. Brother,
If he but wink, not brooking the foul object,
Let our two other hands tear up his lids
And make his eyes like comets shine through blood;
When the bad bleeds, then is the tragedy good.

HIPPOLITO: Whist, brother, music's at our ear; they come.

(*Enter the bastard,* SPURIO *meeting the* DUCHESS)

SPURIO: Had not that kiss a taste of sin, 'twere sweet.

DUCHESS: Why, there's no pleasure sweet, but it is sinful.

SPURIO: True, such a bitter sweetness fate hath given,
Best side to us is the worst side to Heaven.

DUCHESS: Pish, come: 'tis the old Duke, thy doubtful father,
The thought of him rubs Heaven in thy way;
But I protest by yonder waxen fire,
Forget him, or I'll poison him.

SPURIO: Madam, you urge a thought which ne'er had life.
So deadly do I loathe him for my birth
That if he took me hasped within his bed,
I would add murder to adultery
And with my sword give up his years to death.

DUCHESS: Why, now thou'rt sociable; let's in and feast
Loud'st music sound: pleasure is Banquet's guest.

(*Exeunt*)

DUKE: I cannot brook—   *(Dies)*

VINDICE: The brook is turned to blood.

HIPPOLITO: Thanks to loud music.

VINDICE: 'Twas our friend indeed.
  'Tis state in music for a duke to bleed.
  The dukedom wants a head, tho' yet unknown;
  As fast as they peep up, let's cut 'em down.

(Exeunt.)

Scene Six

Enter the DUCHESS' *two sons,* AMBITIOSO *and* SUPERVACUO.

AMBITIOSO: Was not his execution rarely plotted?
  We are the Duke's sons now.

SUPERVACUO: Ay, you may thank my policy for that.

AMBITIOSO: Your policy for what?

SUPERVACUO: Why, was't not my invention, brother,
  To slip the judges? And in lesser compass,
  Did not I draw the model of his death,
  Advising you to sudden officers
  And e'en extemporal execution?

AMBITIOSO: Heart, 'twas a thing I thought on, too.

SUPERVACUO: You thought on't too? 'Sfoot, slander not your thoughts
  With glorious untruth; I know 'twas from you.

AMBITIOSO: Sir, I say 'twas in my head.

SUPERVACUO: Ay, like your brains then,
  Ne'er to come out as long as you lived.

AMBITIOSO: You'd have the honor on't, forsooth, that your wit
  Led him to the scaffold.

SUPERVACUO: Since it is my due,
  I'll publish 't, but I'll ha' 't in spite of you.

AMBITIOSO: Methinks you're much too bold; you should a little
  Remember us, brother, next to be honest Duke.

SUPERVACUO *(aside)*: Ay, it shall be as easy for you to be Duke
  As to be honest, and that's never, i'faith.

AMBITIOSO: Well, cold he is by this time, and because
  We're both ambitious, be it our amity
  And let the glory be sharèd equally.

SUPERVACUO: I am content to that.

AMBITIOSO: This night our younger brother shall out of prison;
  I have a trick.

SUPERVACUO: A trick! Prithee, what is't?

AMBITIOSO: We'll get him out by a wile.

SUPERVACUO: Prithee, what wile?

AMBITIOSO: No sir, you shall not know it till't be done;
  For then, you'd swear't were yours.

(Enter OFFICER, *bearing a head)*

SUPERVACUO: How now, what's he?

AMBITIOSO: One of the officers.

SUPERVACUO: Desirèd news.

AMBITIOSO: How now, my friend?

OFFICER: My lords, under your pardon, I am allotted

To that desertless office to present you
With the yet bleeding head.

SUPERVACUO *(aside):*   Ha, ha, excellent.

AMBITIOSO: *(aside):* All's sure our own: brother, canst weep, think'st
    thou?
'Twould grace our flattery much; think of some dame,
'Twill teach thee to dissemble.

SUPERVACUO: *(aside):* I have thought;—now for yourself.

AMBITIOSO: Our sorrows are so fluent,
    Our eyes o'erflow our tongues: words spoke in tears
Are like the murmurs of the waters, the sound
Is loudly heard, but cannot be distinguished.

SUPERVACUO: How died he, pray?

OFFICER: O, full of rage and spleen.

SUPERVACUO: He died most valiantly then; we're glad to hear it.

OFFICER: We could not woo him once to pray.

AMBITIOSO: He showed himself a gentleman in that:
    Give him his due.

OFFICER: But in the stead of prayer
He drew forth oaths.

SUPERVACUO: Then did he pray, dear heart,
Although you understood him not.

OFFICER: My lords,
E'en at his last, with pardon be it spoke,
He cursed you both.

SUPERVACUO: He cursed us? 'Las, good soul.

AMBITIOSO: It was not in our powers, but the Duke's pleasure.

(Aside) Finely dissembled o'both sides, sweet fate—
O, happy opportunity!

(Enter LUSSURIOSO)

LUSSURIOSO: Now my lords.

BOTH: Oh!

LUSSURIOSO: Why do you shun me, brothers?
You may come nearer now;
The savor of the prison has forsook me.
I thank such kind lords as yourselves, I'm free.

AMBITIOSO: Alive!

SUPERVACUO: In health!

AMBITIOSO: Released!
We were both e'en amazed with joy to see it.

LUSSURIOSO: I am much to thank you.

SUPERVACUO: 'Faith, we spared no tongue unto my lord the Duke.

AMBITIOSO: I know your delivery, brother,
Had not been half so sudden but for us.

SUPERVACUO: O how we pleaded!

LUSSURIOSO: Most deserving brothers,
In my best studies I will think of it.

(Exit LUSSURIOSO)

AMBITIOSO: O death and vengeance!

SUPERVACUO: Hell and torments!

AMBITIOSO: Slave, cam'st thou to delude us?

OFFICER: Delude you my lords?

SUPERVACUO: Ay, villain, where's this head now?

OFFICER: Why here, my lord;
    Just after his delivery, you both came
    With warrant from the Duke to behead your brother.

AMBITIOSO: Ay, our brother, the Duke's son.

OFFICER: The Duke's son, my lord, had his release before you came.

AMBITIOSO: Whose head's that then?

OFFICER: His whom you left command for, your own brother's.

AMBITIOSO: Our brother's? O furies!

SUPERVACUO: Plagues!

AMBITIOSO: Confusions!

SUPERVACUO: Darkness!

AMBITIOSO: Devils!

SUPERVACUO: Fell it out so accursedly?

AMBITIOSO: So damnedly?

SUPERVACUO: Villain, I'll brain thee with it.

OFFICER: O, my good lord!

(*Exit* OFFICER)

SUPERVACUO: The Devil overtake thee.

AMBITIOSO: O fatal!

SUPERVACUO: O, prodigious to our bloods!

AMBITIOSO: Did we dissemble—

SUPERVACUO: Did we make our tears women for thee?

AMBITIOSO: Laugh and rejoice for thee?

SUPERVACUO: Bring warrant for thy death?

AMBITIOSO: Mock off thy head?

SUPERVACUO: You had a trick, you had a wile, forsooth!

AMBITIOSO: A murrain meet 'em!
   There's none of these wiles that ever come to good:
   I see now there's nothing sure in mortality but mortality.
   Well, no more words,—'t shall be revenged i'faith
   Come, throw off clouds now, brother; think of vengeance
   And deeper settled hate; sirrah, sit fast,
   We'll pull down all, but thou shalt down at last.

(Exeunt.)

ACT FOUR

Scene One

Enter LUSSURIOSO *with* HIPPOLITO.

LUSSURIOSO: Hippolito.

HIPPOLITO: My lord—
   Has your good lordship aught to command me in?

LUSSURIOSO: I prithee leave us.

HIPPOLITO: How's this?—Come, and leave us?

LUSSURIOSO: Hippolito.

HIPPOLITO: Your honor, I stand ready for any duteous employment.

LUSSURIOSO: Heart, what mak'st thou here?

HIPPOLITO: *(aside):* A pretty lordly humor;
   He bids me to be present to depart;
   Something has stung his honor.

LUSSURIOSO: Be nearer, draw nearer:
   You are not so good, methinks, I'm angry with you.

HIPPOLITO: With me, my lord? I'm angry with myself for't.

LUSSURIOSO: You did prefer a goodly fellow to me,
   'Twas wittily elected, 'twas; I thought
   'Had been a villain, and he proves a knave—
   To me a knave.

HIPPOLITO: I chose him for the best, my lord,
   'Tis much my sorrow if neglect in him
   Breed discontent in you.

LUSSURIOSO: Neglect? 'Twas will: judge of it—
    Firmly to tell of an incredible act,
    Not to be thought, less to be spoken of,
    'Twixt my stepmother and the bastard—oh!
    Incestuous sweets between 'em.

HIPPOLITO: Fie my lord!

LUSSURIOSO: I, in kind loyalty to my father's forehead,
    Made this a desperate arm, and in that fury
    Committed treason on the lawful bed
    And with my sword e'en razed my father's bosom
    For which I was within a stroke of death.

HIPPOLITO: Alack! I'm sorry. (Aside) 'Sfoot! Just upon the stroke
    Jars in my brother; 'twill be villainous music.

(Enter VINDICE)

VINDICE: My honored lord—

LUSSURIOSO: Away, prithee forsake us! Hereafter we'll not know thee.

VINDICE: Not know me, my lord! Your lordship cannot choose.—

LUSSURIOSO: Begone I say; thou art a false knave.

VINDICE: Why, the easier to be known, my lord.

LUSSURIOSO: Pish, I shall prove too bitter with a word,
    Make thee a perpetual prisoner
    And lay this ironage upon thee.

VINDICE (aside): Mum
    —For there's a doom would make a woman dumb.—
    Missing the bastard next him, the wind's come about;
    Now 'tis my brother's turn to stay, mine to go out.

(Exit VINDICE)

LUSSURIOSO: H' 'as greatly moved me.

HIPPOLITO: Much to blame i'faith.

LUSSURIOSO: But I'll recover, to his ruin.—'Twas told me lately—
  I know not whether falsely—that you'd a brother.

HIPPOLITO: Who, I? Yes my good lord, I have a brother.

LUSSURIOSO: How chance the court ne'er saw him? Of what nature?
  How does he apply his hours?

HIPPOLITO: 'Faith, to curse fates,
  Who, as he thinks, ordained him to be poor—
  Keeps at home, full of want and discontent.

LUSSURIOSO *(aside):* There's hope in him, for discontent and want
  Is the best clay to mold a villain of.—
  Hippolito, wish him repair to us;
  If there be aught in him to please our blood
  For thy sake we'll advance him and build fair
  His meanest fortunes: for it is in us
  To rear up towers from cottages.

HIPPOLITO: It is so, my lord; he will attend your honor,
  But he's a man in whom much melancholy dwells.

LUSSURIOSO: Why, the better: bring him to court.

HIPPOLITO: With willingness and speed.
  (Aside) Whom he cast off e'en now must now succeed;
  Brother, disguise must off,
  In thine own shape now I'll prefer thee to him:
  How strangely does himself work to undo him.

(Exit)

LUSSURIOSO: This fellow will come fitly; he shall kill
  That other slave that did abuse my spleen
  And made it swell to treason. I have put
  Much of my heart into him, he must die.
  He that knows great men's secrets and proves slight,
  That man ne'er lives to see his beard turn white.

Ay, he shall speed him: I'll employ thee, brother;
Slaves are but nails to drive out one another.
He, being of black condition, suitable
To want and ill content, hope of preferment
Will grind him to an edge.

(*The* NOBLES *enter*)

FIRST NOBLE: Good days unto your honor.

LUSSURIOSO: My kind lords, I do return the like.

SECOND NOBLE: Saw you my lord, the Duke?

LUSSURIOSO: My lord and father—is he from court?

FIRST NOBLE: He's sure from court,
   But where, which way his pleasure took we know not;
Nor can we hear on 't.

(*Enter more* NOBLES)

LUSSURIOSO: Here come those should tell.
   Saw you my lord and father?

THIRD NOBLE: Not since two hours before noon, my lord,
   And then he privately rid forth.

LUSSURIOSO: Oh, he's rid forth.

FIRST NOBLE: 'Twas wondrous privately.

SECOND NOBLE: There's none i'th'court had any knowledge on't.

LUSSURIOSO: His Grace is old and sudden; 'tis no treason
   To say the Duke my father has a humor
   Or such a toy about him; what in us
   Would appear light, in him seems virtuous.

THIRD NOBLE: 'Tis oracle, my lord.

(Exeunt.)

Scene Two

Enter VINDICE *and* HIPPOLITO, VINDICE *out of his disguise.*

HIPPOLITO: So so, all's as it should be, y'are your self.

VINDICE: How that great villain puts me to my shifts!

HIPPOLITO: He that did lately in disguise reject thee
    Shall, now thou art thy self, as much respect thee.

VINDICE: 'Twill be the quainter fallacy; but brother
    'Sfoot, what use will he put me to now, think'st thou?

HIPPOLITO: Nay you must pardon me in that, I know not:
    H' 'as some employment for you, but what 'tis
    He and his secretary the Devil knows best.

VINDICE: Well, I must suit my tongue to his desires,
    What color so e'er they be, hoping at last
    To pile up all my wishes on his breast.

HIPPOLITO: 'Faith brother, he himself shows the way.

VINDICE: Now the Duke is dead, the realm is clad in clay:
    His death being not yet known, under his name
    The people still are governed. Well, thou his son
    Art not long-lived; thou shalt not 'joy his death.
    To kill thee then I should most honor thee;
    For 'twould stand firm in every man's belief,
    Thou'st a kind child and only diedst with grief.

HIPPOLITO: You fetch about well, but let's talk in present;
    How will you appear in fashion different
    As well as in apparel, to make all things possible;
    If you be but once tripped, we fall for ever.

It is not the least policy to be doubtful;
You must change tongue—familiar was your first.

VINDICE: Why, I'll bear me in some strain of melancholy
And string myself with heavy-sounding wire,
Like such an instrument that speaks merry things sadly.

HIPPOLITO: Then 'tis as I meant;
I gave you out at first in discontent.

VINDICE: I'll turn myself, and then—

HIPPOLITO: 'Sfoot here he comes; hast thought upon't?

VINDICE: Salute him, fear not me.

(*Enter* LUSSURIOSO)

LUSSURIOSO: Hippolito.

HIPPOLITO: Your lordship—

LUSSURIOSO: What's he yonder?

HIPPOLITO: 'Tis Vindice, my discontented brother,
Whom, 'cording to your will I've brought to court.

LUSSURIOSO: Is that thy brother? Beshrew me, a good presence;
I wonder h' 'as been from the court so long.
Come nearer.

HIPPOLITO: Brother, Lord Lussurioso, the Duke's son.

LUSSURIOSO: Be more near to us, welcome, nearer yet.

VINDICE: How don you? God you god den.

(*Snatches off his hat and makes legs to him*)

LUSSURIOSO: We thank thee.
How strangely such a coarse-homely salute

Shows in the palace, where we greet in fire,
Nimble and desperate tongues. Should we name God in a
salutation, 'twould ne'er be stood on't—Heaven!
Tell me what has made thee so melancholy.

VINDICE: Why, going to law.

LUSSURIOSO: Why, will that make a man melancholy?

VINDICE: Yes, to look long upon ink and black buckram. I went me to law
in *Anno Quadragesimo Secundo*, and I waded out of it in *Anno
Sextagesimo Tertio*.

LUSSURIOSO: What, three and twenty years in law?

VINDICE: I have known those that have been five and fifty, and all about
poultry and pigs.

LUSSURIOSO: May it be possible such men should breathe
To vex the terms so much?

VINDICE: 'Tis food to some, my lord. There are old men at the present
that are so poisoned with the affectation of law-words—having had
many suits canvassed—that their common talk is nothing but Barbary
Latin: they cannot so much as pray but in law, that their sins may be
removed with a writ of error, and their souls fetched up to Heaven
with a sasarara.

LUSSURIOSO: It seems most strange to me,
Yet all the world meets round in the same bent:
Where the heart's set, there goes the tongue's consent.
How dost apply thy studies, fellow?

VINDICE: Study? Why, to think how a great rich man lies a-dying, and a
poor cobbler tolls the bell for him. How he cannot depart the world,
and see the great chest stand before him; when he lies speechless,
how he will point you readily to all the boxes; and when he is past all
memory—as the gossips guess—then thinks he of forfeitures and ob-
ligations; nay, when to all men's hearings he whirls and rattles in the
throat, he's busy threatening his poor tenants; and this would last me
now some seven years' thinking or thereabouts. But I have a conceit

a-coming in picture upon this—I draw it myself—which i'faith, la, I'll present to your honor; you shall not choose but like it, for your lordship shall give me nothing for it.

LUSSURIOSO: Nay, you mistake me then,
For I am published bountiful enough.
Let's taste of your conceit.

VINDICE: In picture, my lord?

LUSSURIOSO: Ay, in picture.

VINDICE: Marry, this it is—'A usuring Father to be boiling in Hell, and his Son and heir with a whore dancing over him.'

HIPPOLITO (aside): H'as pared him to the quick.

LUSSURIOSO: The conceit's pretty, i'faith,
But take't upon my life 'twill ne'er be liked.

VINDICE: No? Why, I'm sure the whore will be liked well enough.

HIPPOLITO (aside): Ay, if she were out o'th'picture he'd like her then himself.

VINDICE: And as for the son and heir, he shall be an eyesore to no young revellers, for he shall be drawn in cloth-of-gold breeches.

LUSSURIOSO: If thou hast put my meaning in the pockets
And canst not draw that out, my thought was this,
To see the picture of a usuring father
Boiling in Hell, our rich men would ne'er like it.

VINDICE: O true, I cry you heart'ly mercy. I know the reason, for some of them had rather be damned indeed than damned in colors.

LUSSURIOSO (aside): A parlous melancholy! H'as wit enough
To murder any man, and I'll give him means.—
I think thou art ill moneyed.

VINDICE: Money, ho, ho!
'T'as been my want so long, 'tis now my scoff.
I've e'en forgot what color silver's of.

LUSSURIOSO *(aside)*: It hits as I could wish.

VINDICE: I get good clothes
  Of those that dread my humor, and for table-room
  I feed on those that cannot be rid of me.

LUSSURIOSO: Somewhat to set thee up withal.

(Gives him gold)

VINDICE: O, mine eyes!

LUSSURIOSO: How now, man?

VINDICE: Almost struck blind;
  This bright unusual shine to me seems proud,
  I dare not look till the sun be in a cloud.

LUSSURIOSO *(aside)*: I think I shall affect his melancholy.—
  How are they now?

VINDICE: The better for your asking.

LUSSURIOSO: You shall be better yet if you but fasten
  Truly on my intent; now y'are both present,
  I will unbrace such a close private villain
  Unto your vengeful swords, the like ne'er heard of,
  Who hath disgraced you much and injured us.

HIPPOLITO: Disgraced us, my lord?

LUSSURIOSO: Ay, Hippolito.
  I kept it here till now that both your angers
  Might meet him at once.

VINDICE: I'm covetous
  To know the villain.

LUSSURIOSO: You know him, that slave pander
  Piato, whom we threatened last
  With irons in perpetual prisonment.

VINDICE *(aside)*: All this is I.

HIPPOLITO: Is't he, my lord?

LUSSURIOSO: I'll tell you—you first preferred him to me.

VINDICE: Did you, brother?

HIPPOLITO: I did indeed.

LUSSURIOSO: And the ungrateful villain,
   To quit that kindness, strongly wrought with me,
   Being—as you see—a likely man for pleasure,
   With jewels to corrupt your virgin sister.

HIPPOLITO: O, villain!

VINDICE: He shall surely die that did it.

LUSSURIOSO: I, far from thinking any virgin harm,
   Especially knowing her to be as chaste
   As that part which scarce suffers to be touched—
   Th'eye—would not endure him.

VINDICE: Would you not, my lord?
   'Twas wondrous honorably done.

LUSSURIOSO: But with some fine frowns kept him out.

VINDICE *(aside)*: Out, slave!

LUSSURIOSO: What did me he? But in revenge of that
   Went of his own free will to make infirm
   Your sister's honor, whom I honor with my soul
   For chaste respect, and not prevailing there
   —As 'twas but desperate folly to attempt it—
   In mere spleen, by the way, waylays your mother,
   Whose honor being coward—as it seems—
   Yielded by little force.

VINDICE: Coward indeed!

LUSSURIOSO: He, proud of this advantage—as he thought—
    Brought me these news for happy; but I—Heaven forgive me for't!

VINDICE: What did your Honor?

LUSSURIOSO: In rage pushed him from me
    Trampled beneath his throat, spurned him, and bruised:
    Indeed, I was too cruel, to say troth.

HIPPOLITO: Most nobly managed!

VINDICE *(aside)*: Has not Heaven an ear? Is all the lightning wasted?

LUSSURIOSO: If I now were so impatient in a modest cause,
    What should you be?

VINDICE: Full mad; he shall not live
    To see the moon change.

LUSSURIOSO: He's about the palace;
    Hippolito, entice him this way, that thy brother
    May take full mark of him.

HIPPOLITO: Heart!—That shall not need, my lord;
    I can direct him so far.

LUSSURIOSO: Yet, for my hate's sake,
    Go wind him this way; I'll see him bleed myself.

HIPPOLITO *(aside)*: What now, brother?

VINDICE *(aside)*: Nay, e'en what you will; y'are put to it, brother.

HIPPOLITO *(aside)*: An impossible task, I'll swear,
    To bring him hither that's already here.

(Exit HIPPOLITO*)*

LUSSURIOSO: Thy name? I have forgot it.

VINDICE: Vindice, my lord.

LUSSURIOSO: 'Tis a good name, that.

VINDICE: Ay, a Revenger.

LUSSURIOSO: It does betoken courage; thou shouldst be valiant
   And kill thine enemies.

VINDICE: That's my hope, my lord.

LUSSURIOSO: This slave is one.

VINDICE: I'll doom him.

LUSSURIOSO: Then I'll praise thee.
   Do thou observe me best, and I'll best raise thee.

(*Enter* HIPPOLITO)

VINDICE: Indeed I thank you.

LUSSURIOSO: Now Hippolito, where's the slave pander?

HIPPOLITO: Your good lordship
   Would have a loathsome sight of him, much offensive;
   He's not in case now to be seen, my lord.
   The worst of all the deadly sins is in him;
   That beggarly damnation, drunkenness.

LUSSURIOSO: Then he's a double slave.

VINDICE (*aside*): 'Twas well conveyed, upon a sudden wit.

LUSSURIOSO: What, are you both
   Firmly resolved? I'll see him dead myself.

VINDICE: Or else let not us live.

LUSSURIOSO: You may direct your brother to take note of him.

HIPPOLITO: I shall.

LUSSURIOSO: Rise but in this and you shall never fall.

VINDICE: Your Honor's vassals.

LUSSURIOSO *(aside):* This was wisely carried;
   Deep policy in us makes fools of such—
   Then must a slave die, when he knows too much.

(Exit LUSSURIOSO*)*

VINDICE: O thou Almighty patience! 'tis my wonder
   That such a fellow, impudent and wicked,
   Should not be cloven as he stood,
   Or with a secret wind burst open!
   Is there no thunder left, or is't kept up
   In stock for heavier vengeance? *(Thunder)* There it goes!

HIPPOLITO: Brother, we lose ourselves.

VINDICE: But I have found it,
   'Twill hold, 'tis sure; thanks, thanks to any spirit
   That mingled it 'mongst my inventions.

HIPPOLITO: What is 't?

VINDICE: 'Tis sound and good, thou shalt partake it:
   I'm hired to kill myself.

HIPPOLITO: True.

VINDICE: Prithee, mark it:
   And the old Duke being dead, but not conveyed,
   For he's already missed too, and you know,
   Murder will peep out of the closest husk.

HIPPOLITO: Most true.

VINDICE: What say you then to this device:
   If we dressed up the body of the Duke—

HIPPOLITO: In that disguise of yours—

VINDICE: Y'are quick, y'ave reached it.

HIPPOLITO: I like it wondrously.

VINDICE: And being in drink, as you have published him,
    To lean him on his elbow, as if sleep had caught him,
    Which claims most interest in such sluggish men.

HIPPOLITO: Good, yet—but here's a doubt:
    We, thought by the Duke's son to kill that pander,
    Shall, when he is known, be thought to kill the Duke.

VINDICE: Neither, O thanks! It is substantial.
    For that disguise being on him which I wore,
    It will be thought I, which he calls the pander,
    Did kill the Duke, and fled away in his
    Apparel, leaving him so disguised
    To avoid swift pursuit.

HIPPOLITO: Firmer and firmer.

VINDICE: Nay doubt not, 'tis in grain, I warrant it
    Hold color.

HIPPOLITO: Let's about it.

VINDICE: But by the way too, now I think on't, brother,
    Let's conjure that base Devil out of our mother.

(Exeunt.)

Scene Three

Enter the DUCHESS arm in arm with the BASTARD: he seemeth lasciviously to
her; after them, enter SUPERVACUO, running with a rapier; his brother, AMBI-
TIOSO stops him.

SPURIO: Madam, unlock yourself; should it be seen
    Your arm would be suspected.

DUCHESS: Who is't that dares suspect or this or these?
   (Kissing him)
   May not we deal our favors where we please?

SPURIO: I'm confident you may.

(Exeunt)

AMBITIOSO: 'Sfoot brother, hold.

SUPERVACUO: Woul't let the bastard shame us?

AMBITIOSO: Hold, hold, brother! There's fitter time than now.

SUPERVACUO: Now, when I see it.

AMBITIOSO: 'Tis too much seen already.

SUPERVACUO: Seen and known.
   The nobler she's, the baser is she grown.

AMBITIOSO: If she were bent lasciviously—the fault
   Of mighty women that sleep soft,—O death,
   Must she needs choose such an unequal sinner,
   To make all worse?

SUPERVACUO: A bastard, the Duke's bastard! Shame heaped on shame!

AMBITIOSO: O our disgrace!
   Most women have small waist the world throughout,
   But their desires are thousand miles about.

SUPERVACUO: Come, stay not here, let's after and prevent,
   Or else they'll sin faster than we'll repent.

(Exeunt)

Scene Four

Enter VINDICE *and* HIPPOLITO *bringing out their mother, one by one shoulder and the other by the other, with daggers in their hands.*

VINDICE: O thou for whom no name is bad enough!

GRATIANA: What means my sons? What, will you murder me?

VINDICE: Wicked, unnatural parent!

HIPPOLITO: Fiend of women!

GRATIANA: Oh, are sons turned monsters? Help!

VINDICE: In vain.

GRATIANA: Are you so barbarous to set iron nipples
    Upon the breast that gave you suck?

VINDICE: That breast
    Is turned to curdled poison.

GRATIANA: Cut not your days for't; am not I your mother?

VINDICE: Thou dost usurp that title now by fraud,
    For in that shell of mother breeds a bawd.

GRATIANA: A bawd? O name far loathsomer than Hell!

HIPPOLITO: It should be so, knew'st thou thy office well.

GRATIANA: I hate it.

VINDICE: Ah, is't possible? Thou only—you powers on high,
    That women should dissemble when they die!

GRATIANA: Dissemble?

VINDICE: Did not the Duke's son direct
A fellow of the world's condition hither,
That did corrupt all that was good in thee,
Made thee uncivilly forget thyself
And work our sister to his lust?

GRATIANA: Who? I?
That had been monstrous! I defy that man
For any such intent; none lives so pure
But shall be soiled with slander.
Good son, believe it not.

VINDICE: Oh, I'm in doubt
Whether I'm myself or no!
Stay, let me look again upon this face.
Who shall be saved when mothers have no grace?

HIPPOLITO: 'Twould make one half despair.

VINDICE: I was the man.
Defy me now, let's see! Do't modestly.

GRATIANA: O, Hell unto my soul!

VINDICE: In that disguise I, sent from the Duke's son,
Tried you, and found you base metal,
As any villain might have done.

GRATIANA: O no, no tongue but yours could have bewitched me so.

VINDICE: O nimble in damnation, quick in tune!
There is no Devil could strike fire so soon.—
I am confuted in a word.

GRATIANA: Oh sons, forgive me! To my self I'll prove more true.
You that should honor me, I kneel to you.

(Kneels, weeping)

VINDICE: A mother to give aim to her own daughter!

HIPPOLITO: True, brother; how far beyond nature 'tis,
    Tho' many mothers do't!

VINDICE: Nay, an you draw tears once, go you to bed;
    Wet will make iron blush and change to red.
    Brother, it rains; 'twill spoil your dagger, house it.

HIPPOLITO: 'Tis done.

VINDICE: I'faith, 'tis a sweet shower, it does much good:
    The fruitful grounds and meadows of her soul
    Has been long dry; pour down, thou blessed dew!
    Rise, mother; troth, this shower has made you higher.

GRATIANA: O you heavens, take this infectious spot out of my soul!
    I'll rinse it in seven waters of mine eyes.
    Make my tears salt enough to taste of grace;
    To weep is to our sex naturally given,
    But to weep truly, that's a gift from Heaven.

VINDICE: Nay, I'll kiss you now. Kiss her, brother,
    Let's marry her to our souls, wherein's no lust,
    And honorably love her.

HIPPOLITO: Let it be.

VINDICE: For honest women are so seld and rare
    'Tis good to cherish those poor few that are.
    Oh you of easy wax! Do but imagine,
    Now the disease has left you, how leprously
    That office would have clinged unto your forehead.
    All mothers that had any graceful hue
    Would have worn masks to hide their face at you.
    It would have grown to this—at your foul name,
    Green-colored maids would have turned red with shame.

HIPPOLITO: And then, our sister full of hire and baseness!

VINDICE: There had been boiling lead again.
    Duke's son's great concubine!

A drab of state, a cloth o'silver slut,
To have her train borne up, and her soul trail i'th'dirt.

HIPPOLITO: Great, too miserably great! Rich to be eternally wretched.

VINDICE: O, common madness!
Ask but the thriving'st harlot in cold blood,
She'd give the world to make her honor good.
Perhaps you'll say: but only to the Duke's son
In private. Why, she first begins with one
Who afterwards to thousand proves a whore:
'Break ice in one place, it will crack in more.'

GRATIANA: Most certainly applied.

HIPPOLITO: Oh brother, you forget our business.

VINDICE: And well remembered; joy's a subtle elf;
I think man's happiest when he forgets himself.
Farewell, once dried, now holy-watered mead,
Our hearts wear feathers, that before wore lead.

GRATIANA: I'll give you this: that one I never knew
Plead better for and 'gainst the Devil, than you.

VINDICE: You make me proud on't.

HIPPOLITO: Commend us in all virtue to our sister.

VINDICE: Ay, for the love of Heaven, to that true maid.

GRATIANA: With my best words.

VINDICE: Why, that was motherly said.

(*Exeunt*)

GRATIANA: I wonder now what fury did transport me.
I feel good thoughts begin to settle in me.
Oh, with what forehead can I look on her

Whose honor I've so impiously beset.
—And here she comes.

(*Enter* CASTIZA)

CASTIZA: Now, mother, you have wrought with me so strongly
   That what for my advancement, as to calm
   The trouble of your tongue, I am content.

GRATIANA: Content to what?

CASTIZA: To do as you have wished me,
   To prostitute my breast to the Duke's son
   And put myself to common usury.

GRATIANA: I hope you will not so.

CASTIZA: Hope you I will not?
   That's not the hope you look to be saved in.

GRATIANA: Truth, but it is.

CASTIZA: Do not deceive yourself.
   I am as you, e'en out of marble wrought.
   What would you now? Are you not pleased yet with me?
   You shall not wish me to be more lascivious
   Than I intend to be.

GRATIANA: Strike not me cold.

CASTIZA: How often have you charged me on your blessing
   To be a cursèd woman? When you knew
   Your blessing had no force to make me lewd,
   You laid your curse upon me. That did more;
   The mother's curse is heavy—where that fights,
   Sons set in storm, and daughters lose their lights.

GRATIANA: Good child, dear maid, if there be any spark
   Of heavenly intellectual fire within thee,
   O let my breath revive it to a flame!
   Put not all out with woman's wilful follies.

I am recovered of that foul disease
That haunts too many mothers; kind, forgive me.
Make me not sick in health. If then
My words prevailed when they were wickedness,
How much more now, when they are just and good!

CASTIZA: I wonder what you mean. Are not you she
For whose infect persuasions I could scarce
Kneel out my prayers, and had much ado
In three hours' reading, to untwist so much
Of the black serpent as you wound about me?

GRATIANA: 'Tis unfruitful, held tedious, to repeat what's past;
I'm now your present mother.

CASTIZA: Pish, now 'tis too late.

GRATIANA: Bethink again, thou know'st not what thou say'st.

CASTIZA: No? Deny advancement, treasure, the Duke's son?

GRATIANA: O see, I spoke those words and now they poison me.
What will the deed do then?
Advancement? True, as high as shame can pitch.
For treasure—whoe'er knew a harlot rich,
Or could build by the purchase of her sin
An hospital to keep their bastards in?
The Duke's son—oh, when women are young courtiers,
They are sure to be old beggars.
To know the miseries most harlots taste,
Thou'dst wish thyself unborn when thou'rt unchaste.

CASTIZA: O mother, let me twine about your neck
And kiss you till my soul melt on your lips.
—I did but this to try you.

GRATIANA: O speak truth.

CASTIZA: Indeed, I did not; for no tongue has force
To alter me from honest.
If maidens would, men's words could have no power;

A virgin honor is a crystal tower
Which, being weak, is guarded with good spirits;
Until she basely yields, no ill inherits.

GRATIANA: O happy child! Faith and thy birth hath saved me.
'Mongst thousand daughters, happiest of all others,
Be thou a glass for maids, and I for mothers.

(Exeunt.)

ACT FIVE

Scene One

Enter VINDICE *and* HIPPOLITO, *with the Duke's corpse.*

VINDICE: So, so, he leans well; take heed you wake him not, brother.

HIPPOLITO: I warrant you my life for yours.

VINDICE: That's a good lay, for I must kill myself. Brother, that's I:
(pointing to corpse) that sits for me: do you mark it. And I must stand
ready here to make away myself yonder. I must sit to be killed, and
stand to kill myself. I could vary it not so little as thrice over again;
't'as some eight returns, like Michaelmas Term.

HIPPOLITO: That's enow, o'conscience.

VINDICE: But sirrah, does the Duke's son come single?

HIPPOLITO: No, there's the Hell on't. His faith's too feeble to go alone; he
brings flesh-flies after him, that will buzz against supper time and
hum for his coming out.

VINDICE: Ah, the fly-flop of vengeance beat 'em to pieces! Here was the
sweetest occasion, the fittest hour to have made my revenge familiar
with him,—show him the body of the Duke his father, and how
quaintly he died, like a politician, in hugger-mugger, made no man
acquainted with it—and in catastrophe slain him over his father's
breast! And oh, I'm mad to lose such a sweet opportunity!

HIPPOLITO: Nay, pish, prithee be content. There's no remedy present. May not hereafter times open in as fair faces as this?

VINDICE: They may, if they can paint so well.

HIPPOLITO: Come now, to avoid all suspicion let's forsake this room and be going to meet the Duke's son.

VINDICE: Content, I'm for any weather. Heart, step close; here he comes.

(Enter LUSSURIOSO*)*

HIPPOLITO: My honored lord.

LUSSURIOSO: Oh, me! You both present?

VINDICE: E'en newly my lord, just as your lordship entered now. About this place we had notice given he should be, but in some loathsome plight or other.

HIPPOLITO: Came your honor private?

LUSSURIOSO: Private enough for this: only a few
   Attend my coming out.

HIPPOLITO *(aside):* Death rot those few.

LUSSURIOSO: Stay, yonder's the slave.

VINDICE: Mass, there's the slave indeed, my lord.
   (Aside) 'Tis a good child; he calls his father slave.

LUSSURIOSO: Ay, that's the villain, the damned villain; softly.
   Tread easy.

VINDICE: Pish, I warrant you, my lord
   We'll stifle in our breaths.

LUSSURIOSO: That will do well.
   Base rogue, thou sleepest thy last. *(Aside)* 'Tis policy

To have him killed in's sleep, for if he waked
He would betray all to them.

VINDICE: But my lord—

LUSSURIOSO: Ha—what say'st?

VINDICE: Shall we kill him now he's drunk?

LUSSURIOSO: Ay, best of all.

VINDICE: Why, then he will ne'er live to be sober.

LUSSURIOSO: No matter, let him reel to Hell.

VINDICE: But being so full of liquor, I fear he will put out all the fire.

LUSSURIOSO: Thou art a mad beast.

VINDICE *(aside)*: And leave none to warm your lordship's paws withal; for
he that dies drunk falls into Hellfire like a bucket o'water, qush, qush.

LUSSURIOSO: Come, be ready; bare your swords, think of your wrongs.
This slave has injured you.

VINDICE: Troth, so he has—and he has paid well for't.

LUSSURIOSO: Meet with him now.

VINDICE: You'll bear us out, my lord?

LUSSURIOSO: Puh, am I a lord for nothing, think you?
Quickly now.

VINDICE *(stabbing Duke's corpse)*: Sa, sa, sa!
                                Thump, there he lies.

LUSSURIOSO: Nimbly done! Ha! Oh villains, murderers!
'Tis the old Duke my father.

VINDICE: That's a jest.

LUSSURIOSO: What—stiff and cold already?
O, pardon me to call you from your names—
'Tis none of your deed. That villain Piato,
Whom you thought now to kill, has murdered him
And left him thus disguised.

HIPPOLITO: And not unlikely.

VINDICE: O rascal, was he not ashamed
To put the Duke into a greasy doublet?

LUSSURIOSO: He has been cold and stiff—who knows how long?

VINDICE (*aside*): Marry, that do I.

LUSSURIOSO: No words, I pray, of any thing intended.

VINDICE: Oh my lord.

HIPPOLITO: I would fain have your lordship think that we
Have small reason to prate.

LUSSURIOSO: 'Faith, thou sayest true. I'll forthwith send to court
For all the nobles, bastard, duchess, all—
How here by miracle we found him dead
And in his raiment that foul villain fled.

VINDICE: That will be the best way my lord, to clear
Us all; let's cast about to be clear.

LUSSURIOSO: Ho, Nencio, Sordido, and the rest!

(*Enter all his* SERVANTS)

FIRST SERVANT: My lord?

SECOND SERVANT: My lord?

LUSSURIOSO: Be witnesses of a strange spectacle.—
Choosing for private conference that sad room,
We found the Duke my father 'gealed in blood.

FIRST SERVANT: My lord the Duke! Run, hie thee, Nencio—
  Startle the court by signifying so much.

(*Exit* NENCIO)

VINDICE (*aside*): Thus much by wit a deep Revenger can,
  When murder's known, to be the clearest man.
  We're farthest off, and with as bold an eye
  Survey his body, as the standersby.

LUSSURIOSO: My royal father, too basely let blood
  By a malevolent slave!

HIPPOLITO (*aside*):   H'as lost, he may.

LUSSURIOSO: Oh sight! Look hither, see, his lips are gnawn
  With poison.

VINDICE: How?—His lips? By th'Mass, they be.
  O villain! O rogue! O slave! O rascal!

HIPPOLITO (*aside*): O good deceit, he quits him with like terms.

VOICES WITHIN: Where? Which way?

(*Enter* AMBITIOSO *and* SUPERVACUO, *with* COURTIERS)

AMBITIOSO: Over what roof hangs this prodigious comet
  In deadly fire?

LUSSURIOSO: Behold, behold, my lords!
  The Duke my father's murdered by a vassal
  That owns this habit and here left disguised.

(*Enter* DUCHESS *and* SPURIO)

DUCHESS: My lord and husband!

FIRST NOBLE: Reverend Majesty.

SECOND NOBLE: I have seen these clothes often attending on him.

VINDICE *(aside)*: That nobleman has been i'th'country, for he does not
   lie.

SUPERVACUO *(aside)*: Learn of our mother, let's dissemble, too.
   I am glad he's vanished; so I hope are you.

AMBITIOSO *(aside)*: Ay, you may take my word for't.

SPURIO *(aside)*: Old dad dead?
   I, one of his cast sins, will send the fates
   Most hearty commendations by his own son;
   I'll tug in the new stream till strength be done.

LUSSURIOSO: Where be those two that did affirm to us
   My Lord the Duke was privately rid forth?

FIRST NOBLE: O pardon us my lords, he gave that charge
   Upon our lives, if he were missed at court
   To answer so; he rode not anywhere.
   We left him private with that fellow here.

VINDICE: Confirmed.

LUSSURIOSO: O, heavens, that false charge was his death!
   Impudent beggars! Durst you to our face
   Maintain such a false answer? Bear him straight
   To execution.

FIRST NOBLE: My lord!

LUSSURIOSO: Urge me no more.
   In this the excuse may be called half the murder.

VINDICE: You've sentenced well. Away, see it be done.

(Exit FIRST NOBLE *under guard)*

VINDICE *(aside)*: Could you not stick? See what confession doth—
   Who would not lie when men are hanged for truth?

HIPPOLITO *(aside)*: Brother, how happy is our vengeance!

VINDICE *(aside):*   Why, it hits
  Past the apprehension of indifferent wits.

LUSSURIOSO: My lord, let posthorse be sent
  Into all places to entrap the villain.

VINDICE *(aside):* Posthorse! Ha, ha!

NOBLE: My lord, we're something bold to know our duty:
  Your father's accidentally departed;
  The titles that were due to him meet you.

LUSSURIOSO: Meet me? I'm not at leisure my good lord,
  I've many griefs to dispatch out o'th'way.
  (Aside) Welcome, sweet titles.—Talk to me, my lords,
  Of sepulchers and mighty emperors' bones;
  That's thought for me.

VINDICE *(aside):*   So, one may see by this
  How foreign markets go:
  Courtiers have feet o'th'nines, and tongues o'th'twelves,
  They flatter dukes and dukes flatter themselves.

NOBLE: My lord, it is your shine must comfort us.

LUSSURIOSO: Alas, I shine in tears, like the sun in April.

NOBLE: You're now my lord's Grace.

LUSSURIOSO: My lord's Grace! I perceive you'll have it so.

NOBLE: 'Tis but your own.

LUSSURIOSO: Then heavens give me grace to be so.

VINDICE *(aside):* He prays well for himself.

NOBLE *(to* DUCHESS): Madam, all sorrows
  Must run their circles into joys; no doubt
  But time will make the murderer bring forth himself.

VINDICE *(aside):* He were an ass then, i'faith.

NOBLE: In the mean season,
   Let us bethink the latest funeral honors
   Due to the Duke's cold body—and withal,
   Calling to memory our new happiness,
   Spread in his royal son;—lords, gentlemen,
   Prepare for revels.

VINDICE *(aside)*:   Revels!

NOBLE: Time hath several falls;
   Griefs lift up joys, feasts put down funerals.

LUSSURIOSO: Come then my lords, my favors to you all.
   (Aside) The Duchess is suspected foully bent;
   I'll begin dukedom with her banishment.

(Exeunt LUSSURIOSO, NOBLES *and* DUCHESS*)*

HIPPOLITO *(aside)*: Revels!

VINDICE *(aside)*:   Ay, that's the word, we are firm yet;
   Strike one strain more, and then we crown our wit.

(Exeunt BROTHERS*)*

SPURIO *(aside)*: Well, have at the fairest mark,
   So said the Duke when he begot me;
   And if I miss his heart or near about
   Then have at any—a bastard scorns to be out.

(Exit)

SUPERVACUO: Not'st thou that Spurio, brother?

AMBITIOSO: Yes, I note him to our shame.

SUPERVACUO: He shall not live; his hair shall not grow much longer.
   In this time of revels, tricks may be set afoot.
   Seest thou yon new moon? It shall outlive
   The new Duke by much; this hand shall dispossess him,
   Then we're mighty.

A mask is treason's licence, that build upon;
'Tis murder's best face when a vizard's on.

(*Exit* SUPERVACUO)

AMBITIOSO: Is't so? 'Tis very good.
  And do you think to be Duke then, kind brother?
  I'll see fair play; drop one, and there lies t'other.

(*Exit* AMBITIOSO.)

Scene Two

Enter VINDICE *and* HIPPOLITO *with* PIERO *and other* LORDS.

VINDICE: My lords, be all of music! Strike old griefs into other
    countries
  That flow in too much milk and have faint livers,
  Not daring to stab home their discontents.
  Let our hid flames break out, as fire, as lightning,
  To blast this villainous dukedom vexed with sin;
  Wind up your souls to their full height again!

PIERO: How?

FIRST LORD: Which way?

SECOND LORD: Any way; our wrongs are such
  We cannot justly be revenged too much.

VINDICE: You shall have all enough: revels are toward,
  And those few nobles that have long suppressed you
  Are busied to the furnishing of a mask
  And do affect to make a pleasant tail on't.
  The masking suits are fashioning; now comes in
  That which must glad us all—we too take pattern
  Of all those suits, the color, trimming, fashion,
  E'en to an undistinguished hair almost:
  Then, entering first, observing the true form,
  Within a strain or two we shall find leisure

To steal our swords out handsomely,
And when they think their pleasure sweet and good,
In midst of all their joys they shall sigh blood.

PIERO: Weightily, effectually!

THIRD LORD: Before the t'other maskers come—

VINDICE: We're gone, all done and past.

PIERO: But how for the Duke's guard?

VINDICE: Let that alone;
By one and one their strengths shall be drunk down.

HIPPOLITO: There are five hundred gentlemen in the action
That will apply themselves, and not stand idle.

PIERO: Oh let us hug our bosoms!

VINDICE: Come my lords,
Prepare for deeds, let other times have words.

(Exeunt)

Scene Three

In a dumb show, the crowning of the young Duke, LUSSURIOSO, *with all his
Nobles: then sounding music. A furnished table is brought forth: then
enters the* DUKE *and his* NOBLES *to the banquet. A blazing star appeareth.*

FIRST NOBLE: Many harmonious hours and choicest pleasures
Fill up the royal numbers of your years.

LUSSURIOSO: My lords, we're pleased to thank you, though we know
'Tis but your duty, now to wish it so.

SECOND NOBLE: That shine makes us all happy.

THIRD NOBLE: His grace frowns.

SECOND NOBLE: Yet we must say he smiles.

FIRST NOBLE: I think we must.

LUSSURIOSO *(aside):* That foul, incontinent Duchess we have banished;
   The bastard shall not live: after these revels
   I'll begin strange ones; he and the stepsons
   Shall pay their lives for the first subsidies.
   We must not frown so soon, else't'ad been now.

FIRST NOBLE: My gracious lord, please you prepare for pleasure,
   The mask is not far off.

LUSSURIOSO: We are for pleasure.
   Beshrew thee! What art thou mad'st me start?
   Thou hast committed treason.—A blazing star!

FIRST NOBLE: A blazing star! O where, my lord?

LUSSURIOSO: Spy out.

SECOND NOBLE: See, see, my lords, a wondrous dreadful one!

LUSSURIOSO: I am not pleased at that ill-knotted fire,
   That bushing-flaring star:—am not I Duke?
   It should not quake me now; had it appeared
   Before then, I might then have justly feared.
   But yet, they say whom art and learning weds,
   When stars wear locks, they threaten great men's heads.
   Is it so? You are read, my lords.

FIRST NOBLE: May it please your Grace,
   It shows great anger.

LUSSURIOSO: That does not please our grace.

SECOND NOBLE: Yet here's the comfort, my lord; many times,
   When it seems most, it threatens farthest off.

LUSSURIOSO: 'Faith, and I think so, too.

FIRST NOBLE: Beside, my lord,
  You're gracefully established with the loves
  Of all your subjects: and for natural death,
  I hope it will be threescore years a-coming.

LUSSURIOSO: True.—No more but threescore years?

FIRST NOBLE: Fourscore I hope, my lord.

SECOND NOBLE: And fivescore, I.

THIRD NOBLE: But 'tis my hope, my lord, you shall ne'er die.

LUSSURIOSO: Give me thy hand, these others I rebuke;
  He that hopes so is fittest for a duke.
  —Thou shalt sit next me. Take your places, lords,
  We're ready now for sports, let 'em set on.
  You thing! We shall forget you quite anon.

THIRD NOBLE: I hear 'em coming, my lord.

(Enter the mask of Revengers, the two Brothers, VINDICE *and* HIPPOLITO *and two* LORDS *more)*

LUSSURIOSO: Ah 'tis well.
  (Aside) Brothers, and bastard, you dance next in Hell.

(The Revengers dance. At the end, steal out their swords, and these four kill the four at the table, in their chairs. It thunders)

VINDICE: Mark, thunder!
  Dost know thy cue, thou big-voiced crier?
  Dukes' groans are thunder's watch words.

HIPPOLITO: So, my lords, you have enough.

VINDICE: Come, let's away—no lingering.

HIPPOLITO: Follow, go!

(Exeunt VINDICE *remains)*

VINDICE: No power is angry when the lustful die:
When thunder claps, Heaven likes the tragedy.

(*Exit* VINDICE)

LUSSURIOSO: Oh! Oh!

(*Enter the other Mask of intended murderers,* STEPSONS, BASTARD, *and a* FOURTH MAN, *coming in dancing;* LUSSURIOSO *recovers a little in voice and groans—calls 'A guard, treason!' At which they all start out of their measure, and turning towards the table, they find them all to be murdered*)

SPURIO: Whose groan was that?

LUSSURIOSO: Treason! A guard!

AMBITIOSO: How now? All murdered!

SUPERVACUO: Murdered!

FOURTH LORD: And those his nobles?

AMBITIOSO (*aside*): Here's a labor saved;
I thought to have sped him. 'Sblood! How came this?

SUPERVACUO: Then I proclaim myself! Now I am Duke.

AMBITIOSO: Thou duke! Brother, thou liest!

(*He slays* SUPERVACUO)

SPURIO: Slave, so dost thou!

(*He slays* AMBITIOSO)

FOURTH LORD: Base villain, hast thou slain my lord and master?
(*He slays* SPURIO. *Enter the first men* VINDICE, HIPPOLITO *and the* TWO LORDS)

VINDICE: Pistols! Treason! Murder! Help, guard my lord the Duke!

(Enter ANTONIO *with a* GUARD)

HIPPOLITO: Lay hold upon this traitor!

(They seize FOURTH LORD)

LUSSURIOSO: Oh!

VINDICE: Alas, the Duke is murdered!

HIPPOLITO: And the nobles.

VINDICE: Surgeons, surgeons! *(Aside)* Heart, does he breathe so long?

ANTONIO: A piteous tragedy! Able to wake
    An old man, 's eyes bloodshot.

LUSSURIOSO: Oh!

VINDICE: Look to my lord the Duke. *(Aside)* A vengeance throttle
    him.—
    Confess, thou murderous and unhallowed man,
    Didst thou kill all these?

FOURTH LORD: None but the bastard, I.

VINDICE: How came the Duke slain then?

FOURTH LORD: We found him so.

LUSSURIOSO: O villain!

VINDICE: Hark!

LUSSURIOSO: Those in the mask did murder us.

VINDICE: Law! You now, sir.
    O marble impudence! Will you confess now?

FOURTH LORD: 'Sblood! Tis all false.

ANTONIO: Away with that foul monster
  Dipped in a prince's blood.

FOURTH LORD: Heart, tis a lie!

ANTONIO: Let him have bitter execution.

(Exit FOURTH LORD *under guard)*

VINDICE *(aside):* New marrow!—No, I cannot be expressed.—
  How fares my lord the Duke?

LUSSURIOSO: Farewell to all:
  He that climbs highest has the greatest fall.
  —My tongue is out of office.

VINDICE: Air, gentlemen, air!

(Whispering to LUSSURIOSO*)* Now thou'lt not prate on't—'twas Vindice
  murdered thee.

LUSSURIOSO: Oh!

VINDICE: Murdered thy father.

LUSSURIOSO: Oh!

VINDICE: And I am he—tell nobody.
  (LUSSURIOSO *dies)*
  So, so, the Duke's departed.

ANTONIO: It was a deadly hand that wounded him.
  The rest, ambitious who should rule and sway
  After his death, were so made all away.

VINDICE: My lord was unlikely.

HIPPOLITO: Now the hope
  Of Italy lies in your reverend years.

VINDICE: Your hair will make the silver age again,
　　When there was fewer but more honest men.

ANTONIO: The burden's weighty and will press age down;
　　May I so rule that Heaven may keep the crown.

VINDICE: The rape of your good lady has been 'quited
　　With death on death.

ANTONIO:　　　　　　　　　Just is the law above.
　　But of all things it puts me most to wonder
　　How the old Duke came murdered.

VINDICE:　　　　　　　　　　　　　Oh my lord.

ANTONIO: It was the strangeliest carried; I not heard of the like.

HIPPOLITO: 'Twas all done for the best, my lord.

VINDICE: All for your Grace's good. We may be bold to speak it now.
　　'Twas somewhat witty carried, though we say it;
　　'Twas we two murdered him.

ANTONIO:　　　　　　　　　You two?

VINDICE: None else i'faith, my lord. Nay, 'twas well managed.

ANTONIO: Lay hands upon those villains!

VINDICE:　　　　　　　　　　　　How! On us?

ANTONIO: Bear 'em to speedy execution.

VINDICE: Heart, was't not for your good, my lord?

ANTONIO: My good? Away with 'em!—Such an old man as he!
　　You that would murder him would murder me.

VINDICE: Is't come about?

HIPPOLITO:　　　　　　　　'Sfoot brother, you begun.

VINDICE: May not we set as well as the Duke's son?
  Thou hast no conscience—are we not revenged?
  Is there one enemy left alive amongst those?
  'Tis time to die when we are ourselves our foes.
  When murd'rers shut deeds close, this curse does seal 'em:
  If none disclose 'em, they themselves reveal 'em.
  This murder might have slept in tongueless brass
  But for ourselves, and the world died an ass.
  Now I remember too, here was Piato
  Brought forth a knavish sentence once:—
  No doubt, said he, but time
  Will make the murderer bring forth himself.
  'Tis well he died, he was a witch.
  And now my lord, since we are in for ever—
  This work was ours, which else might have been slipped,
  And if we list, we could have nobles clipped
  And go for less than beggars; but we hate
  To bleed so cowardly. We have enough
  I'faith, we're well, our mother turned, our sister true,
  We die after a nest of dukes.—Adieu.

(Exeunt VINDICE *and* HIPPOLITO *under guard)*

ANTONIO: How subtly was that murder closed. Bear up
  Those tragic bodies. 'Tis a heavy season;
  Pray Heaven their blood may wash away all treason.

(Exeunt OMNES.*)*

THE TRAGICAL HISTORY OF HAMLET

PRINCE OF DENMARK

The 1603 Version

William Shakespeare

The fervor of Jacobean tragedy was too white-hot to last. As critic Robert B. Heilman observes, "The failure to carry moral insight beyond (an) oversimplified black-and-white view is the essential mark of melodrama." As early as 1603, dramatic alternatives to unthinking revenge began to occur in such plays as George Chapman's *The Revenge of Bussy D'Ambois*, Cyril Tourneur's *The Atheist's Tragedy* and the unarguable capstone of the genre, a play that is both revenge tragedy and counterattack, *Hamlet* by WILLIAM SHAKESPEARE (1564–1616).

Though I try to avoid well-known, easy-to-find compositions in my anthologies, I could not justify ignoring Shakespeare, so I have elected to include the obscure 1603 *Hamlet,* a version that will be unfamiliar to most readers. Prior to the famous 1623 folio edition of The Bard's works, *Hamlet* was twice published: the variant, yet essentially familiar Second Quarto printed in 1604 and the so-called "bad" or "foul" quarto of 1603.

A body of questionable scholarship contends that the First Quarto of *Hamlet* is either an example of publisher theft or stenographic piracy in the playhouse, theories which Albert B. Weiner thoroughly explodes in his critical introduction to the play in the Barron's Educational Series edition of the script. Weiner argues persuasively that the "original" *Hamlet* may have been prepared and condensed from Shakespeare's own manuscript in order to "take the show on the road" with an understaffed touring company.

A glance at the cast list may disorient some readers, and at least one scene is thoroughly foreign, but the 1603 *Hamlet* still makes for brisk reading and . . . who knows? It just might be an authentic over-the-shoulder peek at the workshop techniques of our greatest dramatist.

DRAMATIS PERSONAE

The King of Denmark
Hamlet
Corambis
Horatio
Leartes
Voltemar
Cornelius
Rossencraft
Gilderstone
A Braggart Gentleman
A Priest

Marcellus
Two Sentinels:
    Bernardo and another
Montano
Four Players
Two clowns: Gravediggers
Fortenbrasse
English Ambassador
Gertred, *Queen of Denmark*
Ofelia
Ghost of Hamlet's father

Enter two SENTINELS.

FIRST SENTINEL: Stand! Who is that?

SECOND SENTINEL: 'Tis I.

FIRST SENTINEL: O, you come most carefully upon your watch.

SECOND SENTINEL: And if you meet Marcellus and Horatio,
The partners of my watch, bid them make haste.

FIRST SENTINEL: I will. See! Who goes there?

(Enter HORATIO *and* MARCELLUS*)*

HORATIO: Friends to this ground.

MARCELLUS: And liegemen to the Dane.
O, farewell, honest soldier. Who hath reliev'd you?

FIRST SENTINEL: Bernardo hath my place. Give you good night.

(Exit)

MARCELLUS: Holla, Bernardo!

SECOND SENTINEL: Say, is Horatio there?

HORATIO: A piece of him.

SECOND SENTINEL: Welcome, Horatio. Welcome, good Marcellus.

MARCELLUS: What, hath this thing appear'd again tonight?

SECOND SENTINEL: I have seen nothing.

MARCELLUS: Horatio says 'tis but our fantasy,
   And will not let belief take hold of him
   Touching this dreaded sight, twice seen by us.
   Therefore I have entreated him along
   With us to watch the minutes of this night,
   That, if again this apparition come,
   He may approve our eyes and speak to it.

HORATIO: Tut, 'twill not appear.

SECOND SENTINEL: Sit down, I pray, and let us once again
   Assail your ears, that are so fortified,
   What we have two nights seen.

HORATIO: Well, sit we down,
   And let us hear Bernardo speak of this.

SECOND SENTINEL: Last night of all,
   When yonder star that's westward from the pole
   Had made his course t'illume that part of Heav'n
   Where now it burns, the bell then tolling one—

(*Enter* GHOST)

MARCELLUS: Break off your talk; see, where it comes again!

SECOND SENTINEL: In the same figure, like the King that's dead.

MARCELLUS: Thou art a scholar; speak to it, Horatio.

SECOND SENTINEL: Looks it not like the King?

HORATIO: Most like. It harrowes me with fear and wonder.

SECOND SENTINEL: It would be spoke to.

MARCELLUS: Question it, Horatio.

HORATIO: What art thou that thus usurps the state
   In which the majesty of buried Denmark
   Did sometimes walk? By Heaven I charge thee speak!

(Exit Ghost)

MARCELLUS: It is offended.

SECOND SENTINEL: See, it stalks away.

HORATIO: Stay! Speak, speak! By heaven I charge thee speak!

MARCELLUS: 'Tis gone and makes no answer.

SECOND SENTINEL: How now, Horatio? You tremble and look pale.
Is not this something more than fantasy?
What think you on't?

HORATIO: Afore my God, I might not this believe
Without the sensible and true avouch
Of my own eyes.

MARCELLUS: Is it not like the King?

HORATIO: As thou art to thyself.
Such was the very armor he had on
When he th'ambitious Norway combated.
So frown'd he once when, in an angry parle,
He smote the leaded pole-axe on the ice.
'Tis strange.

MARCELLUS: Thus twice before, and jump at this dead hour,
With martial stalk he passèd through our watch.

HORATIO: In what particular work I do not know,
But in the gross and scope of my opinion,
This bodes some strange eruption to the state.

MARCELLUS: Good now, sit down, and tell me he that knows,
Why this same strict and most observant watch
So nightly toils the subject of the land,
And why such daily cast of brazen cannon
And foreign mart for implements of war;
Why such impress of shipwrights, whose sore task
Does not divide the Sunday from the week.

What might be toward, that this sweaty march
Doth make the night joint-laborer with the day?
Who is't that can inform me?

HORATIO: Marry, that can I;
   At least the whisper goes so: Our late King
Was, as you know, by Fortenbrasse of Norway,
Thereto prick'd on by a most emulous cause,
Dar'd to the combat; in which our valiant Hamlet
(For so this side of our known world esteem'd him)
Did slay this Fortenbrasse, who, by a seal'd compact,
Well ratified by law and heraldry,
Did forfeit with his life all those his lands
Which he stood seiz'd of to the conqueror;
Against the which a moiety competent
Was gaged by our king.
Now sir, young Fortenbrasse
Of unimprovèd mettle hot and full,
Hath in the skirts of Norway here and there
Shark'd up a list of lawless resolutes
For food and diet, to some enterprise
That hath a stomach in't. And this, I take it,
Is the chief head and ground of this our watch.

(Enter the GHOST)

But lo, behold! see where it comes again!
I'll cross it, though it blast me. Stay, illusion!

(It spreads its arms)

If there be any good thing to be done,
That may do ease to thee and grace to me,
Speak to me.
If thou art privy to thy country's fate,
Which haply foreknowing may prevent,
O, speak to me.
Or if thou hast uphoardèd in thy life
Extorted treasure in the womb of earth,
For which, they say, you spirits oft walk in death,

(The cock crows)

Speak to me, stay and speak! Stop it, Marcellus.

SECOND SENTINEL: 'Tis here!

HORATIO: 'Tis here!

(Exit GHOST*)*

MARCELLUS: 'Tis gone!
  O, we do it wrong, being so majestical,
  To offer it the show of violence;
  For it is, as the air, invulnerable,
  And our vain blows malicious mockery.

SECOND SENTINEL: It was about to speak when the cock crew.

HORATIO: And then it faded, like a guilty thing
  Upon a fearful summons. I have heard,
  The cock, that is the trumpet to the morn,
  Doth with his early and shrill-crowing throat,
  Awake the god of day; and at his sound,
  Whether in earth or air, in sea or fire,
  Th'extravagant and erring spirit hies
  To his confines; and of the truth hereof
  This present object made probation.

MARCELLUS: It faded on the crowing of the cock.
  Some say that ever 'gainst that season comes
  Wherein our Saviour's birth is celebrated,
  The bird of dawning singeth all night long;
  And then, they say, no spirit dare walk abroad.
  The nights are wholesome; then no planets strike,
  No fairy takes, nor witch hath power to charm,
  So gracious and so hallow'd is that time.

HORATIO: So have I heard and do in part believe it.
  But see, the sun, in russet mantle clad,
  Walks o'er the dew of yon high mountain top.
  Break we our watch up; and by my advice

Let us impart what we have seen tonight
Unto young Hamlet; for, upon my life,
This spirit, dumb to us, will speak to him.
Do you consent we shall acquaint him with it,
As needful in our loves, fitting our duty?

MARCELLUS: Let's do't, I pray; and I this morning know
Where we shall find him most conveniently.

(Exeunt)

(Enter KING, QUEEN, HAMLET, LEARTES, CORAMBIS *and the two* AMBASSADORS, *with* ATTENDANTS*)*

KING: Lords, we here have writ
To Fortenbrasse, nephew of old Norway,
Who impotent and bedrid, scarcely hears
Of this his nephew's purpose. And we here dispatch
Yon good Cornelius, and you, Voltemar,
For bearers of these greetings to old Norway,
Giving to you no further personal power
To business with the King
Than these related articles do show.
Farewell, and let your haste commend your duty.

COR., VOLT: In this and all things will we show our duty.

KING: We doubt it nothing; heartily farewell.

(Exit VOLTEMAR *and* CORNELIUS*)*

And now, Leartes, what's the news with you?
You said you had a suit. What is't Leartes?

LEARTES: My gracious lord, your favorable license,
Now that the funeral rites are all perform'd,
I may have leave to go again to France.
For though the favor of your grace might stay me,
Yet something is there whispers in my heart,
Which makes my mind and spirits bend all for France.

KING: Have you your father's leave, Leartes?

CORAMBIS: He hath, my lord, wrung from me a forc'd grant,
    And I beseech you grant Your Highness' leave.

KING: With all our heart, Leartes; fare thee well.

LEARTES: I in all love and duty take my leave.

(Exit)

KING: And now princely son Hamlet,
    What means these sad and melancholy moods?
    For your intent going to Wittenberg,
    We hold it most unmeet and unconvenient,
    Being the joy and half heart of your mother;
    Therefore let me entreat you stay in court,
    All Denmark's hope, our cousin, and dearest son.

HAMLET: My lord, 'tis not the sable suit I wear,
    No, nor the tears that still stand in my eyes,
    Nor the distracted havior in the visage,
    Nor all together mix'd with outward semblance,
    Is equal to the sorrow of my heart.
    Him have I lost I must of force foregoe;
    These but the ornaments and suits of woe.

KING: This shows a loving care in you, son Hamlet;
    But you must think, your father lost a father;
    That father dead lost his, and so shall be
    Until the general ending. Therefore cease laments;
    It is a fault 'gainst heaven, fault 'gainst the dead,
    A fault 'gainst nature;
    And in reason's common course most certain,
    None lives on earth, but he is born to die.

QUEEN: Let not thy mother lose her prayers, Hamlet;
    Stay here with us, go not to Wittenberg.

HAMLET: I shall in all my best obey you, madam.

KING: Spoke like a kind and a most loving son.
  And there's no health the King shall drink today,
  But the great canon to the clouds shall tell
  The rouse the King shall drink unto Prince Hamlet.

(*Exeunt all but* HAMLET)

HAMLET: O that this too much griev'd and solid flesh
  Would melt to nothing; or that the universal
  Globe of heav'n would turn all to a chaos!
  O God! Within two months! no not two; married
  Mine uncle. O let me not think of it.
  My father's brother, but no more like my father
  Than I to Hercules. Within two months,
  Ere yet the salt of most unrighteous tears
  Had left their flushing in her gallèd eyes,
  She married. O God! a beast devoid of reason
  Would not have made such speed.—Frailty thy name is woman.
  Why, she would hang on him as if increase
  Of appetite had grown by what it looked on.
  O wicked, wicked speed to make such
  Dexterity to incestuous sheets.
  Ere yet the shoes were old
  With which she follow'd my dear father's corse,
  Like Niobe, all tears—married!
  Well it is not, nor it cannot come to good.
  But break my heart, for I must hold my tongue.

(*Enter* HORATIO *and* MARCELLUS)

HORATIO: Health to your lordship!

HAMLET: I'm very glad to see you.
  Horatio!—or I much forget myself.

HORATIO: The same, my lord, and your poor servant ever.

HAMLET: O, my good friend; I change that name with you.
  But what make you from Wittenberg, Horatio?
  Marcellus?

MARCELLUS: My good lord.

HAMLET: I am very glad to see you; good even sirs.
But what is your affair in Elsinore?
We'll teach you to drink deep ere you depart.

HORATIO: A truant disposition, my good lord.

HAMLET: Nor shall you make me truster of your own report
Against yourself. Sir, I know you're no truant.
But what is your affair in Elsinore?

HORATIO: My good lord, I came to see your father's funeral.

HAMLET: O, I prithee, do not mock me, fellow student.
I think it was to see my mother's wedding.

HORATIO: Indeed, my lord, it followed hard upon.

HAMLET: Thrift, thrift, Horatio! The funeral bak'd meats
Did coldly furnish forth the marriage tables.
Would I had met my dearest foe in Heaven
For ever I had seen that day, Horatio!
O, my father—methinks I see my father.

HORATIO: Where my lord!

HAMLET: Why, in my mind's eye, Horatio.

HORATIO: I saw him once; he was a gallant king.

HAMLET: He was a man, take him for all in all.
I shall not look upon his like again.

HORATIO: My lord, I think I saw him yesternight.

HAMLET: Saw? Who!

HORATIO: My lord, the King your father.

HAMLET: Ha, ha, the King my father, say you?

HORATIO: Season your admiration for a while
  With an attentive ear, till I may deliver,
  Upon the witness of these gentlemen,
  This wonder to you.

HAMLET: For God's love let me hear it.

HORATIO: Two nights together had these gentlemen
  (Marcellus and Bernardo), on their watch
  In the dead vast and middle of the night
  Been thus encount'red by a figure like your father,
  Armed to point exactly, cap-a-pe,
  Appears before them; thrice he walks
  Before their weak and fear-oppressed eyes,
  Within his truncheon's length, while they, distill'd
  Almost to jelly with the act of fear,
  Stand dumb and speak not to him. This to me
  In dreadful secrecy impart they did;
  And I with them the third night kept the watch;
  Where, as they had deliver'd, both in time,
  Form of the thing, each part made true and good,
  The apparition comes. I knew your father;
  These hands are not more like.

HAMLET: 'Tis very strange.

HORATIO: As I do live, my honor'd lord, 'tis true;
  And we did think it writ down in our duty
  To let you know it.

HAMLET: Where was this?

MARCELLUS: My lord, upon the platform where we watch'd.

HAMLET: Did you not speak to it?

HORATIO: My lord, we did;
  But answer made it none. Yet once methought
  It was about to speak, and lifted up
  His head to motion, like as he would speak,
  But even then the morning cock crew loud,

And in all haste it shrunk in haste away
And vanishèd our sight.

HAMLET: Indeed, indeed, sirs. But this troubles me.
Hold you the watch tonight?

ALL: We do, my lord.

HAMLET: Arm'd, say ye?

ALL: Armed, my good lord.

HAMLET: From top to toe?

ALL: My good lord, from head to foot.

HAMLET: Why, then saw you not his face?

HORATIO: O yes, my lord, he wore his beaver up.

HAMLET: How look'd he? frowningly?

HORATIO: A countenance more in sorrow than in anger.

HAMLET: Pale or red?

HORATIO: Nay, very pale.

HAMLET: And fix'd his eyes upon you?

HORATIO: Most constantly.

HAMLET: I would I had been there.

HORATIO: It would 'a' much amaz'd you.

HAMLET: Yea, very like, very like. Stay'd it long?

HORATIO: While one with moderate pace might tell a hundred.

MARCELLUS: O longer, longer.

HAMLET: His beard was grizzled, no?

HORATIO: It was as I have seen it in his life:
A sable silver.

HAMLET: I will watch tonight.
Perchance 'twill walk again.

HORATIO: I warrant it will.

HAMLET: If it assume my noble father's person,
I'll speak to it if Hell itself should gape
And bid me hold my peace. Gentlemen,
If you have hitherto conceal'd this sight,
Let it be tenable in your silence still;
And whatsoever else shall chance tonight,
Give it an understanding but no tongue.
I will requite your loves. So fare you well.
Upon the platform, 'twixt eleven and twelve,
I'll visit you.

ALL: Our duty's to your honor.

HAMLET: O your loves, your loves, as mine to you. Farewell.

(*Exeunt* HORATIO *and* MARCELLUS)

My father's spirit in arms! Well, all's not well.
I doubt some foul play. Would the night were come!
Till then sit still my soul. Foul deeds will rise,
Though all the world o'erwhelm them, to men's eyes.

(*Exit*)

(*Enter* LEARTES *and* OFELIA)

LEARTES: My necessaries are embark'd, I must aboard;
But ere I part, mark what I say to thee:
I see Prince Hamlet makes a show of love.
Beware, Ofelia, do not trust his vows.
Perhaps he loves you now, and now his tongue

Speaks from his heart; but yet take heed, my sister:
The chariest maid is prodigal enough
If she unmask her beauty to the moon.
Virtue itself scapes not calumnious thoughts.
Believe't Ofelia; therefore keep aloof,
Lest that he trip thy honor and thy fame.

OFELIA: Brother, to this I have lent attentive ear,
And doubt not but to keep my honor firm;
But my dear brother,
Do not you, like to a cunning sophister,
Teach me the path and ready way to Heaven,
While you, forgetting what is said to me,
Yourself, like to a careless libertine,
Doth give his heart his appetite at full,
And little recks how that his honor dies.

LEARTES: No, fear it not, my dear Ofelia.

(Enter CORAMBIS)

Here comes my father;
Occasion smiles upon a second leave.

CORAMBIS: Yet here, Leartes? Aboard, aboard, for shame!
The wind sits in the shoulder of your sail,
And you are stay'd for. There—my blessing with thee!
And these few precepts in thy memory:
Be thou familiar, but by no means vulgar;
Those friends thou hast, and their adoptions tried,
Grapple them to thee with a hoop of steel,
But do not dull the palm with entertain
Of every new, unfledg'd corrage. Beware
Of entrance into a quarrel; but being in,
Bear't that th'opposed may beware of thee.
Costly thy apparel as thy purse can buy,
But not express'd in fashion,
For the apparel oft proclaims the man,
And they of France of the best rank and station
Are most select and general, chief in that.
This above all: to thine own self be true,

And it must follow, as the night the day,
Thou canst not then be false to anyone.
Farewell. My blessing with thee.

LEARTES: I humbly take my leave. Farewell, Ofelia;
And remember well what I have said to you.

OFELIA: It is already lock'd within my heart,
And you yourself shall keep the key of it.

(*Exit* LEARTES)

CORAMBIS: What is't, Ofelia, he hath said to you?

OFELIA: Something touching the Prince Hamlet.

CORAMBIS: Marry, well thought on!
'Tis given me to understand that you
Have been too prodigal of your maiden presence
Unto Prince Hamlet.
If it be so—as so 'tis given to me,
And that in way of caution—I must tell you
You do not understand yourself so well
As befits my honor and your credit.

OFELIA: My lord, he hath made many tenders
Of his love to me.

CORAMBIS: Tenders! ay, ay, tenders you may call them.

OFELIA: And withal, such earnest vows.

CORAMBIS: Springes to catch woodcocks.
What! Do not I know when the blood doth burn,
How prodigal the tongue lends the heart vows?
In brief,
Be more scanter of your maiden presence,
Or tend'ring thus you'll tender me a fool.

OFELIA: I shall obey, my lord, in all I may.

CORAMBIS: Ofelia, receive none of his letters;
  For lover's lines are snares to entrap the heart.
  Refuse his tokens; both of them are keys
  To unlock chastity unto desire.
  Come in, Ofelia. Such men often prove
  Great in their words, but little in their love.

OFELIA: I will, my lord.

(Exeunt)

(Enter HAMLET, HORATIO *and* MARCELLUS*)*

HAMLET: The air bites shrewd;
  It is an eager and a nipping wind.
  What hour is't?

HORATIO: I think it lacks of twelve.

MARCELLUS: No, 'tis struck.

HORATIO: Indeed? I heard it not.

HORATIO *(sound trumpets)*:
  What doth this mean, my lord?

HAMLET: O, the King doth wake tonight and takes his rouse,
  Keeps wassail, and the swagg'ring upspring reels,
  And as he drains his draughts of Rhenish down,
  The kettledrum and trumpet thus bray out
  The triumphs of his pledge.

HORATIO: Is it a custom here?

HAMLET: Ay, marry, is't, and though I'm native here,
  And to the manner born, it is a custom
  More honor'd in the breach than in th'observance.

(Enter the GHOST*)*

HORATIO: Look, my lord, it comes!

HAMLET: Angels and ministers of grace defend us!
   Be thou a spirit of health or goblin damn'd
   Bring with thee airs from Heaven or blasts from Hell,
   Be thy intents wicked or charitable,
   Thou comest in such questionable shape
   That I will speak to thee: I'll call thee Hamlet,
   King, father, royal Dane. O, answer me!
   Let me not burst in ignorance, but say
   Why thy canoniz'd bones, hearsed in death,
   Have burst their cerements; why thy sepulchre
   In which we saw thee quietly interr'd,
   Hath burst his ponderous and marble jaws
   To cast thee up again. What may this mean
   That thou, dead corse, again in complete steel,
   Revisits thus the glimpses of the moon,
   Making night hideous, and we fools of nature
   So horridly to shake our disposition
   With thoughts beyond the reaches of our souls?
   Say, speak.

   (GHOST *beckons* HAMLET)

Wherefore? What may this mean?

HORATIO: It beckons you, as though't had something t'impart
   To you alone.

MARCELLUS: Look with what courteous action
   It waves you to a more removed ground;
   But do not go with it.

HORATIO: No, by no means, my lord.

HAMLET: It will not speak; then will I follow it.

HORATIO: What if it tempt you toward the flood, my lord,
   Or to the dreadful summit of the cliff
   That beetles o'er his base into the sea,
   And there assume some other, horrible shape
   Which might deprive your sovereignty of reason
   And drive you into madness? Think of it!

HAMLET: Still am I call'd.—Go on, I'll follow thee.

HORATIO: My lord, you shall not go.

HAMLET: Why, what should be the fear?
  I do not set my life at a pin's fee;
  And for my soul, what can it do to that,
  Being a thing immortal like itself?
  Go on, I'll follow thee.

MARCELLUS: My lord, be rul'd; you shall not go.

HAMLET: My fate cries out, and makes each petty artery
  As hardy as the Nemean lion's nerve.
  Still am I call'd. Unhand me gentlemen.
  By Heaven, I'll make a ghost of him that lets me!
  Away, I say. Go on, I'll follow thee.

(*Exeunt* GHOST *and* HAMLET)

HORATIO: He waxeth desperate with imagination.

MARCELLUS: Something is rotten in the state of Denmark.

HORATIO: Have after. To what issue will this sort?

MARCELLUS: Let's follow; 'tis not fit thus to obey him.

(*Exit* HORATIO *and* MARCELLUS. *Enter* GHOST *and* HAMLET)

HAMLET: I'll go no farther! Whither wilt thou lead me?

GHOST: Mark me.

HAMLET: I will.

GHOST: I am thy father's spirit,
  Doom'd for a time to walk the night,
  And all the day confin'd in flaming fire,
  Till the foul crimes done in my days of nature
  Are purg'd and burnt away.

HAMLET: Alas, poor ghost!

GHOST: Nay, pity me not, but to my unfolding
Lend thy listening ear. But that I am forbid
To tell the secrets of my prison house,
I would a tale unfold whose lightest word
Would harrow up thy soul, freeze thy young blood,
Make thy two eyes, like stars, start from their spheres,
Thy knotted and combined locks to part,
And each particular hair to stand on end
Like quills upon the fretful porpentine.
But this same blazon must not be to ears
Of flesh and blood. Hamlet, if ever thou
Didst thy dear father love—

HAMLET: O God!

GHOST: Revenge his foul and most unnatural murder.

HAMLET: Murder!

GHOST: Yea, murder in the highest degree,
As in the least 'tis bad; but mine most foul,
Beastly, and unnatural.

HAMLET: Haste me to know't, that I, with wings as swift
As meditation or the thought of it,
May sweep to my revenge.

GHOST: O, I find thee apt;
And duller shouldst thou be than the fat weed
Which roots itself in ease on Lethe wharf—
Brief let me be.
'Tis given out that, sleeping in my orchard,
A serpent stung me. So the whole ear of Denmark
Is with a forged process of my death
Rankly abus'd. But know, thou noble youth,
He that did sting thy father's heart now wears
His crown.

HAMLET: O my prophetic soul! My uncle!
   My uncle!

GHOST: Yea, he;
   That incestuous wretch, won to his will with gifts—
   O wicked will and gifts that have the power
   So to seduce!—my most seeming-virtuous queen.
   But virtue, as it never will be mov'd
   Though lewdness court it in a shape of Heaven,
   So lust, though to a radiant angel link'd
   Would sate itself from a celestial bed
   And prey on garbage.
   But soft! methinks I scent the morning's air;
   Brief let me be. Sleeping within my orchard,
   My custom always in the afternoon,
   Upon my secure hour thy uncle came,
   With juice of cursèd hebona in a vial,
   And through the porches of my ears did pour
   The leprous distilment, whose effect
   Holds such an enmity with blood of man
   That swift as quicksilver it posteth through
   The natural gates and alleys of the body,
   And turns the thin and wholesome blood
   Like eagle droppings into milk,
   And all my smooth body bark'd and tetter'd o'er.
   Thus was I, sleeping, by a brother's hand
   Of crown, of queen, of life, of dignity,
   At once deprived, no reckoning made of,
   But sent unto my grave with all my accompts
   And sins upon my head.
   O horrible! most horrible!

HAMLET: O God!

GHOST: If thou hast nature in thee, bear it not;
   But howsoe'er, let not thy heart conspire
   Against thy mother aught; leave her to Heaven
   And to the burden that her conscience bears.
   I must be gone;
   The glow-worm shows the matin to be near,

And 'gins to pale his uneffectual fire.
Hamlet, adieu, adieu! Remember me.

(Exit)

HAMLET: O all you host of Heaven! O earth! What else!
And shall I couple Hell? Remember thee?
Yes, thou poor ghost!
From the tables of my memory I'll wipe away
All saws of books, all trivial fond conceits
That ever youth or else observance noted,
And thy remembrance all alone shall sit.
Yes, yes, by Heav'n! A damn'd pernicious villain!
Murderous, bawdy, smiling, damned villain!
My tables—meet it is I set it down
That one may smile, and smile, and be a villain;
At least I am sure it may be so in Denmark.

(Writes in his tablets)

So, uncle, there you are, there you are.
Now to the words: it is "Adieu, adieu;
Remember me." So, 'tis enough; I've sworn.

(Enter HORATIO *and* MARCELLUS*)*

HORATIO: My lord, my lord!

MARCELLUS: Lord Hamlet!

HORATIO: Illo, lo, lo, ho, ho!

HAMLET: Illo, lo, so, ho, so! come, boy, come.

HORATIO: Heavens secure him.

MARCELLUS: How is't, my noble lord?

HORATIO: What news, my lord?

HAMLET: O, wonderful, wonderful.

HORATIO: Good my lord, tell it.

HAMLET: No, not I, you'll reveal it.

HORATIO: Not I, my lord, by Heaven.

MARCELLUS: Nor I, my lord.

HAMLET: How say you then; would heart of man once think it?
But you'll be secret?

BOTH: Ay, by Heaven, my lord.

HAMLET: There's never a villain dwelling in all Denmark
But he's an arrant knave.

HORATIO: There needs no ghost come from the grave to tell
You this.

HAMLET: Right! You are in the right.
I hold it meet without more circumstance at all,
Meet we shake hands and part,
You, as your business and desires shall lead you,
For every man hath business and desires,
Such as it is; and for my own poor part,
Look you, I'll go pray.

HORATIO: These are but wild and whirling words, my lord.

HAMLET: I am sorry they offend you, heartily;
Yes, faith, heartily.

HORATIO: There's no offense, my lord.

HAMLET: Yes, by Saint Patrick, but there is, Horatio,
And much offense too. Touching this vision,
It is an honest ghost, that let me tell you.
For your desires to know what is between us,
O'ermaster't as you may. And now, kind friends,
As you are friends, scholars, and gentlemen,
Grant me one poor request.

BOTH: What is't, my lord?

HAMLET: Never make known what you have seen tonight.

BOTH: My lord, we will not.

HAMLET: Nay, but swear.

HORATIO: In faith,
   My lord, not I.

MARCELLUS: Nor I, my lord, in faith.

HAMLET: Nay, upon my sword; indeed, upon my sword.

(The GHOST *under the stage)*

GHOST: Swear.

HAMLET: Ha, ha! Come! You hear this fellow in the cellarage?
   Here consent to swear.

HORATIO: Propose the oath, my lord.

HAMLET: Never to speak what you have seen tonight.
   Swear by my sword.

GHOST: Swear.

HAMLET: *Hic et ubique?* Nay, then we'll shift our ground.
   Come hither, gentlemen, and lay your hands
   Again upon this sword. Never to speak
   Of that which you have seen; swear by my sword.

GHOST: Swear.

HAMLET: Well said, old mole! Canst work i' th'earth so fast?
   A worthy pioneer! Once more remove.

HORATIO: Day and night, but this is wondrous strange.

HAMLET: And therefore as a stranger give it welcome.
  There are more things in Heaven and earth, Horatio,
  Than are dreamt of in your philosophy.
  But come; here, as before, you never shall,
  How strange or odd soe'r I bear myself—
  As I perchance hereafter shall think meet
  To put an antic disposition on—
  That you, at such times seeing me, never shall
  With arms encumb'red thus, or this head-shake,
  Or by pronouncing some undoubtful phrase,
  As "Well, well, we know," or "We could and if we would,"
  Or "There be, and if they might,"
  Or such ambiguous giving out, to note
  That you know aught of me: this not to do,
  So grace and mercy at your most need help you,
  Swear.

GHOST: Swear.

HAMLET: Rest, rest, perturbed spirit! So, gentlemen,
  In all my love I do commend me to you;
  And what so poor a man as Hamlet may
  To pleasure you, God willing, shall not want.
  Nay, come, let's go together;
  But still your fingers on your lips, I pray.
  The time is out of joint. O cursed spite
  That ever I was born to set it right.
  Nay, come, let's go together.

(Exeunt. Enter CORAMBIS *and* MONTANO*)*

CORAMBIS: Montano, here, these letters to my son,
  And this same money with my blessings to him;
  And bid him ply his learning, good Montano.

MONTANO: I will, my lord.

CORAMBIS: You shall do very well, Montano, to say thus: "I knew the
  gentleman" or "know his father"; to inquire the manner of his life as
  thus. Being amongst his acquaintance, you may say you saw him at

such a time, mark you me, at game, or drinking, swearing or drabbing.
You may go so far.

MONTANO: My lord, that will impeach his reputation.

CORAMBIS: I'faith, not a whit, no, not a whit, not disparage him a jot.
Now happily he closeth with you in this consequence—What was I
about to say?

MONTANO: He closeth with him in this consequence.

CORAMBIS: Ay, you say right, he closeth with him thus: this will he say—
let me see what he will say—Marry this: I saw him yesterday or t'other
day, or then or at such a time, a-dicing, or at tennis, ay, or drinking
drunk, or ent'ring of a house of lightness, *videlicet*, brothel. Thus, sir,
do we that know the world, being men of reach, by indirections find
directions forth; and so shall you my son. You ha' me, ha' you not?

MONTANO: I have, my lord.

CORAMBIS: Well, fare you well; commend me to him.

MONTANO: I will, my lord.

CORAMBIS: And bid him ply his music.

MONTANO: My lord, I will.

(Exit)

CORAMBIS: Farewell.   *(Enter* OFELIA*)*

How now, Ofelia! what's the news with you?

OFELIA: O, my dear father, such a change in nature,
So great an alteration in a prince,—
So pitiful to him, fearful to me,—
A maiden's eye ne'er looked on—

CORAMBIS: Why, what's the matter, my Ofelia?

OFELIA: O, young prince Hamlet, the only flower of Denmark:
    He is bereft of all the wealth he had.
    The jewel that adorn'd his feature most
    Is filcht and stol'n away; his wit's bereft him.
    He found me walking in the gallery all alone;
    There comes he to me with a distracted look,
    His garters lagging down, his shoes untied,
    And fix'd his eyes so steadfast on my face,
    As if they had vow'd this is their latest object.
    Small while he stood, but grips me by the wrist,
    And there he holds my pulse, till, with a sigh,
    He doth unclasp his hold, and parts away,
    Silent as is the midtime of the night.
    And as he went his eye was still on me,
    For thus his head over his shoulder looked;
    He seemed to find the way without his eyes,
    For out of doors he went without their help,
    And so did leave me.

CORAMBIS: Mad for thy love!
    What, have you giv'n him any cross words of late?

OFELIA: I did repel his letters, deny his gifts,
    As you did charge me.

CORAMBIS: Why, that hath made him mad.
    By Heav'n, 'tis as proper for our age to cast
    Beyond ourselves, as 'tis for the younger sort
    To leave their wantonness. Well, I am sorry
    That I was so rash; but, what remedy?
    Let's to the king. This madness may prove
    Though wild awhile, yet more true to thy love.

(Exeunt. Enter KING *and* QUEEN, ROSSENCRAFT, *and* GILDERSTONE)

KING: Right noble friends, that our dear cousin Hamlet
    Hath lost the very heart of all his sense,
    It is most right, and we most sorry for him.
    Therefore we do desire, even as you tender
    Our care to him and our great love to you,
    That you will labor but to wring from him

The cause and ground of his distemperancy.
Do this. The King of Denmark shall be thankful.

ROSSENCRAFT: My lord, whatsoe'er lies within our power
Your Majesty may more command in words
Than use persuasions to your liege men, bound
By love, by duty, and obedience.

GILDERSTONE: What we may do for both Your Majesties,
To know the grief troubles the Prince your son,
We will endeavor all the best we may.
So in all duty do we take our leave.

KING: Thanks, Gilderstone and gentle Rossencraft.

QUEEN: Thanks, Rossencraft and gentle Gilderstone.

(*Exeunt* ROSSENCRAFT *and* GILDERSTONE. *Enter* CORAMBIS *and* OFELIA)

CORAMBIS: My lord, the ambassadors are joyfully
Return'd from Norway.

KING: Thou still hast been the father of good news.

CORAMBIS: Have I, my lord? I assure your grace
I hold my duty as I hold my life,
Both to my God and to my sovereign King;
And I believe, or else this brain of mine
Hunts not the train of policy so well
As it had wont to do, but I have found
The very depth of Hamlet's lunacy.

QUEEN: God grant he hath.

(*Enter the* AMBASSADORS)

KING: Now Voltemar, what from our brother Norway?

VOLTEMAR: Most fair returns of greetings and desires.
Upon our first he sent forth to suppress
His nephew's levies, which to him appear'd

To be a preparation 'gainst the Polack,
But better look'd into, he truly found
It was against Your Highness; whereat griev'd
That so his sickness, age and impotence
Was falsely borne in hand, sends out arrests
On Fortenbrasse, which he, in brief, obeys,
Receives rebuke from Norway, and, in fine,
Makes vow before his uncle never more
To give th'assay of arms against Your Majesty.
Whereon old Norway, overcome with joy,
Gives him three thousand crowns in annual fee
And his commission to employ those soldiers
So levied as before, against the Polack,
With an entreaty, herein further shown,
That it would please you to give quiet pass
Through your dominions for that enterprise,
On such regards of safety and allowances
As therein are set down.

KING: It likes us well, and at fit time and leisure
We'll read and answer these his articles.
Meantime we thank you for your well-took labor.
Go to your rest; at night we'll feast together.
Right welcome home.

(*Exeunt* AMBASSADORS)

CORAMBIS: This business is very well dispatched.
Now, my lord,
Touching the young Prince Hamlet, certain it is
That he is mad; mad let us grant him then.
Now, to know the cause of this effect,
Or else to say, the cause of this defect,
For this effect defective comes by cause—

QUEEN: Good my lord, be brief.

CORAMBIS: Madam, I will. My lord, I have a daughter
(Have while she is mine), for that we think
Is surest we often lose. Now to the Prince:
My lord, but note this letter,

The which my daughter in obedience
Deliver'd to my hands.

KING: Read it, my lord.

CORAMBIS: Mark, my lord:
   Doubt that in earth is fire;
      Doubt that the stars do move;
   Doubt truth to be a liar;
      But do not doubt I love.
   To the beautiful Ofelia.
   Thine ever, the most unhappy Prince Hamlet.

   My lord, what do you think of me?
   Ay, or what might you think when I saw this?

KING: As of a true friend and a most loving subject.

CORAMBIS: I would be glad to prove so.
   Now when I saw this letter, thus I bespake my maiden:
   Lord Hamlet is a prince, out of your star,
   And one that is unequal for your love.—
   Therefore I did command her refuse his letters,
   Deny his tokens, and to absent herself.
   She, as my child, obediently obey'd me.
   Now since which time, seeing his love thus cross'd,
   Which I took to be idle and but sport,
   He straightway grew into a melancholy,
   From that unto a fast, then unto distraction,
   Then into a sadness, from that unto a madness,
   And so by continuance and weakness of the brain
   Into this frenzy which now possesseth him.
   And if this be not true, take this from this.

KING: Think you 'tis so?

CORAMBIS: How? So? My lord, I would very fain know
   That thing that I have positively said,
   ' 'Tis so,' and it hath fallen out otherwise.
   Nay, if circumstances lead me on,

I'll find it out, if it were hid as deep
As the center of the earth.

KING: How should we try this same?

CORAMBIS: Marry, my good lord, thus:
The Prince's walk is here in the gallery;
There let Ofelia walk until he comes;
Yourself and I will stand close in the study.
There shall you hear the effect of all his heart;
And if it prove any otherwise than love,
Then let my censure fail another time.

(*Enter* HAMLET)

KING: See where he comes, poring upon a book.

CORAMBIS: Madam, will it please your grace to leave us here?

QUEEN: With all my heart.

(*Exit*)

CORAMBIS: And here, Ofelia, read you on this book,
And walk aloof; the King shall be unseen.

(*The* KING *and* CORAMBIS *retire behind a curtain*)

HAMLET: To be, or not to be—ay, there's the point:
To die, to sleep—is that all? ay, all. No;
To sleep, to dream—ay, marry, there it goes;
For in that dream of death, when we awake,
And borne before an everlasting judge,
From whence no passenger ever return'd,
The undiscovered country, at whose sight
The happy smile, and the accursed damn'd.
But for this, the joyful hope of this,
Who'd bear the scorns and flattery of the world,
Scorn'd by the right rich, the rich cursed of the poor,
The widow being oppressed, the orphan wrong'd,
The taste of hunger, or a tyrant's reign,

And thousand more calamities besides,
To grunt and sweat under this weary life,
When that he may his full quietus make
With a bare bodkin? Who would this endure,
But for a hope of something after death,
Which puzzles the brain and doth confound the sense;
Which makes us rather bear those evils we have
Than fly to others that we know not of?
Ay, that! O this conscience makes cowards of us all.
Lady, in thy orisons be all my sins rememb'red.

OFELIA: My lord, I have sought opportunity,
Which now I have, to redeliver to
Your worthy hands, a small remembrance,
Such tokens which I have received of you.

HAMLET: Are you fair?

OFELIA: My lord?

HAMLET: Are you honest?

OFELIA: What means my lord?

HAMLET: That if you be fair and honest, your beauty should admit no discourse to your honesty.

OFELIA: My lord, can beauty have better privilege than with honesty?

HAMLET: Yea, marry, may it; for beauty may transform honesty from what she was into a bawd than honesty can transform beauty. This was sometimes a paradox, but now the time gives it scope. I never gave you nothing.

OFELIA: My lord, you know right well you did,
And with them such earnest vows of love
As would have mov'd the stoniest breast alive;
But now too true I find, rich gifts wax poor
When givers grow unkind.

HAMLET: I never lov'd you.

OFELIA: You made me believe you did.

HAMLET: O, thou shouldst not 'a' believed me. Go to a nunnery, go. Why shouldst thou be a breeder of sinners? I am myself indifferent honest, but I could accuse myself of such crimes it had been better my mother had ne'er borne me. O, I am very proud, ambitious, disdainful, with more sins at my back than I have thoughts to put them in. What should such fellows as I do, crawling between Heaven and earth? To a nunnery, go! We are arrant knaves all; believe none of us. To a nunnery, go!

OFELIA: O heavens, secure him!

HAMLET: Where's thy father?

OFELIA: At home, my lord.

HAMLET: For God's sake, let the doors be shut on him, that he may play the fool nowhere but in his own house. To a nunnery, go.

OFELIA: Help him, good God.

HAMLET: If thou dost marry, I'll give thee this plague to thy dowry: be thou as chaste as ice, as pure as snow, thou shalt not scape calumny. To a nunnery, go!

OFELIA: Alas, what change is this?

HAMLET: But if thou wilt needs marry, marry a fool; for wise men know well enough what monsters you make of them. To a nunnery, go!

OFELIA: Pray God restore him.

HAMLET: Nay, I have heard of your paintings, too; God hath given you one face, and you make yourselves another. You jig, and you amble, and you nickname God's creatures, making your wantonness your ignorance. A pox, 'tis scurvy! I'll no more of it; it hath made me mad. I'll no more marriages; all that are married, but one, shall live; the rest shall keep as they are. To a nunnery, go; to a nunnery, go!

(Exit)

OFELIA: Great God of Heaven, what a quick change is this!
The courtier, scholar, soldier, all in him;
All dash'd and splinter'd thence. O, woe is me,
To 'a' seen what I have seen, see what I see!

(*Exit. Enter* KING *and* CORAMBIS)

KING: Love? No, no, that's not the cause.
Some deeper thing it is that troubles him.

CORAMBIS: Well, something it is, my lord; content you a while;
I will myself go feel him. Let me work,
I'll try him every way.
(*Enter* HAMLET)
               See where he comes.
Send you those gentlemen. Let me alone
To find the depth of this; away, be gone!
(*Exit* KING)
Now, my good lord, do you know me?

HAMLET: Yea, very well; you're a fishmonger.

CORAMBIS: Not I, my lord.

HAMLET: Then, sir, I would you were so honest a man; for to be honest,
as this age goes, is one man to be pick'd out of ten thousand.

CORAMBIS: What do you read, my lord?

HAMLET: Words, words.

CORAMBIS: What's the matter, my lord?

HAMLET: Between who?

CORAMBIS: I mean the matter you read, my lord?

HAMLET: Marry, most vile heresy; for here the satirical satire writes that
old men have hollow eyes, weak backs, gray beards, pitiful weak hams,
gouty legs; all which, sir, I most potently believe not; for, sir, yourself
shall be old as I am if, like a crab, you could go backward.

CORAMBIS *(aside):* How pregnant his replies are, and full of wit; yet at first he took me for a fishmonger. All this comes by love, the vehemency of love. And when I was young I was very idle, and suffered much ecstacy in love, very near this.—Will you walk out of the air, my lord?

HAMLET: Into my grave?

CORAMBIS: By the mass, that's out of the air, indeed. *(aside)* Very shrewd answers.—My lord, I will take my leave of you.

(Enter GILDERSTONE *and* ROSSENCRAFT*)*

HAMLET: You can take nothing from me, sir, I will more willingly part withal. Old doting fool!

CORAMBIS: You seek Prince Hamlet. See, there he is.

(Exit)

GILDERSTONE: Health to your lordship!

HAMLET: What, Gilderstone and Rossencraft! Welcome, kind schoolfellows, to Elsinore.

GILDERSTONE: We thank your grace, and would be very glad you were as when we were at Wittenberg.

HAMLET: I thank you; but is this visitation free of yourselves, or were you not sent for? Tell me true. Come, I know the good King and Queen sent for you; there is a kind of confession in your eye. Come, I know you were sent for.

GILDERSTONE: What say you?

HAMLET: Nay, then I see how the wind sits. Come, you were sent for.

ROSSENCRAFT: My lord, we were; and willingly if we might know the cause and ground of your discontent.

HAMLET: Why, I want preferment.

ROSSENCRAFT: I think not so, my lord.

HAMLET: Yes, faith, this great world you see contents me not; no, nor the spangled heavens, nor earth nor sea; no, nor man, that is so glorious a creature, contents not me—no, nor woman too, though you laugh.

GILDERSTONE: My lord, we laugh not at that.

HAMLET: Why did you laugh, then, when I said man did not content me?

GILDERSTONE: My lord, we laughed when you said man did not content you to think what entertainment the players shall have. We boarded them on the way. They are coming to you.

HAMLET: Players? What players be they?

ROSSENCRAFT: My lord, the tragedians of the city; those that you took delight to see so often.

HAMLET: How comes it that they travel? Do they grow resty?

GILDERSTONE: No, my lord; their reputation holds as it was wont.

HAMLET: How then?

GILDERSTONE: I'faith, my lord, novelty carries it away; for the principal public audience that came to them are turned to private plays and to the humor of children.

HAMLET: I do not greatly wonder of it, for those that would make mops and mows at my uncle when my father lived, now give a hundred, two hundred pounds for his picture. But they shall be welcome. He that plays the king shall have tribute of me; the adventurous knight shall use his foil and target; the lover shall sigh gratis; the clown shall make them laugh that are tickled in the lungs or the blank verse shall halt for't, and the lady shall have leave to speak her mind freely.

(The Trumpets sound. Enter CORAMBIS)

Do you see yonder great baby? He is not yet out of his swaddling clouts.

GILDERSTONE: That may be, for they say an old man is twice a child.

HAMLET: I'll prophesy to you he comes to tell me a' the players—
You say true; a Monday last, 'twas so, indeed.

CORAMBIS: My lord, I have news to tell you.

HAMLET: My lord, I have news to tell you. When Roscius was an actor in
Rome—

CORAMBIS: The actors are come hither, my lord.

HAMLET: Buzz, buzz!

CORAMBIS: The best actors in Christendom, either for comedy, tragedy,
history, pastoral, pastoral-historical, historical-comical, comical-his-
torical-pastoral, tragedy-historical; Seneca cannot be too heavy, nor
Plautus too light. For the whole that's written deliberately, these are
the only men.

HAMLET: O Jephthah, judge of Israel, what a treasure hadst thou!

CORAMBIS: Why, what a treasure had he, my lord?

HAMLET: Why,
                            One fair daughter, and no more,
                            The which he loved passing well.

CORAMBIS (*aside*): Ah, still harping a' my daughter!—Well, my lord, if
you call me Jephthah, I have a daughter that I love passing well.

HAMLET: Nay, that follows not.

CORAMBIS: What follows then, my lord?

HAMLET: Why,
                            As by lot, God wot,

    or,
                            It came to pass, and so it was.

The first verse of the godly ballad will tell you all; for look you where my abridgement comes.

(Enter PLAYERS*)*

Welcome, masters; welcome all.—What, my old friend? Thy face is valanced since I saw thee last. Com'st thou to beard me in Denmark? My young lady and mistress! Burlady, but your ladyship is grown by the altitude of a chopine higher than you were. Pray God, sir, your voice, like a piece of uncurrent gold, be not crack'd in the ring.— Come on, masters, we'll even to't like French falconers, fly at anything we see. Come, a taste of your quality; a speech, a passionate speech.

FIRST PLAYER: What speech, my good lord?

HAMLET: I heard thee speak a speech once, but it was never acted; or if it were, never above twice; for as I remember, it pleased not the vulgar, it was caviary to the million; but to me and others that received it in the like kind, cried in the top of their judgments, an excellent play, set down with as great modesty as cunning. One said there was no sallets in the lines to make the savory, but called it an honest method, as wholesome as sweet.—Come, a speech in it I chiefly remember was Aeneas' tale to Dido, and then especially where he talks of Priam's slaughter. If it live in thy memory, begin at this line—let me see:

> The rugged Pyrrhus, like th'Hyrcanian beast

No, 'tis not so. It begins with Pyrrhus. O, I have it:

> The rugged Pyrrhus, he whose sable arms,
> Black as his purpose did the night resemble
> When he lay couched in the ominous horse,
> Hath now his black and grim complexion smeared
> With heraldry more dismal. Head to foot
> Now is he total gules, horridly tricked
> With blood of fathers, mothers, daughters, sons,
> Bak'd and imparched in coagulate gore,
> Rifted in earth and fire, old grandsire Priam seeks.

So, go on.

CORAMBIS: Afore God, my lord, well spoke, and with good accent.

FIRST PLAYER: Anon he finds him, striking too short at Greeks.
 His antique sword, rebellious to his arm,
 Lies where it falls, unable to resist.
 Pyrrhus at Priam drives, but all in rage
 Strikes wide; but with the whiff and wind
 Of his fell sword th'unnerved father falls.

CORAMBIS: Enough, my friend; 'tis too long.

HAMLET: It shall to the barbers with your beard. A pox, he's for a jig or a
 tale of bawdry, or else he sleeps.—Come, on to Hecuba, come.

FIRST PLAYER: But who, O, who had seen the mobled queen—

CORAMBIS: Mobled queen is good, faith, very good.

FIRST PLAYER: All in th'alarum and fear of death rose up,
 And o'er her weak and all o'erteeming loins
 A blanket, and a kercher on that head
 Where late the diadem stood; who this had seen,
 With tongue in venom steep'd, would treason have pronounced.
 For if the gods themselves had seen her then,
 When she saw Pyrrhus with malicious strokes
 Mincing her husband's limbs,
 'Twould have made milch the burning eyes of Heaven,
 And passion in the gods.

CORAMBIS: Look, my lord, if he hath not chang'd his color, and hath tears
 in his eyes. No more, good heart, no more.

HAMLET: 'Tis well, 'tis very well. I pray, my lord, will you see the players
 well bestowed? I tell you they are the chronicles and brief abstracts of
 the time. After your death, I can tell you, you were better have a bad
 epitaph than their ill report while you live.

CORAMBIS: My lord, I will use them according to their deserts.

HAMLET: O, far better, man! Use every man after his deserts, then who
 should scape whipping? Use them after your own honor and dignity.
 The less they deserve, the greater credit's yours.

CORAMBIS: Welcome, my good fellows.

(Exit)

HAMLET: Come hither, masters. Can you not play *The Murder of Gonzago?*

FIRST PLAYER: Yes, my lord.

HAMLET: And could'st not thou for a need study me some dozen or sixteen lines, which I would set down and insert?

FIRST PLAYER: Yes, very easily, my good lord.

HAMLET: 'Tis well; I thank you. Follow that lord; and, do you hear, sirs? take heed you mock him not.

(Exeunt PLAYERS. *To* ROSSENCRAFT *and* GILDERSTONE) Gentlemen, for your kindness I thank you; and for a time I would desire you leave me.

GILDERSTONE: Our love and duty is at your command.

(Exeunt all but HAMLET)

HAMLET: Why, what a dunghill idiot slave am I!
  Why, these players here draw water from eyes
  For Hecuba.
  Why, what is Hecuba to him, or he to Hecuba?
  What would he do and if he had my loss?
  His father murd'red and a crown bereft him?
  He would turn all his tears to drops of blood,
  Amaze the standersby with his laments,
  Strike more than wonder in the judicial ears,
  Confound the ignorant, and make mute the wise;
  Indeed, his passion would be general.
  Yet I, like to an ass and John-a-dreams,
  Having my father murd'red by a villain,
  Stand still and let it pass. Why, sure, I am a coward!
  Who plucks me by the beard, or twits my nose?
  Gives me the lie i'th' throat, down to the lungs?
  Sure, I should take it! Or else I have no gall,
  Or by this I should 'a' fatted all the region kites
  With this slave's offal; this damned villain!

Treacherous, bawdy, murderous villain!
Why, this is brave, that I, the son of my dear father,
Should, like a scullion, like a very drab,
Thus rail in words. About my brain—I have heard
That guilty creatures, sitting at a play,
Hath, by the very cunning of the scene,
Confess'd a murder committed long before.
This spirit that I have seen may be the devil,
And out of my weakness and my melancholy
(As he is very potent with such men),
Doth seek to damn me.
I will have sounder proofs. The play's the thing
Wherein I'll catch the conscience of the King.

(*Exit. Enter the* KING, QUEEN, CORAMBIS *and* ROSSENCRAFT *and* GILDERSTONE)

KING: Lords, can you by no means find
    The cause of our son Hamlet's lunacy?
    You being so near in love even from his youth,
    Methinks should gain more than a stranger should.

GILDERSTONE: My lord, we have done all the best we could,
    To wring from him the cause of all his grief,
    But still he puts us off, and by no means
    Would make an answer to that we expos'd.

ROSSENCRAFT: Yet was he something more inclin'd to mirth
    Before we left him, and, I take it, he
    Hath given order for a play tonight,
    At which he craves Your Highness' company.

KING: With all our heart; it likes us very well.
    Gentlemen, seek still to increase his mirth;
    Spare for no cost; our coffers shall be open;
    And we unto yourselves will still be thankful.

BOTH: In all we can, be sure you shall command.

QUEEN: Thanks, gentlemen; and what the Queen of Denmark
    May pleasure you, be sure you shall not want.

GILDERSTONE: We'll once again unto the noble Prince.

KING: Thanks to you both.—Gertred, you'll see this play?

QUEEN: My lord, I will; and it joys me at the soul
   He is inclin'd to any kind of mirth.

CORAMBIS: Madam, I pray, be ruled by me.
   And my good sovereign, give me leave to speak.
   We cannot yet find out the very ground
   Of his distemperance; therefore I hold it meet,
   If so it please you (else they shall not meet),
   And thus it is.

KING: What is't, Corambis?

CORAMBIS: Marry, my good lord, this:
   Soon, when the sports are done,
   Madam, send you in haste to speak with him;
   And I myself will stand behind the arras.
   There question you the cause of all his grief,
   And then, in love and nature unto you,
   He'll tell you all. My lord, how think you on't?

KING: It likes us well. Gertred, what say you?

QUEEN: With all my heart. Soon will I send for him.

CORAMBIS: Myself will be that happy messenger,
   Who hopes his grief will be reveal'd to her.

(Exeunt omnes. Enter HAMLET *and the* PLAYERS*)*

HAMLET: Pronounce me this speech trippingly a' the tongue, as I taught
   thee. Marry, and you mouth it, as a many of your players do, I'd
   rather hear a town bull bellow than such a fellow speak my lines. Nor
   do not saw the air thus with your hands, but give everything his
   action with temperance. O, it offends me to the soul to hear a
   robustious, periwig fellow to tear a passion in tatters, into very rags, to
   split the ears of the ignorant, who, for the most part, are capable of

nothing but dumb shows and noises. I would have such a fellow whipp'd for o'erdoing Termagant; it outherods Herod.

FIRST PLAYER: My lord, we have indifferently reformed that among us.

HAMLET: The better, the better; mend it all together. There be fellows that I have seen play, and heard others commend them, and that highly, too, that having neither the gait of Christian, pagan, nor Turk, have so strutted and bellowed that you would 'a' thought some of nature's journeymen had made men, and not made them well, they imitated humanity so abominable. Take heed; avoid it.

FIRST PLAYER: I warrant you, my lord.

HAMLET: And do you hear? let not your clown speak more than is set down. There be of them, I can tell you, that will laugh themselves to set on some quantity of barren spectators to laugh with them, albeit there is some necessary point in the play then to be observed. O, 'tis vile, and shows a pitiful ambition in the fool that useth it. And then you have some again that keeps one suit of jests, as a man is known by one suit of apparel; and gentlemen quote his jests down in their tables before they come to the play, as thus: "Cannot you stay till I eat my porridge?" and "You owe me a quarter's wages," and "My coat wants a cullison," and "Your beer is sour," and blabbering with his lips, and thus keeping in his cinquepace of jests, when God knows, the warm clown cannot make a jest unless by chance, as a blind man catcheth a hare. Masters, tell him of it.

FIRST PLAYER: We will, my lord.

HAMLET: Well, go make you ready.

(*Exeunt* PLAYERS)

What, ho, Horatio!

HORATIO (*entering*): Here, my lord.

HAMLET: Horatio, thou art even as just a man
    As e'er my conversation cop'd withal.

HORATIO: O, my lord!

HAMLET: Nay, why should I flatter thee?
  Why should the poor be flattered?
  What gain should I receive by flattering thee,
  That nothing hath but thy good mind?
  Let flattery sit on those time-pleasing tongues
  To gloze with them that love to hear their praise,
  And not with such as thou, Horatio.
  There is a play tonight, wherein one scene
  They have comes very near the murder of
  My father. When thou shalt see that act afoot,
  Mark thou the King; do but observe his looks;
  For I mine eyes will rivet to his face,
  And if he do not bleach and change at that,
  It is a damned ghost that we have seen.
  Horatio, have a care, observe him well.

HORATIO: My lord, mine eyes shall still be on his face,
  And not the smallest alteration
  That shall appear in him but I shall note it.

HAMLET: Hark, they come.

(Enter KING, QUEEN, CORAMBIS and other LORDS)

KING: How now, son Hamlet, how fare you?

HAMLET: Excellent, i'faith; of the chameleon's dish. I eat the air, prom-
ise-cramm'd. You cannot feed capons so.—My lord, you play'd in the
university?

CORAMBIS: That I did, my lord, and I was counted a good actor.

HAMLET: What did you enact there?

CORAMBIS: My lord, I did act Julius Caesar; I was killed in the Capitol;
Brutus killed me.

HAMLET: It was a brute part of him to kill so capital a calf. Come, be
these players ready?

QUEEN: Hamlet, come sit down by me.

HAMLET: No, by my faith, mother. Here's a metal more attractive.—
Lady, will you give me leave and so forth to lay my head in your lap?

OFELIA: No, my lord.

HAMLET: Upon your lap. What, do you think I meant contrary manners?

(Enter in a dumb show the KING *and the* QUEEN. *He sits down in an arbor;
she leaves him. Then enters* LUCIANUS *with poison in a vial, and pours it in
his ears, and goes away. Then the* QUEEN *cometh and finds him dead, and
goes away with the other)*

OFELIA: What means this, my lord?

HAMLET: This is mychief mallecho; that means mischief.

(Enter the PROLOGUE*)*

OFELIA: What doth this mean, my lord?

HAMLET: You shall hear anon; this fellow will tell you all.

OFELIA: Will he tell us what this show means?

HAMLET: Ay, or any show you'll show him. Be not afeard to show, he'll
not be afeard to tell. O, these players cannot keep counsel; they'll tell
all.

PROLOGUE: For us and for our tragedy,
            Here stooping to your clemency,
            We beg your hearing patiently.

HAMLET: Is't a prologue or a posy for a ring?

OFELIA: 'Tis short, my lord.

HAMLET: As women's love.

(Enter the PLAYER DUKE *and* DUCHESS)

DUKE: Full forty years are past, their date is gone
   Since happy time join'd both our hearts as one.
   And now the blood that fill'd my youthful veins
   Runs weakly in their pipes, and all the strains
   Of music which whilom pleas'd mine ear
   Is now a burden that age cannot bear.
   And therefore, sweet, nature must pay his due;
   To Heaven must I, and leave the earth with you.

DUCHESS: O, say not so, lest that you kill my heart;
   When death takes you let life from me depart.

DUKE: Content thyself; when ended is my date,
   Thou mayst, perchance, have a more noble mate,
   More wise, more youthful, and one—

DUCHESS: O speak no more, for then I am accurst;
   None weds the second, but she kills the first;
   A second time I kill my lord that's dead,
   When second husband kisses me in bed.

HAMLET *(aside):* O, wormwood, wormwood!

DUKE: I do believe you, sweet, what now you speak,
   But what we do determine oft we break;
   For our devices still are overthrown;
   Our thoughts are ours, their end's none of our own.
   So think you will no second husband wed,
   But die thy thoughts when thy first lord is dead.

DUCHESS: Both here and there pursue me lasting strife,
   If, once a widow, ever I be a wife.

HAMLET: If she should break now!

DUKE: 'Tis deeply sworn. Sweet, leave me here awhile.
   My spirits grow dull, and fain I would beguile
   The tedious time with sleep.

DUCHESS: Sleep rock thy brain
And never come mischance between us twain.

(*He sleeps. Exit* LADY)

HAMLET: Madam, how do you like this play?

QUEEN: The lady protests too much.

HAMLET: O, but she'll keep her word.

KING: Have you heard the argument? Is there no offense in it?

HAMLET: No offense in the world; poison in jest, poison in jest.

KING: What do you call the name of the play?

HAMLET: Mousetrap. Marry, how? Tropically. This play is the image of a murder done in Guyana. Albertus was the Duke's name; his wife, Baptista. Father, it is a knavish piece a' work; but what a that? It toucheth not us, you and I, that have free souls. Let the gall'd jade wince.

(*Enter* LUCIANUS)

This is one Lucianus, nephew to the King.

OFELIA: You're as good as a chorus, my lord.

HAMLET: I could interpret the love you bear, if I saw the poopies dallying.

OFELIA: You're very pleasant, my lord.

HAMLET: Who, I? Your only jigmaker! Why, what should a man do but be merry? For look how cheerfully looks my mother, and my father died within these two hours.

OFELIA: Nay, 'tis twice two months, my lord.

HAMLET: Two months! Nay then, let the devil wear black, for I'll have a suit of sables. Jesus! Two months dead, and not forgotten yet? Nay, then there's some likelihood a gentleman's death may outlive memory. But by my faith, he must build churches, then, or else he must follow the old epitaph, "With ho, with ho, the hobbyhorse is forgot."

OFELIA: Your jests are keen, my lord.

HAMLET: It would cost you a groaning to take them off.

OFELIA: Still better, and worse.

HAMLET: So you must take your husband.—Begin, Modred, begin. A pox, leave thy damnable faces and begin. Come, the croaking raven doth bellow for revenge.

LUCIANUS: Thoughts black, hands apt, drugs fit, and time agreeing;
Confederate season, else no creature seeing;
Thou mixture rank, of midnight weeds collected,
With Hecate's bane thrice blasted, thrice infected,
Thy natural magic and dire property
One wholesome life usurps immediately.

(Exit)

HAMLET: He poisons him for his estate!

KING: Lights! I will to bed!

CORAMBIS: The King rises! Lights, ho!

(Exeunt KING and LORDS)

HAMLET: What, frighted with false fires?

Then let the stricken deer go weep,
    The hart ungalled play,
For some must laugh, while some must weep;
    Thus runs the world away.

HORATIO: The King is moved, my lord.

HAMLET: Ay, Horatio, I'll take the ghost's word for more than all the coin in Denmark.

(*Enter* ROSSENCRAFT *and* GILDERSTONE)

ROSSENCRAFT: Now, my lord, how is't with you?

HAMLET: And if the King like not the tragedy,
  Why then, belike, he likes it not, perdy.

ROSSENCRAFT: We are very glad to see your grace so pleasant.
  My good lord,
  Let us again entreat to know of you
  The ground and cause of your distemperature.

GILDERSTONE: My lord, your mother craves to speak with you.

HAMLET: We shall obey, were she ten times our mother.

ROSSENCRAFT: But my good lord, shall I entreat thus much—

HAMLET: I pray, will you play upon this pipe?

ROSSENCRAFT: Alas, my lord, I cannot.

HAMLET: Pray, will you?

GILDERSTONE: I have no skill, my lord.

HAMLET: Why, look; it is a thing of nothing; 'tis but stopping of these holes, and with a little breath from your lips it will give most delicate music.

GILDERSTONE: But this cannot we do, my lord.

HAMLET: Pray now; pray, heartily. I beseech you.

ROSSENCRAFT: My lord, we cannot.

HAMLET: Why, how unworthy a thing would you make of me! You would seem to know my stops; you would play upon me; you would search

the very inward part of my heart, and dive into the secret of my soul.
Zounds, do you think I am easier to be play'd on than a pipe? Call me
what instrument you will, though you can fret me, yet you cannot
play upon me. Besides, to be demanded by a sponge—

ROSSENCRAFT: How? A sponge, my lord?

HAMLET: Ay, sir, a sponge that soaks up the King's countenance, favors
and rewards; that makes his liberality your storehouse. But such as
you do the King in the end best service; for he doth keep you as an
ape doth nuts: in the corner of his jaw; first mouths you, then swallows you. So, when he hath need of you 'tis but squeezing of you,
and, sponge, you shall be dry again, you shall.

ROSSENCRAFT: Well, my lord, we'll take our leave.

HAMLET: Farewell, farewell, God bless you.

(Exit ROSSENCRAFT and GILDERSTONE. Enter CORAMBIS)

CORAMBIS: My lord, the Queen would speak with you.

HAMLET: Do you see yonder cloud in the shape of a camel?

CORAMBIS: 'Tis like a camel, indeed.

HAMLET: Now methinks it's like a weasel.

CORAMBIS: 'Tis back'd like a weasel.

HAMLET: Or like a whale.

CORAMBIS: Very like a whale.

HAMLET: Why, then tell my mother I'll come by and by.

(Exit CORAMBIS)

Good night, Horatio.

HORATIO: Good night unto your lordship.

(*Exit* HORATIO)

HAMLET: My mother, she hath sent to speak with me.
O, God! Let ne'er the heart of Nero enter
This soft bosom.
Let me be cruel, not unnatural.
I will speak daggers; those sharp words being spent,
To do her wrong my soul shall ne'er consent.

(*Exit. Enter the* KING)

KING: O, that this wet that falls upon my face
Would wash the crime clear from my conscience!
When I look up to Heaven, I see my trespass;
The earth doth still cry out upon my act,
"Pay me the murder of a brother and a king";
And the adulterous fault I have committed.
O, these are sins that are unpardonable!
Why, say thy sins were blacker than is jet,
Yet may contrition make them as white as snow.
Ay, but still to persever in a sin:
It is an act 'gainst the universal power.
Most wretched man, stoop, bend thee to thy prayer,
Ask grace of Heaven to keep thee from despair.

(*He kneels. Enters* HAMLET)

HAMLET: Ay, so (*drawing his dagger*)
Come forth and work thy last, and thus he dies;
And so am I revenged. No, not so.
He took my father sleeping, his sins brim full;
And how his soul stood to the state of Heaven,
Who knows save the immortal powers? And shall
I kill him now, when he is purging of his soul,
Making his way for Heaven?
This is a benefit and not revenge.
No. Get thee up again; when he's at game,
Swearing, taking his carouse, drinking drunk,
Or in th'incestuous pleasure of his bed,
Or at some act
That hath no relish of salvation in't.

Then trip him that his heels may kick at Heaven
And fall as low as Hell.—My mother stays.
This physic but prolongs thy weary days.

(Exit HAMLET*)*

KING *(rising):* My words fly up, my sins remain below.
No king on earth is safe if God's his foe.

(Exit KING*. Enter* QUEEN *and* CORAMBIS*)*

CORAMBIS: Madam, I hear young Hamlet coming. I'll shroud
Myself behind th'arras.

QUEEN: Do so, my lord.

(Exit CORAMBIS*. Enter* HAMLET*)*

HAMLET: Mother, mother!
O, are you here? How is't with you, mother?

QUEEN: How is't with you?

HAMLET: I'll tell you, but first we'll make all safe.

QUEEN: Hamlet, thou hast thy father much offended.

HAMLET: Mother, you have my father much offended.

QUEEN: How now, boy?

HAMLET: How now, mother?
Come here; sit down, for you shall hear me speak.

QUEEN: What wilt thou do? Thou wilt not murder me?
Help, ho!

CORAMBIS: Help for the Queen!

HAMLET *(draws)*: Ay; a rat?   *(Stabs through the arras)*
    Dead for a ducat. Rash intruding fool,
    Farewell. I took thee for thy better.

QUEEN: Hamlet, what hast thou done?

HAMLET: Not so much harm, good mother, as to kill
    A king and marry with his brother.

QUEEN: How? Kill a king!

HAMLET: Ay, a king. Nay, sit you down; and ere you part,
    If you be made of penetrable stuff,
    I'll make your eyes look down into your heart,
    And see how horrid there and black it shows.

QUEEN: Hamlet, what mean'st thou by these killing words?

HAMLET: Why, this I mean: See here, behold this picture.
    It is the portraiture of your deceased husband.
    See here a face to outface Mars himself;
    An eye at which his foes did tremble at;
    A front wherein all virtues are set down,
    For to adorn a king and gild his crown;
    Whose heart went hand in hand even with that vow
    He made to you in marriage. And he is dead;
    Murd'red, damnably murd'red. This was your husband.
    Look you now: here is your husband;
    With a face like Vulcan;
    A look fit for a murder and a rape,
    A dull, dead hanging look, and a hellbred eye,
    To affright children and amaze the world.
    And this same have you left to change with this.
    What devil thus hath cozened you at hoodman blind?
    Ah, have you eyes, and can you look on him
    That slew my father and your dear husband,
    To live in the incestuous pleasure of his bed?

QUEEN: O Hamlet, speak no more.

HAMLET: To leave him that bare a monarch's mind
    For a king of clouts, of very shreds!

QUEEN: Sweet Hamlet, cease.

HAMLET: Nay, but still to persist and dwell in sin,
    To sweat under the yoke of infamy,
    To make increase of shame, to seal damnation.

QUEEN: Hamlet, no more.

HAMLET: Why, appetite with you is in the wane;
    Your blood runs backward now from whence it came;
    Who'll chide hot blood within a virgin's heart,
    When lust shall dwell within a matron's breast?

QUEEN: Hamlet, thou cleavest my heart in twain.

HAMLET: O, throw away the worser part of it,
    And keep the better.

(Enter the GHOST *in his nightgown)*

    Save me, save me, you gracious powers above,
    And hover over me with your celestial wings.
    Do you not come your tardy son to chide,
    That I thus long have let revenge slip by?
    O, do not glare with looks so pitiful,
    Lest that my heart of stone yield to compassion,
    And every part that should assist revenge
    Forego their proper powers, and fall to pity.

GHOST: Hamlet, I once again appear to thee,
    To put thee in remembrance of my death.
    Do not neglect, nor long time put it off.
    But I perceive by her distracted looks
    Thy mother's fearful, and she stands amaz'd.
    Speak to her, Hamlet, for her sex is weak;
    Comfort thy mother, Hamlet; think on me.

HAMLET: How is't with you, lady?

QUEEN: Nay, how is't with you,
That thus you bend your eyes on vacancy,
And hold discourse with nothing but with air?

HAMLET: Why, do you nothing hear?

QUEEN: Not I.

HAMLET: Nor do you nothing see?

QUEEN: No; neither.

HAMLET: No? Why, see the King my father!
My father in the habit as he lived!
Look you how pale he looks!
See how he steals away, out of the portal!
Look, there he goes!

(*Exit* GHOST)

QUEEN: Alas, it is the weakness of thy brain,
Which makes thy tongue to blazon thy heart's grief;
But as I have a soul I swear by Heaven
I never knew of this most horrid murder.
But Hamlet, this is only fantasy,
And for my love forget these idle fits.

HAMLET: Idle? No, mother, my pulse doth beat like yours;
It is not madness that possesseth Hamlet.
O mother, if ever you did my dear father love,
Forbear the adulterous bed tonight,
And win yourself by little, as you may;
In time it may be you will loath him quite.
And, mother, but assist me in revenge,
And in his death your infamy shall die.

QUEEN: Hamlet, I vow by that majesty
That knows our thoughts and looks into our hearts,
I will conceal, consent and do my best,
What stratagem soe'er thou shalt devise.

HAMLET: It is enough. Mother, good night.
   Come sir, I'll provide for you a grave,
   Who was in life a foolish, prating knave.

(*Exit* QUEEN *and* HAMLET *with the dead body. Enter the* KING, *the* QUEEN,
ROSSENCRAFT *and* GILDERSTONE)

KING: Now, Gertred, what says our son? How do you find him?

QUEEN: Alas, my lord, as raging as the sea.
   Whenas he came, I first bespake him fair;
   But then he throws and tosses me about,
   As one forgetting that I was his mother.
   At last I call'd for help, and as I cried
   Corambis call'd; which Hamlet no sooner heard,
   But whips me out his rapier and cries,
   "A rat, a rat!"
   And in his rage the good old man he kills.

KING: Why, this his madness will undo our state.
   Lords, go to him; inquire the body out.

GILDERSTONE: We will, my lord.

(*Exeunt* ROSSENCRAFT *and* GILDERSTONE)

KING: Gertred, your son shall presently to England.
   His shipping is already furnished,
   And we have sent by Rossencraft and Gilderstone
   Our letters to our dear brother of England,
   For Hamlet's welfare and his happiness.
   Haply the air and climate of the country
   May please him better than his native home.
   See, where he comes.

(*Enter* HAMLET, ROSSENCRAFT *and* GILDERSTONE)

GILDERSTONE: My lord, we can by no means know of him
   Where the body is.

KING: Now, son Hamlet,
Where is this dead body?

HAMLET: At supper; not where he is eating, but where he is eaten. A
certain company of politic worms are even now at him. Father, your
fat king and your lean beggar are but variable services—two dishes to
one mess. Look you, a man may fish with that worm that hath eaten
of a king, and a beggar eat that fish which that worm hath caught.

KING: What of this?

HAMLET: Nothing, father, but to tell you how a king may go a progress
through the guts of a beggar.

KING: But, son Hamlet, where is this body?

HAMLET: In Heav'n. If you chance to miss him there, father, you had
best look in the other parts below for him; and if you cannot find him
there, you may chance to nose him as you go up the lobby.

KING: Make haste, and find him out.

HAMLET: Nay, do you hear? Do not make too much haste;
I'll warrant you he'll stay till you come.

(*Exeunt* ROSSENCRAFT *and* GILDERSTONE)

KING: Well, son Hamlet,
We, in care of you, but specially
In tender preservation of your health,
The which we price e'en as our proper self—
It is our mind you forthwith go for England.
The wind sits fair; you shall aboard tonight.
Lord Rossencraft and Gilderstone shall go
Along with you.

HAMLET: O, with all my heart.
Farewell, mother.

KING: Your loving father, Hamlet.

HAMLET: My mother, I say! You married my mother; my mother is
your wife; man and wife is one flesh; and so, my mother. Farewell;
for England, ho!

(Exeunt all but the KING *and the* QUEEN*)*

KING: Gertred, leave me; *(Exit* QUEEN*)* and take your leave of Hamlet.
To England is he gone ne'er to return.
Our letters are unto the King of England,
That on the sight of them, on his allegiance,
(He, presently, without demanding why)
That Hamlet lose his head, for he must die.
There's more in him than shallow eyes can see;
He once being dead, why, then our state is free.

(Exit. Enter FORTENBRASSE, *drum and* SOLDIERS*)*

FORTENBRASSE: Captain, from us go greet the King of Denmark.
Tell him that Fortenbrasse, nephew to old Norway,
Craves a free pass and conduct over his land,
According to the articles agreed on.
You know our rendezvous; go, march away.

(Exeunt all. Enter KING *and* QUEEN*)*

KING: Hamlet is shipp'd for England; fare him well;
I hope to hear good news from thence ere long,
If everything fall out to our content,
As I do make no doubt but so it shall.

QUEEN: God grant it may; heav'ns keep my Hamlet safe;
But this mischance of old Corambis' death
Hath pierced so the young Ofelia's heart,
That she, poor maid, is quite bereft her wits.

KING: Alas, dear heart! And on the other side,
We understand her brother's come from France;
And he hath half the heart of all our land;
And hardly he'll forget his father's death,
Unless by some means he be pacified.

QUEEN: O, see, where the young Ofelia is!

(Enter OFELIA *playing on a lute, and her hair down, singing)*

OFELIA:

> How should I your true love know
>   From another man?
> By his cockle hat and staff
>   And his sandal shoon.
>
> White his shroud as mountain snow,
>   Larded with sweet flowers;
> That bewept to the grave did not go
>   With true lovers' showers.
>
> He is dead and gone, lady,
>   He is dead and gone;
> At his head a grass-green turf,
>   At his heels a stone.

KING: How is't with you, sweet Ofelia?

OFELIA: Well, God yield you. It grieves me to see how they laid him in
   the cold ground; I could not choose but weep.

> *(Sings)*   And will he not come again?
> And will he not come again?
>   No, no, he's gone,
>   And we cast away moan,
> And he never will come again.
>
> His beard as white as snow,
> All flaxen was his poll;
>   He is dead, he is gone,
>   And we cast away moan.
> God 'a' mercy on his soul.

And of all Christian souls, I pray God. God be with you ladies! God
be with you!

(*Exit* OFELIA)

KING: A pretty wretch! This is a change, indeed.
O Time, how swiftly runs our joys away!
Content on earth was never certain bred;
Today we laugh and live, tomorrow dead.

(*A noise within*)

How now, what noise is that!

LEARTES (*within*): Stay there until I come!

(*Enter* LEARTES)

                                                    O, thou vile king,
Give me my father! Speak! Say, where's my father?

KING: Dead.

LEARTES: Who hath murd'red him? Speak, I'll not
Be juggled with; for he is murd'red.

QUEEN: True; but not by him.

LEARTES: By whom? By Heav'n, I'll be resolved.

KING: Let him go, Gertred; away! I fear him not.
There's such divinity doth wall a king
That treason dares not look on.
Let him go, Gertred! That your father is murd'red,
'Tis true; and we most sorry for it,
Being the chiefest pillar of our state.
Therefore will you, like a most desperate gamester,
Swoopstake-like, draw at friend, and foe and all?

LEARTES: To his good friends thus wide I'll ope mine arms,
And lock them in my heart; but to his foes
I will no reconcilement but by blood.

KING: Why, now you speak like a most loving son;
And that in soul we sorrow for his death,

Yourself ere long shall be a witness;
Meanwhile be patient, and content yourself.

(Enter OFELIA *as before)*

LEARTES: Who's this? Ofelia! O, my dear sister!
Is't possible a young maid's life
Should be as mortal as an old man's saw?
O heav'ns themselves! How now, Ofelia?

OFELIA: Well, God a' mercy. I a' been gathering of flowers; here, here is
rue for you. You may call it herb a grace a Sundays; here's some for
me too. You must wear your rue with a difference. There's a daisy.
Here, love, there's rosemary for you for remembrance; I pray, love,
remember. And there's pansy for thoughts.

LEARTES: A document in madness! Thoughts! Remembrance!
O God, O God!

OFELIA: There is fennel for you; I would a' giv'n you some violets, but
they all withered when my father died. Alas, they say the owl was a
baker's daughter. We see what we are but cannot tell what we shall
be. *(Sings)*

> For bonny sweet Robin is all my joy.

LEARTES: Thoughts and afflictions; torments worse than Hell.

OFELIA: Nay, love, I pray you make no words of this now. I pray now, you
shall sing a-down, and you a-down-a. 'Tis a' the King's daughter and
the false steward; and if anybody ask you of anything, say you this:
(Sings)

> Tomorrow is Saint Valentine's day,
>   All in the morning betime,
> And I a maid at your window,
>   To be your Valentine.
>
> The young man rose, and don'd his clothes,
>   And dupp'd the chamber door,
> Let in the maid, that out a maid
>   Never departed more.

Nay, I pray, mark now:

> By Gis, and by Saint Charity,
>   Away, and fie for shame!
> Young men will do't when they come to't;
>   By Cock, they are to blame.

> Quoth she, before you tumbled me,
>   You promis'd me to wed.
> So would I a' done, by yonder sun,
>   If thou hadst not come to my bed.

So God be with you all; God b'wi' you ladies; God b'wi' you, love.

(*Exit* OFELIA)

LEARTES: Grief upon grief! My father murdered;
My sister thus distracted. Cursed be
His soul that wrought this wicked act.

KING: Content you,
Good Leartes, for a time. Although
I know your grief is as a flood, brim full
Of sorrow, but forbear a while, and think
Already the revenge is done on him
That makes you such a hapless son.

LEARTES: You have prevail'd, my lord; a while I'll strive
To bury grief within a tomb of wrath,
Which once unhearsed, then the world shall hear
Leartes had a father he held dear.

KING: No more of that. Ere many days be done
You shall hear that you do not dream upon.

(*Exeunt omnes. Enter* HORATIO *and the* QUEEN)

HORATIO: Madam, your son is safe arriv'd in Denmark.
This letter I e'en now receiv'd of him,
Whereas he writes how he escap'd the danger
And subtle treason that the King had plotted.

Being crossed by the contention of the winds,
He found the packet sent to the King of England,
Wherein he saw himself betray'd to death;
As at his next converging with your grace
He will relate the circumstance at full.

QUEEN: Then I perceive there's treason in his looks,
That seem'd to sugar o'er his villany.
But I will soothe and please him for a time,
For murderous minds are always jealous.
But know not you, Horatio, where he is?

HORATIO: Yes, madam; and he hath appointed me
To meet him on the east side of the city
Tomorrow morning.

QUEEN: O, fail not, good Horatio;
And withal, commend me a mother's care to him;
Bid him a while be wary of his presence,
Lest that he fail in that he goes about.

HORATIO: Madam,
Never make doubt of that. I think by this
The news be come to court he is arriv'd.
Observe the King, and you shall quickly find,
Hamlet being here, things fall not to his mind.

QUEEN: But what became of Gilderstone and Rossencraft?

HORATIO: He being set ashore, they went for England;
And in the packet there writ down that doom
To be perform'd on them 'pointed for him;
And by great chance he had his father's seal,
So all was done without discovery.

QUEEN: Thanks be to Heaven for blessing of the Prince.
Horatio, once again I take my leave
With thousand mother's blessings to my son.

HORATIO: Madam, adieu.

(Exeunt. Enter KING *and* LEARTES)

KING: Hamlet from England! is it possible?
    What chance is this? They are gone, and he come home?

LEARTES: O, he is welcome; by my soul he is.
    At it my jocund heart doth leap for joy,
    That I shall live to tell him thus he dies.

KING: Leartes, content yourself; be rul'd by me,
    And you shall have no let for your revenge.

LEARTES: My will, not all the world.

KING: Nay; but Leartes, mark the plot I've laid:
    I've heard him often with a greedy wish,
    Upon some praise that he hath heard of you,
    Touching your weapon, wish with all his heart
    He might be once task'd for to try your cunning.

LEARTES: And how for this?

KING: Marry, Leartes, thus: I'll lay a wager,
    Shall be on Hamlet's side, and you shall give the odds,
    The which will draw him with a more desire
    To try the mast'ry, that in twelve venies
    You gain not three of him. Now this being granted,
    When you are hot in midst of all your play,
    Among the foils shall a keen rapier lie,
    Steep'd in a mixture of deadly poison,
    That if it draws but the least dram of blood
    In any part of him, he cannot live.
    This being done will free you from suspicion,
    And not the dearest friend that Hamlet lov'd
    Will ever have Leartes in suspect.

LEARTES: My lord, I like it well;
    But say Lord Hamlet should refuse this match.

KING: I'll warrant you. We'll put on you
    Such a report of singularity

Will bring him on, although against his will.
And lest that all should miss,
I'll have a potion that shall ready stand,
In all his heat when that he calls for drink,
Shall be his period and our happiness.

LEARTES: 'Tis excellent; O, would the time were come!
Here comes the Queen.

(Enter the QUEEN*)*

KING: How now, Gertred, why look you heavily?

QUEEN: O, my lord, the young Ofelia,
Having made a garland of sundry sorts of flowers,
Sitting upon a willow by a brook,
The envious sprig broke, into the brook she fell.
And for a while her clothes, spread wide abroad,
Bore the young lady up; and there she sat,
Smiling, even mermaid like, twixt Heaven and earth,
Chanting old, sundry tunes, uncapable, as it were,
Of her distress. But long it could not be
Till that her clothes, being heavy with their drink,
Dragg'd the sweet wretch to death.

LEARTES: So she is drown'd!
Too much of water hast thou, Ofelia;
Therefore I will not drown thee in my tears.
Revenge it is must yield this heart relief,
For woe begets woe, and grief hangs on grief.

(Exeunt. Enter CLOWN *and another)*

FIRST CLOWN: I say no. She ought not to be buried in Christian burial.

SECOND CLOWN: Why, sir?

FIRST CLOWN: Marry, because she's drown'd.

SECOND CLOWN: But she did not drown herself.

FIRST CLOWN: No, that's certain; the water drown'd her.

SECOND CLOWN: Yea, but it was against her will.

FIRST CLOWN: No, I deny that; for look you, sir: I stand here; if the water come to me, I drown not myself. But if I go to the water, and am there drown'd, ergo I am guilty of my own death. Y'are gone; go, y'are gone, sir.

SECOND CLOWN: I but see she hath Christian burial because she is a great woman.

FIRST CLOWN: Marry, more's the pity that great folk should have more authority to hang or drown themselves more than other people. Go fetch me a stoup of drink; but before thou goest, tell me one thing: Who builds strongest of a mason, a shipwright or a carpenter?

SECOND CLOWN: Why, a mason, for he builds all of stone, and will endure long.

FIRST CLOWN: That's pretty; to't again, to't again.

SECOND CLOWN: Why then, a carpenter, for he builds the gallows, and that brings many a one to his long home.

FIRST CLOWN: Pretty again. The gallows doth well; marry, how does it well? The gallows does well to them that do ill. Go, get thee gone; and if anyone ask thee hereafter, say a gravemaker, for the houses he builds last till doomsday. Fetch me a stoup of beer, go.

(*Exit* SECOND CLOWN. *Enter* HAMLET *and* HORATIO)

FIRST CLOWN (*sings*): A pickaxe and a spade, a spade,
                For and a winding sheet;
           Most fit it is, for 'twill be made
               For such a "ghost" most meet.

(*He throws up a shovel*)

HAMLET: Hath this fellow any feeling of himself, that is thus merry in making of a grave? See how the slave jowls their heads against the earth.

HORATIO: My lord, custom hath made it in him seem nothing.

FIRST CLOWN (*sings and digs*):

> A pickaxe and a spade, a spade,
>   For and a winding sheet;
> Most fit it is for to be made
>   For such a ghost most meet.

HAMLET: Look you, there's another, Horatio. Why, may't not be the skull of some lawyer? Methinks he should indict that fellow of an action of battery for knocking him about the pate with's shovel. Now where is your quirks and quillets now, your vouchers and double vouchers, your leases, and freehold and tenements? Why, that same box there will scarce hold the conveyance of his land; and must his honor lie there? O, pitiful transformance! I prithee, tell me, Horatio, is parchment made of sheepskins?

HORATIO: Ay, my lord, and of calfskins too.

HAMLET: I'faith, they prove themselves sheep and calves that deal with them, or put their trust in them. There's another. Why, may not that be Such-a-one's skull, that praised my Lord Such-a-one's horse when he meant to beg him? Horatio, I prithee, let's question yonder fellow. (*Stepping forward*) Now, my friend, whose grave is this?

FIRST CLOWN: Mine, sir.

HAMLET: But who must lie in it?

FIRST CLOWN: If I should say I should, I should lie in my throat, sir.

HAMLET: What man must be buried here?

FIRST CLOWN: No man, sir.

HAMLET: What woman?

FIRST CLOWN: No woman, neither, sir; but, indeed, one that was a woman.

HAMLET: An excellent fellow! By the Lord, Horatio, this seven years have I noted it, the toe of the peasant comes so near the heel of the courtier, that he galls his kibe. I prithee, tell me one thing. How long will a man lie in the ground before he rots?

FIRST CLOWN: I'faith, sir, if he be not rotten before he be laid in, as we have many pocky corses, he will last you eight years; a tanner will last you eight years full out, or nine.

HAMLET: And why a tanner?

FIRST CLOWN: Why, his hide is so tanned with his trade that it will hold out water; that's a parlous devourer of your dead body, a great soaker. Look you, here's a skull hath been here this dozen year,—let me see— ay, ever since our last King Hamlet slew Fortenbrasse in combat, young Hamlet's father, he that's mad.

HAMLET: Ay, marry, how came he mad?

FIRST CLOWN: I'faith, very strangely, by losing of his wits.

HAMLET: Upon what ground?

FIRST CLOWN: A' this ground, in Denmark.

HAMLET: Where is he now?

FIRST CLOWN: Why, now they sent him to England.

HAMLET: To England? Wherefore?

FIRST CLOWN: Why, they say he shall have his wits there; or if he have not, 'tis no great matter there; it will not be seen there.

HAMLET: Why not there?

FIRST CLOWN: Why, there, they say, the men are as mad as he.

HAMLET: Whose skull was this?

FIRST CLOWN: This?—A plague on him—a mad rogue's it was. He poured once a whole flagon of Rhenish on my head. Why, do not you know him? This was one Yorick's skull.

HAMLET: Was this? I prithee, let me see it. Alas, poor Yorick! I knew him, Horatio; a fellow of infinite mirth. He hath carried me twenty times upon his back. Here hung those lips that I have kissed a hundred times, and to see, now they abhor me. Where's your jests now, Yorick? Your flashes of merriment? Now go to my lady's chamber, and bid her paint herself an inch thick, to this she must come, Yorick. Horatio, I prithee tell me one thing: Dost thou think that Alexander looked thus?

HORATIO: Even so, my lord.

HAMLET: And smelt thus?

HORATIO: Ay, my lord, no otherwise.

(*The* CLOWN *exits down the trap*)

HAMLET: No? Why might not imagination work as thus of Alexander: Alexander died, Alexander was buried, Alexander became earth; of earth we make clay; and Alexander being but clay, why might not time bring to pass that he might stop the bunghole of a beer barrel? Imperious Caesar, dead and turn'd to clay, Might stop a hole to keep the wind away.

(*Enter* KING *and* QUEEN, LEARTES *and other* LORDS, *with a* PRIEST *after the coffin*)

What funeral's this that all the court laments? It shows to be some noble parentage. Stand by a while.

LEARTES: What ceremony else? Say, what ceremony else?

PRIEST: My lord, we have done all that lies in us, And more than well the Church can tolerate;

She hath had a dirge sung for her maiden soul;
And but for favor of the King and you,
She had been buried in the open fields,
Where now she is allowed Christian burial.

LEARTES: So? I tell thee, churlish priest,
A minist'ring angel shall my sister be,
When thou liest howling.

HAMLET: The fair Ofelia dead!

QUEEN: Sweets to the sweet; farewell!
I had thought t'adorn thy bridal bed, fair maid,
And not to follow thee unto thy grave.

LEARTES: Forbear the earth awhile. Sister, farewell!

(LEARTES *leaps into the grave*)

Now pour your earth on Olympus high,
And make a hill t'o'ertop old Pelion.
What's he that conjures so?

HAMLET: Behold, 'tis I,
Hamlet the Dane!

(HAMLET *leaps in after* LEARTES)

LEARTES: The Devil take thy soul!

(They grapple)

HAMLET: O, thou prayest not well.
I prithee take thy hand from off my throat,
For there is something in me dangerous,
Which let thy wisdom fear. Hold off thy hand!
I lov'd Ofelia as dear as twenty brothers
Could. Show me what thou wilt do for her;
Wilt fight? Wilt fast? Wilt pray?
Wilt drink up vessels? Eat a crocodile?
I'll do't. Com'st thou here to whine?

And where thou talk'st of burying thee alive,
Here let us stand, and let them throw on us
Whole hills of earth, till with the height thereof
Make Ossa as a wart.

KING: Forbear, Leartes;
Now is he mad as is the sea,
Anon as mild and gentle as a dove;
Therefore a while give his wild humor scope.

HAMLET: What is the reason, sir, that you wrong me thus?
I never gave you cause. But stand away;
A cat will mew, a dog will have a day.

(*Exit* HAMLET *and* HORATIO)

QUEEN: Alas, it is his madness makes him thus,
And not his heart, Leartes.

KING: My lord, 'tis so.
(*To* LEARTES) But we'll no longer trifle;
This very day shall Hamlet drink his last;
For presently we mean to send to him.
Therefore, Leartes, be in readiness.

LEARTES: My lord, till then my soul will not be quiet.

KING: Come, Gertred; we'll have Leartes and our son
Make friends and lovers, as befits them both,
Even as they tender us, and love their country.

QUEEN: God grant they may.

(*Exeunt omnes. Enter* HAMLET *and* HORATIO)

HAMLET: Believe me, it grieves me much, Horatio,
That to Leartes I forgot myself;
For by myself methinks I feel his grief,
Though there's a difference in each other's wrong.

(*Enter a* BRAGGART GENTLEMAN)

Horatio, but mark yon waterfly;
The court knows him, but he knows not the court.

GENTLEMAN: Now God save thee, sweet Prince Hamlet.

HAMLET: And you, sir. *(Aside)* Foh, how the musk cod smells!

GENTLEMAN: I come with an embassage from His Majesty to you.

HAMLET: I shall, sir, give you attention. By my troth, methinks it is very cold.

GENTLEMAN: It is, indeed, very rawish cold.

HAMLET: 'Tis hot methinks.

GENTLEMAN: Very swoltery hot. The King, sweet Prince, hath laid a wager on your side, six Barbary horse against six French rapiers, with all their accoutrements, too, a' the carriages. In good faith, they are very curiously wrought.

HAMLET: The carriages, sir? I do not know what you mean.

GENTLEMAN: The girdles and hangers, sir, and such like.

HAMLET: The word had been more cousin-german to the phrase if he could have carried the cannon by his side. And how's the wager? I understand you now.

GENTLEMAN: Marry, sir, that young Leartes in twelve venies at rapier and dagger do not get three odds of you; and on your side the King hath laid, and desires you to be in readiness.

HAMLET: Very well; if the King dare venture his wager, I dare venture my skull. When must this be?

GENTLEMAN: My lord, presently. The King and Her Majesty with the rest of the best judgment in the court are coming down into the outward palace.

HAMLET: Go tell His Majesty I will attend him.

GENTLEMAN: I shall deliver your most sweet answer.

(Exit)

HAMLET: You may, sir; none better, for y'are spiced, else he had a bad
nose could not smell a fool.

HORATIO: He will disclose himself without inquiry.

HAMLET: Believe me, Horatio, my heart is on the sudden very sore all
here about.

HORATIO: My lord, forbear the challenge then.

HAMLET: No, Horatio, not I; if danger be now, why, then it is not to
come. There's a predestinate providence in the fall of a sparrow.—
Here comes the King.

(Enter KING, QUEEN, LEARTES, LORDS *with foils and gauntlets; a table and
flagons of wine on it)*

KING: Now, son Hamlet, we have laid upon your head,
And make no question but to have the best.

HAMLET: Your Majesty hath laid a' the weaker side.

KING: We doubt it not. Deliver them the foils.

HAMLET: First, Leartes, here's my hand and love,
Protesting that I never wrong'd Leartes.
If Hamlet in his madness did amiss,
That was not Hamlet but his madness did it;
And all the wrong I e'er did to Leartes
I here proclaim was madness. Therefore let's be at peace,
And think I have shot mine arrow o'er the house
And hurt my brother.

LEARTES: Sir, I am satisfied
In nature, but in terms of honor
I'll stand aloof, and will no reconcilement

Till by some elder masters of our time
I may be satisfied.

KING: Give them the foils.

HAMLET: I'll be your foil, Leartes. These foils have all a length?
Come on, sir.   *(Here they play)*
        A hit!

LEARTES: No, none.

HAMLET: Judgment!

GENTLEMAN: A hit, a most palpable hit.

LEARTES: Well, come again.

(They play again)

HAMLET: Another! Judgment.

LEARTES: Ay, I grant; a touch, a touch.

KING: Here, Hamlet, the King doth drink a health to thee.

QUEEN: Here, Hamlet, take my napkin, wipe thy face.

KING: Give him the wine.

HAMLET: Set it by; I'll have another bout first.
I'll drink anon.

QUEEN: Here, Hamlet, thy mother drinks to thee.

(She drinks)

KING: Do not drink, Gertred. O, 'tis the pois'ned cup!

HAMLET: Leartes, come; you dally with me.
I pray you, pass with your most cunningst play.

LEARTES: Ay! say you so? Have at you!
   I'll hit you now, my lord.
   (Aside) And yet it goes almost against my conscience.

HAMLET: Come on, sir.

(They catch one another's rapiers, and both are wounded. LEARTES *falls down; the* QUEEN *falls down and dies)*

KING: Look to the Queen!

QUEEN: O, the drink, the drink, Hamlet, the drink!

HAMLET: Treason, ho! Keep the gates!

GENTLEMAN: How is't, my lords? Leartes?

LEARTES: Even as a coxcomb should;
   Foolishly slain with my own weapon. Hamlet,
   Thou hast not in thee half an hour of life;
   The fatal instrument is in thy hand,
   Unbated and invenomed; thy mother's pois'ned.
   That drink was made for thee.

HAMLET: The pois'ned instrument within my hand?
   Then venom to thy venom! Die damn'd villain!
   Come, drink! Here lies thy union, here!

(The KING *dies)*

LEARTES: O, he is justly served.
   Hamlet, before I die, here take my hand
   And, withal, my love. I do forgive thee.

*(*LEARTES *dies)*

HAMLET: And I thee.
   O, I am dead Horatio; fare thee well.

HORATIO: No, I am more an antique Roman than a Dane;
   Here is some poison left.

HAMLET: Upon my love I charge thee, let it go.
  O, fie, Horatio, and if thou shouldst die,
  What a scandal wouldst thou leave behind!
  What tongue should tell the story of our deaths,
  If not from thee? O, my heart sinks, Horatio;
  Mine eyes have lost their sight, my tongue his use.
  Farewell, Horatio. Heaven receive my soul!

(HAMLET *dies. Enter the* AMBASSADORS *from England; enter* FORTENBRASSE
with his train)

FORTENBRASSE: Where is this bloody sight?

HORATIO: If aught of woe or wonder you'd behold,
  Then look upon this tragic spectacle.

FORTENBRASSE: O, imperious Death! how many princes
  Hast thou at one draft bloodily shot to death!

AMBASSADOR: Our embassy that we have brought from England,
  Where be these princes that should hear us speak?
  O, most unlooked for time! Unhappy country!

HORATIO: Content yourselves; I'll show to all the ground,
  The first beginning of this tragedy.
  Let there a scaffold be rear'd up in the market place
  And let the State of the world be there,
  Where you shall hear such a sad story told
  That never mortal man could more unfold.

FORTENBRASSE: I have some rights of memory to this kingdom,
  Which now to claim my leisure doth invite me.
  Let four of our chiefest captains
  Bear Hamlet, like a soldier, to his grave;
  For he was likely, had he lived, to a' prov'd
  Most royal.
  Take up the body. Such a fight as this
  Becomes the field, but here doth much amiss.

(*Exeunt.*)

THE CHANGELING

Thomas Middleton and William Rowley

THOMAS MIDDLETON (1580–1627), the son of a wealthy London brick-layer, wrote several plays including A *Game of Chess* and *Women Beware Women*, but his masterpiece is surely *The Changeling*, which he wrote in collaboration with William Rowley (1585?–1626), a professional drama-tist who often contributed comic subplots to collaborative dramas.

According to the list of characters, the changeling is the secondary character, Antonio, who feigns madness in order to try the virtue of the wife of the asylum chief, but in fact, the title of the play applies to the characters of the main plot and especially Beatrice-Joanna, who, in com-promising her better nature, condemns herself to terrible moral degra-dation.

The Changeling, licensed for performance in 1623 and first printed thirty years later, contains a minimum of onstage grisliness and is re-markably easy to read. In my opinion, it is the ethical pinnacle of the early English revenge drama.

DRAMATIS PERSONAE

VERMANDERO, *Father to Beatrice.*

TOMAZO DE PIRACQUO, *a Noble Lord.*

ALONZO DE PIRACQUO, *his brother, suitor to Beatrice.*

ALSEMERO, a Nobleman, *afterwards married to Beatrice.*

JASPERINO, *his friend.*

ALIBIUS, *a jealous doctor.*

LOLLIO, *his man.*

PEDRO, *friend to Antonio.*

ANTONIO, *the Changeling.*

FRANCISCUS, *the counterfeit madman.*

DE FLORES, *servant to Vermandero.*

Madmen, servants.

BEATRICE-JOANNA, *daughter to Vermandero.*

DIAPHANTA, *her waiting-woman.*

ISABELLA, *wife to Alibius.*

Scene: The Spanish seaport of Alicante.

ACT ONE

Scene One

Enter ALSEMERO.

ALSEMERO: 'Twas in the temple where I first beheld her,
 And now again the same; what omen yet
 Follows of that? None but imaginary;
 Why should my hopes or fate be timorous?
 The place is holy, so is my intent:
 I love her beauties to the holy purpose,
 And that, methinks, admits comparison
 With man's first creation, the place blest,
 And is his right home back, if he achieve it.
 The church hath first begun our interview,
 And that's the place must join us into one,
 So there's beginning and perfection, too.

(Enter JASPERINO*)*

JASPERINO: Oh sir, are you here? Come, the wind's fair with you,
 Y'are like to have a swift and pleasant passage.

ALSEMERO: Sure y'are deceived, friend, 'tis contrary
 In my best judgment.

JASPERINO: What, for Malta?
 If you could buy a gale amongst the witches,
 They could not serve you such a lucky pennyworth
 As comes a'God's name.

ALSEMERO: Even now I observed
 The temple's vane to turn full in my face;
 I know 'tis against me.

JASPERINO: Against you?
 Then you know not where you are.

ALSEMERO: Not well indeed.

JASPERINO: Are you not well, sir?

ALSEMERO: Yes, Jasperino,
   —Unless there be some hidden malady
   Within me, that I understand not.

JASPERINO: And that
   I begin to doubt, sir; I never knew
   Your inclinations to travels at a pause
   With any cause to hinder it, till now.
   Ashore, you were wont to call your servants up
   And help to trap your horses for the speed;
   At sea, I have seen you weigh the anchor with'em,
   Hoist sails for fear to lose the foremost breath,
   Be in continual prayers for fair winds,—
   And have you changed your orisons?

ALSEMERO: No, friend,
   I keep the same church, same devotion.

JASPERINO: Lover I'm sure y'are none, the Stoic
   Was found in you long ago; your mother
   Nor best friends, who have set snares of beauty—ay,
   And choice ones too—could never trap you that way.
   What might be the cause?

ALSEMERO: Lord, how violent
   Thou art; I was but meditating of
   Somewhat I heard within the temple.

JASPERINO: Is this violence? 'Tis but idleness
   Compared with your haste yesterday.

ALSEMERO: I'm all this while a-going, man.

(*Enter* SERVANTS)

JASPERINO: Backwards I think, sir. Look, your servants.

FIRST SERVANT: The seamen call; shall we board your trunks?

ALSEMERO: No, not today.

JASPERINO: 'Tis the critical day it seems, and the sign in Aquarius.

SECOND SERVANT *(aside):* We must not to sea today; this smoke will bring
    forth fire.

ALSEMERO: Keep all on shore; I do not know the end
    (Which needs I must do) of an affair in hand
    Ere I can go to sea.

FIRST SERVANT: Well, your pleasure.

SECOND SERVANT *(aside):* Let him e'en take his leisure too; we are safer
    on land.

(Exeunt SERVANTS. *Enter* BEATRICE, DIAPHANTA *and* SERVANTS. ALSEMERO *greets
and kisses* BEATRICE)

JASPERINO *(aside):* How now! The laws of the Medes are changed, sure.
    Salute a woman? He kisses too—wonderful! Where learnt he this?
    And does it perfectly too—in my conscience, he ne'er rehearsed it
    before. Nay, go on, this will be stranger and better news at Valencia
    than if he had ransomed half Greece from the Turk.

BEATRICE: You are a scholar, sir.

ALSEMERO: A weak one, lady.

BEATRICE: Which of the sciences is this love you speak of?

ALSEMERO: From your tongue I take it to be music.

BEATRICE: You are skillful in't, can sing at first sight.

ALSEMERO: And I have showed you all my skill at once.
    I want more words to express me further
    And must be forced to repetition:
    I love you dearly.

BEATRICE: Be better advised, sir:

Our eyes are sentinels unto our judgments
And should give certain judgment what they see;
But they are rash sometimes, and tell us wonders
Of common things, which when our judgments find,
They can then check the eyes, and call them blind.

ALSEMERO: But I am further, lady; yesterday
Was mine eyes' employment, and hither now
They brought my judgment, where are both agreed.
Both houses then consenting, 'tis agreed;
Only there wants the confirmation
By the hand royal, that's your part, lady.

BEATRICE: Oh, there's one above me, sir. *(Aside)* For five days past
To be recalled! Sure, mine eyes were mistaken,
This was the man was meant me; that he should come
So near his time, and miss it!

JASPERINO *(aside):* We might have come by the carriers from Valencia, I
see, and saved all our sea-provision; we are at farthest, sure. Methinks
I should do something too.
I meant to be a venturer in this voyage.
Yonder's another vessel, I'll board her,
If she be lawful prize, down goes her topsail.

(Greets DIAPHANTA. *Enter* DE FLORES*)*

DE FLORES: Lady, your father—

BEATRICE: Is in health, I hope.

DE FLORES: Your eye shall instantly instruct you, lady.
He's coming hitherward.

BEATRICE: What needed then
Your duteous preface? I had rather
He had come unexpected; you must 'stall
A good presence with unnecessary blabbing.—
And how welcome for your part you are
I'm sure you know.

DE FLORES *(aside)*: Wilt never mend, this scorn,
   One side nor other? Must I be enjoined
   To follow still whilst she flies from me? Well,
   Fates do your worst, I'll please myself with sight
   Of her, at all opportunities,
   If but to spite her anger; I know she had
   Rather see me dead than living, and yet
   She knows no cause for't, but a peevish will.

ALSEMERO: You seem'd displeased, lady, on the sudden.

BEATRICE: Your pardon sir, 'tis my infirmity,
   Nor can I other reason render you
   Than his or hers, or some particular thing
   They must abandon as a deadly poison,
   Which to a thousand other tastes were wholesome;
   Such to mine eyes is that same fellow there,
   The same that report speaks of the basilisk.

ALSEMERO: This is a frequent frailty in our nature;
   There's scarce a man amongst a thousand sound,
   But hath his imperfection: one distastes
   The scent of roses, which to infinites
   Most pleasing is, and odoriferous;
   One oil, the enemy of poison;
   Another wine, the cheerer of the heart
   And lively refresher of the countenance.
   Indeed this fault, if so it be, is general;
   There's scarce a thing but is both loved and loathed,—
   Myself, I must confess, have the same frailty.

BEATRICE: And what may be your poison, sir? I am bold with you.

ALSEMERO: What might be your desire perhaps, a cherry.

BEATRICE: I am no enemy to any creature
   My memory has, but yon gentleman.

ALSEMERO: He does ill to tempt your sight, if he knew it.

BEATRICE: He cannot be ignorant of that, sir,

I have not spared to tell him so; and I want
To help myself, since he's a gentleman
In good respect with my father, and follows him.

ALSEMERO: He's out of his place then, now.

(They talk apart)

JASPERINO: I'm a mad wag, wench.

DIAPHANTA: So methinks; but for your comfort I can tell you, we have a
doctor in the city that undertakes the cure of such.

JASPERINO: Tush, I know what physic is best for the state of mine own
body.

DIAPHANTA: 'Tis scarce a well-governed state, I believe.

JASPERINO: I could show thee such a thing with an ingredient that we two
would compound together, and if it did not tame the maddest blood
i'th'town for two hours after, I'll ne'er profess physic again.

DIAPHANTA: A little poppy, sir, were good to cause you sleep.

JASPERINO: Poppy? I'll give thee a pop i'th'lips for that first, and begin
there: *(kisses her)* poppy is one cure, indeed, and cuckoo what-you-
call't another: I'll discover no more now, another time I'll show thee
all.

BEATRICE: My father, sir.

(Enter VERMANDERO *and servants)*

VERMANDERO: Oh, Joanna, I came to meet thee,—
Your devotion's ended?

BEATRICE: For this time, sir.
   (Aside) I shall change my saint, I fear me; I find
   A giddy turning in me. *(To* VERMANDERO) Sir, this while
   I am beholding to this gentleman
   Who left his own way to keep me company,

And in discourse I find him much desirous
To see your castle: he hath deserved it, sir,
If ye please to grant it.

VERMANDERO: With all my heart, sir.
Yet there's an article between, I must know
Your country; we use not to give survey
Of our chief strengths to strangers; our citadels
Are placed conspicuous to outward view
On promonts' tops; but within are secrets.

ALSEMERO: A Valencian, sir.

VERMANDERO: A Valencian?
That's native, sir; of what name, I beseech you?

ALSEMERO: Alsemero, sir.

VERMANDERO: Alsemero? Not the son
Of John de Alsemero?

ALSEMERO: The same, sir.

VERMANDERO: My best love bids you welcome.

BEATRICE *(aside)*:   He was wont
To call me so, and then he speaks a most
Unfeigned truth.

VERMANDERO: Oh sir, I knew your father;
We two were in acquaintance long ago,
Before our chins were worth Iulan down,
And so continued till the stamp of time
Had coined us into silver: well, he's gone—
A good soldier went with him.

ALSEMERO: You went together in that, sir.

VERMANDERO: No, by Saint Jacques, I came behind him.
Yet I have done somewhat too; an unhappy day
Swallowed him at last at Gibraltar

In fight with those rebellious Hollanders,
Was it not so?

ALSEMERO: Whose death I had revenged
Or followed him in fate, had not the late league
Prevented me.

VERMANDERO: Ay, ay, 'twas time to breathe:
Oh, Joanna, I should ha'told thee news,
I saw Piracquo lately.

BEATRICE *(aside)*:   That's ill news.

VERMANDERO: He's hot preparing for this day of triumph,
Thou must be a bride within this sevennight.

ALSEMERO *(aside)*:   Ha!

BEATRICE: Nay, good sir, be not so violent, with speed
I cannot render satisfaction
Unto the dear companion of my soul,
Virginity, whom I thus long have lived with,
And part with it so rude and suddenly;
Can such friends divide, never to meet again,
Without a solemn farewell?

VERMANDERO: Tush, tush, there's a toy.

ALSEMERO *(aside)*: I must now part, and never meet again
With any joy on earth. *(To* VERMANDERO*)* Sir, your pardon,
My affairs call on me.

VERMANDERO: How, sir? By no means;
Not changed so soon, I hope? You must see my castle
And her best entertainment, ere we part;
I shall think myself unkindly used else.
Come, come, let's on; I had good hope your stay
Had been a while with us in Alicant;
I might have bid you to my daughter's wedding.

ALSEMERO *(aside):* He means to feast me, and poisons me beforehand.
　(To VERMANDERO*)* I should be dearly glad to be there, sir,
　Did my occasions suit as I could wish.

BEATRICE: I shall be sorry if you be not there
　When it is done, sir—but not so suddenly.

VERMANDERO: I tell you sir, the gentleman's complete,
　A courtier and a gallant, enriched
　With many fair and noble ornaments;
　I would not change him for a son-in-law
　For any he in Spain, the proudest he,—
　And we have great ones, that you know.

ALSEMERO:　　　　　　　　　　　　　　　　　He's much
　Bound to you, sir.

VERMANDERO:　　　　　He shall be bound to me
　As fast as this tie can hold him; I'll want
　My will else.

BEATRICE *(aside):* I shall want mine if you do it.

VERMANDERO: But come, by the way I'll tell you more of him.

ALSEMERO *(aside):* How shall I dare to venture in his castle,
　When he discharges cannonballs at the gate?
　But I must on, for back I cannot go.

BEATRICE *(aside):* Not this serpent gone yet?　　　　　*(Drops glove)*

VERMANDERO:　　　　　　　　　　　Look girl, thy glove's fall'n;
　Stay, stay, —De Flores, help a little.

(Exeunt VERMANDERO, ALSEMERO, JASPERINO *and* SERVANTS*)*

DE FLORES *(offering glove):*　　　　　　Here, lady.

BEATRICE: Mischief on your officious forwardness!
　Who bade you stoop? They touch my hand no more:
　There, for t'other's sake I part with this;

(Takes off and throws down second glove)
Take 'em and draw thine own skin off with 'em.
(Exeunt all but DE FLORES*)*

DE FLORES: Here's a favor come—with a mischief! Now I know
  She had rather wear my pelt tanned in a pair
  Of dancing pumps, than I should thrust my fingers
  Into her sockets here; I know she hates me,
  Yet cannot choose but love her;
  No matter; if but to vex her, I'll haunt her still,
  Though I get nothing else, I'll have my will.

(Exit.)

Scene Two

Enter ALIBIUS *and* LOLLIO.

ALIBIUS: Lollio, I must trust thee with a secret,
  But thou must keep it.

LOLLIO: I was ever close to a secret, sir.

ALIBIUS: The diligence that I have found in thee,
  The care and industry already past,
  Assures me of thy good continuance.
  Lollio, I have a wife.

LOLLIO: Fie sir, 'tis too late to keep her secret, she's known to be married
  all the town and country over.

ALIBIUS: Thou goest too fast, my Lollio; that knowledge
  I allow no man can be barred it;
  But there is a knowledge which is nearer,
  Deeper and sweeter, Lollio.

LOLLIO: Well sir, let us handle that between you and I.

ALIBIUS: 'Tis that I go about, man; Lollio,
  My wife is young.

LOLLIO: So much the worse to be kept secret, sir.

ALIBIUS: Why now thou meet'st the substance of the point:
I am old, Lollio.

LOLLIO: No, sir, 'tis I am old Lollio.

ALIBIUS: Yet why may not this concord and sympathize?
Old trees and young plants often grow together,
Well enough agreeing.

LOLLIO: Ay sir, but the old trees raise themselves higher and broader
than the young plants.

ALIBIUS: Shrewd application! There's the fear, man;
I would wear my ring on my own finger;
Whilst it is borrowed it is none of mine,
But his that useth it.

LOLLIO: You must keep it on still, then; if it but lie by, one or other will
be thrusting into it.

ALIBIUS: Thou conceiv'st me, Lollio; here thy watchful eye
Must have employment; I cannot always be
At home.

LOLLIO: I dare swear you cannot.

ALIBIUS: I must look out.

LOLLIO: I know't, you must look out, 'tis every man's case.

ALIBIUS: Here I do say must thy employment be,
To watch her treadings, and in my absence
Supply my place.

LOLLIO: I'll do my best, sir, yet surely I cannot see who you should have
cause to be jealous of.

ALIBIUS: Thy reason for that, Lollio? 'Tis a comfortable question.

LOLLIO: We have but two sorts of people in the house, and both under the whip—that's fools and madmen; the one has not wit enough to be knaves, and the other not knavery enough to be fools.

ALIBIUS: Ay, those are all my patients, Lollio.
I do profess the cure of either sort:
My trade, my living 'tis, I thrive by it;
But here's the care that mixes with my thrift:
The daily visitants, that come to see
My brainsick patients, I would not have
To see my wife: gallants I do observe
Of quick enticing eyes, rich in habits,
Of stature and proportion very comely.—
These are most shrewd temptations, Lollio.

LOLLIO: They may be easily answered, sir; if they come to see the fools and madmen, you and I may serve the turn, and let my mistress alone —she's of neither sort.

ALIBIUS: 'Tis a good ward; indeed, come they to see
Our madmen or our fools, let 'em see no more
Than what they come for; by that consequent
They must not see her; I'm sure she's no fool.

LOLLIO: And I'm sure she's no madman.

ALIBIUS: Hold that buckler fast, Lollio; my trust
Is on thee, and I account it firm and strong.
What hour is't, Lollio?

LOLLIO: Towards belly-hour, sir.

ALIBIUS: Dinner time? Thou mean'st twelve o'clock.

LOLLIO: Yes sir, for every part has his hour; we wake at six and look about us, that's eye-hour; at seven we should pray, that's knee-hour; at eight walk, that's leg-hour; at nine gather flowers and pluck a rose, that's nose-hour; at ten we drink, that's mouth-hour; at eleven lay about us for victuals, that's hand-hour; at twelve go to dinner, that's belly-hour.

ALIBIUS: Profoundly, Lollio! It will be long
  Ere all thy scholars learn this lesson, and
  I did look to have a new one entered; —stay,
  I think my expectation is come home.

(Enter PEDRO *and* ANTONIO *like an Idiot)*

PEDRO: Save you, sir; my business speaks itself,
  This sight takes off the labor of my tongue.

ALIBIUS: Ay, ay, sir;
  'Tis plain enough, you mean him for my patient.

PEDRO: And if your pains prove but commodious, to give but some little
  strength to his sick and weak part of nature in him, these *(giving him
  money)* are but patterns to show you of the whole pieces that will
  follow to you, beside the charge of diet, washing and other necessaries
  fully defrayed.

ALIBIUS: Believe it sir, there shall no care be wanting.

LOLLIO: Sir, an officer in this place may deserve something; the trouble
  will pass through my hands.

PEDRO: 'Tis fit something should come to your hands then, sir.

(Gives him money)

LOLLIO: Yes sir, 'tis I must keep him sweet, and read to him. What is his
  name?

PEDRO: His name is Antonio; marry, we use but half to him, only Tony.

LOLLIO: Tony, Tony, 'tis enough, and a very good name for a fool; what's
  your name, Tony?

ANTONIO: He, he, he! Well, I thank you, cousin; he, he, he!

LOLLIO: Good boy! Hold up your head: he can laugh, I perceive by that
  he is no beast.

PEDRO: Well, sir,
  If you can raise him but to any height,
  Any degree of wit, might he attain,
  As I might say, to creep but on all four
  Towards the chair of wit, or walk on crutches,
  'Twould add an honor to your worthy pains,
  And a great family might pray for you,
  To which he should be heir, had he discretion
  To claim and guide his own; assure you, sir,
  He is a gentleman.

LOLLIO: Nay, there's nobody doubted that; at first sight I knew him for a gentleman, he looks no other yet.

PEDRO: Let him have good attendance and sweet lodging.

LOLLIO: As good as my mistress lies in, sir; and as you allow us time and means, we can raise him to the higher degree of discretion.

PEDRO: Nay, there shall no cost want, sir.

LOLLIO: He will hardly be stretched up to the wit of a magnifico.

PEDRO: Oh no, that's not to be expected, far shorter will be enough.

LOLLIO: I'll warrant you I'll make him fit to bear office in five weeks; I'll undertake to wind him up to the wit of constable.

PEDRO: If it be lower than that it might serve turn.

LOLLIO: No, fie, to level him with a headborough, beadle or watchman were but little better than he is; constable I'll able him: if he do come to be a justice afterwards, let him thank the keeper. Or I'll go further with you; say I do bring him up to my own pitch, say I make him as wise as myself.

PEDRO: Why, there I would have it.

LOLLIO: Well, go to; either I'll be as arrant a fool as he, or he shall be as wise as I, and then I think 'twill serve his turn.

PEDRO: Nay, I do like thy wit passing well.

LOLLIO: Yes, you may, yet if I had not been a fool, I had had more wit than I have too; remember what state you find me in.

PEDRO: I will, and so leave you: your best cares, I beseech you.

ALIBIUS: Take you none with you, leave 'em all with us.

(*Exit* PEDRO)

ANTONIO: Oh, my cousin's gone, cousin, cousin, oh!

LOLLIO: Peace, peace, Tony, you must not cry, child, you must be whipped if you do; your cousin is here still, I am your cousin, Tony.

ANTONIO: He, he, then I'll not cry, if thou be'st my cousin, he, he, he.

LOLLIO: I were best try his wit a little, that I may know what form to place him in.

ALIBIUS: Ay do, Lollio, do.

LOLLIO: I must ask him easy questions at first; —Tony, how many true fingers has a tailor on his right hand?

ANTONIO: As many as on his left, cousin.

LOLLIO: Good; and how many on both?

ANTONIO: Two less than a deuce, cousin.

LOLLIO: Very well answered. I come to you again, cousin Tony: how many fools equals a wise man?

ANTONIO: Forty in a day sometimes, cousin.

LOLLIO: Forty in a day? How prove you that?

ANTONIO: All that fall out amongst themselves and go to a lawyer to be made friends.

LOLLIO: A parlous fool! He must sit in the fourth form at least, I perceive that. I come again, Tony: how many knaves make an honest man?

ANTONIO: I know not that, cousin.

LOLLIO: No, the question is too hard for you: I'll tell you, cousin; there's three knaves may make an honest man, —a sergeant, a jailor and a beadle; the sergeant catches him, the jailor holds him, and the beadle lashes him; and if he be not honest then, the hangman must cure him.

ANTONIO: Ha, ha, ha, that's fine sport, cousin!

ALIBIUS: This was too deep a question for the fool, Lollio.

LOLLIO: Yes, this might have served yourself, tho' I say't; once more and you shall go play, Tony.

ANTONIO: Ay, play at push-pin, cousin, ha, he!

LOLLIO: So thou shalt; say how many fools are here—

ANTONIO: Two, cousin, thou and I.

LOLLIO: Nay, y'are too forward there, Tony; mark my question: how many fools and knaves are here? —A fool before a knave, a fool behind a knave, between every two fools a knave. —How many fools, how many knaves?

ANTONIO: I never learnt so far, cousin.

ALIBIUS: Thou putt'st too hard questions to him, Lollio.

LOLLIO: I'll make him understand it easily; cousin, stand there.

ANTONIO: Ay, cousin.

LOLLIO: Master, stand you next the fool.

ALIBIUS: Well, Lollio?

LOLLIO: Here's my place: mark now, Tony, there a fool before a knave.

ANTONIO: That's I, cousin.

LOLLIO: Here's a fool behind a knave, that's I; and between us two fools, there's a knave, that's my master; 'tis but we three, that's all.

ANTONIO: We three, we three, cousin!

(Madmen within)

FIRST WITHIN: Put's head i'th' pillory, the bread's too little.

SECOND WITHIN: Fly, fly, and he catches the swallow.

THIRD WITHIN: Give her more onion, or the Devil put the rope about her neck.

LOLLIO: You may hear what time of day it is, the chimes of Bedlam goes.

ALIBIUS: Peace, peace, or the lash comes!

THIRD WITHIN: Cat-whore, cat-whore, her Parmesan, her Parmesan!

ALIBIUS: Peace, I say! Their hour's come, they must be fed, Lollio.

LOLLIO: There's no hope of recovery of that Welsh madman, was undone by a mouse that spoiled him a Parmesan; lost his wits for't.

ALIBIUS: Go to your charge, Lollio, I'll to mine.

LOLLIO: Go you to your madmen's ward, let me alone with your fools.

ALIBIUS: And remember my last charge, Lollio.

(Exit)

LOLLIO: Of which your patients do you think I am? Come, Tony, you must amongst your school-fellows now; there's pretty scholars amongst 'em, I can tell you; there's some of 'em at *stultus, stulta, stultum.*

ANTONIO: I would see the madmen, cousin, if they would not bite me.

LOLLIO: No, they shall not bite thee, Tony.

ANTONIO: They bite when they are at dinner, do they not, coz?

LOLLIO: They bite at dinner indeed, Tony. Well, I hope to get credit by
thee; I like thee the best of all the scholars that ever I brought up, and
thou shalt prove a wise man, or I'll prove a fool myself.

(Exeunt.)

ACT TWO

Scene One

Enter BEATRICE *and* JASPERINO *severally.*

BEATRICE: Oh, sir, I'm ready now for that fair service
Which makes the name of friend sit glorious on you.
Good angels and this conduct be your guide,—
(Gives him a paper)
Fitness of time and place is there set down, sir.

JASPERINO: The joy I shall return rewards my service.

(Exit)

BEATRICE: How wise is Alsemero in his friend!
It is a sign he makes his choice with judgment.
Then I appear in nothing more approved,
Than making choice of him;
For 'tis a principle, he that can choose
That bosom well, who of his thoughts partakes,
Proves most discreet in every choice he makes.
Methinks I love now with the eyes of judgment,
And see the way to merit, clearly see it.
A true deserver like a diamond sparkles,
In darkness you may see him, that's in absence,
Which is the greatest darkness falls on love;

Yet is he best discerned then
With intellectual eyesight; what's Piracquo
My father spends his breath for? And his blessing
Is only mine as I regard his name,
Else it goes from me, and turns head against me,
Transformed into a curse. Some speedy way
Must be remembered; he's so forward too,
So urgent that way, scarce allows me breath
To speak to my new comforts.

(*Enter* DE FLORES)

DE FLORES (*aside*):   Yonder's she.
　Whatever ails me, now o'late especially,
　I can as well be hanged as refrain seeing her;
　Some twenty times a day, nay, not so little,
　Do I force errands, frame ways and excuses
　To come into her sight, and I have small reason for't,
　And less encouragement; for she baits me still
　Every time worse than other, does profess herself
　The cruellest enemy to my face in town,
　At no hand can abide the sight of me,
　As if danger, or ill luck hung in my looks.
　I must confess my face is bad enough,
　But I know far worse has better fortune,
　And not endured alone, but doted on;
　And yet such pick-haired faces, chins like witches',
　Here and there five hairs, whispering in a corner,
　As if they grew in fear one of another,
　Wrinkles like troughs, where swine deformity swills
　The tears of perjury that lie there like wash
　Fallen from the slimy and dishonest eye,—
　Yet such a one plucked sweets without restraint,
　And has the grace of beauty to his sweet.
　Though my hard fate has thrust me out to servitude,
　I tumbled into th'world a gentleman.—
　She turns her blessed eye upon me now,
　And I'll endure all storms before I part with't.

BEATRICE *(aside):* Again!
This ominous ill-faced fellow more disturbs me
Than all my other passions.

DE FLORES *(aside):*   Now't begins again;
I'll stand this storm of hail though the stones pelt me.

BEATRICE: Thy business? What's thy business?

DE FLORES *(aside):*   Soft and fair,
I cannot part so soon now.

BEATRICE *(aside):*   The villain's fixed—
(To DE FLORES*)* Thou standing toad-pool!

DE FLORES *(aside):*   The shower falls amain now.

BEATRICE: Who sent thee? What's thy errand? Leave my sight.

DE FLORES: My lord your father charged me to deliver
A message to you.

BEATRICE: What, another since?
Do't and be hanged then, let me be rid of thee.

DE FLORES: True service merits mercy.

BEATRICE: What's thy message?

DE FLORES: Let beauty settle but in patience,
You shall hear all.

BEATRICE: A dallying, trifling torment!

DE FLORES: Signor Alonzo de Piracquo, lady,
Sole brother to Tomazo de Piracquo—

BEATRICE: Slave, when wilt make an end?

DE FLORES *(aside):*   Too soon I shall.

BEATRICE: What all this while of him?

DE FLORES: The said Alonzo,
    With the foresaid Tomazo—

BEATRICE: Yet again?

DE FLORES: Is new alighted.

BEATRICE: Vengeance strike the news!
    Thou thing most loathed, what cause was there in this
    To bring thee to my sight?

DE FLORES: My lord your father
    Charged me to seek you out.

BEATRICE: Is there no other
    To send his errand by?

DE FLORES: It seems 'tis my luck
    To be i'th'way still.

BEATRICE: Get thee from me!

DE FLORES: So;—
    (Aside) Why, am not I an ass, to devise ways
    Thus to be railed at? I must see her still.
    I shall have a mad qualm within this hour again,
    I know't; and like a common Garden-bull,
    I do but take breath to be jogged again.
    What this may bode I know not; I'll despair the less,
    Because there's daily precedents of bad faces
    Belov'd beyond all reason; these foul chops
    May come into favor one day, 'mongst his fellows:
    Wrangling has proved the mistress of good pastime;
    As children cry themselves asleep, I ha'seen
    Women have chid themselves abed to men.

(Exit DE FLORES)

BEATRICE: I never see this fellow, but I think
  Of some harm towards me, danger's in my mind still,
  I scarce leave trembling of an hour after.
  The next good mood I find my father in,
  I'll get him quite discarded;—oh, I was
  Lost in this small disturbance, and forgot
  Affliction's fiercer torrent, that now comes
  To bear down all my comforts.

(*Enter* VERMANDERO, ALONZO, TOMAZO)

VERMANDERO: Y'are both welcome,
  But an especial one belongs to you, sir,
  To whose most noble name our love presents
  The addition of a son, our son Alonzo.

ALONZO: The treasury of honor cannot bring forth
  A title I should more rejoice in, sir.

VERMANDERO: You have improved it well; daughter, prepare,
  The day will steal upon thee suddenly.

BEATRICE (*aside*): Howe'er, I will, be sure, beware the night,
  If it should come so near me.

(BEATRICE *and* VERMANDERO *talk apart*)

TOMAZO: Alonzo.

ALONZO: Brother?

TOMAZO: In troth I see small welcome in her eye.

ALONZO: Fie, you are too severe a censurer
  Of love in all points, there's no bringing on you.
  If lovers should mark everything a fault,
  Affection would be like an ill-set book
  Whose faults might prove as big as half the volume.

BEATRICE: That's all I do entreat.

VERMANDERO: It is but reasonable:
  I'll see what my son says to't: son Alonzo,
  Here's a motion made but to reprieve
  A maidenhead three days longer; the request
  Is not far out of reason, for indeed
  The former time is pinching.

ALONZO: Though my joys
  Be set back so much time as I could wish
  They had been forward, yet since she desires it,
  The time is set as pleasing as before,
  I find no gladness wanting.

VERMANDERO: May I ever meet it in that point still:
  Y'are nobly welcome, sirs.

(Exeunt VERMANDERO *and* BEATRICE)

TOMAZO: So; did you mark the dullness of her parting now?

ALONZO: What dullness? Thou art so exceptious still.

TOMAZO: Why, let it go then, I am but a fool
  To mark your harms so heedfully.

ALONZO: Where's the oversight?

TOMAZO: Come, your faith's cozened in her, strongly cozened:
  Unsettle your affection with all speed
  Wisdom can bring it to, your peace is ruined else.
  Think what a torment 'tis to marry one
  Whose heart is leapt into another's bosom:
  If ever pleasure she receive from thee,
  It comes not in thy name, or of thy gift;
  She lies but with another in thine arms,
  He the half-father unto all thy children
  In the conception; if he get'em not,
  She helps to get'em for him, in his passions, and how dangerous
  And shameful her restraint may go in time to,
  It is not to be thought on without sufferings.

ALONZO: You speak as if she loved some other, then.

TOMAZO: Do you apprehend so slowly?

ALONZO: Nay, if that
   Be your fear only, I am safe enough.
   Preserve your friendship and your counsel, brother,
   For times of more distress; I should depart
   An enemy, a dangerous, deadly one
   To any but thyself, that should but think
   She knew the meaning of inconstancy,
   Much less the use and practice; yet w'are friends.
   Pray let no more be urged; I can endure
   Much, till I meet an injury to her,
   Then I am not myself. Farewell, sweet brother,
   How much w'are bound to Heaven to depart lovingly.

(Exit)

TOMAZO: Why, here is love's tame madness, thus a man
   Quickly steals into his vexation.

(Exit.)

Scene Two

Enter DIAPHANTA *and* ALSEMERO.

DIAPHANTA: The place is my charge, you have kept your hour,
   And the reward of a just meeting bless you.
   I hear my lady coming; complete gentlemen,
   I dare not be too busy with my praises,
   Th'are dangerous things to deal with.

(Exit)

ALSEMERO: This goes well;
   These women are the ladies' cabinets,
   Things of most precious trust are locked into'em.

(*Enter* BEATRICE)

BEATRICE: I have within mine eye all my desires;
 Requests that holy prayers ascend Heaven for,
 And brings'em down to furnish our defects,
 Come not more sweet to our necessities
 Than thou unto my wishes.

ALSEMERO: W'are so like
 In our expressions, lady, that unless I borrow
 The same words, I shall never find their equals.

(*They embrace*)

BEATRICE: How happy were this meeting, this embrace,
 If it were free from envy! This poor kiss,
 It has an enemy, a hateful one,
 That wishes poison to't: how well were I now
 If there were none such name known as Piracquo,
 Nor no such tie as the command of parents.
 I should be but too much blessed.

ALSEMERO: One good service
 Would strike off both your fears, and I'll go near it too,
 Since you are so distressed; remove the cause,
 The command ceases, so there's two fears blown out
 With one and the same blast.

BEATRICE: Pray let me find you, sir.
 What might that service be, so strangely happy?

ALSEMERO: The honorablest piece 'bout man, valor.
 I'll send a challenge to Piracquo instantly.

BEATRICE: How? Call you that extinguishing of fear,
 When 'tis the only way to keep it flaming?
 Are not you ventured in the action
 That's all my joys and comforts? Pray, no more, sir.
 Say you prevailed, you're danger's and not mine then;
 The law would claim you from me, or obscurity
 Be made the grave to bury you alive.

I'm glad these thoughts come forth; oh keep not one
Of this condition, sir; here was a course
Found to bring sorrow on her way to death:
The tears would ne'er ha'dried till dust had choked'em.
Blood-guiltiness becomes a fouler visage,—
(*Aside*) And now I think on one,—I was to blame,
I ha'marred so good a market with my scorn;
'T had been done questionless; the ugliest creature
Creation framed for some use, yet to see
I could not mark so much where it should be!

ALSEMERO: Lady—

BEATRICE (*aside*): Why, men of art make much of poison,
    Keep one to expel another; where was my art?

ALSEMERO: Lady, you hear not me.

BEATRICE: I do especially, sir;
    The present times are not so sure of our side
    As those hereafter may be; we must use'em then
    As thrifty folks their wealth, sparingly now,
    Till the time opens.

ALSEMERO: You teach wisdom, lady.

BEATRICE: Within there—Diaphanta!

(*Enter* DIAPHANTA)

DIAPHANTA: Do you call, madam?

BEATRICE: Perfect your service and conduct this gentleman
    The private way you brought him.

DIAPHANTA: I shall, madam.

ALSEMERO: My love's as firm as love e'er built upon.

(*Exeunt* DIAPHANTA *and* ALSEMERO. *Enter* DE FLORES)

DE FLORES *(aside):* I have watched this meeting, and do wonder much
   What shall become of t'other; I'm sure both
   Cannot be served unless she transgress; happily
   Then I'll put in for one: for if a woman
   Fly from one point, from him she makes a husband,
   She spreads and mounts then like arithmetic,
   One, ten, a hundred, a thousand, ten thousand,
   Proves in time sutler to an army royal.
   —Now do I look to be most richly railed at,
   Yet I must see her.

BEATRICE *(aside):*   Why, put case I loathed him
   As much as youth and beauty hates a sepulchre,
   Must I needs show it? Cannot I keep that secret
   And serve my turn upon him? See, he's here.
   —De Flores.

DE FLORES *(aside):* Ha, I shall run mad with joy!
   She called me fairly by my name, De Flores,
   And neither rogue nor rascal.

BEATRICE: What ha' you done
   To your face a-late? Y'ave met with some good physician;
   Y'ave pruned yourself methinks, you were not wont
   To look so amorously.

DE FLORES: Not I.—
   (Aside) 'Tis the same phys'nomy to a hair and pimple,
   Which she called scurvy scarce an hour ago:
   How is this?

BEATRICE: Come hither; nearer, man.

DE FLORES *(aside):* I'm up to the chin in Heaven!

BEATRICE: Turn, let me see;
   Faugh, 'tis but the heat of the liver, I perceive't.
   I thought it had been worse.

DE FLORES *(aside):*   Her fingers touched me!
   She smells all amber.

BEATRICE: I'll make a water for you shall cleanse this
  Within a fortnight.

DE FLORES: With your own hands, lady?

BEATRICE: Yes, mine own, sir, in a work of cure
  I'll trust no other.

DE FLORES *(aside):*   'Tis half an act of pleasure
  To hear her talk thus to me.

BEATRICE: When we are used
  To a hard face, 'tis not so unpleasing;
  It mends still in opinion, hourly mends,
  I see it by experience.

DE FLORES *(aside):*   I was blest
  To light upon this minute; I'll make use on't.

BEATRICE: Hardness becomes the visage of a man well;
  It argues service, resolution, manhood,
  If cause were of employment.

DE FLORES: 'Twould be soon seen,
  If e'er your ladyship had cause to use it.
  I would but wish the honor of a service
  So happy as that mounts to.

BEATRICE: We shall try you—
  Oh my De Flores!

DE FLORES *(aside):*   How's that?
  She calls me hers already, *my* De Flores!
  —You were about to sigh out somewhat, madam.

BEATRICE: No, was I? I forgot,—Oh!

DE FLORES: There 'tis again,
  The very fellow on't.

BEATRICE: You are too quick, sir.

DE FLORES: There's no excuse for't, now I heard it twice, madam;
That sigh would fain have utterance, take pity on't,
And lend it a free word; 'las, how it labors
For liberty! I hear the murmur yet
Beat at your bosom.

BEATRICE: Would creation—

DE FLORES: Ay, well said, that's it.

BEATRICE: Had formed me man.

DE FLORES: Nay, that's not it.

BEATRICE: Oh, 'tis the soul of freedom!
I should not then be forced to marry one
I hate beyond all depths; I should have power
Then to oppose my loathings, nay, remove'em
For ever from my sight.

DE FLORES: Oh blest occasion! —
Without change to your sex, you have your wishes.
Claim so much man in me.

BEATRICE: In thee, De Flores?
There's small cause for that.

DE FLORES: Put it not from me,
It's a service that I kneel for to you.

(Kneels)

BEATRICE: You are too violent to mean faithfully;
There's horror in my service, blood and danger,
Can those be things to sue for?

DE FLORES: If you knew
How sweet it were to me to be employed
In any act of yours, you would say then
I failed, and used not reverence enough
When I receive the charge on't.

BEATRICE *(aside)*:   This is much, methinks;
  Belike his wants are greedy, and to such
  Gold tastes like angels' food. *(To* DE FLORES*)*—Rise.

DE FLORES: I'll have the work first.

BEATRICE *(aside)*:   Possible his need
  Is strong upon him; *(Giving him money)*—there's to encourage
    thee:
  As thou art forward and thy service dangerous,
  Thy reward shall be precious.

DE FLORES: That I have thought on;
  I have assured myself of that beforehand,
  And know it will be precious—the thought ravishes!

BEATRICE: Then take him to thy fury.

DE FLORES: I thirst for him.

BEATRICE: Alonzo de Piracquo.

DE FLORES: His end's upon him,
  He shall be seen no more.

(Rises)

BEATRICE: How lovely now
  Dost thou appear to me! Never was man
  Dearlier rewarded.

DE FLORES: I do think of that.

BEATRICE: Be wondrous careful in the execution.

DE FLORES: Why, are not both our lives upon the cast?

BEATRICE: Then I throw all my fears upon thy service.

DE FLORES: They ne'er shall rise to hurt you.

BEATRICE: When the deed's done,
  I'll furnish thee with all things for thy flight;
  Thou may'st live bravely in another country.

DE FLORES: Ay, ay, we'll talk of that hereafter.

BEATRICE *(aside):*   I shall rid myself
  Of two inveterate loathings at one time,
  Piracquo, and his dog-face.

(Exit)

DE FLORES: Oh my blood!
  Methinks I feel her in mine arms already,
  Her wanton fingers combing out this beard,
  And being pleased, praising this bad face.
  Hunger and pleasure—they'll commend sometimes
  Slovenly dishes, and feed heartily on 'em,
  Nay, which is stranger, refuse daintier for 'em.
  Some women are odd feeders. —I'm too loud.
  Here comes the man goes supperless to bed,
  Yet shall not rise tomorrow to his dinner.

(Enter ALONZO*)*

ALONZO: De Flores.

DE FLORES: My kind, honourable lord?

ALONZO: I am glad I ha' met with thee.

DE FLORES: Sir.

ALONZO: Thou canst show me
  The full strength of the castle?

DE FLORES: That I can, sir.

ALONZO: I much desire it.

DE FLORES: And if the ways and straits
Of some of the passages be not too tedious for you,
I will assure you, worth your time and sight, my lord.

ALONZO: Pish, that shall be no hindrance.

DE FLORES: I'm your servant, then:
'Tis now near dinner-time; 'gainst your lordship's rising
I'll have the keys about me.

ALONZO: Thanks, kind De Flores.

DE FLORES (*aside*): He's safely thrust upon me beyond hopes.

(*Exeunt.*)

ACT THREE

Scene One

Enter ALONZO *and* DE FLORES. *In the interval, between acts,* DE FLORES *hides a naked rapier.*

DE FLORES: Yes, here are all the keys; I was afraid, my lord,
I'd wanted for the back door, this is it.
I've all, I've all, my lord: this for the ford.

ALONZO: 'Tis a most spacious and impregnable fort.

DE FLORES: You'll tell me more, my lord: this descent
Is somewhat narrow, we shall never pass
Well with our weapons, they'll but trouble us.

ALONZO: Thou say'st true.

DE FLORES: Pray let me help your lordship.

ALONZO: 'Tis done. Thanks, kind De Flores.

DE FLORES: Here are hooks, my lord,
  To hang such things on purpose.

(He hangs up the swords)

ALONZO: Lead, I'll follow thee.

(Exeunt at one door and enter at the other)

Scene Two

DE FLORES: All this is nothing; you shall see anon
  A place you little dream on.

ALONZO: I am glad
  I have this leisure; all your master's house
  Imagine I ha'taken a gondola.

DE FLORES: All but myself, sir, *(Aside)* which makes up my safety.
  —My lord, I'll place you at a casement here
  Will show you the full strength of all the castle.
  Look, spend your eye awhile upon that object.

ALONZO: Here's rich variety, De Flores.

DE FLORES: Yes, sir.

ALONZO: Goodly munition.

DE FLORES: Ay, there's ordnance, sir,
  No bastard metal, will ring you a peal like bells
  At great men's funerals; keep your eye straight, my lord,
  Take special notice of that sconce before you,
  There you may dwell awhile.

(Takes hidden rapier)

ALONZO: I am upon't.

DE FLORES: And so am I.

(Stabs him)

ALONZO: De Flores! Oh, De Flores,
   Whose malice hast thou put on?

DE FLORES: Do you question
   A work of secrecy? I must silence you.

(Stabs him)

ALONZO: Oh, oh, oh.

DE FLORES: I must silence you.
   (Stabs him)
   So, here's an undertaking well accomplished.
   This vault serves to good use now. —Ha, what's that
   Threw sparkles in my eye? Oh, 'tis a diamond
   He wears upon his finger: it was well found,
   This will approve the work. What, so fast on?
   Not part in death? I'll take a speedy course then,
   Finger and all shall off. *(Cuts off finger)* So, now I'll clear
   The passages from all suspect or fear.

(Exit with body.)

                          Scene Three

Enter ISABELLA *and* LOLLIO.

ISABELLA: Why, sirrah? Whence have you commission
   To fetter the doors against me?
   If you keep me in a cage, pray whistle to me,
   Let me be doing something.

LOLLIO: You shall be doing, if it please you; I'll whistle to you if you'll
   pipe after.

ISABELLA: Is it your master's pleasure or your own,
   To keep me in this pinfold?

LOLLIO: 'Tis for my master's pleasure, lest being taken in another man's corn, you might be pounded in another place.

ISABELLA: 'Tis very well, and he'll prove very wise.

LOLLIO: He says you have company enough in the house, if you please to be sociable, of all sorts of people.

ISABELLA: Of all sorts? Why, here's none but fools and madmen.

LOLLIO: Very well: and where will you find any other, if you should go abroad? There's my master and I to boot, too.

ISABELLA: Of either sort one, a madman and a fool.

LOLLIO: I would ev'n participate of both then, if I were as you; I know y'are half mad already,—be half foolish, too.

ISABELLA: Y'are a brave saucy rascal! Come on, sir,
Afford me then the pleasure of your bedlam;
You were commending once today to me
Your last-come lunatic, what a proper
Body there was, without brains to guide it,
And what a pitiful delight appeared
In that defect, as if your wisdom had found
A mirth in madness; pray sir, let me partake
If there be such a pleasure.

LOLLIO: If I do not show you the handsomest, discreetest madman, one that I may call the understanding madman, then say I am a fool.

ISABELLA: Well, a match, I will say so.

LOLLIO: When you have a taste of the madman, you shall, if you please, see Fools' College, o'th'side; I seldom lock there, 'tis but shooting a bolt or two, and you are amongst'em.
(Exit. Enter presently)
Come on sir, let me see how handsomely you'll behave yourself now.

(Enter FRANCISCUS*)*

FRANCISCUS: How sweetly she looks! Oh, but there's a wrinkle in her brow as deep as philosophy. Anacreon, drink to my mistress' health, I'll pledge it; stay, stay, there's a spider in the cup. No, 'tis but a grape-stone, swallow it, fear nothing, poet; so, so, lift higher.

ISABELLA: Alack, alack, 'tis too full of pity
To be laughed at; how fell he mad? Canst thou tell?

LOLLIO: For love, mistress; he was a pretty poet, too, and that set him forwards first; the muses then forsook him, he ran mad for a chamber-maid, yet she was but a dwarf, neither.

FRANCISCUS: Hail, bright Titania!
Why stand'st thou idle on these flow'ry banks?
Oberon is dancing with his Dryades;
I'll gather daisies, primrose, violets,
And bind them in a verse of poesy.

LOLLIO: Not too near; you see your danger.

(Shows whip)

FRANCISCUS: Oh hold thy hand, great Diomed,
Thou feed'st thy horses well, they shall obey thee;
Get up, Bucephalus kneels.

(Kneels)

LOLLIO: You see how I awe my flock; a shepherd has not his dog at more obedience.

ISABELLA: His conscience is unquiet, sure that was
The cause of this. A proper gentleman.

FRANCISCUS: Come hither, Esculapius; hide the poison.

LOLLIO: Well, 'tis hid.

(Lowers whip)

FRANCISCUS *(rising)*: Didst thou never hear of one Tiresias,
  A famous poet?

LOLLIO: Yes, that kept tame wild-geese.

FRANCISCUS: That's he; I am the man.

LOLLIO: No!

FRANCISCUS: Yes; but make no words on't, I was a man
  Seven years ago.

LOLLIO: A stripling I think you might.

FRANCISCUS: Now I'm a woman, all feminine.

LOLLIO: I would I might see that.

FRANCISCUS: Juno struck me blind.

LOLLIO: I'll ne'er believe that; for a woman, they say, has an eye more
  than a man.

FRANCISCUS: I say she struck me blind.

LOLLIO: And Luna made you mad; you have two trades to beg with.

FRANCISCUS: Luna is now big-bellied, and there's room
  For both of us to ride with Hecate;
  I'll drag thee up into her silver sphere,
  And there we'll kick the dog and beat the bush,
  That barks against the witches of the night;
  The swift lycanthropi that walks the round,
  We'll tear their wolvish skins, and save the sheep.

(Tries to seize LOLLIO*)*

LOLLIO: Is't come to this? Nay, then my poison comes forth again, mad
  slave; indeed, abuse your keeper!

(Showing whip)

ISABELLA: I prithee hence with him, now he grows dangerous.

FRANCISCUS (*sings*):

> *Sweet love, pity me,*
> *Give me leave to lie with thee.*

LOLLIO: No, I'll see you wiser first: to your own kennel.

FRANCISCUS: No noise, she sleeps, draw all the curtains round,
  Let no soft sound molest the pretty soul
  But love, and love creeps in at a mouse-hole.

LOLLIO: I would you would get into your hole.
  (*Exit* FRANCISCUS)
  Now mistress, I will bring you another sort, you shall be fooled another while. Tony, come hither Tony, look who's yonder, Tony.

(*Enter* ANTONIO)

ANTONIO: Cousin, is it not my strumpet?

LOLLIO: Yes, 'tis one of'em, Tony.

ANTONIO: He, he, how do you, uncle?

LOLLIO: Fear him not, mistress, 'tis a gentle idiot; you may play with him, as safely with him as with his bauble.

ISABELLA: How long hast thou been a fool?

ANTONIO: Ever since I came hither, cousin.

ISABELLA: Cousin? I'm none of thy cousins, fool.

LOLLIO: Oh mistress, fools have always so much wit as to claim their kindred.

MADMAN (*within*): Bounce, bounce, he falls, he falls!

ISABELLA: Hark you, your scholars in the upper room
  Are out of order.

LOLLIO: Must I come amongst you there? Keep you the fool, mistress; I'll
  go up and play left-handed Orlando amongst the madmen.

(Exit)

ISABELLA: Well, sir.

ANTONIO: 'Tis opportuneful now, sweet lady! Nay,
  Cast no amazing eye upon this change.

ISABELLA: Ha!

ANTONIO: This shape of folly shrouds your dearest love,
  The truest servant to your powerful beauties,
  Whose magic had this force thus to transform me.

ISABELLA: You are a fine fool, indeed!

ANTONIO: Oh, 'tis not strange:
  Love has an intellect that runs through all
  The scrutinous sciences, and like
  A cunning poet, catches a quantity
  Of every knowledge, yet brings all home
  Into one mystery, into one secret
  That he proceeds in.

ISABELLA: Y'are a parlous fool.

ANTONIO: No danger in me: I bring nought but Love,
  And his soft-wounding shafts to strike you with:
  Try but one arrow; if it hurt you,
  I'll stand you twenty back in recompense.

(Kisses her)

ISABELLA: A forward fool, too!

ANTONIO: This was love's teaching:
  A thousand ways he fashioned out my way,

And this I found the safest and the nearest
To tread the Galaxia to my star.

ISABELLA: Profound, withal! Certain you dreamed of this;
Love never taught it waking.

ANTONIO: Take no acquaintance
Of these outward follies; there is within
A gentleman that loves you.

ISABELLA: When I see him,
I'll speak with him; so in the meantime, keep
Your habit, it becomes you well enough.
As you are a gentleman, I'll not discover you;
That's all the favor that you must expect:
When you are weary, you may leave the school,
For all this while you have but played the fool.

(*Enter* LOLLIO)

ANTONIO: And must again.—He, he, I thank you, cousin;
I'll be your valentine tomorrow morning.

LOLLIO: How do you like the fool, mistress?

ISABELLA: Passing well, sir.

LOLLIO: Is he not witty pretty well, for a fool?

ISABELLA: If he hold on as he begins, he is like
To come to something.

LOLLIO: Ay, thank a good tutor. You may put him to't; he begins to
answer pretty hard questions.—Tony, how many is five times six?

ANTONIO: Five times six, is six times five.

LOLLIO: What arithmetician could have answered better?
How many is one hundred and seven?

ANTONIO: One hundred and seven, is seven hundred and one, cousin.

LOLLIO: This is no wit to speak on; will you be rid of the fool now?

ISABELLA: By no means, let him stay a little.

MADMAN *(within):* Catch there, catch the last couple in Hell!

LOLLIO: Again? Must I come amongst you? Would my master were come
   home! I am not able to govern both these wards together.

(Exit)

ANTONIO: Why should a minute of love's hour be lost?

ISABELLA: Fie, out again! I had rather you kept
   Your other posture: you become not your tongue
   When you speak from your clothes.

ANTONIO: How can he freeze,
   Lives near so sweet a warmth? Shall I alone
   Walk through the orchard of the Hesperides,
   And cowardly not dare to pull an apple?
   This with the red cheeks I must venture for.

(Tries to kiss her. Enter LOLLIO above)

ISABELLA: Take heed, there's giants keep'em.

LOLLIO *(aside):* How now, fool, are you good at that? Have you read
   Lipsius? He's past *Ars Amandi*; I believe I must put harder questions
   to him, I perceive that—

ISABELLA: You are bold without fear, too.

ANTONIO: What should I fear,
   Having all joys about me? Do you smile,
   And love shall play the wanton on your lip,
   Meet and retire, retire and meet again:
   Look you but cheerfully, and in your eyes
   I shall behold mine own deformity
   And dress myself up fairer; I know this shape

Becomes me not, but in those bright mirrors
I shall array me handsomely.

LOLLIO: Cuckoo, cuckoo!

(*Exit. Enter* MADMEN *above, some as birds, others as beasts*)

ANTONIO: What are these?

ISABELLA: Of fear enough to part us;
Yet are they but our schools of lunatics,
That act their fantasies in any shapes
Suiting their present thoughts; if sad, they cry;
If mirth be their conceit, they laugh again.
Sometimes they imitate the beasts and birds,
Singing, or howling, braying, barking, all
As their wild fancies prompt'em.

(*Exeunt* MADMEN *above. Enter* LOLLIO)

ANTONIO: These are no fears.

ISABELLA: But here's a large one, my man.

ANTONIO: Ha, he, that's fine sport indeed, cousin.

LOLLIO: I would my master were come home, 'tis too much for one
shepherd to govern two of these flocks; nor can I believe that one
churchman can instruct two benefices at once; there will be some
incurable mad of the one side, and very fools on the other. Come,
Tony.

ANTONIO: Prithee cousin, let me stay here still.

LOLLIO: No, you must to your book now, you have play'd sufficiently.

ISABELLA: Your fool is grown wondrous witty.

LOLLIO: Well, I'll say nothing; but I do not think but he will put you
down one of these days.

(Exeunt LOLLIO *and* ANTONIO)

ISABELLA: Here the restrained current might make breach,
   Spite of the watchful bankers; would a woman stray,
   She need not gad abroad to seek her sin,
   It would be brought home one ways or other:
   The needle's point will to the fixed north,
   Such drawing arctics women's beauties are.

(Enter LOLLIO)

LOLLIO: How dost thou, sweet rogue?

ISABELLA: How now?

LOLLIO: Come, there are degrees, one fool may be better than another.

ISABELLA: What's the matter?

LOLLIO: Nay, if thou giv'st thy mind to fool's-flesh, have at thee.

(Tries to kiss her)

ISABELLA: You bold slave, you!

LOLLIO: I could follow now as t'other fool did—
   'What should I fear,
   Having all joys about me? Do you but smile,
   And love shall play the wanton on your lip,
   Meet and retire, retire and meet again:
   Look you but cheerfully, and in your eyes
   I shall behold my own deformity
   And dress myself up fairer; I know this shape
   Becomes me not—'
   And so, as it follows; but is not this
   the more foolish way? Come, sweet rogue, kiss me, my
   little Lacedemonian. Let me feel how thy pulses beat;
   thou hast a thing about thee would do a man pleasure,—
   I'll lay my hand on't.

ISABELLA: Sirrah, no more! I see you have discovered
   This love's knight-errant, who hath made adventure

For purchase of my love. Be silent, mute,
Mute as a statue, or his injunction
For me enjoying, shall be to cut thy throat:
I'll do it, though for no other purpose,
And be sure he'll not refuse it.

LOLLIO: My share, that's all; I'll have my fool's part with you.

ISABELLA: No more! Your master.

(*Enter* ALIBIUS)

ALIBIUS: Sweet, how dost thou?

ISABELLA: Your bounden servant, sir.

ALIBIUS: Fie, fie, sweetheart,
   No more of that.

ISABELLA: You were best lock me up.

ALIBIUS: In my arms and bosom, my sweet Isabella,
   I'll lock thee up most nearly. Lollio,
   We have employment, we have task in hand;
   At noble Vermandero's, our castle-captain,
   There is a nuptial to be solemnized—
   Beatrice-Joanna, his fair daughter, bride,—
   For which the gentleman hath bespoke our pains:
   A mixture of our madmen and our fools
   To finish, as it were and make the fag
   Of all the revels, the third night from the first;
   Only an unexpected passage over,
   To make a frightful pleasure, that is all,
   But not the all I aim at; could we so act it,
   To teach it in a wild, distracted measure,
   Though out of form and figure, breaking time's head,
   —It were no matter, 'twould be healed again
   In one age or other, if not in this,—
   This, this, Lollio; there's a good reward begun,
   And will beget a bounty, be it known.

LOLLIO: This is easy, sir, I'll warrant you: you have about you fools and
   madmen that can dance very well; and 'tis no wonder, your best
   dancers are not the wisest men; the reason is, with often jumping they
   jolt their brains down into their feet, that their wits lie more in their
   heels than in their heads.

ALIBIUS: Honest Lollio, thou giv'st me a good reason,
   And a comfort in it.

ISABELLA: Y'ave a fine trade on't,
   Madmen and fools are a staple commodity.

ALIBIUS: Oh wife, we must eat, wear clothes, and live;
   Just at the lawyer's haven we arrive,
   By madmen and by fools we both do thrive.

(Exeunt.)

Scene Four

Enter VERMANDERO, ALSEMERO, JASPERINO *and* BEATRICE.

VERMANDERO: Valencia speaks so nobly of you, sir,
   I wish I had a daughter now for you.

ALSEMERO: The fellow of this creature were a partner
   For a king's love.

VERMANDERO: I had her fellow once, sir,
   But Heaven has married her to joys eternal;
   'Twere sin to wish her in this vale again.—
   Come sir, your friend and you shall see the pleasures
   Which my health chiefly joys in.

ALSEMERO: I hear the beauty of this seat largely.

VERMANDERO: It falls much short of that.

(Exeunt. BEATRICE *remains)*

BEATRICE: So, here's one step
Into my father's favor; time will fix him.
I have got him now the liberty of the house:
So wisdom by degrees works out her freedom;
And if that eye be darkened that offends me,—
I wait but that eclipse,—this gentleman
Shall soon shine glorious in my father's liking
Through the refulgent virtue of my love.

(*Enter* DE FLORES)

DE FLORES (*aside*): My thoughts are at a banquet; for the deed,
I feel no weight in't, 'tis but light and cheap
For the sweet recompense that I set down for't.

BEATRICE: De Flores.

DE FLORES: Lady.

BEATRICE: Thy looks promise cheerfully.

DE FLORES: All things are answerable—time, circumstance,
Your wishes and my service.

BEATRICE: Is it done then?

DE FLORES: Piracquo is no more.

BEATRICE: My joys start at mine eyes; our sweet'st delights
Are evermore born weeping.

DE FLORES: I've a token for you.

BEATRICE: For me?

DE FLORES: But it was sent somewhat unwillingly,—
I could not get the ring without the finger.

(*Shows her* ALONZO's *finger*)

BEATRICE: Bless me! What hast thou done?

DE FLORES: Why, is that more
  Than killing the whole man? I cut his heartstrings.
  A greedy hand thrust in a dish at court,
  In a mistake, hath had as much as this.

BEATRICE: 'Tis the first token my father made me send him.

DE FLORES: And I made him send it back again
  For his last token; I was loath to leave it,
  And I'm sure dead men have no use of jewels.
  He was as loath to part with't, for it stuck
  As if the flesh and it were both one substance.

BEATRICE: At the stag's fall the keeper has his fees:
  'Tis soon applied—all dead men's fees are yours, sir;
  I pray, bury the finger, but the stone
  You may make use on shortly; the true value,
  Take't of my truth, is near three hundred ducats.

DE FLORES: 'Twill hardly buy a capcase for one's conscience, though,
  To keep it from the worm, as fine as 'tis.
  Well, being my fees, I'll take it;
  Great men have taught me that, or else my merit
  Would scorn the way on't.

BEATRICE: It might justly, sir:
  Why, thou mistak'st, De Flores, 'tis not given
  In state of recompense.

DE FLORES: No, I hope so, lady,
  You should soon witness my contempt to't then.

BEATRICE: Prithee, thou look'st as if thou wert offended.

DE FLORES: That were strange, lady; 'tis not possible
  My service should draw such a cause from you.
  Offended? Could you think so? That were much
  For one of my performance, and so warm
  Yet in my service.

BEATRICE: 'Twere misery in me to give you cause, sir.

DE FLORES: I know so much, it were so—misery
  In her most sharp condition.

BEATRICE: 'Tis resolved, then;
  Look you, sir, here's three thousand golden florins:
  I have not meanly thought upon thy merit.

DE FLORES: What, salary? Now you move me.

BEATRICE: How, De Flores?

DE FLORES: Do you place me in the rank of verminous fellows,
  To destroy things for wages? Offer gold?
  The lifeblood of man!—Is anything
  Valued too precious for my recompense?

BEATRICE: I understand thee not.

DE FLORES: I could ha' hired
  A journeyman in murder at this rate,
  And mine own conscience might have slept at ease,
  And have had the work brought home.

BEATRICE *(aside):*   I'm in a labyrinth;
  What will content him? I would fain be rid of him.
  (To DE FLORES*)* I'll double the sum, sir.

DE FLORES: You take a course
  To double my vexation, that's the good you do.

BEATRICE *(aside):* Bless me! I am now in worse plight than I was;
  I know not what will please him. *(To* DE FLORES*)*—For my fear's
    sake,
  I prithee make away with all speed possible.
  And if thou be'st so modest not to name
  The sum that will content thee, paper blushes not;
  Send thy demand in writing, it shall follow thee,—
  But prithee, take thy flight.

DE FLORES: You must fly too, then.

BEATRICE: I?

DE FLORES: I'll not stir a foot else.

BEATRICE: What's your meaning?

DE FLORES: Why, are not you as guilty, in, I'm sure,
As deep as I? And we should stick together.
Come, your fears counsel you but ill, my absence
Would draw suspect upon you instantly;
There were no rescue for you.

BEATRICE (aside):   He speaks home.

DE FLORES: Nor is it fit we two, engaged so jointly,
Should part and live asunder.   (Tries to kiss her)

BEATRICE: How now, sir?
This shows not well.

DE FLORES: What makes your lip so strange?
This must not be betwixt us.

BEATRICE (aside):   The man talks wildly.

DE FLORES: Come, kiss me with a zeal now.

BEATRICE (aside):   Heaven! I doubt him.

DE FLORES: I will not stand so long to beg 'em shortly.

BEATRICE: Take heed, De Flores, of forgetfulness,
'Twill soon betray us.

DE FLORES: Take you heed first;
Faith, y'are grown much forgetful, y'are to blame in't.

BEATRICE (aside): He's bold, and I'm blamed for't!

DE FLORES: I have eased you
Of your trouble—think on't,—I'm in pain,

And must be eased of you; 'tis a charity;
Justice invites your blood to understand me.

BEATRICE: I dare not.

DE FLORES: Quickly!

BEATRICE: Oh I never shall!
  Speak it yet further off, that I may lose
  What has been spoken, and no sound remain on't.
  I would not hear so much offense again
  For such another deed.

DE FLORES: Soft, lady, soft,—
  The last is not yet paid for. Oh, this act
  Has put me into spirit, I was as greedy on't
  As the parched earth of moisture, when the clouds weep.
  Did you not mark, I wrought myself into't,
  Nay, sued and kneeled for't: why was all that pains took?
  You see I have thrown contempt upon your gold,
  Not that I want it not, for I do piteously;
  In order I will come unto't, and make use on't,
  But 'twas not held so precious to begin with;
  For I place wealth after the heels of pleasure,
  And were I not resolved in my belief
  That thy virginity were perfect in thee,
  I should but take my recompense with grudging,
  As if I had but half my hopes I agreed for.

BEATRICE: Why, 'tis impossible thou canst be so wicked,
  Or shelter such a cunning cruelty,
  To make his death the murderer of my honor?
  Thy language is so bold and vicious,
  I cannot see which way I can forgive it
  With any modesty.

DE FLORES: Pish, you forget yourself!
  A woman dipped in blood, and talk of modesty?

BEATRICE: Oh misery of sin! Would I had been bound
  Perpetually unto my living hate

In that Piracquo, than to hear these words.
Think but upon the distance that creation
Set 'twixt thy blood and mine, and keep thee there.

DE FLORES: Look but into your conscience, read me there,
'Tis a true book, you'll find me there your equal:
Pish, fly not to your birth, but settle you
In what the act has made you; y'are no more now.
You must forget your parentage for me.
Y'are the deed's creature; by that name
You lost your first condition; and I challenge you,
As peace and innocency has turned you out,
And made you one with me.

BEATRICE: With thee, foul villain?

DE FLORES: Yes, my fair murd'ress; do you urge me?
Though thou writ'st maid, thou whore in thy affection!
'Twas changed from thy first love, and that's a kind
Of whoredom in thy heart; and he's changed now,
To bring thy second on, thy Alsemero,
Whom—by all sweets that ever darkness tasted—
If I enjoy thee not, thou ne'er enjoy'st;
I'll blast the hopes and joys of marriage,
I'll confess all—my life I rate at nothing.

BEATRICE: De Flores!

DE FLORES: I shall rest from all lovers' plagues then;
I live in pain now: that shooting eye
Will burn my heart to cinders.

BEATRICE: Oh sir, hear me!

DE FLORES: She that in life and love refuses me,
In death and shame my partner she shall be.

BEATRICE: Stay, hear me once for all; (Kneeling) I make thee master
Of all the wealth I have in gold and jewels:
Let me go poor unto my bed with honor,
And I am rich in all things.

DE FLORES: Let this silence thee:
  The wealth of all Valencia shall not buy
  My pleasure from me;
  Can you weep fate from its determined purpose?
  So soon may you weep me.

BEATRICE: Vengeance begins;
  Murder I see is followed by more sins.
  Was my creation in the womb so cursed,
  It must engender with a viper first?

DE FLORES: Come, rise, and shroud your blushes in my bosom;
  (Raises her)
  Silence is one of pleasure's best receipts.
  Thy peace is wrought for ever in this yielding.
  'Las, how the turtle pants! Thou'lt love anon
  What thou so fear'st and faint'st to venture on.

(Exeunt.)

ACT FOUR

Scene One

In a dumb show, Enter GENTLEMEN, VERMANDERO *meeting them with action of wonderment at the flight of* PIRACQUO. *Enter* ALSEMERO *with* JASPERINO *and* GALLANTS; VERMANDERO *points to him, the* GENTLEMEN *seeming to applaud the choice; Exeunt* VERMANDERO, ALSEMERO, JASPERINO, *and* GENTLEMEN; BEATRICE *the bride following in great state, accompanied with* DIAPHANTA, ISABELLA *and other* GENTLEWOMEN: DE FLORES *after all, smiling;* ALONZO's *ghost appears to* DE FLORES *in the midst of his smile, startles him, showing him the hand whose finger he had cut off. They pass over in great solemnity. Enter* BEATRICE.)

BEATRICE: This fellow has undone me endlessly,
  Never was bride so fearfully distressed;
  The more I think upon th'ensuing night,
  And whom I am to cope with in embraces,
  One that's ennobled both in blood and mind,
  So clear in understanding,—that's my plague now—

Before whose judgment will my fault appear
Like malefactors' crimes before tribunals;
There is no hiding on't, the more I dive
Into my own distress; how a wise man
Stands for a great calamity! There's no venturing
Into his bed, what course soe'er I light upon,
Without my shame, which may grow up to danger;
He cannot but in justice strangle me
As I lie by him, as a cheater use me;
'Tis a precious craft to play with a false die
Before a cunning gamester. Here's his closet,
The key left in't, and he abroad i'th'park—
Sure 'twas forgot,—I'll be so bold as look in't.
(*Opens closet*)
Bless me! A right physician's closet 'tis,
Set round with vials, every one her mark too.
Sure he does practise physic for his own use,
Which may be safely called your great man's wisdom.
What manuscript lies here? 'The Book of Experiment,
Called Secrets in Nature'; so 'tis, 'tis so;
'How to know whether a woman be with child or no'.
I hope I am not yet; if he should try though!
Let me see—folio forty-five. Here 'tis;
The leaf tucked down upon't, the place suspicious.
'If you would know whether a woman be with child or
not, give her two spoonfuls of the white water in glass C—'
Where's that glass C? Oh yonder I see't now,—
'and if she be with child, she sleeps full twelve hours
after, if not, not.'
None of that water comes into my belly.
I'll know you from a hundred; I could break you now,
Or turn you into milk, and so beguile
The master of the mystery, but I'll look to you.
Ha! That which is next is ten times worse:—
'How to know whether a woman be a maid or not';
If that should be applied, what would become of me?
Belike he has a strong faith of my purity,
That never yet made proof; but this he calls
'A merry, slight but true experiment, the author Antonius
Mizaldus. Give the party you suspect the quantity of a spoonful of
the water in the glass M, which upon her that is a maid makes

three several effects: 'twill make her incontinently gape, then fall
into a sudden sneezing, last into a violent laughing; else dull, heavy
and lumpish.'
Where had I been?
I fear it, yet 'tis seven hours to bedtime.

(Enter DIAPHANTA)

DIAPHANTA: Cuds, madam, are you here?

BEATRICE *(aside):*   Seeing that wench now,
   A trick comes in my mind; 'tis a nice piece
   Gold cannot purchase; *(To* DIAPHANTA) I come hither, wench,
   To look my lord.

DIAPHANTA *(aside):* Would I had such a cause to look him, too.
   (To BEATRICE) Why, he's i'th'park, madam.

BEATRICE: There let him be.

DIAPHANTA: Ay, madam, let him compass
   Whole parks and forests, as great rangers do;
   At roosting time a little lodge can hold 'em.
   Earth-conquering Alexander, that thought the world
   Too narrow for him, in the end had but his pithole.

BEATRICE: I fear thou art not modest, Diaphanta.

DIAPHANTA: Your thoughts are so unwilling to be known, madam;
   'Tis ever the bride's fashion towards bedtime,
   To set light by her joys, as if she ow'd 'em not.

BEATRICE: Her joys? Her fears, thou would'st say.

DIAPHANTA: Fear of what?

BEATRICE: Art thou a maid, and talk'st so to a maid?
   You leave a blushing business behind,
   Beshrew your heart for't!

DIAPHANTA: Do you mean good sooth,
  madam?

BEATRICE: Well, if I'd thought upon the fear at first,
  Man should have been unknown.

DIAPHANTA: Is't possible?

BEATRICE: I will give a thousand ducats to that woman
  Would try what my fear were, and tell me true
  Tomorrow, when she gets from't: as she likes,
  I might perhaps be drawn to't.

DIAPHANTA: Are you in earnest?

BEATRICE: Do you get the woman, then challenge me,
  And see if I'll fly from't; but I must tell you
  This by the way, she must be a true maid,
  Else there's no trial, my fears are not hers else.

DIAPHANTA: Nay, she that I would put into your hands, madam,
  Shall be a maid.

BEATRICE: You know I should be shamed else,
  Because she lies for me.

DIAPHANTA: 'Tis a strange humor:
  But are you serious still? Would you resign
  Your first night's pleasure, and give money, too?

BEATRICE: As willingly as live; *(aside)* alas, the gold
  Is but a by-bet to wedge in the honor.

DIAPHANTA: I do not know how the world goes abroad
  For faith or honesty, there's both required in this.—
  Madam, what say you to me, and stray no further?
  I've a good mind, in troth, to earn your money.

BEATRICE: Y'are too quick, I fear, to be a maid.

DIAPHANTA: How? Not a maid? Nay, then you urge me, madam;

Your honorable self is not a truer
With all your fears upon you—

BEATRICE *(aside)*:   Bad enough, then.

DIAPHANTA: Than I with all my lightsome joys about me.

BEATRICE: I'm glad to hear't then; you dare put your honesty
Upon an easy trial?

DIAPHANTA: Easy? —Anything.

BEATRICE: I'll come to you straight.

(Goes to closet)

DIAPHANTA *(aside)*:   She will not search me, will she
Like the forewoman of a female jury?

BEATRICE: Glass M: ay, this is it;—look, Diaphanta,
You take no worse than I do.

(Drinks)

DIAPHANTA: And in so doing,
I will not question what 'tis, but take it.

(Drinks)

BEATRICE *(aside)*: Now, if the experiment be true, 'twill praise itself
And give me noble ease:—begins already;
(DIAPHANTA *gapes*)
There's the first symptom; and what haste it makes
To fall into the second, there by this time!
(DIAPHANTA *sneezes*)
Most admirable secret! On the contrary,
It stirs not me a whit, which most concerns it.

DIAPHANTA: Ha, ha, ha!

BEATRICE *(aside)*: Just in all things and in order

As if 'twere circumscribed; one accident
Gives way unto another.

DIAPHANTA: Ha, ha, ha!

BEATRICE: How now, wench?

DIAPHANTA: Ha, ha, ha! I am so—so light at heart, ha, ha, ha,—so
   pleasurable!
But one swig more, sweet madam.

BEATRICE: Ay, tomorrow;
   We shall have time to sit by't.

DIAPHANTA: Now I'm sad again.

BEATRICE (aside): It lays itself so gently too! (To DIAPHANTA) Come,
   wench,
Most honest Diaphanta, I dare call thee now.

DIAPHANTA: Pray tell me, madam, what trick call you this?

BEATRICE: I'll tell thee all hereafter; we must study
The carriage of this business.

DIAPHANTA: I shall carry't well,
   Because I love the burthen.

BEATRICE: About midnight
   You must not fail to steal forth gently,
   That I may use the place.

DIAPHANTA: Oh fear not, madam,
   I shall be cool by that time;—the bride's place!
   And with a thousand ducats! I'm for a justice now,
   I bring a portion with me; I scorn small fools.

(Exeunt.)

Scene Two

Enter VERMANDERO *and* SERVANT.

VERMANDERO: I tell thee, knave, mine honor is in question,
　A thing till now free from suspicion,
　Nor ever was there cause; who of my gentlemen
　Are absent? Tell me, and truly, how many and who.

SERVANT: Antonio, sir, and Franciscus.

VERMANDERO: When did they leave the castle?

SERVANT: Some ten days since, sir, the one intending to
　Briamata, th'other for Valencia.

VERMANDERO: The time accuses 'em; a charge of murder
　Is brought within my castle gate, Piracquo's murder;
　I dare not answer faithfully their absence:
　A strict command of apprehension
　Shall pursue 'em suddenly, and either wipe
　The stain off clear or openly discover it.
　Provide me winged warrants for the purpose.
　(*Exit* SERVANT)
　See, I am set on again.

(*Enter* TOMAZO)

TOMAZO: I claim a brother of you.

VERMANDERO:　　　　　　　　　　Y'are too hot,
　Seek him not here.

TOMAZO:　　　　　　　Yes, 'mongst your dearest bloods,
　If my peace find no fairer satisfaction;
　This is the place must yield account for him,
　For here I left him, and the hasty tie
　Of this snatched marriage gives strong testimony
　Of his most certain ruin.

VERMANDERO: Certain falsehood!
This is the place indeed; his breach of faith
Has too much marred both my abused love,
The honorable love I reserved for him,
And mocked my daughter's joy. The prepared morning
Blushed at his infidelity; he left
Contempt and scorn to throw upon those friends
Whose belief hurt 'em: oh 'twas most ignoble
To take his flight so unexpectedly,
And throw such public wrongs on those that loved him.

TOMAZO: Then this is all your answer?

VERMANDERO: 'Tis too fair
For one of his alliance; and I warn you
That this place no more see you.

(*Exit. Enter* DE FLORES)

TOMAZO: The best is,
There is more ground to meet a man's revenge on.
Honest De Flores!

DE FLORES: That's my name, indeed.
Saw you the bride? Good sweet sir, which way took she?

TOMAZO: I have blest mine eyes from seeing such a false one.

DE FLORES (*aside*): I'd fain get off, this man's not for my company,
I smell his brother's blood when I come near him.

TOMAZO: Come hither, kind and true one; I remember
My brother loved thee well.

DE FLORES: Oh purely, dear sir,
(*aside*)—methinks I am now again a-killing on him,
He brings it so fresh to me.

TOMAZO: Thou canst guess, sirrah,
—One honest friend has an instinct of jealousy,—
At some foul guilty person?

DE FLORES: 'Las sir, I am so charitable, I think none
Worse than myself.—You did not see the bride then?

TOMAZO: I prithee name her not. Is she not wicked?

DE FLORES: No, no, a pretty, easy, round-packed sinner,
As your most ladies are, else you might think
I flattered her; but sir, at no hand wicked,
Till th'are so old their sins and vices meet,
And they salute witches. I am called I think, sir:
(aside)—his company ev'n o'erlays my conscience.

(Exit)

TOMAZO: That De Flores has a wondrous honest heart;
He'll bring it out in time, I'm assured on't.
—Oh, here's the glorious master of the day's joy.
'Twill not be long till he and I do reckon.
(Enter ALSEMERO)
Sir.

ALSEMERO: You are most welcome.

TOMAZO: You may call that word back,
I do not think I am, nor wish to be.

ALSEMERO: 'Tis strange you found the way to this house, then.

TOMAZO: Would I'd ne'er known the cause! I'm none of those, sir,
That come to give you joy, and swill your wine;
'Tis a more precious liquor that must 'lay
The fiery thirst I bring.

ALSEMERO: Your words and you
Appear to me great strangers.

TOMAZO: Time and our swords
May make us more acquainted; this the business:
I should have a brother in your place;
How treachery and malice have disposed of him,

I'm bound to inquire of him which holds his right,
Which never could come fairly.

ALSEMERO: You must look
  To answer for that word, sir.

TOMAZO: Fear you not,
  I'll have it ready drawn at our next meeting.
  Keep your day solemn. Farewell, I disturb it not;
  I'll bear the smart with patience for a time.

(Exit)

ALSEMERO: 'Tis somewhat ominous, this: a quarrel entered
  Upon this day; my innocence relieves me,
  (Enter JASPERINO)
  I should be wondrous sad else.—Jasperino,
  I have news to tell thee, strange news.

JASPERINO: I ha' some too,
  I think as strange as yours; would I might keep
  Mine, so my faith and friendship might be kept in't!
  Faith, sir, dispense a little with my zeal,
  And let it cool in this.

ALSEMERO: This puts me on,
  And blames thee for thy slowness.

JASPERINO: All may prove nothing;
  Only a friendly fear that leapt from me, sir.

ALSEMERO: No question it may prove nothing; let's partake it, though.

JASPERINO: 'Twas Diaphanta's chance—for to that wench
  I proffer honest love, and she deserves it—
  To leave me in a back part of the house,
  A place we chose for private conference;
  She was no sooner gone, but instantly
  I heard your bride's voice in the next room to me;
  And lending more attention, found De Flores
  Louder than she.

ALSEMERO: De Flores? Thou art out now.

JASPERINO: You'll tell me more anon.

ALSEMERO: Still I'll prevent thee;
  The very sight of him is poison to her.

JASPERINO: That made me stagger too, but Diaphanta
  At her return confirmed it.

ALSEMERO: Diaphanta!

JASPERINO: Then fell we both to listen, and words passed
  Like those that challenge interest in a woman.

ALSEMERO: Peace, quench thy zeal, tis dangerous to thy bosom!

JASPERINO: Then truth is full of peril.

ALSEMERO: Such truths are.
  —Oh, were she the sole glory of the earth,
  Had eyes that could shoot fire into kings' breasts,
  And touched, she sleeps not here! Yet I have time,
  Though night be near, to be resolved hereof;
  And prithee do not weigh me by my passions.

JASPERINO: I never weighed friend so.

ALSEMERO: Done charitably.
  That key will lead thee to a pretty secret,
  (Gives key)
  By a Chaldean taught me, and I've made
  My study upon some; bring from my closet
  A glass inscribed there with the letter M,
  And question not my purpose.

JASPERINO: It shall be done, sir.

(Exit)

ALSEMERO: How can this hang together? Not an hour since,
  Her woman came pleading her lady's fears,
  Delivered her for the most timorous virgin

That ever shrunk at man's name, and so modest,
She charged her weep out her request to me,
That she might come obscurely to my bosom.

(Enter BEATRICE)

BEATRICE (aside): All things go well; my woman's preparing yonder
    For her sweet voyage, which grieves me to lose;
    Necessity compels it; I lose all else.

ALSEMERO (aside): Pish, Modesty's shrine is set in yonder forehead.—
    I cannot be too sure though. (To her)—My Joanna!

BEATRICE: Sir, I was bold to weep a message to you,—
    Pardon my modest fears.

ALSEMERO (aside):   The dove's not meeker,
    She's abused, questionless.
    (Enter JASPERINO with glass)
                                —Oh, are you come, sir?

BEATRICE (aside): The glass, upon my life! I see the letter.

JASPERINO: Sir, this is M.

ALSEMERO: 'Tis it.

BEATRICE (aside):   I am suspected.

ALSEMERO: How fitly our bride comes to partake with us!

BEATRICE: What is't, my lord?

ALSEMERO: No hurt.

BEATRICE: Sir, pardon me,
    I seldom taste of any composition.

ALSEMERO: But this, upon my warrant, you shall venture on.

BEATRICE: I fear 'twill make me ill.

ALSEMERO: Heaven forbid that.

BEATRICE *(aside):* I'm put now to my cunning; th'effects I know
  If I can now but feign 'em handsomely.

(Drinks)

ALSEMERO *(to* JASPERINO): It has that secret virtue, it ne'er missed, sir,
  Upon a virgin.

JASPERINO: Treble qualitied?

(BEATRICE *gapes, then sneezes*)

ALSEMERO: By all that's virtuous, it takes there, proceeds!

JASPERINO: This is the strangest trick to know a maid by.

BEATRICE: Ha, ha, ha!
  You have given me joy of heart to drink, my lord.

ALSEMERO: No, thou hast given me such joy of heart
  That never can be blasted.

BEATRICE: What's the matter, sir?

ALSEMERO *(to* JASPERINO): See, now 'tis settled in a melancholy,—
  Keep both the time and method;—my Joanna!
  Chaste as the breath of Heaven, or morning's womb,
  That brings the day forth; thus my love encloses thee.

(Embraces her. Exeunt.)

Scene Three

Enter ISABELLA *and* LOLLIO.

ISABELLA: Oh Heaven! Is this the waiting moon?
  Does love turn fool, run mad, and all at once?

Sirrah, here's a madman, a-kin to the fool too,
A lunatic lover.

LOLLIO: No, no, not he I brought the letter from?

ISABELLA: Compare his inside with his out, and tell me.

(Gives him letter)

LOLLIO: The out's mad, I'm sure of that, I had a taste on't. *(Reads)* 'To
the bright Andromeda, chief chambermaid to the Knight of the Sun,
at the sign of Scorpio, in the middle region, sent by the bellows-
mender of Aeolus. Pay the post.' This is stark madness.

ISABELLA: Now mark the inside. *(Takes letter and reads)* 'Sweet lady, having now cast off this counterfeit cover of a madman, I appear to your
best judgment a true and faithful lover of your beauty.'

LOLLIO: He is mad still.

ISABELLA: 'If any fault you find, chide those perfections in you which
have made me imperfect; 'tis the same sun that causeth to grow,
and enforceth to wither—'

LOLLIO: Oh rogue!

ISABELLA: '—Shapes and transshapes, destroys and builds again; I come
in winter to you, dismantled of my proper ornaments: by the sweet
splendor of your cheerful smiles, I spring and live a lover.'

LOLLIO: Mad rascal still!

ISABELLA: ''Tread him not under foot, that shall appear an honor to your
bounties. I remain—mad till I speak with you, from whom I expect
my cure. Yours all, or one beside himself, FRANCISCUS.'

LOLLIO: You are like to have a fine time on't; my master and I may give
over our professions, I do not think but you can cure fools and
madmen faster than we, with little pains too.

ISABELLA: Very likely.

LOLLIO: One thing I must tell you, mistress: you perceive that I am privy
to your skill; if I find you minister once and set up the trade, I put in
for my thirds—I shall be mad or fool else.

ISABELLA: The first place is thine, believe it, Lollio;
    If I do fall—

LOLLIO: I fall upon you.

ISABELLA: So.

LOLLIO: Well, I stand to my venture.

ISABELLA: But thy counsel now, how shall I deal with 'em?

LOLLIO: Why, do you mean to deal with 'em?

ISABELLA: Nay, the fair understanding, how to use 'em.

LOLLIO: Abuse 'em! That's the way to mad the fool and make a fool of
the madman, and then you use 'em kindly.

ISABELLA: 'Tis easy, I'll practise; do thou observe it.
    The key of thy wardrobe.

LOLLIO: There—fit yourself for 'em, and I'll fit 'em both for you.

(Gives her key)

ISABELLA: Take thou no further notice than the outside.

(Exit)

LOLLIO: Not an inch; I'll put you to the inside.

(Enter ALIBIUS*)*

ALIBIUS: Lollio, art there? Will all be perfect, think'st thou.
    Tomorrow night, as if to close up the solemnity,
    Vermandero expects us.

LOLLIO: I mistrust the madmen most; the fools will do well enough; I have taken pains with them.

ALIBIUS: Tush, they cannot miss; the more absurdity,
The more commends it—so no rough behaviors
Affright the ladies; they are nice things, thou know'st.

LOLLIO: You need not fear, sir; so long as we are there with our commanding pizzles, they'll be as tame as the ladies themselves.

ALIBIUS: I will see them once more rehearse before they go.

LOLLIO: I was about it, sir; look you to the madmen's morris, and let me alone with the other; there is one or two that I mistrust their fooling; I'll instruct them, and then they shall rehearse the whole measure.

ALIBIUS: Do so; I'll see the music prepared. But Lollio,
By the way, how does my wife brook her restraint?
Does she not grudge at it?

LOLLIO: So, so. She takes some pleasure in the house, she would abroad else; you must allow her a little more length, she's kept too short.

ALIBIUS: She shall along to Vermandero's with us;
That will serve her for a month's liberty.

LOLLIO: What's that on your face, sir?

ALIBIUS: Where, Lollio? I see nothing.

LOLLIO: Cry you mercy sir, 'tis your nose; it showed like the trunk of a young elephant.

ALIBIUS: Away, rascal! I'll prepare the music, Lollio.

(*Exit* ALIBIUS)

LOLLIO: Do, sir, and I'll dance the whilst; Tony, where art thou, Tony?

(*Enter* ANTONIO)

ANTONIO: Here, cousin—where art thou?

LOLLIO: Come, Tony, the footmanship I taught you.

ANTONIO: I had rather ride, cousin.

LOLLIO: Ay, a whip take you; but I'll keep you out. Vault in; look you,
Tony,—fa, la la, la la.

(Dances)

ANTONIO: Fa, la la, la la.

(Dances)

LOLLIO: There, an honor.

ANTONIO: Is this an honor, coz?

(Bows)

LOLLIO: Yes, if it please your worship.

ANTONIO: Does honor bend in the hams, coz?

LOLLIO: Marry does it, as low as worship, squireship, nay, yeomanry
itself sometimes, from whence it first stiffened. There, rise, a caper.

ANTONIO: Caper after an honor, coz?

LOLLIO: Very proper, for honor is but a caper, rises as fast and high, has a
knee or two, and falls to th' ground again. You can remember your
figure, Tony?

(Exit)

ANTONIO: Yes, cousin, when I see thy figure, I can remember mine.

(Enter ISABELLA *like a madwoman)*

ISABELLA: Hey, how he treads the air! Shough, shough,
t'other way! He burns his wings else; here's wax enough
below, Icarus, more than will be canceled these eighteen moons;
He's down, he's down, what a terrible fall he had!

Stand up, thou son of Cretan Dedalus,
And let us tread the lower labyrinth;
I'll bring thee to the clue.

ANTONIO: Prithee, coz, let me alone.

ISABELLA: Art thou not drowned?
About thy head I saw a heap of clouds,
Wrapped like a Turkish turban; on thy back
A crook'd chameleon-coloured rainbow hung
Like a tiara down unto thy hams.
Let me suck out those billows in thy belly;
Hark, how they roar and rumble in the straits!
Bless thee from the pirates!

ANTONIO: Pox upon you, let me alone!

ISABELLA: Why shouldst thou mount so high as Mercury,
Unless thou hadst reversion of his place?
Stay in the moon with me, Endymion,
And we will rule these wild rebellious waves
That would have drowned my love.

ANTONIO: I'll kick thee if again thou touch me,
Thou wild, unshapen antic; I am no fool,
You bedlam!

ISABELLA: But you are, as sure as I am, mad.
Have I put on this habit of a frantic,
With love as full of fury to beguile
The nimble eye of watchful jealousy,
And am I thus rewarded?

(Reveals herself)

ANTONIO: Ha! Dearest beauty!

ISABELLA: No, I have no beauty now,
Nor never had, but what was in my garments.
You a quick-sighted lover? Come not near me!

444 *Thomas Middleton and William Rowley*

Keep your caparisons, y'are aptly clad;
I came a feigner, to return stark mad.

(Exit. Enter LOLLIO*)*

ANTONIO: Stay, or I shall change condition
And become as you are.

LOLLIO: Why, Tony, whither now? Why, fool?

ANTONIO: Whose fool, usher of idiots? You coxcomb!
I have fooled too much.

LOLLIO: You were best be mad another while, then.

ANTONIO: So I am, stark mad! I have cause enough,
And I could throw the full effects on thee,
And beat thee like a fury!

LOLLIO: Do not, do not; I shall not forbear the gentleman under the fool
if you do; alas, I saw through your foxskin before now: come, I can
give you comfort; my mistress loves you, and there is as arrant a
madman i'th'house as you are a fool, your rival, whom she loves not; if
after the masque we can rid her of him, you earn her love, she says,
and the fool shall ride her.

ANTONIO: May I believe thee?

LOLLIO: Yes, or you may choose whether you will or no.

ANTONIO: She's eased of him; I have a good quarrel on't.

LOLLIO: Well, keep your old station yet, and be quiet.

ANTONIO: Tell her I will deserve her love.

(Exit)

LOLLIO: And you are like to have your desire.

(Enter FRANCISCUS*)*

FRANCISCUS (*sings*): 'Down, down, down a-down a-down,
    and then with a horse-trick,
To kick Latona's forehead, and break her bowstring.'

LOLLIO: This is t'other counterfeit; I'll put him out of his humor. (*Takes out letter and reads*) 'Sweet lady, having now cast this counterfeit cover of a madman, I appear to your best judgment a true and faithful lover of your beauty.' This is pretty well for a madman.

FRANCISCUS: Ha! What's that?

LOLLIO: 'Chide those perfections in you, which made me imperfect.'

FRANCISCUS: I am discovered to the fool.

LOLLIO (*aside*): I hope to discover the fool in you ere I have done with you.—'Yours all, or one beside himself, Franciscus.' This madman will mend, sure.

FRANCISCUS: What? Do you read, sirrah?

LOLLIO: Your destiny, sir; you'll be hanged for this trick, and another that I know.

FRANCISCUS: Art thou of counsel with thy mistress?

LOLLIO: Next her apron strings.

FRANCISCUS: Give me thy hand.

LOLLIO: Stay, let me put yours in my pocket first; (*puts away letter*) your hand is true, is it not? It will not pick? I partly fear it, because I think it does lie.

FRANCISCUS: Not in a syllable.

LOLLIO: So; if you love my mistress so well as you have handled the matter here, you are like to be cured of your madness.

FRANCISCUS: And none but she can cure it.

LOLLIO: Well, I'll give you over then, and she shall cast your water next.

FRANCISCUS: Take for thy pains past.

(Gives him money)

LOLLIO: I shall deserve more, sir, I hope; my mistress loves you, but must have some proof of your love to her.

FRANCISCUS: There I meet my wishes.

LOLLIO: That will not serve—you must meet her enemy and yours.

FRANCISCUS: He's dead already.

LOLLIO: Will you tell me that, and I parted but now with him?

FRANCISCUS: Show me the man.

LOLLIO: Ay, that's a right course now, see him before you kill him in any case, and yet it needs not go so far neither; 'tis but a fool that haunts the house and my mistress in the shape of an idiot; bang but his fool's coat well-favoredly, and 'tis well.

FRANCISCUS: Soundly, soundly!

LOLLIO: Only reserve him till the masque be past; and if you find him not now in the dance yourself, I'll show you. In! In! My master!

FRANCISCUS: He handles him like a feather. Hey!

(Exit dancing. Enter ALIBIUS)

ALIBIUS: Well said; in a readiness, Lollio?

LOLLIO: Yes, sir.

ALIBIUS: Away then, and guide them in, Lollio;
Entreat your mistress to see this sight.
(Exit LOLLIO)

Hark, is there not one incurable fool
That might be begged? I have friends.

LOLLIO *(within)*: I have him for you, one that shall deserve it, too.

ALIBIUS: Good boy, Lollio.

(Enter ISABELLA, *then* LOLLIO *with* MADMEN *and* FOOLS. *The* MADMEN *and*
FOOLS *dance)*

'Tis perfect; well, fit but once these strains,
We shall have coin and credit for our pains.

(Exeunt.)

ACT FIVE

Scene One

Enter BEATRICE. *A clock strikes one.*

BEATRICE: One struck, and yet she lies by't—oh my fears!
   This strumpet serves her own ends, 'tis apparent now,
   Devours the pleasure with a greedy appetite
   And never minds my honor or my peace,
   Makes havoc of my right; but she pays dearly for't:
   No trusting of her life with such a secret,
   That cannot rule her blood to keep her promise.
   Beside, I have some suspicion of her faith to me
   Because I was suspected of my lord,
   And it must come from her.—Hark by my horrors!
   Another clock strikes two.

(Strikes two. Enter DE FLORES)

DE FLORES: Psst, where are you?

BEATRICE: De Flores?

DE FLORES: Ay; is she not come from him yet?

BEATRICE: As I am a living soul, not.

DE FLORES: Sure the Devil
　Hath sowed his itch within her; who'd trust
　A waiting-woman?

BEATRICE: I must trust somebody.

DE FLORES: Push, they are termagants,
　Especially when they fall upon their masters,
　And have their ladies' first-fruits; th'are mad whelps,
　You cannot stave 'em off from game royal; then
　You are so harsh and hardy, ask no counsel,
　And I could have helped you to an apothecary's daughter,
　Would have fall'n off before eleven, and thank you, too.

BEATRICE: Oh me, not yet! This whore forgets herself.

DE FLORES: The rascal fares so well; look, y'are undone,
　The day-star, by this hand! See Phosphorus plain yonder.

BEATRICE: Advise me now to fall upon some ruin,
　There is no counsel safe else.

DE FLORES: Peace, I ha't now,
　For we must force a rising, there's no remedy.

BEATRICE: How? Take heed of that.

DE FLORES: Tush, be you quiet,
　Or else give over all.

BEATRICE: Prithee, I ha'done then.

DE FLORES: This is my reach: I'll set some part a-fire
　Of Diaphanta's chamber.

BEATRICE: How? Fire, sir?
　That may endanger the whole house.

DE FLORES: You talk of danger when your fame's on fire.

BEATRICE: That's true—do what thou wilt now.

DE FLORES: Pish, I aim
At a most rich success, strikes all dead sure;
The chimney being a-fire, and some light parcels
Of the least danger in her chamber only,
If Diaphanta should be met by chance then,
Far from her lodging, which is now suspicious,
It would be thought her fears and affrights then
Drove her to seek for succor; if not seen
Or met at all, as that's the likeliest,
For her own shame she'll hasten towards her lodging;
I will be ready with a gun high-charged,
As 'twere to cleanse the chimney: there 'tis proper now,
But she shall be the mark.

BEATRICE: I'm forced to love thee now,
'Cause thou provid'st so carefully for my honor.

DE FLORES: 'Slid, it concerns the safety of us both,
Our pleasure and continuance.

BEATRICE: One word now, prithee—
How for the servants?

DE FLORES: I'll dispatch them,
Some one way, some another in the hurry,
For buckets, hooks, ladders; fear not you;
The deed shall find its time—and I've thought since
Upon a safe conveyance for the body too.
How this fire purifies wit! Watch you your minute.

BEATRICE: Fear keeps my soul upon't, I cannot stray from't.

(Enter ALONZO's *ghost)*

DE FLORES: Ha! What art thou that tak'st away the light
'Twixt that star and me? I dread thee not;
'Twas but a mist of conscience.—All's clear again.

(Exit)

BEATRICE: Who's that, De Flores? Bless me! It slides by,
  (Exit ghost)
  Some ill thing haunts the house; 't has left behind it
  A shivering sweat upon me: I'm afraid now.
  This night hath been so tedious—oh, this strumpet!
  Had she a thousand lives, he should not leave her
  Till he had destroyed the last.—List, oh my terrors!
  Three struck by Saint Sebastian's!

(Struck three o'clock. VOICES *within, "Fire, fire, fire!")*

BEATRICE: Already? How rare is that man's speed!
  How heartily he serves me! His face loathes one,
  But look upon his care, who would not love him?
  The east is not more beauteous than his service.

*(*VOICES *within, "Fire, fire, fire!" Enter* DE FLORES; SERVANTS *pass over, ring a bell)*

DE FLORES: Away, dispatch! Hooks, buckets, ladders; that's well said—
  The firebell rings, the chimney works—my charge;
  The piece is loaded.

(Exit)

BEATRICE: Here's a man worth loving!—
  (Enter DIAPHANTA*)*
  Oh, y'are a jewel!

DIAPHANTA: Pardon frailty, madam,
  In troth I was so well, I ev'n forgot myself.

BEATRICE: Y'have made trim work.

DIAPHANTA: What?

BEATRICE: Hie quickly to your chamber—
  Your reward follows you.

DIAPHANTA: I never made
  So sweet a bargain.

(Exit. Enter ALSEMERO)

ALSEMERO: Oh my dear Joanna,
  Alas, art thou risen too? I was coming,
  My absolute treasure.

BEATRICE: When I missed you,
  I could not choose but follow.

ALSEMERO: Th'art all sweetness!
  The fire is not so dangerous.

BEATRICE: Think you so, sir?

ALSEMERO: I prithee tremble not: believe me, 'tis not.

(Enter VERMANDERO, JASPERINO)

VERMANDERO: Oh bless my house and me!

ALSEMERO: My lord your father.

(Enter DE FLORES *with a piece)*

VERMANDERO: Knave, whither goes that piece?

DE FLORES: To scour the chimney.

(Exit)

VERMANDERO: Oh well said, well said;
  That fellow's good on all occasions.

BEATRICE: A wondrous necessary man, my lord.

VERMANDERO: He hath a ready wit, he's worth 'em all, sir;
  Dog at a house a-fire; I ha' seen him singed ere now.
  (The weapon goes off)
  Ha, there he goes.

BEATRICE *(aside):*   'Tis done.

ALSEMERO: Come, sweet, to bed now;
  Alas, thou wilt get cold.

BEATRICE: Alas, the fear keeps that out;
  My heart will find no quiet till I hear
  How Diaphanta, my poor woman, fares;
  It is her chamber sir, her lodging chamber.

VERMANDERO: How should the fire come there?

BEATRICE: As good a soul as ever lady countenanced,
  But in her chamber negligent and heavy;
  She 'scaped a'mine twice.

VERMANDERO: Twice?

BEATRICE: Strangely twice, sir.

VERMANDERO: Those sleepy sluts are dangerous in a house,
  And they be ne'er so good.

(*Enter* DE FLORES)

DE FLORES: Oh poor virginity!
  Thou hast paid dearly for't.

VERMANDERO: Bless us! What's that?

DE FLORES: A thing you all knew once—Diaphanta's burnt.

BEATRICE: My woman, oh my woman!

DE FLORES: Now the flames
  Are greedy of her—burnt, burnt, burnt to death, sir.

BEATRICE: Oh my presaging soul!

ALSEMERO: Not a tear more!
  I charge you by the last embrace I gave you
  In bed before this raised us.

BEATRICE: Now you tie me;
  Were it my sister, now she gets no more.

(Enter SERVANT*)*

VERMANDERO: How now?

SERVANT: All danger's past, you may now take your rests, my lords; the
  fire is thoroughly quenched; ah, poor gentlewoman, how soon was she
  stifled!

BEATRICE: De Flores, what is left of her inter,
  And we as mourners all will follow her:
  I will entreat that honor to my servant,
  Ev'n of my lord himself.

ALSEMERO: Command it, sweetness.

BEATRICE: Which of you spied the fire first?

DE FLORES: 'Twas I, madam.

BEATRICE: And took such pains in't too? A double goodness!
  'Twere well he were rewarded.

VERMANDERO: He shall be.
  De Flores, call upon me.

ALSEMERO: And upon me, sir.

(Exeunt all but DE FLORES*)*

DE FLORES: Rewarded? Precious, here's a trick beyond me!
  I see in all bouts, both of sport and wit,
  Always a woman strives for the last hit.

(Exit.)

Scene Two

Enter TOMAZO.

TOMAZO: I cannot taste the benefits of life
   With the same relish I was wont to do.
   Man I grow weary of, and hold his fellowship
   A treacherous bloody friendship; and because
   I am ignorant in whom my wrath should settle,
   I must think all men villains, and the next
   I meet (whoe'er he be) the murderer
   Of my most worthy brother.—Ha! What's he?
   (Enter DE FLORES, *passes over the stage)*
   Oh, the fellow that some call honest De Flores;
   But methinks honesty was hard bestead
   To come there for a lodging—as if a queen
   Should make her palace of a pesthouse.
   I find a contrariety in nature
   Betwixt that face and me: the least occasion
   Would give me game upon him; yet he's so foul,
   One would scarce touch him with a sword he loved
   And made account of; so most deadly venomous,
   He would go near to poison any weapon
   That should draw blood on him; one must resolve
   Never to use that sword again in fight
   In way of honest manhood, that strikes him;
   Some river must devour't, 'twere not fit
   That any man should find it.—What, again?
   (Enter DE FLORES*)*
   He walks o'purpose by, sure, to choke me up,
   To infect my blood.

DE FLORES: My worthy noble lord.

TOMAZO: Dost offer to come near and breathe upon me?

(Strikes him)

DE FLORES: A blow!

(Draws sword)

TOMAZO: Yea, are you so prepared?
  I'll rather like a soldier die by th'sword,
  Than like a politician by thy poison.

(Draws)

DE FLORES: Hold, my lord, as you are honorable.

TOMAZO: All slaves that kill by poison are still cowards.

DE FLORES *(aside):* I cannot strike, I see his brother's wounds
  Fresh bleeding in his eye, as in a crystal.
  (To him)—I will not question this, I know y'are noble;
  I take my injury with thanks given, sir,
  Like a wise lawyer; and as a favor,
  Will wear it for the worthy hand that gave it.
  (Aside)—Why this from him, that yesterday appeared
  So strangely loving to me?
  Oh but instinct is of a subtler strain,
  Guilt must not walk so near his lodge again;
  He came near me now.

(Exit)

TOMAZO: All league with mankind I renounce for ever,
  'Till I find this murderer; not so much
  As common courtesy but I'll lock up:
  For in the state of ignorance I live in,
  A brother may salute his brother's murderer,
  And wish good speed to the villain in a greeting.

(Enter VERMANDERO, ALIBIUS *and* ISABELLA)

VERMANDERO: Noble Piracquo!

TOMAZO: Pray keep on your way, sir,
  I've nothing to say to you.

VERMANDERO: Comforts bless you, sir.

TOMAZO: I have forsworn compliment, in troth I have, sir;
   As you are merely man, I have not left
   A good wish for you, nor any here.

VERMANDERO: Unless you be so far in love with grief,
   You will not part from't upon any terms,
   We bring that news will make a welcome for us.

TOMAZO: What news can that be?

VERMANDERO: Throw no scornful smile
   Upon the zeal I bring you, 'tis worth more, sir.
   Two of the chiefest men I kept about me
   I hide not from the law, or your just vengeance.

TOMAZO: Ha!

VERMANDERO: To give your peace more ample satisfaction,
   Thank these discoverers.

TOMAZO: If you bring that calm,
   Name but the manner I shall ask forgiveness in
   For that contemptuous smile upon you:
   I'll perfect it with reverence that belongs
   Unto a sacred altar.

(Kneels)

VERMANDERO: Good sir, rise;
   Why, now you overdo as much o'this hand
   As you fell short o't'other. Speak, Alibius.

ALIBIUS: 'Twas my wife's fortune—as she is most lucky
   At a discovery—to find out lately
   Within our hospital of fools and madmen,
   Two counterfeits slipped into these disguises,
   Their names, Franciscus and Antonio.

VERMANDERO: Both mine, sir, and I ask no favor for 'em.

ALIBIUS: Now that which draws suspicion to their habits,
   The time of their disguisings agrees justly
   With the day of the murder.

TOMAZO: Oh blest revelation!

VERMANDERO: Nay more, nay more, sir—I'll not spare mine own
   In way of justice—they both feigned a journey
   To Briamata, and so wrought out their leaves;
   My love was so abused in't.

TOMAZO: Time's too precious
   To run in waste now; you have brought a peace
   The riches of five kingdoms could not purchase.
   Be my most happy conduct, I thirst for 'em;
   Like subtle lightning will I wind about 'em,
   And melt their marrow in 'em.

(Exeunt.)

Scene Three

Enter ALSEMERO *and* JASPERINO.

JASPERINO: Your confidence, I'm sure, is now of proof.
   The prospect from the garden has showed
   Enough for deep suspicion.

ALSEMERO: The black mask
   That so continually was worn upon't
   Condemns the face for ugly ere't be seen—
   Her despite to him, and so seeming bottomless.

JASPERINO: Touch it home then: 'tis not a shallow probe
   Can search this ulcer soundly, I fear you'll find it
   Full of corruption. 'Tis fit I leave you;
   She meets you opportunely from that walk;
   She took the back door at his parting with her.

(Exit JASPERINO*)*

ALSEMERO: Did my fate wait for this unhappy stroke
At my first sight of woman?—She's here.

(*Enter* BEATRICE)

BEATRICE: Alsemero!

ALSEMERO: How do you?

BEATRICE: How do I?
Alas! How do you? You look not well.

ALSEMERO: You read me well enough, I am not well.

BEATRICE: Not well, sir? Is't in my power to better you?

ALSEMERO: Yes.

BEATRICE: Nay, then y'are cured again.

ALSEMERO: Pray resolve me one question, lady.

BEATRICE: If I can.

ALSEMERO: None can so sure. Are you honest?

BEATRICE: Ha, ha, ha! That's a broad question, my lord.

ALSEMERO: But that's not a modest answer, my lady—
Do you laugh? My doubts are strong upon me.

BEATRICE: 'Tis innocence that smiles, and no rough brow
Can take away the dimple in her cheek.
Say I should strain a tear to fill the vault,
Which would you give the better faith to?

ALSEMERO: 'Twere but hypocrisy of a sadder color,
But the same stuff; neither your smiles nor tears
Shall move or flatter me from my belief:
You are a whore!

BEATRICE: What a horrid sound it hath!
It blasts a beauty to deformity;
Upon what face soever that breath falls,
It strikes it ugly: oh, you have ruined
What you can ne'er repair again.

ALSEMERO: I'll all demolish and seek out truth within you,
If there be any left; let your sweet tongue
Prevent your heart's rifling; there I'll ransack
And tear out my suspicion.

BEATRICE: You may, sir,
'Tis an easy passage; yet, if you please,
Show me the ground whereon you lost your love;
My spotless virtue may but tread on that
Before I perish.

ALSEMERO: Unanswerable!
A ground you cannot stand on: you fall down
Beneath all grace and goodness, when you set
Your fickle heel on't; there was a visor
O'er that cunning face, and that became you;
Now impudence in triumph rides upon't.—
How comes this tender reconcilement else
'Twixt you and your despite, your rancorous loathing,
De Flores? He that your eye was sore at sight of,
He's now become your arm's supporter, your
        lip's saint!

BEATRICE: Is there the cause?

ALSEMERO: Worse—your lust's devil,
Your adultery!

BEATRICE: Would any but yourself say that,
'Twould turn him to a villain.

ALSEMERO: 'Twas witnessed
By the counsel of your bosom, Diaphanta.

BEATRICE: Is your witness dead then?

ALSEMERO: 'Tis to be feared
  It was the wages of her knowledge; poor soul,
  She lived not long after the discovery.

BEATRICE: Then hear a story of not much less horror
  Than this your false suspicion is beguiled with:
  To your bed's scandal, I stand up innocence,
  Which even the guilt of one black other deed
  Will stand for proof of: your love has made me
  A cruel murd'ress.

ALSEMERO: Ha!

BEATRICE: A bloody one—
  I have kissed poison for't, stroked a serpent;
  That thing of hate, worthy in my esteem
  Of no better employment, and him most worthy
  To be so employed, I caused to murder
  That innocent Piracquo, having no
  Better means than that worst, to assure
  Yourself to me.

ALSEMERO: Oh, the place itself e'er since
  Has crying been for vengeance, the temple
  Where blood and beauty first unlawfully
  Fired their devotion, and quenched the right one;
  'Twas in my fears at first, 'twill have it now—
  Oh, thou art all deformed!

BEATRICE: Forget not, sir,
  It for your sake was done; shall greater dangers
  Make the less welcome?

ALSEMERO: Oh thou shouldst have gone
  A thousand leagues about to have avoided
  This dangerous bridge of blood. Here we are lost.

BEATRICE: Remember I am true unto your bed.

ALSEMERO: The bed itself's a charnel, the sheets shrouds
  For murdered carcases; it must ask pause

What I must do in this—meantime you shall
Be my prisoner only: enter my closet;
(*Exit* BEATRICE)
I'll be your keeper yet. Oh, in what part
Of this sad story shall I first begin?
(*Enter* DE FLORES)

          Ha!
This same fellow has put me in.—De Flores!

DE FLORES: Noble Alsemero?

ALSEMERO: I can tell you
 News, sir; my wife has her commended to you.

DE FLORES: That's news indeed, my lord; I think she would
 Commend me to the gallows if she could,
 She ever loved me so well—I thank her.

ALSEMERO: What's this blood upon your band, De Flores?

DE FLORES: Blood? No, sure, 'twas washed since.

ALSEMERO: Since when, man?

DE FLORES: Since t'other day I got a knock
 In a sword and dagger school; I think 'tis out.

ALSEMERO: Yes, 'tis almost out, but 'tis perceived, though.
 I had forgot my message; this it is:
 What price goes murder?

DE FLORES: How, sir?

ALSEMERO: I ask you, sir;
 My wife's behindhand with you, she tells me,
 For a brave bloody blow you gave for her sake
 Upon Piracquo.

DE FLORES: Upon? 'Twas quite through him, sure;
 Has she confessed it?

ALSEMERO: As sure as death to both of you,
And much more than that.

DE FLORES: It could not be much more;
'Twas but one thing, and that—she's a whore.

ALSEMERO: It could not choose but follow—oh cunning devils!
How should blind men know you from fair-faced saints?

BEATRICE *(within)*: He lies, the villain does belie me!

DE FLORES: Let me go to her, sir.

ALSEMERO: Nay, you shall to her.
Peace, crying crocodile, your sounds are heard!
Take your prey to you,—get you in to her, sir.
(Exit DE FLORES*)*
I'll be your pander now; rehearse again
Your scene of lust, that you may be perfect
When you shall come to act it to the black audience
Where howls and gnashings shall be music to you.
Hug your adult'ress freely, 'tis the pilot
Will guide you to the Mare Mortuum
Where you shall sink to fathoms bottomless.

(Enter VERMANDERO, ALIBIUS, ISABELLA, TOMAZO, FRANCISCUS *and* ANTONIO*)*

VERMANDERO: Oh, Alsemero, I have a wonder for you.

ALSEMERO: No sir, 'tis I, I have a wonder for you.

VERMANDERO: I have suspicion near as proof itself
For Piracquo's murder.

ALSEMERO: Sir, I have proof
Beyond suspicion for Piracquo's murder.

VERMANDERO: Beseech you hear me, these two have been disguised
E'er since the deed was done.

ALSEMERO: I have two other
  That were more close disguised than your two could be,
  E'er since the deed was done.

VERMANDERO: You'll hear me! These mine own servants—

ALSEMERO: Hear me! Those nearer than your servants,
  That shall acquit them and prove them guiltless.

FRANCISCUS: That may be done with easy truth, sir.

TOMAZO: How is my cause bandied through your delays!
  'Tis urgent in blood, and calls for haste;
  Give me a brother alive or dead—
  Alive, a wife with him; if dead, for both
  A recompense, for murder and adultery.

BEATRICE *(within)*: Oh, oh, oh!

ALSEMERO: Hark, 'tis coming to you.

DE FLORES *(within)*: Nay, I'll along for company.

BEATRICE *(within)*:   Oh, oh!

VERMANDERO: What horrid sounds are these?

ALSEMERO: Come forth, you twins of mischief!

(Enter DE FLORES *bringing in* BEATRICE *wounded)*

DE FLORES: Here we are; if you have any more
  To say to us, speak quickly, I shall not
  Give you the hearing else; I am so stout yet,
  And so, I think, that broken rib of mankind.

VERMANDERO: An host of enemies entered my citadel
  Could not amaze like this. Joanna, Beatrice-Joanna!

BEATRICE: Oh come not near me, sir, I shall defile you;
  I am that of your blood was taken from you

For your better health; look no more upon't,
But cast it to the ground regardlessly—
Let the common sewer take it from distinction.
Beneath the stars, upon yon meteor
Ever hung my fate, 'mongst things corruptible;
I ne'er could pluck it from him; my loathing
Was prophet to the rest, but ne'er believed—
Mine honor fell with him, and now my life.
Alsemero, I am a stranger to your bed,
Your bed was cozened on the nuptial night,
For which your false bride died.

ALSEMERO: Diaphanta!

DE FLORES: Yes, and the while I coupled with your mate
At barley-brake; now we are left in Hell.

VERMANDERO: We are all there, it circumscribes us here.

DE FLORES: I loved this woman in spite of her heart;
Her love I earned out of Piracquo's murder.

TOMAZO: Ha! My brother's murderer!

DE FLORES: Yes, and her honor's prize
Was my reward; I thank life for nothing
But that pleasure, it was so sweet to me
That I have drunk up all, left none behind
For any man to pledge me.

VERMANDERO: Horrid villain!
Keep life in him for further tortures.

DE FLORES: No!
I can prevent you; here's my penknife still.
It is but one thread more, (*Stabs himself*)—and now 'tis cut.
Make haste, Joanna, by that token to thee:
Canst not forget, so lately put in mind,
I would not go to leave thee far behind.

(*Dies*)

BEATRICE: Forgive me, Alsemero, all forgive:
'Tis time to die, when 'tis a shame to live.

(*Dies*)

VERMANDERO: Oh, my name is entered now in that record
Where till this fatal hour 'twas never read.

ALSEMERO: Let it be blotted out, let your heart lose it,
And it can never look you in the face,
Nor tell a tale behind the back of life
To your dishonor. Justice hath so right
The guilty hit, that innocence is quit
By proclamation, and may joy again.
Sir, you are sensible of what truth hath done,
'Tis the best comfort that your grief can find.

TOMAZO: Sir, I am satisfied, my injuries
Lie dead before me; I can exact no more,
Unless my soul were loose, and could o'ertake
Those black fugitives that are fled from thence,
To take a second vengeance; but there are wraths
Deeper than mine, 'tis to be feared, about 'em.

ALSEMERO: What an opacous body had that moon
That last changed on us! Here's beauty changed
To ugly whoredom; here, servant obedience
To a master sin, imperious murder:
I, a supposed husband, changed embraces
With wantonness, but that was paid before.
Your change is come too, from an ignorant wrath
To knowing friendship. Are there any more on's?

ANTONIO: Yes, sir; I was changed too, from a little ass as I was, to a great
fool as I am, and had like to ha' been changed to the gallows, but that
you know my innocence always excuses me.

FRANCISCUS: I was changed from a little wit to be stark mad,
Almost for the same purpose.

ISABELLA (*to* ALIBIUS):   Your change is still behind,
But deserve best your transformation:

You are a jealous coxcomb, keep schools of folly,
And teach your scholars how to break your own head.

ALIBIUS: I see all apparent, wife, and will change now
   Into a better husband, and never keep
   Scholars that shall be wiser than myself.

ALSEMERO: Sir, you have yet a son's duty living,
   Please you accept it; let that your sorrow
   As it goes from your eye, go from your heart:
   Man and his sorrow at the grave must part.

EPILOGUE

ALSEMERO: All we can do to comfort one another,
   To stay a brother's sorrow for a brother,
   To dry a child from the kind father's eyes,
   Is to no purpose, it rather multiplies:
   —Your only smiles have power to cause relive
   The dead again, or in their rooms to give
   Brother a new brother, father a child:
   If these appear, all griefs are reconciled.

(Exeunt omnes.)

THE BASTARD OF BOLOGNA

A TRAGEDIE

Paula Volsky

It is a medical fact that tears and mirth involve nearly identical physiological processes. Laughter is capable of turning into tears, but in the following play, it is definitely vice versa as Paula Volsky nearly kids revenge tragedies—well, to death.

Theatrical literature contains few first-rate parodies. Drydenesque heroic drama was effectively quelled by George Villiers's *The Rehearsal* and other tub-thumping propensities of "high drama" were lambasted in Sheridan's *The Critic* and lampooned in Fielding's *Tom Thumb*. But the best parodies, I contend, are those that border on pastiche: a faithful recreation of style and tone. That is the approach taken here.

Ms. Volsky, a resident of Alexandria, Va., is one of America's preeminent fantasists. Her novels include *Illusion*, *The Luck of Relian Kru*, *Curse of the Witch Queen*, *The Sorcerer's Lady*, *The Sorcerer's Heir* and *The Sorcerer's Curse*.

The Bastard of Bologna was first performed at Vassar College with the following cast:

DUKE OF BOLOGNA: Esther Friesner
ARIOSTO: Harriett Hawkins
CESARE: Karen Markeloff
GOFFREDO: Jane Bishop
NICCOLO: James Berry
ENRICO: Gale Justin
SIMONE: James Weiss
APOTHECARY: Joanne Citron
UMBERTO: Katherine Teyler
CUSTOMERS: J. Sinder, Karen Markeloff
NOBLES: J. Sinder, Jane Bishop
DUCHESS: J. Sinder
GRAZIELLA: Delia Sherman
LUCREZIA: Paula Volsky

DRAMATIS PERSONAE

DUKE OF BOLOGNA

ARIOSTO,
CESARE, } *Sons to the Duke*
GOFFREDO,

NICCOLO SPARVIERO, *Bastard son to the Duke*
ENRICO DISPADA, *An impoverished gentleman*
APOTHECARY
UMBERTO, *Apprentice to Apothecary*
FIRST CUSTOMER
SECOND CUSTOMER
FIRST NOBLE
SECOND NOBLE

DUCHESS
LUCREZIA VELENA, *Widow to the Duke's oldest son*
GRAZIELLA, *Waiting-woman to Lucrezia Velena*

Scene: Bologna

ACTUS PRIMUS

Scene One

A hall in the DUKE's *palace. A corse lies in state. Enter* ARIOSTO *and* GOFFREDO.

GOFFREDO: Dead! Our brother dead! I know not how it came to pass. But last night walked he well mailed i' the armor of youth and strength.

ARIOSTO: 'Sfoot, Brother, 'tis so. Yet the dawn discover'd him weltering in a bed whose disorder bore grim witness to the violence of his last agonies. Already stiff, his limbs lay frozen in a still convulsion. His lips were rent, his visage bloodied. A blackened tongue sought escape from the ruins of his mouth, while his wide eyes gazed roundly upon the other world.

GOFFREDO: Alack that he should suffer so, whose life was a fair, unblemished page whereon Nature penned her sweetest sonnets.

ARIOSTO: A page torn too early from the book by unlettered Death's rough, envious hand.

GOFFREDO: Truly, we may mourn his loss. Few men could boast his nobleness of mind, his elevation of soul.

ARIOSTO: We may sigh indeed that he is dead, i'faith—and weep that he did not choose to die the sooner.

GOFFREDO: Ariosto!

ARIOSTO: Come, sir, we are alone. In truth, my very liver was ofttimes sickened by his vaunting gravity—

GOFFREDO: His enforced virtue—

ARIOSTO: His double-faced piety—

GOFFREDO: And the ostentation of his modesty. Well, he's gone—and happily for us twain. 'Twill swell the inheritance of each when his Grace our father finally breathes his last.

ARIOSTO: You say true. Yet my mind misgives me. Of late has our father wandered fondly. He has admitted to the court his bastard Niccolo Sparviero—

GOFFREDO: O, speak not that loathed name! A hell of hatred fires my breast at the sound of't. Niccolo, a base-born slave begotten by our father of a French whore—

ARIOSTO: Tainted, no doubt, with the French sickness—

GOFFREDO: And now that human hawk, that carrion bird of prey, that Niccolo—has sunk his 'fouled talons i' the heart of the Duke, who comes to dote on him. That silver age could show so green!

ARIOSTO: Heart! The villain seeks to supplant us in our father's affections, sure. Look to your patrimony, Goffredo. The bastard will trim it finely for you.

GOFFREDO: He'll die, first. Yet why mark you my patrimony alone? Yours is equally at hazard.

ARIOSTO: Not so. Of us two, our father holds me the dearer. I am riper in years, riper in reason. He shall not touch my inheritance.

GOFFREDO: I' faith, you lie!

ARIOSTO: No.

GOFFREDO: Pish, but I say you do—

ARIOSTO: Beloved Goffredo, when common danger threatens, 'tis not the moment to quarrel. Rather must we strengthen the bond of our mutual love, that united we may defeat the enemy bastard. Troth, we shall clip the wings of that hawk.

GOFFREDO: Good, Brother, we'll lure him, then hood him.

ARIOSTO: Nor shall he slip his jesses—ha! The fancy's a pretty one. And yet the choler rises i' my throat. The old man stoops too far, to this dishonored blood.

GOFFREDO: Mark you, 'tis his own dishonored blood. Yet 'tis said that bleeding's a sovereign physic—

ARIOSTO: And we shall prove brave leeches, Brother. Ah—comes the Duke.

(Enter the DUKE, *borne in a chair. With him, the* DUCHESS, CESARE *(bearing a crutch),* NICCOLO, LUCREZIA VELENA, SIMONE, NOBLES *and* ATTENDANTS)

ARIOSTO: 'Tis but a sorry greeting we extend upon this melancholy occasion, your Grace.

DUKE: We have come to pay our last of farewells to our first-born of sons. Attend us. *(Rises, with* CESARE's *assistance. Accepts crutch, approaches bier)* So.

DUCHESS *(weeps)*: O, me! O, my sweet son!

DUKE: Silence! Weep when I give you leave.

DUCHESS: I will, my lord.

DUKE: Now I bethink me we might have called a priest. He had need of it, for he was putrid with sin. I have ever loathed the sins of the flesh. He has sinned, and see, he is dead. Fie on luxury! 'Tis the Devil's vice!

CESARE: The eye of wisdom beholds the fair visage of truth, Father.

DUKE: Silence! *(Beats* CESARE *with crutch)* I gave you no leave to speak!

SIMONE: Grandfather, forbear, I pray!

DUKE: I am old, but not yet toothless, and I will be obeyed. Down, sirrah! *(Beats* SIMONE) Lucrezia Velena, as widow of our son, you have our permission to approach the bier.

LUCREZIA: I humbly thank your Grace. *(Approaches the bier, places a ring upon the finger of the corse)* My loved and honored husband, I pray God that your rest be a peaceful one. May your soul rise to Heaven, and its eternal joys. I remain below, to languish in lonely sorrow until we are reunited.

ARIOSTO *(aside):* 'S Blood! A fine wench, that. 'Tis a form most excellent beneath that robe of mourning. Marry, we'll discover how long her chaste resolution endure, now that its foundation and support—her husband—is gone.

LUCREZIA: O! Darkness engulfs my soul, and faintness clouds my vision. I pray your Grace, dismiss me.

DUKE: I will. Assist her.

DUCHESS: Poor soul! This grief undoes her. My clamorous sorrows are awed into silence by this, her illimitable woe. Come, Lucrezia, get us hence.

LUCREZIA: Madame, you are good. *(Exeunt* LUCREZIA VELENA *and the* DUCHESS, *supporting her)*

SIMONE: How shall that frail spirit survive this, Father?

CESARE: Silence, Simone. Do not, O, do not arouse the Duke's easy wrath.

DUKE: Tomorrow, the earth will cover him, his bones will corrupt. *Requiescat in pace.* Yet must not our thoughts bide with our son in the grave. Gentlemen, now would we bespeak a matter whereon long our thoughts have dwelt. Our firstborn son is dead, yet is there a consolation. We falter beneath the weight of paternal sorrow, yet is there comfort. Of late have we admitted to our court duteous Niccolo Sparviero—

NICCOLO: Your Grace too greatly honors my unworthiness.

ARIOSTO *(aside):* I'faith, he does.

GOFFREDO *(aside):* O black presentiment! What comes?

DUKE: And now have we chosen to acknowledge this *novus homo* as our rightful son, the equal of you all in honors and inheritance.

NICCOLO: Your Grace, this is a blessing most unexpected, and most undeserved—

CESARE: Most undeserved.

NICCOLO: Sir, I've ne'er aspired to high estate. You have raised me beyond ambition's height in allowing me the court. Let it rest there.

ARIOSTO: Let it rest there.

DUKE: Peace, I'll brook no contradiction. You are my son.

NICCOLO: Your Grace's condescension o'erwhelms me, freezing my tongue. Beseech you, think hardly upon't.

DUKE: These admonitions are not to your advantage. Forbear. I will not hear them, my son.

ARIOSTO: Son! You had but four sons, and one lies dead. Three remain, and they are here before you. Why enrich you this ignoble slave with the name of son? Beshrew me if I don't eclipse such a son!

DUKE: Do you dare—

GOFFREDO: Yes, by God! This Niccolo is a bastard, a thing of contemptible mean stature, engendered of a whore—

NICCOLO: This I will not suffer.

GOFFREDO: Peace, bastard. Get you gone from the court, get you gone from Bologna. Y'are like to pay for your presumption with your life— though troth, I'm loath to soil my blade with such stale as runs in your veins.

DUKE: Slanderer! Unnatural son! Oh, you shameless villain, you swinish traitor, you walking infection! Get you from my sight, you shall bleed for this. Look to it!

CESARE: Your Grace, I prythee, think on what you do. Would you elevate shame, enshrine dishonor? Consider well.

DUKE: I consider your deaths! Traitors, all! Who defies me attacks the state. Well might I choose to hang you all, to draw and to quarter, to burn your bowels before your face.

CESARE: Passion masters you. You court the apoplexy.

GOFFREDO: Spare us your palsied rages! And spare us your bastard, conceived in secret lust, and nurtured in shame. Let him return to the shadows that spawned him, and do you act as befits your ancient dignity.

DUKE: There is my dignity! (*Strikes* GOFFREDO) And there it is again, take it! (*Kicks him*)

GOFFREDO: Plague take you, old man! Will you parade your sins, to our detriment?

CESARE (*aside*): Peace, fool, you grow too hot.

GOFFREDO: Think you our spirits will submit to such insult? Shall we deign to call that bastard brother? Pox rot my soul if he lives another instant. (*Draws sword*)

DUKE: Your wish is my own. (*Strike* GOFFREDO *senseless with crutch*)

ARIOSTO: Your Grace! Father, you do wrong my brother—

DUKE: Silence! You sharp-fanged serpent, filthied o'er with base ingratitude and disobedience! You foul, dark-visaged slave, I rue the day I begot you!

ARIOSTO: Your Grace, do but consider—

DUKE: I will not hear you.

ARIOSTO: But a moment. You wrong the sons that honor you—

DUKE: Not another word!

ARIOSTO: Ud's death, but you will hear me, Father!

DUKE: Is't so? *(Strikes* ARIOSTO *senseless with crutch)* Now, Cesare, do you follow the path of your rebellious brothers?

CESARE: No, your Grace! Take my oath upon it!

DUKE: Your oath—alack, what faith may I place in that slender reed? Bologna would benefit were I to kill you.

CESARE *(kneels):* Mercy, I prythee—

DUKE: Granted. And no—I know not. I'll think on't.

CESARE: O, pity, I beseech you! Soften your heart. Pity!

DUKE: Perhaps.

NICCOLO: Your Grace, they have impiously scorned your reverend years.

DUKE: So. You see, Niccolo, the baseness of these rebels who flout their father and their duke. And I a tired old man! 'Twould crack a hardened heart. Come, we've done here. *(Exeunt omnes save* NICCOLO; *attendants bearing* ARIOSTO *and* GOFFREDO)

NICCOLO: Marry, this exceeds my expectations by far. Long have I striven to assure myself a hold upon the parched affections of the humorous Duke, and to that end have I shown the world an honorable face. The old man has been deceived. Pox on't, he of all should know better. Am I not his son? His blood runs rank in my veins. Does he not know himself?

It might be reckoned that I must hate the Duke for the brand of shame he has set upon me, and yet it is not so. Nay, he has my gratitude, even my affection, for he has bequeathed a most precious commodity—opportunity. A Duke's base-born eagle soars higher than your well-mewed tercel, has he but wit to spread his pinions and dare the sky. I revel in royal blood, for all its soilure.

Now, to the Duke's sons. Were they but cold in their graves, I must succeed my father. To think is to act. Already have I poisoned the eldest, who shrieked his life to a halt yesternight upon venom'd sheets. There remains cowardly Cesare. Incontinent Ariosto. And corpulent Goffredo, that fleshly mountain. They will die, soon and secretly. The old Duke will scarcely mourn 'em.

I require a trusty villain to aid me, and such a one I believe I can buy. He comes well-praised, and he comes anon.

But for that, I would not stay. I would yon cold fellow were deep in his grave. That dead face accuses me; all moist as it is with the rain of the widow's tears. Heart! In the midst of grief, her virtue ennobles her beauty, her beauty warms her virtue. Such a visage, fair as victory itself, owns power to enslave minds—yet her purity and chaste innocence possess a greater power yet, to cleanse the souls of all beholders. Sure, she is the paragon of her sex.

Who comes?

(*Enter* DISPADA)

DISPADA: I seek one Niccolo, surnamed Sparviero.

NICCOLO: You have found him. Your business, sir?

DISPADA: I am that Enrico DiSpada who has been preferred to you.

NICCOLO: I do recall it. You are welcome, *signor*. You have been praised for secrecy, so I'll state my purpose plainly.

DISPADA: 'Tis business that demands secrecy?

NICCOLO: 'Twould discover your want of understanding to seek aught other, at court.

DISPADA: So much I feared.

NICCOLO: You fear? Then it may be, you are not the man for me.

DISPADA: Nay, then, say—so much I apprehend.

NICCOLO: I think it well. Yet let this still enfeebling conscience—in my service, you will go far.

DISPADA: You mean, I shall be banished Bologna?

NICCOLO: Nay, sir, be ruled by me, and you will climb—

DISPADA: The gallows stair?

NICCOLO: You jest, yet you doubt. Prove but a constant villain, and you will rise. My star is ascendant at last. Follow me, and you'll traverse the heavens. *(Aside)* I'll have him.

DISPADA: And mingle with angels, my lord?

NICCOLO: Why, man, you'd scatter them, you'd flutter 'em like haloed pigeons. Fix your thoughts upon earthly angels. A court beauty may well transport you to a paradise of your own devising. Consider the enjoyment of privilege, power, endless festivity, infinite opulence. Think of the changing splendor, the brilliance, the enchanting variety of the palace. Don a cloak of velvet, and dance three ells above the ground. Come, DiSpada, come and lead a life of gold.

DISPADA: Speak not to me of courtly pleasures. I know them well.

NICCOLO: Truly?

DISPADA: Troth, having known them and lost them. I was born a gentleman, and as a gentleman came I to the palace. Alas for a young man's folly! I squandered my fortune, I gamed and lusted it away. The last of my inheritance tumbled into the hands of the Duke's sons, upon the rattle of bad dice, upon the fall of marked cards. As a beggar stole I hence. At my nativity, sir, Sagittarius was in the House of Mars, beneath the tail of the Dragon. I was created to be dogged by misfortune, and it has proved so.

NICCOLO: The Duke's sons, say you? Then must your task prove a pleasant one. Come, sir, be merry. I've aught to cheer your melancholy humor. *(Gives him money)*

DISPADA: So. Banish all thoughts of honor! Away with pride, and set your mind on villainy. 'Sfoot my lord, you've made a poor bargain.

NICCOLO: How so?

DISPADA: The gold you give could well have kept you brave,
              Yet with it have you purchased but a knave.

(Exeunt.)

Scene Two

The apartment of LUCREZIA VELENA. *Enter* SIMONE *and* GRAZIELLA, *severally.*

SIMONE: O, my sweet Graziella! 'Twas a sorry sight! O, me!

GRAZIELLA: How now, gentle Simone? Whence such storms of grief? The sight of your dead uncle's ashen visage has riven your heart?

SIMONE: 'Twas not Uncle's face. 'Twas my father's face. Alas!

GRAZIELLA: My sweet love, what's this? You weep. Heaven, but these tears are vitriol to my soul. What ails your father?

SIMONE: The Duke has owned the legitimacy of my uncle Niccolo Sparviero, yet Father and my remaining uncles are loath to acknowledge him. I know not why.

GRAZIELLA: No more can I fathom it. He is a well-favored, most proper man. Who could hate him?

SIMONE: Marry, Father could. He made protest, and the Duke's choler grew apace, until at last he belabored Father with his crutch 'fore the eyes of the court. Nor did his fury abate until he had struck Uncle Goffredo and Uncle Ariosto such blows that the two of them fell like dead men. O!

GRAZIELLA: 'Tis a fierce and unrelenting old man.

SIMONE: Generous soul of sympathy! Your sweet pity is balm to my wounded spirit.

GRAZIELLA: Most beloved Simone! Hark! The Duchess sooths my distempered lady in the next room, but now they come. Away, lest they think me wanton. (*Exit* SIMONE)

Enter DUCHESS *and* LUCREZIA VELENA. DUCHESS *and* GRAZIELLA *help* LUCREZIA VELENA *to a bed*)

DUCHESS: She fails sadly. I fear she cannot live.

GRAZIELLA: Mistress! Courage, I prythee!

LUCREZIA: You are faithful, Graziella. *(To* DUCHESS*)* And you, Madam—
your sweet charity enthrones you among the saints of Heaven.

DUCHESS: Peace, Lucrezia. You tax yourself o'ermuch.

LUCREZIA: Madame, I will live. Together we shall spend our lives in mutual sorrow, prayer, and fasting.

DUCHESS: 'Tis a noble widow.

LUCREZIA: Eternal love and shared grief will bond our hearts forever.

DUCHESS: My daughter! Come, Graziella. Sleep must sooth your lady's
pain. *(Exeunt* DUCHESS *and* GRAZIELLA. LUCREZIA VELENA *rises)*

LUCREZIA: O, damnation! A plague upon the indifferent stars! Was ever
another as unfortunate as I? My loathed husband dead, leaving me
penniless and alone, bound to a living death in a nest of venomous
fools. I have youth and beauty—shall I be chained to a corse? Shall I
sink a daily inch into the grave? Shall I wear black weeds, eye the
cobbles, mumble psalms and eat the stale bread of charity?
I had rather bathe in Hell's fiery floods.
I scorn a humble dependency in this house. Had my husband
lived, I must have been Duchess in time. Yet nothing awaits me now
but miserable, everlasting tedium. I must escape it, an I would live. I
must marry me again to some great man ere bright youth greys and
chills. Haste!
What chance have I? To marry high, needs must I appear honest.
To carry that seeming, must I dwell in sad widowhood, nor go abroad.
So must I look to the palace.
O, that the bastard Niccolo might succeed! Despite the shame of
his conception, he alone among this crawling palace breed displays
high honor, gentleness and constancy. Oft has his valor moved me.
Would that my dingy soul might rise to his honesty! Would that his
tainted blood might rise to my station!
Enough. My heart is set upon the Duke himself, I do resolve. I
am absolute that he shall make me great. The tearful Duchess shall

not block my path, I promise.
    Her death will put his Grace's heart to test.
    I'll trust my wit and form to do the rest.   *(Exit.)*

ACTUS SECUNDUS

Scene One

An Apothecary's Shop. Enter APOTHECARY *and* UMBERTO.

APOTHECARY: Umberto, 'tis said that gold is a sort of poison. Yet my trade
has proved of a surety that poison's gold.

UMBERTO: Poison is poison, sir. 'Tis not so certain as a poniard.

APOTHECARY: Tut, man, you've a beast's taste for blood.

UMBERTO: So you say. Yet I warrant 'tis a taste to your purse's profit.

APOTHECARY: Would that you had an eye to subtler deeds! Look you,
Umberto. Ranged about us on every shelf are ancient potions, flasks
of poison, and sovereign remedies for all ills. Roots and herbs have we
aplenty. Spring waters gathered at midnight beneath a full moon.
Bats' eyes and rats' brains seethed to a cullis. Rare minerals and earths
ground to powder. Consecrated bones, and thrice-accursed stones. A
blessed virgin's blood, infectious graveyard mud. Oriental jade, a human infant flayed.
    Yet among our wares, canst tell me what fills our pockets? Why, 'tis
not the cures. They languish unnoticed throughout the years, their
virtues mantled in dust. Nay, 'tis the poison that keeps us, Umberto.
We live by poison. Mass, we batten on death, the two of us, like
scavengers.

UMBERTO: 'Tis a full-bellied scavenger.

APOTHECARY: Do not interrupt, sirrah. I say, 'tis the poison that keeps us.
'Tis our arsenic, antimony, quicksilver, copperas, henbane; the night-
shade, La Cantarella, poppy-juice, mandragora, and the old nux vomica. Every deadly plant and herb blossoms by night, withers and fades,
then brings forth a fruit of gold—which we do pluck.

UMBERTO: Ha, ha, ha!

APOTHECARY: 'Tis my pride to devise quaint executions. I have been known to poison the lip of a goblet, but not the wine within, and so lull all suspicion. I once poisoned a young maid's wedding veil. She was modest, and so died. I imbued a courtesan's fan with deadly vapors—and she coquetted herself to the Devil.

UMBERTO: Very pretty, i'faith. Yet is steel swifter, truer.

APOTHECARY: You are not deep—but you are young. Anon, you'll bend to poison, it will creep upon your spirit. What do you wager that some high patron will fill our pockets today?

UMBERTO: A poor wager, sir. Look you, they come.

(*Enter* GOFFREDO *and* CESARE)

CESARE: (*to* GOFFREDO) I do fear me. Shall we be known?

GOFFREDO: Good morrow, Apothecary. (*To* CESARE) Never.

APOTHECARY (*to* UMBERTO): The Duke's sons, as I live! Your pleasure, my lords?

GOFFREDO: Marry, 'tis no pleasure draws us hither. We are aplagued with rats, sir.

APOTHECARY: No rare complaint.

CESARE: We'd have a poison to make our house clean.

APOTHECARY: Most excellent, my lord. Here's what you seek. (*Hands* CESARE *poison*) Rest assured, 'twill kill rats of all shapes, sizes and colors. 'Twill kill any rat of your choice. The price is twenty scudi.

GOFFREDO: Twenty! The charge is excessive, man!

APOTHECARY: The charge is fixed. 'Tis your choice to purchase if you will.

GOFFREDO: Reduce the quantity. Half will suffice.

APOTHECARY: Your pardon, *signor*, it will not. A house plagued with vermin is a parlous matter. 'Twould differ indeed had you but a single rat, but you have named an infestation, have you not? The quantity is fixed.

CESARE *(aside):* Plague take a usurer! Your payment. *(Gives money)*

APOTHECARY: I thank you, sir. May your rats die in pain.

CESARE *(aside):* 'Twould shame Niccolo sadly, methinks, to be called a rat, as well as a bastard. *(Exeunt* GOFFREDO *and* CESARE*)*

APOTHECARY: Their minds are set on murder, 'tis plain.

UMBERTO: The old Duke, think you?

APOTHECARY: Nay, for then the title would fall to their brother Ariosto, and they would gain naught thereby.

UMBERTO: An their courage fail not, we'll soon know.

APOTHECARY: Perhaps. Sure, they'll boggle. I hate an amateur. Who's this?

(Enter NICCOLO *and* DISPADA*)*

NICCOLO *(To* DISPADA*):* Here shall we purchase the means whereby you'll dispatch mine enemies.

DISPADA: Poison, sir! Why must we employ a method so crafty and vile?

NICCOLO: Because 'tis a method so crafty and vile. Now peace, sirrah.

APOTHECARY *(To* UMBERTO*):* Bless me, 'tis the Duke's newly-acknowledged, Niccolo Sparviero.

UMBERTO: Salute him.

APOTHECARY: My customers are all strangers. Your will, gentlemen?

NICCOLO: Faith, 'tis a filthy grievance!

APOTHECARY: Which is—?

NICCOLO: Rats. Ah, me! My home is overrun with rats, they haunt me. I do abominate rats, is't not so, DiSpada?

DISPADA: Truly, sir. They are a breed you would exterminate.

NICCOLO: O, think me not cruel. Yet these rats impede me, and that I cannot abide. I am of the tenderest nature, the most profound sentiment, and yet—

APOTHECARY: I understand, sir. You wish poison?

NICCOLO: Of the deadliest.

DISPADA: Yet swift and painless.

APOTHECARY: You shall be answered. Here it is. *(Hands him poison)* The price is twenty-five scudi.

NICCOLO: Very good. Pay him, DiSpada.

DISPADA: I, my lord?

NICCOLO: Enough, ungrateful man! I've no small coins about me.

DISPADA *(pays)*: Thus, thus pass the wages of infamy. Alas! *(Exeunt NIC-COLO and DISPADA)*

APOTHECARY: Why, there's a noble gentleman! Sure, the Duke's high stature reveals itself in his son's largesse.

UMBERTO: We are benefited should he prove a constant customer.

APOTHECARY: If he but live, he may well. Heart! 'Tis a fat day. Comes another.

(Enter LUCREZIA VELENA, vizarded)

APOTHECARY: Gi' you good den. Fair one, you enter like the sun in eclipse —your glory shielded, but scarcely hid.

LUCREZIA: Thus yields the sun by day to the whims of the wayward moon; and by night, the silvery harlot queens it unrivalled.

APOTHECARY: Nay—the cold white punk's but a beast of burden, bearing the sun's triumphant luster to a darkling world.

LUCREZIA: And yet her beauty's killed by clouds, which are but insubstantial mist.

APOTHECARY *(aside):* Heart! This one escapes me.

UMBERTO: Know you not her? Who could mistake that carriage? 'Tis Lucrezia Velena, widow to the Duke's oldest son.

APOTHECARY: Your business, lady?

LUCREZIA: You'll take me for a sloven, sir, yet needs must I confess—I am troubled with rats.

APOTHECARY: Lady, say no more. I've a poison here will put your woe to flight. Its price is thirty scudi.

LUCREZIA: As to that, sir, I have no need. Yet must I plead a woman's frailty. My soft heart shrinks from cruel deeds, and therefore seek I manly assistance. I am told you will furnish it.

APOTHECARY: For a price, Madam, for a price.

LUCREZIA: 'Tis meet. I am much troubled with an aged she-rat—

APOTHECARY: My apprentice Umberto will play the confessor.

UMBERTO: Fair lady, 'twill ravish me to serve you.

LUCREZIA: Come, sir, I'll acquaint you with the matter. *(Exeunt* LUCREZIA *and* UMBERTO)

APOTHECARY: 'Tis a plague of rats, sure, in the Duke's palace.
　　　When consciences grow rank and black as pitch,
　　　Then do I wax fat, well-clothed and rich.　　　　　　　*(Exit.)*

Scene Two

A room in the DUKE's *palace, with table and chairs. Enter* ARIOSTO, CESARE *and* GOFFREDO, *bearing wine. They sit and drink.*

CESARE: Goffredo, you disgrace the name of temperance. Thus do you also, Ariosto.

ARIOSTO: 'S Blood, you sniveling pedant, d'you school me?

GOFFREDO: Ho, Brother, some sack! 'Las, 'tis finished. Broach a new cask.

CESARE: Brothers, let me entreat you. Prudence.

ARIOSTO: Silence, you.

CESARE: Do but think where you are.

GOFFREDO: Why, in his Grace's palace, to be sure. His Grace's now, and mine hereafter.

ARIOSTO: Yours, sirrah? You lie.

GOFFREDO: What say you?

ARIOSTO: You lie shamefully, dog.

GOFFREDO: I do not.

ARIOSTO: Troth, you do indeed.

GOFFREDO: Slander! Dirt-tongued villain!

CESARE: Peace, sweet brothers, peace. Think on our task.

GOFFREDO: Marry, have we a task?

CESARE: Marry, but we do. Soon comes Niccolo, upon our invitation—

ARIOSTO: O, aye, Niccolo. Misbegotten, thievish, most despised Niccolo.

CESARE: Of an apothecary have we acquired the deadliest poison, will speed him to his tomb—

ARIOSTO: Brave! Ravishing thought!

GOFFREDO: 'Tis true, 'tis very true, 'tis true indeed.

CESARE: Anon he comes, and we shall greet him fairly. We'll carouse, and he'll pledge our health in venomed wine.

ARIOSTO: Ha, limed twigs for a daw.

GOFFREDO: Poisoned bait to lure a carrion-crow, ha!

CESARE: Brothers, on guard! Take heed—we must take a falcon unaware. You are o'erfilled with sack, and claret, and march beer. Fie!

ARIOSTO: Braying ass! *(Strikes* CESARE*)*

CESARE: Mercy!

ARIOSTO: Canting knave! The scoundrel waxes insolent, does he not? I will not suffer him. When I am Duke—

GOFFREDO: You—Duke? Traitor, never!

CESARE: Brothers, you forget our purpose!

GOFFREDO: Pish, not so.

CESARE: Prythee, remember—

ARIOSTO: Troth, we do recall—

(Enter NICCOLO *and* DISPADA*)*

GOFFREDO: Niccolo!

ARIOSTO: Dearest companion!

CESARE: Beloved brother!

NICCOLO *(to* DISPADA*)*: You have the poison ready? This night, in the midst of their drunken rout, a member of that hated trio will die. Gentlemen, what cheer?

GOFFREDO: Faith, none but the brightest, sweet Brother. For now do you merit that loving title.

NICCOLO: Rest assured, Brother, your devotion is returned in equal bounteous measure. To join in our revel have I carried hither the valiant Enrico DiSpada.

CESARE: DiSpada. Methinks I recall the name and countenance.

DISPADA: And well you might, my lord. You three once did cozen me of a fortune in gold at the gaming table.

CESARE: Cozen! A harsh word, *signor.*

ARIOSTO: Methinks an overly-harsh word, *signor.*

NICCOLO: O, friends! Loving brothers! Let no cloud of dissension darken the perfect amity of our gathering. *(They drink)*

ARIOSTO: You say true. 'Tis well. The wine is plentiful, the company merry. Yet we are sadly lacking here!

GOFFREDO: Lacking what?

ARIOSTO: Why, women, by Venus!

GOFFREDO: Scoundrel!

NICCOLO: Faith, Brother, a jest to fire our father's choler.

GOFFREDO: Aye—for he would hide his own lusts behind closed doors, that the foul stench of 'em might not o'erspread the palace. He perfumes his sins all o'er with piety, yet are they rank. Marry, he's a goatish sinner, will still cut a caper i' the dark!

NICCOLO *(to* DISPADA*)*: The time is almost come. They reel and stagger. O, witty Brother!

CESARE *(to* ARIOSTO*)*: The time is almost come. Make him merry, Brother.

ARIOSTO: Why, what should we do without women? Shall we burn with the fever of an unslaked thirst? Set virtue to war with flesh? Tell our beads and mortify our bodies? Pox upon piety! 'Tis the pallid and tremorous virtue. Where's Cytherea's true votary, would not die for his goddess?

GOFFREDO: To die the gentler way! Oh, sweet, delicious death! Ha!

DISPADA *(aside)*: His wit's a blunted, rusty blade, indeed.

ARIOSTO: 'Twould be a pleasant jaunt, methinks, to snap at the widow's young wench Graziella one night. There's a morsel, there's a sweet maidenhead.

GOFFREDO: Brave! A eulogy to her maidenhead!

ALL: Graziella! *(Drink)*

ARIOSTO: But for myself, would I frolic in the bed of the widow herself, Lucrezia Velena. She's the flesh to feed my lechery. Faith, my culverin could salute her five times a night.

GOFFREDO: Aye, she's the quean of 'em all, ha!

NICCOLO: Enough, sir! I'll not have that mirror of sweet purity spotted.

GOFFREDO: There's a damper!

CESARE *(aside)*: Now. *(Fills goblet with wine, secretly adds poison. Hands wine to* NICCOLO*)* Here, dear Brother, be merry. Carouse to the lady's white name.

GOFFREDO *(snatches goblet)*: My need's the greater. The bastard's thrown cold water on my fire. *(Drinks)*

CESARE: No! No, Goffredo! O, God! Lightning, strike! *(Exit, running)*

NICCOLO: Why, what ails him?

GOFFREDO: I know not, and I care not. Marry, I am suddenly faint.

ARIOSTO: You cannot drink. A small capacity.

NICCOLO: What do I see? He grows most exceedingly pale.

DISPADA: His eyes dull. This is beyond drunkenness.

GOFFREDO: O, I am passing weary.

NICCOLO: O, rare illumination! I have it—he is poisoned. 'Twas meant for me. The treacherous, conscienceless villains!

GOFFREDO: A coldness steals upon my limbs. I fear I am not well.

ARIOSTO: Pish, Goffredo, y'are drunk. Always have you fretted o'er trifles.

GOFFREDO: God! I feel death within me!

ARIOSTO: Tut, a bagatelle. You dream.

NICCOLO: Why sit, sweet brother, 'twill soon pass, I'll assure you.

GOFFREDO: Help! Ariosto, I am dying. Send you for a physician!

ARIOSTO: Drunken fool. Coward! Away with your fearful clamorings, my head doth pain me.

GOFFREDO: Fatal woe! I beg, I pray, send you for a priest!

ARIOSTO: Ass! You have no need.

NICCOLO: At least, could do you no good.

DISPADA: Terror! The fog of wine has lifted from him. His last moments are unsoftened.

GOFFREDO: Hell gapes! The jaws of demons spread wide, I writhe impaled upon their fangs. Absolution—a priest! A rosary!

ARIOSTO: Trouble me not. *(Sleeps)*

NICCOLO: I have a rosary.

GOFFREDO: Give it me!

NICCOLO: Alas, 'twas the gift of my mother, and I promised the whore it should never pass from my hands.

GOFFREDO: Mocking hellhound! Hell's curse upon you!

NICCOLO: You will soon know it, sweet Brother.

GOFFREDO: O, for absolution! My soul would rise, yet it sinks in flames, weighted with a burden of sin. Agony of spirit! The darkness claims me. *(Dies)*

NICCOLO: Unequaled joy of victory!

DISPADA: A horror, my lord.

NICCOLO: We may thank the brothers, i' truth. Why, they themselves had grace to supply the festive poison. They've saved my pocket, and I am grateful. Come, we've done here. *(Exeunt* NICCOLO *and* DISPADA*)*

ARIOSTO *(wakes):* Vanished! The bastard's nowhere to be seen. Alas, our scheme has failed. Goffredo? Goffredo? *(Shakes him)* Stupid with wine, a drugged slumber. So weak shall I ne'er prove. Come, fool.
    May Satan claim me if I ever sink
    To let myself be conquered by a drink.

(Exit, dragging GOFFREDO.*)*

Scene Three

The DUCHESS' *apartment. Night. Enter* DUCHESS *and* GRAZIELLA.

DUCHESS: Tell me, dear child, the condition of your mistress.

GRAZIELLA: Her looks are pale and downcast, Madam, her hands meekly folded, her head bowed. Yet oft do I perceive in her eyes flashes of the noble courage that strengthens her to cling to a sad existence. At times, her gaze e'en sparkles with a fervor that can but spring from her faith in Heaven.

DUCHESS: Such tidings cheer me. I perceive in 'em hope for the distressed lady. You may leave me, Graziella.

GRAZIELLA: Your Grace. *(Exit)*

*(*DUCHESS *prepares for sleep. Knocking without)*

DUCHESS: Enter.

(Enter LUCREZIA VELENA *and* UMBERTO, *disguised as a priest)*

DUCHESS: Why, Lucrezia—here, at this hour!

LUCREZIA: Dearest Madam—my heart's mother—I pray you will forgive me.

DUCHESS: Nay, I am rejoiced to see you abroad and vigorous. There is a liveliness in your carriage, a contentment in your visage that I have not beheld there since you were made a widow.

LUCREZIA: Duchess, 'tis the blessed Church hath wrought this change.

DUCHESS: Ah, happiness.

LUCREZIA: See, here is good Father Umberto, come to hurl a divine thunderbolt at my soul's oppressors.

DUCHESS: Father, you are a light to mine eyes. You are God's chosen teacher.

UMBERTO: My lady, you elevate me in your thoughts. I am all unworthy, believe it.

LUCREZIA: Madam, too well I know you've lately lacked confession's solace. So have I carried hither the Father Umberto to hear your slight list of tiny sins.

DUCHESS: This is balm to my soul! Dearest Lucrezia, your sweet thoughts ever anchor upon the joy of others.

LUCREZIA: I'll withdraw. Fare you well, gentle Duchess. *(Exit)*

UMBERTO: Speak, Daughter.

DUCHESS *(kneels)*: Bless me, Father, for I have sinned. I last confess'd upon the tenth October. Since then, my transgressions have been many and grievous. Three nights ago, my lord the Duke once again beat me, and—O, holy Father—I thought upon rebellion. My soul was stained with anger, for I have ever failed in that perfect love, honor and submission to my lord that marks the dutiful wife. I have concealed my faults as best I may, yet 'tis folly to shun God's vision.

I am guilty of sloth. I grow old, fail in the management of my household, thus through my weakness heaping a cruel burden upon the shoulders of others.

I do not practice the charity of the true Christian. Our Savior gave his life for mankind—yet I live in sinful plenty, while others perish of want. My sins are black. Shall I find forgiveness?

UMBERTO: Daughter, I absolve you in the name of the Father, and of the Son, and of the Holy Ghost.

DUCHESS: Father, shall I pay a penance?

UMBERTO: Daughter, you shall.

DUCHESS: What must I do?

UMBERTO: You must die.

DUCHESS: So must we all.

UMBERTO: May that thought comfort you.

DUCHESS: Come, speak plainly.

UMBERTO: Plainly, then—I am no priest.

DUCHESS: What, then? And why come hither? Methinks I fear you.

UMBERTO: Yet you should not, for I am come to deliver you of your frailties. No more will you fail in your wifely duties. No more will your feebleness burden your intimates. No more will you glut worldly hungers. I am come to serve as executioner. Are you not grateful?

DUCHESS: Help! Help! A murder!

UMBERTO: Silence!

DUCHESS: Help! Lucrezia! Lucrezia!

UMBERTO: Call her not. 'Twas that fair devil hired me.

DUCHESS: No! O, no!

UMBERTO: I say to you, I am no priest. Yet take comfort, your death shall be a most holy one. *(Strangles her with rosary)* Well. Do you pray for me.

Re-enter LUCREZIA VELENA)

LUCREZIA: Is't done, then?

UMBERTO: See, there she lies.

LUCREZIA: Valiant Umberto! I prize you above rubies for this deed.

UMBERTO: 'Tis well. You are content?

LUCREZIA: More than content. O, when she cried out, I feared exceedingly; thought to see all the palace upon us, the both of us taken, and

the old woman speaking out loud to condemn us. 'Tis past now—
fortunate circumstance!—and naught remains but the savor of victory's fruits.

UMBERTO: Aye. So please you with my service, lady, 'tis time to think on
reward.

LUCREZIA: That I'd ne'er prove so churlish as to dispute. Here. *(Gives
him money)* A heavy sum.

UMBERTO: I thank you.

LUCREZIA: Now, get you gone from my lady's chamber. Take my gold and
my gratitude with you.

UMBERTO: Not yet.

LUCREZIA: Did you not hear me, man? I tell you go, else face the consequences of your deed.

UMBERTO: Our deed, rather. Here I remain for a season.

LUCREZIA: Alone, then. I do not choose to venture my life upon the
wanton spin of your fancy. *(Offers to leave. He detains her)*

UMBERTO: 'Tis a matter that's passed beyond your choice. I'll be brief.
Your gold does not satisfy me.

LUCREZIA: 'Tis the sum agreed upon.

UMBERTO: So.

LUCREZIA: There must be no contention betwixt us here and now. My
very blood cries out to quit this place. Swiftly, ere we are discovered—

UMBERTO: Thus I foresaw. I can gauge your thoughts to a nicety.

LUCREZIA: Here, then, grasping villain. *(Gives him money)* Take your hire-
ling's reward, and leave my sight.

UMBERTO: My thanks. You are bountiful, lady.

LUCREZIA: Why do you tarry? Go! Never let me clap eyes upon your dog-face again. Mark that well.

UMBERTO: Marked. *(Sits)*

LUCREZIA: Madman! Get you hence!

UMBERTO: Lady, I've no power to stir. The brilliance of your jewels hath dazzled mine eyes.

LUCREZIA *(gives him her jewelry)*: Here, take them, take them all. But away, I prythee. Away, for the sake of our lives!

UMBERTO: I thank you. You've a fine spirit of Christian charity.

LUCREZIA: What, here yet? And will not move? Name your sum, and I'll undertake to furnish it. Yet go. Methinks I hear footsteps in the gallery. They draw near, they are upon us. Away, or let me go! *(He detains her)* May you choke on your damnable greed!

UMBERTO: Fie, lady! This, to a holy father!

LUCREZIA: To a villain, you blasphemer. Your price, I beg you.

UMBERTO: You beg—good, now we come upon't, and by the shortest route. In brief then, lady, I'd have you my mistress.

LUCREZIA: I'll not brook your knavish jests. Come, your price in gold.

UMBERTO: I do not jest. What gold follows we'll sort hereafter. For now, I'll tax your labors.

LUCREZIA: Presumptuous slave! Brutish murderer! What prompts this insolence to me? To me! Go while you may, and thank your good fortune.

UMBERTO: I stand upon my condition. Trust me to stand right truly, lady. 'Twill be a wondrous pleasant thing, methinks, to enjoy a dame of high station. Know you, I've never jounced but the jade was hatted—

LUCREZIA: Filthy villain!

UMBERTO: —And troth, you're of a novel flavor.

LUCREZIA: Aye, the flavor o' gall, sirrah. What proofs would you bring against me? You've none.

UMBERTO: And require none. A motiveless accusation carries weight to sink you. 'Tis your unblemished name that masks your wickedness. That gone, or suspected, and you are undone.

LUCREZIA: Graveyard maggot! Verminous mongrel cur!

UMBERTO: Soft, lady. Leave off your railing, else my price rises.

LUCREZIA: Think you I'd soil my sheets with such foulness?

UMBERTO: Why, such a furious pother over a trifle! 'Tis but the act of an instant, performed in the dark with the world's eyes averted. An act you've performed a thousand times. Tut, 'tis less than nothing.

LUCREZIA: Your impudence warrants the whip, the rack, the strappado. I myself could gouge out your eyes and trample 'em underfoot like grapes pressed for wine. That you should raise those eyes to me!

UMBERTO: I need not raise my eyes, I could look to the gutter and find you. You louse-crawling brach, had best be in season for me—

LUCREZIA: O!

UMBERTO: Venomous you may be, and top-full of guile, but you've been cloistered, lady. In this, you knew not whither you ventured. Learn, then. Submit, play Briseis to my Achilles, else I'll turn such a tide of suspicion upon you shall sweep you to the headman within the month. Mark me, lady, you'll bleed. Your head will sit atop a pike i' the sun, the sport o' the times. The crows will strip the beauty from your cheek, e'en the flesh from your bones, and the common folk will mock your naked grinning, crying out, *There flaunts the great courtesan of Bologna.*

LUCREZIA: O, forbear!

UMBERTO: I will. Heaven knows I'd not affright you. So. You'll grant my desire.

LUCREZIA: Yes.

UMBERTO: You'll receive me in your chamber tomorrow night.

LUCREZIA: Yes.

UMBERTO: A bargain, then.

LUCREZIA: Agreed.

UMBERTO: Most faithfully. 'Tis well. Why tarry you then, Madam? You invite discovery. *(Exit* LUCREZIA*)* Why, she's compromised beyond hope, and 'tis I reaps the benefit of it. Rare fortune!
    There are no heights to which I may not climb
    When arm'd with knowledge of a great one's crime.   *(Exit.)*

ACTUS TERTIUS

Scene One

A *hall in the* DUKE's *palace. The* DUCHESS *lies in state. Enter* GRAZIELLA *and* SIMONE.

SIMONE: O, fatal hour!

GRAZIELLA: Insupportable woe!

SIMONE: Sweet Graziella, sure our house is accursed. But yesterday saw interred my Uncle Goffredo, dead of a shameful drunken surfeit. And now, here lies the blameless Duchess, my loved granddam, kill'd by a villain surprised in the midst of his thieveries.

GRAZIELLA: Alas! What hand so cruel, what heart so pitiless? Can such wickedness exist?

SIMONE: O, Graziella, would that I could shield you from it! 'Tis a world too harsh.

GRAZIELLA: Do not weep, gentle love. Yet yours is a noble grief.

SIMONE: When we are wed, we'll flee this den of horror.

GRAZIELLA: Nay, surely now are all our sorrows ended.

(Enter the DUKE, CESARE, NICCOLO *and* ATTENDANTS)

DUKE: Thus are we assembled to mourn the dead, as is fitting. Yet is there one made conspicuous by his unfeeling absence. Where is my other son? Where is Ariosto?

CESARE: Your Grace—

DUKE: I am here.

CESARE: My lord—Father—

DUKE: Speak, sirrah.

CESARE: He is not well.

DUKE: What ails him?

CESARE: He is exceedingly ill.

DUKE: You dog! You lie scurvily. He is not in his apartment, I know. If he can stir abroad, why comes he not hither? Well, sirrah?

CESARE: Father, I would not brave your anger—

DUKE: That I know well, coward that you are! Speak, where is Ariosto? Speak, ere my tranquil humor fail me.

CESARE: Father, mercy! No one knows where he is. I say to you that he is vanished.

DUKE: Would it were so! Who has seen him last?

NICCOLO: That I have. Last night revel'd he in drunken, furious riot. He entreated me fair to join him, but I soon departed, sickened by his excesses.

DUKE: Such would I look for from you, virtuous exemplar to all.

NICCOLO: Marry, your Grace, he drank himself into a vile sort of delirium, and in this shameful frenzy wandered off, I know not whither. By now, his condition no doubt verges upon madness. O, alas!

DUKE: He deserves no better. Fie on his incontinence!

SIMONE: Your Grace, who knows what injury he may not do himself or others in this unhappy state?

DUKE: I care not. Death rot him!

SIMONE: Your Grace—

CESARE *(to* SIMONE*)*: Silence, lest his anger blast and consume us all.

DUKE: Away, all of you. Go, grant me a final moment alone with my Duchess.

NICCOLO: Sir, we bow to your grief. *(Exeunt omnes, save the* DUKE*)*

DUKE: Aye, a final moment I have long awaited; for you afflicted me with a tedium endless and inexpressible. God's blood, old woman, how your stale piety wearied me! Another crime I might have pardoned, but yours defies absolution. Well, go you now and wander the pale realm alone. Tell your ghostly beads, old abbess, babble your paternosters. Weep holy water if you will—there's a pure cold trickle will never douse my fire. Fare you well, saintly Duchess; I'll console me for your loss. 'Tis a fresh young wife I must have to renew my youth.
Gaunt I may be, and old, and sick, and frail;
But once more shall I live ere life must fail.   *(Exit.)*

Scene Two

A room in the palace. Night. Enter NICCOLO *and* DISPADA.

DISPADA: Yet another bloody crime? The night closes about us. O sir, think well on this.

NICCOLO: Pish, DiSpada, you prate like a woman. Courage, sirrah, 'tis all
but done. You are well readied for Cesare?

DISPADA: I bear the Duke's son no such mortal enmity. Why shall I bear
the lawless burden of your hatred?

NICCOLO: Not of my hatred, but rather, my high ambition. Dolt! Marry,
to what other end would I hire you? You are armed?

DISPADA: Formidably. Look you, here's a pistol of antique workmanship,
formerly the property of a most fantastical pedagogue at the University of Padua. 'Twas kept in open air as a chamber's ornament, until
that pedagogue published a curious treatise, waxed rich and assured
in position, and bestowed the quaint device 'pon me. Faith, I've re-
kindled its fire.

NICCOLO: 'Tis well. Y'are a credit to your teacher. Now, do you likewise
credit your chosen profession.

DISPADA: 'Tis not of my choosing.

NICCOLO: Beware, then. The friendship that festers is breeding ground to
direst hatred. Woulds't turn from me now? Consider well.

DISPADA: O, fear me not. I am more close-bound by your gold than your
threats.

NICCOLO: Perform your task without complaint, lest I doubt you.

DISPADA: I will, sir. Cesare now roams the palace, seeking his death.

NICCOLO: He has found it. Look you, he's upon us. *(They conceal themselves. Enter* CESARE*)*

CESARE: Blacken the old devil's soul! This afternoon, my father's cate-
chism confounded me sadly. Where is Ariosto, he asked. Troth, I
know not. But I'd venture he now sprawls senseless in some unswept
corner. Else quenches his eternal lusts upon some dirty wench. Or
perchance his brain burns in a drunkard's heated ecstasy. Heart, the
fellow has slain Goffredo, and knows it not. And 'tis he will be Duke
at last! 'Tis an honor he scarce befits. Were he but remov'd, I should

come upon the dukedom myself. I—Duke! A single impediment in want of disposal—But where is Ariosto now? Indeed, where? (NICCOLO *and* DISPADA *discover themselves*) The bastard! God save me!

NICCOLO: God may save you, Brother, but I will not do't.

CESARE: O, what do you intend?

NICCOLO: Your death. Make ready.

CESARE: Mercy! O, mercy! Sweet Brother, harm not your own flesh and blood!

NICCOLO: Trifles.

CESARE: Yet have pity, I beseech you! *(Retreats)* Help! Murder! Help! A rescue!

NICCOLO: Now, ere he escape us! To him, DiSpada! (DISPADA *shoots.* CESARE *falls*) There, he is finished.

DISPADA: O, how his ending 'compassed fear and horror! Alas! The death of his body marks the death of my soul. I am lost to Heaven and earth.

NICCOLO: Cease your plaint, 'tis a moment of triumph. Come, this corse must be hid. *(They attempt to lift* CESARE*)*

CESARE: O!

DISPADA: Here's life yet! He moves, he breathes, he speaks! Piteous spectacle! This o'ercomes all fell resolution.

CESARE: Heaven pity me! My very life floats upon the tide of blood that gushes to the ground. Alas, the tide ebbs. I am racked with pain unspeakable. O, bind this grievous wound, I implore you!

DISPADA: Niccolo! This is horror too great to bear! See—ah, see how he suffers!

NICCOLO: Why then, 'twere cruelty in the basest degree to prolong his misery. I am merciful. *(Strangles* CESARE *with cord)*

DISPADA: Now he is past pain. Peace smooths his features, and death seals his countenance with a dignity that life ne'er lent it.

NICCOLO: 'Tis well. Come, bear we him hence. Our handiwork, howe'er noble, demands concealment. *(They attempt to lift* CESARE*)*

CESARE: O!

DISPADA: What, again? He lives yet! The black clouds are driven from my muddied soul. And yet, must he die. O, my conscience, peace! Peace!

CESARE: Grace for my affliction! Do not, O do not kill me! Yet may I be saved. My fearful soul seeks exit, do you bar its passage!

NICCOLO: Down with him!

DISPADA: It must be. Come, hellfire, and cleanse my mind of all remorse! O, but pity for this sad wretch wrings my heart. Of all my crimes, is this the blackest. *(Tramples upon* CESARE*)*

NICCOLO: Good!

CESARE: Help!

DISPADA: That I could aid you, Cesare! O, the pity of it! Alas, poor slaughtered wretch! I weep for you, mine eyes are moist and aflame. *(Beats* CESARE *with cudgel)*

NICCOLO: That's kill'd him, sure. He was fast bound to life.

DISPADA: We have cut the threads. *(They attempt to lift* CESARE*)*

CESARE: O!

DISPADA: Again!

NICCOLO: O, damnation!

CESARE: I am dying. Terror freezes my soul. Death hovers, her dark pinions o'erspreading me. I lie in the sightless shadow of her wings.

DISPADA: O, woe! Woe! Heavy hour! Forgive me, Cesare! Alas, my pangs of guilt! *(Stabs* CESARE *with poniard)*

NICCOLO: He's finished. Come, DiSpada, be of good cheer. Your stealthy, subtle arts have silenced him. But come away, stand not agape like one amazed. We dare no longer stay. Go we now to Ariosto, where e'er he may hide. My ambition thirsts for his blood as he himself thirsts for wine.

DISPADA: I follow ever. *(Exeunt. Enter* SIMONE*)*

SIMONE: I do fear me much that grief hath o'erta'en my unhappy Uncle Ariosto. None can say where he has taken himself—*(Sees* CESARE*)* Father! Dead! O, Father! Dead, dead, dead! Alas, what sorrow! He lies before me, pierced, riddled, strangled and bruised. All the torments of man's devising have racked this hapless form. O, my father! If you but wanted a warming balm, then would my flowing tears restore you! I perish in agony! What monster has used you thus barbarously? O, who has done this deed?

CESARE: Niccolo.

SIMONE: He speaks! He lives!

CESARE: But for a moment.

SIMONE: A physician!

CESARE: Useless. 'Twas Niccolo killed me. Avenge me, my son. An arrow for that hawk's heart. *(Dies)*

SIMONE: Gone! And seeking vengeance! Break, heart! I know not where to go, nor what to do. Shall I seek vengeance indeed? What if he but raved in fevered fancy? Why, then I should damn myself perpetually! Fearful thought! Dreadful deed! Awful peril to my soul! Aye, but my father's mortal command! What shall I do? What? What? Alas, grief has mull'd my mind. I am quite distracted!

I'll yield to Father's will if but I dare—
Yet, spake he false, then shall I court despair.   *(Exit.)*

Scene Three

GRAZIELLA's *apartment. Enter* GRAZIELLA.

GRAZIELLA: Misfortune dogs us all. Yet do I pray that this last double
death may finally purge the court of grief. What, are we condemned
to suffer eternally? Must my blameless Simone suffer such agonies of
sorrow as rend my heart to behold? If it were so, then has the
perfum'd air o' the court bred a plague has kill'd all justice. *(Knocking
without)* Who comes? Enter.

(Enter ARIOSTO, *drunk)*

ARIOSTO: All joy to you, wench.

GRAZIELLA: Lord Ariosto! Alas, sir, you are sought. All the court wonders
at your absence. His Grace your father, much alarmed, demands your
attendance hour upon hour.

ARIOSTO: Doubtless.

GRAZIELLA: My lord, where have you lain?

ARIOSTO: Ask, rather, where would I lie?

GRAZIELLA: In Bologna?

ARIOSTO: Aye, if she's handsome.

GRAZIELLA: My lord?

ARIOSTO: Troth, I do not recall. All is befogged. Here, wench, drink. *(Offers wine)*

GRAZIELLA: Nay, sir. Unwatered wine becomes neither my years nor my
sex.

ARIOSTO: Light objections. Drink.

GRAZIELLA: I do not wish it.

ARIOSTO: I'faith, I say you shall. Deny me not.

GRAZIELLA: Sir, you are unwell. I prythee, take you to your bed.

ARIOSTO: Lady, I had rather take me to your bed.

GRAZIELLA: Fie! Such looseness befits not mine ears.

ARIOSTO: Sweet Graziella, whence comes this strangeness? 'Sblood, but the sight of you stirs my senses. That sparkling eye, that pretty lip, that fair form, each part exact and inviting—all inflame my blood. I must have my will.

GRAZIELLA: Heaven defend me! Sir, forbear, I entreat you.

ARIOSTO: 'Tis useless.

GRAZIELLA *(kneels)*: On bended knee, I implore you. Leave me.

ARIOSTO: In vain. What I desire, that must I have.

GRAZIELLA: Lightning consume me where I stand! Earth swallow me alive! Or let the sea engulf me, that I perish shrieking—yet mar not mine honor!

ARIOSTO: Insolent punk! Is not my favor an honor? I am the next of Bologna.

GRAZIELLA: God preserve mine innocence! Shield me from the lustful ravisher!

ARIOSTO: A pretty slut! Troth, a shy, modest firker!

GRAZIELLA: Such injury is no desert of mine. Base, uncivil man, you fill me with loathing.

ARIOSTO: Will I endure your insults? Here, taste the fruit of insolence. *(Strikes her)*

GRAZIELLA: O! O, I beseech you, beat me, dismember me, or tear the flesh piecemeal from my bones, if that may assuage your passion. Such pain would I greet with rapture.

ARIOSTO: Give over. Have done with these clamorous complaints. They spoil my pleasure. *(Seizes her)*

GRAZIELLA: O, Justice, where is your sword? Help! Alas!

ARIOSTO: Come, this coyness becomes you not. Well I know 'tis a woman's sly trick to sharpen my desire.

GRAZIELLA: Where is death? Why does my suffering spirit still cling to this body?

ARIOSTO: Silence! Rest assured on't, your flesh must serve to feed my lust —*(Knocking without)*

SIMONE *(without)*: Graziella! What are these fearful cries?

ARIOSTO: One calls! Pox rot him, who e'er he may be! Do jealous fiends conspire to rob me of all harmless pleasure? O, fury! *(Exit)*

(Enter SIMONE*)*

GRAZIELLA: Simone! Heaven has heard my prayers!

SIMONE: Graziella! What means this distress?

GRAZIELLA: 'Twas Ariosto. Heated with wine, and half-maddened with lechery, did he enter in upon me, offering the greatest indecency.

SIMONE: O, vile! Vile! Unspeakably vile! Foulness beyond expression! Discourteous villain!

GRAZIELLA: Your approach delivered me.

SIMONE: I breathe again.

GRAZIELLA: Satan guided him sure.

SIMONE: Such evil as this, my mind scarce comprehends.

GRAZIELLA: 'Tis past. And yet, methinks your pallid visage discovers the ravages of new and corrosive sorrow.

SIMONE: My father is slain.

GRAZIELLA: Your valiant father! O, my Simone! Who is the impious criminal?

SIMONE: I know not. I doubt me. I am uncertain, perplexity blights my soul. What shall I do? Whither shall I turn? Confusion and just wrath war within me.

GRAZIELLA: Alas!

SIMONE: Yet is there another woe hard upon us. Uncle Ariosto must be apprehended ere wreaking his insensate rage upon the innocent. We two must seek out assistance.
  Upon my heart has anguish set its brand,
  But sorrow yields to grief more close at hand.   *(Exeunt.)*

Scene Four

The apartment of LUCREZIA VELENA. *Enter* LUCREZIA.

LUCREZIA: The night wears on. Anon comes Umberto to claim his vile reward. How little dreamt I that he could prove so bold! The peasant thinks to bleed me. He'd be the leech to suck my fortune dry. Beyond this, he has dared demand the privilege of my bed. Secure in the knowledge of my guilt, he aspires to rule me. Hellfire consume him! Shall Lucrezia Velena live a slave's slave? My spirit disdains to stoop thus. 'Twere a hundred times better that I die; but a hundred thousand times better that he should die. To this fatal purpose have I o'ersmeared the flesh of neck and breast with poison; harmless to the outer skin, yet instant deadly if ta'en within. When the base ravisher offers his slobbering kisses, 'tis then that vengeance takes him; his lust the instrument of his damnation. I'll pierce him then with bitter words, sharper than any poison's pang. He'll know my hatred ere dying, and my joy in his destruction thrives in his knowledge that I am the author of't. Faith, 'twill be sweet as forbidden love to view his pain; a pleasure to all the senses. And when 'tis done, none bars my path to greatness as the old Duke's consort. *(Knocking without)* Bless me, he comes early. Enter, I await you.

(Enter ARIOSTO*)*

ARIOSTO: You await me? Y'are merciful indeed, lady.

LUCREZIA: Ariosto—you here! What can this mean? *(Aside)* Heaven! What if Umberto now comes?

ARIOSTO: Nay, think it not strange. The adamant of your beauty has drawn me hither.

LUCREZIA *(aside):* Reeking, amorous sot! Sir, you've outpaced my comprehension. Pray leave me.

ARIOSTO: My gallantry decrees otherwise. 'Twere a pity, lady, that you grow cold and stale for lack of fellowship. Faith, the fairest field decays for want of ploughing.

LUCREZIA: Sir, what seek you here?

ARIOSTO: Marry, I am grown wanton and lascivious. I'll tarry no longer. Must I pay you soft and silly court? You are no virgin. Come to bed.

LUCREZIA: O, brazen sin! This to your brother's wife!

ARIOSTO: Aye, but the fool is dead now.

LUCREZIA: Incest! Vile incest!

ARIOSTO: Lady, 'tis sure his horse grows not sluggish for want of riding. Then, 'twere folly to neglect his wife.

LUCREZIA: Chaste innocence ought not suffer this most loathsome familiarity. I am all amazed. Have done.

ARIOSTO: I will indeed. Talk is cheap, 'tis action called for here. *(Seizes her)*

LUCREZIA: Cruel barbarity! Release me!

ARIOSTO: To bed, wench!

LUCREZIA: Touch me at your peril!

ARIOSTO: 'Tis a sweet peril. O, my amorous blood! *(Kisses her throat)*

LUCREZIA: O, fool! Most damned, miserable, braying ass! Drunken oaf! What have you done?

ARIOSTO: Here's a spirit, here's a tempest. *(Releases her)* Marry, I am suddenly ill. I'm all fire. The tongue chars within my mouth.

LUCREZIA: Worse, much worse.

ARIOSTO: All is mist about me. What mean you?

LUCREZIA: Why, dull Ariosto, you are fitly poisoned with your own profane kiss.

ARIOSTO: Alas, no!

LUCREZIA: 'Tis so, I swear it. You are an animate corpse, beyond all human aid. And who knows what a task 'twill prove to conceal it!

ARIOSTO: Wicked, vile woman! Perfumed breath and poisoned flesh! O, I burn!

LUCREZIA: Silence, screech owl. Woulds't draw all the court upon me? Your earthly cares are finished. Have a thought to mine.

ARIOSTO: O, infamy! Help! Help, ho! My mouth, my throat, are filled with smouldering coals.

LUCREZIA: Then will the wagging of your tongue fan them to a blaze. Silence, I say!

ARIOSTO: Incarnate venom, why have you done this?

LUCREZIA: Ask me not. Do you still hear?

ARIOSTO: Would that I could not! O, is this just punishment for my innocent pleasantries?

LUCREZIA: Answer if you can. Know you how I may secretly transport your mortal remains from the palace?

ARIOSTO: O! O, the Devil! The Angel of Death's upon me.

LUCREZIA: He's of no use. Sure, the man raves. Fool! What a coil he's wound!

ARIOSTO: She-wolf, would you might know my pain! (Dies)

LUCREZIA: O, what devilish malice! Well, he's gone, but his earthly substance remains. How to dispose it? Beneath the bed. (Hides ARIOSTO under bed. Knocking without) Darkness shield me, I am discovered! A moment!

(Enter UMBERTO)

UMBERTO: What, shall I meanly sue where I can enter at will? I'll not wait.

LUCREZIA: Umberto! By Heaven, I had forgot you.

UMBERTO: Your memory is somewhat short.

LUCREZIA: So. No matter, you are here. (Aside) I tremble.

UMBERTO: You've a curious air of distraction, lady. Your eye, shunning mine, wanders restlessly about the chamber. What is amiss here?

LUCREZIA: O, nothing.

UMBERTO: Something will come of nothing. Speak again.

LUCREZIA: Modesty compels my silence. Do not my blushes answer?

UMBERTO: Madam, you do not blush. Through long disuse, the blood has forgot the path to your cheek.

LUCREZIA: I protest, sweet Umberto, you do me much wrong.

UMBERTO: How—sweet Umberto, she says! What trickery does this complaisance mask?

LUCREZIA: None. None. Come, have you forgot your purpose?

UMBERTO: What, so sudden eager?

LUCREZIA: To so sweet a yoke, do I willingly bend my neck.

UMBERTO: Why so?

LUCREZIA: For the answer, look you into mine eyes. They mirror your face and shape.

UMBERTO: Your eyes, Madam, yet dart about the room. What do they seek? I'll discover't. *(Searches)*

LUCREZIA: Hold!

UMBERTO: Ha—what's this? A foot, a hand—some knave lies concealed beneath the bed. Come forth, sirrah! *(Drags* ARIOSTO *forth)* How now, 'tis a dead man!

LUCREZIA: Death freeze my blood, I am lost!

UMBERTO: His lips are burnt and bloodied, horror shapes those lifeless features, pain sears 'em—familiar portrait! He has tasted poison.

LUCREZIA *(aside)*: Aye, so must you, as well.

UMBERTO: This is your murderous work.

LUCREZIA: I cannot deny it.

UMBERTO: Belike you purposed the same for me.

LUCREZIA: Never, O, never! Sooner would I brand my face with red hot irons, pluck out my tongue by the roots, or crush my joints to powder. For by all that's marvelous, methinks I grow to love you.

UMBERTO: You are the living breath of falsehood.

LUCREZIA: Nay, Umberto. Look on me. Am I not young? Am I not fair?

UMBERTO: Aye. And?

LUCREZIA: I long to share with you all the warm pleasure that ever night witnessed. Come, we'll frolic until morning, tasting the sweetness of every wanton sport. Venus herself, envying the luxury of our dalliance, must henceforth scorn Mars as a dullard. Come then, Umberto, let us set the Cyprian to school. Come.

UMBERTO: I'm not so easily gull'd. Poisonous woman, I'll go—

LUCREZIA: To noise my crimes abroad? Not so, dog. (Draws poniard, stabs him)

UMBERTO: O, treachery!

LUCREZIA: Thus do you deserve, who would murder mine honor.

UMBERTO: Your honor! Ha, ha, ha! (Dies)

LUCREZIA: Damned villain. I'd hurl your stinking carcass out upon a dungheap, a tribute to the flies—yet must I conceal it. (Hides ARIOSTO and UMBERTO under bed. Knocking without) Out, alas! What shall I do? My life is finished!

(Enter GRAZIELLA, SIMONE, NICCOLO, DISPADA, the DUKE and ATTENDANTS)

SIMONE: Madam! Dear Aunt! We have roused all the court to search the palace for the desperate, frenzied Ariosto. In his rage, has he assaulted sweet Graziella.

GRAZIELLA: Happily, Madam, am I delivered.

DISPADA: Methinks I read in your face, lady, the signs of recent terror and alarm. Is't possible you have met him?

LUCREZIA: O—I tremble to confess it—Ariosto was but lately here. Upon pretext gained he entrance to my chamber, and then did he—did he —attempt my virtue. O! *(Weeps)*

NICCOLO: Excellent, wronged lady! Of what blackness is that miscreant's heart compounded!

GRAZIELLA: That he used me thus was criminal. That he should offer such treatment unto you, Madam—O, that was sacrilege. *(Weeps)*

LUCREZIA: Gentle maid! *(Weeps)*

DUKE: Enough! Away, all of you. My outlaw son must be ta'en. I myself will stay to console Lucrezia Velena.

LUCREZIA: You are good, sir. *(Exeunt all save LUCREZIA and the DUKE)*

DUKE *(aside)*: 'Sdeath, she's handsome. Dearest Lucrezia, for this outrage has my son Ariosto earned my undying enmity.

LUCREZIA: As he is yours, my lord, I cannot hate him.

DUKE: Lady, perhaps 'tis not the time or place to speak, yet this night's work has prov'd all too plain that you are in want of a husband's protection.

LUCREZIA *(aside)*: Now, is my fortune fair or foul? My lord?

DUKE: Will you be ruled by me in this?

LUCREZIA: Your Grace's merest suggestions are my commands from Heaven.

DUKE: So. 'Tis best your safety were soon guarded. I have decided upon a match for you.

LUCREZIA: I am all obedience. *(Aside)* But shall I be Duchess?

DUKE: I bestow you upon one who would gladly offer his heart as well as his title. I give you to one who is high in name, and holds you most high in affection. In giving greatly, I receive beyond measure. Lady, I take you unto myself.

LUCREZIA *(aside)*: O, rare! Ravishing! Your Grace, the honor and the joy confound my tongue. 'Tis a happiness so unlooked for—

DUKE: You'll do't?

LUCREZIA: Most gratefully, my loved lord.

DUKE: There's a wench! Come, we'll inform the court on't. And should we discover the villainous Ariosto, our nuptials may be brightened with his death.

LUCREZIA: Alas, say not so, your Grace!
   On death and vengeance sorrow ever feeds.
   My woman's heart cannot endure fell deeds.   *(Exeunt.)*

ACTUS QUARTUS

The battlements of the palace. Enter DISPADA.

DISPADA: Goffredo and Cesare have both been slain. Thus, 'tis Ariosto alone stands between Niccolo and the ducal throne. When he's found, 'tis sure he'll straight follow his brothers. In these deeds of blood, have I proved the dagger in the bastard's fist. Much has it gone against my nature, yet have wealth, ease, and position lured me. Now, methinks 'twere time to look to the future. When all's done, and he is Duke, what further need of my service? Beyond that, I am privy to his secrets. What, do I serve as a bridge to power for one who would burn his bridges behind him? Yet I dare not desert him. Where e'er I turn, 'twould seem that danger threatens. But no more. I am not alone. *(Conceals himself)*

(Enter SIMONE *and* GRAZIELLA*)*

SIMONE: Indecision racks my soul. Confusion batters my heart.

GRAZIELLA: Gentle love, I conceive you not. Much do I share in your noble sorrow. Yet wherefore confusion?

SIMONE: Ah, Graziella, you know not all! What a hideous secret lies heavy and black upon my mind!

GRAZIELLA: How, Simone!

SIMONE: My father was slain. Ere his soul took flight, he uttered his murderer's name; bade me seek vengeance; and died.

DISPADA *(aside):* O fatal error! We left him too early!

GRAZIELLA: Whom did he name?

SIMONE: Niccolo.

DISPADA *(aside):* The bastard discovered!

GRAZIELLA: O, my Simone! Sure it is not so! Named he none other?

SIMONE: None.

DISPADA *(aside):* So. I am safe, for the present.

GRAZIELLA: Can it be? Can it be his own brother? That name was not, you are certain, the fruit of his dying delirium?

SIMONE: Aye, 'tis that very fear tortures me! He bade me seek vengeance. What if I destroy mine uncle, and he prove innocent? Or what if I do nothing, and he is guilty? A whirlwind buffets me. O, what shall I do?

GRAZIELLA: That I could aid you!

SIMONE: 'Tis beyond your power. 'Tis beyond the power of all save angel or demon. I must think on't. Pray leave me.

GRAZIELLA: O, me miserable! *(Exit)*

SIMONE: Her sweet pity makes me love her. Yet I burden her with a thousand miseries. Those in my bosom take the contagion o' my sorrows. Were I to fling myself from these battlements, rendering this weak vessel unto the spirits of the airy void, surely 'twere a charitable flight. Surrounded on all sides by evil and corruption, I know not where to turn. All the torments of the damned oppress me—unbearable woe! *(Mounts parapet)* Night spreads her sable cloak o'er the world below. There lies an end to my confusion. But is't a path I may follow with honor? Alack, what shall I do? What shall I do? *(Weeps)*

DISPADA *(aside)*: Why, he would destroy himself, who may prove my assurance of salvation. Simone!

SIMONE: Who's there?

DISPADA *(discovers himself)*: 'Tis I.

SIMONE: A spy, sirrah?

DISPADA: You do me great wrong, sir. I have lain here asleep.

SIMONE: You sleep up here?

DISPADA: Occasionally. And you, sir? What do you here?

SIMONE: Cultivate my melancholia, sir; tend black humors like rare blossoms o' the night.

DISPADA: How, sir?

SIMONE: Know you that my father is slain, murdered by stealth.

DISPADA: I know't. 'Tis a cursed villain indeed would bleed that noble gentleman.

SIMONE: A pitiless monster.

DISPADA: A graceless fiend, Acheron's foulest spawn.

SIMONE: You strengthen my spirits, good DiSpada.

DISPADA *(aside)*: I'll work this Simone to friendship. Marry sir, your dark humor breeds apace in the night air.

SIMONE: Aye, I would I were hence.

DISPADA: Come, then. We'll drink, sir. *(Aside)*
    Toward safety now my fortunes should I bend,
    Were I to make this weak youth my fast friend.   *(Exeunt.)*

Scene One

The APOTHECARY'S *shop. Enter* NICCOLO *and* DISPADA.

NICCOLO: This apothecary must die, there's no help for't. 'Twas he that
    sold me poison, and the late death of the Duke's two sons may well
    prick him on to conclusions would prove my undoing. Haply, I'll
    dodge that peril.

DISPADA: A politic foresight, sir.

NICCOLO: Foresight owns its limits. Ariosto's absence puzzles me. Days
    have passed, and he's not shown his face. If he is fled Bologna, I am
    defeated.

DISPADA: I think not so.

NICCOLO: Perhaps. So. You do venture yet upon the confidence of the
    young prince Simone?

DISPADA: For your profit and benefit, my lord.

NICCOLO: 'Tis well, continue then. Bless me, comes the apothecary. You
    know your task?

DISPADA: Too well.

(Enter APOTHECARY*)*

APOTHECARY: Ah, gentlemen, I beg your indulgence. All here's in disarray,
    since my apprentice departed. 'Sfoot, I believe the incontinent young
    rogue has achieved favor of a certain great court lady. If it were so, 'tis
    a vice to be envied. 'Tis a codpiece filled with gold, and the wench is

fair, to boot. I mourn the loss of his services; sure, 'tis the lady's gain. Well, pardon my pleasantries. How may I serve you?

NICCOLO: I require poison.

APOTHECARY: Bless me, 'tis not your first visit.

NICCOLO: No?

APOTHECARY: I ask no questions. You desire poison for—?

NICCOLO: A rat.

APOTHECARY: What, another? Your pardon, beseech you—I ask no questions. *(Aside)* This fellow will make my fortune. *(Hands* NICCOLO *poison)* You know the price.

NICCOLO: Experience breeds knowledge. *(Pays, and stands aside)*

DISPADA: Apothecary—

APOTHECARY: Sir?

DISPADA: Apothecary, beware. 'Tis a notorious rogue, will cozen you if he can.

APOTHECARY: How—cozen!

DISPADA: Soft, man. I say he will. He's been known a thousand times to pass on gilded lead as gold. 'Tis wretched gulls will fill his treasury. Look to it. *(Exit)*

APOTHECARY: Only fools are cheated so.

NICCOLO: What has that crawling knave advised you?

APOTHECARY: In brief, sir, he questions the weight of your gold.

NICCOLO: Ha—a villain! Stinking slave! I'll cut his dissembling tongue out, and force him to swallow it whole.

APOTHECARY: He's moved you.

NICCOLO: Bane to his lying existence! I and my gold are honest.

APOTHECARY: I'll prove these coins, then.

NICCOLO: No need.

APOTHECARY: My lord is vexed?

NICCOLO: An insult. I say you shall not do it.

APOTHECARY: Pardon me, my lord, but I will. *(Bites coin)* 'Tis true gold.

NICCOLO: Aye.

APOTHECARY: Marry, I am not well. I am sudden sick unto death.

NICCOLO: True. You have gi'en't the tang.

APOTHECARY: It comes to me—I am poisoned! 'Lack, who should know the fatal signs better than I?

NICCOLO: Who indeed?

APOTHECARY: Murderer! You led me to bite the poisoned gold!

NICCOLO: Alas, alas, the root of all evil.

APOTHECARY: Vile assassin! Poisoned gold to steal my life! Yet must I concede—'tis a most ingenious conceit; cunning, rare, and deadly withal.

NICCOLO: Y'are kind.

APOTHECARY: Fain would I profit by your wisdom. O viper in human form, how cruelly have you used me! A curse upon you! And yet, must I commend your method. What poison employed?

NICCOLO: Antimony.

APOTHECARY: You had done better with La Cantarella. 'Tis faster.

NICCOLO: Aye, but costlier.

APOTHECARY: Nay, but surer.

NICCOLO: Truly?

APOTHECARY: I warrant you.

NICCOLO: My thanks. I'll recall your counsel upon the next necessity.

APOTHECARY: Do. O, my end is upon me! 'Tis only fitting that I, who lived by poison, should die thus. *(Dies)*

NICCOLO: Well done, Apothecary. Now must I hasten away —but no, here's a customer.

(Enter LUCREZIA VELENA, *armed and attired as a man)*

LUCREZIA: My former crimes drive me to new ones. Soon, this apothecary will think on his apprentice, and wonder. He'll remember my last visit. He'll divine the truth, seek me out, force my subjection. He is older, wiser, richer in experience than the other—altogether a more formidable foe. Best to stop his mouth ere the poison flood of words spurt from it. *(Sees* APOTHECARY*)* Heaven, he lies here asleep. All to the best, he'll not defend himself. *(Draws, and runs him through)* What, no cry, no struggle, no hint of movement? By all that's murderous, methinks he was already slain!

NICCOLO *(aside):* The Devil protects his own. Sure, this bloodthirsty youth was sent for my benefit. 'Tis his head shall fall for this murder. *(Discovers himself)* Hold, foul criminal! Assassin! Here you have slain my friend, the good apothecary. Beardless villain!

LUCREZIA: Niccolo!

NICCOLO: So, you know me. That will not save you.

LUCREZIA: He was dead ere I came. And you hid yourself here—'twas you killed him!

NICCOLO: Lies, and you shall pay for 'em. The headsman will welcome your acquaintance.

LUCREZIA: Never shall I suffer for another's crime. Touch me not.

NICCOLO: I shall, and bear you to a dungeon.

LUCREZIA: Not while I may defend me, lying hypocrite. O, how your wonted mask hangs in tatters!

(He disarms her, discovering her disguise)

NICCOLO: O, just Heavens! Lucrezia Velena!

LUCREZIA: I am past speech.

NICCOLO: You, here—and a murderess!

LUCREZIA: 'Tis false, I killed him not. You have done this deed.

NICCOLO: You attempted as much, and intention is but the deed without labor. 'Twas chance alone forestalled you.

LUCREZIA: Nay, 'twas you forestalled me.

NICCOLO: Lady, I see you are not what you seem.

LUCREZIA: But you, sir, fulfill every base promise of your birth.

NICCOLO: Rich-gowned in false virtue, visage daubed like a whore's in false fair colors of white piety and rose innocence—thus 'tired, you'd commit the blackest of crimes.

LUCREZIA: You, and not I, shall pay for't.

NICCOLO: Never a julio. And yet, what boots this tradesman's talk of reckoning? 'Twere grossest folly to prove our own most importunate creditors. Look you, Madam, our common intent is accomplished. What matter how, why, and by whom? 'Tis done. Be content.

LUCREZIA: There is much i'that.

NICCOLO: Lady, I must tender thanks. You've served me well.

LUCREZIA: How—served you?

NICCOLO: 'Sblood, a lone lingering illusion burthened me, and you have broken it. Now am I free of 'em altogether.

LUCREZIA: Even thus have you favored me.

NICCOLO: Our mutual debts are cleared.

LUCREZIA: I would not betray you, Niccolo.

NICCOLO: Enough, we are not alone. Away with this carrion. *(They conceal APOTHECARY, and hide themselves. Enter two CUSTOMERS)*

FIRST CUSTOMER: Apothecary! What ho!

SECOND CUSTOMER: Absent.

FIRST CUSTOMER: Never. Apothecary! I've need of a remedy. I've gold for you. That will lure the knave.

SECOND CUSTOMER: But he comes not.

LUCREZIA: O, I would the fools were under earth.

NICCOLO: Peace.

SECOND CUSTOMER: For what do you seek a remedy, sir?

FIRST CUSTOMER: Tell no one—

SECOND CUSTOMER: No indeed.

FIRST CUSTOMER: Why, for a fit o' the mother.

SECOND CUSTOMER: Y'are taken with the fits?

FIRST CUSTOMER: Not I, sir; but my wench, sir. She is so deep i' the mother that I am like to shake with the ague of paternity, an ailment whose sovereign remedy is golden. My purse is certain to take fever on't.

SECOND CUSTOMER: Be at ease, sir. The apothecary's your man to cure her swelling affliction, else kill her. Either will equally serve your turn.

LUCREZIA: Beasts!

NICCOLO: Silence.

FIRST CUSTOMER: Pish, we'll wait for him. Tell me, for I am fresh from abroad—what news of the court?

SECOND CUSTOMER: It has been given out that the Duke is betrothed to Lucrezia Velena, widow to his eldest son.

FIRST CUSTOMER: Why, 'tis incest!

SECOND CUSTOMER: Nay, no blood relation there.

FIRST CUSTOMER: An old capon for a young hen.

SECOND CUSTOMER: He's no mummy, 'tis said, e'en yet.

LUCREZIA: Troth he is not, the grey and furrowed luxur!

NICCOLO: Fie, lady—your royal intended. Ha, ha, ha!

LUCREZIA: O, silence, for modesty's sake!

SECOND CUSTOMER: The good Duchess is mysteriously killed. Two of the Duke's sons have died, and the third is missing.

NICCOLO: 'Sdeath, he is vanished indeed.

SECOND CUSTOMER: And the Duke has declared the legitimacy of his bastard Niccolo Sparviero.

LUCREZIA: He must, else lack for heirs. Niccolo, why kill'd you the apothecary?

NICCOLO: Of a sudden, in a quarrel.

LUCREZIA: Nay, to silence him, I warrant. And wherefore? Methinks 'twas much to your profit that Cesare and Goffredo should so sudden die.

FIRST CUSTOMER: Sure, 'tis a profligate court.

SECOND CUSTOMER: Infested with knaves and whores, wastrels and debauchees.

FIRST CUSTOMER: A nest of vipers, a pit of depravity, the shame of Bologna. Fie upon't!

NICCOLO: Well might I inquire then, why you sought to kill him?

LUCREZIA: O, for a vile insult to mine honor, which I'd fain forget.

NICCOLO: Troth, the Duchess' death gilded your fortunes. Did you render your thanks unto God—or unto the apothecary?

SECOND CUSTOMER: Good friend, once more treading your native soil, now seek you an office at court?

FIRST CUSTOMER: Assuredly. Faith, 'tis plain the apothecary will not come today. I've no stomach to wait upon this base fellow's pleasure. Let's away. (*Exeunt*)

LUCREZIA: They're gone, and my heart eases.

NICCOLO: And mine. For lady, from the splendor of your eyes no longer fly the resistless shafts that formerly stabbed my conscience. Those lucent missiles have altered quality, and now, potent still, pierce with sweetness where once they wounded.

LUCREZIA: Faith, Niccolo, so far you surpass the court in knowledge as I once dreamt you surpassed in honesty.

NICCOLO: Aforetimes reverenced I your beauty and piety. Now do I glory in your beauty and your guile. Methinks 'tis no unhappy change. Come, Madam, let us fly this unlucky spot.

LUCREZIA: Whither?

NICCOLO: Will not my chamber conceal us?

LUCREZIA: I pray that it might.

NICCOLO: There may we privily continue our discourse.
　　My chamber shields us from the prying court,
　　And none to interrupt us at our sport.   *(Exeunt.)*

ACTUS QUINTUS

The apartment of LUCREZIA VELENA. *Night. Enter* GRAZIELLA.

GRAZIELLA: Heaven grant my lady discover me not! She has forbidden me
　　her chamber in her absence, yet I disobey. I have lost a token gi'en me
　　by Simone, and I must recover it. Alas, of late has my lady grown
　　viperish, I know not why. Sure, if she enters in upon me, that sharp
　　tongue will pierce a thousand bloody wounds in my soul. No matter.
　　For Simone's treasured token, will I brave all. Now, where has it
　　fallen? On the floor—beneath the bed? *(Searches, and discovers corses
　　beneath the bed)* What's this? O, horrible! Most horrible! 'Tis two
　　dead, cold bodies—one a stranger, the other Lord Ariosto! Dead, O,
　　dead! Piteous and terrible spectacle! My spirit faints! I must straight
　　inform the Duke on't—alas! *(Exit)*

(Enter LUCREZIA VELENA *and* NICCOLO*)*

NICCOLO: Marry, my Lucrezia, I am much troubled at the thought of
　　your approaching nuptials.

LUCREZIA: No need. The fond, ancient Duke shall not spoil our choicest
　　pleasures.

NICCOLO: Beyond that, I would not see you his wife.

LUCREZIA: Nor I, i'faith.

NICCOLO: For I find that I must love you, though 'tis much against my
　　nature and purposes.

LUCREZIA: And I you. For 'tis with you alone may I be true to myself. Before all others must I counterfeit honor, modesty, faint-spirited submission.

NICCOLO: Virtues of foolish women, and I should despise you for 'em. Lucrezia, the Duke hinders us. Let him die.

LUCREZIA: O, my Niccolo, I'd not expose you to needless peril. Be satisfied, your succession is assured.

NICCOLO: Not so. The Duke's second-born Ariosto yet lives. Be certain he'll return to claim his inheritance.

LUCREZIA: Ha, ha, ha!

NICCOLO: Wherefore laughter?

LUCREZIA: Why, now must you own my politic wit. Behold your good fortune! *(Reveals dead men beneath the bed)*

NICCOLO: How now! Two corses! 'Tis Ariosto and another!

LUCREZIA: Pish, the apothecary's knavish apprentice. A slave who's paid the price of his presumption.

NICCOLO: Ariosto dead! O, my Lucrezia, what a rare, precious treasure are you! How subtly was this carried, my sweet love! Yet for your safety and ease must these cold meats be carried straight away.

LUCREZIA: 'Tis true, and quickly. Alas, they have lain some days, and the weather continues warm. This secret will soon discover itself.

NICCOLO: Rare wench! *(Kisses her. Enter the* DUKE, *locking door behind him)*

DUKE: Traitors!

NICCOLO and LUCREZIA: O!

DUKE: Incestuous adulterers! Traitors! Vile traitors! *(Aside)* Unhappy man! And you believed yours such a pure and immaculate lily!

NICCOLO: I warrant your Grace, this can be explained—

DUKE: Only too well! Never seek to escape my wrath, lecherous, filthy serpent! O, bastard, misbegotten, despised bastard! Hated all the more because 'tis mine!

LUCREZIA: Sir, but hear us. Appearances accuse us, yet are we innocent. Never have we offended—

DUKE: Silence! I'll ne'er hear a word more from your wanton, false lips, loathed whore! Away, away, come not near. You have betrayed me shamefully.

LUCREZIA: No, never, I swear! *(Kneels)* Beseech you, listen—

DUKE: Silence! *(Spurns her)* Niccolo, I have raised you high, yet may I fling you back unto the depths. It will be my pleasure to do't—but first must I look to the tale told me by the wench Graziella. *(Approaches bed)*

LUCREZIA: No!

NICCOLO: I implore your Grace—Father—

DUKE: Never speak that detested word! *(Strikes him with crutch)*

NICCOLO: Blackest catastrophe!

DUKE *(discovers dead men)*: O! My son Ariosto! O!

LUCREZIA: Corses beneath my bed! Alas, how came they hither?

DUKE: Lying brach! Murderess! Both of you will die—yet first know the most cunning, ingenious tortures. Guards! To me!

LUCREZIA: I am innocent, innocent as a fluttering dove. Mercy!

DUKE: Death! And death! *(Beats her with crutch)*

LUCREZIA: Help!

NICCOLO: Strike a woman! Forbear!

DUKE: Nay then, I'll strike you instead! *(Beats him)* Guards! To me! Lay hands upon them, to the dungeons with them!

LUCREZIA: Alas, we are lost!

DUKE: You are, 'tis true! *(Pursues them, striking with crutch)*

NICCOLO: He's lost all reason—

DUKE: Poisonous serpents, I'll crush you both beneath my heel!

FIRST NOBLE *(without):* Your Grace, admit us!

SECOND NOBLE *(without):* 'Sfoot, the door is barred against us!

LUCREZIA: Heaven's vengeance upon us! Help!

FIRST NOBLE *(without):* What violence rages within?

DUKE: I am old, and cannot o'ertake you. But never hope to outpace a bullet. *(Draws pistol)*

NICCOLO: Nor you to dodge a blade, old man. *(Draws sword, wounds DUKE)*

DUKE: O! Y'are a dutiful son in one respect—you'll soon follow your father. *(Dies)*

NICCOLO: I've killed the Duke himself!

SECOND NOBLE *(without):* Break ope the door! *(Pounding without)*

LUCREZIA: O, my Niccolo, no escape! On whom can we fix these murders?

NICCOLO: On Simone, perhaps? 'Tis a hopeful victim—

FIRST NOBLE *(without):* The door gives way!

LUCREZIA: Whither shall we turn our desperate steps, but to each other?

NICCOLO: My gentle Lucrezia! We are broken on Fortune's wheel. *(The door gives way)*

(Enter SIMONE, GRAZIELLA, DISPADA, NOBLES and ATTENDANTS)

FIRST NOBLE: The Duke lies but newly slain! And here is murdered Ariosto! Fearful sight!

NICCOLO: DiSpada—

DISPADA *(aside):* If he speaks, I am lost. *(To SIMONE)* My lord, there stands the red-handed slayer of your father, grandfather, and loving uncles. Avenge yourself.

SIMONE: Uncle Niccolo! Alas, I know not what to do!

DISPADA: I do. *(Draws pistol, fires. NICCOLO falls)*

LUCREZIA: Niccolo! Niccolo!

SECOND NOBLE: And thus the murderous bastard is repayed.

DISPADA: A just reward for his misdeeds.

LUCREZIA: Niccolo, do not die! O, does no breath linger in this dear form?

NICCOLO: But breath to bid farewell.

LUCREZIA: You, of all, should have triumphed.

NICCOLO: Sweet Lucrezia! Alas, had I to do all over again, how differently would I carry it! Now would I know not to tarry so long 'fore killing the Duke. *(Dies)*

DISPADA: He is dead. *(Aside)* And I am safe.

FIRST NOBLE *(to LUCREZIA):* Lady, you'll pay the price of these bloody deeds.

LUCREZIA: Murderers! Murderers all! He was more valiant, more noble than the best of you. You have killed one was born to make you all his slaves. And now would you wreak your paltry vengeance upon me? This shall prevent you. *(Draws poniard, stabs herself)* Dogs, I fly where you dare not follow. *(Dies)*

DISPADA: Aye, to Hell. A fury!

SIMONE: O, my Aunt! Heavy hour! *(Weeps)*

GRAZIELLA: Alas, my love, do not weep. Assume the dignity that befits you, for now must you be Duke.

FIRST NOBLE: Aye, naught remains but to repair the wrongs done by this accursed pair, and establish the young prince Simone in his grandfather's right.

SECOND NOBLE: Now do we require a firm hand to guide Bologna from out this morass of woe.

SIMONE: O! To assume the bloodstained throne of power—a prospect dark and terrifying! Alas!

SECOND NOBLE: Come, sir, courage.

SIMONE: I will, sir. I am the last of my line. Upon wedding sweet Graziella, will I seek to reestablish my family. And may my issue prove worthy of the valiant kinsmen so lately slain!

DISPADA: I have no doubt they will so, my lord.

SIMONE: And as my chief advisor, my counsellor, my second-in-command, name I my true and trusted friend, faithful Enrico DiSpada.

DISPADA: Your Grace, my thanks.

FIRST NOBLE: 'Tis well. Bear up these lifeless bodies, then, and pray that such deeds will ne'er be repeated.

SECOND NOBLE: Aye. The young prince will guide us well.
Despite these crimes, the city wall yet stands.
Bologna's rule is left in worthy hands.   *(Exeunt omnes.)*

FRANCESCA DA RIMINI

George Henry Boker

The fifth canto of Dante's *Inferno* describes a region of Hell where a whirlwind eternally buffets the carnal. Here, the poet shows unusual compassion for Paolo and Francesca, a pair of doomed lovers whose poignant story culminates in a famous passage that (freely rendered) declares that

> The double anguish of a pleasure that is fled
> Is remembering its joys in the hour of pain.

This sentiment inspired Tschaikovsky to compose his tone poem, *Francesca Da Rimini*, a powerful orchestral depiction of damnation, and also stimulated GEORGE HENRY BOKER (1823–1890) to write a splendid verse drama that recreates the Paolo-Francesca legend with a sweeping command of human emotion that Shakespeare himself might have admired. Though Boker's masterpiece is unjustly obscure today, theatre scholars generally acknowledge it to represent the pinnacle of romantic tragedy in America.

Its Philadelphia-born author, a distinguished career diplomat, was a poet and fairly prolific playwright who saw several of his scripts, including *The Betrothal, Calaynos, Leonor de Guzman* and *The World a Mask*, produced on Broadway, in Philadelphia and in London.

Francesca Da Rimini was first performed in New York on September 26, 1855, and revived in Philadelphia in 1882 with Otis Skinner in the role of Paolo. In 1901, it was revived in Chicago, this time with Otis Skinner playing the part of Lanciotto.

Because Boker revised the play several times, there is no definitive final version. I have elected to follow the 1853 acting edition, with generous additions. (For further details, see Appendix.)

DRAMATIS PERSONAE

MALATESTA, *Lord of Rimini*

PAOLO,

LANCIOTTO, } *Malatesta's sons*

GUIDO DAPOLENTA, *Lord of Ravenna*

FRANCESCA, *Guido's daughter*

RITTA, *her maid*

PEPE, *Malatesta's jester*

CARDINAL, *Friend to Guido*

RENÉ, *a troubadour*

Nobles, ladies, knights, priests, soldiers, pages and attendants

Scene: Rimini, Ravenna and the neighborhood.
Time: About 1300 A.D.

ACT FIRST

Rimini. The garden of the palace. PAOLO *and a number of* NOBLEMEN *are discovered, seated under an arbor, surrounded by* RENÉ *and other* TROUBADOURS *and* ATTENDANTS.

PAOLO: I prithee, René, charm our ears again
　　With the same song you sang me yesterday.
　　Here are fresh listeners.

RENÉ: 　　　　　　Really, my good lord,
　　My voice is out of joint. A grievous cold—　　　　　　*(Coughs)*

PAOLO: A very grievous, but convenient cold,
　　Which always racks you when you would not sing.

RENÉ: O, no, my lord! Besides, I hoped to hear
　　My ditty warbled into fairer ears,
　　By your own lips; to better purpose, too.

(The NOBLEMEN *all laugh)*

PAOLO: But, hark! here comes the fool! Fit company
　　For this most noble company of wits!
　　(Enter PEPE, *laughing violently)*
　　Why do you laugh?

PEPE: 　　　　　　I'm laughing at the world.
　　It has laughed long enough at me; and so
　　I'll turn the tables. Ho! ho! ho! I've heard
　　A better joke of Uncle Malatesta's
　　Than any I e'er uttered.　　　　　　*(Laughing)*

ALL: 　　　　　　Tell it, fool.

PEPE: Why, do you know—upon my life, the best
　　And most original idea on earth:
　　A joke to put in practice, too. By Jove!
　　I'll bet my wit 'gainst the stupidity
　　Of the best gentlemen among you all,
　　You cannot guess it.

ALL: Tell us, tell us, fool.

PEPE: Guess it, guess it, fools.

PAOLO: Come, disclose, disclose!

PEPE: He has a match afoot.—

ALL: A match!

PEPE: A marriage.

ALL: Who?—Who?

PEPE: A marriage in his family.

ALL: But, who?

PEPE: Ah! there's the point.

ALL: Count Paolo?

PEPE: No.

FIRST N: The others are well wived.
    Shall we turn Turks?

PEPE: Why, there's the summit of his joke, good sirs.
    By all the sacred symbols of my art—
    By cap and bauble, by my tinkling bell—
    He means to marry Lanciotto!

(Laughs violently)

ALL (laughing): Ho!—

PAOLO: Peace! peace! What tongue dare echo yon fool's laugh?
    Nay, never raise your hands in wonderment;
    I'll strike the dearest friend among ye all
    Beneath my feet, as if he were a slave,
    Who dares insult my brother with a laugh!   (Exit.)

The same. A hall in the castle. Enter MALATESTA *and* LANCIOTTO.

MALATESTA: Guido, ay, Guido of Ravenna, son—
  Down on his knees, as full of abject prayers
  For peace and mercy as a penitent.

LANCIOTTO: His old trick, father. While his wearied arm
  Is raised in seeming prayer, it only rests.
  Anon, he'll deal you such a staggering blow,
  With its recovered strength, as shall convert
  You, and not him, into a penitent.

MAL: No, no; your last bout leveled him. He reeled,
  Into Ravenna, from the battlefield,
  Like a stripped drunkard, and there headlong fell—
  I pity Guido.

LAN: 'S death! Go comfort him!
  I pity those who fought, and bled and died,
  Before the armies of this Ghibelin.
  I pity those who halted home with wounds
  Dealt by his hand. I pity widowed eyes
  That he set running; maiden hearts that turn,
  Sick with despair, from ranks thinned down by him;
  Mothers that shriek, as the last stragglers fling
  Their feverish bodies by the fountain side,
  Dumb with mere thirst, and faintly point to him,
  Answering the dame's quick questions. I have seen
  Unburied bones, and skulls—that seemed to ask,
  From their blank eyeholes, vengeance at my hand—
  Shine in the moonlight on old battlefields;
  And even these—the happy dead, my lord—
  I pity more than Guido of Ravenna!

MAL: What would you have?

LAN: I'd see Ravenna burn,
  Flame into Heaven, and scorch the flying clouds;
  I'd choke her streets with ruined palaces;
  I'd hear her women scream with fear and grief,
  As I have heard the maids of Rimini.

All this I'd sprinkle with old Guido's blood,
And bless the baptism.

MAL: You are cruel.

LAN: Not I;
But these things ache within my fretting brain.
The sight I first beheld was from the arms
Of my wild nurse, her husband hacked to death
By the fierce edges of these Ghibelins.
One cut across the neck—I see it now,
Ay, and have mimicked it a thousand times,
Just as I saw it, on our enemies.—
Why, that cut seemed as if it meant to bleed
On till the judgment. My distracted nurse
Stooped down, and paddled in the running gore
With her poor fingers; then a prophetess,
Pale with the inspiration of the god,
She towered aloft, and with her dripping hand
Three times she signed me with the holy cross.
'T is all as plain as noonday. Thus she spake—
"May this spot stand till Guido's dearest blood
Be mingled with thy own!" The soldiers say,
In the close battle, when my wrath is up,
The dead man's blood flames on my vengeful brow
Like a red planet; and when war is o'er,
It shrinks into my brain, defiling all
My better nature with its slaughterous lusts.
Howe'er it be, it shaped my earliest thought,
And it will shape my last.

MAL: You moody churl!
You dismal knot of superstitious dreams!
I'll get a wife to teach you common sense.

LAN: A wife for me!   (Laughing)

MAL: Ay, sir, a wife for you.

LAN: 'T is not your wont to mock me.

MAL: I have chosen
The fairest wife in Italy for you.
If you will plead, I ween, she dare not say—
No, by your leave. I have made her hand
The price and pledge of Guido's future peace.

LAN: All this is done!

MAL: Done, out of hand; and now
I wait a formal answer, nothing more.

LAN: Who is the lady I am bartered for?

MAL: Francesca, Guido's daughter.—Never frown;
It shall be so!

LAN: By Heaven, it shall not be!
My blood shall never mingle with his race.

MAL: According to your nurse's prophecy,
Fate orders it.

LAN: Ha!

MAL: Now, then, I have struck
The chord that answers to your gloomy thoughts.
Bah! on your sibyl and her prophecy!
Lanciotto, look ye! You brave gentlemen,
So fond of knocking out poor people's brains,
In time must come to have your own knocked out:
What, then, if you bequeath us no new hands,
To carry on your business, and our house
Die out for lack of princes?

LAN: Wed my brothers:
They'll rear you sons, I'll slay you enemies.
Paolo and fair Francesca! Note their names;
They chime together like sweet marriage-bells.
A proper match. 'T is said she's beautiful;
And he is the delight of Rimini,—
The pride and conscious center of all eyes,

The theme of poets, the ideal of art,
The earthly treasury of Heaven's best gifts!
I am a soldier; from my very birth,
Heaven cut me out for terror, not for love.

MALATESTA: Pshaw! son, no more: I'll have it so!   (*Exit*)

LAN: Curses upon my destiny! What, I—
Ho! I have found my use at last—
What. I.   (*Laughing*)
I, the great twisted monster of the wars,
The brawny cripple, the herculean dwarf,
The spur of panic, and the butt of scorn—
I be a bridegroom! Heaven, was I not cursed
More than enough, when thou didst fashion me
To be a type of ugliness,—a thing
By whose comparison all Rimini
Holds itself beautiful? Lo! here I stand,
A gnarlèd, blighted trunk! There's not a knave
So spindle-shanked, so wry-faced, so infirm,
Who looks at me, and smiles not on himself.
Pah! it is nauseous! Must I further bear
The sidelong shuddering glances of a wife?
The degradation of a showy love,
That overacts, and proves the mummer's craft
Untouched by nature? And a fair wife, too!—
Francesca, whom the minstrels sing about!
Now, in the battle, if a Ghibelin
Cry, "Wry-hip! Hunchback!" I can trample him
Under my stallion's hoofs; or haggle him
Into a monstrous likeness of myself:
But to be pitied,—to endure a sting
Thrust in by kindness, with a sort of smile!—
'S death! it is miserable!

(*Enter* PEPE)

PEPE: My lord—

LAN: My fool!

PEPE: We'll change our titles when your bride's bells ring—

LAN: Who told you of my marriage?

PEPE: Rimini!
  A frightful liar; but true for once, I fear.
  The messenger from Guido has returned,
  And the whole town is wailing over him.
  Some pity you, and some the bride; but I,
  Being more catholic, I pity both.

LAN *(aside)*: Still, pity, pity! *(Bells toll)* Ha! whose knell is that?

PEPE: Lord Malatesta sent me to the tower,
  To have the bells rung for your marriage news.
  How, he said not; so I, as I thought fit,
  Told the deaf sexton to ring out a knell.
  (Bells toll)
  How do you like it?

LAN: Varlet, have you bones,
  To risk their breaking? I have half a mind
  To thrash you from your motley coat!

(Seizes him)

PEPE: Pardee!
  Respect my coxcomb, cousin. Hark! Ha, ha!
  (Laughing. Bells ring a joyful peal)
  Some one has changed my music. Heaven defend!
  How the bells jangle! Yonder graybeard, now.
  Rings a peal vilely. Only give him time,
  And, I'll be sworn, he'll ring your knell out yet.

LAN: I shook you rudely; here's a florin.

(Offers money)

PEPE: No:
  My wit is merchandise, but not my honor.

LAN: Your honor, sirrah!

PEPE: Why not? You great lords
Have something you call lordly honor; pray,
May not a fool have foolish honor too?
Cousin, you laid your hand upon my coat—
'T was the first sacrilege it ever knew—
And you shall pay it. Mark! I promise you.

LAN *(laughing):* Ha, ha! You bluster well. Upon my life,
You have the tiltyard jargon to a breath.
Pepe, if I should smite you on the cheek—
Thus, gossip, thus—*(Strikes him)* what would you then demand?

PEPE: Your life!

LAN *(laughing):* Ha, ha! There is the campstyle, too—
A very cutthroat air! How this shrewd fool
Makes the punctilio of honor show!
Change helmets into coxcombs, swords to baubles,
And what a figure is poor chivalry!
Thanks for your lesson, Pepe.   *(Exit)*

PEPE: Ere I'm done,
You'll curse as heartily, you limping beast!
(Bells ring)
There go the bells rejoicing over you:
I'll change them back to the old knell again.
You marry, faugh! Beget a race of elves;
Wed a shecrocodile, and keep within
The limits of your nature! Here we go,
Tripping along to meet our promised bride,
Like a rheumatic elephant!—ha, ha!

(A clash of arms without. Enter LANCIOTTO*)*

LAN: Was that a signal, made by Heaven itself
To warn my soul against this coming marriage?
I like it not. My father named this match
While I boiled over with vindictive wrath
Towards Guido and Ravenna. Straight my heart

Sank down like lead; a weakness seized on me,
A dismal gloom that I could not resist;
I lacked the power to take my stand, and say—
Bluntly, I will not! Would that I
Were in the wars again! These mental weeds
Grow on the surface of inactive peace.
I'm haunted by myself. Thought preys on thought.
My mind seems crowded in the hideous mold
That shaped my body. What a fool am I
To bear the burden of my wretched life,
To sweat and toil under the world's broad eye,
Climb into fame, and find myself—O, what?—
A most conspicuous monster! Crown my head,
Pile Caesar's purple on me—and what then?
My hump shall shorten the imperial robe,
And pomp, instead of dignifying me,
Shall be by me made quite ridiculous.
The faintest coward would not bear all this:
Prodigious courage must be mine, to live;
To die asks nothing but weak will.
(Draws and gazes upon his dagger)
                                    What floods
Of joy might enter through the wound thou'dst give
Had I but hardihood.

(Enter PAOLO*)*

PAOLO *(seizing his hand):* Brother! what is this?
    Lanciotto, are you mad? Kind Heaven! look here—
    Straight in my eyes. Now answer, do you know
    How near you were to murder? Dare you bend
    Your wicked hand against a heart I love?
    Were it for you to mourn your wilful death,
    With such a bitterness as would be ours,
    The wish would ne'er have crossed you. Shame,
    Brother, shame! I thought you better metal.

LANCIOTTO: I know the seasons of our human grief,
    And can predict them without almanac.
    A few sobs o'er the body, and a few
    Over the coffin; then a sigh or two,

Whose windy passage dries the hanging tear;
Perchance, some wandering memories, some regrets;
Then a vast influx of consoling thoughts—
Based on the trials of the sadder days
Which the dead missed; and, then a smiling face
Turned on tomorrow. Such is mortal grief.
It writes its histories within a span,
And never lives to read them.

PAOLO: Lanciotto,
    I heard the bells of Rimini, just now,
    Exulting o'er your coming marriage day.
    Why are you sad?

LAN: Paolo, I am wretched;
    Sad's a faint word. But of my marriage bells—
    Heard you the knell that Pepe rang?

PAOLO: 'T was strange.

LAN: It was portentous. All dumb things find tongues
    Against this marriage. As I passed the hall,
    My armor glittered on the wall, and I
    Paused by the harness, as before a friend
    Whose well-known features slack our hurried gait;
    Francesca's name was fresh upon my mind,
    So I half-uttered it. Instant, my sword
    Leaped from its scabbard, as with sudden life,
    Plunged down and pierced into the oaken floor,
    Shivering with fear! Lo! While I gazed upon it—
    Doubting the nature of the accident—
    Around the point appeared a spot of blood,
    Oozing upon the floor, that spread and spread—
    As I stood gasping by in speechless horror—
    Ring beyond ring, until the odious tide
    Crawled to my feet, and lapped them, like the tongues
    Of angry serpents! Go—you may see—go to the hall!

PAOLO (goes to the door, and returns): There sticks the sword, indeed,
    Just as your tread detached it from its sheath;
    Looking more like a blessed cross, I think,

Than a bad omen. As for blood—Ha, ha!   (*Laughing*)
It sets mine dancing. Pshaw! Away with this!
Deck up your face with smiles. Go trim yourself
For the young bride. New velvet, gold and gems,
Do wonders for us. Brother, come; I'll be
Your tiring-man, for once.

LAN: Array this lump—
  Paolo, hark! There are some human thoughts
Best left imprisoned in the aching heart,
Lest the freed malefactors should dispread
Infamous ruin with their liberty.
There's not a man—the fairest of ye all—
Who is not fouler than he seems. This life
Is one unending struggle to conceal
Our baseness from our fellows. Here stands one
In vestal whiteness with a lecher's lust;—
There sits a judge, holding law's scales in hands
That itch to take the bribe he dare not touch;—
Here goes a priest with heavenward eyes, whose soul
Is Satan's council chamber;—there a doctor,
With nature's secrets wrinkled round a brow
Guilty with conscious ignorance;—and here
A soldier rivals Hector's bloody deeds—
Outdoes the devil in audacity—
With craven longings fluttering in a heart
That dares do aught but fly! Thus are we all
Mere slaves and almsmen to a scornful world,
That takes us at our seeming.

PAOLO: Say 't is true;
  What do you drive at?

LAN: At myself, full tilt.
  I, like the others, am not what I seem.
Men call me gentle, courteous, brave.—They lie!
I'm harsh, rude and a coward. Had I nerve
To cast my devils out upon the earth,
I'd show this laughing planet what a Hell
Of envy, malice, cruelty, and scorn,

It has forced back to canker in the heart
Of one poor cripple!

PAOLO: Cripple!

LAN: Ay, now 't is out!
A word I never breathed to man before.
Can you, who are a miracle of grace,
Feel what it is to be a wreck like me?
Paolo, look at me. Is there a line,
In my whole bulk of wretched contraries,
That nature in a nightmare ever used
Upon her shapes till now? Find me the man,
Or beast, or tree, or rock or nameless thing,
So out of harmony with all things else,
And I'll go raving with bare happiness,—
Ay, and I'll marry Helena of Greece,
And swear I do her honor!

PAOLO: Let me beseech you, brother,
To look with greater favor on yourself;
Go to Ravenna, wed your bride, and lull
Your cruel delusions in domestic peace.

LAN: To Ravenna?—no!
In Rimini they know me; at Ravenna
I'd be a newcome monster, and exposed
To curious wonder, and when they look,
How can I tell if 't is the bridegroom's face
Or hump that draws their eyes? I will not go.
To please you all, I'll marry; but to please
The wondermongers of Ravenna—Ha!
Dear Paolo, now I have it. You shall go,
To bring Francesca; and you'll speak of me,
Not as I ought to be, but as I am.
If she draw backward, give her rein; and say
That neither Guido nor herself shall feel
The weight of my displeasure. You may say,
I pity her—

PAOLO: For what?

LAN: For wedding me.
   In sooth, she'll need it. Say—

PAOLO: Nay, Lanciotto,
   I'll be a better orator in your behalf,
   Without your promptings.

LAN: She is fair, 't is said;
   And, my dear Paolo, if she please your eye,
   And move your heart to anything like love,
   Wed her yourself. The peace would stand as firm
   By such a match.

PAOLO *(laughing)*: Ha! That is right: be gay!
   Ply me with jokes! I'd rather see you smile
   Than see the sun shine.

LAN: I am serious,
   I'll find another wife, less beautiful,
   More on my level, and—

PAOLO: An empress, brother,
   Were honored by your hand. You are by much
   Too humble in your reckoning of yourself.
   I can count virtues in you, to supply
   Half Italy, if they were parcelled out.
   Look up!

LAN: I cannot: Heaven has bent me down.
   But to you, Paolo, I could look, however,
   Were my hump made a mountain. Bless him, God!
   Pour everlasting bounties on his head!
   Round his fair fortune to a perfect end!
   O, you have dried the sorrow of my eyes;
   My heart is beating with a lighter pulse;
   The air is musical; the total earth
   Puts on new beauty, and within the arms
   Of girdling ocean dreams her time away,
   And visions bright tomorrows!

(*Enter* MALATESTA *and* PEPE)

MALATESTA: Mount, to horse!
   Lanciotto, you are waited for. The train
   Has passed the gate, and halted there for you.

LAN: I go not to Ravenna.

MAL: Hey! Why not?

PAOLO: For weighty reasons, father. Will you trust
   Your greatest captain, hope of all the Guelfs,
   With crafty Guido? Should the Ghibelins
   Break faith, and shut Lanciotto in their walls—
   Sure the temptation would be great enough—
   What would you do?

MAL: I'd eat Ravenna up!

PEPE: Lord! What an appetite!

PAOLO: But Lanciotto
   Would be a precious hostage.

MAL: True; you're wise;
   Guido's a fox. Well, have it your own way.
   What is your plan?

PAOLO: I go there in his place.

MAL: Good! I will send a letter with the news.

LAN: I thank you, brother. (*Apart to* PAOLO)

PEPE: Ha! ha! ha!—O! O!   (*Laughing*)

MAL: Pepe, what now?

PEPE: O! lord, O!—ho! ho! ho! (*Laughing*)

PAOLO: 'S death! fool, I'll have you in the stocks.
   Father, your fool exceeds his privilege.

PEPE *(apart to* PAOLO): Keep your own bounds.
  But, cousin, don't forget
  To take Lanciotto's picture to the bride.
  Ask her to choose between it and yourself.
  I'll count the moments, while she hesitates,
  And not grow gray at it.

PAOLO: Here's for your counsel!

(Strikes PEPE, *who runs behind* MALATESTA)

MAL: Son, son, have a care!
  We who keep pets must bear their pecks sometimes.
  Poor knave! Ha! ha! thou 'rt growing villainous. *(Laugh and pats* PEPE)

PEPE *(aside)*: Another blow! another life for that!

PAOLO: Farewell, Lanciotto. You are dull again.

LAN: Nature will rule.

MAL: Come, come!

LAN: God speed you, brother!
  I am too sad; my smiles all turn to sighs.

PAOLO: More cause to haste me on my happy work.

(Exit with MALATESTA)

PEPE: I'm going, cousin.

LAN: Go.

PEPE: Pray, ask me where.

LAN: Where, then?

PEPE: To have my jewel carried home:
  And, as I'm wise, the carrier shall be
  A thief, a thief, by Jove! The fashion's new.   *(Exit)*

LAN: In truth, I am too gloomy and irrational.
  And Paolo must be right. I always had
  These moody hours and dark presentiments,
  Without mischances following after them.
  The camp is my abode. A neighing steed,
  A fiery onset and a stubborn fight,
  Rouse my dull blood, and tire my body down
  To quiet slumbers when the day is o'er,
  And night above me spreads her spangled tent,
  Lit by the dying cresset of the moon.
  Ay, that is it; I'm homesick for the camp.   *(Exit.)*

ACT SECOND

Ravenna. A room in GUIDO's *palace. Enter* GUIDO *and a* CARDINAL.

CARDINAL: I warn thee, Count.

GUIDO: I'll take the warning, father,
  On one condition: show me but a way
  For safe escape.

CARDINAL: I cannot.

GUIDO: There's the point.
  The Guelfs are masters, we their slaves; it is well
  To say you love Francesca. So do I;
  But neither you nor I have any voice
  For or against this marriage.

CARDINAL: 'Tis too true.

GUIDO: Say we refuse: why, then, before a week,
  We'll hear Lanciotto rapping at our door,
  With twenty hundred ruffians at his back.
  What's to say then? My lord, we waste our breath.

CARDINAL: And yet I fear—

GUIDO: You fear! and so do I.

I fear Lanciotto as a soldier, though,
More than a son-in-law.

CARDINAL: But have you seen him?

GUIDO: Ay, ay, and felt him, too. I've seen him ride
The best battalions of my horse and foot
Down like mere stubble: I have seen his sword
Hollow a square of pikemen, with the ease
You'd scoop a melon out.

CARDINAL: Report declares him
A prodigy of strength and ugliness.

GUIDO: Were he the Devil—but why talk of this?—
Here comes Francesca. Add your voice to mine,
Or woe to poor Ravenna!

(*Enter* FRANCESCA *and* RITTA)

FRANCESCA: Ha! my lord—
And you, my father!—But do I intrude
Upon your counsels? How severe you look!
Shall I retire?

GUIDO: No, no. We spoke of you,
Francesca, your betrothed is on the way:
Perhaps, even now, he's riding toward Ravenna.
Count Lanciotto is not used to wait,
And looks to find you in your fairest trim.
I have his father's hand—

FRANCESCA: You moody men
Seem leagued against me. As I passed the hall,
I met your solemn Dante, with huge strides
Pacing in measure to his stately verse.
Thinking to pass, without disturbing him,
I stole on tiptoe, but the poet paused,
Subsiding into man, and steadily
Bent on my face the luster of his eyes.
Then, taking both my trembling hands in his—

You know how his God-troubled forehead awes—
He looked into my eyes, and shook his head,
As if he dared not speak of what he saw,
Then muttered, sighed and slowly turned away
The weight of his intolerable brow.
Indeed, my lord, he should not do these things:
They strain the weakness of mortality
A jot too far. As for poor Ritta, she
Fled like a doe, the truant.

RITTA: Yes, forsooth:
There's something terrible about the man.
Ugh! if he touched me, I should turn to ice.
I wonder if Count Lanciotto looks—

GUIDO: Ritta, come here. *(Takes her aside)*

RITTA: My lord.

GUIDO: 'Twas my command,
You should say nothing of Count Lanciotto.

RITTA: Nothing, my lord.

GUIDO: You have said nothing, then?

RITTA: Indeed, my lord.

GUIDO: 'Tis well. Some years ago,
My daughter had a very silly maid,
Who told her sillier stories. So, one day,
This maiden whispered something I forbade—
In strictest confidence, for she was sly:
What happened, think you?

RITTA: I know not, my lord.

GUIDO: I boiled her in a pot.

RITTA: Good heaven! my lord.

GUIDO: She did not like it. I shall keep that pot
  Ready for the next boiling.   *(Walks back to the others)*

RITTA: Saints above!
  I wonder if he ate her! Boil me—me!
  I'll roast or stew with pleasure; but to boil
  Implies a want of tenderness—or rather
  A downright toughness—in the matter boiled,
  That's slanderous to a maiden. What, boil me—
  Boil me! O! mercy, how ridiculous!   *(Retires, laughing)*

(Enter a MESSENGER*)*

MESSENGER: Letters, my lord, from great Prince Malatesta.

(Presents them to GUIDO *and exits)*

GUIDO *(reads)*: "Fearing our treachery,"—by heaven, that's blunt,
  And Malatesta-like!—"he will not send
  His son, Lanciotto, to Ravenna, but"—
  But what?—a groom, a porter? Or will he
  Have his prey sent him in an iron cage?
  By Jove, he shall not have her! O! no, no;
  "He sends his younger son, the Count Paola,
  To fetch Francesca back to Rimini."
  That's well, if he had left his reasons out.
  And, in a postscript—by the saints, 'tis droll!—
  "'Twould not be worth your lordship's while, to shut
  Paola in a prison; for, my lord,
  I'll only pay his ransom in plain steel:
  Besides, he's not worth having." Is there one,
  Save this ignoble offshoot of the Goths,
  Who'd write such garbage to a gentleman?
  Take that, and read it.   *(Gives letter to* CARDINAL*)*

CARDINAL: I have done the most.
  She seems suspicious.

GUIDO: Ritta's work.

CARDINAL: Farewell!   *(Exit)*

FRANCESCA: Father, you seem distempered.

GUIDO: No, my child,
I am but vexed. Your husband's on the road,
Close to Ravenna. We must be stirring, then.

FRANCESCA: I do not like this marriage.

GUIDO: But I do.

FRANCESCA: But I do not. Poh! to be given away,
Like a fine horse or falcon, to a man
Whose face I never saw!

RITTA: That's it, my lady.

GUIDO: Ritta, run down, and see if my great pot
Boils to your liking.

RITTA (aside):   O! that pot again!
My lord, my heart betrays me; but you know
How true 'tis to my lady.   (Exit)

FRANCESCA: What ails Ritta?

GUIDO: The ailing of your sex, a running tongue.
Francesca, 'tis too late to beat retreat.
Old Malatesta has me—you, too, child—
Safe in his clutch. Poh, poh! have a soul
Equal with your estate. A prince's child
Cannot choose husbands. Her desires must aim,
Not at herself, but at the public good.

FRANCESCA: Is Lanciotto handsome—ugly—fair—
Black—sallow—crabbèd—kind—or what
Is he? You always put me off;
You never have a whisper in his praise.

GUIDO: The world reports it.—Count my soldier's scars,
And you may sum Lanciotto's glories up.

FRANCESCA: I shall be dutiful, to please you, father.
   My part has been obedience; and now
   I play it over to complete my task;
   And it shall be with smiles upon my lips—
   Heaven only knows with what a sinking heart!   *(Exeunt.)*

The same. Before the gates of the city. The walls hung with banners and
flowers are crowded with citizens. At the side of the scene is a canopied
dais, with chairs of state upon it. Music, bells, shouts and other sounds of
rejoicing are occasionally heard. Enter GUIDO, CARDINAL, *Nobles, knights,*
guards, with banners and arms.

GUIDO: My lord, I'll have it so. You talk in vain.
   Paola is a marvel in his way:
   I've seen him often. If Francesca take
   A fancy to his beauty, all the better;
   For she may think that he and Lanciotto
   Are as like as blossoms of one parent branch.
   The fraud cannot last long; but long enough
   To win her favor to the family.

CARDINAL: I'll neither help nor countenance a fraud.
   You crafty men take comfort to yourselves,
   Saying, deceit dies with discovery.
   'Tis false; each wicked action spawns a brood,
   And lives in its succession. You, who shake
   Man's moral nature into storm, should know
   That the last wave which passes from your sight
   Rolls in and breaks upon eternity!   *(Exits)*

GUIDO: Why, that's a very grand and solemn thought:
   I'll mention it to Dante. Gentlemen,
   What see they from the wall?

NOBLEMAN: The train, my lord.

GUIDO: Inform my daughter.

NOBLEMAN: She is here, my lord.

(Enter FRANCESCA, RITTA, LADIES *and* ATTENDANTS*)*

FRANCESCA: See, father, what a merry face I have,
And how my ladies glisten! I will try
To do my utmost, in my love for you
And the good people of Ravenna. Now,
As the first shock is over, I expect
To feel quite happy. I will wed the Count,
Be he whate'er he may. One pang remains.
Parting from home and kindred is a thing
None but the heartless, or the miserable,
Can do without a tear. This home of mine
Has filled my heart with twofold happiness,
Taking and giving love abundantly.
Farewell, Ravenna! If I bless thee not,
'T is that thou seem'st too blessed; and 't were strange
In me to offer what thou'st always given.
(Shouts and music within)
Ha! there's the van just breaking through the wood!
Music! that's well; a welcome forerunner.
Now, Ritta—here—come talk to me. Alas!
How my heart trembles! What a world to me
Lies 'neath the glitter of yon cavalcade!
Is that the Count?

RITTA: Upon the dapple-gray?

FRAN: Yes, yes.

RIT: No; that's his—

GUI *(apart to her):*   Ritta!

RIT: Ay; that's—that's—

GUI: Ritta, the pot!   *(Apart to her)*

RIT *(aside):*   O! but this lying chokes!
Ay, that's Count Somebody, from Rimini.

FRAN: I knew it was. Is that not glorious?

RIT: My lady, what?

FRAN: To see a cavalier
Sit on his steed with such familiar grace.

RIT: To see a man astraddle on a horse!
It don't seem much to me.

FRAN: Fie! stupid girl!
If that's the gentleman my father chose,
He must have picked him out from all the world.
The Count alights. Why, what a noble grace
Runs through his slightest action! Are you sad?
You, too, my father? Have I given you cause?
I am content. If Lanciotto's mind
Bear any impress of his fair outside,
We shall not quarrel ere our marriage-day.

RITTA *(aside):* Alas! Dear lady!

GUIDO: Come, come;
Get to your places. See, the Count draws nigh.

*(GUIDO and FRANCESCA seat themselves upon the dais, surrounded by RITTA,
ladies, attendants and guards. Music, shouts, ringing of bells. Enter men-
at-arms, with banners; pages bearing costly presents on cushions; then
PAOLO, surrounded by noblemen, knights, minstrels and followed by other
men-at-arms. They range themselves opposite the dais)*

GUI: Ravenna welcomes you, my lord, and I
Add my best greeting to the general voice.
This peaceful show of arms from Rimini
Is a new pleasure, stranger to our sense
Than if the East blew zephyrs.

PAOLO: Noble sir,
We looked for welcome from your courtesy,
Not from your love. I need not ask, my lord,
Where bides the precious object of my search;
For I was sent to find the fairest maid
Ravenna boasts, among her many fair.
I might extend my travel many a league,
And yet return, to take her from your side.

I blush to bear so rich a treasure home,
As pledge and hostage of a sluggish peace;
For beauty such as hers was meant by Heaven
To spur our race to gallant enterprise,
And draw contending deities around
The dubious battles of a second Troy.

GUI: Sir Count, you please to lavish on my child
The high-strained courtesy of chivalry.

PAOLO: I must suppose so rare a tabernacle
Was framed for rarest virtues. Pardon me.
When I have brushed my travel from my garb,
I'll pay my court in more befitting style.

(Music. Exit with his train)

GUI (advancing): Now, by the saints, Lanciotto's deputy
Stands in this business with a proper grace,
Stretching his lord's instructions till they crack.
I but half like it!

FRAN (advancing): Father?

GUI: Well, my child.

FRAN: How do you like—

GUI: The coxcomb! I've done well!

FRAN: No, no; Count Lanciotto?

GUI: Well enough.
But hang this fellow—hang your deputies!
I'll never woo by proxy.

FRAN: Deputies!
And woo by proxy!

GUI: Come to me anon.
I'll strip this cuckoo of his gallantry!

(Exit with guards)

FRAN: Ritta, my father has strange ways of late.

RIT: I wonder not.

FRAN: You wonder not?

RIT: No, lady:
  (Aside) Plague on his boiling! I will out with it.
  Lady, the gentleman who passed the gates—

FRAN: Count Lanciotto? As I hope for grace,
  A gallant gentleman! How well he spoke!
  With what sincere and earnest courtesy
  The rounded phrases glided from his lips!
  He spoke in compliments that seemed like truth.
  Methinks I'd listen through a summer's day,
  To hear him woo.—And he must woo to me—
  I'll have our privilege—he must woo a space,
  Ere I'll be won, I promise.

RIT: But, my lady,
  He'll woo you for another.

FRAN: He?—Ha! ha!   *(Laughing)*
  I should not think it from the prologue, Ritta.

RIT: Nor I.

FRAN: Nor any one.

RIT: 'T is not the Count—
  'T is not Count Lanciotto.

FRAN: Gracious saints!
  Have you gone crazy? Ritta, speak again,
  Before I chide you.

RIT: 'Tis the solemn truth.
  That gentleman is the Count Paolo, lady,

Brother to Lanciotto, and no more
Like him than—than—

RAN: Than what?

RIT: Count Guido's pot,
For boiling waiting maids, is like the bath
Of Venus on the arras.

FRAN: But are you mad—
Quite mad, poor Ritta?

RIT: By the mass,
They shall not cozen you. Boldly I repeat,
That he who looked so fair, and talked so sweet,
Who rode from Rimini upon a horse
Of dapple-gray, and walked through yonder gate,
Is not Count Lanciotto.

FRAN: This you mean?

RIT: I do, indeed!

FRAN: Then I am more abused—
More tricked, more trifled with, more played upon—
By him, my father, and by all of you,
Than anything, suspected of a heart,
Was ever yet!

RIT: But in Count Paolo, lady,
Perchance there was no meditated fraud.

FRAN: How, dare you plead for him?

RIT: I but suppose:
Though in your father—O! I dare not say.

FRAN: I dare. It was ill usage, gross abuse,
Treason to duty, meanness, craft—dishonor!
What if I'd thrown my heart before the feet
Of this sham husband! Cast my love away

Upon a counterfeit! I was prepared
To force affection upon any man
Called Lanciotto. O! what a fool—
Trapped by mere glitter! What an easy fool!
Ha! ha! I'm glad it went no further, girl;   (*Laughing*)
I'm glad I kept my heart safe, after all.
There was my cunning. I have paid them back,
I warrant you! I'll marry Lanciotto;
I would not live another wicked day
Here, in Ravenna, only for the fear
That I should take to lying, with the rest.
Ha! ha! It makes me merry, when I think
How safe I kept this little heart of mine!

(*Laughing. Exit, with* ATTENDANTS)

RITTA: So, 'tis all ended—all except my boiling,
And that will make a holiday for some.
Perhaps I'm selfish. Fagot, axe and gallows,
They have their uses, after all. They give
The lookers-on a deal of harmless sport.
Though one may suffer, twenty hundred laugh—
I wonder if they'll put me in a bag,
Like a great suet-ball? I'll go and tell
Count Guido, on the instant: How he'll laugh
To think his pot has got an occupant!
I only said the man was not Lanciotto;
No word of Lanciotto's ugliness.
I may escape the pot, for all. Pardee!
I wonder if they'll put me in a bag.

(*Exit, laughing*)

The same. A room in GUIDO's *palace. Enter* GUIDO *and* RITTA.

RITTA: There now, my lord, this is the whole of it:
I love my mistress more than I fear you.
If I could save her finger from the axe,
I'd give my head to do it. So, my lord,
I am prepared to stew.

GUIDO: Boil, Ritta, boil.

RITTA: No; I prefer to stew.

GUIDO: And I to boil.

RITTA: 'Tis very hard, my lord, I cannot choose
My way of cooking. I shall laugh, I vow,
In the grim headsman's face, when I remember
That I am dying for my lady's love.
I leave no one to shed a tear for me;
Father nor mother, kith nor kin, have I,
To say, "Poor Ritta!" o'er my lifeless clay.
They all have gone before me, and 'twere well
If I could hurry after them.

GUIDO *(aside)*:   Poor child!
But, baggage, said you aught of Lanciotto?

RITTA: No, not a word; and he's so ugly, too!

GUIDO: Is he so ugly?

RITTA: Ugly! He is worse
Than Pilate on the hangings.

GUIDO: Hold your tongue
Here, and at Rimini, about the Count,
And you shall prosper.

RITTA: Am I not to boil?

GUIDO: No, child. But be discreet at Rimini.
Old Malatesta is a dreadful man—
Far worse than I—he bakes his people, Ritta;
Lards them, like geese, and bakes them in an oven.

RITTA: Fire is my fate, I see that.

GUIDO: Have a care

It do not follow you beyond this world.
Where is your mistress?

RITTA: In her room, my lord.
  After I told her of the Count Paolo,
  She flew to have an interview with you;
  But on the way—I know not why it was—
  She darted to her chamber, and there stays
  Weeping in silence. It would do you good—
  More than a hundred sermons—just to see
  A single tear, indeed it would, my lord.

GUIDO: Ha! You are saucy. I have humored you
  Past prudence, malpert! Get you to your room!
  (Exit RITTA*)*
  More of my blood runs in yon damsel's veins
  Than the world knows. Her mother to a shade;
  The same high spirit, and strange martyr-wish
  To sacrifice herself, body and soul,
  For some loved end. All that she did for me;
  And yet I loved her not. O! memory!
  The darkest future has a ray of hope,
  But thou art blacker than the sepulcher!
  Thy horrid shapes lie round, like scattered bones,
  Hopeless forever! I am sick at heart.
  The past crowds on the present: as I sowed,
  So am I reaping. Shadows from myself
  Fall on the picture, as I trace anew
  These rising specters of my early life,
  And add their gloom to what was dark before.
  O! Memory, memory! How my temples throb!

(Sits. Enter FRANCESCA, *hastily)*

FRANCESCA: My lord, this outrage— *(He looks up)* Father, are you ill?
  You seem unhappy. Have I troubled you?
  You heard how passionate and bad I was,
  When Ritta told me of the Count Paolo.
  Dear father, calm yourself; and let me ask
  A child's forgiveness. 'T was undutiful
  To doubt your wisdom. It is over now,

I only thought you might have trusted me
With any counsel.

GUI (*aside*): Would I had!

FRAN: Ah! well,
I understand it all, and you were right.
Only the danger of it. Think, my lord,
If I had loved this man at the first sight:
We all have heard of such things. Think, again,
If I had loved him—as I then supposed
You wished me to—'t would have been very sad.
But no, dear sir, I kept my heart secure,
Nor will I loose it till you give the word.
I'm wiser than you thought me, you perceive.
But when we saw him, face to face, together,
Surely you might have told me then.

GUI: Francesca,
My eyes are old—I did not clearly see—
Faith, it escaped my thoughts. Some other things
Came in my head. I was as ignorant
Of Count Paolo's coming as yourself.
The brothers are so like.

FRAN: Indeed?

GUI: Yes, yes,
One is the other's counterpart, in fact;
And even now it may not be—O! shame!
I lie by habit.   (*Aside*)

FRAN: Then there is hope? Ritta may be deceived.
He may be Lanciotto, after all?
O! joy—

(*Enter a* SERVANT)

SERVANT: The Count Paolo.   (*Exit*)

FRAN: Ah. Misery!
   That name was not Lanciotto!

GUI: Farewell, child.
   I'll leave you with the Count: he'll make it plain.
   It seems 't was Count Paolo.   *(Going)*

FRAN: Father!

GUI: Well.

FRAN: You knew it from the first!
   (Exit GUIDO*)*
   Worse cannot fall me. Though my husband lack
   A parent's tenderness, he yet may have
   Faith, truth, and honor—the immortal bonds
   That knit together honest hearts as one.
   Let me away to Rimini. Alas!
   It wrings my heart to have outlived the day
   That I can leave my home with no regret!

(Weeps. Enter PAOLO*)*

PAOLO: Pray, pardon me.   *(Going)*

FRAN: You are quite welcome, Count.
   A foolish tear, a weakness, nothing more:
   But present weeping clears our future sight.
   They tell me you are love's commissioner,
   A kind of broker in the trade of hearts:
   Is it your usual business? Or may I
   Flatter myself, by claiming this essay
   As your first effort?

PAOLO: Lady, I believed
   My post, at starting, one of weight and trust;
   When I beheld you, I concluded it
   A charge of honor and high dignity.
   I did not think to hear you underrate
   Your own importance, by dishonoring me.

FRAN: Your brother—my good lord that is to be—
    Stings me with his neglect; and in the place
    He should have filled, he sends a go-between,
    A common carrier of others' love;
    How can the sender, or the person sent,
    Please overmuch? Now, were I such as you,
    I'd be too proud to travel round the land
    With other people's feelings in my heart;
    Even to fill the void which you confess
    By such employment.

PAOLO: Lady, 't is your wish
    To nettle me, to break my breeding down,
    And see what natural passions I have hidden
    Behind the outworks of my etiquette.
    I neither own nor feel the want of heart
    With which you charge me. You are more than cruel;
    My task is odious to me. Since I came,
    Heaven bear me witness how my traitor heart
    Has fought against my duty; and how oft
    I wished myself in Lanciotto's place,
    Or him in mine.

FRAN: You riddle.

PAOLO: Do I? Well,
    Let it remain unguessed. My duty waits.

FRAN: My future lord's affairs? I quite forgot
    Count Lanciotto.

PAOLO *(aside):* I, too, shame upon me.

FRAN: Does he resemble you?

PAOLO: Pray, drop me, lady.

FRAN: Nay, answer me.

PAOLO: Somewhat—in feature.

FRAN: Ha!
   Is he so fair?

PAOLO: No, darker. He was tanned
In long campaigns, and battles hotly fought,
While I lounged idly with the troubadours,
Under the shadow of his watchful sword.

FRAN: In person?

PAOLO: He is shorter, I believe,
But broader, stronger, more compactly knit.

FRAN: What of his mind?

PAOLO: Ah, now you strike the key!
A mind just fitted to his history,
An equal balance 'twixt desert and fame.
My love might weary you, if I rehearsed
The simple beauty of his character;
His grandeur and his gentleness of heart,
His warlike fire and peaceful love, his faith,
His courtesy, his truth. He graspeth crowns
While I pick at the laurel.

FRANCESCA: Stay, my lord!
I asked your brother's value, with no wish
To hear you underrate yourself. Your worth
May rise in passing through another's lips.
Lanciotto is perfection, then?

PAOLO: To me:
Others may think my brother over-nice
Upon the point of honor; over-keen
To take offense where no offense is meant;
A thought too prodigal of human life,
Holding it naught when weighed against a wrong;
Perhaps I throw these points too much in shade,
By catching at an enemy's report.
But, then, Lanciotto said, "You'll speak of me,

Not as I ought to be, but as I am."
He loathes deceit.

FRAN: That's noble! Have you done?
  I have observed a strange reserve, at times,
  Both in my father and his nearest friends,
  When speaking of your brother; as if they
  Picked their way slowly o'er rocky ground,
  These things have troubled me. From you I look
  For perfect frankness. Is there naught withheld?

PAOLO: All that my honor calls for I have said.

FRANCESCA: You know, my lord, that, once at Rimini,
  There can be no retreat for me. By you,
  Here at Ravenna, in your brother's name,
  I shall be solemnly betrothed. And now
  I thus extend my maiden hand to you;
  If you are conscious of no secret guilt,
  Take it.

PAOLO: I do.   *(Takes her hand)*

FRAN: You tremble!

PAOLO: With the hand,
  Not with the obligation.

FRAN: Farewell, Count!
  T' were cruel to tax your stock of compliments,
  That waste their sweets upon a trammelled heart;
  Go fly your fancies at some freer game.

(Exit)

PAOLO: O, heaven, if I have faltered and am weak,
  'T is from my nature! Fancies, more accursed
  Than haunt a murderer's bedside, throng my brain—
  Temptations, such as mortal never bore
  Since Satan whispered in the ear of Eve.
  Sing in my ear—and all, all are accursed!

At heart I have betrayed my brother's trust,
Francesca's openly. Turn where I will.
As if enclosed within a mirrored hall,
I see a traitor. Now to stand erect,
Firm on my base of manly constancy;
Or, if I stagger, let me never quit
The homely path of duty, for the ways
That bloom and glitter with seductive sin!   (*Exit.*)

Rimini. A room in the castle. LANCIOTTO *discovered reading.*

LANCIOTTO: O! Fie, philosophy! This Seneca
  Revels in wealth, and whines about the poor!
  Talks of starvation while his banquet waits,
  And fancies that a two hours' appetite
  Throws light on famine! Doubtless he can tell,
  As he skips nimbly through his dancing-girls,
  How sad it is to limp about the world
  A sightless cripple! Let him feel the crutch
  Wearing against his heart, and then I'd hear
  This sage talk glibly; or provide a pad,
  Stuffed with his soft philosophy, to ease
  His aching shoulder. Pshaw; he never felt,
  Or pain would choke his frothy utterance.
  Show me philosophy in rags, in want,
  Sick of a fever, with a back like mine,
  Creeping to wisdom on these legs, and I
  Will drink its comforts. Out! away with you!
  There's no such thing as real philosophy!
  (*Throws down the book. Enter* PEPE)
  Here is a sage who'll teach a courtier
  The laws of etiquette, a statesman rule,
  A soldier discipline, a poet verse,
  And each mechanic his distinctive trade;
  Yet bring him to his motley, and how wide
  He shoots from reason! We can understand
  All business but our own, and thrust advice
  In every gaping cranny of the world;
  While habit shapes us to our own dull work,
  And reason nods above his proper task.
  Just so philosophy would rectify

All things abroad, and be a jade at home.
This jester is a rare philosopher.
Teach me philosophy, good fool.

PEPE: No need.
You'll get a teacher when you take a wife.
If she do not instruct you in more arts
Than Aristotle ever thought upon,
The good old race of woman has declined
Into a sort of male stupidity.

(*Trumpet sounds within*)

Hist! my lord.

LAN: That calls me to myself.

PEPE: At that alarm,
All Rimini leaped up upon its feet.
Cousin, your bridal train. You groan! 'Ods wounds!
Here is the bridegroom sorely malcontent—
The sole sad face in Rimini. Since morn,
A quiet man could hardly walk the streets,
For flowers and streamers. All the town is gay.
Perhaps 't is merry o'er your misery.

LAN: Perhaps; but that it knows not.

PEPE: Yes, it does:
It knows that when a man's about to wed,
He's ripe to laugh at. Cousin, tell me, now,
Why is Count Paolo on the way so long?
Ravenna's but eight leagues from Rimini—

LAN: That's just the measure of your tongue, good fool.
You trouble me. I've had enough of you—
Begone!

MALATESTA (*without*): Come, Lanciotto!

LAN: Hark!
My father calls.

PEPE: If he were mine, I'd go—
That's a good boy!

(Pats LANCIOTTO's *back)*

LAN *(starting)*:   Hands off! you'll rue it else!   *(Exit)*

PEPE *(laughing)*: Ha! ha! I laid my hand upon his hump!
Heavens, how he squirmed! And what a wish I had
To cry, Ho! Camel! leap upon his back,
And ride him to the Devil! Ho, my bird,
I can toss lures as high as any man.
So, I amuse you with my harmless wit?
Pepe's your friend now—you can trust in him—
An honest, simple fool! Just try it once,
You ugly, misbegotten clod of dirt!
Ay, but the hump—the touch upon the hump—
The start and wriggle—that was rare! Ha! ha!   *(Exit, laughing.)*

ACT THIRD

Rimini. The Grand Square before the castle. SOLDIERS *on guard, with banners.* CITIZENS, *in holiday dress, cross the scene. The houses are hung with trophies, banners and garlands. Enter* MALATESTA, *with* GUARDS, ATTENDANTS.

MALATESTA: Captain, take care the streets be not choked up
By the rude rabble. Send to Caesar's bridge
A strong detachment of your men, and clear
The way before them. Make all things look bright;
As if we stood in eager readiness,
And high condition, to begin a war.

CAPTAIN: I will, my lord.

MAL: Keep Guido in your eye;
And if you see him looking overlong

On any weakness of our walls, just file
Your bulkiest fellows round him. You conceive?

CAPTAIN: Trust me, my lord.   *(Exit with* GUARDS. *Enter* PEPE)

PEPE: Room, room! A hall; a hall!
I pray you, good man, has the funeral passed?

MAL: Who is it asks?

PEPE: Pepe of Padua,
A learned doctor of uncivil law.

MAL: But how a funeral?

PEPE: You are weak of wit.
Francesca of Ravenna's borne to church,
And never issues thence.

MAL: How, doctor, pray?

PEPE: Now, for a citizen of Rimini,
You're sadly dull. Does she not issue thence.
Fanny of Rimini? A glorious change,—
A kind of resurrection in the flesh!

(Distant shouts and music)

MAL: Hark! here comes Jeptha's daughter, jogging on
With timbrels and with dances.

MAL: Jeptha's daughter!
How so?

PEPE: Her father's sacrifice.

MAL: Here comes the vanguard. Where,
where is that laggard?

PEPE: At the mirror, uncle,
Making himself look beautiful. He comes,   *(Looking out)*

Fresh as a bridegroom! Mark his doublet's fit
Across the shoulders, and his hose!—
By Jove, he nearly looks like any other man!

MAL: You'd best not let him hear you. Sirrah, knave,
I have a mind to swing you!

(Seizes his ear)

PEPE: You're unjust.
Being his father, I was fool sufficient
To think you fashioned him to suit yourself,
By way of a variety. The thought
Was good enough, the practice damnable.

MAL: Hush! or I'll clap you in the pillory. You're a raven, croaker.

PEPE: And you no white crow, to insure us luck.

MAL: There's matter in his croak.

PEPE: There always is;
But men lack ears.

MAL: Then eyes must do our work.
I do not like this flight of eagles more
Than Pepe. 'S death! Guido was ever treacherous.

PEPE: Guido was ever treacherous?—So—so!

MAL: So—so! How so?

PEPE: What if this treachery
Run in the blood? We'll tap a vein then—so!

MAL: Sew up your mouth, and mind your fooling, fool!

PEPE: Am I not fooling? Why, my lord, I thought
The fooling exquisite.
(Shouts and music within)
Look! here's the whole parade! Mark old Guido, too!

He looks like Judas with his silver. Ho!
Here's news from sweet Ravenna!

MAL *(laughing)*:   Ha! ha! ha!

PEPE: Ah! Now the bride!—that's something—she is toothsome.
Look you, my lord—now, while the progress halts—
Cousin Paolo, has he got the dumps?
Mercy! To see him, one might almost think
'T was his own marriage. What a doleful face!
The boy is ill. He caught a fever, uncle,
Traveling across the marshes. Physic! physic!

MAL: For heaven's sake, cease your clamor! I shall have
No face to meet them else. 'T is strange, for all:
What ails poor Paolo?

PEPE: Dying, by this hand!

MAL: Then I will hang you.

PEPE: Don't take up my craft.
Wit's such a stranger in your brain that I
Scarce knew my lodger venturing from your mouth.
Now they come on again.

MAL: Stand back!

(Music, shouts, ringing of bells. Enter MEN-AT-ARMS, *with banners,* GUIDO,
CARDINAL, KNIGHTS, ATTENDANTS; *then* PAOLO, *conducting* FRANCESCA, *followed
by* RITTA, LADIES, PAGES *and other* MEN-AT-ARMS. *They file around the stage,
and halt)*

MAL: Welcome to Rimini, Count Guido! Welcome.
And fair impressions of our poor abode,
To you, my daughter! You are well returned,
My dear son, Paolo! Let me bless you, son.
(PAOLO *approaches)*
How many spears are in old Guido's train?   *(Apart to* PAOLO)

PAOLO: Some ten-score.

MAL: Footmen?

PAOLO: Double that.

MAL: 'T is well.
  Again I bid you welcome! Make no show
Of useless ceremony with us. Friends
Have closer titles than the empty name.
Let us drop Guelf and Ghibelin henceforth,
Coupling the names of Rimini and Ravenna
As bridegroom's to his bride's.

GUIDO: Count Malatesta,
  simply, I thank you. With an honest hand
I take the hand which you extend to me,
And hope our grasp may never lose its warmth.—
You marked the bastion by the waterside?
Weak as a bulrush.   *(Apart to a* KNIGHT*)*

KNIGHT: Tottering weak, my lord.

GUI: Remember it; and when you're private, sir,
  Draw me a plan.

KNIGHT: I will, my lord.

GUI: How's this?
  I do not see my future son-in-law.

MAL: Lanciotto!

LANCIOTTO *(entering):* I am here, my lord.

FRANCESCA *(starting):*   O! heaven!
  Is that my husband, fair Count Paolo? You,
You then, among the rest, have played me false!
He is—   *(Apart to* PAOLO*)*

PAOLO: My brother.

LAN *(aside):*   Ha! she turns from me.

Turns off with horror; as if she had seen—
What?—Simply me. For, am I not enough,
And something over, to make ladies quail,
Start, hide their faces, whisper to their friends,
Point at me—dare she?—and perform such tricks
As women will when monsters blast their sight?
O! saints above me, have I come so low?
I must be patient. They have trifled with her:
Lied to her, lied!
They're all aghast—all looking at me, too.
Francesca's whiter than the brow of fear:
What if I draw my sword, and fight my way
Out of this cursed town? 'T would be relief.
By Heaven, I'll brave this business out! Shall they
Say at Ravenna that Count Lanciotto,
Who's driven their shivering squadrons to their homes,
Haggard with terror turned before their eyes
And slunk away? They'll look me from the field,
When we encounter next. Why should not I
Strut with my shapeless body, as old Guido
Struts with his shapeless heart? I'll do it!   *(Offers, but shrinks back)*
          'S death!
                Lady Francesca!

(Approaches FRANCESCA)

FRAN: Sir—my lord—

LAN: Dear lady,
    I have a share in your embarrassment,
    And know the feelings that possess you now.

FRAN: O! you do not.

PAOLO *(advancing):*   My lady—

LAN: Gentle brother,
    Leave this to me.   (PAOLO *retires)*

FRAN: Pray do not send him off.

LAN: 'T is fitter so.

FRAN: He comforts me.

LAN: Indeed?
  Do you need comfort?

FRAN: No, no—pardon me!
  But then—he is—you are—

LAN: Take breath, and speak.

FRAN: I am confused, 't is true. But, then, my lord,
  You are a stranger to me; and Count Paolo
  I've known so long!

LAN: Since yesterday.

FRAN: Ah! well:
  But the relationship between us two
  Is of so close a nature, while the knowledge,
  That each may have of each, so slender is
  That the two jar. Besides, Count Paolo is
  Nothing to me, while you are everything.
  (Aside) Can I not act?

LAN: I scarcely understand.
  You say your knowledge of me, till today,
  Was incomplete. Has naught been said of me
  Either by Count Paolo or your father?

FRAN: Yes;
  But nothing definite.

LAN: Perchance, no hint
  As to my ways, my feelings, manners, or—
  Or—or—as I was saying—ha! ha!—or—   *(Laughing)*
  As to my person?

FRAN: Nothing, as to that.

LAN: To what?

FRAN: Your—person.

LAN: That's the least of all.
   (Turns aside)
   Now, had I Guido of Ravenna's head
   Under this heel, I'd grind it into dust!
   Lady Francesca, when my brother left,
   I charged him, as he loved me, to conceal
   Nothing from you that bore on me: and now
   That you have seen me, and conversed with me,
   If you object to anything in me—
   Go, I release you.

FRAN: But Ravenna's peace?

LAN: Shall not be periled.

GUI *(coming behind, whispers her):* Trust him not, my child;
   I know his ways; he'd rather fight than wed.
   'Tis but a wish to have the war afoot.
   Stand firm for poor Ravenna!

LAN: Well, my lady,
   Shall we conclude a lasting peace between us
   By truce or marriage rites?

GUI *(whispers her):* The Devil tempts thee:
   Think of Ravenna, think of me!

LAN: My lord,
   I see my father waits you.

(GUIDO *retires*)

FRAN: Gentle sir,
   You do me little honor in the choice.

LAN: My aim is justice.

FRAN: Would you cast me off?

LAN: Not for the world, if honestly obtained;
  Not for the world would I obtain you falsely.

FRAN: The rites were half concluded ere we met.

LAN: Meeting, would you withdraw?

FRAN: No. *(Aside)* Bitter word!

LAN: No! Are you dealing fairly?

FRAN: I have said.

LAN: O! rapture, rapture! Can it be that I—
  Now I'll speak plainly; for a choice like thine
  Implies such love as woman never felt.
  Love me! Then monsters beget miracles,
  And Heaven provides where human means fall short.
  Lady, I'll worship thee! I'll line thy path
  With suppliant kings! Thy waiting-maids shall be
  Unransomed princesses! Mankind shall bow
  One neck to thee, as Persia's multitudes
  Before the rising sun! From this small town,
  This center of my conquests, I will spread
  An empire touching the extremes of earth!
  I'll raise once more the name of ancient Rome;
  And what she swayed she shall reclaim again!
  If I grow mad because you smile on me,
  Think of the glory of thy love; and know
  How hard it is, for such an one as I,
  To gaze unshaken on divinity!
  There's no such love as mine alive in man.
  From every corner of the frowning earth,
  It has been crowded back into my heart.
  Now, take it all! If that be not enough,
  Ask, and thy wish shall be omnipotent!
  Your hand. *(Takes her hand)* It wavers.

FRAN: So does not my heart.

LAN: Bravo! Thou art every way a soldier's wife;
    Thou shouldst have been a Caesar's! Father, hark!
    I blamed your judgment, only to perceive
    The weakness of my own.

MAL: What means all this?

LAN: It means that this fair lady—though I gave
    Release to her, and to Ravenna—placed
    The liberal hand, which I restored to her,
    Back in my own, of her own free goodwill.
    Is it not wonderful?

MAL: How so?

LAN: How so!
    No matter, father, I am happy; you,
    As the blessed cause, shall share my happiness.
    Let us be moving. Revels, dashed with wine,
    Shall multiply the joys of this sweet day!
    There's not a blessing in the cup of life
    I have not tasted of within an hour!

FRAN (aside): Thus I begin the practice of deceit,
    Taught by deceivers, at a fearful cost.
    The bankrupt gambler has become the cheat,
    And lives by arts that erewhile ruined me.
    Where it will end, Heaven knows; but I—
    I have betrayed the noblest heart of all!

LAN: Draw down thy dusky vapors, sullen night—
    Refuse, ye stars, to shine upon the world—
    Let everlasting blackness wrap the sun,
    And whisper terror to the universe!
    We need ye not! We'll blind ye, if ye dare
    Peer with lackluster on our revelry!
    I have at heart a passion, that would make
    All nature blaze with recreated light!

(Exeunt.)

ACT FOURTH

The same. An apartment in the castle. Enter LANCIOTTO.

LANCIOTTO: It cannot be that I have duped myself,
  That my desire has played into the hand
  Of my belief; yet such a thing might be.
  We palm more frauds upon our simple selves
  Than knavery puts upon us. Could I trust
  The open candor of an angel's brow,
  I must believe Francesca's. But the tongue
  Should consummate the proof upon the brow,
  And give the truth its word. The fault lies there.
  I've tried her. Press her as I may to it,
  She will not utter those three little words—
  "I love thee." She will say, "I'll marry you;—
  I'll be your duteous wife;—I'll cheer your days;—
  I'll do whate'er I can." But at the point
  Of present love, she ever shifts the ground,
  Winds round the word, laughs, calls me "Infidel!—
  How can I doubt?" So, on and on. But yet,
  For all her dainty ways, she never says,
  Frankly, I love thee. I am jealous—true!
  Suspicious—true! Distrustful of myself:—
  Perhaps she loves another? No; she said,
  "I love you, Count, as well as any man";
  Sweeter than slumber to the lids of pain,
  To fancy that a shadow of true love
  May fall on this God-stricken mold of woe.

(*Enter* PEPE)

PEPE: Good morning, cousin!

LAN: Good morning to your foolish majesty!

PEPE: The same to your majestic foolery!

LAN: You compliment!

PEPE: I am a troubadour,
  A ballad monger of fine mongrel ballads,
  And therefore running o'er with elegance.
  Wilt hear my verse?

LAN: With patience?

PEPE: No, with rapture.
  You must go mad—weep, rend your clothes, and roll
  Over and over, like the ancient Greeks,
  When listening to the Iliad.

LAN: Sing, then, sing!
  And if you equal Homer in your song,
  Why, roll I must, by sheer compulsion.

PEPE: Nay,
  You lack the temper of the fine-eared Greek.
  You will not roll; but that shall not disgrace
  My gallant ballad, fallen on evil times.

(Sings)

    My father had a blue-black head,
        My uncle's head was reddish—maybe,
      My mother's hair was noways red,
        Sing high ho! the pretty baby!

  Mark the simplicity of that! 'T is called
  "The Babe's Confession," spoken just before
  His father strangled him.

LAN: Most marvellous!
  You struggle with a legend worth your art.

PEPE: Now to the second stanza. Note the hint
  I drop about the baby's parentage:
  So delicately too! A maid might sing,
  And never blush at it. Girls love these songs
  Of sugared wickedness. They'll go miles about,
  To say a foul thing in a cleanly way.
  A decent immorality, my lord,

Is art's specific. Get the passions up,
But never wring the stomach.

LAN: Triumphant art!

(PEPE *sings*)

> My father combed his blue-black head,
>   My uncle combed his red head—maybe,
> My mother combed my head, and said,
>   Sing high ho! My red-haired baby.

LAN: Fie, fie! Go comb your hair in private.

PEPE: What!
Will you not hear? Now comes the tragedy.   *(Sings)*

> My father tore my red, red head,
>   My uncle tore my father's—maybe,
> My mother tore both till they bled—
>   Sing high ho! Your brother's baby!

LAN: Why, what a hair-rending!

PEPE: Thence wigs arose;
A striking epoch in man's history.
It has a moral, fathers should regard—
A black-haired dog breeds not a red-haired cur.

LAN: So all this cunning thing was wound about,
To cast a jibe at my deformity?
(Tears off PEPE's *cap)*
There lies your cap, the emblem that protects
Your head from chastisement. Now, Pepe, hark!
Of late you've taken to reviling me;
Under your motley, you have dared to jest
At God's inflictions. Let me tell you, fool,
No man e'er lived, to make a second jest
At me, before your time!

PEPE: Boo! Bloody-bones!

If you're a coward—which I hardly think—
You'll have me flogged, or put into a cell,
Or fed to wolves. If you are bold of heart,
You'll let me run. Do not; I'll work you harm!
I, Beppo Pepe, standing as a man,
Without my motley, tell you, in plain terms,
I'll work you harm—I'll do you mischief, man!

LAN: I, Lanciotto, Count of Rimini,
Will hang you, then. Put on your jingling cap;
You please my father. But remember, fool,
No jests at me!

PEPE: I will try earnest next.

LAN: And I the gallows.

PEPE: Well; cry quits, cry quits!
I'll stretch your heart, and you my neck—quits, quits!

LAN: Go, fool! Your weakness bounds your malice.

PEPE: Yes.
So you all think, you savage gentlemen,
Until you feel my sting. Hang, hang away!
It is an airy, wholesome sort of death,
Much to my liking. When I hang, my friend,
You'll be chief mourner, I can promise you.
Hang me! I've quite a notion to be hung:
I'll do my utmost to deserve it. Hang!

(Exit)

LAN: I am bemocked on all sides. My sad state
Has given the licensed and unlicensed fool
Charter to challenge me at every turn.
The jester's laughing bauble blunts my sword,
His gibes cut deeper than its fearful edge;
And I, a man, a soldier, and a prince,
Before this motley patchwork of a man,
Stand all appalled, as if he were a glass

Wherein I saw my own deformity.
O Heaven! A tear—one little tear—to wash
This aching dryness of the heart away!

(*Enter* PAOLO)

PAOLO: What, Lanciotto, art thou sad again!
    Where has the rapture gone of yesterday?

LAN: Where are the leaves of summer? Where the snows
    Of last year's winter? Where the joys and griefs
    That shut our eyes to yesternight's repose,
    And woke not on the morrow?

PAOLO: Arouse yourself.
    Balance your mind more evenly, and hunt
    For honey in the wormwood.

LAN: Or find gall
    Hid in the hanging chalice of the rose:
    Which think you better? If my mood offend,
    We'll turn to business.
    When at Ravenna, did you ever hear
    Of any romance in Francesca's life?
    A love-tilt, gallantry, or anything
    That might have touched her heart?

PAOLO: Not lightly even.
    I think her heart as virgin as her hand.

LAN: Then there is hope.

PAOLO: Of what?

LAN: Of winning her.

PAOLO: Grammercy! Lanciotto, are you sane?
    You boasted yesterday—

LAN: And changed today.
    Is that so strange? I always mend the fault

Of yesterday with wisdom of today.
She does not love me.

PAOLO: Pshaw! She marries you:
  'T were proof enough for me.

LAN: Perhaps, she loves you.

PAOLO: Me, Lanciotto, me! For mercy's sake,
  Blot out such thoughts—they madden me! What, love—
  She love—yet marry you!

LAN: It moves you much.
  'T was but a fleeting fancy, nothing more.

PAOLO: You have such wild conjectures!

LAN: Well, to me
  They seem quite tame; they are my bedfellows.
  Think, to a modest woman, what must be
  The loathsome kisses of an unloved man—
  A gross, coarse ruffian!

PAOLO: O, good heavens, forbear!

LAN: What shocks you so?

PAOLO: The picture which you draw,
  Wronging yourself by horrid images.

LAN: Until she love me, till I know, beyond
  The cavil of a doubt, that she is mine—
  Wholly, past question—do you think that I
  Could so afflict the woman whom I love?

PAOLO: You love her, Lanciotto!

LAN: Next to you,
  Dearer than anything in nature's scope.

PAOLO *(aside)*: O! Heaven, that I must bear this! Yes, and more,—

LAN: You and I, perchance,
  Joining our forces, may prevail at last.
  They call love like a battle. As for me,
  I'm not a soldier equal to such wars,
  Despite my arduous schooling. Tutor me
  In the best arts of amorous strategy.
  I am quite raw, Paolo. Glances, sighs,
  Sweets of the lip, and arrows of the eye,
  Shrugs, cringes, compliments, are new to me;
  And I shall handle them with little art.
  Will you instruct me?

PAOLO: Conquer for yourself.
  Two captains share one honor: keep it all.
  What if I ask to share the spoils?

LAN *(laughing)*:   Ha! ha!

PAOLO: But this is idle talk. *(Bells ring)* Your marriage bells
  Are pealing on the air. The guests attend.
  Bestir you, if you are not yet attired
  Quite to your liking.

LANCIOTTO *(aside)*: Does he mock me, too?
  Nay, I more wrong myself in wronging him.

(Enter RENÉ, TROUBADOURS *and* NOBLEMEN*)*

RENÉ: Bestir yourselves, good gentlemen. The church
  Awaits your presence, Count Lanciotto, come!
  Can you be slow to win so fair a prize?

FIRST NOBLEMAN: Go fetch the bride, Count Paolo. This command
  Your father bade me bear you.

PAOLO *(aside)*:   Break, my heart!
  Why stretch the torture through another day?
  Come, brother, hasten!   *(Exit)*

LANCIOTTO: As you will. In sooth,
  You all look joyous. Are you honest, then,

To urge this marriage? If I once say, no!
Not all the fathers that begot their kind
Since man was man can shake my uttered will.

FIRST NOBLEMAN: Think of the bride, my lord.

RENÉ: Oh! Such a slight,
   To hurl your *no* against her whispered *yes*.

LAN: So be it then, I have called in the world
   To counsel with me, and you all approve
   The lovesick yearnings of my heart. O God,
   I trust I do no creature shaped by thee,
   In thy own image—not in mine—a wrong
   By mating with the fairest of them all!
   Marriage! Why, marriage is, like birth and death
   The common lot of all. Then why should I,
   Who never feared the sternest mood of man,
   Fear woman at her tenderest? Gently, sirs:
   Let us walk softly to the sacred church;
   Mindful that other rites than marriages
   Make it a portal opening into Heaven.

(Exeunt.)

The same. A chamber in the same. FRANCESCA *and* RITTA *discovered at the bridal toilet.*

RIT: I'm weary of this wreath. These orange-flowers
   Will never be adjusted to my taste:
   Strive as I will, they ever look awry.

FRAN: Not more than my poor head.
   There, leave them so.

RIT: That's better, yet not well.

FRAN: They are but fading things, not worth your pains:
   They'll scarce outlive the marriage merriment.
   Ritta, these flowers are hypocrites; they show
   An outside gaiety, yet die within,

Minute by minute. You shall see them fall,
Black with decay, before the rites are o'er.

RIT: How beautiful you are!

FRAN: Fie, flatterer!
White silk and laces, pearls and orange-flowers,
Would do as much for any one.

RIT: No, no!
You give them grace, they nothing give to you.
Ah! well, your Count should be the proudest man
That ever led a lady into church,
Were he a modern Alexander. Poh!
What are his trophies to a face like that?

FRAN: I seem to please you, Ritta.

RIT: Please yourself,
And you will please me better. You are sad:
I marked it ever since you saw the Count.
I fear the splendor of his victories,
And his sweet grace of manner—for, in faith,
His is the gentlest, grandest character,
Despite his—

FRAN: Well?

RIT: Despite his—

FRAN: Ritta, what?

RIT: Despite his difference from Count Paolo, lady—
   (FRANCESCA *staggers*)
   What is the matter?   (*Supporting her*)

FRAN: Nothing; mere fatigue.
Hand me my kerchief. I am better now.
What were you saying?

RITTA: That I fear the Count
   Has won your love.

FRANCESCA *(laughing):* Would that be cause for fear?

RIT: O! yes, indeed! Once—long ago—I was
   Just fool enough to tangle up my heart
   With one of these same men. 'T was terrible!
   Morning or evening, waking or asleep,
   I had no peace. Sighs, groans, and standing tears,
   Counted my moments through the blessed day.
   And then to this there was a dull, strange ache
   Forever sleeping in my breast,—a numbing pain,
   That would not for an instant be forgot.
   O! but I loved him so, that very feeling
   Became intolerable. And I believed
   This false Giuseppe, too, for all the sneers,
   The shrugs and glances, of my intimates.
   They slandered me and him, yet I believed.
   He was a noble, and his love to me
   Was a reproach, a shame, yet I believed.
   He wearied of me, tried to shake me off,
   Grew cold and formal, yet I would not doubt.
   O! lady, I was true! Nor till I saw
   Giuseppe walk through the cathedral door
   With Dora, the rich usurer's niece, upon
   The very arm to which I clung so oft,
   Did I so much as doubt him. Even then—
   More is my shame—I made excuses for him.
   "Just this or that had forced him to the course:
   Perhaps, he loved me yet—a little yet.
   His fortune, or his family, had driven
   My poor Giuseppe thus against his heart.
   The low are sorry judges for the great.
   Yes, yes, Giuseppe loved me!" But at last
   I did awake. It might have been with less:
   There was no need of crushing me, to break
   My silly dream up. In the street, it chanced,
   Dora and he went by me, and he laughed—
   A bold, bad laugh—right in my poor pale face,
   And turned and whispered Dora, and she laughed.

Ah! then I saw it all. I've been awake,
Ever since then, I warrant you. And now
I only pray for him sometimes, when friends
Tell his base actions towards his hapless wife.
O! I am lying—I pray every night!

(Weeps)

RIT: Poor Ritta.   *(Weeping)*

RIT: No! Blest Ritta! Thank kind Heaven,
That kept me spotless when he tempted me,
And my weak heart was pleading with his tongue,
Pray, do not weep. You spoil your eyes for me.
But never love; oh! it is terrible!

(Enter PAOLO, *with* PAGES *bearing torches)*

FRANCESCA: Gracious saints! My lord What brought you here?

PAOLO: The bridegroom waits.

FRAN: He does?
Let him wait on forever! I'll not go!
O! dear dear Paolo—

PAOLO: Sister!

FRAN: It is well.
I have been troubled with a sleepless night.
My brain is wild. I know not what I say.
Pray; do not call me sister; it is cold.
Call me Francesca.

PAOLO: You shall be obeyed.

FRAN: I would not be obeyed. I'd have you do it
Because—because you love me—as a sister—
And of your own good will, not my command,
Would please me.—Do you understand?

PAOLO *(aside)*: Too well!
  'T is a nice difference.

FRAN: Yet you understand?
  Say that you do.

PAOLO: I do.

FRAN: That pleases me.
  'T is flattering if our—friends appreciate
  Our nicer feelings.

PAOLO: I await you, lady.

FRAN: Ritta, my gloves.—Ah, yes, I have them on;
  Though I'm not quite prepared. Arrange my veil;
  It folds too closely. That will do; retire.
  (RITTA *retires*)
  and so, Count Paolo, you have come, hot haste,
  To lead me to the church,—to have your share
  In my undoing? And you came, in sooth,
  Because they sent you? You are very tame!
  And if they sent, was it for you to come?

PAOLO: Lady, I do not understand this scorn.
  I came, as is my duty, to escort
  My brother's bride to him. When next you're called,
  I'll send a lackey.

FRAN: Count, you are cruel!   *(Weeps)*

PAOLO: O! no; I would be kind.
  In Heaven's name, come!

FRAN: One word—one question more:
  Is it your wish this marriage should proceed?

PAOLO: It is.

FRAN: Come on! You shall not take my hand:
  I'll walk alone—now, and forever!

PAOLO *(taking her hand):*   Sister!

(Exeunt PAOLO *and* FRANCESCA, *with* PAGES.*)*

The same. Interior of the cathedral. LANCIOTTO, FRANCESCA, PAOLO, MA-
LATESTA, GUIDO, RITTA, PEPE, LORDS, KNIGHTS, PRIESTS, PAGES, *a bridal-train of*
LADIES, SOLDIERS, CITIZENS, ATTENDANTS, *discovered before the high altar.*
Organ music. The rites being over, they advance.

MALATESTA: By Heaven—

PEPE: O! uncle, uncle, you're in church!

MAL: I'll break your head, knave!

PEPE: I claim sanctuary.

MAL: Why, bridegroom, will you never kiss the bride?
   We all are mad to follow you.

PEPE: Yes, yes; give us room.

MAL: You heaven-forsaken imp, be quiet now!

PEPE: Then there'd be naught worth hearing.

MAL: Bridegroom, come!

PEPE: Lord! He don't like it! Hey!—I told you so—
   He backs at the first step. Does he not know
   His trouble's just begun?

LANCIOTTO: Gentle Francesca,
   Custom imposes somewhat on thy lips:
   I'll make my levy.   *(Kisses her. The others follow. Aside)* Ha! she
         shrank! I felt
   Her body tremble, and her quivering lips
   Seemed dying under mine! I heard a sigh,
   Such as breaks hearts—O! No, a very groan;
   And then she turned a sickly, miserable look
   On pallid Paolo, and he shivered, too!

There is a mystery hangs around her,—ay,
And Paolo knows it, too.—By all the saints,
I'll make him tell it, at the dagger's point!
Paolo!—Here! here! I do adjure you, brother,
By the great love I bear you, to reveal
The secret of Francesca's grief.

PAOLO: I cannot.

LAN: She told you nothing?

PAOLO: Nothing.

LAN: Not a word?

PAOLO: Not one.

LAN: What heard you at Ravenna, then?

PAOLO: Nothing.

LAN: Here?

PAOLO: Nothing.

LAN: Not the slightest hint?—
Don't stammer, man! Speak quick! I am in haste.

PAOLO: Never.

LAN: What know you?

PAOLO: Nothing that concerns
Your happiness, Lanciotto. If I did,
Would I not tell unquestioned?

LAN: Would you not?
You ask a question for me: answer it.

PAOLO: I have.

LAN: You juggle, you turn deadly pale,
   Fumble your dagger, stand with head half round,
   Tapping your feet.—You dare not look at me!
   By Satan! now, Count Paolo, let me say,
   You look much like a full-convicted thief!

PAOLO: Brother!—

LAN: Pshaw! brother! You deceive me, sir:
   You and that lady have a devil's league,
   To keep a devil's secret. Is it thus
   You deal with me? Now, by the light above,
   I'd give a dukedom for some fair pretext
   To fly you all! She does not love me? Well,
   I could bear that, and live away from her.
   Love would be sweet, but want of it becomes
   An early habit to such men as I.
   But you—ah! there's the sorrow—whom I loved
   An infant in your cradle; you who grew
   Up in my heart, with every inch you gained;
   You whom I loved for every quality,
   Good, bad, and common, in your natural stock;
   Ay, for your very beauty! It is strange, you'll say,
   For such a crippled horror to do that,
   Against the custom of his kind! O! yes,
   I love, and you betray me!

PAOLO: Lanciotto,
   This is sheer frenzy. Join your bride.

LAN: I'll not!
   What, go to her, to feel her very flesh
   Crawl from my touch? To hear her sigh and moan,
   As if God plagued her? Must I come to that?
   No, no! until I go to her, with confident belief
   In her integrity and candid love,
   I'll shun her as a leper.

(Alarm-bells toll)

MAL: What is that?

(Enter, hastily, a MESSENGER *in disorder)*

MESSENGER: My lord, the Ghibelins are up—

LAN: And I
  Will put them down again! *(Aside)* I thank thee, Heaven,
  For this unlooked-for aid!

GUIDO: My lord, believe
  I had no hand nor heart in this new trial.

MALATESTA: We do not doubt you.

GUIDO: Else I must depart.

MAL: Pray you remain. He longs to lead the war
  Despite his protest. Friend, what force have they?   *(To* MESSENGER*)*

LAN: It matters not,—nor yet the time, place, cause,
  Of their rebellion. I would throttle it,
  Were it a riot, or a drunken brawl!

MAL: Nay, son, your bride—

LAN: My bride will pardon me;
  Bless me, perhaps, as I am going forth:—
  Thank me, perhaps, if I should ne'er return.   *(Aside)*
  A soldier's duty has no bridals in it.

PAOLO: Lanciotto, this is folly. Let me take
  Your usual place of honour.

LAN *(laughing)*:   Ha! ha! ha!
  What! thou, a tiltyard soldier, lead my troops!
  My wife will ask it shortly. Not a word
  Of opposition from the new-made bride?
  Nay, she looks happier. O! Accursed day,
  That I was mated to an empty heart!
  You, soldiers, who are used to follow me,
  And front our charges, emulous to bear
  The shock of battle on your forward arms,—

Why stand ye in amazement? Do your swords
Stick to their scabbards with inglorious rust?
Or has repose so weakened your big hearts,
That you can dream with trumpets at your ears?
Out with your steel! It shames me to behold
Such tardy welcome to my war-worn blade!
(Draws. The KNIGHTS *and* SOLDIERS *draw)*
Ho! Draw our forces out! Strike camp, sound drums,
And set us on our marches! As I live,
I pity the next foeman who relies
On me for mercy! Farewell! To you all—
To all alike—a soldier's short farewell!
(Going. PAOLO *stands before him)*
Out of my way, thou juggler!   *(Exit)*

PAOLO: He is gone!

ACT FIFTH

The same. The garden of the castle. Enter PEPE, *singing.*

PEPE:
       'T is jolly to walk in the shady greenwood
         With a damsel by your side;
       'T is jolly to walk from the chapel-door,
         With the hand of your pretty bride;
       'T is jolly to rest your weary head,
      When life runs low and hope is fled,
         On the heart where you confide:
       'T is jolly, jolly, jolly, they say,
         They say—but I never tried.

Nor shall I ever till they dress their girls
In motley suits, and pair us, to increase
The race of fools. 'T would be a noble thing,
A motley woman, had she wit enough
To bear the bell. But there's the misery:
You may make princes out of any stuff;
Fools come by nature. She'll make fifty kings—
Good, hearty tyrants, sound, cruel governors—
For one fine fool. There is Paolo, now,
A sweet-faced fellow with a wicked heart—
Talk of a flea, and you begin to scratch.
Lo! here he comes. And there's fierce crookback's bride
Walking beside him—O, how gingerly!
Take care, my love! that is the very pace
We trip to Hell with. Hunchback is away—
That was a fair escape for you; but, then,
The Devil's ever with us, and that's worse.
See, the Ravenna gigglet, Mistress Ritta,
And melancholy as a cow.—How's this?
I'll step aside, and watch you, pretty folks.

(Hides behind the bushes. Enter PAOLO *and* FRANCESCA, *followed by* RITTA.
He seats himself in an arbor, and reads)

FRANCESCA: Ritta.

RITTA: My lady.

FRAN: You look tired.

RIT: I'm not.

FRAN: Go to your chamber.

RIT: I would rather stay,
  If it may please you. I require a walk
  And the fresh atmosphere of breathing flowers,
  To stir my blood. I am not very well.

FRAN: I knew it, child. Go to your chamber, dear.
  Paolo has a book to read to me.

RIT: What, the romance? I should so love to hear!
  I dote on poetry; and Count Paolo
  Sweetens the Tuscan with his mellow voice.
  I'm weary now, quite weary, and would rest.

FRAN: Just now you wished to walk.

RIT: Ah! did I so?
  Walking, or resting, I would stay with you.

FRAN: The Count objects. He told me, yesterday,
  That you were restless while he read to me;
  And stirred your feet amid the grass, and sighed,
  And yawned, until he almost paused.

RIT: Indeed
  I will be quiet.

FRAN: But he will not read.

RIT: Let me go ask him.

(*Runs toward* PAOLO)

FRAN: Stop! Come hither, Ritta.
(She returns)
I saw your new embroidery in the hall—
The needle in the midst of Argus' eyes;
It should be finished.

RIT: I will bring it here—
O, no! My finger's sore; I cannot work.

FRAN: Go to your room.

RIT: Let me remain, I pray.
'T is better, lady; you may wish for me;
I know you will be sorry if I go.

FRAN: I shall not, girl. Do as I order you.
Will you be headstrong?

RIT: Do you wish it, then?

FRAN: Yes, Ritta.

RIT: Yet you made pretexts enough,
Before you ordered.

FRAN: You are insolent.
Will you remain against my will?

RIT: Yes, lady;
Rather than not remain.

FRAN: Ha! Impudent!

RIT: You wrong me, gentle mistress.
Love like mine
Does not ask questions of propriety,
Nor stand on manners. I would do you good,
Even while you smote me; I would push you back,
With my last effort, from the crumbling edge
Of some high rock o'er which you toppled me.

FRAN: What do you mean?

RIT: I know.

FRAN: Know what?

RIT: Too much
Pray, do not ask me.

FRAN: Speak!

RIT: I know—dear lady,
Be not offended—

FRAN: Tell me, simpleton!

RIT: You know I worship you; you know I'd walk
Straight into ruin for a whim of yours;
You know—

FRAN: I know you act the fool. Talk sense!

RIT: I know Paolo loves you.

FRAN: Should he not?
He is my brother.

RIT: More than brother should.

FRAN: Ha! are you certain?

RIT: Yes, of more than that.

FRAN: Of more?

RIT: Yes, lady; for you love him, too.
I've said it! Fling me to the carrion crows,
Kill me by inches, boil me in the pot
Count Guido promised me—but, O, beware!
Back, while you may! Make me the sufferer,
But save yourself!

FRAN: Now, are you not ashamed
   To look me in the face with that bold brow?
   I am amazed!

RIT: I am a woman, lady;
   I too have been in love; I know its ways,
   Its arts and its deceits. Your frowning face,
   And seeming indignation, do not cheat.
   Your heart is in my hand.

PAOLO *(calls):*   Francesca!

FRAN: Hence,
   Thou wanton-hearted minion! Hence, I say!—
   And never look me in the face again!—
   Hence, thou insulting slave!

RIT *(clinging to her):* O lady, lady—

FRAN: Begone.   *(Throws her off)*

RIT: I have no friends—no one to love—
   O, spare me!

FRAN: Hence!

RIT: Was it for this I loved—
   Cared for you more than my own happiness—
   Ever at heart your slave—without a wish
   For greater recompense than your stray smiles?

PAOLO *(calls):* Francesca!

FRAN: Hurry!

RIT: I am gone. Alas!
   God bless you, lady! God take care of you,
   When I am far away! Alas, alas!

(Exit weeping)

FRAN: Poor girl!—but were she all the world to me,
    And held my future in her tender grasp,
    I'd cast her off, without a second thought,
    To savage death, for dear Paolo's sake!
    Paolo, hither! Now he comes to me;
    I feel his presence, though I see him not,
    Stealing upon me like the fervid glow
    Of morning sunshine. Now he comes too near—
    He touches me—O Heaven!

PAOLO: Our poem waits.
    I have been reading while you talked with Ritta.
    How did you get her off?

FRAN: By some device.
    She will not come again.

PAOLO: I hate the girl:
    She seems to stand between me and the light.
    And now for the romance. Where left we off?

FRAN: Where Lancelot and Queen Guenevra strayed
    Along the forest, in the youth of May.
    You marked the figure of the birds that sang
    Their melancholy farewell to the sun—
    Rich in his loss, their sorrow glorified—
    Like gentle mourners o'er a great man's grave.
    Was it not there? No, no; 't was where they sat
    Down on the bank, by one impulsive wish
    That neither uttered.

PAOLO (*turning over the book*): Here it is.   (*Reads*)
                          "So sat
    Guenevra and Sir Lancelot"—'T were well
    To follow them in that.

(*They sit upon a bank*)

FRAN: I listen: read.
    Nay, do not; I can wait, if you desire.

PAOLO: My dagger frets me; let me take it off.   *(Rises)*
      In thoughts of love, we'll lay our weapons by.
      (Lays aside his dagger, and sits again)
      Draw closer: I am weak in voice today.
      (Reads)
      "So sat Guenevra and Sir Lancelot,
            Under the blaze of the descending sun,
      But all his cloudy splendors were forgot.
            Each bore a thought, the only secret one,
      Which each had hidden from the other's heart,
            That with sweet mystery well-nigh overrun.
      Anon, Sir Lancelot, with gentle start,
            Put by the ripples of her golden hair,
      Gazing upon her with his lips apart.
            He marveled human thing could be so fair;
      Essayed to speak; but, in the very deed,
            His words expired of self-betrayed despair.
      Little she helped him, at his direst need,
            Roving her eyes o'er hill, and wood, and sky,
      Peering intently at the meanest weed;
            Ay, doing aught but look in Lancelot's eye.
      Then, with the small pique of her velvet shoe,
            Uprooted she each herb that blossomed nigh;
      Or strange wild figures in the dust she drew;
            Until she felt Sir Lancelot's arm around
      Her waist, upon her cheek his breath like dew.
            While through his fingers timidly he wound
      Her shining locks; and, haply, when he brushed
            Her ivory skin, Guenevra nearly swound:
      For where he touched, the quivering surface blushed,
            Firing her blood with most contagious heat,
      Till brow, cheek, neck and bosom, all were flushed.
            Each heart was listening to the other beat.
      As twin-born lilies on one golden stalk,
            Drooping with Summer, in warm languor meet,
      So met their faces. Down the forest walk
            Sir Lancelot looked—he looked east, west, north, south—
      No soul was nigh, his dearest wish to balk:
            She smiled; he kissed her full upon the mouth."
      (Kisses FRANCESCA*)*
      I'll read no more!

(Starts up, dashing down the book)

FRAN: Paolo!

PAOLO: I am mad!
   The torture of unnumbered hours is o'er,
   The straining cord has broken, and my heart
   Riots in free delirium! O, Heaven!
   I struggled with it, but it mastered me!
   I fought against it, but it beat me down!
   I prayed, I wept, but Heaven was deaf to me;
   And every tear rolled backward on my heart,
   To blight and poison!

FRAN: And dost thou regret?

PAOLO: The love? No, no! I'd dare it all again,
   Its direst agonies and meanest fears,
   For that one kiss. Away with fond remorse!
   Here, on the brink of ruin, we two stand;
   Lock hands with me, and brave the fearful plunge!
   Thou canst not name a terror so profound
   That I will look or falter from. Be bold!
   I know thy love—I knew it long ago—
   Trembled and fled from it. But now I clasp
   The peril to my breast, and ask of thee
   A kindred desperation.

FRAN *(throwing herself into his arms)*: Take me all—
   Body and soul. The women of our clime
   Do never give away but half a heart:
   I have not part to give, part to withhold,
   In selfish safety. When I saw thee first,
   Riding alone amid a thousand men,
   Sole in the luster of thy majesty,
   And Guido da Polenta said to me,
   "Daughter, behold thy husband!" with a bound
   My heart went forth to meet thee. He deceived,
   He lied to me—ah! that's the aptest word—
   And I believed. Shall I not turn again,
   And meet him, craft with craft? Paolo, love,

Thou'rt dull—thou'rt dying like a feeble fire
Before the sunshine. Was it but a blaze,
A flash of glory, and a long, long night?

PAOLO: No, darling, no! You could not bend me back;
My course is onward; but my heart is sick
With coming fears.

FRAN: Away with them! Must I
Teach thee to love? And reinform the ear
Of thy spent passion with some sorcery
To raise the chilly dead?

PAOLO: Thy lips have not
A sorcery to rouse me as this spell.

(Kisses her)

FRAN: I give thy kisses back to thee again:
And, like a spendthrift, only ask of thee
To take while I can give.

PAOLO: Give, give forever!
Have we not touched the height of human bliss?
And if the sharp rebound may hurl us back
Among the prostrate, did we not soar once?—
Taste heavenly nectar, banquet with the gods
On high Olympus? If they cast us, now,
Amid the furies, shall we not go down
With rich ambrosia clinging to our lips,
And richer memories settled in our hearts?
Francesca.

FRAN: Love?

PAOLO: The sun is sinking low
Upon the ashes of his fading pyre,
And gray possesses the eternal blue;
The evening star is stealing after him,
Fixed, like a beacon, on the prow of night;
The world is shutting up its heavy eye

Upon the stir and bustle of today—
On what shall it awake?

FRAN: On love that gives
Joy at all seasons, changes night to day,
Makes sorrow smile, plucks out the barbèd dart
Of moaning anguish, pours celestial balm
In all the gaping wounds of earth, and lulls
The nervous fancies of unsheltered fear
Into a slumber sweet as infancy's!
On love that laughs at the impending sword.
And puts aside the shield of caution: cries,
To all its enemies, "Come, strike me now!—
Now, while I hold my kingdom, while my crown
Of amaranth and myrtle is yet green,
Undimmed, unwithered; for I cannot tell
That I shall e'er be happier!" Dear Paolo,
Would you lapse down from misery to death,
Tottering through sorrow and infirmity?
Or would you perish at a single blow,
Cut off amid your wildest revelry,
Falling among the wine-cups and the flowers,
And tasting Bacchus when your drowsy sense
First gazed around eternity? Come, love!
The present whispers joy to us; we'll hear
The voiceless future when its turn arrives.

PAOLO: Thou art a siren. Sing, forever sing;
Hearing thy voice, I cannot tell what fate
Thou hast provided when the song is o'er;—
But I will venture it.

FRAN: In, in, my love!

(*Exeunt.* PEPE *steals from behind the bushes*)

PEPE: O, brother Lanciotto!—O, my stars!—
If this thing lasts, I simply shall go mad!
(*Laughs, and rolls on the ground*)
O Lord! to think my pretty lady puss
Has tricks like this, and we ne'er know of it!

I tell you, Lanciotto, you and I
Must have a patent for our foolery!
"She smiled; he kissed her full upon the mouth!"—
There's the beginning; where's the end of it?
O poesy! Debauch thee only once,
And thou'rt the greatest wanton in the world!
O cousin Lanciotto—ho, ho, ho!
(Laughing)
Can a man die of laughter? Here we sat;
Mistress Francesca so demure and calm;
Paolo grand, poetical, sublime!—
Eh! what is this? Paolo's dagger? good!
Here is more proof, sweet cousin broken-back.
"In thoughts of love, we'll lay our weapons by!"
(Mimicking PAOLO*)*
That's very pretty! Here's its counterpart:
In thoughts of hate, we'll pick them up again!   *(Takes the dagger)*
Now for my soldier, now for crook-backed Mars!
Ere long all Rimini will be ablaze.
He'll kill me? Yes: what then? That's nothing new,
Except to me: I'll bear for custom's sake.
More blood will follow; like the royal sun,
I shall go down in purple. Fools for luck;
The proverb holds like iron. I must run,
Ere laughter smother me.—O, ho, ho, ho!

(Exit, laughing.)

A *camp among the hills. Before* LANCIOTTO's *tent. Enter, from the tent,*
LANCIOTTO.

LANCIOTTO: The camp is strangely quiet. Not a sound
Breaks nature's high solemnity. How grand and vast
Is yonder show of heavenly pageantry!
How mean and narrow is the earthly stand
From which we gaze on it!
What heart in Rimini is softened now,
Towards my defects, by this grand spectacle?
Perchance, dear Paolo now forgives the wrong
Of my hot spleen. Perchance, Francesca now
Wishes me back, and turns a tenderer eye

On my poor person and ill-mannered ways;
Fashions excuses for me, schools her heart
Through duty into love, and ponders o'er
The sacred meaning in the name of wife.
Dreams, dreams! Poor fools, we squander love away
On thankless borrowers; when bankrupt quite,
We sit and wonder of their honesty.
Love, take a lesson from the usurer,
And never lend but on security.
What, Marco! ho!   *(To* PAGE *who enters)*
Have Pluto shod; he cast a shoe today:
Let it be done at once. My helmet, too,
Is worn about the lacing; look to that.
My sword-hilt feels uneasy in my grasp.
(Gives his sword)
Have it repaired; and grind the point.

(Exit PAGE. *Enter hastily* PEPE, *tattered and travel stained)*

PEPE: News from Rimini!

(Falls exhausted)

LAN: Is that you, Pepe?
  I never saw you in such straits before.
  Wit without words!

PEPE: That's better than—O!—O!—
  (Panting)
  Words without wit.

LAN *(laughing)*: You'll die a jester, Pepe.

PEPE: If so, I'll leave the needy all my wit.
  You, you shall have it, cousin. —O! O! O!
  (Panting)
  Those devils in the hills, the Ghibelins,
  Ran me almost to death. My lord—ha! ha!   *(Laughing)*
  It all comes back to me—O! Lord a' mercy—
  The garden, and the lady, and the Count!
  Not to forget the poetry—ho! ho!

(Laughing)
O! cousin Lanciotto, such a wife,
And such a brother! Hear me, ere I burst!

LAN: You're pleasant, Pepe!

PEPE: Am I?—Ho! ho! ho!
(Laughing)
You ought to be; your wife's a—

LAN: What?

PEPE: A lady—
A lady, I suppose, like all the rest.
I am not in their secrets. Such a fellow
As fine Count Paolo is your man for that.
I'll tell you something, if you'll swear a bit.

LAN: Swear what?

PEPE: First, swear to listen till the end.—
O! you may rave, curse, howl, and tear your hair;
But you must listen.

LAN: For your jest's sake? Well.

PEPE: You swear?

LAN: I do.

PEPE: Next, swear to know the truth.

LAN: The truth of a fool's story!

PEPE: You mistake.
Now, look you, cousin! You have often marked—
I know, for I have seen—strange glances pass
Between Count Paolo and your lady wife.—

LAN: Ha! Pepe!

PEPE: Now I touch you to the quick.
I know the reason of those glances.

LAN: Ha!
  Speak! or I'll throttle you!

(Seizes him)

PEPE: Your way is odd.
  Let go my throat then and I'll talk you deaf.
  Swear my last oath: only to know the truth.

LAN: But that may trouble me.

PEPE: Your honor lies—
  Your precious honor, cousin Chivalry—
  Lies bleeding with a terrible great gash,
  Without its knowledge. Swear!

LAN: My honor? Speak!

PEPE: You swear?

LAN: I swear. Your news is ill, perchance?

PEPE: Ill! Would I bring it else? Am I inclined
  To run ten leagues with happy news for you?
  O, Lord, that's jolly!

LAN: You infernal imp,
  Out with your story, ere I strangle you!

PEPE: Then take a fast hold on your two great oaths,
  To steady tottering manhood, and attend.
  Last eve, about this hour, I took a stroll
  Into the garden.—Are you listening, cousin?

LAN: I am all ears.

PEPE: Why, so an ass might say.

LAN: Will you be serious?

PEPE: Wait a while, and we
Will both be graver than a churchyard. Well,
Down the long walk, towards me, came your wife,
With the Count Paolo walking at her side.
It was a pretty sight, and so I stepped
Into the bushes. Ritta came with them;
And lady Fanny had a grievous time
To get her off. That made me curious.
Anon, the pair sat down upon a bank,
To read a poem;—the tenderest romance,
All about Lancelot and Queen Guenevra.
The Count read well—I'll say that much for him—
Only he stuck too closely to the text,
Got too much wrapped up in the poesy,
And played Sir Lancelot's actions, out and out,
On Queen Francesca. Nor in royal parts
Was she so backward. When he struck the line—
"She smiled; he kissed her full upon the mouth;"
Your lady smiled, and, by the saints above,
Count Paolo carried out the sentiment!
Can I not move you?

LAN: With such trash as this?
And so you ran ten leagues to tell a lie?—
Run home again.

PEPE: I am not ready yet.
After the kiss, up springs our amorous Count,
Flings Queen Guenevra and Sir Lancelot
Straight to the Devil; growls and snaps his teeth,
Laughs, weeps, howls, dances; talks about his love,
His madness, suffering and the Lord knows what,
Bullying the lady like a thief. But she,
All this hot time, looked cool and mischievous;
And when he calmed a little, up she steps
And takes him by the hand. You should have seen
How tame the furious fellow was at once!
How he came down, snivelled, and cowed to her,
And fell to kissing her again! It was

A perfect female triumph! Such a scene
A man might pass through life and never see.
More sentiment then followed,—buckets full
Of washy words, not worth my memory.
But all the while she wound his Countship up,
Closer and closer; till at last—tu!—wit!—
She scoops him up, and off she carries him,
Fish for her table!
All this time you smile!

LAN: You should have been a poet, not a fool.

PEPE: I might be both.

LAN: You made no record, then?
Must this fine story die for want of ink?
Left you no trace in writing?

PEPE: None.

LAN: Alas!
Then you have told it? 'T is but stale, my boy;
I'm second hearer.

PEPE: You are first, in faith.

LAN: In truth?

PEPE: In sadness. You have got it fresh.
Now go to Rimini, and see yourself.
You'll find them in the garden. Lovers are
Like walking ghosts, they always haunt the spot
Of their misdeeds.

LAN: But have I heard you out?
You told me all?

PEPE: All; I have nothing left.

LAN: Why, you brain-stricken idiot, to trust
Your story and your body in my grasp!

(Seizes him)

PEPE: Unhand me, cousin!

LAN: When I drop you, Pepe,
    You'll be at rest.

PEPE: I will betray you—O!

LAN: Not till the judgment day.

(They struggle)

PEPE *(drawing* PAOLO's *dagger):* Take that!

LAN *(wresting the dagger from him):* Well meant,
    But poorly done! Here's my return.

(Stabs him)

PEPE: O! beast!   *(Falls)*
    This I expected; it is naught—Ha! ha!
    (Laughing)
    I'll go to sleep; but you—what you will bear!
    Hunchback, come here! Hark, hark!
    Your brother hired me, swine, to murder you.

LAN: That is a lie; you never cared for gold.

PEPE: He did, I say! I'll swear it, by Heaven!
    Do you believe me?

LAN: No!

PEPE: You lie! you lie!
    Look at the dagger, cousin—Ugh!—good night!   *(Dies)*

LAN: O! horrible! It was a gift of mine—
    He never laid it by. Speak, speak, fool, speak!   *(Shakes the body)*
    How didst thou get it?—Speak! Thou'rt warm—not dead—
    Thou hast a tongue—O! speak! Come, come, a jest—

Another jest from those thin mocking lips!
Call me a cripple—hunchback—what thou wilt;
But speak to me! He cannot. Now, by Heaven,
I'll stir this business till I find the truth!
Am I a fool? It is a silly lie,
Coined by yon villain with his last base breath.
What ho! without there!

(Enter CAPTAIN *and Soldiers)*

CAPTAIN: Did you call, my lord?

LAN: Did Heaven thunder? Are you deaf, you louts?
    Saddle my horse! Black Pluto—stir! Bear that assassin hence.
    Chop him to pieces, if he move. My horse!
    (Exeunt Soldiers with the body)
    By Jupiter, I shall go mad, I think!

(Walks about)

CAPT: Something disturbs him. Do you mark the spot
    Of purple on his brow?   *(Apart to a Soldier)*

SOLDIER: Then blood must flow.

LAN: Boy, boy! *(Enter a* PAGE*)* My cloak and riding staff. Quick, quick!
    How you all lag! *(Exit* PAGE*)* I ride to Rimini.
    Skirmish tomorrow. Wait till my return—
    I shall be back at sundown. You shall see
    What slaughter is then!

CAPT: Ho! turn out a guard!—

LAN: I wish no guard; I ride alone.

(Enter a SOLDIER*)*

SOLDIER: Pluto is saddled—

LAN: 'T is a damned black lie!

SOL: Indeed, my lord—

LAN: O! comrade, pardon me:
I talk at random. Am I quite calm?

CAPTAIN: Quite calm, my lord.

LANCIOTTO: I wish no guard, I ride alone. My Paolo—
A boy whom I have trotted on my knee;
And young Francesca with her angel face!—
Ah, but I saw the signals of your eyes
Made and returned. Now, if there be one grain
Of solid truth in all this hideous lie,
I cannot answer for the work thou'lt do
(To the dagger)
Thou edged and pointed instrument of wrath
Laid in my hand by Justice! Glorious race
Of iron men, and women far too proud
To be unchaste, ye whisper in my ear
The vengeance due to your dishonored son!
Let me embrace it, lest your scornful hiss,
Drive your degraded offspring from your tombs,
And cast him on a dunghill! Must I lash
My broken spirit into flame with dreams?
No, no! O mighty ancestry, your words,
Erewhile a whisper, tear the vault of Heaven,
With thunder upon thunder. Blood, blood, blood!
Ye shout, and I re-echo it! To horse!—
O, give me wings, not feet, to make my way;
That like a famished eagle scenting blood,
I may swoop down on sleeping Rimini!

(Exeunt omnes)

Rimini. The garden of the castle. Enter PAOLO *and* FRANCESCA.

FRANCESCA: Thou hast resolved.

PAOLO: I've sworn it.

FRAN: Ah, you men

Can talk of love and duty in a breath;
Love while you like, forget when you are tired,
And salve your falsehood with some wholesome saw;
But we, poor women, when we give our hearts,
Give all, lose all, and never ask it back.

PAOLO: What couldst thou ask for that I have not given?
With love I gave thee manly probity,
Innocence, honor, self-respect and peace.
Lanciotto will return, and how shall I—
O! shame, to think of it!—how shall I look
My brother in the face? Take his frank hand?
Return his tender glances? I should blaze
With guilty blushes.

FRAN: Thou canst forsake me, then,
To spare thyself a little bashful pain?
But Paolo, dost thou know what 't is for me,
Have I no secret pangs, no self-respect,
No husband's look to bear? O! worse than these,
I must endure his loathsome touch; be kind
When he would dally with his wife, and smile
To see him play thy part. Pah! Sickening thought!
From that thou art exempt. Thou shalt not go.
Thou dost not love me!

PAOLO: Love thee! Standing here,
With countless miseries upon my head,
I say, my love for thee grows day by day.
It palters with my conscience, blurs my thoughts
Of duty, and confuses my ideas
Of right and wrong. Ere long, it will persuade
My shaking manhood that all this is just.

FRAN: Let it! I'll blazon it to all the world,
Ere I will lose thee. Nay, if I had choice,
Between our love and my lost innocence,
I tell thee calmly, I would dare again
The deed which we have done. O! thou art cruel
To fly me, like a coward, for thine ease.
When thou art gone, thou'lt flatter thy weak heart

With hopes and speculations; and thou'lt swear
I suffer naught, because thou dost not see.
I will not live to bear it.

PAOLO: Die—'t were best;
'T is the last desperate comfort of our sin.

FRAN: I'll kill myself!

PAOLO: And so would I, with joy;
But crime has made a craven of me. O!
For some good cause to perish in! Something
A man might die for, looking in God's face;
Not slinking out of life with guilt like mine
Piled on the shoulders of a suicide!

FRAN: Where wilt thou go?

PAOLO: I care not; anywhere
Out of this Rimini. The very things
That made the pleasures of my innocence
Have turned against me. There is not a tree,
Nor house, nor church, nor monument, whose face
Took hold upon my thoughts, that does not frown
Balefully on me. From their marble
My ancestors scowl at me; and the night
Thickens to hear their hisses. I would pray,
But Heaven jeers at it. Turn where'er I will,
A curse pursues me. Ay, thy very face
Is black with curses.

FRAN: Heavens! O, say not so!
I never cursed thee, love.

PAOLO: But thy gentleness
Seems to reproach me; and, instead of joy,
It whispers horror!

FRAN: Cease! cease!

PAOLO: I must go.

FRANCESCA: And I must follow. All that I call life
  Is bound in thee. I could endure for thee
  More agonies than thou canst catalogue—
  For thy sake, love—bearing the ill for thee!
  With thee, the devils could not so contrive
  That I would blench or falter from my love!
  Without thee, Heaven were torture!

PAOLO: I must go.   *(Going)*

FRAN: O! no, no,—Paolo—dearest!—

(Clinging to him)

PAOLO: Loose thy hold!
  'T is for thy sake, and Lanciotto's; I
  Am as a cipher in the reckoning.
  I have resolved. Thou canst but stretch the time.
  Keep me today, and I will fly tomorrow—
  Steal from thee like a thief.

(Struggles with her)

FRAN: Ah, Paolo—love—
  Kill me, but do not leave me. I will laugh—
  A long, gay, ringing laugh—if thou wilt draw
  Thy pitying sword, and stab me to the heart!
  (Enter LANCIOTTO *behind)*
  Nay, then, one kiss!

LANCIOTTO *(advancing between them)*:
                    Take it: 't will be the last.

PAOLO: Lo! Heaven is just!

FRANCESCA: The last! So be it.   *(Kisses* PAOLO)*

LANCIOTTO: Ha!
  Dare you these tricks before my very face?

FRAN: Why not? I've kissed him in the sight of Heaven;
Are you above it?

PAOLO: Peace, Francesca, peace!

LAN: Count Paolo—why, thou sad and downcast man,
Look up! I have some words to speak with thee.
Thou art not guilty?

PAOLO: Yes, I am. But she
Has been betrayed; so she is innocent.
Her father tampered with her. I—

FRAN: 'T is false!
The guilt is mine. Paolo was entrapped
By love and cunning. I am shrewder far
Than you suspect.

PAOLO: Lanciotto, shut thy ears;
She would deceive thee.

LAN: Silence, both of you!
Is guilt so talkative in its defense?
Then, let me make you judge and advocate
In your own cause. You are not guilty?

PAOLO: Yes.

LAN: Deny it—but a word—say no. Lie, lie!
And I'll believe.

PAOLO: I dare not.

LAN: Lady, you?

FRAN: If I might speak for him—

LAN: It cannot be:
Speak for yourself. Do you deny your guilt?

FRAN: No! I assert it; but—

LAN: In Heaven's name, hold!
Will neither of you answer no to me?
A nod, a hint, a sign, for your escape.
Bethink you, life is centered in this thing.
Speak! I will credit either. No reply?
What does your crime deserve?

PAOLO: Death.

FRAN: Death to both.

LAN: Well said! You speak the law of Italy;
And by the dagger you designed for me,
In Pepe's hand—your bravo?

PAOLO: It is false!
If you received my dagger from his hand,
He stole it.

LAN: There, sweet Heaven, I knew! And now
You will deny the rest? You see, my friends,
How easy of belief I have become!—
How easy 't were to cheat me!

PAOLO: No; enough!
I will not load my groaning spirit more;
A lie would crush it.

LANCIOTTO: Then this nameless deed—
At which our nature cannot even blush,
So pale is she with horror—is confessed?
Alas! Francesca, whom I loved at sight!
(*Turns to her*)
Why, woman, what harm did I do to thee—
What else but love thee—when I saw thee come,
Like a descending angel bearing peace
Into my lonely life? Wouldst thou convert
My very virtues into crime? Make love
Do murder, tempted by thy loveliness?
Fool that I was to credit thee! Thy lies,
Fair-faced deluder, in the sight of Heaven,

Make thee more monstrous than this blighted trunk!
Speak! Is the Devil that inspires thee dumb?
Cast out thy Devil! Speak, speak, for your lives!
She cannot! *(Turns to* PAOLO) Paolo, is there aught to say,—
In thy boy's voice, as thou hast often hung
With silken arms about my armed neck,
In days, oh! Not forgotten, let me trust?
Brother, my brother, it must be that I
Am ill, bewildered, in a nightmare,—Speak!
Say but a word, and wake me to myself!
He too is speechless! Yet there sails the moon;
And this is earth beneath me; and there stands
A misty shape that one time was my wife;
And there a shade that personates the man
Whom I loved most of men; and only I
Ah! Only I am changed so horribly!
For if I be not mad, I am in a hell
To which sin's vision were a paradise!
(A pause, during which he looks from one to the other)
Now, look ye! there is not one hour of life
Among us three. Count Paolo, you are armed—
You have a sword, I but a dagger: see!
I mean to kill you.

PAOLO: I will never lift
This wicked hand against thee.

LAN: Coward, slave!
Art thou so faint? Does Malatesta's blood
Run in thy puny veins? Take that!

(Strikes him)

PAOLO: And more:
Thou canst not offer more than I will bear.

LAN: Oh, Paolo, what a craven has thy guilt
Transformed thee to! Why, I have seen the time
When thou'dst have struck at Heaven for such a thing!
Art thou afraid?

PAOLO: I am.

LAN: O! Infamy!
  Can man sink lower? I will wake thee, though:—
  Thou shalt not die a coward. See! look here!

(Stabs FRANCESCA*)*

FRAN: O!—O!—   *(Falls)*

PAOLO: Remorseless man, dare you do this,
  And hope to live? Die, murderer!

(Draws, rushes at him, but pauses)

LAN: Strike, strike!
  Ere thy heart fail.

PAOLO: I cannot.

(Throws away his sword)

LANCIOTTO: Dost thou see
  Yon dusky cloud that slowly steals along;
  Like a shrewd thief upon a traveler,
  To blot the glory of the jocund moon?
  When it has dimmed the luster of her edge,
  She'll shrink behind it to avoid the sight
  She else might see on this disfigured earth,
  When it has crossed her, one of us, who now
  Is touched to wonder by her radiance
  Shall gaze upon her with an altered face—
  As pale, and cold and vacant as her own.

PAOLO: O, Heaven!

LAN: 'T is done!

PAOLO *(struggling with him)*: O! Lanciotto, hold!
  Hold, for thy sake. Thou wilt repent this deed.

LAN: I know it.

FRAN *(rising)*: Help!—O! murder!—help, help, help!

(She totters towards them, and falls)

MALATESTA *(without)*: Help! This way,—this way—help! Help! Help!

LAN: Our honor, boy!

(Stabs PAOLO, he falls)

FRAN: Paolo!

PAOLO: Hark! She calls.
   I pray thee, brother, help me to her side.

(LANCIOTTO helps him to FRANCESCA)

LAN: Why, there!

PAOLO: God bless thee!

LAN: Have I not done well?
   What were the honor of the Malatesti,
   With such a living slander fixed to it?
   You blame me?

PAOLO: No.

LAN: You, lady?

FRAN: No, my lord.

LAN: May God forgive you. We are even now:
   Your blood has cleared my honor, and our name
   Shines to the world as ever.

PAOLO: O!—O!—

FRAN: Love,
  Art suffering?

PAOLO: But for thee.

FRAN: Here, rest thy head
  Upon my bosom. Fie upon my blood!
  It stains thy ringlets. Ha! He dies! Kind saints,
  I was first struck, why cannot I die first?
  Paolo, wake!—God's mercy! Wilt thou go
  Alone—without me? Prithee, strike again!
  Nay, I am better—love—now—O!

(Dies)

LAN *(sinks upon his knees):*   Great Heaven!

MALATESTA *(without):* This way, I heard the cries.

(Enter with GUIDO, *and attendants)*

GUIDO: O! horrible!

MAL: O! bloody spectacle! Where is thy brother?

LAN: So Cain was asked. Father, here it is—
  The blood of Guido mingled with our own,
  As my old nurse predicted. And the spot
  Of her infernal baptism burns my brain
  Till reason shudders! Down, upon your knees!
  Ay, shake them harder, and perchance they'll wake.

MALATESTA: What hast thou done?

GUIDO: Francesca!—O! my child!

LANCIOTTO: Be satisfied with what you see. You two
  Began this tragedy, I finished it.
  Here, by these bodies, let us reckon up
  Our crimes together. Why, how still they lie!
  A moment since, they walked, and talked and kissed!

Defied me to my face, dishonored me!
They had the power to do it then; but now,
Poor souls, who'll shield them in eternity?
Father, the honor of our house is safe;
I have the secret. I will to the wars,
And do more murders, to eclipse this one.
Back to the battles; there I breathe in peace;
And I will take a soldier's honor back.—
Honor! What's that to me now? Ha! ha! ha!   *(Laughing)*

I killed thy son for honor: thou mayst chide.
O God! I cannot cheat myself with words!
I loved him more than honor—more than life—
This man, my Paolo—this stark, bleeding corpse!
(Falls on PAOLO's *body)*
Here let me rest, till all together wake!
(Curtain)

SWEENEY TODD

THE DEMON BARBER
OF FLEET STREET

George Dibdin Pitt
Revised and Restructured
by Marvin Kaye

The origins of the Sweeney Todd legend are obscure. Though I once read an article that attributed it to a novel by Thomas Peckett Prest (who also wrote the endless penny-dreadful *Varney the Vampire*), the author to whom the tale is usually attributed is a now-obscure Victorian dramatist, George Dibdin Pitt (? –1854? 1855?). Pitt called his play a "legendary drama," but so far, no historical evidence has surfaced to link its dark deeds to any real haircutter.

Though many of Pitt's plays were published, the playwright did not survive to see *Sweeney Todd, the Demon Barber of Fleet Street* in print and since at least one other wholly disparate version appeared and individual managers mounted their own idiosyncratic productions, the surviving script is now hopelessly muddled. (For details on the ensuing reconstructed version, see Appendix.)

In spite of this textual corruption, there is no question that the original Sweeney Todd bears little resemblance to the wronged convict in the Christopher Bond version that Stephen Sondheim based his opera upon. That character was reportedly patterned on the vengeful protagonist of an unrelated nineteenth century melodrama, but Pitt's Sweeney is not driven by a thirst for revenge. His motive is pure mad avarice, as was depicted by the wonderfully hammy Tod Slaughter (!) in the 1936 British film version of Pitt's guignol.

As in most nineteenth century "mellerdrammers," *Sweeney Todd, the Demon Barber of Fleet Street* is loaded with emotional excesses and bombastic language. But it also has a vigorously energetic plot with moments of true horror, graveyard humor, a Moliere-ish canting hypocrite and even one or two instances of genuine human warmth.

DRAMATIS PERSONAE

SWEENEY TODD
MR. SMITH, *a mechanic*
TOBIAS RAGG, *an apprentice*
MARK INGESTRIE, *a sea captain*
JEAN PARMINE, *a jeweler*
JASPER OAKLEY, *Johanna's father*
COLONEL JEFFERY, *a friend to Mark Ingestrie*
DR. LUPIN, *a parson*
JARVIS WILLIAMS, *an indigent*
JONAS FOGG, *asylum director*
SIR WILLIAM BRANDON, *a judge*
FIRST WARDEN
SECOND WARDEN
PRISONERS

MRS. RAGG, *Tobias' mother*
JOHANNA, *Mark Ingestrie's fiancée*
MRS. OAKLEY, *Johanna's mother*
MRS. LOVETT, *a piemaker*
MRS. POORLEAN, *an alewife*

POLICEMAN
KEEPERS OF MADMEN
SPECTATORS IN THE COURTROOM
PRISON IDLERS

ACT ONE

Scene One

Fleet Street, outside SWEENEY TODD's *Shop—part of St. Dunstan's church-yard is visible. The shop window is back center, the inside of the shop being hidden by a curtain which covers in the back of the window. The window contains a dusty wig on a block and several bottles. On the curtain there is the shadow of a barber's chair. Enter* SWEENEY TODD *dressed in the fashion of the time of George II. He is wearing his barber's apron and carries a razor in his right hand, which however he usually conceals behind his back. From time to time he turns away from his interlocutor and whets the razor on the palm of his hand. With him is* MR. SMITH, *a mechanic, who is dressed in rough homespun.*

SWEENEY: Soh—Mr. Smith, you are come on the matter of that leetle consideration owing to you in respect of your mechanical toy?

SMITH: Yes, Mr. Todd, I have brought with me an account for seven pounds eighteen shillings and ninepence ha'penny.

SWEENEY: And what may the ninepence ha'penny be for, Mr. Smith?

SMITH: For one pound of ten-inch nails, Mr. Todd.

SWEENEY: And has it occurred to you, Mr. Smith, that some parties might consider ninepence ha'penny a leetle excessive for a pound of ten-inch nails?

SMITH: It has occurred to me that I do not like your manner of haggling, Mr. Todd. Do you be pleased to pay me and let me go.

SWEENEY (*going towards the door of the shop*): Come a leetle nearer, Mr. Smith. What would you say to a guinea and a half, Mr. Smith? And perhaps a free shave, too—afterwards.

SMITH: I would say you are a rogue, Mr. Todd.

SWEENEY (*aside*): This individual annoys me. I dislike his method of grabbing money. My gorge rises. I think him mean. With all the pleasure in the world I would shave him—shave him very close.

(*Aloud—at the door*) I will make it thirty shillings, Mr. Smith. A mere one and sixpence will scarcely embarrass an individual in such a prosperous way of business as yourself. Come now, let us say thirty shillings, Mr. Smith.

SMITH (*going towards the door and speaking in a very earnest manner*): Has it occurred to you that certain parties not very far up this street—certain legal parties as you might phrase it—might gain a good deal of profit and instruction from a perusal of some of the items and specifications in this little account of mine? Has it occurred to you that there is what you might call a school a little higher up this street where a number of individuals keep little bills like this for their school books? I mean—the Old Bailey, Mr. Todd. (*Aside*) That will quieten him, I think. (*Aloud*) I think the amount we mentioned was seven eighteen nine and a half, Mr. Todd.

SWEENEY: I was speaking about a free shave, Mr. Smith. I discern a roughness about the region of your lower lip and a hairiness about your throat that makes my razor long to be at it. Pray come in and take a seat, Mr. Smith . . . Ha—but here comes Mrs. Ragg. (*Calling off*) Good morning, Mrs. Ragg. So you have brought the leetle whelp!

(*Enter* MRS. RAGG *with her son* TOBIAS. SMITH *steps aside*)

MRS. RAGG: He ain't a little whelp, Mr. Todd, and I don't have you call him so.

SWEENEY: But it was only fun, Mrs. Ragg. You know that I dearly love a jest.

MRS. RAGG: And I ax you to remember that he's very delicite and not to work him too hard. He comes of a very delicite family and is easily upset. Aren't you, my lamb?

TOBIAS: Yes, please ma.

MRS. RAGG: And I ax you to remember likewise, Mr. Todd, that my Tobias has been tenderly nurtured and to treat him as sich. With which I says, Good morning, and leaves you to him, Mr. Todd.

SWEENEY: Come, my young friend.

(Seizes TOBIAS *by the wrist and leads him to the shop door. Exit* MRS. RAGG)

SWEENEY: You will remember now, Tobias Ragg, that you are my apprentice; that you have had of me board, lodging and washing, save that
you take your meals at home, that you don't sleep here, and that your
mother gets up your linen. *(Fiercely)* Now, are you not a fortunate,
happy dog?

TOBIAS *(timidly):* Yes, sir.

SWEENEY: You will acquire a first-rate profession, quite as good as the
law, which your mother tells me that she would have put you to, only
that a little weakness of the head-piece unqualified you. And now
Tobias, listen.

TOBIAS *(trembling):* Yes, sir.

SWEENEY: I'll cut your throat from ear to ear if you repeat one word of
what passes in this shop, or dare to make any supposition, or draw any
conclusion from anything you may see or hear, or fancy you see or
hear. Do you understand me?

TOBIAS: I wouldn't say anything, Mr. Todd; if I do, may I be made into
veal pies at Lovett's in Bell Yard.

SWEENEY *(starts):* How dare you mention veal pies in my presence? Do
you suspect?

TOBIAS: Oh, sir; I don't suspect—indeed I don't! I meant no harm in
making the remark.

SWEENEY *(eyes* TOBIAS *narrowly):* Very good. I'm satisfied—quite satisfied!
and, mark me, the shop, and the shop only, is your place.

TOBIAS: Yes, sir.

SWEENEY: And if any customer gives you a penny, you can keep it, so
that if you get enough of them you will become a rich man; only I'll
take care of them, and when I think you require any— Ay, who's this?
His dress and manners bespeak him a seafaring man and a stranger in
these parts.

(Enter MARK INGESTRIE *dressed as a sea captain of the period. He walks round the stage, looking about him and examining the names above the shops.* TOBIAS *goes up to him. They converse)*

SWEENEY *(to* SMITH*):* I fancy, Mr. Mechanic, that I have business with this gentleman. If you will call again some time next week, we may find time to discuss that leetle matter. Thirty shillings, I think, was the sum mentioned between us. In the meantime, I dare swear that you have a great deal of business on hand in other parts of the city. I wish you good morning.

SMITH: I will go now, but I will be back before next week, Mr. Todd— considerably before next week.

*(*SMITH *exits.* SWEENEY *watches* TOBIAS *from the shop door)*

MARK *(to* TOBIAS*):* I thank you, my good boy, for the information you have so kindly afforded me. You say that you know Miss Johanna Oakley?

TOBIAS: Yes, sir. I am acquainted with Miss Johanna. She is a kind-hearted lady. Shortly after my father's death, sickness and sorrow overcame my poor mother and myself. Had it not been for Miss Oakley's timely aid, both of us might have perished for want.

MARK *(aside):* How it gladdens a person's heart to hear his sweetheart so highly esteemed. *(Aloud)* Miss Johanna Oakley is my affianced bride. For five years have I been absent from the country that gave me birth and from the home I love so well. My vessel unexpectedly arrived at this port this morning, and no sooner did I place my foot on shore but I naturally felt a desire to seek out my old friends. Judge of my mortification and surprise when I was told they were not known at their former address, but had removed no one knew whither. Heaven only knows how I should have discovered them, had it not been for the valuable information with which you have supplied me.

TOBIAS: How I should love to become a sailor! Happy and joyous in my freedom, breathing the fresh pure air of liberty!

MARK: The sea has its perils and its chances. I have been captain of the good ship *Star* for five years. During that time, I have saved ten thousand pounds, besides being the possessor of a string of pearls—

(Chord)

SWEENEY *(aside):* A string of pearls!

MARK: . . . worth twelve thousand more!

SWEENEY *(coming down between them):* Ah, Toby, my dear—what a time you have been. What has detained you, my darling boy?

TOBIAS *(retreating fearfully):* Sir—Mr. Todd—I—

SWEENEY: Has Captain Pearson's peruke been sent home, my dear?

TOBIAS: I—I—I don't know, sir.

SWEENEY *(getting close to* TOBIAS *and speaking fiercely):* I thought I gave you instructions never to speak to any person when out of my sight—eh?

TOBIAS: You may have done, sir—I—

SWEENEY *(strikes him):* Take that—and remember for the future what it was for. Now go into your shop and attend to your business. The next time you disobey me, I'll cut your throat from ear to ear.

MARK: Your pardon, sir—I am to blame. I asked him for the address of a particular old friend—we got into conversation—and—

SWEENEY: No apologies, I beg. Boys will be boys, and a little mild chastisement from time to time does them no harm.

MARK: Perhaps you are right, but I must protest always against unnecessary severity towards young persons, who can scarcely be expected to answer for every little fault when hardly capable of judging which is right and wrong. Though hasty, you are no doubt possessed of a generous heart, and hang me if I don't patronise you this very moment. I am going to meet my sweetheart presently, and I think a clean face will become so important an occasion.

SWEENEY: Happy to be of service to you, good gentleman. Is it a shave you need? What am I here for but to give you a shave—to give you a closer shave than you have ever had before?

TOBIAS *(signalling behind* SWEENEY'*s back)*: You mustn't go in . . . don't go—don't go!

SWEENEY *(turning suddenly)*: By the way, Tobias, while I am operating on this gentleman's . . . chin . . . the figures at St. Dunstan's are about to strike; the exhibition will excite your curiosity and allow me time to shave our customer without interruption.

TOBIAS: Please, Mr. Todd, can't I stay and lather him?

SWEENEY *(fiercely)*: Get out, I tell you—get out.

*(*TOBIAS *goes out reluctantly)*

SWEENEY *(to* MARK*)*: I am quite a father to that boy, sir. I love him—positively dote on him—so much, sir, that I feel I could—*(Aside)*—polish him off. *(Aloud)* Dear me—I had quite forgotten that you are perhaps in a hurry, sir. This way, if you please—pray come in.

(Slow music. SWEENEY *stands bowing at the door.* MARK *enters the shop.* SWEENEY *pauses a moment and whets his razor on the palm of his hand. Then he follows. Re-enter* MR. SMITH, *finger on lips. He goes to St. Dunstan's churchyard, looks round him carefully, then touches a concealed spring and one of the gravestones slowly moves, revealing a secret staircase.* MR. SMITH *begins to descend; pauses)*

SMITH: I have come back, Mr. Todd . . . considerably before next week . . .

Scene Two

Interior of SWEENEY TODD'S *shop. Window in center; two curtains; door on right; two pistols hanging over fireplace; benches, cupboards, stools ranged round stage, together with the necessary articles appertaining to a barber's shop. There are three shaving chairs, one of which is fixed center stage to a revolving trap.* SWEENEY TODD *and* MARK INGESTRIE *are discovered.*

SWEENEY *(indicates center chair):* Will you be pleased to seat yourself? Just turn your head a little on one side, sir. That will do. *(Brushes* MARK'S *hair)* You've been to sea, sir?

MARK: Yes; and I have only now lately come up the river from an Indian voyage.

SWEENEY: You carry some treasures, I presume?

MARK: Among others, this small casket. (MARK *produces it.)*

SWEENEY: A piece of exquisite workmanship.

MARK: It is not the box, but its contents that must cause you wonder, for in confidence, I tell you it contains a string of veritable pearls of the value of twelve thousand pounds.

(Music tremuloso. SWEENEY *addresses* MARK *through music, which continues through following scene)*

SWEENEY *(chuckling aside, and whetting his razor on his hand):* I shall have to polish him off. Ha, ha, ha! heugh!

MARK: What the devil noise was that?

SWEENEY: It was only me. I laughed.

MARK: Laugh! Humph! Do you call that a laugh? I suppose you caught it of somebody who died. If that is your way of laughing, I beg you won't do it any more.

SWEENEY: You will find me all attention to your orders, good sir. (SWEENEY *prepares his apparatus for shaving*) Now sir, we can proceed to business, if it so please you; it's well you came here, sir, for though I say it, there isn't a shaving shop in the City of London that ever thinks upon polishing off a customer as I do—ha, ha, ha! heugh!

MARK: Shiver the main-balance! I tell you what it is, Master Barber: if you come that laugh again I will get up and go. I don't like it, I tell you, and there's an end of it.

SWEENEY: Very good, it won't occur again. (*Commences to mix up a lather*) If I may be so bold, who are you?—where did you come from? —and whither are you going?

MARK: Humph! that's cool, at all events. Mind, you'll put the brush in my mouth. You seem fond of asking questions, my friend; perhaps before I answer them, you will reply to one I'm about to put?

SWEENEY: Oh yes, of course; what is it?

MARK: Do you know a Mr. Oakley, who lives somewhere hereabouts? He is a spectacle maker.

SWEENEY: Yes, to be sure I do—Jasper Oakley, in Fore Street. He has a daughter called Johanna, that the young bloods call the flower of Fore Street. Bless me, where can my strop be? I had it this minute—I must have lain it down somewhere. What an odd thing I can't see it; it's very extraordinary, what can have become of it? Oh, I recollect—I took it into the parlor. Sit still, sir, I shan't be a minute; you can amuse yourself with the newspaper. I shall soon polish him off!

(SWEENEY *hands paper and goes out. A rushing noise heard, and* MARK *seated on the chair sinks through stage. After a pause, the chair rises vacant, and* SWEENEY *enters. He examines the string of pearls which he holds in his hand. As he stands watching, the chair turns over again of its own accord. He starts*)

SWEENEY: What is this? Can I believe my eyes? Some ghostly trick? (*Passes his hand across his brow*) The chair has life of its own. Terror bedews my forehead. No, no, no—courage, Sweeney. It is only that the mechanism is disorganised. And remember—the string of pearls, the string of pearls! . . . When a boy, the thirst of avarice was first awakened by the fair gift of a farthing: that farthing soon became a pound; the pound a hundred—so to a thousand, till I said to myself, I will possess a hundred thousand. This string of pearls will complete the sum. Who's there? (SWEENEY *pounces upon* TOBIAS, *who has cautiously opened the door*) Speak—and speak the truth, or your last hour has come! How long were you peeping through the door before you came in?

TOBIAS *(alarmed):* Peeping, sir?

SWEENEY: Yes, peeping; don't repeat my words, but answer at once; you'll find it better for you in the end.

TOBIAS: Please, sir, I wasn't peeping at all.

(SWEENEY *scrutinizes* TOBIAS, *and then alters his manner*)

SWEENEY: Well, well, if you did peep, what then?—it's no matter. I only wanted to know, that's all. It was quite a joke, wasn't it?—quite funny, though rather odd, eh? Why don't you laugh, you dog? Come now, there's no harm done, tell me what you thought about, at once; we'll be merry over it—very merry.

TOBIAS *(puzzled):* Yes, very merry; but I really, sir, don't know what you mean.

SWEENEY: I mean nothing at all—eh?—what—who's that at the door? *(Looks through window)*

TOBIAS: It's only the black servant of the gentleman who came here to be shaved, this morning.

SWEENEY: Tell the fellow his master's not here; go—let him seek elsewhere, do you hear? I know I shall have to polish that boy off! *(Whets his razor in his hand. As* SWEENEY *concludes this speech,* TOBIAS *discovers the hat worn by* MARK; *this he hides)*

TOBIAS *(aside):* 'Tis improbable that he would go without giving notice to his servant. *(Aloud)* Suppose the man won't go?

SWEENEY (*forgetting himself*): Well then, I shall have to polish him off, too. (TOBIAS *goes out,* SWEENEY *looks out at the door*) If my memory does not deceive me, this should be Jean Parmine, the famous lapidary, the very man I need—fortune is evidently favoring me.

(*Enter* JEAN PARMINE)

PARMINE: Good evening neighbor; I would have you shave me. (*Sits in chair*)

SWEENEY: Your servant, Mr. Parmine—you deal in precious stones?

PARMINE: Yes, I do; but it's rather late for a bargain. Do you want to buy or sell?

SWEENEY: To sell.

PARMINE: Hum! I dare say it's something not in my line, the only order I get is for pearls, and they are not in the market.

SWEENEY: I have nothing but pearls to sell. I mean to keep all my diamonds, garnets and rubies.

PARMINE: The deuce you do! What, do you mean to say you have any of them; be off with you, I'm too old to joke, and am waiting for my supper.

SWEENEY: Will you look at the pearls I have?

PARMINE: Where are they?

SWEENEY: Here! (*Produces a casket and gives it to* PARMINE)

PARMINE: Real, by Heaven—all real.

SWEENEY: I know they are real. Will you deal with me or not?

PARMINE: I'm not quite sure that they are real; let me look at them again. Oh, I see, counterfeit; but so well done that really for the curiosity of the thing I will give you fifty pounds.

SWEENEY: Fifty pounds? Who is joking now, I wonder? We cannot deal tonight.

PARMINE: Stay—I will give you a hundred.

SWEENEY: Hark ye, friend, it neither suits my inclination or my time to stand haggling with you. I know the value of the pearls, and as a matter of ordinary business I will sell them to you so that you may get a handsome profit.

PARMINE: Well, since you know more than I gave you credit for, and this is to be a downright business transaction, I think I can find a customer who will pay eleven thousand pounds for them; if so, I have no objection to advance the sum of eight thousand pounds.

SWEENEY: I am content—let me have the money early tomorrow.

PARMINE: Stop a bit; there are some rather important things to consider —you must know that a string of pearls is not to be bought like a few ounces of old silver, and the vendor must give every satisfaction as to how he came by them.

SWEENEY *(aside)*: I am afraid I shall have to polish him off. *(Aloud)* Psha, man, who will question you, who are known to be in the trade?

PARMINE: That's all very fine; but I don't see why I should give you the full value of an article without evidence to prove your title to it.

SWEENEY: Or, in other words, you don't care how I possess the property provided I sell it to you at a thief's price; but if, on the contrary, I want their real value, you mean to be particular.

PARMINE: I suspect you have no right to dispose of the pearls, and to satisfy myself I shall insist upon your accompanying me to a magistrate.

SWEENEY: And what road shall you take?

PARMINE: The right road!

SWEENEY (*who has edged towards the door, springs into the next room; shouts off*): Then off you go, Mr. Parmine; goodbye, goodbye, goodbye!

(*The chair sinks;* SWEENEY *breaks into demoniacal laughter*)

SMITH (*entering by secret door*): Not at all, Mr. Todd; not goodbye, but how d'ye do, *dear* Mr. Todd!

SWEENEY (*stands aghast, then speaking very slowly*): So you know that secret, too. It is enough. Your bill is paid.

SMITH: But it has to be receipted yet, Mr. Todd.

SWEENEY: And it was you, too, that was responsible for the sudden liveliness of my chair just now, eh? You are a leetle too clever, Mr. Smith. I do not like to have such a clever mechanic in my confidence. It does not altogether suit. (*He draws a pistol quickly from his breast and fires.* SMITH *falls.* SWEENEY *goes up to him and lifts him into the chair*) Ha! Mr. clever Smith—you won't do much thinking now, I suppose, with that bleeding head. You can take all your cleverness down below now; you can have a little ride in this very particular chair of yours . . . it ought to work well now that its master is sitting in it. (*Goes towards the door.*)

Scene Three

Breakfast parlor in the house of JASPER OAKLEY. *Enter* JOHANNA.

JOHANNA: Oh, Mark, Mark! why do you thus desert me when I have relied so abundantly on your true affection? Oh, why have you not sent me some token of your existence and of your continual love? The merest, slightest word would have been sufficient, and I should have been happy! Hark, what was that? I'm sure I heard footsteps beneath the chamber window. As I live, a man in the garden! He holds a white rose in his hand; that should be an emblem of faith and purity. At every hazard, I will address the stranger; he may bring tidings of him I so well love!

(JOHANNA *opens the door, and* COLONEL JEFFERY, *enveloped in a cloak, enters*)

JEFFERY: I have the honor of speaking to Miss Johanna Oakley?

JOHANNA: Yes, sir; and you are Mark Ingestrie's messenger?

JEFFERY: I am.

JOHANNA: Oh, sir, your looks are sad and serious! You seem about to announce some misfortune; tell me if it is not so. Speak to me at once, or my heart will break!

JEFFERY: Let me pray you, lady, to subdue this passion of grief, and listen with patience to what I shall unfold. There is much to hear and much to speculate upon, and if from all that I have learnt, I cannot, dare not tell you Mark Ingestrie lives, I shrink likewise from telling you he is no more!

JOHANNA: Speak again!—say those words again!—there is hope then— there is hope!

JEFFERY: There is hope, and it is better that your mind should receive the first shock of the probability of the death of your lover than that from the first you should expect too much, and then have those expectations rudely destroyed.

JOHANNA: This is kind of you, and if I cannot thank you as I ought, you will know that it is because I am in a state of too great affliction to do so.

JEFFERY: You are aware that a quarrel with his uncle caused him to embark in an adventure in the Indian Seas?

JOHANNA: Too well. Alas! it was on my account he sacrificed himself.

JEFFERY: Nay, good fortune attended that enterprise; and Mark Ingestrie, among others, returned to his native land a wealthy and prosperous merchant. He showed me on our homeward voyage a string of pearls of immense value, which he said he intended for you.

JOHANNA: He was to have presented them yesterday.

JEFFERY: When we reached the River Thames, only three days since, he left the vessel for that purpose.

JOHANNA: Alas! he never came.

JEFFERY: No; from all inquiries we can make, and from all information we can obtain, it seems that he disappeared somewhere in Fleet Street.

JOHANNA: Disappeared!

JEFFERY: We can trace him to Temple Stairs, and from thence to a barber's shop kept by a man named Sweeney Todd; but beyond, we have no clue.

JOHANNA: Hush! someone is coming—'tis my mother's voice. You had better not be seen at present; conceal yourself till I can speak further with you.

(JOHANNA *removes a sliding panel, through which* JEFFERY *passes. Enter* JASPER *and* MRS. OAKLEY)

MRS. OAKLEY: How is this, child—you look pale? If you are ill, I must speak positively about you to Dr. Lupin.

JASPER: Dr. Lupin may be all very well in his way as a parson, but I really don't see what he can have to do with Johanna looking pale.

MRS. OAKLEY: A pious man, Mr. O., has to do with everything and everybody.

JASPER: Then he must be the most intolerable bore in existence, and I don't wonder at his being kicked out of some people's houses, as I have heard this same Dr. Lupin has been.

MRS. OAKLEY: If the sainted man has been kicked, Mr. O., he glories in it. Dr. Lupin likes to suffer for the faith, and if he were made a martyr, it would give him much pleasure.

JASPER: It would not give him half the pleasure it would me.

MRS. OAKLEY: I understand your insinuation, Mr. O., you would like to see him murdered on account of his holiness; but though you say these words now, you won't say as much to the lamb of peace when he comes to tea this afternoon.

JASPER: To tea, Mrs. O.! Haven't I told you over and over again that I won't have that man in my house?

MRS. OAKLEY: And haven't I told you, Mr. O., twice that number of times, that he *shall* come to tea? I've asked him now, and it can't be altered.

JASPER: But my dear—

MRS. OAKLEY: It's no use your talking. Johanna, I think my old complaint, the beating of the heart, is coming on. I know what produced it— your father's brutality. I must retire and compose my nerves with a little cherry brandy. *(Exit)*

JASPER: Bless my soul, I've been too precipitate; my violent temper will cause the death of the poor woman. I must offer her crumbs of comfort, as Dr. Lupin would say. Damn Dr. Lupin!

(Goes out after MRS. OAKLEY. JEFFERY *comes through panel)*

JEFFERY: It is necessary, Miss Oakley, that I now leave you, but you must promise to meet me—

JOHANNA: When and where?

JEFFERY: At the hour of six this day week, in the Temple Gardens. I ask this of you because I am resolved to make all the exertion in my power to discover what has become of Mark Ingestrie, in whose fate I am sure I have succeeded in interesting you, although you care so little for the string of pearls he intended for you.

JOHANNA: I do, indeed, care little for them—so little, that it may be said to amount to nothing.

JEFFERY: Yet it is well not to despise a gift so precious; if you can yourself do nothing with them, there are surely some others than you upon whom they would bestow great happiness.

JOHANNA: A string of pearls, great happiness!

JEFFERY: Your mind is so occupied by your grief, Miss Oakley, that you quite forget such strings are of great value. I've seen the pearls we speak of, and can assure you they are in themselves a fortune.

JOHANNA: I suppose it is too much for human nature to expect two blessings at once. I had the fond warm heart that loved me, without the fortune that would have enabled us to live in comfort, and now, when that is, perchance, within my grasp, the heart which was by far the more costly possession lies buried in a grave—its bright influences, its glorious aspirations quenched for ever.

JEFFERY: You will meet me, then, as I request, to hear if I have any news for you?

JOHANNA: I have the will to do so, but Heaven knows only if I may have the power.

JEFFERY: What do you mean?

JOHANNA: I cannot tell what a week's anxiety may do. I do not know but a sick bed may be my resting place till I exchange it for a coffin. I feel now my strength fail me, and am scarcely able to totter to my chamber. Farewell, sir, I owe you my best thanks, as well as for the trouble you have taken as for the kindly manner in which you have detailed to me what has passed.

JEFFERY: Remember, I bid you adieu, with the hope of meeting you again.

(JEFFERY *by this time has reached the door of the apartment. He hears some one without, and conceals himself behind it as* DR. LUPIN *enters*)

JOHANNA: Lupin here! (*Aside*) How unfortunate!

LUPIN: Yes, maiden. I am that chosen vessel whom the profane call "Mealy Mouth." I come hither at the bidding of thy respected mother to partake of a vain mixture which rejoiceth in the name of "tea." (LUPIN *detains* JOHANNA, *who is going*)

JOHANNA: You will allow me a free passage from this room, if you please, Dr. Lupin.

LUPIN: Thou art disrespectful, but I will not snub thee, virgin, because thou knowest not the honor that's intended thee.

JOHANNA: What do you mean?

LUPIN: Thy mother hath decided that I take thee unto my bosom, even as a wedded wife.

JOHANNA: Absurd! Have you been drinking?

LUPIN: I never drink, save when the spirit waxeth faint. *(Takes a bottle from his pocket, and drinks)* 'Tis an ungodly practice. *(Drinks again)* Thou wilt shortly become as bone of my bone, flesh of my flesh. Thou dost not deserve such an honor. *(Drinks)*

JOHANNA: We don't get all we deserve in this world, Dr. Lupin.

LUPIN *(offering* JOHANNA *the bottle)*: Let me offer you *spiritual* consolation—hum! ha!

JOHANNA: Bless me! You have the hiccups.

LUPIN: Yes; I—I rather think I have a little. Isn't it a shame that one so pious should have the hiccups? Hum—ha! hum—ha! Damn the hiccups—that is, I mean damn all backsliders!

JOHANNA: The miserable hypocrite!

LUPIN: The fire of love rageth—it consumeth my very vitals. Peradventure I may extinguish the flame by the moisture of those ruby lips— nay, I am resolved. *(Seizes* JOHANNA*)*

JOHANNA: Unhand me, ruffian, or repent it!

*(*JEFFERY *rushes forward and belabors* LUPIN *with scabbard of his sword.* JEFFERY *escapes through door.* JOHANNA *secures key)*

LUPIN: Help! verily I am assailed. Robbers! fire! help!

(The household run in, armed with brooms, mops and a warming-pan.

LUPIN *exhibits a black eye. On perceiving this,* MRS. OAKLEY *screams and faints. Picture of consternation. Curtain.)*

ACT TWO

Scene One

The parlor behind MRS. LOVETT's *pie shop, in Bell Yard, Temple Bar.* MRS. LOVETT *is discovered knitting. She is a tall, gaunt woman of middle age and forbidding appearance.*

BOY *(shouts from the shop at the top of his voice)*: I want two twopenny pies for Mrs. Widdle-Waddle.

MRS. LOVETT: You're too late—all sold—not one left. Go away. *(Aside)* Heigho, I feel lonely. I wish at this moment one of my many admirers would call upon me, just to while away the tedious moments. I wonder what the prospects of Major Bounce are? He's tolerably good-looking, although middle-aged. Then there's Mr. Lupin—a very nice man, it is true—but he will persist in talking of such melancholy subjects. *(Looks out of window)* What a sharp shower, to be sure! Fortunate for me that I did not pay my intended visit to Mr. Sweeney Todd; I should have caught my death of cold. *(A knock outside)* Another knock! Some of those troublesome customers again. *(Peers outside)* Why, if it isn't Mr. Lupin! I must make haste and let him in, or the poor gentleman will be wet through. *(She exits, but soon returns with* MR. LUPIN, *who is shaking his umbrella)* A thousand pardons, Mr. Lupin, for keeping you outside so long. But the fact is, I took you for a customer. Give me your umbrella—sit down and take something warm, or you will die of cold.

LUPIN: Yes, dear sister, I bear this misfortune, like all others, with fortitude, believing that our sufferings here will in a future world be changed to peace and happiness. Yea, verily, and the acts of the wicked will call forth the wrath they deserve.

MRS. LOVETT: Certainly; therefore I beg you will take a little drop of tea, with something in it just to keep out the cold.

(They take tea: business with bottle)

LUPIN: Dear sister, you are indeed an angel. Ah me, tea is a blessing, Mrs. L. What should we do without it, sister?

MRS. LOVETT: Ah, indeed, Mr. Lupin.

LUPIN: Call me brother, dear sister, for we are all brothers and sisters in this wicked world, are we not?

MRS. LOVETT: Oh—Mr. Lupin . . . won't you draw your chair a little closer?

LUPIN: And is it true, dear sister, that thou hast gathered unto thyself much of the mammon of unrighteousness by the sale of these same pieces of manna which the ungodly call dough, wrapped round the flesh of the fatted calf?

MRS. LOVETT *(coyly):* Oh, mister—brother, what a lovely "why" of saying pies!

LUPIN: Call me brother, my sister. Verily, "mister brother" is an abomination. But sayest thou, is there much of the mammon of unrighteousness in what thou callest pie? Dost keep what the wicked call a stocking?

MRS. LOVETT: Oh, brother, let us not talk of pies. Remember that all day and all night I think of nothing but pies, and sometimes pies haunt my dreams; remember that all day I smell pies, and knead dough for pies and take tuppences for pies.

LUPIN: Verily, sister, it is a delicious text. Lo, the smell of gravy haunteth my nostrils and my soul quivers with delight.

MRS. LOVETT *(moving very close):* Then would you like a pie—brother?

LUPIN: My soul fainteth, yea, my stomach crieth out, oh, my sister, oh, my beloved, verily I would partake of thy pies! (MRS. LOVETT *brings a pie.* LUPIN *rolls up sleeves and ties a kerchief round his neck)* Nay, sister, of a surety this is not a tuppenny pie?

MRS. LOVETT: No, Mr. Lupin, that is a very special pie, such as I keep for callers and friends.

LUPIN: And tell me, sister—is there great profit on a tuppenny pie? Dost thou put in a pennyworth of the fat of calf?

MRS. LOVETT: Now, Mr. Lupin, how do you imagine I live? I put in a farthing's worth, no more.

LUPIN (*smacking his lips*): Verily, a magnificent pie. Of a truth, thou art a woman in a thousand. And how much flour puttest thou in a tuppenny pie?

MRS. LOVETT: A ha'porth, Mr. Lupin.

LUPIN: And whence comest thy flour, my beloved?

MRS. LOVETT: I buy it from Miller Brown.

LUPIN: And Brown has nearby his mill certain cavities in the earth containing chalk, hath he not, sister?

MRS. LOVETT: Miller Brown is a highly respectable merchant, Mr. Lupin.

LUPIN: Hoity-toity, did I say aught else? Ah, sister—what a pie, what a pie was that! Behold my heart yearneth after thy beauty; behold a great love welleth up in my soul. Wilt thou take my hand? And hast a stocking, sayest thou? Hark—I will whisper—is it near thy bed?

MRS. LOVETT: Oh—brother, brother, you mustn't . . . Mr. Lupin, you are a naughty man.

LUPIN: Hsst, my beloved, wilt call me Lupy now? (*Holding her hand*) And wilt meet me at twelve o'clock near Temple Bar? For the work of the Lord calleth his servant and I must begone. (*Whispers as he goes*) Twelve o'clock, then, lovey, near Temple Bar.

MRS. LOVETT: Oh . . . Lupy!!!

Scene Two

SWEENEY's *shop. Enter* LUPIN. *Looks about him in trepidation.*

LUPIN: Verily, I believe this Sweeney to be a man of sin. I have a mind to test his wickedness. Yes, I believe that he has secrets that he will buy at a great price, for it is said that his wealth is very great: and of a surety, it is well that the children of the Lord should partake of the illgotten gains of the wicked and strip the robber of his spoil. *(Enter* SWEENEY*)* Good evening, Mr. Todd. I would have you shave me.

SWEENEY: Certainly. Pray sit down. *(Aside)* I wonder if he's worth polishing off? *(As* LUPIN *sits down)* No, not that chair, please—this one over here. *(As* LUPIN *sits in another chair)* No, that one, either—this one. Better light.

(LUPIN *crosses to center chair, treading cautiously.* SWEENEY *begins to lather him furiously)*

LUPIN: P-p-p-lease, Mr. Todd, not so hard, not so hard.

SWEENEY *(lathers harder)*: What?

LUPIN: Pray, Mr. Todd, remember that we had a beautiful collection at the meeting yestereve, and that the man of God can well afford that gracious offering known to the righteous as a tip.

SWEENEY *(aside)*: Dear me. Perhaps he is worth polishing off!

LUPIN: Pray shave me carefully, Mr. Todd, for I am to meet a wealthy heiress I would fain make the wife of my bosom.

SWEENEY: A wealthy heiress, eh? And what's her name, may I ask?

LUPIN: Of a surety, she is not unknown to you—Mrs. Lovett, who owns a pie shop, that the Lord hath blessed with a trade bountiful and everflowing?

SWEENEY *(in consternation)*: What d'ye say? Then you *are* going to be polished off!

(SWEENEY *hurries into the next room.* LUPIN, *his face covered with lather, bib round his neck, leaps out of the chair and watches it turn over)*

LUPIN: So that's how you do it! You'll pay blood money for this, Mr. Todd!

(SWEENEY *comes back and rushes at* LUPIN *in a rage.* LUPIN *screams and runs off,* SWEENEY *chasing after him. While the shop is empty, the chair slowly begins to move and a hand, red with blood, pushes up the trap. With great difficulty,* MARK INGESTRIE *struggles out. He is pale and his clothes are torn. His face is bloody. He staggers)*

MARK: Have my senses left me? Do I dream of horrors unparalleled or is my existence a reality? I remember this place; the man who invited me in stood yonder and this is the chair on which I sat—afterwards falling to the depths below. Merciful Heaven! This piece of machinery to which a chain is fixed either side is a contrivance for the purpose of murder and robbery. My pocketbook gone—my string of pearls—all lost! The facts are clear enough. The owner of this shop is a robber and an assassin, but I have not quite fallen victim to his inhuman designs, for though weak and defenseless, I will sell my life dearly. *(Tries to open the door)* It will not yield. I'll find an instrument fit for the purpose and soon force it open. What is here? Another door? This leads to the room into which the scoundrel entered before I was thrown into the cellar below. *(Examines the trap)* The mystery is explained. A bolt that is here communicates with a spring from yonder room, and at the murderer's will, the unsuspecting victims are launched into eternity. Someone is at the door. Perhaps it is the assassin himself. Murderer, I am prepared for you.

(TOBIAS *enters.* MARK *springs out at him)*

TOBIAS: Merciful Heaven! The sailor—the owner of the pearls!

MARK: Silence—another word and 'tis the last you will utter. I am determined to leave this murderer's den, but not until I have dragged the owner to prison. Where is he?

TOBIAS: I know not. I expected to find him here.

MARK: I believe you to be in league with the villain.

TOBIAS: Indeed, I am not! Say rather that I am in his power.

MARK: Then assist me to bring him to the hands of Justice!

TOBIAS: I will, I will! Only tell me how to act!

MARK: Fetch the police officers here. I will await the murderer's coming and secure him till assistance arrives. (TOBIAS *runs off*)

MARK (*alone*): I think I hear footsteps. He is coming. No—they have gone past. My head is swimming, my heart beats fast, but it is not fear. Spring together all my senses, there is still work to do! Steel yourselves, sinews, there is fighting to come. (*His voice trembles*) Only . . . it's growing dark . . . I can't see. There's blood dripping in front of my eyes. Where has all the light gone? I must sit down. I must rest . . . (*He staggers about the stage*) Which chair is this . . . why is it dark? . . . it may be the fatal chair. Why have my eyes gone dark? I think I hear him . . . but I can't see . . . I can't see . . . for blood.

(*Sinister music.* MARK *stumbles into the chair, which slowly sinks. He falls below with a dull thud*)

DUMB SHOW: LUPIN *runs across the stage,* SWEENEY *chases after him.* TOBIAS *appears, points out* SWEENEY *to a* POLICEMAN. TOBIAS *hangs back as* POLICEMAN *stops* SWEENEY. *They converse in pantomime.* SWEENEY *shows the empty shop to* POLICEMAN, *who shakes his head and leaves.* SWEENEY *is left alone*)

SWEENEY: That ranting parson has escaped me, but I fear no man of his kidney. A little money—an offering, he will call it—blackmail, I should say—but merely a temporary disbursement to be returned along with all the other effects of the legator! Ha! ha! A pretty jest. And when he has been polished off, poor Lupin, I will also stop the babbling tongue of Tobias Ragg . . .

(*Enter* MRS. LOVETT)

MRS. LOVETT: Mister Todd . . .

TODD: Mrs. Lovett! Rather late for a call! Still, as a mere matter of friendship, I'll overlook the indiscretion. What do you want?

MRS. LOVETT: My mind is disturbed, Todd. The wicked manner of our lives darkens every hour and colors all my dreams with blood. Can there not be a change? Can we not reform our ways and live good righteous lives? (SWEENEY *seizes her wrist in an iron grip. She whimpers*) Don't, Todd! You hurt me.

SWEENEY: Now tell me exactly what you are talking about?

MRS. LOVETT *(trembling)*: William Grant died last night.

SWEENEY: And who may William Grant be?

MRS. LOVETT: But you know him—he was my baker, Mr. T.

SWEENEY: But my dear Mrs. L., your baker's name was Jones.

MRS. LOVETT *(bursts into tears)*: He had a nice face, that Jones had, Mr. T. But he got discontented. Surely you remember.

SWEENEY: There are so many of your bakers who get discontented. One gets confused, Mrs. L. But never mind; you'll find a new baker. Dry those tears—little crybaby!

MRS. LOVETT: Todd—I have not come here to be called a crybaby. I come here to tell you there has to be an end; to tell you that the pie shop in Bell Yard is going to be closed. My conscience is aroused. I have bad dreams. I tell you, Sweeney Todd, demon in human shape that you are, that you and I shall shortly see the last of each other.

SWEENEY: My heart goes out to you in sympathy, my dear Mrs. L. You must be tired of standing. *(Indicating the center chair)* Let me implore you to take a seat.

MRS. LOVETT: In *that* chair? Do you think I am *such* a fool, Todd? *(He deliberately begins to twist her wrist)* Please, please, Todd, my dear . . . *(She writhes in agony)*

SWEENEY: Funny, is it not, that I being so much smaller than you, Mrs. L., should yet know the way to control you. Believe me, my dear, the management of women is much like the management of horses— force judiciously applied. *(He drags her to the side of the stage and pulls up two loose chairs)* Come, let us sit down, my dear, and talk like old friends. You know you did not mean what you said just now. Come, come, think a little, be reasonable, Mrs. L.

MRS. LOVETT: Pray, leave go my hand. You are crushing it. Almost I can hear the bones crackle.

SWEENEY: I have always been noted for my strength.

MRS. LOVETT: Release me! I want to go out, I must breathe the clean air; let me go, let me go.

SWEENEY: Air, did you say? Come, I will open a window.

MRS. LOVETT: Let me go, let me go—I must go outside.

SWEENEY: Why this hurry to go out at this time of evening, Mrs. L.?

MRS. LOVETT: Let me go, I say—unhand me!

SWEENEY: Nay, nay—we shall sit here quietly and talk of your troubles. You were speaking of the unexpected demise of your baker . . . let me see—what was his name? Not Jones. What was it now? . . . Ay, cry, cry on. It'll do you good. *(St. Dunstan's clock strikes twelve)* Ha! Midnight. Now is the time for a heart-to-heart talk. *(A brief silence. He releases her)* You are not still thinking of going?

MRS. LOVETT *(aside):* Too late. Lupy will have gone by now. *(Aloud)* It is too late now.

SWEENEY: Why, then—let me hold your hand again—*(She trembles)*—and we will sit here holding hands—like lovers.

Scene Three

MRS. LOVETT's *pie shop, the next morning. Enter* MRS. LOVETT, *disheveled, nursing her bruised hand. Enter* JARVIS WILLIAMS, *in rags.*

MRS. LOVETT: Go away, my good fellow. We never give anything to beggars.

JARVIS: I ain't no beggar, mum, but a young man who is on the lookout for a situation. I thought as how you might recommend me to some light employment where they puts the heavy coin out.

MRS. LOVETT: Recommend you! Recommend a ragged wretch like you?

JARVIS: Bless your innocent heart, mum, it's the conduct, it ain't the toggery as makes the gentleman. There's often vice in velvet and virtue in velveteen. I've seen better days, mum, I have. I kept a vehicle.

MRS. LOVETT: A vehicle?

JARVIS: Yes, you never saw such a barrow of greens and taters as I used to turn out, but monopoly made me a bankrupt. The big shops ruins the little ones, and starves the coster. Blowed shame, ain't it?

MRS. LOVETT: I daresay when you get into better case you will have quite sufficient insolence to make you unbearable. But what employment can we have but piemaking? (*Aside*) If he be unknown, he is the very man for our purpose. (*Aloud*) You have solicited employment of me. If I give it you, you must furnish me with a reference.

JARVIS: Reference, mum? I haven't got one about me. Mayhap this toothpick as I've just found may do; it's real German silver.

MRS. LOVETT: Fool, I am speaking as to character!

JARVIS: Character—um—that's one of them things as I told you I'd lost. Besides, character ain't no use nowadays. There is always sufficient argument by the rich against the poor and destitute to keep 'em so. But argifying don't mend the matter. I'll look after another job. (*Starts to leave*)

MRS. LOVETT: You are ingenuous, and I don't see why I should not make a trial of you. Follow me.

JARVIS: Where to?

MRS. LOVETT: To the bakehouse, where I will show you what you have to do. You must promise never to leave it on any pretense.

JARVIS: Never to leave it!

MRS. LOVETT: Never, unless you leave it for good and all. If upon those conditions you choose to accept the situation, you may; if not, you can depart and leave it alone.

JARVIS: As Shakespeare says, "My poverty and not my will consents."

MRS. LOVETT *(raises a trapdoor and points to the descent)*: By this passage, young man, we must descend to the furnace and ovens, where I will show you how to manufacture the pies, feed the fires and make yourself generally useful.

(Music. They descend. The trap closes.)

Scene Four

The bakehouse. A gloomy cellar of vast extent. A fitful glare issues from various low arches in one of which a huge oven is placed. A flight of stone steps in the center leads to a doorway at top. There are sacks of flour, also a counter, with pies on tray. Enter MRS. LOVETT *and* JARVIS *down the steps.*

JARVIS: I suppose I'm to have someone to assist me in this situation? One pair of hands could never do the work in such a place.

MRS. LOVETT: Are you not content? Now say the word and let me know if you have any scruples.

JARVIS: No scruples, but one objection.

MRS. LOVETT: And that is?

JARVIS: I should like to leave when I please.

MRS. LOVETT: Make your mind easy on that score. I never *keep* anybody after they begin to feel uncomfortable. But now I must leave you for a time. As long as you are industrious, you will get on very well, but as soon as you begin to grow idle and neglect my orders, you will receive a piece of information that may—

JARVIS: What is it? I am of an inquiring disposition. You may as well give it to me now.

MRS. LOVETT: No. I seldom find there is occasion for it at first; but after a time, when you get well fed, you are pretty sure to want it. (*Aside*) Everybody who relinquishes this situation goes to his old friends— friends that he has not seen for years. (*To* JARVIS) I shall return anon. (MRS. LOVETT *exits*)

JARVIS: What a strange manner of talking that respectable middle-aged female has! There seems to be something very singular in all she utters! What the deuce does she mean by a communication being made to me? It's very strange! And what a singular looking place, too —nothing visible but darkness. I think it would be quite unbearable if it wasn't for the delicious odor of the pies. Talking of pies, I fancy I could eat one. (*Takes a pie off tray and eats voraciously*) Beautiful! Delicious! Lots of gravy! (*He suddenly discovers a long hair. He winds it round his finger*) Somebody's been combing their hair. I don't think that pie's a nice 'un. (*Puts eaten pie back and takes another*) This is better! Done to a turn! Extremely savory! (*Puts hand in mouth*) What's this? A bone? No—a button. How did that button get into that pie? I don't think I like pies now. Oh, la! I'm very poorly! (*A portion of the wall gives way.* MARK INGESTRIE, *with an iron bar, forces a passage through the aperture*) Oh, la! Here's one of the murdered ghosts come to ax for his body, and it's been made into pies. Please, it wasn't me. I was only engaged today.

MARK: Hush, friend, you have nothing to fear. I see, like myself, you have been lured into this den.

JARVIS: I hope, Mr. Ghost, that they ain't a-going to murder me as they did you afore me.

MARK: I have escaped the fate the assassins intended for me, and have learnt that of unfortunate men who have for some years past disappeared from their families in London, one after the other.

JARVIS: Since you are flesh and blood, and not a ghost, perhaps you can inform me why such wholesale butchery has been indulged in.

MARK: The object of the wretches has solely been robbery, and their victims people of supposed wealth. They have in all cases been inveigled into the shop of an infamous monster named Sweeney Todd, a barber residing in Fleet Street. Here, by an ingenious contrivance, the unfortunate sufferers were lowered to the cellars below, murdered and conveyed to this retreat, where a glowing furnace destroyed every trace of the crime.

JARVIS: Now I am brought to believe that if anyone had the assistance of the Devil in conducting human affairs, I should say by some means the parties in question have made it worth the while of his Satanic Majesty to join in the concern.

MARK: We have no time to lose in idle discourse, but must strike out some plan for our mutual deliverance. We are in Bell Yard, and to my certain knowledge the houses right and left have cellars. Now surely, with a weapon such as this bar, willing hearts and arms that have not quite lost their powers, we may make our way from this horrible abode. Hark! Someone is approaching. I must not be seen. Follow me. Leave the matter in my hands and see if I cannot thwart those who are engaged in this disgusting speculation.

(*Music.* MARK *and* JARVIS *retire through aperture. After a pause,* SWEENEY *enters*)

SWEENEY: Gathering clouds warn the mountaineer of the approaching storm; let them now warn me to provide against danger. I have too many enemies to be safe. I will dispose of them one by one, till no evidence of my guilt remains. My first step must be to silence Tobias Ragg. I need not take his life, for that may be of service to me hereafter, but a close confinement in the lunatic asylum of Jonas Fogg will effectually quell him. Mrs. Lovett, too, grows scrupulous and dissatisfied; I've had my eyes on her for some time, and fear she intends mischief. A little poison, skillfully administered, may remove any unpleasantness in that quarter. Hum!—ha—heugh! Who's there? (SWEENEY *turns suddenly and discovers* MRS. LOVETT *standing at his elbow. She points to two chairs. They both sit down*)

MRS. LOVETT: Sweeney Todd!

SWEENEY (*calmly*): Well?

MRS. LOVETT: Since I discover that you intend treachery, I shall on the instant demand my share of the booty—aye, an equal share of the fruits of our mutual bloodshed.

SWEENEY: Well, you shall have it.

MRS. LOVETT: I will! Every shilling, every penny!

SWEENEY: So you shall, if you are patient. I will balance accounts with you in a minute. (He takes book from pocket and runs a finger down the account) Twelve thousand pounds, to a fraction.

MRS. LOVETT: That is just six thousand pounds for each person, there being two of us.

SWEENEY: But, Mistress Lovett, I must first have you to know that before I hand you a coin, you will have to pay me for your support, lodging and clothes.

MRS. LOVETT: Clothes?!

SWEENEY: I repeat the word—clothes!

MRS. LOVETT: Why, I haven't had a new dress for these six months!

SWEENEY: Besides, am I to have nothing for your education? (Draws his finger significantly across his throat) Yes, for some years you have been totally provided for by me; and after deducting that and the expenses of erecting furnaces, purchasing flour for your delicious pies, and cetera, I find it leaves a balance of sixteen shillings four and three-quarters pence in my favor, and I don't intend you to budge an inch till it is paid.

MRS. LOVETT: You want to rob me; but you shall find, to your sorrow, I will have my due. (She secretly draws a knife. He confronts her, but starts back as he sees the weapon) Now, villain, who triumphs? Put your name to a deed consigning the whole of the wealth blood has purchased, or you perish where you stand!

SWEENEY: Idiot! You should have known Sweeney Todd better and learnt that he is a man to calculate his chances. Behold! (He draws a pistol.

MRS. LOVETT *flings herself at his feet)* Now say your prayers. Your last hour has come. *(He takes knife away from her)*

MRS. LOVETT: Spare my life, for the love of Heaven, as I spared yours! You cannot have the heart to kill me. *(Clinging to him)* I will not loose my hold—you cannot throw me off. Oh, stop, before you spill my blood. Upon my guilty soul, I have been true to you!

SWEENEY: Off! Off!

MRS. LOVETT: I will enter a holy order and end my days in solitude and peace. Let us both lead better lives and forget we have ever lived except in prayer!

SWEENEY *(brandishing the knife):* You will not loose your hold?

MRS. LOVETT: It is never too late to repent—never—

SWEENEY: Damnation! *(He stabs her to death, then stands motionless for a time)* There is blood upon my hands—and she is dead . . . *(SWEENEY passes a hand across his brow, then opens the furnace door. A fierce glare lights the stage)* Now let the furnace consume the body, as it would wheaten straw, and destroy all evidence of my guilt in this, as it has in my manifold deeds of blood!

(SWEENEY drags the body of MRS. LOVETT to the oven. Curtain.)

ACT THREE

Scene One

SWEENEY's *shop.* TOBIAS *and* MARK *on.*

MARK: At last, Tobias, I fancy I have got to the bottom of this mystery. This house communicates with the next door, and in it Sweeney Todd hides his victims until he gets rid of them in the shape of his juicy confectionary—pies, all hot! By touching a spring in the mantel-piece, the opening to Lovett's house is discovered, but it is very difficult to remove alone. I needn't ask you if you will lend me a hand?

TOBIAS: I will, indeed, but we must use caution in the proceeding and watch our opportunity. Most likely, tomorrow I shall be able to frame some excuse by which I may get Sweeney Todd out of the way and we shall have plenty of time to make the venture. At present, it would be dangerous, as I expect his return every minute.

MARK: Then I'll make myself scarce at once.

TOBIAS: Hush! I hear footsteps.

MARK: Talk of the Devil, and he's at your elbow. I wonder how he'd taste in one of his own pies!

(MARK *exits. He is scarcely gone when* SWEENEY TODD *enters carrying box of pearls. He regards* TOBIAS *suspiciously*)

SWEENEY: What are you staring at, boy?

TOBIAS: I wasn't staring, sir!

SWEENEY: Don't be impertinent! Now tell me what are you doing?

TOBIAS: Nothing.

SWEENEY: Then finish the job at once and begin something else.

TOBIAS: Shall I put away the casket you have in your hand?

SWEENEY *(striking him):* There's a lesson for you; it will teach you to make no remarks about what don't concern you. You may think what you like, but you shall only say what *I* like, Tobias Ragg.

TOBIAS: I won't be knocked about in this way, I won't!

SWEENEY: You won't, eh? Ha, ha, heugh! Have you forgotten your mother?

TOBIAS: You say you have power over her, but I don't know what it is. I cannot and will not believe it. I'll leave you, come of it what may. I'll go to sea—anywhere, rather than stay in such a place as this.

SWEENEY: Oh, you will, will you? Then, Tobias Ragg, I'll tell you what power I have over your mother.

TOBIAS: You can do her no injury while I live to protect her!

SWEENEY: Last winter, when the frost continued eight weeks, you were starving and Mrs. Ragg was employed to attend the chambers of a lawyer in the Temple. He was a coldhearted, severe man who never forgave anything in his life and never will.

TOBIAS: Our home was indeed desolate. A guinea was owing for rent, but mother got the money, paid it and obtained the situation where she now is.

SWEENEY: Ah, you think so. The rent was paid, but Tobias, my boy, a word in your ear—she took a candlestick from her employer to pay it. I know it—can prove it! and I will hang her if you force me by your conduct.

TOBIAS: Liar and calumniator! This infamous charge against an innocent woman has given me a nerve of iron. I utterly throw off the yoke imposed by you upon me and—

SWEENEY: Where are you going?

TOBIAS: To the nearest magistrate—there to denounce Sweeney Todd and deliver into the hands of justice a designing, cruel and cold-blooded murderer!

SWEENEY: You have sealed your fate!

(A *desperate struggle takes place between* SWEENEY *and* TOBIAS, *who is ultimately overpowered.* SWEENEY *drags* TOBIAS *out.* JARVIS *emerges through the secret door and follows after.*)

Scene Two

A chamber in the Madhouse at Peckham. Enter JONAS FOGG.

FOGG: Five o'clock and not arrived. Mr. Todd is late. He is generally a very punctual man. *(Takes out memorandum book)* Let me see. "R. S. T.—Todd, Fleet Street, London, paid one year's keep and burial of Thomas Simkins, aged fifteen, found dead in his bed after a residence in the asylum of ten months and four days." I think that was our last transaction. Some of our patients do die very suddenly, and somehow or other we never know how it happens. It must be some sort of fit, for they are found dead in the morning, and in their beds; then I bury them quietly and privately, without anyone knowing anything about it. *(A knock)* 'Tis he—I said he was a very punctual man. *(Enter* SWEENEY*)* Mr. Sweeney Todd, I think, if my memory don't deceive me?

SWEENEY: You are right, Mr. Jonas Fogg. I believe I am not easily forgotten by those who have once seen me.

FOGG *(pointedly)*: True, sir. You are not easily forgotten. What can I do for you now?

SWEENEY: I am rather unfortunate with my boys. I have got another here who has shown such decided symptoms of insanity that it becomes, I regret to say, absolutely necessary to put him under your care.

FOGG: Indeed—does he rave?

SWEENEY: Oh, yes, he does, and about the most absurd nonsense in the world. To hear him, one would really think that instead of being one of the most humane of men I am, in point of fact, an absolute murderer.

FOGG: A murderer?

SWEENEY: Yes. Could anything be more absurd than such an accusation? I, that have the milk of human kindness flowing in every vein, and whose very appearance ought to be sufficient to convince anybody at once of my sweet and considerate disposition.

FOGG: For how long do you think, Mr. Todd, this malady will continue?

SWEENEY: I will pay for twelve months; but I do not think, between you and me, that the case will last anything like so long. I think he will die like Simkins—suddenly.

FOGG: I shouldn't wonder if he did.

SWEENEY: It is decidedly the best way, because it saves a great deal of trouble and annoyance to friends and relatives, as well as preventing expense which otherwise might be foolishly gone into.

FOGG: We make no remarks, and we ask no questions; those are the principles on which we have conducted this establishment so successfully and so long; those are the principles upon which we shall continue to conduct it, and to merit, we hope, the patronage of the public.

SWEENEY: Unquestionably.

FOGG: You may as well introduce me to your patient at once.

SWEENEY: Certainly. I shall have great pleasure in showing him to you. *(Goes to door)* Tobias Ragg, come into the room directly!

(Enter TOBIAS, pale and dejected)

FOGG: Quite young!

SWEENEY: Yes, more's the pity, and of course we deeply lament his present position.

FOGG: Of course. But see, he raises his eyes. He will speak directly.

SWEENEY: Rave, you mean—don't call it speaking; it's not entitled to the name. Hush! Listen!

TOBIAS: Sweeney Todd is a murderer, and I denounce him!

SWEENEY: You hear him?

FOGG: Mad, indeed!

TOBIAS: Oh, save me—save me from him; it is my life he seeks, because I know his secret. He is a murderer, and many a person comes into his shop who never leaves it again in life.

SWEENEY: Could anyone but a maniac make so absurd an assertion?

FOGG: No; it's insanity in its most terrible form. I shall be under the necessity of putting him into a strait-waistcoat.

SWEENEY: I'm afraid mild treatment, which I have tried, only irritates the disease; therefore I must leave you, as a professional man, to deal with the case as you deem fit. But as time presses and I have an important engagement, good evening. I have no doubt the patient will be properly attended to. (SWEENEY *shakes hands with* FOGG, *then speaks quietly to* TOBIAS) Ha, ha! Tobias, how do you feel now? Shall I hang, or will you die in the cell of a madhouse? *(Exits)*

TOBIAS: I don't know who you are, sir, or where I am, but let me beg of you to have the house of Sweeney Todd, in Fleet Street, searched and you will find that he is a murderer. There are at least a hundred watches, rings and trinkets, all belonging to the unfortunate persons who from time to time have met their deaths through him.

FOGG: How uncommonly mad!

TOBIAS: No, no; indeed, I am not mad. Why call me so, when the truth or falsehood of what I say can so easily be ascertained? Search his house and if those things be not found, then say I am mad and have but dreamt of them.

(JONAS *rings a loud bell.* KEEPERS *enter*)

FOGG: You will take this lad under your care, as he seems extremely feverish and unsettled—shave his head and put a strait-waistcoat on him. Let him be conveyed to one of the dark damp cells, as too much light encourages his wild delirium.

TOBIAS: Oh, no, no, no! What have I done that I should be subjected to such cruel treatment? If this be a madhouse, I am not mad—oh, have mercy on me!

FOGG: Give him nothing but bread and water, and the first symptoms of his recovery, which will produce better treatment, will be his exonerating his master from what he has said about him, for he must be mad so long as he continues to accuse such a gentleman as Mr. Todd of such things.

TOBIAS: Then I shall continue mad, for be it madness to know and aver that Sweeney Todd is an assassin—mad I am, for it is true!

FOGG: Take him away; he is more vicious than any patient we have had here for a considerable time.

TOBIAS: I will die ere I submit to you or your vile myrmidons!

FOGG: Then die, for no power can aid you.

TOBIAS: Yes, there is one! *(Points upward)* Heaven, which fails not to succor the helpless and persecuted.

(Music. FOGG *and his men advance to seize* TOBIAS. *The window shatters and* JARVIS WILLIAMS *dashes through it and confronts the villains with his fists)*

JARVIS: Stand off, you cowardly rascals! Tobias, assist me! We'll lock these rascals in their own madhouse!

*(*JARVIS *seizes* FOGG *by the throat, shakes him violently and throws him to the ground. He and* TOBIAS *fight off others and, after sending one through the window, make their escape.)*

Scene Three

Temple Stairs. Enter COLONEL JEFFERY.

JEFFERY: Johanna will be true to her appointment, I have no doubt, though I have little to make known to her with respect to her missing lover. Since our last interview, a feeling to which I have been hitherto a stranger has assailed me—is it love? If Mark Ingestrie be dead, there is no dishonor in the acknowledgment, and a beautiful girl is not to be shut out from the pale of all affection because the first person to whom her heart has warmed is no more; it may be that she is incapable of experiencing a sentiment which can at all approach that which she once felt, but still she may be happy and pass many joyous hours as the wife of another. *(Enter* JOHANNA*)* Ah, she is here! Your servant, Miss Oakley, I rejoice again to meet you.

JOHANNA: Pardon me if I dispense with the common observances of courtesy, as my mind is ill at ease. Tell me at once, I pray you, if you bring sad or gladsome tidings.

JEFFERY: I have heard nothing, my good young lady, that can give you satisfaction concerning the fate of Mark Ingestrie, but I have suspicion that something serious must have happened to him.

JOHANNA: I do sincerely hope from my heart that such a suspicion may be dissipated. I hope it, because I tell you freely and frankly, dim and obscure as the hope is, that Mark has escaped the murderous hands raised against him.

JEFFERY: If the sacrifice, Miss Oakley, of my life would be a relief, and save you from the pains you suffer, believe me, it should be made.

JOHANNA: No, no! Heaven knows enough has been sacrificed already— more than enough— much more than enough—but do not suppose that I am ungrateful for the generous interest you have taken in me. No, believe me, Colonel Jeffery, among the few names that are enrolled in my breast, remember, yours will be found while I live, but that will not be long.

JEFFERY: Do not speak despairingly.

JOHANNA: Have I not cause for despair?

JEFFERY: You have cause for grief, but scarcely for despair; you are yet young, and let me entertain a hope—

JOHANNA: I know your words are kindly spoken and kindly meant. But alas! Colonel Jeffery, I cannot endure this dreadful suspense.

JEFFERY: It is too common an affliction on human nature, Johanna. Pardon me for using that name.

JOHANNA: It requires no excuse; I am accustomed to be so addressed by all who feel a kindly interest in me. Call me Johanna, if you will, as a greater assurance of your friendship and esteem.

JEFFERY: I will avail myself, then, of that permission, and again entreat you to leave the task to me of discovering your lover's destiny. If there has been any foul play, there must be danger even in inquiring for him, and therefore I ask you to let that danger be mine alone.

JOHANNA: I will accord with your wishes thus far, and promise that I will attempt nothing that shall not have the possibility of success attending it. Return here tomorrow at the same hour and I will divulge to you the scheme I have in view with regard to this terrible mystery. (JOHANNA *goes out*)

JEFFERY: I love her, but she seems in no respect willing to enchain her heart. Alas! how sad it is for me that the woman who above all others I could wish to call my own, instead of being a joy to me, I have only encountered that she might impart a pang to my soul. Beautiful and excellent Johanna, I love you, but I see that your affections are withered for ever.

(*Enter* SWEENEY *in a mask and cloak*)

SWEENEY: Colonel Jeffery, you are in danger, or I am much mistaken.

JEFFERY: Indeed! From whom, may I ask?

SWEENEY: Follow me, and you will soon find out your enemy.

JEFFERY: I must first know who and what you are before I consent to be guided by a man who disguises his features by wearing a mask.

SWEENEY: I wear this mask for other purposes than concealment, which it is not judicious to explain at the present moment.

JEFFERY: Unless you are more explicit, I cannot consider with safety to myself to accompany you. What is your name?

SWEENEY: I am a man, and friendly disposed towards you.

JEFFERY: Nevertheless, this assertion fails to move my scruples.

SWEENEY: Why should it do so? But since you distrust me, I must leave, and you will remain without the information I was about to afford. (SWEENEY *begins to exit*)

JEFFERY: Can it be? I am in doubt and fear how to act in this strange intercourse. Stay, my friend; since you say you are a friend to me, have you no token by which I may recognize amity?

SWEENEY: Yes, an undeniable one.

(SWEENEY *hands him the pearls. A chord of music*)

JEFFERY: Great Heaven! The string of pearls!

SWEENEY: Hasten with me to the shop of Sweeney Todd, the barber of Fleet Street, and you will there learn who and what I am, and more of the owner of the gems than I can tell you here.

JEFFERY: Say you so? Then I have tarried too long; my impatience to fathom the mystery is so great that I wish our onward speed could leave the wind behind us. Come, let no further time be lost by discourse. (*He rushes out*)

SWEENEY: So he has the pearls in his possession—good! I can now denounce him, and remove the grave suspicion that attaches itself to the name of Sweeney Todd.

(*He blows a whistle. A policeman appears and* SWEENEY *hustles him off in the direction that* COLONEL JEFFERY *took.*)

Scene Four

A courtroom. A high range of seats at back. A high dark window of gauze over judge's seat. The judge, SIR WILLIAM BRANDON, *is discovered. The court is full of spectators. The prisoner is* COLONEL JEFFERY.

JUDGE: That the prisoner at the bar is either an accomplice in the murder of the unfortunate man, or the actual perpetrator, there is strong evidence—his absence from his home without any special reason and the discovery of the pearls on his person, can lead to no other supposition than he must be in some way connected with the mysterious affair upon which we are adjudicating. What your motive was, prisoner, can be clearly conceived—your victim was the only bar between you and the object of your affection, Johanna Oakley.

JEFFERY: My lord, circumstances are against me. I can make no defense, can call no witness to prove my innocence. The stranger from whom I received those pearls has failed to make his appearance, and my bare word is nothing—

JUDGE: The statement that you received those pearls from an unknown person in a public thoroughfare is so improbable that it cannot for a moment be accepted as truth.

JEFFERY: Then I must sink into the grave with ignominy, and my name, which has been hitherto untarnished by dishonor, become the scorn of all honest men.

JUDGE: The only chance of life left you, prisoner, hangs on this mysterious letter, but its purpose is so vague that I cannot offer you any hope on that score. *(Reads letter)* "Let the hand of justice for a moment be arrested. Ere sentence is pronounced, a witness will appear and confound the guilty in their hour of triumph." That witness has not appeared, and there is but one other to examine. Let him stand forth.

(SWEENEY *ascends witness box*)

JEFFERY: My lord, you will not take evidence of this man, who—

JUDGE: Silence! Make your deposition.

SWEENEY: My lord, I cannot but express my deep regret at being called to testify against one who has held the good opinion of the world, but duty and justice compel me to speak. I had taken into my service a fatherless lad named Tobias Ragg—

JUDGE: So it has been stated in the earlier stages of the trial. Is that boy here?

SWEENEY: No, my lord! Since the murder of Mark Ingestrie, he can be found nowhere, though a diligent search has been made by the officers. It is supposed that, being an accomplice of the prisoner, he has—

JEFFERY: My lord, surely the unsupported testimony of this designing man will not be suffered to condemn me, and—

JUDGE: This interruption augurs ill for your judgment, prisoner. You will have an opportunity of replying in due season and receive every advantage justice can yield. Witness, proceed with your attestation.

(A *green light burns at the gauze window and the form of* MARK INGESTRIE *appears for an instant.* SWEENEY *stands transfixed*)

SWEENEY: Can the dead rise? 'Tis his form—I see it distinctly! Ah! the yawning grave yields up its ghastly inmate to fix my guilt! Blood will have blood!

JUDGE: Why do you pause, witness? The Court is waiting.

SWEENEY: My lord, it is impossible that I can give evidence whilst that figure is gleaming upon me from yonder window. (MARK *vanishes*) Gone! 'Twas the picture of a distraught brain. Your pardon, my lord— a sudden giddiness, nothing more.

JUDGE: Produce the string of pearls stated to have been taken from the murdered man. (*Casket is produced*) Can you swear to them?

SWEENEY: Yes. The clasp is so curiously and cleverly devised, you might distinguish it amongst a thousand.

JUDGE: And you have seen it in the possession of Mark Ingestrie? (MARK *appears again behind the* JUDGE)

SWEENEY: Have I seen it in his possession? Shame, shame—why do you ask such a question? Do you not see him coming to claim it? Ask him, I say—he is coming towards the judgment seat. See, he is there—he

comes to accuse me of the murder. Oh, save me! 'Twas not I that slew
him. Look, my Lord Judge, Mark Ingestrie is by your side! Do not
whisper to him. Your ermine robe is stained with blood! Let me
hence, or it will kill me—ha, ha, ha! (MARK *vanishes*)

JUDGE: Witness, your words are incoherent and wild; your frantic gesture
would lead us to suppose that reason has resigned her throne to mad
despair. If your nerves are unstrung by the painful office you undertake, retire awhile to recover self-possession.

SWEENEY: Yes, it was a dark, foul deed; but heed not what you hear, Lord
Judge. The prisoner has brought his victim! (SWEENEY *points to window, though* MARK *is no longer visible through it*) What! Do you still
remain? I feared it would come to this, and through accursèd gold, for
which men sell their souls and barter their eternal salvation! Ha, ha!
'tis useless to deny my guilt; the dead rise from their cerements to
prove Sweeney Todd a murderer!

(SWEENEY *collapses. Sensation in the courtroom. Curtain.*)

ACT FOUR

Scene One

The entrance to Newgate Prison. On the left, MRS. POORLEAN *at a table with
bottles, glasses and quart pots. Three or four idlers and* PRISON WARDERS
await the opportunity of seeing the new prisoner, SWEENEY TODD.

FIRST WARDER: Sorry to keep you waiting, gentlemen; Sweeney Todd will
be moving shortly.

(*Enter* LUPIN)

LUPIN (*aside*): Verily, hypocrisy is the ladder by which to mount. From
the lowest step did I begin, till I reached the topmost; it hath made a
man of me, and that carcass which was as lank as a herring is now
round and comely to look upon. Ah, 'tis a sinful world! (*To* WARDERS)
Brethren, I am told that in this den of thieves you have a wondrous
expert fellow worth seeing. Canst thou oblige me?

FIRST WARDER: Have you any business with him?

LUPIN: Yea, to rebuke him. My spirit is full of exhortations.

FIRST WARDER: Why, let your heart be full of generosity or he'll laugh at you and your exhortations, too. If you'll contribute something in charity towards his upkeep, give it to me and I'll pass it on.

LUPIN: Verily, I would give anything to save his soul, but for his body I can give no more than a sixpenny piece.

FIRST WARDER: Well, everything helps. You must wait here.

(A sound of rattling chains)

SECOND WARDER: Note the free entertainment we give you, gentlemen.

(A chorus of chained prisoners enters. They sing)

PRISONERS: In a cell of the stone jug, I was born;
Of a hempen widow, the kid forlorn,

                                 Carry on!

And my noble father, as I've heard say,
Was a famous swindler of capers gay.

                 Nix, my dolly pals, carry on!

But my amorous lady one fine day
To the judge did her gentleman betray,

                                 Carry on!

And so I was bolted up at last
And into the jug a convict was cast.

                 Nix, my dolly pals, carry on!

But I slipped my irons one fine day
And gave the turnkeys a holiday,

                                 Carry on!

And here I am, pals, merry and free,
A regular rollicking gypsy I be!

                 Nix, my dolly pals, carry on!

FIRST WARDER (marching prisoners off): I am not pleased with the sentiment of that song. It seems to smack of danger. (Exeunt)

LUPIN *(aside)*: I find that my outward man, after so much psalm singing, wanteth refreshment. I will therefore confabulate with that well-grown damsel. *(Approaches* MRS. POORLEAN*)* Wife, virgin, thou hast an abundance of oil in thy lamp, if I am not mistaken. The morning being cold, I would willingly qualify it with something comforting and refreshing. What hast thou got?

MRS. POORLEAN: Sir, because you are a friend, I will entertain you with my own favorite bottle. *(They drink together)*

LUPIN: Pray, do the frogs of this lake of darkness regale with such choice liquors?

MRS. POORLEAN: Some of the better sort that can afford it, do; but they are for the generality such poor rogues. My service to you.

LUPIN: Thou needest not say that; thy love is enough. *(Drinks)* Thou art as round as a full moon and as fleshy as the goats that wanton on the delectable mountain. Thy tabernacle is full with mammon. Hast thou not an idol in thy inward woman to whom thou sacrificest day and night, as of old the heathen gave up their babes to be devoured by Moloch?

MRS. POORLEAN: Ha, ha, you are a comical gent! No, no, mine is nothing but sheer fat; you may feel it, if you please. I have neither Pope nor idol in my belly. Pure sheer fat. Grief and brandy, indeed, sir, nothing else. You don't drink, sir?

LUPIN: Verily, fill unto me. I am a righteous person and never fall above seven times a day. Vouchsafe me the kiss of peace.

MRS. POORLEAN: Nay, nay, sir, it is more than I allow to any stranger. None but the gentlemen of the jail ever presume to kiss me.

LUPIN: Verily, thou art a most delightful piece of flesh; if thou wert well fructified thou mightest raise up seed unto the righteous.

MRS. POORLEAN: Ah, sir, I have been as well fructified as any woman but am very unfortunate in my husbands. I lost two of them in one sessions. So I'll marry no more, but take my chance like any other honest woman. Come, sorrow's dry. My love, as thou sayest!

LUPIN: I greet thee. Verily, flesh is prevailing. Woman, I shall come and see thee pretty often. But no more now. We may be observed by the profane.

SECOND WARDER: Well, gentlemen, if you will follow me, I can now take you to see this famous prisoner, Sweeney Todd, in his cell. Follow me, please.

(WARDERS, *the idlers and* LUPIN *all exit. The prisoners sing from offstage*)

PRISONERS: And when we come unto the jug
        Our irons to behold,
        Our lodging is on the cold, cold ground
        And we booze the water cold.

        But if we live to come out again,
        And the jolly old Peachum I meet,
        I'll cut out his heart and murder his tart
        As he walks along the street.

(FIRST WARDER *runs across the stage*)

FIRST WARDER: Hi, hi, Lockfast, the bird is flown! Sweeney Todd has escaped! Hi, hi—tell the governor! Ring the bells.

(*He exits. A clamor of bells. Enter* LUPIN)

LUPIN: Verily, Todd is fled! He is gone like the flower of the field, and the flower fadeth and the man vanisheth, and then shall be said in those days, "Woe to England, for Todd is escaped! Woe, woe, woe for the roaring lion is abroad and no throats shall remain of a piece." Oh, that my head were a fountain to weep salt tears for the crying sins of this nation!

(JARVIS WILLIAMS *comes on slowly behind him*)

JARVIS: That's my man, sure enough. Now to treat him with a surprise he little expects. Um—hollo, my tulip!

LUPIN: Tulip! Avaunt! Of a verity, my name is Lupin.

JARVIS: Any fool knows a tulip and a lupin ain't the same plant. You're a *rum* 'un, you are!

LUPIN: Rum? Peradventure, I may have partaken of that carnal fluid in a cup of tea with the pious dame who vends the article at yonder sinful public-house, but medicinally only, for spasms sorely afflict this rebellious stomach of mine.

JARVIS: I want a word with you, since I see you are of a sanctimonious turn.

LUPIN: I despise not the ungodly, that I may teach them the errors of their ways, but I may not like thy company, for—

JARVIS: I see you are not comfortable in the company of respectable people.

LUPIN: Thy wit is thrown away.

JARVIS: It generally is on a fool.

LUPIN: Fool! Thou knowest me not! I'm an honest man.

JARVIS: How folks are deceived by appearances! You look for all the world like a rogue.

LUPIN: I like not this unseemly fellow. The spirit moveth me to depart.

JARVIS: Stop, stop! I've not done with you yet, old sobersides; I've a few more questions to ax. Were you ever in the West Indies?

LUPIN: Yes—that is, no!

JARVIS: Yes—no? Mind what you are about, Mr. Honest Man, or you'll get into hot water. I say again, were you ever in the West Indies?

LUPIN: Why askest thou?

JARVIS: Because here's a family that claim some relationship.

(A *black woman and five black children run on*)

LUPIN: By all that's damnable, my wife Chloe! I will gird up my loins and
flee!

(LUPIN *runs off, followed by his family.* JARVIS *follows them out, laughing.*)

Scene Two

The bakehouse. SWEENEY *alone. He is pale and distraught.*

SWEENEY: I think I have given them the slip now . . . but I am weary
and would fain rest a while. What happened? They were crying after
me down Ludgate Hill . . . yes, I remember now. I ran! Straight and
swift I ran, and no one dare stop me. I heard the noise of feet behind
and redoubled my speed. It grew fainter and fainter in the distance
and at length died away altogether, but on I bounded, through marsh
and rivulet, over fence and wall, with a wild shout, which was taken
up by the strange beings that flocked around me on every side and
swelled the sound till it pierced the air. I was borne upon the arms of
demons who swept along upon the wind, and bore down bank and
hedge before them and spun me round and round with a rustle and a
speed that made my head swim, until at last they threw me from
them with a violent shock and I fell heavily upon the earth . . . and
then I woke and crawled back here. What was it I came for? My head
aches. I cannot remember . . . for now I mix up realities with my
dreams, and having so much to do, and being always hurried hither
and thither, have no time to separate the two from some strange
confusion in which they get involved . . . I remember now—it was
money—and some jewels . . . but not here. Yes, the money was
here. And the jewels—oh, my poor head. Have I forgotten where I hid
them? Was it in the shop? (*He listens*) Footsteps! I can hear somebody on the stairs. (*Shouts*) You can't come down those stairs. Only
Mrs. Lovett and Sweeney Todd know of those stairs—and that Smith.
But he's dead. Go away! You can't come down! (*After a pause,* SWEE-
NEY *talks to himself*) Quietly, quietly—it was only the wind. (*He moves
about the cellar, stopping at the open door to the furnace. He peers
inside*) Ah—there you are, Mrs. Lovett. Somebody's cut your throat.
Tell me who did it. Tell Sweeney . . . he'll revenge you . . . he'll
cut their throats, too. Are you burning down there in Hell? Never
mind, crybaby, never mind, Mrs. L. You shall have your share, to the
last farthing. Look, dear, I'll count it out for you!

(He finds and opens the money box. While he counts the money, MARK *enters)*

MARK *(quietly):* Your trade was a paying one, Mr. Todd.

SWEENEY *(screams):* Go away! Go away! You're dead! You're dead!

MARK *(making for him):* No, not dead, Mr. Todd. Not quite dead yet.

SWEENEY *(raising his pistol):* Well, Mr. Sailor, Sweeney Todd has never been known to miss yet. You'll be quite dead this time.

*(*JARVIS *springs out from a dark corner)*

JARVIS: Not this time, Sweeney, not this time. *(Knocks the pistol out of his hand)*

MARK: Now, Mr. Todd, it's your turn to swing low. With my own hands, I shall drag you to the gallows and the end you have so richly deserved.

SWEENEY *(crouching in a corner):* Very well. The fortune of war. Take me alive, if you can. But remember, Mr. Sailor, that you're in my prison yet. *(Turns suddenly and runs through a secret door, shouting as he goes)* You're fast now! All the doors are locked! One lever locks them all! You're fast now!

(Both rush to the door and try to force it open in vain. They hear SWEENEY *laughing as he mounts the stairs.)*

Scene Three

Inside the barber shop. SWEENEY *is searching furiously.*

SWEENEY: Was it here I hid them? Or there? Or there? No. Lost. Forgotten. *(Holds his head in his hands)* I will sit quietly and I will remember soon.

(As SWEENEY *sits down,* SIR WILLIAM BRANDON *enters in his judge's robes.* SWEENEY *starts up)*

JUDGE: I would like a shave, Mr. Barber, and a quick one, if you don't mind. I have to go and try a case at half-past three.

SWEENEY *(his voice trembling)*: Y-y-y-es, sir. But the shop is not really open, sir.

JUDGE *(sternly)*: Never mind, the door was open. Give me a shave.

SWEENEY: P-p-pray sit down, sir. N-n-no, this way, sir.

JUDGE: I beg your pardon. I am very short-sighted. I cannot see your face properly, but haven't I heard your voice before?

SWEENEY: I was once a foreman on the jury, sir.

JUDGE: Ah, that must have been it.

(SWEENEY, *distraught, goes into the next room. He returns, sighing*)

SWEENEY: There! Polished him off! *(Not seeing the* JUDGE, *he continues his search)* I think I remember now. They were in the other room, under the loose plank.

JUDGE *(testily)*: Barber, what about my shave? Am I to sit here all night?

SWEENEY *(starts)*: I beg your p-p-pardon, sir. I am a little absent-minded this afternoon. *(Hurries out)*

JUDGE: Get on with it, man, get on with it!

(The chair turns over, dumping him below. SWEENEY *returns)*

SWEENEY: Blast that mechanic, Mr. Smith! His tricks with the mechanism outlive him! *(He continues with his search)* There were other necklaces as well—some garnets, I seem to remember. Oh, my head, my head. *(A knocking from below)* Ah—knock away, knock away, Mr. Sailor! My doors are as strong as the Bank of England. Ha! I had forgotten again. Must lock the front door!

(He hurries to the door, but it is thrown open by COLONEL JEFFERY *and* TOBIAS)

JEFFERY: Here he is, Tobias, here he is! St. George for England!

(*He rushes at him.* SWEENEY *flings him aside and rushes towards the secret door, but thunderous knocking comes from near at hand*)

SWEENEY: Trapped!

(*He flings himself at* JEFFERY *and* TOBIAS. *They struggle and gradually over-power* SWEENEY)

JEFFERY: Hang on, Tobias. One foot apiece. Hang on! To the chair, Tobias, to the chair.

(*They force* SWEENEY *into the chair. The knocking from below redoubles*)

TOBIAS: Now, Colonel, the lever!

JEFFERY: No, no, Tobias—'twould be murder and we should all be hanged!

(*Louder knocking. Enter* JOHANNA, *followed by police and warders*)

JOHANNA: Here he is! I can see him in his shop! Todd, the murderer!

(*The secret door bursts open. Enter* JARVIS *and* MARK)

ALL: Mark Ingestrie alive!

MARK: Yes! Mark Ingestrie, who, preserved from death by a miracle, returns to confound the guilty and protect the innocent!

(JOHANNA *throws herself into his arms.* SWEENEY *throws up his arms and screams. Slowly the chair turns over of its own accord and* SWEENEY *falls into the depths below. Final curtain.*)

MURDERER

Anthony Shaffer

For the past twenty-plus years, the New York professional theatre has enjoyed a renewed interest in gruesome thrillers, thanks chiefly to the success of *Sleuth* by the British playwright, Anthony Shaffer. The theatrical trickery of that script influenced several other notable playwrights to try hoodwinking their audiences, including Ira Levin in *Deathtrap*, Gerald Moon in *Corpse* and Rupert Holmes in *Accomplice*. But perhaps the cruelest theatrical trick was devised by Shaffer in *Murderer*, which its original publisher describes as "opening with one of the most truly horrifying scenes ever devised for the stage."

This is not hyperbolic. Frankly, as much as I love the literature of the macabre, I am not sure my nerves are equal to a performance of *Murderer*. Reading it was quite harrowing enough, thank you.

Murderer was first performed in 1975 in London.

CAST OF CHARACTERS

Norman Bartholomew

Sergeant Stenning

Millie Sykes

Elizabeth Bartholomew

ACT ONE

Scene One

Thirty minutes should elapse between the start of the play and the first spoken words, "Open up. Police."

The artist's studio cum living room of NORMAN BARTHOLOMEW, *in a small village in Dorset, England. The usual painter's paraphernalia litters the place and many canvases lie against the walls. Upstage left is the kitchen area containing inter alia, a gas stove. Next to the stove is a sink. Upstage right of kitchen is a passage leading off to an unseen hallway. Center stage is the living area containing a sofa, sofa table with lamp and a large pot-bellied stove, vigorously alight. Center stage is a divan. Above this is a staircase leading to a bathroom and offstage bedroom. The double frosted glass doors leading into the bathroom are closed. (NB. An alternative and effective way of showing the bathroom is to have walls of gauze, so that when it is in use it can be lit and visible to the whole auditorium, and when not in use it would be opaque.) Downstage right is a desk and desk chair. Positioned with its back to us in front of the stove is an armchair and foot stool. The time is about five o'clock on a winter's evening. A winter sunset highlights statues and withered pot plants, in an outside garden room. As the curtain rises* NORMAN BARTHOLOMEW, *a good-looking smooth man dressed casually in slacks and jumper is standing at an easel painting, standing behind him, watching him paint is an attractive girl in her early twenties. Threatening music can either come from a radio or, perhaps better, be overlaid at appropriate moments throughout the scene to highlight the tension. She leaves him and gets a magazine from the sofa and sits in the armchair facing up towards* NORMAN. *He stops painting and goes to pour two drinks, the bottle is empty, he gets another one from the cellar, pours the drinks and goes to the kitchen to put water in them. He gives the girl her drink and returns to his easel. He regards her slyly from time to time as she starts to sip her drink. Finally she drains it and after a pause there is a crash as the glass slips from her fingers and she slumps unconscious. He crosses rapidly to the chair and takes a scarf from the back of it. This he puts carefully round the girl's throat and pulls it tight. With much grunting and straining he maintains the pressure for a full minute.*

BARTHOLOMEW *examines her critically, taking her pulse, listening to her heart etc. Satisfied that she is dead, he delicately picks out the scarf from the folds of the neck, burns it in the stove. He then takes the body from the chair and carries it to the sofa stage right, where he lays it carefully face down. Suddenly he stiffens, as if hearing a noise, and stands still listening. He goes quietly through to the front door and opens it. After a long moment, he closes it and locks it and returns to the body.*

One by one he removes the shoes, stockings, skirt, blouse and underclothes, and takes them into the bedroom.

He returns with a blanket in which he wraps the corpse.

His next action is to take a pair of pliers and remove a number of teeth from the head. These he puts in a glass dish and pours acid on them from a glass-stoppered bottle. Fumes rise from the dish.

Now he picks up the blanket-wrapped corpse and carries it up the stairs to the bathroom. We see him tip it out into the bath, with a dull, soft thud. He then folds the blanket neatly and descends the stairs with it, closing the door behind him, and disappears into the bedroom.

A few moments pass and he re-appears stripped off down to his shorts, in which state he crosses the stage into the dining area where he puts on a full chef's apron. He also selects a butcher's knife and a meat saw and places them on a central table.

He then descends to the cellar and returns with half a dozen sacks which he places next to them. A car light passes the window and we hear the car slow and stop. In a sudden panic he rushes to the window and looks out. After a long moment the car starts and the lights move on. With a sigh of relief he leaves the window and moves back to the kitchen where he gives himself a large whisky and smokes a calming cigarette. He examines his hand which is shaking. Gradually it stops.

Now he takes the knife, saw and sack upstairs to the bathroom and gets to work on the body in the bath. He begins with the knife and then changes to the saw and we hear the very explicit noise of it cutting through bone. Eventually we see him straighten up holding an arm which he puts in a sack. He then starts on the other arm, using first the knife, and then the saw. Eventually he succeeds in detaching it and, holding up the hand, he takes off the ring from the ring finger. He then puts the arm in another sack.

Carrying the two sacks he leaves the bathroom and crosses to the stove. He throws them in, where they start to sizzle furiously. Suddenly we see his apron is covered in blood, as are his hands. He now lights a blow torch and melts the ring in a pestle. He throws the mess in the stove.

Suddenly a newspaper is pushed abruptly through the letter box and slaps on the floor. He jumps and stoops to pick it up. The headline reads 'Torso Found In Tea Chest.' The photograph is of the accused with a coat over his head being escorted by Police Officers. He sits down to read it with evident pleasure. After a moment or two he rises and throws down the paper, now bloodstained.

He now returns to the bathroom, taking up to it an electric drill with garden saw attachment and goes to work on a leg. The task is extremely strenuous, but he finally succeeds in detaching it with much cracking and whirring from the electric saw and puts it in a sack. He crosses again to the furnace and throws it in.

A timer clock rings, startling him. Wiping his sweating brow with the back of his forearm, he crosses to the kitchen and puts on the kettle. He then opens the oven and takes out a spit on which is a roast of beef. He detaches the meat and puts it on a plate. The spit and prongs he washes, dries and replaces in the oven. He regards the roast of rare beef fondly, comparing its color and texture with his own dripping hands. Fastidiously he washes them under a tap before carving off a decent slice and making himself a neat sandwich which he seasons elaborately with salt, pepper and mustard. Primly he cuts off all the crusts. He starts to eat it as he saunters back to the bathroom to start work on the last limb.

Before picking up the knife, he carefully props the plate with the sandwich on the side of the bath, takes a bite and munches cheerfully as he cuts. Putting down the knife, he starts sawing, but the vibrations succeed in tipping his sandwich and plate into the bath. He retrieves the plate and then the sandwich, which he is about to take a bite out of, when he sees it saturated with blood. Briefly he debates eating it, but reluctantly rejects the idea, replaces it on the plate and puts it on the floor. He continues with the sawing until he achieves a successful severance, whereupon he puts the leg in a sack and once again walks down the stairs to the stove.

Halfway across the room there is a sudden piercing shriek. Involuntarily he drops the sack and whirls round to face the bathroom, as if fearing the corpse had come alive. Almost immediately he realises it is only the kettle and grins ruefully to himself. He picks up the sack with the leg in it and tosses it into the stove before crossing to the kettle and turning it off. He makes himself a cup of instant coffee, and lights a cigarette which he inhales deeply.

Now he picks up a chopper from the wood basket and returns to the bathroom where he sets to work to cut off the head. The blows are deliberate and sickening. After three or four he straightens up, holding the head by its hair. He examines it closely, then kisses it playfully on the nose.

Suddenly the telephone shrills. He drops the head back in the bath and takes some involuntary running steps down the stairs towards the instrument. Then he pauses, listening to it ring, goes to it and is about to lift the receiver when he stops himself. In an agony of indecision he stands with his bloody hand held out above the telephone. Finally it stops and he retraces his steps to the bathroom where he packs both the torso and the head in sacks and carries them over to the stove and throws them in.

Returning to the bathroom he scrubs the floor round the bath, then cleans the electric saw, handsaw, knife and hatchet in the bath and walks downstairs to replace them in their original places—the chopper in the wood basket and the saws and knife in the kitchen.

Now he goes back to the bathroom to scrub out the bath meticulously and then strips himself for an intensive wash. He dries himself and then walks down into the bedroom to dress, hanging the blood-stained apron over the banisters as he goes. In the bedroom we hear him whistling cheerfully as he dresses.

Suddenly the doorbell sounds. The whistling stops abruptly. He emerges from the bedroom wearing sweater and slacks, and looks anxiously towards the front door and then at the stove. He stands indecisively doing nothing. It sounds again, impatiently. Slowly he goes towards the front door and is about to open it when he checks himself and looks round to examine the room for any signs of his recent activity. As the door bell sounds again, he sees the bloodstained apron hanging over the banisters.

SERGEANT STENNING *(off):* Open up! Police!

(*He runs quickly across stage and up the stairs to retrieve the apron and then down again to thrust it into the stove. He then runs to the front door and throws it open*)

BARTHOLOMEW (*off*): Sorry to keep you. I was in the bath.

STENNING (*off*): Is that so, sir? In the bath, eh? Would you mind if I stepped inside?

BARTHOLOMEW (*off*): Why should I?

STENNING (*off*): I think it would be better, sir?

BARTHOLOMEW (*off*): I mean mind. Come in.

STENNING (*off*): Thank you, sir.

(STENNING *enters, removing his cap as he does so and putting it down. He is somewhat younger than* BARTHOLOMEW *and a good deal heavier*)

It is Mr. Bartholomew, isn't it? Mr. Norman Bartholomew?

BARTHOLOMEW: Mr. Norman Cresswell Bartholomew actually. And you're Sergeant Stenning, aren't you? How can I help you?

(STENNING *looks slowly round the room. He is obviously uncomfortable*)

STENNING: It's a little difficult to explain, sir, and I trust you won't take offense, but well, you see, we've got to investigate all complaints, even if they are . . .

BARTHOLOMEW: Yes?

STENNING: Well, fanciful like.

BARTHOLOMEW: Fanciful like?

STENNING: Well, barmy, sir. You know—a bit out to lunch.

BARTHOLOMEW: I can quite see that Sergeant, but I do hope nobody has been making fanciful, barmy, or out to lunch statements about me.

STENNING: I'm afraid as a matter of fact they have, sir.

BARTHOLOMEW: I'm sorry to hear that. Nothing serious I trust.

STENNING: Very serious, I'm sorry to say. Very serious indeed.

BARTHOLOMEW: I know. I've been pissing on Mrs. Green's sunflowers again?

STENNING: I did say it was extremely serious.

BARTHOLOMEW: The vicar's found the fly buttons I put in the plate last Sunday?

(STENNING *stares at* BARTHOLOMEW *blank-eyed.* BARTHOLOMEW *continues somewhat discomforted*)

BARTHOLOMEW: Perhaps he's put them on that old grey suit of his. They've been missing for the last couple of years. As a matter of fact it's him you ought to be interrogating. I'm absolutely convinced he spends his afternoons on the common disguised as a tramp, flashing the secondary-school girls.

STENNING: I haven't come about the vicar, sir.

BARTHOLOMEW: Well, what the devil have you come about?

STENNING: Mrs. Ramage who, as you know, has the cottage behind you, called the station a few minutes ago and said she saw you through that big window there, acting in a highly suspicious manner.

(BARTHOLOMEW *looks uneasily at the window, as if he'd forgotten it*)

BARTHOLOMEW: Suspicious manner?

STENNING: Criminal would be nearer the mark.

BARTHOLOMEW: Bomb making or buggery?

STENNING: Strangling a woman.

BARTHOLOMEW: A woman . . . but I've been all alone here this evening . . .

STENNING: She couldn't be sure, but she thought it might be your wife. After which, she said she saw you take the clothes off the body and then get undressed yourself.

BARTHOLOMEW: My God, who'd have thought old Mrs. Ramage was a peeping Tom?

STENNING: She further said she saw you carry the body into another room and return to get a saw and later a hatchet, for the purpose, she presumes, of dismembering it.

BARTHOLOMEW *(singing)*: I'll dismember you in all the old familiar places.

STENNING: Would you mind *not* singing, sir.

BARTHOLOMEW: Why not? Both Wood and Billings were recorded as having sung mightily after they were apprehended for hewing up John Hayes.

STENNING: What are you talking about?

BARTHOLOMEW: The pawnbroker, John Hayes. Killed with a coal hatchet under the Brawn's Head Inn, New Bond Street, at the instigation of his wife.

STENNING: I've never heard of the case.

BARTHOLOMEW: It was all a bit before your time I expect—1725. His wife Catherine boiled the flesh off the decapitated head to make it unrecognizable and Messrs Wood and Billings carried it in a bucket to the Thames near Lambeth Bridge where they threw it in. It was all to no avail, however. The head was recognized and they were caught. Which only goes to show, Sergeant, that if you want to get away with spouse-disposal, you've simply got to make the body unrecognizable.

STENNING *(stolidly)*: Exactly so, sir. Mrs. Ramage also said she saw you carrying a number of sacks.

BARTHOLOMEW: You know the strangest thing is that anyone should actually recognize a pawnbroker. I mean you know—you shuffle in rather embarrassed, not looking him in the face, and muttering " 'ow much'll yer give me for this lot, guvner. It's been in the family 150 years. It's me great grandmother's twenty-four carat, solid gold dilldoll . . . must be worth a packet." . . . You know the sort of thing. But you certainly don't go in for much eyeball contact, do you now?

STENNING: Sir! Would you please give me your attention.

BARTHOLOMEW: I assure you, you have it. You were telling me an improbable tale of me quartering my wife and gift-wrapping her in sacking. What exactly was I meant to have done with these parcels?

STENNING: She didn't know. Apparently you passed out of her line of vision.

BARTHOLOMEW: How strange. I always thought Mrs. Ramage had X-ray eyes.

STENNING: I'd rather like to take a look round, if you don't mind. Let's see if we can't find a boiled head or two.

BARTHOLOMEW: Now look here, Sergeant, you really can't believe all this rubbish. I mean, do I look the sort of bloke who'd carve up his missus?

STENNING: In my opinion there's no one who couldn't answer to that description.

BARTHOLOMEW: In full sight of the neighbors?

STENNING: As I said before, it all does sound a bit far-fetched, but I have to check. I'm sure you understand.

BARTHOLOMEW: I'm not sure that I do. As you can see this room is devoted to the gentle pursuit of the Arts, Sergeant.

STENNING: Some people believe that murder is an art, sir. Excuse me.

(STENNING *walks over to the kitchen area and starts to examine the saw and the knives which are arrayed on a magnetised steel bar on the wall.* BARTHOLOMEW *suddenly sees the bloodstained evening newspaper. He picks it up, folds it inside out and nonchalantly starts to read it.* STENNING *shoots him a suspicious look, then glances at the portrait of* MRS. BARTHOLOMEW *on the wall*)

By the way, where exactly is your wife?

BARTHOLOMEW: She's away.

STENNING: Away? . . . Where?

BARTHOLOMEW: I don't know exactly. Some hospital outside Birmingham, I think she said.

STENNING: You mean she's ill?

BARTHOLOMEW: I mean she's a gynecological surgeon. She's doing some operations there.

STENNING: But you are expecting her back fairly shortly?

BARTHOLOMEW: Frankly, I'm not sure that I'm expecting her back at all.

(STENNING *shoots* BARTHOLOMEW *a curious glance*)

STENNING: Oh?

BARTHOLOMEW: Well, I suppose it's no secret in the village that my wife and I don't particularly get on. Recently she's been hinting that she's found another feller and is thinking of leaving me.

STENNING: I see. And may I ask what your attitude was to what she told you.

BARTHOLOMEW (*simulated passion*): Blind brute jealousy. I'd rather cut her up in the bath than let another man possess her.

(STENNING *regards him levelly. Suddenly* BARTHOLOMEW *bursts out laughing*)

STENNING (*affronted*): Which way *is* the bathroom?

BARTHOLOMEW: Up there.

(STENNING *brushes past* BARTHOLOMEW *and makes his way across the room and up the stairs to the bathroom.* BARTHOLOMEW *watches his progress with some trepidation, crossing to the bottom of the stairs for a closer view as* STENNING *kneels to examine the bath with minute care. After a long moment he straightens up, apparently satisfied*)

BARTHOLOMEW: No grimy ring, Sergeant? Would even my mother-in-law approve as they say in those craven commercials?

STENNING: Of your bath, sir, yes. But not, I think, of your eating habits. I found this under it.

(*He produces the bloodsodden sandwich.* BARTHOLOMEW *stares at it, then slowly walks up the stairs, as if mesmerized.* BARTHOLOMEW *and* STENNING *look at each other in silence, then the former bends to peer at the sandwich*)

BARTHOLOMEW: I'm afraid I like my roast beef rare, Sergeant. A crime I know, in most English restaurants, but surely not in common law.

(STENNING *sniffs the sandwich gingerly and then opens it*)

STENNING: It really is very bloody, sir. Quite sodden with it in fact.

BARTHOLOMEW: I shouldn't waste time in idle speculation if I were you, Sergeant. Thanks to the invention of the spectroscope, it has been possible to distinguish between animal and human blood for the past eighty-four years.

(BARTHOLOMEW *takes the sandwich from the plate and takes a bite. He gags on it.* STENNING *grasps his wrist like lightning and retrieves the remains of the sandwich, which he then places in a small cellophane bag, and pockets it*)

BARTHOLOMEW: If you want a snack, Sergeant, you only have to ask. Didn't your mummy ever tell you it's very rude to grab?

(BARTHOLOMEW *stalks down the stairs.* STENNING *follows him down and starts prowling round the room looking in chests and cupboards for signs of the body. Near the stove he suddenly stops and sniffs. His face wrinkles in disgust and he takes a hard look at the stove which he transfers to* BARTHOLOMEW, *who flinches away from it. Briskly he steps forward, preparatory to throwing open the door*)

(*involuntary*) No!

(STENNING *opens the door of the stove and peers inside. He recoils almost instantly*)

STENNING: My God!

(STENNING *reaches in and tries to extract something with his naked hands, but it is too hot. He looks round desperately for some implement and he grabs a pair of fire tongs standing up against the wall. With these he drags out the head and lets it fall on the floor, where it rolls about smoking horribly. He manages to beat out the sparks in the hair which are causing the smoke and then drags out a partially burnt leg.* BARTHOLOMEW *watches him horror-struck, backed up against a wall, apparently incapable of speech. But suddenly he starts babbling wildly*)

BARTHOLOMEW: I had to do it, Sergeant. Can't you see that . . . she was always on at me, nagging . . . never leaving me alone . . . insanely jealous of everybody I might happen to speak to . . . night after night, never any sleep . . . who was I with? . . . who was my lover? . . . creating scenes in public . . . hounding me wherever I went . . . making me a laughing stock . . . you do see, don't you. I had no choice.

(BARTHOLOMEW *falls on to his knees sobbing.* STENNING *who has been examining the head and leg, regards him curiously, then turns back to the task of removing parts of the body from the furnace. Eventually he picks up the head by the hair and holds it aloft. Very deliberately he takes a palette knife from a side table and knocks the skull with it. It gives off a dull, hollow sound. Alternatively he can pop out a glass eye so that it rolls across the floor*)

STENNING: Is this some sort of sick joke? This isn't a body. It's some kind of dummy or waxwork.

BARTHOLOMEW: To be exact, it's wood. But the limbs are made of expanded polystyrene stiffened with wire and filled with stage blood—what film stuntmen refer to as Kensington Gore—made it myself, as a matter of fact.

(STENNING *puts the head down on a table and turns very deliberately to face* BARTHOLOMEW)

STENNING *(coldly)*: I think you owe me an explanation, sir?

BARTHOLOMEW: No, I don't think I *owe* you anything, Sergeant. But because I'm a genial, gregarious sort of fellow, I'll supply you with one. Why not take a seat and make yourself comfortable.

STENNING: No, I don't believe I will. You've been making a right pillock out of me.

BARTHOLOMEW: Not at all. I may have been making a right pillock out of myself, but that's surely up to me.

STENNING: And what's more, you've been obstructing me in the performance of my duties. All that stuff about murdering your wife because she was jealous.

BARTHOLOMEW: A little play-acting, that's all. The end of the fantasy has surely got to be self-justification.

STENNING: Now you look here, Mr. Bartholomew. You'd better start making some sense or I'll take you down to the station and have the Inspector sort it out.

BARTHOLOMEW *(resignedly)*: Oh alright!

STENNING: To begin with—what's this here fantasy you're talking about?

BARTHOLOMEW: Why, that I was Bukhtyar Rustomji Ratanji Hakim, of course.

STENNING: Eh?

BARTHOLOMEW: Better known as Buck Ruxton the Parsee doctor who in 1935 murdered his mistress and spent a whole night carefully cutting her up in a bath, draining her of blood and making her up into neat little bundles for disposal.

STENNING (*incredulous*): You mean you've been play-acting you were him?

BARTHOLOMEW: Exactly.

STENNING: What in the world for?

BARTHOLOMEW: It's very simple. I wanted to know what it felt like actually doing it—you know—the fear of a sudden caller, of telltale blood on clothes, of identification through teeth or jewelry.

(STENNING *shakes his head in bewilderment*)

STENNING: But you weren't actually doing it. You were just pretending. That's hardly the same thing.

BARTHOLOMEW: I have a very vivid imagination, Sergeant. What I may lose in moribund verisimilitude, I gain in inventive artistry.

STENNING: Here, now hang on a minute. Just let me get all this straight. You actually made this dummy and filled it with—with stage blood and then hacked it up in the bath simply in order to reproduce the crime of this Doctor Buxton?

BARTHOLOMEW: Ruxton. Yes, I've already said so.

STENNING: But in God's name why?

BARTHOLOMEW: It gives me a thrill, that's why. Oh don't look so disapproving, Sergeant. It takes all kinds, you know. Some people can't live without the excitements of hang gliding or drag racing. Me, I like to play famous murderers. So far I've been Frederick Henry Seddon, the Tollington Park killer who disposed of his tenant with arsenic, and George Chapman, who poisoned three of his so-called wives with strychnine, and Henry Wainwright, the Whitechapel Road murderer.

STENNING: What did he do?

BARTHOLOMEW: Silly man, he made the most fearsome mistake, using chloride of lime instead of quicklime. You see it had the effect of preserving the body of his mistress whom he had concealed under some floorboards, rather than destroying it.

STENNING: And you reconstructed that?

BARTHOLOMEW: Indeed I did. But that wasn't the best bit. That came when, like him, I took a cab across London with the disinterred remains wrapped in brown paper, in the company of an unsuspecting ballet dancer, smoking a cigar to disguise the smell. Well, in my case, I actually used five pounds of ancient bloaters to simulate the odor of human putrefaction and the ballet dancer was really more of your Soho stripper, but the effect was much the same.

(STENNING *looks at him aghast*)

STENNING: You actually did that?

BARTHOLOMEW: Certainly I did. I took the exact route he did. Down Whitechapel Street, over London Bridge to the Borough High Street, though I'm afraid the actual Ironmonger's shop where Wainwright was arrested has been demolished. It's such a shame when these old landmarks get torn down, don't you think, Sergeant? Perhaps I'll found a society for the Preservation of Murder's Monuments.

(STENNING *shakes his head dumbly.* BARTHOLOMEW *chuckles delightedly as he moves to pour himself a large glass of whisky*)

Will you join me?

STENNING: Not just now. Listen, are you a bloody nutter or something?

BARTHOLOMEW: A nutter? I don't think so. I just like to pay homage to the great murderers of the past . . . to Doctor Neil Cream, who prowled Lambeth in the nineties, cross-eyed and top-hatted, dispatching ladies of the evening with *nux vomica* . . . to Louis Voisin, the Charlotte Street butcher who minced his paramour into trays of offal . . . to Florence Maybrick who, it was said, turned her husband's stomach into a druggist's drainpipe . . . why, the very names should bring tears of grateful nostalgia to your eyes.

STENNING: They sound like a right load of villains to me.

BARTHOLOMEW: On the contrary, they were heroes, every one—master practitioners in the world of bizarre homicide. Take the case of Patrick Mahon, for example. He's particularly apropos. Surely you remember the Crumbles Bungalow murder case?

STENNING: I can't say I can, no.

BARTHOLOMEW: How strange. I do think that a young man with his way to make in the police force should take more interest in these things. He was a classic dismemberer. Sliced up his ladylove, Emily Kaye, in 1924 and dropped pieces of her from the train between Waterloo and Richmond Stations. I think I might have a go at him next week, though I don't suppose the exercise will do a lot for keeping Britain tidy.

STENNING: I'm afraid I just don't understand you, sir. I don't understand you at all.

BARTHOLOMEW: That's because you don't understand the true nature of murder—that once a man has killed deliberately, his inhibitions are destroyed, because he has truly looked on mortality. "He has joined the alien clan, of which no member knows the other, and has set his face against the world. Thereafter he is alone magnificent in his belief in the impossibility of divine forgiveness."

STENNING: That's as may be, but for me murder is a shocking crime—the most shocking–and I certainly can't see any fun in it.

BARTHOLOMEW: It's not a question of fun exactly, but how it enables you to look at life. Can't you see that life is beautiful and that murder is the most extreme form of the denial of man's potential to see that beauty? As such its study is of compelling interest to a curious chap like me.

STENNING: Is it? Well, while you've been studying it, I have had to deal with it—as it is in the flesh. At various times and in various places, I have seen the agony of murdered people and I've smelled the odor of murdered people and I've touched the skin of murdered people and I can tell you there's nothing compelling about it in any way.

BARTHOLOMEW: Yes, but can't you see that . . .

STENNING: Do not continue to play with death, Mr. Bartholomew. I know beyond a shadow of doubt that most murder victims spend all their lives searching for their murderers. Be warned. You do not know the game you play at all well. Stop in time.

(An uneasy silence)

I'll go over to Mrs. Ramage's now and set her mind at rest. She was highly disturbed.

BARTHOLOMEW: Mrs. Ramage is a tiresome old fart who richly deserves the attentions of Jack the Ripper. Just imagine finding a piece of her pancreas wrapped up in a cardboard box, waiting for you when you get back to the Station accompanied by a bloodstained note reading *(Jack the Ripper voice)*, "Today her pancreas. Tomorrow all twenty-six feet of her intestines."

(BARTHOLOMEW's *forced laugh falls on stony ground*)

STENNING: You won't be warned, will you sir? I can see that.

(He walks out slamming the front door)

(Thoughtfully, BARTHOLOMEW *returns to the main room and pulls down the blind to cover the window, then his face breaks into a broad smile and he launches himself into a delighted caper of self-congratulation. Eventually he stops to examine himself in the mirror)*

Mirror mirror on the wall
Who is the wiliest murderer of them all?
Unquestionably it is I—Norman Cresswell
Bartholomew, the Dorchester Dismemberer
and noted Cop Kidder.

(He preens himself, striking some more attitudes and making faces)

BARTHOLOMEW: Well I suppose even self-congratulation must have a stop. To our muttons.

(He exits up the stairs and after a short pause returns with the inert body of MILLIE. *She is still naked. He lays her on the couch. A pause. He contemplates her, thoughtfully toying with a kitchen knife, as if about to start cutting her up. Suddenly she starts to stir. He drops the knife and gets her a glass of water and, sitting her up, forces her to drink it)*

Here, drink this. You can't sleep your whole life away you know.

MILLIE *(drugged voice)*: What? . . . What happened?

(She looks about herself and finds that she is naked)

Where are my clothes? . . . What am I doing here?

BARTHOLOMEW: Surely you mean, "Where am I?"

MILLIE *(recovering full consciousness)*: What the hell's been going on?

BARTHOLOMEW: Quite a lot actually. A whole rather touching charade, in fact. I must say that your performance, though lacking somewhat in animation was most convincing.

*(*MILLIE *rises and starts to dress)*

MILLIE: What are you talking about? One moment I was sitting in that chair— the next I'm over here with all my clothes off.

BARTHOLOMEW: Don't you remember? We were playing strip poker and you had rather a run of bad luck . . .

MILLIE: Norman! Don't be tiresome.

BARTHOLOMEW: What can I say? You passed out.

MILLIE: What? Just like that?

BARTHOLOMEW: Well, with the help of a Mickey Finn I slipped you.

MILLIE: What! You mean you drugged me?

BARTHOLOMEW: Absolutely.

MILLIE: Whatever for?

BARTHOLOMEW: I needed your passive co-operation in a little game I was playing.

MILLIE: Really? What was it called—Hunt The Necrophiliac?

BARTHOLOMEW: No. It was called Sergeant Stenning Meets the Cry-Wolf Syndrome.

MILLIE: Do you think we might take it from the top?

BARTHOLOMEW: Surely. A drink?

MILLIE: O.K.

BARTHOLOMEW: Champagne?

MILLIE: Fine.

(BARTHOLOMEW *fetches the wine and starts to open it*)

BARTHOLOMEW: Here we are, Veuve Cliquot.

MILLIE: I wonder if they make a Veuf Cliquot.

BARTHOLOMEW: H'm?

MILLIE: Widower as opposite to widow. It's what you're aiming to become, isn't it?

BARTHOLOMEW: Oh I see. Yes, of course it is. I'm sorry darling, I haven't had the advantage of your Berlitz education. (*He fills the glasses and hands her one*) But I do know a little Latin. To uxoricide!

MILLIE: It sounds like a venereal disease.

BARTHOLOMEW: It means to wife-murder.

(MILLIE *raises her glass gravely*)

MILLIE: To wife-murder!

(They drink)

MILLIE: I only hope the little game you've been playing has something to do with the subject.

BARTHOLOMEW: Oh, it had everything. You could say that I have been arranging the enabling factor, with you standing in for Elizabeth.

MILLIE: Will you explain or do I have to play twenty questions?

BARTHOLOMEW: Patience, my sweet. Patience. You see, using your body I staged a strangulation, stripping and dismemberment in full view of Mrs. Ramage next door. She not unnaturally called Sergeant Stenning at the station and he not unnaturally raced up here, only to find bits of a rather peachy little dummy I'd prepared bubbling away in the stove. I not unnaturally told him I was playing Buck Ruxton.

MILLIE: Good God, you didn't tell him about the games.

BARTHOLOMEW: It was necessary to mention a few. I told him I'd done Seddon, Chapman and Wainwright, and that I was thinking of doing Patrick Mahon.

MILLIE: Jesus. How did he take it?

BARTHOLOMEW: He wasn't a hundred per cent beatified by the experience, but the point is it worked. Sergeant Stenning is now unquestionably in the crushing grip of the deadly Cry-Wolf syndrome.

MILLIE: So you said before, but what the hell does that mean?

BARTHOLOMEW: It means that now I could disembowel seventy-three whirling dervishes in full sight of the neighbors and the police wouldn't interfere. (MRS. RAMAGE's *voice*) "Please, officer, come at once. That dreadful Mr. Bartholomew is at it again. He seems to be cutting up a spinning man dressed in a funny hat and white pyjamas." (SERGEANT STENNING'*s voice*) "Oh we know all about that, mum. It's quite in order. He's just re-creating the Mysterious Mevlevi Murders." *(Own voice)* No, I think I can safely say that in future any odd happenings around this house will be discounted. I could murder anyone here without attracting the least suspicion or interference. The police would just think it was one of my games.

MILLIE: It all seems a rather elaborate way of going on to me.

BARTHOLOMEW: Elaborate. Effective and above all enjoyable.

MILLIE: Ah, now we come to it.

BARTHOLOMEW: I may have pleasured myself a little in the doing, but why not?

MILLIE: And me too possibly.

BARTHOLOMEW: Tut! Tut! You were the merest object—a necessary prop.

MILLIE: That's what I object to. Why did you have to knock me out?

BARTHOLOMEW: Don't you see? You had to be inert. If I'd stuck a stiff dummy in the chair, Mrs. Ramage would never have believed it was a real body and she would never have called Sergeant Stenning.

MILLIE: I could have acted it.

BARTHOLOMEW: I didn't think you'd have wanted to.

MILLIE: Why not? I've helped you before, haven't I? You've obviously forgotten that only last week I spent a whole afternoon in a half gale on Henley Common, dressed in stays and crinoline as Mary Blandy, yelling "Gentlemen, don't hang me high for the sake of decency." And the previous weekend you had me dressed in an ancient nursing costume pushing a two-hundred-and-forty-pound weight round the suburbs of Nottingham playing that hideous poisoner Dorothea Waddingham.

BARTHOLOMEW: I assure you I haven't forgotten. Both were very affecting portrayals, my darling.

(He goes to kiss her. She avoids it)

MILLIE: Well then, that only makes it worse. To think you had this game all worked out and didn't say a single word to me about it. I don't think I like that very much, Norman. After all I've done for you, it's decidedly mean spirited.

BARTHOLOMEW: Millie, my angel, you must realise that this was one game I didn't want you involved in.

MILLIE: Exactly how much more involved can I get than being stripped and strangled in full view of the neighbors.

BARTHOLOMEW: Oh much more. Mrs. Ramage didn't really see your face. In fact, she thought you were Elizabeth. You see I took special care that under no circumstances in the future could you be labeled a willing accomplice.

MILLIE: Gallant but unconvincing. I'd have adored to have heard that chat with Stenning.

BARTHOLOMEW: I'm sorry. Actually, I really needed to be alone to get the full flavor of Ruxton.

MILLIE: Yes, I rather suspected that was the truth. It doesn't matter. But you don't really believe that that crazy hoax will avert suspicion from this house, do you?

BARTHOLOMEW: Of course it will. I mean, Stenning might be a bit sniffy. It's only natural. Promotion prospects dashed. No pictures in the paper, no dramatic appearance in the witness box, but on the whole he took it very well and he certainly isn't going to come leaping up here the next time Mrs. Ramage reports the thud of axe on bone, or what have you. *(He puts his arm round her)* Look I'll make it up to you, I promise. There's a marvelous part for you in the Long Compton Witchcraft Murders. You see, the mistress of this randy old farmer was found in a pig's trough with a pentacle cut into each kneecap. It'll make a lovely day out in the Cotswolds.

MILLIE *(she draws away)*: You know what worries me most about your tales, Norman, is how poorly mistresses seem to come off.

BARTHOLOMEW: Don't you think you're being a trifle over sensitive?

MILLIE: Not really. It's just that I'd like to hear about wives getting it once in a while—particularly your wife. I've noticed you've been a bit evasive about the whole subject.

BARTHOLOMEW: Evasive?

MILLIE: Non specific. Neglectful. Omissive.

BARTHOLOMEW: Oh! You think that, do you?

MILLIE: I'm afraid I do, yes. For instance, when is she back?

BARTHOLOMEW: Tomorrow night.

MILLIE: And you'll do it then?

BARTHOLOMEW: Absolutely. One more night of that road drill voice will drive me into a strait jacket.

MILLIE: I doubt whether it will drive you into being a murderer however. And I really wonder whether you think it should.

BARTHOLOMEW: Of course I do. We both know very well why I'm killing her. She won't agree to divorce and we can't wait five years to prove irretrievable breakdown unilaterally.

MILLIE: I know all that, but I still don't believe you've actually formed the intention to do it.

BARTHOLOMEW: What on earth do you mean?

MILLIE: Simply that *au fond* you're just a child who loves to play mad, off-beat games. Admittedly you do them with great thoroughness and panache, but they've got absolutely nothing to do with solving the real problems in your life whatever. I mean, look at this murder. You've been playing with the idea for ages, wondering whether you can actually "cross the great divide between fantasy and reality," but you're no nearer doing it now than you were a month ago. Old books and famous trials and playing at murderers are one thing, but they're a pretty far cry from actually bumping someone off yourself. I'm sorry Norman, but I've got to say it. I don't think you're the stuff of which real murderers are made.

BARTHOLOMEW: For Christ's sake, Millie, shut up! I know I may have been a bit dilatory, but these things need working out. I've already taken the first step this evening. The second I will execute tomorrow night and I can assure you it is a plan of mind-shattering cunning and imagination.

MILLIE: Oh, I'm sure it is . . . the broken neck induced by a dislodged stair rod or piece of invisible twine tied to the banister; electrocution by impaired iron or tampered toaster; poisoning by small doses of antimony administered over a long period as in the Charles Bravo case, disposal in a carboy of sulphuric acid as used by George Haig in his garage and so on and so forth; but I'll bet my sainted Aunt Harriet's amber bangle that you've got nothing practical worked out that won't have me visiting you in Parkhurst within the month.

BARTHOLOMEW: God, you really are a bitch sometimes.

(They glare at each other for a moment)

MILLIE: Alright then, supposing you tell me what you have in mind.

BARTHOLOMEW *(slowly, still furious)*: Well, if you must know, basically I am planning to use Christie's trick with the deck chair and gas pipe. It proved very effective with those half a dozen drabs he built into the wallpaper of ten Rillington Place.

MILLIE: What was it?

BARTHOLOMEW: It's really quite simple. I'll show you.

(He dives down into the cellar and emerges with a deck chair which he proceeds to erect near the stove but facing away from it. He then takes up the gas poker which is lying nearby attached to a long piece of rubber

tubing and unfastens it. The tubing he uncoils and leads over to the deck chair)

Now, if you'll just come here and make yourself comfortable.

MILLIE: Wouldn't an armchair do as well? Do you have to use a deck chair?

BARTHOLOMEW: Well, Christie did.

MILLIE: Can you possibly see Elizabeth accepting a deck chair in the middle of her living room without asking a few questions?

BARTHOLOMEW: It's a good point. *(Reluctantly)* I suppose I could bring myself to use the armchair.

(He collapses the deck chair and then faces the armchair away from the stove and indicates that MILLIE should sit in it. She does so. He gives her a bowl and covers her head with a cloth. He then turns on the gas and tiptoes up behind her, holding the tube which now stretches halfway across the room and slowly advances it under her nose)

BARTHOLOMEW: Old Christie used to pretend he was a doctor and could cure women's ailments. Muriel Eady, his second victim, and a lifetime catarrh sufferer thought that she was inhaling Friar's Balsam. Actually it was mixed with coal gas and when she became unconscious he had intercourse with her while at the same time strangling her.

(MILLIE, who has been struggling during this speech to avoid the gas, now goes limp, unnoticed by the enthusiastic BARTHOLOMEW)

Looking at the body afterwards he said, "Once again I experienced that quiet peaceful thrill. I had no regrets."

(He suddenly notices MILLIE's condition)

Here, are you alright?

(He removes the cloth and turns the gas off. She returns to full consciousness, choking)

MILLIE: Well, I must say that's the nearest thing to a lethal act you've perpetrated all month.

BARTHOLOMEW: Sorry. I didn't notice. I'll get you some water.

(He pours a glass of water and brings it to her, drinking some himself before handing over the glass. She drinks greedily)

MILLIE: I seem to be spending most of this evening unconscious.

BARTHOLOMEW: Alright, I've said I'm sorry.

MILLIE: Look, I don't care how you kill your wife, as long as you don't kill me practising for it.

BARTHOLOMEW: I got a bit carried away, that's all.

MILLIE: Lucky I wasn't—in a coffin . . . it was a damn fool scheme in the first place. Elizabeth knows you're not a doctor . . . and she certainly wouldn't sit here calmly while you farted around with that ludicrous length of tubing.

BARTHOLOMEW: I know all that. Can't you see I was only having a bit of fun.

MILLIE: Fun?

BARTHOLOMEW: Well, getting even with you for sending me up. I'm sorry it went so far.

(He kisses her)

MILLIE: Alright.

BARTHOLOMEW: I really do have an absolutely foolproof scheme, you know.

(He starts to change into evening dress)

MILLIE: Reading her your collected volumes of Famous British Trials and boring her to death, I suppose?

BARTHOLOMEW (*sourly*): Very droll.

MILLIE: O.K. What is it?

BARTHOLOMEW: I don't think I'll tell you now.

MILLIE: Oh come on.

BARTHOLOMEW: No. You're altogether too untrusting.

MILLIE: Now don't play hard to get, Norman.

BARTHOLOMEW: Sorry, old bean. You'll just have to content your probing little soul in peace.

MILLIE: Norman, I want to know.

BARTHOLOMEW: Well, you'll have to wait and see, I'm afraid. For one thing, as I said, I've no intention of making you an accessory before the fact.

MILLIE: Oh pooh!

BARTHOLOMEW: Sorry, my mind's made up. And now I must be off, I'm afraid. It's the Dorchester Water Color Society's annual cook-in tonight.

MILLIE: I suppose you'll be back late and pissed?

BARTHOLOMEW: I hope so.

MILLIE: Well, I don't think I'll wait around for that.

BARTHOLOMEW: How wise, darling. Besides I'm sure it would be just as well if you kept out of the way until after I'd done it.

MILLIE: Why?

BARTHOLOMEW: To paraphrase Lady Macbeth, She that's coming must be provided for and I'd like to make all my preparations without distraction.

MILLIE: You mean you still won't tell me your plan?

(He kisses her)

BARTHOLOMEW: I love you.

MILLIE: Answer me.

BARTHOLOMEW: Why is it that women don't realise that No *is* an answer?

(He puts his overcoat on)

MILLIE: Strange. In my experience it's men who don't.

BARTHOLOMEW: I suppose both sexes have a recurring deafness. The Male through ennobling passion. The Female through ineradicable curiosity. I'll phone you tomorrow. O.K.?

MILLIE: Look, why don't you just admit you simply haven't got the guts to do it?

BARTHOLOMEW *(grimly)*: You'll see.

MILLIE: Arrogant sod! You've no more got a plan for killing Elizabeth than I have for becoming World Tree Felling Champion.

BARTHOLOMEW *(tight)*: Jolly witty. Goodnight.

MILLIE *(half mocking, half seductive)*: Don't be cross Tiger. Look, why don't you try it on me? I'll play Elizabeth and you can show me how you're going to do it.

(She pulls up her skirt and sits 1950s pin-up style)

No? Too tarty for a Professional Woman? Well then, how about this?

(She changes her pose to a more demure one)

Demure but affectionate. Feminine yet responsible. Yes, I think that's it . . . now let me see . . . she would be reading *Diseases of the Scrotal Sack* or some other learned medical tome while you cooked the evening meal. *(Imitating* ELIZABETH's *voice)* "Din-dins ready, darling," she says or rather, "Is dinner ready, Norman?"—that's more her, isn't it? Yes. "Is dinner ready, Norman?" And suddenly you take the carving knife or rather it being you, the seventeenth-century Chinese Executioner's sword and creep up . . .

BARTHOLOMEW *(tight)*: Goodnight Millie.

MILLIE: Have a lovely time, darling, with all your clever Bohemian painter chumsies.

BARTHOLOMEW: Oh piss off.

MILLIE *(derisively)*: My hero.

(She storms out banging the door behind her)

BARTHOLOMEW: Well . . . I've got to do it now.

(He draws himself up and toasts himself in the mirror)

Norman Cresswell Bartholomew—what a marvelous name for a Murderer! . . . but how?

SLOW BLACKOUT.

Scene Two

The time is later the same evening.

The stage is in darkness, except for the bathroom which is lit. Through the semi-opaque glass of the door we can see the distorted shadow of ELIZABETH *moving round inside. The taps are running and she walks from the wash basin to the bath carrying a bottle. She shakes the contents into the bath and stirs the contents around violently before turning off the taps. The radio is playing 'My Way.'*

We hear a car arrive and then we hear the front door open and close. BARTHOLOMEW *enters in evening dress. He is somewhat drunk. He crosses to center stage, turns on a light and removes his overcoat. He mimes to the song 'My Way.'*

BARTHOLOMEW: Yes, and I'll do it my way!

(Suddenly he stops in his tracks as he sees his wife's fur coat and hat lying on a chair. Next to them is her suitcase. His gaze moves upwards to the bathroom where we can see the shadow of ELIZABETH *putting on her bath-cap. He scowls and turns off the radio)*

BARTHOLOMEW *(to himself)*: Oh shit! . . . she's back a night early.

(Angrily he throws his overcoat into a chair making a clatter. The louvred door opens a fraction to emit a great gust of steam. [Or alternatively if the gauzed bathroom is used, we can see a bath-capped figure moving about in it or getting into the bath])

ELIZABETH *(voice from bathroom)*: Hullo . . . is that you Norman?

BARTHOLOMEW *(forcing himself to speak pleasantly)*: Oh hullo dear, I wasn't expecting you home till tomorrow.

ELIZABETH *(voice from bathroom)*: I had a change of plan. Bring me a brandy, will you?

BARTHOLOMEW: O.K.

(He crosses to the kitchen area and pours out the brandy. He is thinking furiously. He crosses the main room and stops at the foot of the stairs. Suddenly he is struck by a thought)

BARTHOLOMEW *(to himself)*: Of course! That's it! George Joseph Smith . . . the Brides in the Bath Murderer . . . perfect! Bessie Munday at Herne Bay. Alice Burnham at Blackpool. Margaret Lofty at Highgate. He crept up behind them and slid their heads down under the water and held them there. Afterwards he played the harmonium. "Nearer My God To Thee." What could have been more tasteful?

(He starts to strip)

ELIZABETH *(voice from bathroom)*: Norman! . . . Where's that drink?

BARTHOLOMEW: Coming.

(He finishes undressing, but retains his shorts. He tosses back the brandy and starts to ascend the stairs flexing his fingers. Slow curtain.)

ACT TWO

Act Two continues where Act One stopped.

BARTHOLOMEW *stands outside the bathroom door, irresolute. With sudden resolve he cautiously opens the bathroom door to its full extent. We see him approach the bath-capped head almost overtopped by bubbles and through the swirling clouds of steam we watch the whole murder—the head pushed under, the wildly thrashing legs—the water slopped over in the struggle and then after an appreciable time, the cessation of all movement.*

BARTHOLOMEW *steps back and stares down at the inert mass of bubbles for a long moment. Satisfied that life is extinct, he takes a towel and leaves the bathroom, closing the door behind him. There is a short satisfied pause. He has actually done it and is filled with great elation.*

BARTHOLOMEW: I've done it . . . I've actually done it! I felt the life force slip away under my hands, I'm a murderer. I've joined the 'alien clan' and set my face against the world . . . *(He examines his face in a mirror)* Norman Bartholomew, are you really one of those very special intrepid men who are prepared to be damned? Have you in fact achieved the most abandoned guilt which is the last and most irresistible challenge to everlasting goodness? . . . I wonder. Perhaps shame will come seeping in as the days pass to erode my belief in the impossibility of forgiveness and truly damn me. I shall have to wait and see.

(He wipes his glasses, then towels himself vigorously and gathering up his clothes he retires to the bedroom whistling cheerfully. After a few moments he returns wearing sweater and slacks and moves downstairs where he sits down at an antique harmonium and starts to sing and play the hymn 'Nearer My God to Thee.')

Not a dry fly in the house as they used to say at the Windmill. *(He rises from the harmonium and returns downstage in a champagne mood)* Now let's see. How to effect the disappearing trick? The remote moorland grave? . . . The weighted corpse in the canal? . . . The unclaimed trunk at Victoria Station? . . . The packing case sent to foreign parts? . . . The corpse in the blazing car? . . . The wrong body in the churchyard? . . . Hell. I suppose the cellar's still the safest.

(He takes a torch and exits stage left. We hear him open and close the back door. After a few moments we again hear the back door open and close and he enters carrying a pickax and spade. He moves over to the cellar door, opens it and descends the steps.

Presently we hear the blows of the pickax striking stone, After a time this noise is replaced by the sound of the spade shoveling earth. Both sounds are interspersed through the ensuing monologue. Off. Parody Q.C's voice)

"Now Inspector Dew, perhaps you would be kind enough to tell the members of the jury exactly what it was you found in the cellar of number thirty-nine Hilldrop Crescent . . ." *(Inspector's voice)* "We found portions of a woman's body wrapped in a piece of pajama jacket. The head was missing and, to the best of my knowledge, still is. Identification however was effected through known physical features and items of personal jewelry and we are positive that the remains are those of Kunigunda Makamotski, otherwise known as Belle Elmore, otherwise known as Cora Crippen." *(The front door bell rings. Q.C.'s voice)* "And have you been able to form any opinion as to the cause of death, Inspector? . . . " *(Inspector's voice)* "Yes, sir, we have. A postmortem revealed the presence of five grains of hyoscine in the stomach. I have been informed that that is far in excess of a fatal dose." *(The front door bell rings again. Judge's voice)* "Hawley Harvey Crippen, it is now my painful duty to pass sentence upon you, but before proceeding to do so, I would ask you whether you have anything to say in your own defense." *The front door opens and* SERGEANT STENNING *enters a trifle hesitantly)*

STENNING: Hullo. Is anyone at home? Mr. Bartholomew?

BARTHOLOMEW *(off from cellar. American-Crippen accent):* "I can only say that I know what I have done cannot be excused—only explained."

STENNING: Hullo. Mr. Bartholomew?

(STENNING *closes the door and moves further into the room to stand by the cellar door*)

BARTHOLOMEW (*off. American-Crippen voice*): "I killed my wife because of my very great love for the lady who honored me by consenting to become my mistress. I expect no mercy and deserve none. I am guilty and now have no recourse other than to accept my fate."

(BARTHOLOMEW *emerges from the cellar, disheveled and dirty from work. He bypasses* STENNING *without seeing him and heads for the drinks in the kitchen area*)

STENNING: What are you guilty of, Mr. Bartholomew?

(BARTHOLOMEW *swings round, startled*)

BARTHOLOMEW: Christ! Where the hell did you spring from?

STENNING: I rang the bell a couple of times, sir, but was unable to attract your attention, so I took the liberty of stepping in.

BARTHOLOMEW: I see.

STENNING: You should keep your door locked, you know.

BARTHOLOMEW: I forgot.

STENNING: I know it's the country and you're supposed to trust people and all, but you'll only have yourself to blame if you get done.

BARTHOLOMEW (*flustered*): Yes, you're quite right. I'm sorry.

(BARTHOLOMEW *pours a shaky drink*)

STENNING: That's alright, sir. Now then, what was it you were saying you were guilty of, just now?

(BARTHOLOMEW *glances involuntarily at the bathroom, and then quickly away again*)

BARTHOLOMEW: Me? . . . Er . . . I 'm not guilty of anything.

STENNING: I thought I heard you say you were, sir.

BARTHOLOMEW: No . . . not me.

STENNING: Well, who were you talking to then?

BARTHOLOMEW: No one . . . I wasn't talking to anyone. I'm . . . I'm alone here.

STENNING: Very strange, sir. I could have sworn when I came in I heard voices. Perhaps in the circumstances I should take a quick look round.

(*He moves away as if to start a search, but* BARTHOLOMEW *forestalls him*)

BARTHOLOMEW: There's no need, Sergeant. What you heard was just another of my little charades. You see I'm digging a grave in the cellar—Crippen actually.

STENNING: Isn't he a bit obvious?

BARTHOLOMEW: Done to death, you might say. Would you care to come down and have a look at it—view the "grisly remains."

STENNING: I've already warned you to stop playing these games, sir. You don't know what trouble you're inviting.

BARTHOLOMEW: Alright, Sergeant. Since it's an official request. (*He places his hand on his heart*) From now on I solemnly promise to give up murder. Though what I shall do in these long winter evenings without my innocent little hobby, I really don't know. Perhaps I'll take up serious drinking.

STENNING (*looking at* NORMAN'S *glass*): I thought you'd already started, sir.

BARTHOLOMEW: Only after I'd got in the house Sergeant, I assure you, so you can forget about your little bag of yellow crystals.

STENNING: Oh, don't worry about that, sir. Though I did happen to notice, as I was passing just now, that you'd left your car headlights on. I took the liberty of turning them off, by the way, you wouldn't want a flat battery in the morning.

(He hands BARTHOLOMEW *the keys)*

BARTHOLOMEW: Thank you very much indeed. Most kind. I was wondering what you'd come about.

(He pours himself a large whisky. STENNING *observes this closely)*

STENNING *(meaningfully):* I'm off duty now myself, as a matter of fact. Just on my way home.

BARTHOLOMEW: Oh, will you have a quick scotch?

STENNING: Very kind of you, but beer's my drink.

BARTHOLOMEW: Beer?

STENNING: Yes. I think I see some there. *(*BARTHOLOMEW *looks at two quart bottles of beer standing among the drinks and makes a feeble gesture towards them)* Don't you trouble, sir. I'll manage. *(He takes the quart bottle and slowly empties it into a quart-sized pewter tankard)*

*(*BARTHOLOMEW *watches the operation with no great enthusiasm. Plainly his visitor is prepared to spend some time consuming his drink and may need to use the facilities of the house, in course of time)*

BARTHOLOMEW: I used to drink a lot of beer, once upon a time, but I gave it up. It was far too much exercise for the bladder.

STENNING: I know what you mean. It's the same for me. In one end and out the other—quick as a flash. But I can't afford shorts on a sergeant's pay, so I don't encourage myself to get the taste for them.

*(*BARTHOLOMEW *shoots an uneasy glance in the direction of the bathroom)*

BARTHOLOMEW: Cheers. *(Both men raise their glasses.* BARTHOLOMEW *takes a sip of his whisky.* STENNING *takes a huge draught of his and then crosses unasked to dump himself in a chair. Reluctantly* BARTHOLOMEW *moves to take a seat opposite him. There is a short silence during which* STENNING *swallows his beer contentedly.* BARTHOLOMEW *forces himself to talk equably)* Well, I'm sorry you've had to come here twice in one day to no real purpose.

STENNING: It's all in the day's work.

BARTHOLOMEW: I'll bet you were really a bit disappointed I wasn't actually a murderer—confess it.

STENNING: I've already told you what I think about murder, sir.

BARTHOLOMEW: Well then, tell me about some of the murder cases you have been involved in, would I recognize them?

STENNING: Some of them, I expect.

BARTHOLOMEW: Any real corkers?

STENNING: Corkers?

BARTHOLOMEW: Well, like Peter Kurten, the Dusseldorf Monster, for example. He actually decapitated a swan and drank its blood when he couldn't find any human beings to stab.

(STENNING *looks coldly at* NORMAN *and shakes his head in reproof*)

STENNING: Did you ever hear of Gerald Sandgate?

BARTHOLOMEW: The Tattooed Galleon Murderer? Of course. Raped and killed four great-grandmothers. Apparently he was just crazy for wizened flesh.

STENNING: I was involved in that. Over nine million fingerprint comparisons were made. I got a commendation from the judge for being thorough. Not much in your line, though, I suppose. Not much to do with denying man's potential to see beauty.

(STENNING *drinks up his beer. He examines the empty tankard suggestively and looks around for a refill*)

BARTHOLOMEW (*suggestively*): Are you sure you won't have a quick scotch before you go?

STENNING: No. If it's all the same to you, I'll stick to the beer. (*He rises and starts to pour beer from another quart bottle. The sound of the beer pouring in the tankard irresistibly suggests urination and* BARTHOLOMEW *glances helplessly in the direction of the bathroom. He crosses and recrosses his legs.* STENNING *sits)* Another one you might have heard of was George Paling.

BARTHOLOMEW: I don't recall him, I'm afraid.

STENNING: R.A.F. Fitter. Ran his wife down in a car—an Austin A40, I think it was—no call me a liar, it was a Morris 1100. Anyway he did it simply because she'd got on a bit and he'd found himself a new fancy piece. To my way of thinking, people like him are the worst. Just cunning and selfish—killing their partners deliberately in cold blood. He was a bit tricky at first, but I had a few minutes alone with him and I soon got to the heart of the matter. *(He drinks deeply)*

BARTHOLOMEW *(alarmed)*: What do you mean, Sergeant? What did you do?

STENNING: I saw to it that he told the truth, sir.

BARTHOLOMEW: Yes. Yes. I see. Of course. One sometimes forgets that the detective is almost as important as the murderer. It is his work which helps the other to immortality. I mean, where would the Yarmouth Beach Murderer be without the pertinacity of Inspector Gough? . . . Or Raymond Morris, the Pixie Hood Murderer, be without the insights of Superintendent Forbes? They complement each other, don't you see.

STENNING: It's not like that sir, at all. But as I said before, you won't be told. *(He rises)* Anyway, that was very pleasant. I must be on my way.

BARTHOLOMEW: Glad you enjoyed it. Goodnight.

STENNING: There's just one thing before I go. I wonder if I could use your toilet?

*(*NORMAN *stands thunderstruck as* STENNING *heads off up the stairs in the direction of the bathroom.* STENNING *is just about at the door when* BARTHOLOMEW *finds his voice)*

BARTHOLOMEW: Hey! Stop! Not in there.

STENNING: Sorry, sir. This is the bathroom, isn't it?

BARTHOLOMEW: Yes, yes of course. But . . . but the loo's blocked, I'm afraid. Helplessly blocked. I've sent for a plumber, but you know how long they take to come round.

(STENNING *again turns to the door*)

STENNING: Oh, I expect I can fix that. I'm a bit of a handyman myself.

(STENNING *opens the door so that the audience can see the legs of the drowned woman hanging over the side of the bath. He, still facing* BAR-THOLOMEW, *cannot see them*)

BARTHOLOMEW (*urgently*): Please, Sergeant, I'd rather you didn't. It's all a bit messy.

(STENNING *debates it for a moment, then shrugs*)

STENNING: Oh, very well sir, if you insist. (*He closes the door and descends the stairs*) I suppose you don't have another toilet, do you?

BARTHOLOMEW: No, I'm afraid we don't, but you are very welcome to use the garden.

STENNING: Then I suppose I better had.

(BARTHOLOMEW *shows him out to the back garden and then returns himself. He is in a high state of excitement and breathes deeply*)

BARTHOLOMEW (*to himself*): This is exactly how Christie must have felt when he discovered the skull of one of his earlier victims had acciden-tally become exposed in the garden where the police were searching for the body of Mrs. Evans. Extraordinary . . . the mind does work extremely swiftly under the circumstances. (STENNING *comes running in, looking very embarrassed*) That was a quick one, Sergeant.

STENNING: On the contrary, sir, just as I was about to . . . er . . . re-lieve myself, your neighbor Mrs. Ramage poked her head out of the window, so I had to desist. We'd never hear the end of it, if she was to catch the Law urinating.

BARTHOLOMEW: That's for certain. Perhaps you'd care to use the Spode potty?

(He offers an old chamber pot which has a flowerpot in it)

STENNING: Everything's a big laugh to you, sir, isn't it? But you'll see it all quite differently one of these days, believe me. *(He starts to leave the room, then stops)* By the way, sir, heard from your wife?

BARTHOLOMEW: Er no. As I told you, I think she's taken off.

STENNING: You don't seem too upset at the prospect.

BARTHOLOMEW: There's more to life than matrimony, Sergeant. Goodnight.

STENNING: Goodnight, sir.

(He gives BARTHOLOMEW *a long look from which the other flinches, then leaves.* BARTHOLOMEW *follows him into the hall. We hear the front door open and close.*

*(*BARTHOLOMEW *re-enters the room and stands weakly against a wall breathing deeply. After a moment he collects himself and advances into the center of the stage)*

BARTHOLOMEW: Now then, where was I? . . . Ah yes. Stage two. The note. *(He takes a sheet of notepaper and inserts it in the typewriter. He types rapidly for a minute, then pulls out the paper and reads it. reading)* My darling Norman. I am going away with the man I love and will never trouble you again. Please try to understand that when love commands, I have no choice but to obey, even if it means hurting the one man who has shown more gentleness, kindness and understanding to me than anyone else in the world. Farewell and try to forget me quickly. Your faithless Elizabeth. *(He grins to himself delightedly and places the note on the easel. He then goes out to the garden and returns staggering under the weight of a large sack of quicklime, so marked)* At least I won't make the same mistake that Wainwright did with Chloride of Lime. I never did like well preserved women. *(He carries the sack down into the cellar. We hear him spreading the lime in the cellar with a spade, whistling cheerfully as he works. slowly as if making it up)*

There was an old doctor called Crippen
Whose ways were really quite rippin.
He took ticket of leave
With Ethel Le Neve
But fell foul of Canadian shippin.

(Chuckling, BARTHOLOMEW *emerges from the cellar, brushing himself down and plainly well satisfied with himself and his work)* Good. Now for the interment. *(He crosses the room and mounts the stairs to the bathroom. He opens the door and is about to go in when the doorbell rings. He stands frozen and indecisive. It rings again more imperiously. Quietly he closes the bathroom door and tiptoes downstairs. It rings again as he exits to the hallway to answer it. We hear him open the door and then, after a substantial pause, he backs slowly into the room. His face wears an expression of cataclysmic shock. We hear the front door close and then, after a further pause, a figure walks into the room, carrying a suitcase. It is his wife* ELIZABETH. *She is about forty, attractive, well turned out, about the same size as* MILLIE. *She has about her an air of great competence and efficiency. She puts down her suitcase)*

BARTHOLOMEW: My God . . . Elizabeth!

ELIZABETH: Well, come on, don't just stand there saying my God Elizabeth, as if you'd seen a ghost. Who the hell did you think it was? One of your silly old murderers come to pay a call? I forgot my key, that's all.

BARTHOLOMEW *(dazedly):* Elizabeth . . . ?

(He looks helplessly upwards towards the bathroom)

ELIZABETH: Exactly . . . your dear wife Elizabeth. I didn't expect a rapturous welcome, but at least you might seem a bit more pleased to see me home.

*(*BARTHOLOMEW *makes a great effort to pull himself together)*

BARTHOLOMEW: But I don't understand. You're a day early. I didn't expect you till tomorrow.

ELIZABETH: I know. But I had to postpone a Caesarian. Give me a hand with the cases, will you?

(*She goes out through the front door. He looks round desperately and sees her fur coat and open suitcase. He closes it and throws both into the cellar*)

BARTHOLOMEW (*looking up to the bathroom*): So you did play Elizabeth after all. Christ! . . . what have I done?

ELIZABETH (*off*): Come on. What's keeping you?

BARTHOLOMEW: N . . . nothing.

ELIZABETH (*off*): Then stop skyving and give me a hand. (*He runs off. After a short pause they both return carrying suitcases which they put down in a corner of the room*) God, I'm tired. It really is a bloody long way. I think I'll have a bath before I unpack.

BARTHOLOMEW (*wildly*): Why not have a drink first . . . do you good.

ELIZABETH: Alright. Give me a brandy.

(ELIZABETH *takes off her coat and puts it away in the hall cupboard.* BARTHOLOMEW *looks agitatedly up the stairs, then moves to make the drink. She returns and he hands it to her*)

ELIZABETH: Didn't you have that painter's dinner tonight?

BARTHOLOMEW: Yes.

ELIZABETH: I thought you had to dress for that.

BARTHOLOMEW: I changed.

ELIZABETH: What on earth for?

BARTHOLOMEW: I wanted to be comfortable.

ELIZABETH: Sloppy, you mean. Like this room. All I have to do is to go away for a couple of days and the whole place looks like a pig sty. You really expect me to clear up after you all the time, don't you?

BARTHOLOMEW: I told you, I didn't expect you back tonight.

ELIZABETH: I tried to phone you earlier, but there was no reply. Anyway, what's that got to do with the price of fish? Does it mean you have to live like a tramp while I'm away?

BARTHOLOMEW: I live as I please.

ELIZABETH: Like a tramp.

(She starts to tidy up the room)

BARTHOLOMEW: If you say so. Personally I think it's better than living like a Prussian Factory Inspector.

ELIZABETH: Why don't you save your wit for that pneumatic little slut, whom I expect you've been seeing every day I've been gone.

BARTHOLOMEW: Don't be ridiculous!

ELIZABETH: Oh? Then has she finally become as bored with your nonsensical games as I did?

BARTHOLOMEW: What?

ELIZABETH: Yes. That's it—or she'd be here now, wouldn't she—since neither of you expected me home tonight? The only thing I can't understand is why it took her so long. I was catatonically uninterested in your homicide capers within a month. It's taken her three.

BARTHOLOMEW: What utter piffle.

ELIZABETH: You may find it peeving that your whore's sussed out she's been playing footsie with a ten-year-old child, but I suspect it certainly isn't piffle.

BARTHOLOMEW: If you only knew how vulgar you looked when you spoke like that.

ELIZABETH: When I speak the truth, you mean.

BARTHOLOMEW: It is not the truth. Millie was not . . . is not bored with me!

ELIZABETH: She's bored alright. Rigidly, sempiternally, paraplegically bored.

BARTHOLOMEW: No!

ELIZABETH: If she wasn't, you'd be out with her now, scampering around tying her to trees or rummaging through abattoirs or throwing blood-stained parcels out of train windows or wasting your time in some equally morbid manner. Why don't you think seriously about growing up, Norman?

BARTHOLOMEW: And why don't you think seriously about shutting up, Elizabeth?

(ELIZABETH *approaches very close to* BARTHOLOMEW)

ELIZABETH: If you want my opinion, giving you and your infantile fanta-sies the push was the best day's work that sleazy little trollop of yours ever did.

BARTHOLOMEW: For Christ's sake, lay off Millie. At least she knows how to have fun. At least she doesn't spend all day with her nose buried in some dry old medical textbook. At least she knows which side is up!

ELIZABETH: Really? I'm surprised that as your girl friend, she ever learnt the meaning of the word up.

(They stare at each other)

BARTHOLOMEW: Thanks a lot. What a charitable lady you are, to be sure.

ELIZABETH: I'm sorry. I'm tired. I'd better have that bath now.

BARTHOLOMEW: Have another drink.

ELIZABETH: Alright. Just one.

(He pours a drink and hands it to her)

Why don't you try with me any more?

BARTHOLOMEW: I do. I do try. But mostly nothing comes. It's as if I'd never known anything in my entire life—not a single physical fact— not a story—not the tiniest scrap of memorabilia. Nothing. . . . *(He laughs)* They do say the memory goes first.

ELIZABETH: Not so. It's the urge to search it that goes first. The trouble is that in the last twelve years I've made you feel so secure, you've gone quite numb. I have the effect on you of six seconal and a comfort blanket. It's my fault, I suppose.

(She reaches to touch his hand. He endures it)

BARTHOLOMEW: No.

ELIZABETH: Yes. It must always be the fault of the ones who suffer— they're such rancidly bloody fools.

BARTHOLOMEW: No more foolish than people trying to protect a pretty ropey investment.

ELIZABETH: By throwing good money after bad, you mean? *(They smile at each other)* Like that time in the South of France when you had to pay for that perfectly foul meal and then fell off the patio and rolled down the hill . . .

BARTHOLOMEW: I know. Into all those hideous thorn bushes.

ELIZABETH: And the goats . . . remember the goats?

BARTHOLOMEW: Do I ever! Between them they cut my silk suit to ribbons. First time on, too.

ELIZABETH: And you hadn't even paid for it . . .

BARTHOLOMEW: It was eighty quid—even in those days.

(*They laugh companionably. Then the laughter subsides*)

ELIZABETH: What was the name of that village—Ouly, Ourly . . .

BARTHOLOMEW: Ouchy sur Fleuve. You know that reminds me of the most extraordinary thing I found out later.

ELIZABETH: Oh, what was that?

BARTHOLOMEW: James Berry, the official English executioner between 1884 and 1892, actually lived there for a while.

ELIZABETH (*stiffening*): Really.

BARTHOLOMEW: Yes. Only the other day I was reading his account of the execution of a Mrs. Jane Cassidy, a woman who murdered her lover during a drunken quarrel. (*Declamatory*) She walked to the scaffold with a free firm stride, defying the world which had so justly punished her. But when the rope touched her neck, she blushed crimson to the very roots of her hair and her lips twitched convulsively. Intense shame and sorrow were never more plainly expressed by any woman. (*Normal voice*) Fantastic, eh?

ELIZABETH: Fantastic! Why don't you try and woo Millie back by asking her to play the part of that woman. I'm sure she'd be only too happy to do it, except of course she's probably not had too much experience of expressing intense shame.

BARTHOLOMEW: Very funny.

ELIZABETH: I really am going to have that bath now. I'm operating at 9 a.m. and, believe it or not, bringing a little life into the world takes even more effort and concentration than bringing a little death.

(*Under* BARTHOLOMEW's *appalled gaze she starts up the stairs towards the bathroom*)

BARTHOLOMEW (*desperate*): Aren't you going to put the car away first?

ELIZABETH: No. I can't be bothered. It can stay out tonight like yours.

BARTHOLOMEW: Mine starts alright. You know you always have trouble.

ELIZABETH: Look, I'm bloody tired. I've just driven all the way down from
Birmingham. If you were any kind of man at all, you'd put the flaming
car in the garage yourself. *(She takes another couple of steps up the
stairs)*

BARTHOLOMEW *(mimicking her)*: It's your car. But of course if you want
me to clear up after you all the time . . .

ELIZABETH: Alright, I'll put the sodding thing away myself. *(She storms
down the stairs, across the room and out of the front door.* BARTHOLOMEW
*runs up the stairs and into the bathroom. We see him scoop the dead
body out of the bath and carry it, wet and still flecked with soap bubbles, to the head of the stairs and start down them. The head falls back
and we see clearly that it is the body of* MILLIE. *We hear the car door
slam furiously outside and footsteps approaching. The front door slams
as* BARTHOLOMEW *retreats hurriedly up the stairs and back into the bathroom, closing the door.* ELIZABETH *enters)* The damned keys are in my
coat. I can't be bothered with it any more . . . *(She sees that* BAR-
THOLOMEW *isn't there and stumps closely into the bedroom)* Norman,
where are you? (BARTHOLOMEW *slips out of the bathroom and down the
stairs, bumping into* ELIZABETH *who comes out of the bedroom)* What
the hell are you doing, capering about all over the place. Out of my
way. *(She pushes him aside and walks up the stairs towards the bathroom. He slowly retreats stage center looking up, petrified. She goes into
the bathroom and closes the door. There is a slight pause, then a sudden
sharp scream. The door of the bathroom is then thrown open and* ELIZA-
BETH *staggers out and totters down the stairs to face* BARTHOLOMEW. *The
bathroom door swings shut behind her. Alternatively, of course, if gauze
is used we will actually see* ELIZABETH *discover the body. There is a long
silence between them.* BARTHOLOMEW *nods his head vigorously)*

BARTHOLOMEW: . . . It was an accident.

ELIZABETH: An accident?

BARTHOLOMEW: Yes.

ELIZABETH: You mean she slipped and struck her head—something like that?

BARTHOLOMEW *(rallying)*: Yes. That's what happened.

ELIZABETH: How do you know?

BARTHOLOMEW: I mean, that's what must have happened.

ELIZABETH: You weren't in the bathroom at the time, though?

BARTHOLOMEW: No.

ELIZABETH: But you heard a crash. A cry?

BARTHOLOMEW: Yes.

ELIZABETH: Which?

BARTHOLOMEW: Er . . . both. I ran up, but I couldn't see her for the bubbles.

ELIZABETH: Bubbles?

BARTHOLOMEW: She had a bubble bath. A huge one. I expect most of them have subsided by now.

ELIZABETH: Yes.

BARTHOLOMEW: And the steam of course. That also made it very difficult to see. There was a lot of steam.

ELIZABETH: And?

BARTHOLOMEW: Her head had gone under the water. Her legs were in the air. I tried to get her out, but the bubbles made it too slippery. I felt her pulse and tried a mirror on her breath, but she was unquestionably dead, so I left her there.

ELIZABETH: How long ago was this?

BARTHOLOMEW: Half an hour.

ELIZABETH: Have you called the police?

BARTHOLOMEW: No.

ELIZABETH: Why not?

BARTHOLOMEW: I don't know.

ELIZABETH: What do you mean . . . you don't know?

BARTHOLOMEW: I don't know.

ELIZABETH: Why haven't you called the police?

BARTHOLOMEW (*shouting*): I don't know!

ELIZABETH: Really? I think I do. It wasn't an accident, was it?

BARTHOLOMEW: Yes. Of course it was.

ELIZABETH: Not the way I see it! You killed her.

BARTHOLOMEW: I . . .

ELIZABETH: What was it? Some wretched little sex romp that went wrong?

BARTHOLOMEW: No . . . no . . . of course not.

ELIZABETH (*with dawning understanding*): Or was it one of your stupid murderer games?

BARTHOLOMEW: No.

ELIZABETH: Yes. That's more like it, isn't it? What were you playing? Brides in the Bath?

BARTHOLOMEW: I told you it was an accident. I didn't mean . . .

ELIZABETH: No, I don't suppose you did. But that's what happens if you don't grow up. You kill people, but you don't mean to. *(Relentless)* In my book that's worse almost than killing people and actually meaning to. At least one is the act of a man who has taken a conscious decision, while the other is just the work of a lunatic child. They'll find out she was your mistress, of course.

BARTHOLOMEW: How? None of her friends knew about me.

ELIZABETH: Your wife away. A naked girl in your bathroom at night. Do you think they'd believe she was the plumber's mate come to fix the U bend?

BARTHOLOMEW: It could still be an accident. What's my motive? I wanted her alive.

ELIZABETH: Many men have killed importuning mistresses with whom they have become bored. Surely I don't have to remind the famous murder expert of that?

BARTHOLOMEW: I suppose you're right.

ELIZABETH: You're not doing very well, really, are you?

BARTHOLOMEW: Sorry. I'm a bit numb—not thinking.

ELIZABETH: So I see. Don't you think it's about time you started?

BARTHOLOMEW: Yes.

ELIZABETH: Well, suppose you begin by telling me what actually did happen.

BARTHOLOMEW: You were right. I was playing George Joseph Smith—The Brides in the Bath Murderer—and I must have gone too far. One minute we were laughing and joking, and the next—well, she was just lying there under the water—dead.

ELIZABETH: Well, it's Life if they believe that you meant to kill her and at least five years if they believe you didn't.

BARTHOLOMEW: And nothing if they believe it was an accident.

ELIZABETH: I don't think it's very likely they'll do that.

BARTHOLOMEW: They will if you support me. I mean you're a doctor. Couldn't you say that it's happened since you've been back. That you returned home unexpectedly . . . that I confessed to you that Millie was upstairs taking a bath and that suddenly we heard a cry, but by the time we'd got the door broken down it was too late.

(ELIZABETH *looks at him thoughtfully for a long moment*)

ELIZABETH: I need a drink.

(BARTHOLOMEW, *a half smile on his face moves to pour her a glass of brandy. She follows him and he gives her the drink which she sips thoughtfully*)

BARTHOLOMEW: Well, what do you say?

ELIZABETH: Would you mind telling me just why I should stick my neck out for you?

BARTHOLOMEW: To protect your name, for one thing. I'm sure future patients won't rush to be treated by a woman doctor whose husband killed his mistress in the course of what they will all take to have been "a wretched little sex romp." You'll have to leave the neighborhood, you know—give up your practice, change your name, go and live in self-enforced obscurity. I can see you now, crouched over the cruet set in the dining room of an Eastbourne boarding house, timidly forking up the tomato sauce-covered rissoles as you wait for the inevitable glance of recognition that will send you on your weary way again.

ELIZABETH: Oh phooey! You don't really think the world's like that any more do you. Much though it may offend against your ridiculous theories, it's got far too violent for people to care all that much about one little murder. It'll probably be tough for a few weeks, but they'll soon forget.

BARTHOLOMEW: Not as quickly as all that. . . . You may be very sure that if I find myself in the dock through your failure to help me, my spicy embellishments will make it not only the murder trial of the century, but also one in which you figure unforgettably. *(Supplicant's voice)* "Ladies and gentlemen of the jury, I must confess that it was my wife who first introduced me to strange and recondite forms of love making, in which bubble baths, rubber wear, and even live dog fish all figured prominently."

ELIZABETH: Can't you shut up fantasizing for a moment? It's not enough, I suppose, that your stupid games have actually led you to kill someone, without your wanking away about what you're going to do at the trial.

BARTHOLOMEW *(hard)*: I'm merely showing you how absolutely intolerable I could make life for you, if I chose.

(They regard each other with mutual loathing. She, recognizing the truth of what he is saying, flinches away and starts to walk abstractedly about the room)

ELIZABETH *(bitterly)*: You'd better let me think. *(After several moments, she moves to stand very close to him, looking into his face)* May I ask what you were planning to do with the body before I got here?

BARTHOLOMEW: The cellar. Quicklime. Pretty old hat, I'm afraid, but serviceable.

ELIZABETH: Serviceable, my arse. A single anxious phone call from one of her relatives and the police would have it up before it had dried. If I go along with it at all, it will have to be the accident.

BARTHOLOMEW: Yes. Alright.

ELIZABETH: And furthermore I shall not expect to hear any further talk of divorce or separation or whatever, and of course there'll be no more mistresses.

BARTHOLOMEW: So that's your price?

ELIZABETH: Yes, and a pretty modest one I'd have thought for making oneself an accessory after the fact of manslaughter. Well, do you agree?

BARTHOLOMEW: A lifetime's representation to the outside world of hard core connubial bliss?

ELIZABETH: Exactly. Together we will uphold the sanctity of the marriage contract.

(BARTHOLOMEW *thinks gloomily about the proposition*)

BARTHOLOMEW *(heavily)*: Alright.

ELIZABETH: Well, you'd better start filling in the cellar. I don't want anything suspicious here when the police come. (ELIZABETH *goes to the cellar door, opens it and peers down into it*) My, you have been a busy little bee here haven't you. That's quite a corking little grave you've dug. *(Her attention is caught by the sight of her case and coat. She ducks down and returns with them)* What on earth are these doing in the cellar! *(She holds up the suitcase and coat for* BARTHOLOMEW *to see)*

BARTHOLOMEW *(uneasily)*: I don't know. You must have put them there.

ELIZABETH: Me? Whatever for?

BARTHOLOMEW: How would I know? *(He starts up the stairs to the bathroom)*

ELIZABETH: Just a minute. There's something very funny going on here. What the devil are my fur coat and suitcase doing in the cellar?

BARTHOLOMEW: Search me.

ELIZABETH: Well, either you put them there or that girl put them there. Which?

BARTHOLOMEW *(shrill)*: I keep telling you, I don't know.

(ELIZABETH *paces up and down, thinking deeply*)

ELIZABETH: It's funny. When I came in tonight, your surprise at seeing me was quite out of proportion to my merely arriving a night early. It wasn't simply distress at having a dead body on your hands. It was surprise . . . no—it was amazement! Now why I ask myself, should you be *amazed* to see me?

(BARTHOLOMEW *is quite unable to move. He makes a helpless gesture*)

ELIZABETH: Obviously you didn't expect to see me again, either then or ever. (BARTHOLOMEW *gives an involuntary cry*) You know what I'm saying, don't you Norman? I'm saying that it wasn't your mistress you meant to kill. It was me!

BARTHOLOMEW: No!

ELIZABETH: How did the mistake happen . . . something, I suppose, to do with the steam . . . the bubble bath . . . the head turned away from you as you entered, wearing my bath cap . . . the body shrouded in bubbles and steam . . . the face invisible under the foamy water . . . my God!!

(BARTHOLOMEW *tries to take hold of her, but she shakes him off fiercely*)

BARTHOLOMEW: Don't be ridiculous, Elizabeth. I know the difference between you and her.

ELIZABETH: Obviously you didn't. I was the person you wanted out of the way, not her.

BARTHOLOMEW: No!

ELIZABETH: Yes. Now let me think exactly how it all came about. You had a dinner date this evening, so you couldn't have had one with Millie. Nor did either of you expect me home tonight. Did she try and play a joke on you—is that it? . . . Did she creep in here and put this case and coat down to make you think as you came in that I had returned? . . . Of course! That's it! It *was* a game she was playing. Oh my God, the old bitch has come back a day early. Surprise, surprise it's your yummy little sex kitten after all, contentedly purring away in the bath tub. But it went wrong, didn't it? You returned, a bit boozed, thought she was me, shot upstairs and shoved her head under the water before she had a chance to show who she was. Jesus Christ!

BARTHOLOMEW: You can't really believe anything as stupid as that.

ELIZABETH: Or was it worse than that? Was she your accomplice in the plan to murder me . . . and had she realised what a feeble partner she'd got, all talk and no do. I wonder—was it that she wanted to try you out—to see whether if she could persuade you that she was me, all helpless in the bath, you actually had the guts to try and do the murder.

BARTHOLOMEW *(realising this might be the truth)*: No! She wouldn't have done that.

ELIZABETH: It doesn't really matter. Either way she got her comeuppance, the poor cow.

BARTHOLOMEW *(desperate)*: I swear to you on my life it wasn't like that. If you want to know, *I* borrowed the case and coat. It was part of my Brides in the Bath charade. Don't you see we were meant to be honeymooners newly arrived at our lodgings. When you went out to the van before, I pushed them into the cellar as obviously I didn't want you to see them.

ELIZABETH: Is that the truth?

BARTHOLOMEW: Yes. Absolutely.

ELIZABETH: Then why didn't you tell me about it before?

BARTHOLOMEW: I don't know . . . I was flustered . . . somehow, I suppose I didn't want to make myself look more of a fool than I already was. Help me now and I promise I'll stay with you and there'll be no more girl friends or talk of divorce. *(She stares at him thoughtfully, evaluating the situation. He moves towards her and holds her by the shoulders looking sincerely into her eyes)*

Look, if you honestly do believe that I am a murderer and that it was you I tried to murder there is no point in our trying to go on together, is there? You must phone Sergeant Stenning now and turn me in.

ELIZABETH *(slowly)*: Alright, Norman. I'll give you the benefit of the doubt. Perhaps there is something we can still make out of this life together—after all, we had it once.

BARTHOLOMEW: Yes, we did, it's true. I promise I'll try.

(*They kiss tenderly.* BARTHOLOMEW *is the first to break*)

BARTHOLOMEW: Perhaps we should call the police soon. They'll be able to tell, won't they, if we delay too long?

ELIZABETH: From the rigor you mean? . . . Yes I suppose so. Will you do it or will I?

BARTHOLOMEW: Perhaps it would come better from you—being a doctor. I'll go up and make poor Millie look a bit decent and then I'll fix the cellar.

ELIZABETH: What strange bargains we strike in our life!

BARTHOLOMEW: Yes. But I swear you won't regret this one.

(*They exchange a fond look, then he moves to take a travelling rug from the back of a sofa and walks up the stairs to the bathroom. His expression changes to one of smug self-satisfaction.* ELIZABETH *moves to the phone, and having selected the police station number from a list on the desk, she dials it. While waiting for an answer she suddenly notices* BARTHOLOMEW'*s "Leaving" note pinned to the easel. She puts the phone down and moves nearer to read it*)

ELIZABETH (*reading*): My darling Norman. I am going away with the man I love and will never trouble you again . . . (*She continues to read silently*) Farewell, and try to forget me quickly. Your faithless Elizabeth.

(BARTHOLOMEW *freezes in horror. Like an automaton he turns to face her. There is a long silence between them.* ELIZABETH *does not immediately turn round to face him*)

So I was right. You bloody bastard!

(*She starts shaking violently and suddenly turns round to show us that she is laughing uncontrollably*)

Well, well, well. If this isn't the best thing ever. The great murder expert plots and plans his first actual crime with fiendish cunning and can't even get the victim right. *(She breaks up laughing hysterically)*

BARTHOLOMEW *(hissing):* Shut up!

ELIZABETH: Oh my dear, it's far too late to tell me to shut up. Everyone's going to hear about this. You'll get your precious notoriety alright—as a laughing stock. They'll probably have a wax effigy of you in The Chamber of Horrors at Madame Tussaud's—Norman Bartholomew, The Bubble Bath Murderer. Drowned his lover in mistake for his wife.

(She resumes laughing. He, now totally out of control, runs down the stairs and flies at her. Grasping her round the throat, he starts to throttle her)

BARTHOLOMEW: Shut up! Shut up! Shut up! *(Suddenly she goes limp and faints to the floor. Dazedly he stands looking down at her, then stoops to check her state of health. To himself)* H'm, only fainted. *(He picks her up and puts her on the sofa)* Oh God, this is a disaster . . . there must be something I can do . . . but what? . . . Now steady . . . think! *(He stands looking down at her, thinking. Gradually light dawns. He turns away and paces. Slowly, thinking it through)* Yes, that's it . . . she had a motive, for getting rid of my mistress . . . but I didn't. . . . So what happend? . . . Let's see now. I'm out taking a walk to clear my head after the alcoholic excess of my dinner . . . While I'm out she comes home unexpectedly—finds Millie making herself at home in *her* bath—she's absolutely livid—a sudden temptation she pushes her under and holds her there . . . and then remorse and suicide . . . yes, that's perfect. *(He crosses to the sofa, and stoops to examine her throat with great attention)* Good. No bruises on the neck. Thank God she fainted when she did. *(He drags her to the stove and lays her down beside it. Then he fetches a cushion from the divan, opens the oven door, and arranges her comfortably with her head in the oven)* Now then, is there anything I've missed? *(He looks around the room, and suddenly sees the note on the easel)* Ha! Glad I spotted you. You could have been the "one mistake all murderers make." *(He burns it in the stove)* Good! . . . Anything else? Of course! Her dress. The sleeves and front would be wet. Good thinking, N.B. You really are behaving like a classic Murderer now. *(He gets a bowl of water from the sink and throws it over her dress. Then he turns on the gas. We hear it hissing loudly for a while.* BARTHOLOMEW *watches delightedly. Suddenly the gas stops)* Damn. The bloody cylinder's empty. *(He runs over to the kitchen area and starts quickly changing over to a full gas cylinder)* Sodding thing . . . I don't know why we can't be on the mains like everybody else. *(At last his job is successfully completed and we hear the hiss of gas start again. Behind his back,* ELIZABETH *has revived and has taken the spit out of the oven. He crosses to the cooker to check that all is well. He kneels down, feeling for her pulse. With a sudden savage movement, she sits up and stabs him in the stomach with the spit. He reels back screaming, leaving the spit in* ELIZABETH'S *hands. Blood pours out through his fingers as he seeks to keep the wound closed.* ELIZABETH *rises from the floor, turns off the gas and runs retching into the kitchen for a glass of water. Recovered, she returns to him)*

BARTHOLOMEW: My God . . . my God, you bitch, what have you done? *(*BARTHOLOMEW *runs to the window. He pulls aside the curtain and opens it)* Mrs. Ramage . . . Mrs. Ramage, help me. I've been stabbed. *(He holds out his bloody hands)* Help . . . help! . . . call an ambulance. *(A long pause. Then he registers hopelessness caused by her rejection and topples back into the room)* Bloody cow!

*(*ELIZABETH *pulls the curtains closed)*

ELIZABETH: Wouldn't she listen to you, Norman? Well, it's hardly surprising, is it? A man wholly obsessed with negative forces like murder and murderers must eventually forfeit all protection and put himself in the way of harm.

BARTHOLOMEW: Help me!

*(*ELIZABETH *opens her suitcase, and takes out a case containing surgeon's scalpels. Very deliberately, she selects one)*

BARTHOLOMEW: What are you doing?

(Slowly she approaches him)

ELIZABETH: I'm doing you a favor, Norman. I'm showing you what the murder game is really all about. *(She slashes him four times with the scalpel across the chest and arms. He screams and tries to protect himself as blood spurts out through the torn shirt)* Well, darling, tell me—

does it represent a mirror image of man's potential to realize bliss? *(She slashes him again. He screams again)* Is it truly our most daring challenge to God? *(Another slash. Another scream)* Is this really a way to salvation? Is it Norman? . . . Is it? . . . Is it? . . . Is it? *(She cuts away at him in a frenzy. Finally he collapses on the floor and she moves away in a daze to sit on the stairs. There is a long silence. She is emotionally drained)* Norman . . . Norman . . . listen to me. . . . It's worth listening to, because you see you've finally made a convert. *(Hysterical laugh)* Do you know what story I'll tell the police when they get here? I'll say I came in and found your mistress in my bath. In a sudden, uncontrollable burst of passion I drowned her and then killed you. It will be *my* murder.

(In his terrible pain, BARTHOLOMEW *somehow realizes the significance of what she is saying)*

BARTHOLOMEW *(very weak):* What!! . . . You can't do that. I killed. It was *my* murder.

*(*ELIZABETH *smiles a wicked smile at him, and slowly shakes her head as she takes away from him all he has left)*

ELIZABETH: No, I think not. Did you really think that an inept little man like you could challenge the great moral laws of this universe. Mediocrity, my darling, has no theological status.

BARTHOLOMEW: I had my vision.

ELIZABETH: Vision! The eye of the heroic murderer does not fall on the wrong person.

(She stirs him with her foot, then slowly, as she speaks, moves to sit on the stairs, still holding the scalpel)

ELIZABETH: You know, this really could be the *crime passionelle* of the century. I can see myself in the witness box now, proud, aloof, mysterious. All eyes will be upon me as I weave my bloody tale of wronged womanhood, omitting no ghastly detail of the drowning of my rival and the slaughter of my husband. Believe me, my own dearest Norman, I will have, what you have always wanted—a true and abiding notoriety.

BARTHOLOMEW *(a great cry)*: No. It's mine!! . . .

(He collapses. There is a sudden loud knocking on the front door)

STENNING: Open up. Police!

(ELIZABETH *looks vaguely in the direction of the door, but being virtually in a state of catatonia, is unable to move. There is further knocking, then* STENNING *comes crashing into the room through the back door. He sees* BARTHOLOMEW *huddled on the floor, but does not at first notice Elizabeth)* Still playing games eh, Mr. Bartholomew? Well . . . this time you've gone too far. You frightened Mrs. Ramage half to death showing yourself to her all covered in blood. She just called me in a fair old state, I can tell you. You may know the difference between Kensington Gore, as you call it, and the real stuff. Old ladies don't. I warned you twice today and that's enough. Do you hear me? Good God, man, look at me when I'm talking to you. I'm arresting you for a breach of the peace. (BARTHOLOMEW *doesn't move) Oh come on!*

(STENNING *grabs* BARTHOLOMEW *and lifts him into a sitting position. Then he sees his hideous mutilations)* Christ Almighty! *(He kneels to examine him, then straightens up.* BARTHOLOMEW's *lifeless body slips from his arms.* ELIZABETH *drops the scalpel with a clatter.* STENNING *turns to look at her. There is a pause. Slowly)* I told him to stop in time. I told him he didn't know the game he was playing. I told him it was the victim who looked for the murderer.

ELIZABETH: You were right, Sergeant. But he didn't have to look very far. We made the appointment—years ago.

(She leans against the banisters sobbing and laughing as the Curtain falls.)

VICTIM

Mario Fratti

Many aspects of Jacobean revenge tragedy appear in thinly disguised fashion in *Victim:* casual murder, infidelity, silent brooding hatred, a putative vengeful spirit and even, in its opening atrocity, an echo of the old Dumb Show.

It is not surprising that these conventions surface in the work of the enormously eclectic and prolific Italian-American playwright-poet-critic Mario Fratti, a distinguished faculty member of Hunter College in New York City. His remarkably disparate short and long plays include such acclaimed comedies and dramas as *The Academy, The Cage, The Chinese Friend, Eleonora Duse, Mafia, The Refrigerators* and many others. Professor Fratti also wrote the book for the hit Broadway musical, *Nine.*

Victim, written in 1978, has been performed in many countries, including America, Austria, Belgium, Brazil, Canada, Germany, India, Israel, Holland, Mexico, Poland, Spain and Uruguay.

CAST OF CHARACTERS

DIANA, *in her early thirties; striking and sensuous; well-bred and sophisticated.*

KIRK, *a tormented man in his early thirties; sensitive and vulnerable, notwithstanding his physical strength.*

WARREN, *Diana's husband; distinguished; he appears to be very sure of himself; in his early fifties.*

THE METER MAN

Time: The Present.
Place: An isolated house in New York State.

ACT ONE

Scene One

A strikingly attractive living room with a very personal quality. Upstage Right: a door that leads to the kitchen. Upstage Center: a door that leads into the bedroom. Upstage Left (in the hall): a screen. Downstage Right: a large comfortable couch; there are also chairs, a coffee table, a desk with a telephone, a television set and a radio. Downstage Left: the door that leads into the hall (we can see the front door and part of the garden). The hall is narrow. It has a beautiful old armoire (downstage) and a screen (upstage). The door from the hall into the living room is downstage left. At rise, it is late afternoon. DIANA is sitting, talking on the telephone.

DIANA: . . . me too, my love. . . . Every minute . . . day and night. . . . Of course, love. . . . I understand. . . . I know. . . . I know, my love, but. . . . Yes. . . . *(with tenderness in her voice)* Thank you. . . . You're sweet . . . *(tender cooing)*. . . . How can I forget?. . . . Never. . . . Always exciting. Always new. . . . Like being born again. . . . Because you love me . . . and because I love you of course. . . . With all my soul. . . . I promise. . . . You know. . . . Of course. . . . I believe you. . . . I trust you, my love . . .

(During this telephone conversation we see KIRK approaching the front door. He stops. It is obvious he has never been to this house. He takes out a slip of paper from a ladies' wallet and checks the address. He nervously looks around to make sure no one has seen him. He is about to ring the bell when the METER MAN from the gas company suddenly appears behind him. He is wearing a cap and carrying a tool bag. Startled—KIRK does not ring the bell. He just fakes it. He is now waiting for someone to open the door. METER MAN, after a few seconds, makes gesture to ring the bell)

KIRK *(stopping him)*: I've got the key. *(He takes the key out of the same wallet and opens the door. KIRK lets the METER MAN walk in first. An embarrassed silence. The METER MAN waits for KIRK to lead the way. Before he can say a word, KIRK stabs him in the back. KIRK catches the body to avoid any noise. He carefully drags the body behind the screen. KIRK comes out from behind the screen wearing the dead man's cap. He puts the knife into the toolbag. He goes to the door which leads into the living room. He listens to DIANA's conversation for a few seconds. KIRK emerges from the hall. There is a moment. Then DIANA notices him. She is surprised, but at the same time thoroughly intrigued by his physical appearance)*

KIRK: Gas company.

DIANA *(surprised):* How did you get in?

KIRK: The door was open.

DIANA *(after a reflection):* The kitchen is over there. *(She indicates the door.* KIRK *disappears into the kitchen. Continuing the phone conversation)* Yes, darling. *(She is more detached. She is trying to conceal her feelings)* What were you saying, darling? Why do I sound different? Because I'm no longer alone. . . . The Man from the gas company is here. . . . Just now . . . How did he get in? . . . *(With some doubt in her voice)* I must have left the door open. . . . You're right. . . . I know, my darling. . . . It won't happen again. . . . I called them this morning and. . . . The door? . . . Maybe, I don't remember. . . . Just now. . . . You know how slow they are. . . . Yes, my love. . . . He's in the kitchen. . . . *(*KIRK *comes out of the kitchen and goes into the bedroom.* DIANA *does not notice it)* Don't worry, he's old and ugly. . . . I swear it. . . . Thank you, darling. . . . That's a beautiful compliment. . . . I'm respectably dressed, yes. . . . I'll tell him to remove his glasses. Only short-sighted men are allowed here. . . . Yes, love. . . . And thank you for being jealous. . . . I mean it. . . . I believe you. . . . My jealous tender lover. . . . Yes. . . . Promise. . . . Cross my heart. . . . I'll call you tomorrow morning, the moment he leaves. . . . I kiss you, my love. . . . *(Tenderly)* Me too. . . . Me too. . . . *(She hangs up and quickly goes toward the kitchen door.* KIRK *comes out of the bedroom)*

DIANA *(surprised):* What are you doing? *(With humor)* Exploring the bedroom?

KIRK: Looking for the meter.

DIANA: There?

KIRK: Mine's in the bathroom.

DIANA: I called about the stove! A stove is in the kitchen!

KIRK: Thanks. They didn't tell me what *your* trouble is. *(He goes back in the kitchen.* DIANA *watches him from the threshold, with suspicion)*

DIANA: . . . it's the front burner. . . . There's no flame. . . . There's a leak. . . . I can smell it. . . . You—you seem confused. . . . Why don't you use your tools?

KIRK *(from the kitchen):* It can't be fixed.

DIANA: It's brand new!

KIRK: It's beyond repair. *(He comes out of the kitchen)*

DIANA: You give up rather easily.

KIRK *(looking straight into her eyes):* Shouldn't I?

DIANA: You didn't even bother to open your bag.

KIRK: I don't need to.

DIANA: Then why carry it around? Anyone else would have made an effort.

KIRK: I don't need to. I always know what's wrong. *(A brief pause)* With people too, when I'm off duty.

DIANA *(her eyes wander to his waistline):* Where is your flashlight?

KIRK *(looking at her):* You don't need flashlights for some jobs.

DIANA: Are you new at this?

KIRK: In a way. How about you?

DIANA: . . . I'd say you're peculiar . . .

KIRK: Am I?

DIANA: No flashlight, no tools . . .

KIRK: Do you want to check? (*He gives her the bag that contains the blood-stained knife.* DIANA *hesitates*)

DIANA (*deciding not to open it*): No thanks. . . .

KIRK: A wise decision. We don't like people nosing around and making complaints.

DIANA: . . . you've put the thought into my head.

KIRK (*with a smirk*): Who would you complain to?

DIANA: The gas company, of course.

KIRK: What would you tell them? That I've forgotten my flashlight?

DIANA: I would tell them you went into my bedroom.

KIRK: Go check your jewels.

DIANA: I'm not implying that you . . .

KIRK: Check. Then you can apologize.

DIANA: I'm sorry. I apologize . . .

KIRK: Anyhow you wouldn't keep them in the bedroom . . .

DIANA: They're in a safe place.

KIRK: That's why you trust me! Because they are not there.

DIANA: You had no business going into the bedroom.

KIRK (*calm and sure of himself*): I'm drawn to bedrooms. Aren't you?

DIANA (*studying him*): You're the strangest man I've ever met . . .

KIRK: That's a compliment.

DIANA: Why?

KIRK: All women say things like that—when they're intrigued.

DIANA: Like what?

KIRK: Like—"You're the strangest man I ever met." It means they want to know more about us.

DIANA *(after studying him with curiosity)*: What's troubling you?

KIRK: Do you want to find out?

DIANA *(trying to be aloof and wise; she is nevertheless intrigued)*: No thanks . . .

KIRK: Not everyone is lucky enough to come across a case like mine.

DIANA: Did you say "case"?

KIRK: That's right. I'm worth knowing.

DIANA: You really think so?

KIRK: I know it. I never lie.

DIANA: Are you really from the gas company?

KIRK: May I sit down?

(A silence)

DIANA: . . . I'm terribly busy. . . . And it's late. . . .

KIRK: Late for what?

DIANA: This is the most hectic time of the day—

KIRK: I have something important to tell you . . .

DIANA *(with curiosity)*: Important?

KIRK: Something that could help you personally.

DIANA: Oh?

(They study each other)

KIRK: May I sit down?

DIANA *(intrigued):* All right. But I'm expecting my husband any moment.

KIRK *(sitting down):* Do you think he ought to find me here?

DIANA: It does not really matter.

KIRK: He's an understanding husband . . .

DIANA: He is.

KIRK: He wouldn't mind seeing a man sitting on his sofa? . . .

DIANA: He might be interested in meeting a type like you.

KIRK *(suspicious):* A type like me? *(Defensive)* What do you mean?

DIANA: The kind of man who *never* lies. It's unusual, you must admit. *(A silence)* Would you care for a drink?

KIRK: I don't drink.

DIANA *(sits down—facing him):* A teetotaller . . . a wild look in your eyes . . . angry with the world. . . . What's your problem?

KIRK: I have no problem.

DIANA: That's a problem too. *(Studying him)* . . . And you *never* lie. Is it really true?

KIRK *(trying to change the subject):* Are you in love with your husband?

DIANA: You wanted to discuss your life—your "case." You had something to tell me—"Something that could help me personally," you said.

KIRK: You'll find out. *(A brief pause)* In due time.

DIANA: I haven't got much time.

KIRK: We have.

DIANA: That's for me to decide.

KIRK: One can't discuss important matters in a few minutes.

DIANA: What are these "important" matters?

KIRK: *Me*—if you show enough interest—and *you*.

DIANA: Go on.

(A brief silence)

KIRK: What do you want to know?

DIANA: I give you the floor. You've made yourself comfortable. *(Indicates the sofa)* Do proceed.

KIRK: You invited me to.

DIANA: Human curiosity.

KIRK: Feminine curiosity.

DIANA: I happen to be a woman. And I'm curious, I admit. I hope I won't regret it.

KIRK: You won't.

DIANA: Who *ARE* you?

KIRK: Kirk is my name.

DIANA: Mine is—

(KIRK cuts in)

KIRK: Diana.

DIANA *(surprised and intrigued)*: How did you know? It's not on the door.
. . . *(Reflecting)* . . . You saw it in the bedroom?

KIRK: No.

DIANA *(scrutinizing him)*: Have we met before? . . .

KIRK: We never met.

DIANA: Why did you come, then?

KIRK: To do a job.

DIANA: You don't really mean it?

KIRK: I mean it.

DIANA *(looking straight into his eyes)*: You're *not* the man from the gas
company.

KIRK *(ironically)*: You're certain?

DIANA: I am.

KIRK: How can you tell?

DIANA: Feminine intuition.

KIRK *(admiring her)*: Very "feminine," I must say.

DIANA: You don't know how to repair the burner. You *don't* even look like
a repair man.

KIRK: Is that a compliment?

DIANA: In a way. *(A brief pause)* . . . Who are you, really? What's on
your mind?

KIRK: A lot of things.

DIANA: Why did you choose to impersonate a repair man?

KIRK: It—it just happened.

DIANA: Like that?

KIRK: "Like that."

DIANA: You're becoming more and more mysterious. . . . (DIANA *studies him*) But I *did* call the "gas company." So you *knew* I was waiting for the "gas man." How did you know?

KIRK: A coincidence. Life is full of coincidences.

DIANA *(humorously)*: Oh—of course—you're actually a door to door salesman!

KIRK *(sarcastically)*: Thank you!

DIANA: Or maybe it was you I talked to when I called the company. You liked my voice—they say I have an intriguing telephone voice.

KIRK: They're right.

DIANA: Thank you. . . . So you decided to come see me.

KIRK: I came to see you, it's true.

DIANA *(intrigued)*: To *see me*. And it must be true because you *never* lie.

KIRK: I am not lying.

DIANA *(after a brief pause)*: Had you ever seen me before?

KIRK: You're more attractive.

DIANA *(puzzled)*: More attractive than what? You saw a photograph?

KIRK: I did.

DIANA: When? Where?

KIRK: Last week. I found it.

DIANA: Where?

KIRK: In the street.

DIANA: You're beginning to lie.

KIRK: I'm not.

DIANA: Then, how could you . . . ? I don't go around dropping photo-
graphs of myself . . .

KIRK: Did you ever lose a wallet?

DIANA *(surprised)*: A wallet yes, but. . . . I don't think there was a picture. . . . Have you by chance . . . ?

KIRK: Look familiar? *(He gives her the wallet)* Photo. Name. Address.
Money. It's all there.

DIANA *(puzzled, opens the wallet)*: You're right! . . . And all my things.
. . . Thank you. . . . The key! That's how you entered! I didn't
leave the door open! I was sure I didn't! . . .

KIRK: I'm sorry. I was just about to ring. Then . . .

DIANA: Then?

KIRK: This idea came to me . . .

DIANA: What idea?

KIRK: Do you want the truth, all the truth, nothing but the truth?

DIANA: I certainly do.

KIRK: I'm just starting to ring the bell. The gas man appears. Behind me.
Like a ghost. I think to myself:—"He's going to spoil my chance to
talk to you alone! To see your smiling reaction, brimming over with
gratitude for my noble gesture. . . ."

DIANA: I'm grateful . . .

KIRK: So. . . . I got rid of him.

DIANA: How?

KIRK: It was easy . . . *(Vague gesture; a brief pause)*

DIANA: What do you mean?

KIRK: I gave him twenty dollars.

DIANA: How generous. . . . I'm very flattered. . . . And you—borrowed his cap and his tools . . .

KIRK: I promised to leave them here. He'll be here tomorrow morning. *(He smiles)*

DIANA: You could have rung the bell all the same, when he left.

KIRK: You're right. I apologize. . . . But. . . . I must confess. . . . There is a wild streak in me. . . . You are so beautiful. . . . I hoped to catch you . . .

DIANA: What do you mean?

KIRK: I'm optimistic by nature. . . . Maybe in the bathtub.

DIANA *(amused)*: You're a child! If I found you watching me in . . . *(Vague gesture)* I'd have you . . . shot.

KIRK: Death. Is that your price?

DIANA: You like to joke. I might have really killed you in a moment of panic. . . . You'd better know. . . . I have a gun.

KIRK: Where?

DIANA: "Never tell a stranger where your weapons are."

KIRK: Am I still a stranger?

DIANA: No, Kirk. I'm grateful. I never thought I would get the wallet back. You're a real gentleman and I . . .

KIRK: And you . . . ?

DIANA: I would like to repay you. . . . How much?

KIRK: No money.

DIANA: At least the twenty dollars you gave the "gas man."

KIRK: It was my pleasure. For the privilege of catching you.

DIANA *(smiling)*: I'm sorry I . . . disappointed you.

KIRK: You didn't. It was worth it.

DIANA: Was it? Thank you. . . . You're a wonderful liar. You give a woman a sense of . . . of existing. Of still being—

KIRK *(cuts in)*: —Beautiful.

DIANA: Thank you, Kirk. But I want to—

KIRK: There's time for that.

DIANA: But I would like to know—

KIRK: You *will* know.

DIANA: . . . How . . . how can I repay you?

KIRK: There are ways.

DIANA: What ways?

KIRK: You can guess.

(Tension; they look at each other)

DIANA: That—no.

KIRK: I like you . . . I like you the way I never liked anyone else.

DIANA: You're exaggerating. You found the wallet only a few days ago. . . . You know nothing about me.

KIRK: From the moment I saw your picture I haven't been able to think of anything else.

DIANA: You're very kind and I'm flattered.

KIRK: Do you want to know why I didn't ring? (DIANA *looks at him with curiosity*) To catch you off guard. I wanted to see you at your worst. Some women are . . . unbeautiful if they're caught at a bad time.

DIANA: I'm one of those and I'm sorry you didn't turn up early this morning . . .

KIRK: I don't believe it.

DIANA: Kirk, be sensible. You were kind to return my wallet and I'm very grateful but . . .

KIRK: I need you, Diana.

(A *pause*)

DIANA: You're very romantic and it's most touching. Thank you. You're very nice but unfortunately my husband will be here soon and . . .

KIRK: "Unfortunately"?

DIANA: —A figure of speech—and we'll tell him.

KIRK: Everything?

DIANA: Of course! That you found my wallet and were kind enough to return it. And—if you like—the story of the "gas man" . . . (KIRK *smiles; a brief silence*) What else?

KIRK: *Everything.*

DIANA: Meaning?

KIRK: It depends.

DIANA: On *what?*

KIRK: It depends.

DIANA: You'd better tell me now. He'll be here in a few minutes and—

KIRK: When a woman says—"I'm waiting for my husband"—she's usually stalling.

DIANA: You'll see. He should call in . . . *(She looks at her wrist watch)* . . . about five minutes. And he'll arrive fifteen minutes later . . .

KIRK *(sarcastic):* A good husband. Why does he call ahead?

DIANA: Because he loves me.

KIRK: Or because he has a weak heart?

(A silence; DIANA *looks at him severely)*

DIANA: His heart is perfect. And you're becoming rude.

KIRK: I merely meant that jealous husbands do this. To avoid the "shock of infidelity."

DIANA: My husband is *not* jealous. He trusts me. I'll tell him what happened. About the wallet. That you entered as the gas man, but couldn't fix the burner; *(Slightly sarcastic)* and that you're a man who can neither steal nor lie. He'll be delighted to meet such an exceptional man.

KIRK: You're lucky to have such an exceptional husband! *(Looking at her with admiration)* And *he* is lucky to have a *woman* like you!

DIANA: I'll tell him what you said. He'll be flattered.

KIRK: Are you really going to tell him everything?

DIANA: Why not?

KIRK: And that I like you?

DIANA: I don't think that's necessary.

KIRK: And that I went into the bedroom—to "feel" your presence there?

DIANA: A detail best left unsaid. Unless you really want me to . . .

KIRK: Will you also tell him that when I came in you were on the phone
. . . calling someone "love"? *(Dead silence. DIANA freezes)* Will you?
. . . What a romantic way to address someone! . . . *(Dead silence;
DIANA does not dare react)* Will you tell him? *(She jumps up. She rum-
mages in her purse)*

DIANA: You have been a gentleman up to now. Let me reimburse you
for . . . *(She pulls out a handful of bills. She realizes they are insuffi-
cient)* I'll give you a check.

KIRK: No money.

DIANA *(pleading)*: Please, my husband will be back and—

KIRK: I like you, Diana.

DIANA: No time to discuss that now. He's on his way and . . . *(Desperate)* Please go!

KIRK: I'm staying.

(A silence)

DIANA: What are you going to tell him?

KIRK: That depends on you.

DIANA: Come back tomorrow. We'll talk about it. I—

KIRK: It's now or never.

DIANA: With my husband coming? You must be crazy.

KIRK *(tense)*: Don't ever say that!

DIANA *(surprised)*: Why?

KIRK: Because I don't like it.

DIANA: I'm sorry. Come tomorrow, around three o'clock. *(Tries to show him door)*

KIRK: I'm staying. *(A silence)* I take my chances in life. I was born lucky. I bet he won't come home tonight.

DIANA: I wouldn't bet on that if I were you. He is punctuality personified. *(She is beginning to worry as she waits for the telephone to ring)*

KIRK *(sarcastic)*: Is he?

DIANA: In seven years he hasn't been late once.

KIRK: We'll see. I trust my luck . . .

DIANA *(she is very nervous)*: Suppose your luck runs out. . . . What will you tell him?

KIRK: I'll be very kind. But let's suppose I'm lucky—as I've always been —could we "talk" tonight instead of tomorrow?

DIANA *(very nervous)*: Of course. . . . Why not? I'm always willing to talk to a reasonable person . . . *(Pleading)* What do you want from me?

KIRK: I want somebody like you to call me "love."

DIANA: Even if she doesn't mean it?

KIRK: I don't expect "burning passion" the first time. Women—like good wine—improve with time. . . . When you said "love" with that melting voice on the telephone—God, I envied him . . .

DIANA (*trying to find a way out*): She just happens to be a friend of mine . . .

KIRK (*ironical*): "She"?

DIANA: Yes. . . . She was my roommate at college. . . . We called each other "love" just to be silly . . .

KIRK: Then why don't you want me to tell your husband?

DIANA: He dislikes her. . . . He'd be furious if he found out I still talk to her . . .

KIRK: Fascinating! . . . How intimate are you?

DIANA: We're just friends.

KIRK: I understand. . . . What do they call such "friends"? Husbands are jealous of men. Not lesbians. You know why?

DIANA (*ironical*): No—do tell me.

KIRK: The Latins have a proverb:—"A kiss does not . . . penetrate . . ."

DIANA: A vulgar proverb. I always thought Latins were so romantic.

KIRK: . . . Meaning: Husbands are not jealous of lesbian love because—

DIANA (*interrupting*): Spare me the details. I only mentioned my roommate who—

KIRK: . . . who happens to have an astonishingly masculine voice.

(DIANA *stares at him*)

KIRK (*indicating the bedroom, imitating another voice*): "I'll call you tomorrow morning, *the moment he goes* out, love. . . . I kiss you, my love. . . ." And he returned your kiss. Those extensions can be very accommodating . . .

DIANA *(furious):* You didn't?!?

KIRK: I *did.* It was so romantic. I envied him. Now—I'd like him to envy me. Will you tell him, when we . . . ?

DIANA *(tense):* When we—*what?!* *(She looks at the telephone again)*

KIRK: You know.

DIANA *(very upset, pleading):* Kirk, please! Will you . . . ?

KIRK *(gets up, playing the gentleman):* What can I do for you Diana? Anything you desire.

DIANA: Please . . .

KIRK: Yes, Diana. I'm at your command.

DIANA: Please go.

KIRK *(indicating the telephone):* First—let's see if he does come home. I'm curious to see if my luck holds out.

DIANA *(relieved and optimistic):* Very well. *(She goes toward the telephone)* And then, please, will you promise to go?

(They study each other)

KIRK: You're a courageous woman.

DIANA: Why do you say that?

KIRK: Three men in your life and . . . in full control.

DIANA: Three?

KIRK: I'm here. I don't like being ignored.

(The telephone rings. DIANA, relieved, rushes to the telephone)

DIANA: You see! He's always—

KIRK: Just a moment! Don't touch that phone! *(He quickly goes into the bedroom and appears in the doorway holding the extension phone. While the telephone continues to ring)* If you tell him one word about me, I'll kill you! *(He takes out a revolver and points it at her)* Now! Pick it up.

(DIANA slowly lifts the receiver. At the same time KIRK slowly lifts the receiver of his telephone. He listens in and begins smiling. He feels victorious)

DIANA: Yes, darling, yes. . . . Yes, Warren. . . . *(Disappointed)* Oh no!. . . . Of all times! . . . I was so sure you would. . . . But. . . . How long will you be? . . . Why? What happened? . . . Can't they? . . . I was sure. . . . I had made plans. . . . How am I feeling? *(She looks at KIRK who threatens her with the revolver)* Fine. Nothing is wrong, no. . . . I don't like being alone, that's all. . . . What time will you be here? . . . *(Disappointment in her face)* But. . . . Can't you really? . . . Then, as soon as possible! Please! . . . Please! . . . Yes. . . . I'll lock all the doors. Yes. . . . But please come home as soon as possible! I'll be up waiting . . . *(DIANA hangs up—very discouraged)*

KIRK: I told you I was born lucky. . . . And you're lucky too. This is your chance to be alone with me and . . . to "talk."

DIANA: With a gun pointed at me? A charming way to converse.

KIRK: I'm sorry. I didn't want you to spoil our beautiful evening. *(He puts the revolver on the coffee table)*

DIANA *(sarcastic):* "Our" evening! *(Desperate)* What do you want to discuss?

KIRK *(sarcastic):* The phone call.

DIANA: You just heard!

KIRK: The *other* call—the tender one.

(A pause)

DIANA: All right—so someone called me and put on an amorous show! Is that a crime?

KIRK: No crime in being amorous. It makes life worth living.

DIANA: Anyway, you have no proof! Did you tape it? (*A brief pause; no answer*) It's my word against yours!

KIRK: If you're kind to me. . . . I won't have to use it.

DIANA: There's nothing to use! I was stupid to let you make an issue of it. As a matter of fact, it was my brother!

KIRK: Come on, Diana. . . . Do you think I'm that naive? Brothers don't talk like that. Besides, why don't you want your husband to know?

DIANA: My husband doesn't approve of him.

KIRK (*ironical*): Really? Why?

DIANA: I don't discuss my family.

KIRK (*tongue-in-cheek*): I like you. I want to know everything about you.

DIANA: My brother is a lazy scoundrel. He likes to blackmail poor defenseless women.

KIRK (*indicating himself*): Interesting coincidence!

DIANA: Since my husband is a. . . . Police Inspector, he is naturally ashamed of him!

KIRK: Your husband's a . . . ?

DIANA: Yes! A *Police Inspector!*

KIRK (*laughing*): What imagination women have!

DIANA: He *is!* You heard. He's detained because they're looking for some criminal.

KIRK *(sarcastic, laughing):* Your husband—a cop!

DIANA: Yes! And you'd better get going before it's too late!

KIRK *(sizing up the room):* This isn't a cop's house. That much I know . . .

DIANA *(interested):* What do you know?!

KIRK: Plenty. . . . Would a cop have a picture like that in his house? *(He goes over and looks admiringly at a Modigliani nude).* . . . More likely you'd see a picture of some saint. Or his grandparents surrounded by dozens of children. . . . Do you like children?

DIANA: I do.

KIRK: So he can't give you any.

DIANA: That's none of your business.

KIRK: He can't.

DIANA: It never happened. That's all.

KIRK: I bet he's lousy in bed.

DIANA: That's none of your business. *(She is looking at the revolver. She is waiting for the right moment to snatch it)*

KIRK: Tell me he is. It will make me feel good. *(Ironical; quoting)* "A woman's needs should be fulfilled through the man she lives with." Does he "fulfill" your needs? I'd like to be that man . . . *(A silence; he studies her)* How do you feel about "your men"? Are they both lousy? I'm sure the other guy is O.K. Why didn't he give you a child?

DIANA *(with defiance):* One can be great in bed without . . . "consequences" . . .

KIRK: So your lover is all right. All the more of a challenge for me!

DIANA: Not a chance—consequently no challenge! *(Calming down)* If you're a gentleman, you will please . . .

KIRK: Even a gentleman can be in love. I love you, Diana.

DIANA: Now you're using "that" word. Don't be ridiculous. How can you . . . ? "Love" is something you shouldn't be flip about.

KIRK: What's the difference? Suppose it's only physical attraction. For me that's "love." I need you. I really do, Diana.

DIANA: Love! Attraction! Need! No matter how you justify it, you can't convince me!

KIRK: Don't you know you're in my hands? And you'll be—

DIANA *(cuts in, sarcastic):* You're getting funnier by the minute!

KIRK: I'm happy to hear that.

DIANA: Even television is funnier. . . . *(DIANA turns on the television set)*

KIRK *(gets up and turns it off):* No television.

DIANA: Why? This is *my* house and I . . .

KIRK: Not tonight!

DIANA: I can't believe it! Is this really happening to me? *(To KIRK, aggressive)* Look! I turn on the news every night! If you don't mind—*(She turns the radio on)*

KIRK *(turns the radio off):* Not tonight.

DIANA *(furious):* How dare you! You can't push me around!

KIRK: Sorry, Diana. . . . Not tonight . . . we've more interesting things to do! *(DIANA gets closer to the revolver)* I've never had a woman like you, Diana. Never . . .

DIANA (*slowly, as she gets closer to the revolver*): Maybe some day you'll meet one—

KIRK: I've met her.

DIANA: Be reasonable. . . . You can't live on fantasies . . .

KIRK: I'll stay here until fantasy becomes reality.

DIANA (*grabs the revolver and threatens him*): You'll go now! Now . . . (*A silence;* KIRK *is very calm*) Take your things and go! . . . (KIRK *does not move*) Go, please, if your life means anything to you . . .

KIRK (*calmly*): It does. It's the only one I have—

DIANA (*who is on the verge of hysteria*): Then, go, go!

KIRK: I'm not leaving.

DIANA (*surprised*): I'll kill you. . . . I will! I will! . . .

KIRK: Let's make a deal.

DIANA (*screaming hysterically*): NO DEAL! Just get out!

KIRK (*very sure of himself*): What's gotten into you, Diana? You *were* so attractive before! (*Starts toward her*)

DIANA: Don't move!

KIRK: Women should not have guns. They lose their femininity . . .

DIANA: I'll kill you! I swear I will!

KIRK (*standing up*): Let's make a deal. (*Starts toward her again*)

DIANA: Don't move! I'll shoot if you take one more step.

KIRK: . . . If you hand over the gun—I promise to be very affectionate . . . very . . . loving . . .

DIANA (*very nervous*): You're really crazy.

KIRK (*freezes*): I don't like that word.

DIANA: You are! You are! (KIRK *advances slowly toward her*) No, no. . . .
Don't come near me! . . . I don't want to kill you. . . . I don't.
. . . Please. . . . Don't force me to. . . . Please! . . . (KIRK *stops
and lights a cigarette*) I beg you! For my sake—stay away from
me. . . . (*Astonished*) You're not afraid?

KIRK (*after taking a long draw from his cigarette*): I'm in love. . . . A
man in love is never afraid. (*He advances toward* DIANA)

DIANA: Stop. . . . I beg you! I implore you! . . . I don't want to. . . .
(DIANA *has not the will or the courage to shoot.* KIRK *takes the revolver
from her hand*)

KIRK (*after a silence, he aims at her and pulls the trigger three times*): It is
not loaded, Diana. . . .

DIANA (*accusingly*): And you knew it all the time.

KIRK: Naturally! . . . A man in love doesn't want to die. . . . He needs
his body.

(DIANA, *discouraged, sits down. She is exhausted, destroyed*)

KIRK: You're lucky, Diana. . . . If you had pulled the trigger I would
have killed you. . . . (*Leaves the revolver near her; a silence; he looks
at her with compassion; he wants to console her*) I'm glad you didn't,
Diana. . . . It means you're a sensitive human being, it means you're
not revolted by me. . . . That's the beginning of love. . . . A good
beginning for us. . . . I don't want to resort to blackmail—I've already forgotten the man you call "love"—I don't want to force myself
physically. . . . I couldn't stand being rejected. I want to be loved.
. . . I need to be loved. . . . If you give me this chance I'll never
bother you again . . . (DIANA *raises her eyes and looks at him with
some hope*) I promise you. . . . No one will ever know. . . . No
one. . . . (*After some hesitation, confessing*) I wouldn't admit this to
anyone else. . . . I. . . . haven't made love for more than two
years . . .

DIANA (*surprised*): Why? Where have you been?

KIRK (*vague*): . . . It was partly my choice. . . . I hate being rejected . . .

DIANA: But— (*a brief pause*) you're handsome . . . young . . .

KIRK: Thank you, Diana. Can I assume then, that you—? . . . Do you mean it?

DIANA: I mean it.

KIRK (*encouraged*): I promise I'll never bother you again if you . . . if you—

DIANA: Be reasonable, Kirk!

KIRK (*interrupting again*): I can't! Even if you reject me, I'll keep trying. . . . I must. . . . I desire you too much . . . (*He paces nervously*) I'm determined, Diana—even if I have to use force. . . . It could be dangerous for you. . . . I might . . . kill you. . . . The women murdered while being raped—they'd be alive today if they had . . . don't force me to use violence. . . . Don't frighten me into killing you. . . . They should make a movie about this, about the value of life. . . .

DIANA (*sarcastic*): How useful!

KIRK: A movie like that could save thousands.

DIANA: It wouldn't be very popular in certain countries.

KIRK: Why?

DIANA: Some prefer martyrdom to . . . "love." (*She smiles faintly*)

KIRK: I like the way you smile, Diana. Are you a Catholic?

DIANA (*warm, serious*): Kirk. . . . I like you as a human being. . . . But can't you understand? I don't love you, I can't . . .

KIRK: No one can until they get to know each other. . . . I'll make you happy, Diana.

DIANA *(looks straight into his eyes; a long silence; she has a new plan)*: Should I run a warm bath?

*(*KIRK *is surprised at her sudden acceptance; maybe he is hurt too; he reflects)*

KIRK *(after a silence, with humor)*: I suppose it's as good a way to start as any . . . "When in Rome, do as the Romans do" . . . *(He accepts* DIANA's *suggestion and gestures her to proceed.* DIANA *goes into the bedroom. From the bathroom we hear the water running. When* KIRK *hears the water, he quickly moves the Modigliani painting. There is a safe hidden behind it. He is relieved to know it is there. He then moves swiftly to a drawer. He pulls out* DIANA's *revolver.* He checks to see whether it is loaded. He puts it back.* DIANA *comes back. She hands him a bathrobe)*

KIRK: Thank you, Diana. *(*KIRK *goes into the bedroom.* DIANA *goes to the drawer and takes her revolver. She looks at it with reluctance. She moves toward the bedroom.* KIRK *emerges—naked from the waist up—in the doorway)* I was just thinking. Why don't you. . . . ? *(He freezes, motionless)*

DIANA *(after a painful silence)*: I'm sorry. . . . I'm really sorry. . . . I'm forced to. *(She pulls the trigger one, two, three times. It clicks. The revolver is unloaded.* KIRK *looks at her with sadistic defiance)*

BLACKOUT.

*The second revolver must be very *different* from the first one.

Scene Two

The same. Two hours later. We see KIRK *coming out of the bedroom and walking quietly to the hall. He is carrying a blue blanket. He opens the armoire to see whether there is space. He goes behind the screen and wraps the body of the* METER MAN *in the blanket. He drags the corpse which is hidden under the blanket and puts it in the armoire.* DIANA *appears in the doorway. She is wearing a smart-looking wrapper which is both subtle and revealing. She seems calmer. She is holding a small transistor radio to her ear. There is a sudden change. Apparently she has just heard something on the radio that frightens her. It is obvious that she is quite upset by this. She quickly tries to hide the radio but* KIRK—*entering from the hall—sees her. He freezes.*

KIRK *(trying to be casual):* I didn't know you had one of those . . .

DIANA: I keep it on my night table . . .

(A silence)

KIRK: You should have told me . . .

DIANA: I'm sorry. . . . I didn't think you would mind . . .

KIRK: I told you before. I don't like my woman listening to the radio, when she is with me.

DIANA: I'm sorry. . . .

(A brief pause)

KIRK: Did I bore you?

DIANA *(she does not want to commit herself):* Oh no. . . . But I listen to the news every night. . . . Forgive me . . .

*(*KIRK *puts out his hand. She hands him the radio)*

KIRK: What station was that?

DIANA: WINS.

KIRK: The same news every five minutes. . . . *(A brief pause)* . . . Anything . . . "unusual"?

DIANA: Not really . . . negotiations, promises . . . talk . . .

KIRK: Any *local* news?

DIANA: Nothing special . . .

KIRK: Any more girls raped and murdered?

DIANA: No . . .

KIRK: Think, Diana. You could have made the headlines. . . . You might be dead now . . . you should be grateful . . .

DIANA: I am . . .

KIRK: It was wiser to give in rather than die.

DIANA: Yes . . .

KIRK: Here you are—"alive" . . . even more beautiful than before. . . . I like you more and more. . . . Thank you, Diana. . . . You've made me very happy. . . . Are *you* happy?

DIANA *(in haste):* I am!

KIRK: Why?

DIANA: Because I'm alive—as you said . . . because . . . *(She indicates him)*

KIRK: *Because?*

DIANA: You should know.

KIRK: Tell me.

DIANA: Because you . . . you made love to me.

KIRK *(with determination):* We made love!

DIANA: That's what I meant . . . *(She looks at her wrist watch)*

KIRK: You're in a hurry?

DIANA: Oh no! . . . No . . .

KIRK: Your future is before you now. . . . Just think. Years and years of love. . . . And I decided that you should be allowed to live. . . . It's thanks to me, that you're alive. . . . Aren't you grateful?

DIANA *(nervously)*: I am, Kirk, I am! *(She is very nervous as she sees* KIRK *put the transistor radio on the coffee-table)*

KIRK: The power of the individual is unlimited. . . . He can extinguish anyone if he so desires. . . . He can also pardon anyone. . . . I've pardoned you because I like you. . . . It's a terrifying thought in a way. . . . You're here now, beautiful and desirable, radiantly alive. . . . You could have been dead these last two hours. . . . Rigid and cold. . . . I can see you—all life gone—gone forever. . . . I often see myself. . . . I see my coffin, my funeral. Here today. Gone to-morrow—gone forever. . . . It's frightening. I shudder at the thought. . . . When you think of how it can happen. . . . In the street. . . . In a car. . . . In a bank—if you accidentally surprise an insecure burglar trying to escape. . . . People who kill don't really start out with that intention—they kill out of fear. . . . Someone sneaks up from behind when you least expect it and ruins your plans. . . . Poor bastard—he probably could have become a friend—even a close friend—The poor guy, there's no alternative but to kill him . . . and the girls who get murdered—screaming and howling. Why? Is it so unbearable?

DIANA: No, Kirk, no!

KIRK: They should be warned! They should be told! I don't want to murder anyone! I don't. . . . I have no desire to go around harming girls . . .

DIANA: You've done this before?

KIRK: Done what?

DIANA: Taken girls by force?

KIRK *(indignant)*: By *force*? Did I take you by force?

DIANA: Oh no! I didn't mean—

KIRK: You wanted it as much as I did. And you liked it. *(Waits)* Didn't you?

DIANA: I did. You know that . . .

KIRK *(after a brief pause)*: Then why did you ask about other girls?

DIANA: I was just curious. Feminine curiosity . . .

KIRK *(looking at the radio)*: What did you hear over the radio?

DIANA: Nothing! Why?

(KIRK *slowly walks behind her and begins to caress her neck.* DIANA *is terrified)*

KIRK *(while caressing her neck)*: I love you, Diana. . . . I really do. . . . Your skin is so smooth. . . . Your neck is so warm, so alive . . . so inviting . . .

(DIANA *can no longer control herself. She jumps up)*

KIRK *(taken aback, suspicious)*: What's the matter, Diana? Don't you like me anymore?

DIANA: I do! I do! . . . But I'm tired. Try to understand. . . . My nerves are on edge. . . . It's—well . . . everything happened so suddenly . . .

KIRK: But you liked it. You were cooing like a dove.

DIANA: That part was fine, I told you. I'm normal and you're a virile young man, but . . .

KIRK: But?

DIANA: Try to understand, Kirk. I don't really know you . . .

KIRK *(with a sarcastic smile)*: You don't?

DIANA: . . . that's only one side of you. And I do like you, but . . .

KIRK: But what? Is there anything else to know?

DIANA: Let's be honest—. . . . I don't know anything about you.

KIRK: I can tell you the story of my life, if you like.

DIANA: No, not now. It's been a trying day for me—for both of us. *(There is a silence:* DIANA *is plagued with fear again as* KIRK *studies her)* Maybe tomorrow.

KIRK: You want to see me again tomorrow?

DIANA: . . . If you still want me.

KIRK: And the day after tomorrow?

DIANA: Yes. . . . Whatever you wish.

KIRK: That's a good girl . . . *(He studies her)* Provided you mean it. . . . Do you?

DIANA: Of course. Whenever you wish.

KIRK: Do you want me to go now?

DIANA: Yes. I mean . . . whenever you want.

KIRK: You seem frightened, Diana. Of me?

DIANA: No!

KIRK: Be honest, Diana.

DIANA: I told you. I like you. It's just that . . . *(She hesitates; humorously)* I've been too . . . reckless. Curious females shouldn't sleep with strangers. They could be . . . sadists.

KIRK: Don't worry, my love. I'd never hurt you, never! You have proof of that.

DIANA: Proof?

KIRK: You pulled the trigger on me. I forgave you because I love you.

DIANA: I know and I'm glad. You understood how . . . how terrified I was.

KIRK: Terrified of *heaven*? (*He goes to her and tries to put his arm around her; she avoids him carefully; she is terrorized*) How can women be so stupid! . . . Afraid of heaven . . . (*He studies her*) It *was* heaven— wasn't it?

DIANA: Yes, yes . . . (*She tries to keep him at a distance*)

KIRK (*puzzled*): . . . What's wrong? You were so loving when. . . . You made me feel "loved." I felt you meant it, with all your body. . . . What's happened "after"? (*Her eye absently falls upon the radio for an instant;* KIRK *catches her eye*) You want to hear the radio?

DIANA: No . . .

KIRK: Should I turn it on? (*No answer*) Maybe we should . . .

DIANA: It's up to you. . . . Whatever you want.

KIRK: That's an obedient woman. I can see why your husband doesn't want to lose you. You're kind and obliging. . . . (*He is playing with the radio*) Let's suppose we hear something wild. . . . That I am a dangerous criminal who escaped from a nearby prison. Would you believe it?

DIANA: No! . . . No . . .

KIRK: Be honest.—I want my woman to be honest.

DIANA: . . . If they said it. . . . I suppose it would mean it's true.

KIRK: That I am a dangerous criminal?

DIANA: No. . . . But that you escaped, that could be true . . .

KIRK: And that would frighten you even more. Right?

DIANA (*hesitant*): I suppose so . . . (*A pause*) But I'm not afraid, Kirk, I know you're gentle and human. I believe you.

KIRK (*after a silence*): Why did you change then?

DIANA: I haven't changed. It's—I've told you! For a woman, making love is important . . .

KIRK: I'm encouraged to hear it was *important* for you.

DIANA: That's why I seem nervous. . . . I discovered a new side to myself.

KIRK: Are you sorry?

DIANA: No. . . . But in a way it's a physical shock.

KIRK: You liked it. You were shaking like a . . . like a virgin. I like thinking of you as a virgin. I read somewhere that when a woman loves a new man she is reborn—new. Do you love your husband?

(*A pause*)

DIANA: He's a good man and he's my husband.

KIRK: What about the other one, (*Sarcastic*) your "love"?

DIANA: An infatuation . . .

KIRK: Do you love him?

DIANA: I suppose so.

KIRK: More than your husband?

DIANA: It's different . . .

KIRK: More than me?

DIANA (*with difficulty*): I've known him longer . . .

KIRK: Is he better than me?

DIANA: No. . . . But I've known him a long time.

KIRK: How long?

DIANA: Six months.

KIRK: Will you see him again?

DIANA: No . . .

KIRK: Is it because of me?

DIANA: Anything you want. But please . . .

KIRK: Please what?

DIANA: I am tired . . .

KIRK: Come over here. *(He indicates his lap)*

DIANA: In a moment . . . *(She is nervous and tries to stall)* Would you care for a drink?

KIRK: Make mine a bourbon. *(Starts toward bar)* To celebrate.

DIANA: Oh dear! We're out! *(With hope)* Why don't I run out and get us a bottle? . . . *(A silence)* Or *you* can go. . . .

KIRK: You're trying to get rid of me.

DIANA: You asked for bourbon!

KIRK: Let's skip the whole thing! I don't really want it. Come here. Sit down. (DIANA *hesitates*) You're very sexy. I'm ready again . . .

DIANA: Please . . . You're stronger than you realize.

KIRK *(with pride)*: I'll be very gentle this time. I love you. . . . *(He gets up and goes toward her. She tries to avoid him. Puzzled)* You're afraid of me . . .

DIANA: Was I afraid before?

KIRK: No. . . . Just shy, adorably shy. But now . . .

DIANA: I'm tired now. . . . Tomorrow. Any other time. . . . Not today, I beg you.

KIRK *(after studying her)*: You've been listening to the radio!

DIANA *(feebly)*: I haven't . . .

KIRK: You *have!*

DIANA *(feebly)*: It's not true . . .

KIRK *(threatening to smash the radio. Going toward her)*: You listened! *(He grabs her)*

DIANA *(screaming with terror)*: No! Don't!

KIRK *(bitterly)*: "Don't!"—she says. Women! You can touch them all you want. The more the better. Then they turn on the radio. They're told there's a maniac around and they believe it! Do you? . . . (DIANA *tries to avoid him*) I haven't changed since you kissed me. Was I a maniac in bed? . . . Maybe I was. I don't know. That kind of madness is accepted. It's *normal.* Look at me, Diana. Do I look crazy to you? . . . (DIANA *does not find the strength to contradict him*) Maybe I do now because I'm angry. . . . Sit down! *(He pummels the pillow near him)* Here, if you don't want to sit on my lap—if you're *afraid.* *(A pause)* Do you know why they locked me up? I'll tell you. (DIANA *sits down, at some distance from* KIRK) . . . The first time was at college. I accused my History Professor of lying. They said I screamed too much—that I even tried to kill him—it's my personality. I just get excited when I know I'm right. After two months they had to release me. The psychiatrist happened to think the way I do about politics. The second time was in Vietnam. They were torturing this prisoner— blood all over—it was the end for him. I couldn't take it. I killed him. They said I was crazy. A prisoner of war cannot be killed. Torture, yes —kill, no! I got one year. I was pardoned when the war was over. . . . I came back, I was lonely and depressed . . . in need of love. I'm very normal, I like women. Grown up women—mature and beautiful like you. I'm normal—I need love. . . . I hadn't had a woman for a long time—I was afraid of those Asian women with their filthy diseases. When I got back I looked for a clean, healthy female. Someone like you. One day, I came across one. . . . I smile timidly, she smiles back. We begin talking, we go for a walk in the country. . . . I get excited—You saw me, I get all excited and nervous. Maybe I frightened her. Did I frighten you?

DIANA: No . . .

KIRK: That stupid bitch began screaming as if I was going to kill her—I wasn't. You know, Diana. You know how I behave. I'm just excitable. But I don't lose my head. I was just overanxious, trying to make her happy. . . . The way she screamed—I should have killed her. . . . A cop arrives—he hits me with all his strength! Here! . . . (*He touches the top of his head*) They accused me of attempted rape. I was in again—for "mental observation." This time in the "hospital". . . . (*He indicates the radio*) Did they mention my name?

DIANA (*after a silence*): Kirk Stiller.

KIRK: What else did they say?

DIANA: . . . they said the chances of finding you were good.

KIRK: Naturally. Anything else? Did they say I was dangerous?

DIANA: They always say that.

KIRK: Do you believe them?

DIANA: No. I believe you and I'll help you . . .

KIRK (*he studies her*): What else did they say?

DIANA: That's all I heard.

KIRK: Did they mention a doctor?

DIANA: They only said that . . . some doctor (*Carefully studying him*)—a Doctor O'Brien is in charge of the search . . . (*She studies his reaction*)

KIRK: That snake. . . . I hate him. *He's* the sick one in that place.

(They look at each other with curiosity)

DIANA: Why?

KIRK: He's the most sadistic one. He tortures everyone.

DIANA: How?

KIRK: Morbid questions. Prying into our subconscious . . .

DIANA: What kind of questions?

KIRK: Mostly sexual. Perversion! That's his specialty! Is he sick! How I hate him!

DIANA: If it's just questions. . . . They all do that—it's their work.

KIRK: Not the kind he asks. He enjoys torturing. If there's a man I'd like to kill, he's the one.

(DIANA *is all attention; she is very interested in this subject*)

DIANA: I don't understand. Were his questions different from the questions you had before—in other hospitals?

KIRK: You better believe it!

(A pause)

DIANA: Are you accusing him of being unprofessional?—Unethical?

KIRK: He's just plain sick, I assure you! He hasn't helped anyone. His morbid needling makes them more insecure than they were before.

DIANA: Did you complain to anyone?

KIRK: Of course not! If you complain that's the end. Only if you keep your mouth shut you have a chance to get out.

DIANA: Then why did you escape instead of—?

KIRK: I couldn't take it. I would have killed him.

DIANA *(after a brief pause):* I don't understand . . . how a doctor can
do this to his patients. Physical torture too?

KIRK: Humiliation—first of all . . .

DIANA: How do you mean?

KIRK: For instance. He is the only doctor who ever demanded an inspection of . . . the genitals. Then questions on alleged homosexual activity. He doesn't let up until you finally admit you had. Of course, it
wasn't true. I hate him for that.

DIANA: In other words—you had to lie.

KIRK: It was my only chance to get out—Then of course we were given
the usual routine. No matter what I dreamt about—it all ended up
with me making love to my mother, my father, my sister. Or all of
them together. They can really drive you crazy—they put things into
your head that can really make you—*(Gesture indicating madness)*
But what the hell—I didn't care. I was used to it. *(With hatred)* Until
he began his "personal" inquiry . . .

DIANA: What do you mean by "personal"?

KIRK: Very intimate. He wanted to "learn."

DIANA: I don't understand . . .

KIRK: He must have quite a complex.

DIANA: A complex?

KIRK: Being inadequate with his wife. He tried to find out from us.

DIANA: Find what out?

KIRK: Details . . .

DIANA *(with curiosity)*: Tell me, Kirk . . .

KIRK: You know—questions young boys ask. How? When? How many times? What's the best position? Kid stuff. Over and over again. Obsessive. With that morbid look on his face. I hate him! I would have killed him if I'd been there another day.

DIANA: The same questions to all the . . . patients?

KIRK: Yes. We talked to each other. They all admitted they'd been through the same thing. Inspection, curiosity about homosexual stories, the mother bit, the wife bit. . . . The same for all of us.

DIANA: Maybe it helps the patient—

KIRK: Maybe it helps *him!*

DIANA: But he does release a few.

KIRK: Only the guys who told him what he wanted to hear.

DIANA: They all lie then—?

KIRK: Yes.

DIANA: I'm truly sorry. . . . What a devastating experience it must have been. I never thought. . . . That man sounds dangerous to me.

KIRK: *He's* the one who's dangerous.

DIANA: And none of you ever tried to rebel?

KIRK: To them a show of anger is pure insanity. You have to suffer inside and button your lip—just to prove you're normal. What's being "normal"? Not to rebel, being silent, complying—the stillness of death? Away from that place you can be yourself—in bed with you or in the streets like other people—There—you cannot be yourself. You must pretend all the time that you're "perfection." That nothing bothers you. Not even the dirty eye of a sick man in your ass!

DIANA: What will he do—if he finds you?

KIRK: Are you thinking of "delivering" me to the executioner?

DIANA: I want to help you, Kirk. You know why.

KIRK: Why?

DIANA: Because I like you. . . . You're my man now.

KIRK: And your husband? And your great "lover"?

DIANA: You are in my blood now. You'll always be. *(Correcting herself)* For as long as *you* want.

KIRK: I had a dream once. That I would have the love of one woman . . . forever.

DIANA: I want to help you. That's why I'm asking these questions. What would they do—if they caught you?

KIRK *(shrugs)*: I'd kill myself first.

DIANA: Would they turn you over to him?

KIRK: He's in charge there. He'd never forgive me for causing so much trouble. He would torture me to death. I can see his eyes—that degenerate bastard.

DIANA *(after reflection)*: Suppose he were to appear at the door—now?

KIRK: Here? Why *that* door?

DIANA: He is looking for you, isn't he?

KIRK: Why would he come to *this* house?

DIANA: I imagine he's searching every house. They said on the radio that he wants to find you personally because he's the only man who can "handle" you. *(A silence)* You'd kill him. . . . *(He nods)* You have a good reason to. What would you do with the body?

KIRK *(studying her)*: The body?

DIANA: We couldn't just pretend it isn't there. . . . If you left it here, I would have to call the police. That would be the end of us.

KIRK *(reflecting)*: You . . . really like me?

DIANA: I told you. A woman doesn't forget the things we did. I'm yours —You're part of my life now. *(Very feminine)* If you still want me.

KIRK: And you're not afraid I might really be . . . off my rocker.

DIANA: No. You've suffered enough. Now you deserve love. What would you do with the body?

KIRK *(studying her with admiration)*: What do you suggest?

DIANA: You could use my husband's car . . .

KIRK: And then?

DIANA: Anything you say.

KIRK *(studying her)*: You're a very practical woman . . .

DIANA: I'm a woman in love.

KIRK: . . . with whom?

DIANA *(very serious)*: You know, Kirk . . .

KIRK *(ironical)*: Your lover?

DIANA: You made me forget him.

KIRK: Your husband? He gave you security and comfort.

DIANA: I despise him.

KIRK *(reflecting)*: "Despise". . . . I know how you feel. . . . When you despise you want to destroy, to kill . . .

(A silence)

DIANA *(slowly):* I'd like to help.

KIRK: Help?

DIANA: Help you kill your enemy.

KIRK: Where is he? *(She shrugs)* Do you think he . . . might really come here?

DIANA: Anything is possible.

KIRK: Would he come . . . alone?

DIANA: I could arrange that. Just the two of you—

KIRK: You're a fascinating woman, Diana. You're beginning to frighten me. . . . You really want me to kill him?

DIANA: He's *your* enemy.

KIRK: And all this because . . . *(He indicates the bedroom)*

DIANA: Because I love you.

KIRK *(with a sense of humor):* Thank you, Diana. I'm getting my confidence back, thanks to you. I didn't know I was that good.

DIANA: It's not just that. I like you for yourself—as a person—as a human being who has suffered. You need someone like me now . . .

KIRK: How would you get him to come here?

DIANA *(slowly):* I must confess something, Kirk . . .

KIRK: I'd like to listen to a confession. For a change.

DIANA: My husband is not a Police Inspector . . .

KIRK: I guessed that.

DIANA: I was afraid to tell you before . . .

(A *silence*)

KIRK (*very calm*): Tell me now.

DIANA (*slowly—word by word*): My husband is . . . the one who's been torturing you. My husband is Dr. O'Brien.

(A *long silence*: KIRK *gets up slowly and looks at her—straight in the eyes*)

KIRK (*with cold calm: distinctively*): I knew it.

(DIANA *freezes, terrorized*)

DIANA: What—what do you mean?

KIRK: I knew this was his house. And that you were his wife.

DIANA (*unbelieving*): And you—

KIRK: HE SENT ME . . . (A *silence*) He sent me here. (*He pauses; she stares*). To see whether you could be faithful, for once. He helped me escape. . . . He gave me your wallet. . . . Revenge? Call it what you like . . . (*From here on the lights begin to fade*) It's a fascinating experience making love to the wife of your torturer . . .

(As *the lights dim—the curtain falls*)

END OF ACT ONE

ACT TWO

The same. Two hours later.
At *rise*, DIANA *is sitting in a chair, tied and gagged. She is alone.* DR. WARREN O'BRIEN *opens the door with his key. He slips chain into bolt and pauses at the door. He comes in cautiously. He sees* DIANA *and is rather surprised. But he does not rush to free her.* DIANA *indicates the bedroom with her head.* WARREN *opens the drawer; takes* DIANA's *revolver and loads it with bullets taken from his pocket. He goes toward the bedroom, cautiously.* KIRK *emerges from the bedroom. A tense silence.* KIRK *looks at the revolver and smiles.*)

KIRK: Hi, Doctor. (He *walks in without giving any importance to the revolver*)

WARREN (*still threatening him with the revolver*): What's going on here?

KIRK: Don't worry. Everything is O.K.

WARREN: What do you mean?

KIRK: You know what I mean. (A *silence*)

WARREN: What about my wife? Why is she—?

KIRK: She's resting.

WARREN: Why?

KIRK: You know why.

WARREN: I do not. What do you mean? (He *threatens him with the revolver*)

KIRK: Put that away. It's not loaded.

WARREN: First, tell me why . . . (He *indicates* DIANA)

KIRK: You *know* why. Don't pretend, Doctor. You always said that some patterns of disease begin with "lies." Are *you* sick?

WARREN: It's *you* they're looking for—

KIRK: We heard all about it on the radio. (He *indicates* DIANA) Diana was shocked. Why are *you*?

WARREN: Nothing shocks me! I want facts.

KIRK: First things first. Have you got the money?

WARREN: First things first. You escaped from the clinic . . .

KIRK: With your help. You're not going to deny that you're involved in this? Are you putting this on to win her back? Forget it. It's too late.

WARREN *(threatening)*: "Too late?"

KIRK: Isn't it what you wanted to hear? I'll give you all the details. But first let's see the money.

WARREN *(vague)*: If you need money, you'll get money.

KIRK *(to DIANA too)*: Like a child. Ashamed to tell the truth. You *promised* to bring the cash. Where is it?

WARREN: In the safe. (KIRK *goes to the painting and removes it)* But first tell me what happened here. *(He threatens KIRK with the revolver)*

KIRK: Stop playing with that gun. I've already made sure it's not loaded. You kept *that* promise.

WARREN: I like playing with it. It makes me feel secure. Now get on with it.

KIRK: All right. So keep your toy if it makes you feel more "masculine." Open the safe. (WARREN *is undecided. Nevertheless he wants to know from KIRK what happened)* Open it and show me the money.

WARREN: Step aside. (KIRK *does so.* WARREN *opens the safe and takes out a stack of bills. While WARREN is taking and counting the money,* DIANA *tries to tell KIRK something)*

KIRK *(to WARREN)*: Your wife seems very upset. They're all stingy, aren't they?

WARREN: Here! *(He throws the money which KIRK catches and counts)*

KIRK: It *is* true! Doctors *do* make money!

WARREN *(indicating his wife)*: Now take that thing off and let her talk.

KIRK: Not yet. She might start screaming and spoil our little deal. Where's your friend's address?

(WARREN *takes a piece of paper out of his pocket and hands it to* KIRK)

KIRK *(reading)*: All neatly typed. . . . You've thought of everything. Congratulations! . . . And where is the letter of introduction to your friend?

WARREN: I called him.

KIRK *(after reflection)*: You typed the address. . . . No letter that could compromise you. . . . You're too shrewd for my taste . . .

WARREN: A call is always more effective than a letter.

KIRK: So, what did he say?

WARREN: He's waiting for you.

KIRK: Suppose you didn't call?

WARREN: You have your choice in New York. Either you trust me and go to this address. Or you don't and use that money to buy *other* friends.

KIRK *(reflecting)*: That's fair.

WARREN: Now—tell me everything. *(He indicates* DIANA)

KIRK: First the car keys.

WARREN *(he hands them)*: Well?

KIRK: Relax! I'm running this show.

WARREN *(ironical)*: Are you? Then talk.

KIRK: You're being over-anxious, Doctor. You'll hear all about it in due time. For once, I'm going to enjoy being the cat! *(A command)* Sit down, mouse! . . .

WARREN: Take that out of her mouth first.

KIRK *(scoldingly)*: I told you. She'll start crying that she's still a virgin
and all that! I'll give you *my* story first.

WARREN *(interrupting)*: But I want to—

KIRK *(interrupting)*: Hold it! Did you allow interruptions when you were
the cat? She'll get her chance. *After* I'm through.

(They both sit down. WARREN *is still threatening* KIRK *with the revolver)*

KIRK *(indicating the revolver)*: You still need your security blanket? It
gives you confidence?

WARREN: Yes. It does.

KIRK: Maybe you should issue one to each of your patients, if they are
that effective. I must confess that you really used to frighten me. We
hated you!

WARREN: This is the last time you'll see me. Forget the past and tell me
how it went.

KIRK: Can't you guess?

WARREN: I didn't pay you so I'd have to "guess"! Tell me what you did.

KIRK: What *I* did or what *she* did?

WARREN: Everything.

KIRK *(keeping him in suspense)*: . . . I got a cab right away and came
here. . . . I ring the bell. . . . She opens the door. . . . Much
more beautiful than the picture. . . . You have a beautiful wife,
Doctor. I compliment you . . .

WARREN *(nervously)*: Go on.

KIRK: Well, she's all smiles and warmth and invites me in. . . . As if she
were waiting for her Prince Charming. . . . Just between you and me
—if I told anyone how easy it was, they'd say I'm crazy and send me
back to your clinic.

WARREN: Go on.

KIRK: She offers me a drink. She sits down and devours me with her eyes. . . . As you suspected, Doctor.

WARREN: Didn't she ask you why you had come?

KIRK: I asked her why she didn't ask. She said it didn't matter. My heart was in my mouth. I'm like a child when a girl says, "It's all right with me."

WARREN: Did she say—"It's all right with me"?

KIRK: I saw it in her eyes. I understood.

WARREN: Facts—I want facts.

KIRK: Don't worry. You'll have them. *Solid* facts. I fooled around a little with her—just to see whether she would discover the "maniac" you doctors saw in me. She didn't. She was kind and feminine. You have a terrific wife, Doctor . . .

WARREN: What did you tell her?

KIRK: Romantic lies. . . . That I dreamt of her every night. That I've been following her for months. That I'd kill myself if she rejected me. . . . She smiled. Your wife has a wonderful smile, Doctor . . .

WARREN: Go on.

KIRK: She said, smiling, "Thank you. You make me feel younger. But *unfortunately* my husband will be back soon." "Unfortunately." I knew then she was ready for it. We went on, talking and flirting— waiting for you to call. When your call came, she was relieved . . .

WARREN: Don't forget, I was at the other end of the line. She urged me to come back. Why?

KIRK (*slightly embarrassed*): She was pretending.—only *pretending* to be disappointed. You know how women are. They all lie.

WARREN: I heard everything she said. She wasn't in the least interested in you.

KIRK: Remember! I was *here*. She was smiling at me. Her eyes were full of promise.

WARREN: Go on.

KIRK: She offered to run a hot bath . . .

WARREN *(ironic)*: Aren't you getting carried away with your fantasy?

KIRK: No.

(DIANA *tries desperately to talk*)

WARREN: Let's hear her version.

KIRK: Not yet. She'd confuse you with silly justifications. You know women.

WARREN: So the moment she hung up, she said, "Let's go to bed!"

KIRK: I only mentioned a hot bath.

WARREN: Maybe you needed one! (KIRK *freezes, offended. He gets up— threateningly.* WARREN *points the revolver again)* Get back! Sit down!

KIRK: I'll break you and your toy.

WARREN: Don't try it! Toys are dangerous.

KIRK: You couldn't frighten me with a loaded machine gun!

WARREN: Sit down and get on with the story. If you want to get out of here alive—

KIRK *(smiling)*: Every detail?

WARREN: Every detail.

KIRK: It'll be a pleasure. . . . *(He sits down)* I know how you like "details." I won't deprive you. . . . *(A silence)* She told me you have to take a bath too, before. . . . *(A silence)*

WARREN: What happened after I called? Did you threaten her with the gun?

KIRK: What? That unloaded gun? *(He indicates* WARREN's *revolver)*

WARREN: She didn't know. It's usually loaded.

KIRK: All right, I'll tell you something . . . favorable about your wife's morality. . . . *She* threatened me with that revolver.

WARREN *(with curiosity)*: Why?

KIRK: Maybe I was too aggressive. Too soon—

WARREN: How did you get out of that? Did you hit her?

KIRK: I apologized. And I handed her the wallet you'd given me. With the picture *you* put in it. She was surprised about the picture, but you know women. They're so scatterbrained. She didn't suspect anything and—as a matter of fact—she was kinder, much kinder . . .

WARREN: How?

KIRK: She offered me more drinks; she began asking intimate questions . . .

WARREN: What sort of questions?

KIRK: —"Are you married?"—"Why not?"—"You look strong and able. How many women have you made happy?"—"Did you return the wallet because you're basically honest or because . . ."

WARREN: Because what?

KIRK: That's what I asked her. Her answer was: ". . . Or because you liked my picture?" She was being coquettish. So I began touching her. . . . I had my hands all over her. *(He studies* WARREN) Everywhere . . .

WARREN: And she?

KIRK: She complained a bit. Pretending I was too strong. . . . You know women. Or let's say, you know your wife . . .

WARREN: Go on.

KIRK: It was then she suggested that I take a bath. She would have joined me . . .

WARREN: Did she?

KIRK: Try to guess.

WARREN *(furious):* Enough of this guessing! Did she? *(He threatens KIRK with the revolver)* Answer!

KIRK *(teasing):* You have a luxurious bathroom. . . . Must have cost a fortune. . . . Such a large sexy tub. . . . She joined me. *(A silence)* She was shy, I must admit. . . . She was wearing her bra and panties. . . . But when she got into that water . . . you could see right through. Very exciting. . . . *(Brief pause)* However. . . . Nothing happened in the water. I wanted to make a good impression the first time. I'm square. I like beds. . . . *(Studying WARREN)* Are you all right, Doctor? . . . You look pale.

WARREN: Go on!

KIRK: I'm sorry, but. . . . you sent me here.

WARREN: Yes! To find out about the other man.

KIRK: I found out.

WARREN: What's his name?

KIRK: I didn't get to that yet.

WARREN: What did she admit?

KIRK: Plenty.

WARREN: Such as?

KIRK: You know how it goes. . . . When I sensed she was "satisfied," I let her rest and then began questioning her. "Are you happy?" "Did you like it?" "Am I only the second man in your life?" She admitted I wasn't.

WARREN: How many others?

KIRK: She didn't give me the exact number.

WARREN: What did she tell you?

KIRK: About her college years—

WARREN: I know all that. What about after our marriage? *Now?*

KIRK: She told me quite frankly . . .

WARREN: What?

KIRK: . . . With you—once a month.

WARREN *(looking at her with hatred)*: The bitch!

KIRK *(innocently)*: She lied? How many times?

WARREN: That's my business! Continue.

KIRK: . . . with the other guy—once a week.

WARREN: Since when?

KIRK: A year. But don't worry. According to her he isn't that good.

WARREN *(after a silence)*: What did she say about me?

KIRK *(slowly)*: . . . That you're a good man after all. . . . Boring, of course. . . . Too busy, of course. . . . Lousy in bed—of course.

WARREN: Bitch! Is that why she's unfaithful?

KIRK: She denied it. Women are ashamed to admit they want sex because they like sex.

WARREN: Is she in love with him?

KIRK: She implied she *was*.

WARREN: And now?

KIRK *(looking at her)*: She says no. *(Pause)* However, I don't believe her.

WARREN: Why?

KIRK: During one of the "breaks," she called him. I overheard. She still calls him "love." *(They both look at* DIANA*)* She says she calls everybody "love": brother, friends, even you. Then she said he's the same as you —not much better. . . . you're both boring, and lousy in bed. Guess who she really likes now?

WARREN *(ironically)*: You—obviously.

KIRK: Good guess. I'm the best in every department. She even proposed we run away together. She's tired of both of you.

WARREN: With women the last man is always the best. Don't flatter yourself.

KIRK: I don't. I learned long ago that all widows and divorcées *had* impotent husbands. *(He looks at* DIANA*)* But it's still flattering. She's great in bed. She really gives all of herself. She made me feel "loved." Do you feel "loved," Doctor? The first Friday of every month?

WARREN *(ignoring)*: If she'd been "happy with you," she wouldn't have called the other one immediately after your. . . . *(Gesture)* A satisfied woman doesn't.

KIRK: I agree. No satisfied woman calls her lover *after* being with me.

WARREN: Did she try to get rid of you as soon as . . . ?

KIRK: No. I never felt she wanted to get rid of me. No. She knew I could go on forever. She could tell I never get tired of making love.

WARREN *(after a pause):* Did she . . . ask for more?

KIRK *(looks at him with irony):* Don't forget who she's married to all these years. She's *your* wife. And don't forget I've been cooped up in that cell for two years. I knew I'd never see her again and. . . . When it's a one-shot deal you do your best. . . . We did everything. . . . On your rug. . . . *(Points to the rug)* the bed, that chair—*everything.*

(A silence. WARREN is hurt. He absentmindedly leaves the revolver near KIRK and goes to DIANA. As he looks at her with contempt, KIRK notices the revolver and, without thinking, picks it up and starts playing around with it. He is still unaware that it is loaded. WARREN is trembling with rage. He goes over to DIANA and stares at her. She ignores him)

WARREN *(with a maniacal look; losing all control for a few moments):* I knew it! I knew it all along! You—you never get enough! There's no limit—you can never—never get enough! You're an insatiable bitch! A dirty whoring bitch! *(Red and convulsed, he is trembling)* You're sick! Yes—sick and depraved! You're a hopeless nymphomaniac! *(Indicates the rug)* Always looking for variety! For something obscene! Dirty! A new twist! You're a rotten bitch! *(He is about to strike her, when he suddenly realizes that he must control his anger. To KIRK)* I know her— that's why—*(Shaking his head hopelessly at her "sickness")* After all these years—I know her better than I know myself . . . *(He cannot speak; he pulls himself together. He succeeds to a certain extent and recovers his "detached" manner. WARREN starts to remove DIANA's gag; she is still tied to the chair)* What have you to say in your defense? *(WARREN removes gag)* Talk!

DIANA *(after catching her breath, looking at WARREN with hatred):* In *my* defense? Aren't you embarrassed?

WARREN: I'm not. What about you?

DIANA: He told you nothing but lies. Can't you tell?

WARREN: Lies?

DIANA: That's right.

(WARREN *turns and sees* KIRK *playing with the revolver. He pretends to ignore it. He goes over to* KIRK, *waiting for the right moment to get the revolver back*)

WARREN *(to* KIRK): Now—what have you got to say?

KIRK: I know every inch of her body. That's enough for me.

WARREN: What proof have you that she . . . ?

KIRK: Please—not in front of a lady. The only thing I'll say is, she's got a perfect body. Like Venus from . . . somewhere in Greece.

DIANA: Thank you.

WARREN: That's a cliché. You can say that about all women.

DIANA *(ironically)*: Thanks! You always spoil everything!

WARREN *(to* KIRK): Did you notice anything unusual? *(He is very near* KIRK, *ready to grab the revolver from him)*

KIRK: Yeah.

WARREN: What?

KIRK: An adorable pink scar, here. . . . *(He indicates the scar with the revolver)* Appendix, I think. . . . And—I forgot something—something which fascinated me. Her left one *(He indicates her nipples)* is longer than the right one. *(Brief pause)* How come?

(WARREN *tries to grab the revolver. He does not succeed*)

KIRK: Calm yourself, Doctor. You don't need it now. You've heard everything.

DIANA: Watch the gun! It's loaded!

WARREN *(to* DIANA): Shut up! *(Threatens her)*

KIRK *(puzzled)*: Loaded? (KIRK *points the revolver at* WARREN *with delibera-tion.* WARREN *is terrorized. Then* KIRK *slowly points it at* DIANA)

DIANA *(frightened)*: Don't! It's loaded!

(KIRK *switches his target. This time to* WARREN. KIRK *fires, but intentionally misses* WARREN)

KIRK *(almost to himself)*: You can't trust anyone in this world. . . . Not even your own doctor. *(To* WARREN) You loaded it! Why?

WARREN *(trying to be calm)*: YOU KNOW WHY.

KIRK: You were going to shoot me?

WARREN: I didn't shoot you.

KIRK: . . . You were pointing it at me.

WARREN *(worried)*: You know I wouldn't. I respect agreements. . . . If you stick to yours, I'll stick to mine.

KIRK: Do you still think I'm "crazy"?

WARREN: No. Do you think I'd have chosen you if I thought you hadn't made a complete recovery?

KIRK: By the way—she never suspected—not for an instant—that I came out of *that* place. Or that I was crazy.

WARREN: You're not. Please put that gun down.

KIRK: Are you nervous, little mouse? *I'll* play with it now. . . . Let me frighten someone for a change. . . . YOU BIG SHOTS always fright-ened me. You and your lying wives. . . . (He points the revolver at DIANA) Did I lie, Lady? Or have you forgotten already?

DIANA *(calm)*: You didn't ring the bell—you know you didn't.

KIRK: What's the difference? *(To* WARREN) I uscd thc kcy you put in the wallet. So what? *(To* DIANA*)* Be careful, Lady. I don't like liars. Tell him the truth.

DIANA: What truth? That you made a dirty agreement to trap me? *(To* WARREN*)* That you lowered yourself to steal my wallet and use it as a cover-up? If only once you had asked me what I felt—what I thought —what I was doing with my life, I might have told you!

WARREN: "Might."

DIANA: Yes, I would have told you. I would have told you that you're selfish, a coward! I despise you!

WARREN: Do you admit all the things he said?

DIANA: What's the difference?

WARREN: Yes or no?

DIANA: With a gun pointed at me? It's all true!

WARREN *(to* KIRK*)*: Put the gun away. (KIRK *puts the revolver in his pocket)* Now?

DIANA: Does it matter?

WARREN: I want to know.

DIANA: Why? Isn't it enough that I hate you now?

WARREN: Did you hate me before?

DIANA: No. You were my husband.

WARREN: Why were you unfaithful?

DIANA: You lock your wife up in a room with someone like that. Then you call her a whore! You're a pervert.

WARREN: What about your other lover? Who's he?

DIANA: You don't know him.

WARREN: Why were you unfaithful?

DIANA: I was bored.

WARREN: How did it begin?

DIANA: He knew how to make me feel like a woman. He seemed more interesting than you.

WARREN: "Seemed"?

DIANA: That's right. I discovered he was as boring as you after a while.

WARREN: All men become "boring" after a while. You're old enough to know that!

DIANA: That's not necessarily so—

WARREN *(indicating* KIRK*)*: What do you think of him?

DIANA *(looking* KIRK *over)*: I didn't like him at first. I didn't like him when he was too aggressive. I even tried to . . .

WARREN: What?

DIANA: I even tried to use the gun *you* emptied for him.

WARREN: Did she?

KIRK: She was pretending. You know women. They pretend not to want it to excite you.

WARREN *(to* DIANA*)*: You were saying, "You didn't like him at first." *(With defiance)* And now?

DIANA: Now I like him.

WARREN *(to* KIRK*)*: Do you believe her?

KIRK: It doesn't really matter. But I'm happy to hear it. Thank you, Diana. I believe you.

WARREN *(to* KIRK*)*: Male ego. That's what ruins us. We believe them while they cheat and destroy us. *(To* DIANA, *teasingly)* Do you think *he* wouldn't bore you after a while?

DIANA: I don't think so. He's more alive and interesting than you.

WARREN: I was more "alive and interesting" than those boys you knew at college.

DIANA: You *were.*

WARREN: This mysterious lover you've been meeting for a year—he must have seemed very "alive"—the first night—or was it afternoon?

DIANA: Afternoon.

WARREN: Bitch! You were born like that. Unfaithful and deceiving. I'm glad I took that mask off.

DIANA: So do I. I feel better now that you know. And now that you know, get out of my life!

WARREN: *You'*ll get out of *my* life.

DIANA: It's all the same. Untie me, Kirk.

WARREN: "Kirk". . . . How romantic!

DIANA: You learn the name in bed. Please, Kirk.

(KIRK *does not move)*

WARREN: Did "Kirk" tell you why he came here?

DIANA *(with sarcasm)*: You amaze me. He gave me *all* the answers. And I enjoyed them.

WARREN: Not all of them.

DIANA *(with defiance)*: All of them.

WARREN: You don't understand. I mean, I don't think he told you everything . . .

DIANA *(puzzled by his insistence)*: I believe he did. He was affectionate
and tender. Like a friend who cares.

WARREN: Friends who care don't tie people up.

DIANA *(after a few seconds of reflection)*: He was carrying out your orders.
You're paying him.

WARREN: Do you know *why* I am paying him?

DIANA: Because you're sick! You paid a man to go to bed with your wife!
Do you realize what you've done?

WARREN: I gave him his freedom, my money, my car, a passport is waiting for him in New York—I gave him all this—

DIANA *(interrupting)*: And your wife, don't forget!

WARREN *(ignoring)*: —all this just to get you into bed with him? *You*'re
too naive, Diana . . .

DIANA *(shaken)*: You gave him all that because you wanted him to trap
me! He did.

WARREN: Not just to trap you. That would have been too generous for
such a small service . . .

DIANA *(frightened)*: What else?

WARREN: You see? He didn't tell you. He isn't such a great friend, after
all. He doesn't really appreciate your "charms" and . . . devotion.

DIANA *(frightened)*: What else, Kirk? You didn't tell me. . . . .(A *silence*)
What else?

KIRK (*resignedly*): All right! Let's get it over with! (*He gets the revolver out.* DIANA *is terrorized*)

DIANA: No, Kirk. . . . No. . . . Be careful. . . . It's loaded . . .

(KIRK *seems undecided. He looks at* WARREN *and notices that he steps back, worried*)

KIRK: Look at the power I have in my hands today. . . . The power to decide. . . . Either way. . . . It makes me nervous. . . . I could kill her. . . . Or you. . . . Or both. . . . Or let you out of it. . . . The power to extinguish a life. . . . No one should have it. . . . (*He points the revolver back and forth from* DIANA *to* WARREN) But I'm stuck with it now. . . . If it's given to you, you're bound to use it. . . . I was paid to kill. . . . (*He points the revolver at* DIANA) I wasn't paid for "nothing". . . . (*He points the revolver at* WARREN)

WARREN (*very nervous*): You know she's been unfaithful. More than once. She must die.

(*A silence*)

KIRK: If I were to follow my instinct. . . .(*To* WARREN) Should I?

WARREN: Kill her and get out. Remember, they're looking for you. They could come here any moment.

KIRK: You're not so dumb, Doctor. You know you can't trust my instinct. . . . *You* tortured me. . . . *You* humiliated me. . . . It's you I should kill.

WARREN: That friend in New York! I told him not to give you the passport unless I call him tomorrow—

DIANA (*to* KIRK): Don't trust him!

KIRK: I don't trust you, Doctor. . . . I have no intention of going to your friend tomorrow. You're too good at setting traps.

WARREN *(going to the safe again):* Look. Here. . . . *(He opens the safe again)* It's all yours. The jewels, the money. . . . Take it. . . . *(He gives* KIRK *a box of jewels and another stack of bills)*

KIRK: Thank you. . . . You're very generous today. . . .
(He looks at DIANA, *undecided)*

DIANA: Kirk—I can make you happy. You know I can . . .

KIRK: Everybody loves me today! It's the first time in my life. And all because I have the power to kill. *(He shows them the revolver)*

DIANA: I've proved I love you, Kirk. . . . You know I love you. Who else would . . . ?

KIRK: What?

DIANA: What we did, I've never done with anyone else. . . . It's love, Kirk, for you—for your eyes, for your body, for you alone . . .

WARREN: She'd say the same things to a freak. She said all those things to all the men she knew. Do you trust her?

*(*KIRK *looks at* DIANA. *Then at* WARREN. *He is enjoying his power. He looks at the jewels)*

DIANA: They belong to me. *I'm* giving them to you.

WARREN: *I* bought them. They're mine. I'm giving them to you, Kirk. And all the money. Everything here is mine.

(A silence. KIRK *is undecided)*

WARREN: You won't get away with it, without my help. . . . We are in this thing together.

KIRK: More than you think. Suppose I had a tape, of this little get-together?

WARREN *(alarmed)*: Nonsense! How? *(He runs to a drawer and opens it. He sees with relief that his tape recorder is there. He shows it to* KIRK*)* I didn't think you would . . .

KIRK: I have it on me.

(A tense silence; both DIANA *and* WARREN *are worried)*

WARREN: On you? *(He looks at* DIANA *for confirmation)* She should know . . .

*(*DIANA *is speechless, noncommittal)*

KIRK: I didn't let her look through my pockets.

WARREN *(to* KIRK*)*: Where did you get it?

KIRK: I know my way around.

WARREN: You told me you took a taxi the moment I left you outside. . . . *(Incredulous)* And how would you know about these new gadgets?

KIRK: I know plenty. I have the tape. Do you still want to help me?

WARREN: Of course. . . . *(Uncertain; unbelieving)* That tape is valuable *only* if I'm alive and can pay for it. Deliver it to my friend in New York and he'll give you an extra ten thousand. I must call him to tell him that you kept your part of the deal. *(He indicates* DIANA*)* I'll tell him to pay you the extra money.

*(*KIRK *is still undecided)*

DIANA: Don't trust him, Kirk! He's a penny-pincher—you can't imagine. Most of those jewels—perhaps all of them—are fakes. The diamond earrings for instance! Glass!

*(*KIRK *takes the diamond earrings and throws them at* WARREN*)*

WARREN: Fool! You just threw away fifty thousand dollars. How can you be so naive to trust her?

DIANA: They're fakes! I had them appraised.

WARREN: She's lying! *(He picks them up and gives them to* KIRK) Deliver them to my friend. He'll give you fifty thousand cash.

DIANA: That friend doesn't even exist, I'm sure!

KIRK *(confused):* With your kind of people—where's the truth?

DIANA: Show me that address.

WARREN *(while* KIRK *is showing the address):* She doesn't know him.

DIANA: Naturally! *(Reads the address)* Never heard of him!

WARREN: You wouldn't know such people!

KIRK: "Such people"?

WARREN: People who help with false passports.

DIANA: He doesn't exist, Kirk. I assure you. I know *all* of Warren's friends. Even the weird ones.

(KIRK *looks again at them both. Puts the revolver in his pocket.* WARREN *is relieved.* DIANA *remains tense.* KIRK *walks slowly to* WARREN *and whispers something to him.* WARREN *nods and goes into the bedroom.* KIRK *kneels down and opens the tool-bag)*

DIANA: What did you tell him?

KIRK: That I'd rather use a knife. *(A tense silence.* DIANA *is speechless.* KIRK *takes out the knife. It is the same one he killed the* METER MAN *with. There is still blood on it.* WARREN *comes back with a blue blanket like the one* KIRK *used to cover the* METER MAN. *With the knife in his hand, to* DIANA *who has not the strength to speak)* Thank you, Diana. . . . You're the first woman who made me feel loved. . . . *(Covering the action with his body, he hits* DIANA *twice. We hear* DIANA's *weak moan)* Blanket!

(WARREN— *at a distance—upset by what he sees—throws the blanket to*

KIRK. KIRK *covers* DIANA *with the blanket and goes behind her to untie her hands from the chair. While he is doing this we see two spots of blood coming through the blanket where* DIANA's *heart is.* WARREN *watches, trying to conceal his own horror)*

KIRK *(who has finished untying* DIANA*)*: Don't just stand there. Give me a hand. *(He indicates to* WARREN *that they should carry the body.* WARREN *does not react. He is numb)* All right. Then take care of this knife. . . . *(He pulls it from under the blanket, wraps it carefully in a newspaper and hands it to* WARREN*)* I'll take care of the body.

*(*WARREN *reluctantly takes the knife. He goes to the kitchen.* KIRK *quickly takes the body, goes to the hall and hides it behind the screen. Then he quickly opens the armoire, carries out the body of the* METER MAN—*which is wrapped in the blue blanket and leaves it at the door. When* KIRK *returns,* WARREN *is still in the kitchen)*

KIRK *(goes to the kitchen door and speaks to* WARREN *from there)*: What are you doing, Doctor? Vomiting? Blood doesn't bite, you know. . . . Why don't you wash it? . . . Be a man, Doctor! *You* asked for blood —you've got it . . .

WARREN *(coming out of the kitchen, pale and tired)*: Later . . .

KIRK: Now, what do we do with the body?

WARREN: Put it in the car and go.

KIRK: You're not coming with me?

WARREN: It's not necessary.

KIRK: The plan was that we'd get rid of it together. Where do I dump it?

WARREN: That's up to you. Along the way.

KIRK: What way?

WARREN *(taking a map from his pocket)*: Here we are. . . . Take Route 22 through Brewster. . . . Then get on the Saw Mill River Parkway . . . to New York.

KIRK: Fine. But where do I dump the body?

WARREN: It's getting dark. It'll be easy. The first chance you get.

KIRK *(taking the map)*: What are you going to do with the knife?

WARREN: I don't know . . .

KIRK: I better take it. I'll throw it away with the body. (KIRK *goes to the kitchen.* WARREN *goes to the hall and stares at the body wrapped in the blue blanket. He starts to bend down as though to lift the blanket.* KIRK *comes back with the knife which is still wrapped in the newspaper;* WARREN *stops)*

KIRK: Well, Doctor, our collaboration is over. . . . Now we take two different paths. . . . Me to the old country where my mother was born. You—a relieved widower—free to do your thing. *(Pause)* Be kind to those poor derelicts who are in your custody. They're not dangerous, believe me. They're victims of people like you. . . . (KIRK *offers him his hand,* WARREN *is reluctant to take it)* Something wrong? You don't want to shake the hand of a "murderer"? They say the "brain" —you, Doctor—is guiltier than the hand.

(They shake hands)

WARREN: Good luck.

KIRK: We'll need it. Take a look outside to see if it's all clear. (As WARREN *goes to the window,* KIRK *puts the package containing the knife behind the screen. Then he takes the body of the* METER MAN, *carrying it on his shoulder)* Clear?

WARREN *(who is watching from the window)*: Hold it! . . . Now. . . . Go!

(KIRK *exits with the body. From the window* WARREN *watches* KIRK *get into the car. We hear the sound of the car leaving)*

WARREN *(picks up the telephone and dials)*: This is Doctor O'Brien. I want to report a. . . . Yes. . . . A murder. . . . Me and my wife, we've been held at gun point by that maniac who escaped. . . . He just left the house. . . . With my gun, my car. . . .(*He pretends grief*) the body of my wife. . . . He killed her. (DIANA *appears from behind the screen, moving slowly, like a ghost. There are two red spots on her dress; she is holding the knife.* DIANA *comes to the door of the living room and listens to* WARREN's *conversation*) Yes—he killed her in front of my eyes and carried the body away. . . . In my car. It's a '79 Cadillac—white with black top—License number 1594. MD 1594. He's armed. He's dangerous. He telephoned an accomplice from here —he's taking Route 22 to Brewster then the Saw Mill River Parkway to New York . . . Shoot him on sight. He's desperate and dangerous. Shoot to kill or your men will pay with their lives. . . . He's violent. A sadistic criminal. . . . I don't care about the car. . . . I don't care about anything, not after what I've been through. (*He pretends grief again*) After what he did to my wife. . . . (*He hangs up and smiles to himself. He is satisfied—relieved. He has not yet seen* DIANA *who now enters slowly, like a terrifying ghost. Sensing someone's presence,* WARREN *turns slowly. The impact on him is tremendous. He is gasping for air. He steps back slowly, shocked.* DIANA *advances implacably with the knife pointed at her husband. Meanwhile we see* KIRK *coming back cautiously. He takes the key from Diana's wallet, opens the door and enters the hall. There is no sound from the living room.* KIRK *takes the gun out of his pocket.* WARREN *takes a few steps backwards, in the direction of the hall. It is* DIANA *who first sees* KIRK. *No reaction. It is clear at this moment that* DIANA *and* KIRK *have an agreement.* WARREN *is near the door and hopes he can escape from the terrifying apparition of this "walking corpse." He backs into* KIRK's *gun. His reaction is violent shock as he turns to see gun and* KIRK *standing there. With gasps, he slumps to the floor. He half turns, stares at* KIRK *and* DIANA. *He dies*)

KIRK (*feeling* WARREN's *heart*): He's dead. (KIRK *stands up and looks at* DIANA *who is no longer playing the role of "ghost." She shows relief*) You were right about his heart condition . . .

DIANA: I expected him to drop dead the moment he saw the "blood". . . . (*She indicates the two spots*)

KIRK (*looking at* DIANA *admiringly*): Diana. . . . (*They look at each other. They kiss*) I love you Diana. . . . You are amazing. . . . The most wonderful woman I ever met . . .

DIANA: I love you too, Kirk. But when you began pointing that gun at me I really thought you had changed your mind.

KIRK: . . . I'll never change my mind about you. You'll be mine forever. I adore you.

DIANA: Me too.

KIRK (*looking up at her with love*): Now I have faith, Diana. In you. When you cooked up the scheme, I thought you were just out for yourself . . .

DIANA: Ourselves. And our love . . .

(A *silence*)

KIRK: Our love. . . . It's beautiful the way you say it. . . . Did you do *this* (*He indicates the body of* WARREN) for our love?

DIANA: Yes, Kirk.

KIRK: Not because you hated him? Not for revenge?

DIANA: Two sentiments can be combined. When you find out that your husband has paid someone to kill you, you hate him and you want him dead. When you find that you are in love with the man your husband sent—you want to escape with him. You must go now, Kirk. It's too dangerous.

KIRK: And you?

DIANA: I'll tell the police a burglar broke in and frightened my husband to death. And that he fled with the money and the jewels. I'll give them the wrong description. They'll never find you. (*She notices that* KIRK *is looking at the knife which she dropped when* WARREN *had the stroke*)

KIRK: I'll take that with me. (*He picks up the knife and puts it into his pocket*)

DIANA: Everything will be all right. (KIRK *is looking at her stained dress*) I'll change, of course. Please go! Before they come!

KIRK: What about us?

DIANA: I'll join you as soon as things calm down. In a few days.

KIRK: How many?

DIANA *(caressing and kissing him)*: Let's say . . . within the week. Maybe sooner, my love . . .

KIRK: Will you see . . . that other guy?

DIANA: You know better than that. *You* made me forget him. Please go. It's not safe for you to be here.

KIRK: Where will we meet?

DIANA: New York, of course.

KIRK: I am not going to that address. . . . (*He touches the pocket where he put the address of* WARREN'*s friend*) I don't trust him. . . . (*He indicates the body*)

DIANA: I wouldn't either! You're wise not to. Let's see. . . . Go to the . . . St. Moritz Hotel. I'll meet you there.

(KIRK *looks at her with love. He is really in love with* DIANA. *He is reluctant to leave*)

KIRK: At the St. Moritz. . . . I'll be waiting. . . . Day and night, for you . . .

DIANA *(kissing him again)*: Go, my love. . . . (*They kiss again*) Please. . . . Only a few days and then. . . . We'll be together . . . for ever.

KIRK *(reluctant to go)*: Thank you, Diana. . . . I'll make you happy. . . .

(DIANA's *smile is full of love. She succeeds in sending him away. He leaves. She double-locks the door and wipes her mouth with her hand. She takes a deep breath—relieved. Then she goes to the telephone, passing near the body of* WARREN *which she ignores.* DIANA *picks up the receiver and dials "information"*)

DIANA: Please, the Police. *(She gets the number and dials)* This is Mrs. Warren O'Brien. . . . Yes. . . . I'm calling to confirm what my husband told you a few minutes ago. . . . No. That was a misunderstanding. But we have been harassed and tortured by the man you're looking for. . . . Yes. . . . I'll explain everything when you get here. . . . It was a nightmare. . . . But what is important now is that you kill him before he kills someone else. . . . He is very dangerous and will shoot anyone who tries to stop him. . . . He's driving my husband's car—a white Cadillac, MD 1594. . . . He's heading for Saw Mill River Parkway. . . . Shoot on sight. He's very dangerous. *(She puts the receiver down and pauses for a few seconds. Then she dials again. With tenderness)* How do you feel, my love? . . . Yes, it's me. . . . I have some incredible news. I'm free. He's dead. Dead. . . . You'll read about it in the papers—tomorrow. . . . Come to the funeral. . . . We'll talk then.

CURTAIN.

APPENDIX

Textual Notes

Two potentially opposing principles guided me in preparing the public domain playscripts for this anthology. Proper "hands-off" respect for the language and dramatic intentions of each playwright occasionally conflicted with the need to convey a meaningful contemporary reading experience. Since my allegiance as a theatre scholar and as an author rests primarily with the former consideration, I have opted for little textual editing except in cases of obvious typographical errors or obsolete words so obscure that their meanings cannot be derived from the context. In the latter instances, I have tried to avoid substituting anachronisms, and have meticulously attempted to preserve the original meter and sonority.

In the following four instances, emendations of a larger scope were required.

THE SPANISH TRAGEDY

Five sequences of varying length were introduced into the text in an edition published in 1602. These additions introduce new characters and sometimes substitute for original dialogue. Though generally attributed to Ben Jonson, these passages add nothing important to the drama and interfere with its structural integrity, dramatic intensity and overall playing time; therefore, I have excised them.

In earlier texts, the framing device of Andrea's ghost and personified Revenge is indicated by the superscription, "Chorus." To offset them more clearly, I have, instead, labelled them functionally: i.e., Prologue, Interlude(s), Epilogue.

Dialogue in Latin. I have excised inessential words and terse phrases, except in one instance when Latin seemed essential to the character's emotional state and I substituted (and noted) an apposite English phrase. I have not altered Hieronimo's elegy near the close of Act Two, Scene Four, but a footnote provides an English gloss that producers may wish to substitute for the original Latin passage.

HAMLET

Generally, I have opted to preserve the mixture of the strange and familiar that one encounters in the 1603 Quarto. I have avoided substitutions from the 1604 Quarto or the First Folio of 1623 except in cases of probable printer errors or wilfully puzzling locutions.

One passage (corresponding to a section of Act Two, Scene Two, in the more familiar version of *Hamlet*)—Corambis's encomium to "The best actors in Christendom"—required special editorial attention.

According to Albert B. Weiner, editor of the Barron's Educational Series edition of the 1603 Quarto, "(The end of) this line is sheer nonsense, and it defies emendation." Perhaps. But the late O. B. Hardison, Jr., former head of The Folger Shakespeare Library in Washington, D.C., once told me that throughout literary history, Shakespearean scholarship has been crippled by the ignorance of scholars to the theatrical ramifications implicit in the texts.

The passage, as it appears in the 1603 Folio, ends thus: ". . . Seneca cannot be too heavy, nor Plautus too light, for the law of Writ, and the Liberty. These are the only men." The emendation of Corambis's speech in the present edition is founded upon the auditory character of the problematic line.

FRANCESCA DA RIMINI

Arthur Hobson Quinn's *Representative American Plays* includes an edition that, according to Quinn, "represents (George Henry) Boker's best judgment of the form in which it should be read." However, the playwright prepared a generally excellent acting version of his great drama in 1853, one which excises lengthy passages and substitutes new material, often of great beauty and dramatic worth.

The script included in *Sweet Revenge* is based on the playwright's 1853 edition, but I have made generous restorations of deleted matter when Boker's cuts obscure vital psychological and thematic issues. In the instance of a few irresistible variant passages, I have knit together parts of *both* of Boker's versions.

The 1853 edition omits much of Ritta's speeches, but I have restored most of this winsome character's dialogue, especially her memorable speech to Francesca on the agonies of love.

SWEENEY TODD

Though George Dibdin Pitt wrote *Sweeney Todd* in 1842, he died in 1855, long before the script was published in a drastically cut edition. Meanwhile, a radically different version attributed to a Frederick Hazleton was mounted in 1862 and later printed. Lacking any copyright protection, the play began to be performed at other playhouses in absurdly bastardized versions that defy dramatic logic.

The four-act version published in England in 1928 is rife with flaws. The sequence of events is thoroughly muddled; patches of irrelevant dialogue intrude on the forward thrust of the action; worst of all, every character murdered by Sweeney miraculously survives the ordeal to come back to life late in the drama. Even Mrs. Lovett, whose body Sweeney is about to dump into the furnace at the end of the second act, somehow ends up as an unburned corpse on the bakehouse floor in Act Four.

I have attempted to turn *Sweeney Todd* into a cohesive script that, hopefully, will not strain audience credibility much more than the average contemporary television soap opera.

The first act seems the least corrupted, therefore, no significant changes have been made in it. The first scenes of the second act likewise have been preserved, although I inserted a brief Dumb Show to account for the fact that Mark sends Tobias off for police, a detail afterward ignored in the 1928 script. In the fourth scene, Jarvis meets up with the resurrected lapidary, Parmine. I have switched Mark Ingestrie for

Parmine, a substitution consistent with Mark's lurking presence in the cellars and elsewhere throughout the rest of the play. Similarly, at the outset of the third act, I have altered the opening sequence between Tobias and Jarvis to replace the latter character with Mark. At the end of the scene, Sweeney is about to stab Tobias when Mark rises like a ghost from the gimmicked chair. This device both diminishes the impact of the sailor's appearance in the later courtroom scene and jars with Sweeney's already announced intention to take Tobias to the asylum, as he does in the next scene. Therefore, I have cut what I believe to be Mark's premature spectral appearance and have transferred the dialogue in which Sweeney expresses his melodramatic reaction to the fourth act courtroom episode.

At the close of the third act, Jarvis encounters the hypocritical Lupin and confounds him with the family he left behind. This episode, a fitting climax to the Lupin subplot, appears out of place here. I have transferred it to the end of the Newgate Prison scene in the fourth act, where its reference to "the pious dame who vends the article at yonder sinful public-house" accords with Lupin's recent tête-à-tête with Mrs. Poorlean.

In the fourth act, the sense of the two prisoner's songs is obscured by slang and antique terms, which I have altered for the sake of comprehensibility. Thus, in the first song, the refrain, "Carry on!" means approximately the same as the original, "Fake away!"; "Darbies" become "irons" ("handcuffs" sound too modern); "my nuttiest lady . . . to the beaks did her gentleman betray" translates to "my amorous lady . . . to the judge . . ." and "a regular rollicking Romany" becomes the admittedly forced "gypsy I be!" Part of the latter stanza of the second song is particularly difficult to render: "If the jolly old Roger I meet, I'll tout his mums and I'll snabble his Poll." A quick glimpse at Eric Partridge's *A Dictionary of Slang and English Usage* first suggested piratical doings, but more careful analysis indicates that a jolly old Roger is an older way of referring to a "stool pigeon." To preserve the meter and diction, I have substituted "Peachum," a generic term deriving, of course, from John Gay's *The Beggar's Opera*.

In the middle of the fourth act, the long-dead mechanic, Mr. Smith, comes to life again. I have substituted Jarvis. This means substituting Jeffery for Jarvis in the final scene, though his declaration, "St. George for England," strikes me as far more likely in the colonel's mouth, so perhaps the change is a proper one.